AL CAPONE – KING OF THE GAN

What was the background of Capone's parents?

His father, Gabriele, was a barber and his mother, Teresina, was a seamstress. They … in Italy (Naples) and immigrated to the U.S. in 1894. Al, their 4th son, was born in 18 … there would be seven brothers and one daughter, Mafalda, being the youngest.

Capone home on Garfield Place in Brooklyn (author col.)

What were Capone's physical features?

At age 29 he was about five feet ten inches tall, bull-necked, 255 pounds, grayish eyes, dark brown hair and had sloping shoulders. His very large head was accented by thick eyebrows.

What was there in Capone's upbringing that led to his criminal behavior as an adult?

According to all accounts, Al grew up in a close-knit, loving, law-abiding family.

Did Al run afoul of the law as a youth?

Al was bored with school and was more interested in roaming the streets with his Italian buddies. He lived in a tough neighborhood and was frequently involved in street brawls with the enemy - Irish youth. He earned mostly Bs in school until his running around resulted in a decline in achievement, causing him to fail the 6th grade. After a fight with a teacher, he dropped out of school at age 14. He soon got involved with the wrong crowd. Al quickly became a member of the South Brooklyn Rippers gang and later joined the Five Pointers. But there were no serious altercations with the law.

Did Capone ever run away from home?

No, but an older brother, Vincenzo, who Americanized his name to Richard Hart, ran away and went out west to Wichita, Kansas, where he became fascinated with six-shooters and Indians. He was the only Capone to serve in World War I, and he received a sharpshooter's medal from General Pershing.

When did Capone contract syphilis?

It is believed Al contracted the disease at an early age, not long after he became sexually active. The disease was quite common back them. Army records indicate that as many as 8 percent of World War I draftees had it. Syphilis is a disease that comes and goes and in its later stages can cause dementia and then death. Capone belonged to the minority 20 percent of cases ravaged by the disease in its final stages.

Capone's mother, Teresina, with a grandchild

How did Capone blow a chance at early detection of his syphilis?

A young Greek girl he kept as a mistress complained of a genital sore that was diagnosed by a doctor who began immediate treatment. When it was suggested to Capone that he take the Wasserman Test to determine if he was infected, he refused, **terrified by the thought of being stuck by a needle** and having blood withdrawn.

How did Capone get introduced to a life of crime?

Al's mentor was **Johnny Torrio**, a vice lord in his neighborhood who hired young teens to do odd jobs and run errands. Torrio was sometimes called "Terrible John" and was once a dreaded member of Manhattan's celebrated Five Points Gang. In later life, Torrio tried to avoid violence and preferred working out solutions to conflicts. When Capone was a teenager he, too, became a member of the Five Pointers, as did **Lucky Luciano**.

One important law official called Torrio the "**Father of Modern Gangsterdom**."

How did Capone get the nickname, **Scarface Al**?

At age 18 Capone began working at a local dance hall as a bartender and bouncer. One night he saw a beautiful Italian girl and went over to her table and made suggestive remarks about her figure. The insult angered her brother, **Frank Galluccio**, who was with her. A vicious fight erupted and Galluccio, who was smaller than Capone, pulled a knife and **slashed Al three times** across the cheek and neck. After the scars healed and turned from red to white, Capone was sensitive to the disfigurement and usually had photographers picture him from his "good" profile. Galluccio was afraid for his life and pleaded his case to Joe "The Boss" Masseria, who arranged a meeting with Galluccio, Capone and Lucky Luciano. Because Capone had insulted Galluccio's sister in public, he was ordered not to seek revenge. In turn, Galluccio had to apologize. Incredibly, Galluccio was later forgiven and became one of Capone's bodyguards. Capone never took revenge on Galluccio and concocted the story that his scars came from service during World War I in France.

Did Capone ever hold down a traditional job?

Yes. Al worked three years in a munitions factory and three more as a paper cutter with United Paper, earning a measly $3 a week.

Capone's attacker, Frank Galluccio

Whom did Al Capone marry?

He married a slim, good-looking blonde Irish girl, **Mae Coughlin,** in December of 1918. She became pregnant before their marriage. Back in those days it was considered an upward move in social mobility for an Italian to marry someone of Irish descent. The baby boy was named Albert Francis Capone, but everybody called him "Sonny." Johnny Torrio became his godfather. Some said Capone had promised to marry Mae as a way to avoid the draft since she gave birth before their nuptials. Mae, who was two years older than Al, turned out to be the perfect wife for him. She didn't complain about his philandering, never gossiped about his business dealings and never talked to newspaper reporters. Al gave her a generous allowance, which she spent on fancy clothes and expensive furs.

Did Capone live anywhere else besides Brooklyn or Chicago?

After his marriage, Al moved his family to Baltimore and left the life of thuggery in favor of home and hearth. He became a bookkeeper for a construction firm and learned to deal with a balance sheet, credits and debits – a skill that came in handy later in life.

How was Capone affected by his father's death in 1920 at the age of fifty-five?

It was profound. Al quit his job after his father's fatal heart attack and resumed his ties with Johnny Torrio. Torrio had left Brooklyn and headed for Chicago where more opportunities seemed to exist. He persuaded Al to come with him and put his street smarts and knack for figures to use in the rackets.

Capone's pretty blonde wife, Mae

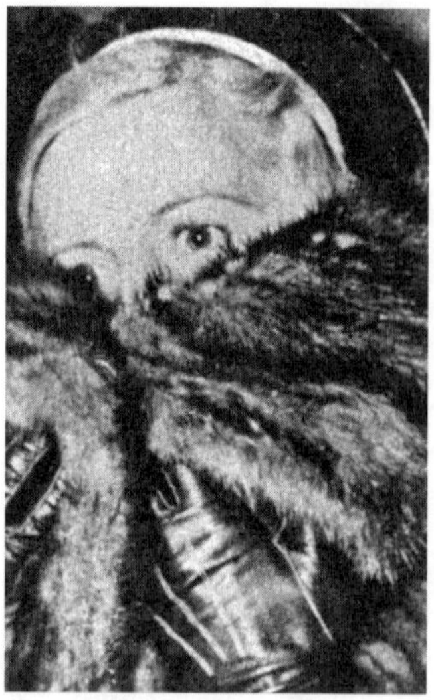

When did the Capones first come to Chicago?

They arrived in 1921 when Al was 22-years-old. Johnnie Torrio saw opportunities in Chicago and had moved there earlier. Torrio's distant cousin, who was married to **Big Jim Colosimo** and a madam of several houses, wrote Torrio a letter asking him to come. After Torrio was established, he recommended Al to Colosimo. Colosimo sent for Al Capone and **Frankie Yale**, both graduates of the Five Points Gang. Al was already suspected of two murders in New York and faced possible indictment for a third, giving him added incentive to leave. Capone worked as a doorman and clean-up man at a Colosimo restaurant, but eventually he became Torrio's most trusted lieutenant. Torrio concentrated his illegal liquor empire in the beer market, getting control of several distilleries and five breweries. Torrio set up roadhouses all over Illinois and soon had an annual income of $100,000. Capone impressed Torrio, who quickly promoted him to manage one of his nightclubs.

There were also other gangs in Chicago who quickly became rivals. Torrio met with other mob leaders and at his suggestion, they divided Chicago and Cicero into small kingdoms. The North Side went to Dion O'Banion. Torrio took the West Side. The South Side was assigned to the six Genna Brothers, the O'Donnells, and several others.

Who was Big Jim Colosimo?

Big Jim Colosimo, a restauranteer and vice lord of the Chicago district known as The Levee, was gunned down in the lobby of his own establishment. Colosimo was Chicago's first great underworld king (1900-1920). His restaurant was frequented by idols of the day, such as **Enrico Caruso**, **George M. Cohan**, **Sophie Tucker** and **Al Jolson**. He was murdered three weeks after his second marriage in April of 1920. Some thought his first wife, Victoria, was responsible for his death, but she was in L.A. at the time of the killing. Colosimo's murder on May 11 enabled Torrio and Capone to enlarge their holdings in vice and racketeering.

Frankie Yale probably murdered Colosimo so he could expand his own empire. But he was charged with the murder, and it was Johnny Torrio who now presided over the operation of countless brothels, speakeasies and gin joints in the old Levee District. Colosimo was Torrio's uncle, and it was he who first persuaded Torrio to leave New York and come to Chicago. Although a Catholic, Colosimo's funeral was conducted by a Protestant clergyman because the local archbishop forbade any diocese priest from performing rites on a gangster.

Some say the cause of his death was his lovely new wife, a former Methodist church choir singer named **Dale Winter**. She was hired as a featured performer at Colosimo's club, and he immediately became moonstruck and she with him, even though Dale was half his age. **Florenz Ziegfield Jr**. heard Winter sing at Colosimo's club and offered her a contract, but she turned him down. Dale said her aspiration was to become a serious opera singer. Colosimo divorced his wife and catered to Dale's every whim and fancy. Colosimo soon lost respect. Everyone in the underworld said Colisimo had "gone soft." To the sharks of gangland Chicago, that was like blood in the water. When Colosimo went daft in the head over a dame, Torrio stepped in and took over operations. Colosimo's murder was never solved.

There were fifty-three pallbearers and honorary pallbearers at his funeral. Nine aldermen, three judges and a couple of Congressmen were there. The grieving Dale Winter soon discovered that technically their nuptuals had no legal basis because they were married before the mandatory year-long waiting period after Jim's divorce from his first wife. The family, however, decided that the happiness she had given to her husband was worth about $6,000. Some say it was Colosimo who laid the foundation for the reign of Al Capone.

Big Jim Colosimo and Dale Winter

Why was Chicago sometimes called **Mud Town**?

In its early years, before the streets were raised, most of the town was barely above the level of the Chicago River, and sanitary conditions were intolerable. The street raising began in 1856 and lasted for nearly twenty years.

East St. Louis underwent a similar costly transformation when it raised its streets back in the late 1880s, nearly bankrupting the town.

How did the term "bootlegging" originate?

Back in the 1890s it was a popular thing for some men to conceal a bottle of liquor in the upper part (the leg) of their boot.

Who were the **Everleigh sisters**?

The Everleigh Club, a posh brothel at 2131 South Dearborn in Chicago, was run by two sisters whose father was a Kentucky lawyer. Their establishment was open 24 hours a day. This splendid place boasted over 50 rooms. It was a formal policy that **Illinois legislators were admitted free**. Marshall Field's son, age 37, died from a fatal gunshot wound, and many believe it happened at the Club. The girls paid protection money and the conduit to the politicians was **Big Jim Colosimo**. A reform mayor closed the club in 1911, so the sisters left Chicago and retired in New York to live in regal splendor. Chicago's segregated red light district was in an area known as The Levee. The madams in the Levee District had an organization called The Friendly Sisters.

What was Al Capone's mansion like in Chicago?

Surprisingly, Capone lived in a slightly upscale, unpretentious two-story brick house with fifteen rooms at 7244 Prairie Avenue. His widowed mother lived upstairs with Mafalda and two younger sons, John and Matthew. A few doors down lived a retired Presbyterian clergyman. Other brothers stayed occasionally with Al and his wife. Inside, the house was handsomely furnished with gilded cornices and adornments imported from Europe. The basement walls were a foot thick to protect from bullets or bombs. The windows had close-set bars to prevent tossed bombs from penetrating.

Capone's Chicago residence at 7244 Prairie Avenue

Who was the first person killed by Capone?

It happened back when Capone was living in New York. Capone was working for **Frankie Yale,** the liquor boss of New York. Yale was also known for bankrolling people in local dice games. A man named Tony Perotta owed Yale $1,500, and Al was sent to collect the sum. An argument ensued, and Capone drew a gun and killed him. It turned out that Perotta was an illegal alien. So the police weren't interested in pursuing the matter.

What precautions did Prohibition era gangsters take when they went to dine at a restaurant?

Bodyguards always checked out the place first, especially bathrooms and rear exits. When eating, mobsters usually sat at the rear of the restaurant with their backs to the wall.

After Capone became famous, what edict was given by baseball commissioner Judge **Kennesaw Mountain Landis** as a result of Chicago Cub players autographing baseballs for Al Capone?

He forbade players to fraternize with the fans. This was the same commissioner who banned eight Chicago White Sox players for life for "throwing" the 1919 World Series. A man named Arnold Rothstein allegedly was behind the fix. **Shoeless Joe Jackson** was one of the players, but he claimed he was innocent until his death in 1951. "Say it isn't so, Joe," was the famous lament of one young boy. Joe's best argument was the fact that he had twelve hits in the series – a record. Chicago reporter **Jake Lingle** was one of the first to know that the fix was on as a result of his underworld contacts.

Some blamed the incident on niggardly owner Charles Comiskey who grew rich off his team and paid his star players half the salary of what other featured players earned.

Gabby Hartnett, Chicago Cub star, autographing a baseball for Sonny Capone

Why was the word "gat" sometimes used by Illinois gangsters in place of the word "gun?"

It was a tribute to **Richard Gatling** who invented the crank-operated, multi-barreled gatling gun in 1862.

If Capone lived in Chicago, how did he get to hobnob with many of the silent screen stars?

In the early silent screen days, Chicago had a budding film industry. The Green Mill Gardens was one of the favorite hangouts of Mary Pickford, Tom Mix, Ben Turpin, Gloria Swanson, Broncho Billy Anderson, and Wallace Beery. It was Pickford who introduced East St. Louisan Lillian Gish to D.W. Griffith. The chorus line at the Mill had 50 beautiful girls.

Were Capone's suits conservative or outlandish?

His tastes were baroque and eclectic. He wore diamond-studded belts, expensive fedoras, diamond cufflinks, and swaggered around in hand-tailored suits in zany colors: tangerine, pea green, mustard yellow, peach, primrose and lavender.

Which brother is known as the "**Lost Capone**?"

It was **Vincenzo Capone**, the oldest, who went west, changed his name to **Richard Hart** and became a married man in Homer, Nebraska. When Prohibition became law, he secured a commission from the governor to become an agent and was given a gun and a badge. He demonstrated his skill with a revolver by shooting cigarettes from the mouths of his three sons. His daring raids and flair for the dramatic soon earned him the ambidextrous nickname, ***Two Gun Hart***. He later became the head of Indian reservation police covering twelve reservations. When **President Calvin Coolidge** took a vacation in South Dakota during the summer of 1927, Two Gun Hart was assigned as one of his bodyguards. Coolidge would have been mortified had he known one of the men protecting him was Capone's brother, but no one knew. Hart died from diabetic complications in 1952. A film called *The Lost Capone*, made some years ago, told the little known story.

Two-gun Hart with chief on reservation

What is the connection of **Mary Hastings** and the **Mann Act** of 1910?

Mary was a Chicago madam dating back to the 1890s. She traveled the Midwest recruiting nubile young girls by promising them work in the big city. Once they were inside her brothel at Custom House Place, they were locked up on the third floor and turned over to professionals who raped the girls and then trained them in the art of prostitution. The white slavery activities of Mary Hastings, and others like her, led to Congress passing the Mann Act, which meted out a five year prison sentence to those found engaging in transporting women across state lines for immoral purposes.

What were Capone's duties in his first job with Johnny Torrio?

Torrio operated a four-story brick building known as the Four Deuces. It was located appropriately at 2222 Wabash Avenue. Capone performed various services – chauffeur, bodyguard, bartender and hustler for the brothel, located on the top floor. Torrio soon made Capone a partner, and his yearly income shot to 25 Gs a year.

What was unusual about the basement of the Four Deuces?

It was where rivals were taken and tortured until they gave up the information that was wanted. They were then killed, and bodies were taken through a tunnel that led to the back of the building. The bodies were transported in the dead of night and either dumped in a field or down an abandoned mine shaft

What did Capone keep on his desk that he considered to be his good luck pieces?

He had a herd of miniature ivory elephants.

Who were Capone's favorite movie stars?

He loved Fatty Arbuckle, **Theda Bara – the "Vamp Girl"** - and Eddie Cantor. He had pictures of them on the wall in his office. Other favorite entertainers included Louis Armstrong, George Jessel, Joe E. Lewis and musician Eddie Condon.

Theda Bara as Salome

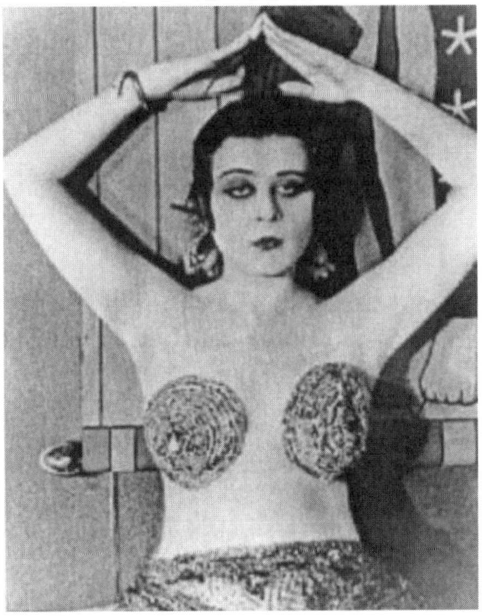

What was Capone's favorite music?

Capone loved opera, but he was also a jazz impresario. In its early years, jazz was derided and called "nigger music." Capone spent a lot of time at his brother Ralph's **Cotton Club** in Cicero. Chicago became famous for jazz and was played by Louis Armstrong, Jelly Roll Morton, Cab Calloway and Duke Ellington. Brother Ralph Capone opened several jazz nightclubs and hired bands to play. By featuring some of the best jazz men of the era at his speakeasies, Capone left one of the few positive influences as a legacy. Al Capone had good rapport with blacks, organized them into bootlegging and protected them from the police. Another famous jazz musician, Bix Beiderbecke, died from the poisonous effects of home brew in 1931 at the age of 28.

Ralph Capone directed a branch of the Chicago syndicate that owned twenty rum-running aircraft, including a tri-motored monoplane with a capacity for fifty cases. Between 1929 and 1930 they transferred nearly a million and a half dollars worth of liquor from Ontario to Chicago. There were some instances where Canadian and American planes avoided customs by transferring liquor in mid-air by using hoses, in the same manner that mid-air refueling was done.

Capone's brother, Ralph

When did Capone get into bootlegging?

Shortly after the Volstead Act became national law, various gang leaders in the Chicago area went into the smuggling business. Capone worked for Johnny Torrio, who found his niche by setting up agreements with the various gang chiefs that parceled out territories over which each group would hold sovereign sway. Torrio, in return, received a certain percentage of the profits for acting as commissioner.

What were the circumstances surrounding the death of **Marshall Field**, the department store mogul?

Field allegedly died while participating in a sex orgy in a very upscale Chicago brothel. It was probably from a heart attack.

Capone's brother, Albert

When did Al Capone first make newspaper headlines?

It was in 1922 when, in a drunken stupor, he rammed one of Torrio's sedans into a parked taxi. An argument ensued, and Capone pulled a gun on the driver. The police arrived on the scene and arrested Alfred "Caponi," as the newspaper spelled it. Torrio greased the palms of a few officials, and the matter was dropped.

What did Capone's business card have printed on it?

His unpretentious cards said he was a used furniture dealer. His shop was next door to the Four Deuces at 2220 South Wabash. But the store was merely a front for his other dealings. In later years, when he went into the racket of "protecting" independent cleaning establishments, he told people he was in the cleaning business.

Why did Torrio and Capone move their base of operations to Cicero?

Around 1924, friendly Big Bill Thompson was succeeded by reform mayor William Dever. Cicero was west of Chicago, but it was still in Cook County. They moved their base of operations to get away from Dever's jurisdiction and his shrill and tiresome rhetoric about efforts to clean up the town. Cicero had a population of nearly 70,000 and was the 5th largest city in Illinois. Although well intentioned, Dever's efforts threw Chicago's underworld into turmoil and made things worse than ever. There were few Negroes there, and most of the town's population hailed from central Europe. The most notable Capone in Torrio's Cicero operation at the time was brother Frank. He used strong-arm tactics to insure that Torrio-backed candidates won all the positions in the elections.

Another brother, Ralph, oversaw the opening of one of the organization's new brothels, **The Stockade**. The large facility had about 60 girls and doubled as a gambling spot. The impressive wooden and stone structure was known as the Maple Inn, but it was also a storehouse for guns and ammo. It had a large secret room where all the girls hid when a raid took place. Capone's headquarters became the Hawthorne Inn at 4833 Twenty-second Street. It was a multi-story structure with bulletproof steel shutters on the windows.

What were *shills* at Torrio's casinos?

These were paid workers whose job it was to attract patrons by acting as if they were big winners.

Johnny Torrio, Capone's mentor

Did Capone ever use an alias?

Yes. His favorite in the early years was Al Brown.

Who was described as "Chicago's arch criminal" and had purportedly killed 27 men?

It was none other than **Dion O'Banion**, the Irish gangster with the cherubic choirboy voice. His gang controlled the northeast side of Chicago, from the Chicago River to Lake Michigan. He always kept one hand free and could shoot a gun with either hand; his suits had extra pockets that concealed pistols.

In earlier times, O'Banion worked as a singing waiter at McGovern's Café on Clark Street, bringing tears to patron's eyes with his syrupy versions of Irish ballads. He never spent any time in jail because he was too useful to politicians in getting out the Irish vote during elections. He loved and was fascinated with flowers and always wore a carnation or a sprig of something else in his lapel. He was part owner with Samuel (tough as) "Nails" Morton in a flower shop on State Street, and soon it became fashionable for all gangsters to order flowers from O'Banion's store when a fellow mobster bit the dust.

O'Banion and his wife were childless, and unlike most other gangsters, he was very devoted to her and didn't carouse around with other women. It was due, in part, to O'Banion's love for formal attire that led many others of his ilk to start dressing fancy.

What Chicagoan minted the phrase, "**You're going for a ride**?"

It was **Hymie Weiss,** a Polish man who worked for O'Banion. The first victim to fall prey to this method of murder was a Polish guy named Steve Wisniewski, who was guilty of hijacking one of O'Banion's trucks. He was lured into the front seat of a car and then a thug in the back seat put a gun to the base of his skull. The victim was then driven to a deserted area, shot in the back of the head and pushed out the door.

Jake "Greasy Thumb" Guzik

What Chicagoan devised the first hit on an enemy, carried out by a string of cars that drove to the victim's house, pouring blistering fire into it as they sped by?

It was none other than **Bugs Moran**. Moran was responsible for twenty-six robberies and was sentenced to jail on three separate occasions prior to his 21st birthday. Moran, who was married to a full-blooded Sioux, usually went along with O'Banion on safe-cracking schemes.

Who was the financial manager of Capone's empire?

It was **Jake "Greasy Thumb" Guzik**, a Russian born Jew. It is thought the nickname went back to his younger days when he worked as a waiter and carelessly allowed his thumb to get in bowls of soup that he carried to patrons. Room 430 at the Lexington Hotel in Chicago was the nerve center of the operations.

What new murder technique was invented by Leland Varain?

Varain was O'Banion's bodyguard. He was the one who invented what came to be known as the "**rented ambush**." The killers would follow their prey and discover what places he frequently visited. Then they rented an apartment directly across from one of the establishments and waited next to a window for the victim to arrive. From their vantage point, they would open fire directly on the unsuspecting target.

What was **Dead Man's Tree**?

In the part of Chicago known as Little Italy, numerous gang wars broke out after Prohibition started. These conflicts were responsible for the deaths of over thirty men. There was a tree on Loomis Street that was used to affix a scrap of paper with a man's name. It sent a signal to everyone that the individual was a dead man walking, and the tactic was used to unnerve the potential victim and make it easier to kill him.

Frank McErlane

What were the **Aldermanic Wars** in Chicago?

This was a series of rivalries and killings between politicians seeking election from around 1913 to 1921. About 30 people were killed in this quest for power, payoffs and patronage.

Where did the expression, "**The Real McCoy**" originate?

Some think it was in reference to a boxer named Kid McCoy back in the 1890s. But it was Captain Bill McCoy, widely known as "The Real McCoy" and the founder of **Rum Row**. McCoy was an upstate New Yorker. In 1925 he was sentenced to nine months in the federal penitentiary in Atlanta. He died in Florida in 1948. His spirits came from wholesalers in Nassau in the Bahamas. Curiously, he had no significant ties with the big bootleg syndicates. It was McCoy who invented the burlock, a new way to stow liquor cargo on ships. The burlock was a package with six straw-jacketed bottles sewed in burlap and stacked like a pyramid with three on the bottom, two in the middle and one on top.

What was the first gang to start using the famous **tommy gun**?

It was the Saltis-McErlane gang. Frank McErlane was described by the Illinois Association for Criminal Justice as "the most brutal gunman who ever pulled a trigger in Chicago." The gun was named for its inventor, **Brigadier General John Thompson,** who was director of arsenals during World War I. Most police forces thought the tommy gun was a danger to pedestrians and were loathe to use it. But gangsters of the twenties and thirties loved "the chopper."

When did the serious gang wars begin in Chicago?

They started in 1923 when Spike O'Donnell, the leader of the South Side Irish gang, got out of prison. They immediately began hijacking Johnny Torrio's beer shipments. Torrio joined forces with the Saltis-McErlane group, and the O'Donnell's were no match for the new coalition. Several of the O'Donnell brothers and numerous associates were killed in this famous "**Beer War**." Casualties from the conflict were often dumped in a ditch that became known locally as "**beer cemetery**."

Spike O'Donnell

How was **Frank Capone** killed?

Al's brother was killed in 1924 during an election dispute in Cicero. Al and Frank were at a polling place with drawn revolvers to intimidate the voters. The police arrived on the scene, and a shooting fracas erupted. Frank was killed by two shotgun blasts while Al and cousin Charlie Fischetti escaped under the cover of darkness. Frank was buried at Mount Olivet Cemetery. There were kidnappings, sluggings and four deaths plus forty wounded on that election day in Cicero. Al ordered all taverns to shut down for two hours and close their blinds out of respect for Frank.

How did most of the mobsters acquire colorful nicknames such as "Nails" Morton or Mike "the devil" Genna?

The vast majority of these nicknames were thought up by reporters to sell more newspapers. It must be remembered that back at the turn of the century there were fractured skulls and killings due to newspaper rivalries in what were called "**circulation wars**." **James Dougherty** of the *Chicago Tribune* and **Clem Lane** of the *Daily News* were two of the best at thinking up the picturesque handles.

Some of the more interesting ones include: "Dingbat" O'Berta, "Polack Joe" Saltis, Joe "Hop Toad" (supposedly a good dancer) Giunta, James "Bozo" Shupe, Enoch "Nucky" Johnson, Max "Boo Hoo" Hoff, James "Shooey" Malone, "Pegleg" Lonergan, William "Three-fingered Jack" White (a Capone enforcer), James "Fur" Sammons, Willie "Potatoes" Daddano, Peter "the Clutching Hand" Morello, Joe "Bananas" Bonanno, Abe "Kid Twist" Reles, Murray "the Camel" Humphreys, Sam "Golf Bag" Hunt (he kept a machinegun in his golfbag), Samuel (tough as) "Nails" Morton, Fred "Killer" Burke, "Banjo Eyes" Smith, "Hinkey Dink" Kenna, Mike "de Pike" Heitler, Vincent "Mad Dog" Coll (I swear, these are all real), Bob "Gimpy" Newberry, Edna "The Kissing Bandit" Murray, Frank

"Blubber" Devlin, Solly "Cutchyer-Head-Off" Weissman, Sam "Googy Eyes" Marcello, "Legs" Diamond and Charles "Limpy" Cleaver.

Why did **Al Capone** pump six bullets into **Joe Howard** in 1924?

Howard got into a barroom argument with **Jake Guzik** and slapped him around. Guzik went running to Al, his close friend, and complained of the maltreatment. Al went to a saloon and confronted Howard about the incident. Instead of apologizing, he smarted off and Capone emptied his gun into the man's head. Capone was arrested, and for the first time got his picture in the paper, although the story referred to him as Tony "Scarface" Capone. Capone escaped prosecution when no one specifically identified him as the shooter at a coroner's inquest.

Frankie "Prince of Darkness" Yale

How was **Dion O'Banion** killed in the infamous "**handshake murder**" on November 10, 1924?

He was shot to death in his flower shop in a mob hit. O'Banion was always wanting to increase the size of his territory. Torrio and Capone found it increasingly difficult to deal with him, and the last straw was when he made some inflammatory remarks about Italians and Sicilians. O'Banion's big mistake was when he dismissed his three bodyguards and started carrying three guns instead for protection.

Three men came to O'Banion's shop to buy flowers for **Mike Merlo's** funeral. Albert Anselmi and John Scalisi were two of the killers. They acted as if they were going to buy some flowers for a funeral. As O'Banion extended his hand to shake on it, one of them grabbed and held it. The other helped immobileized him while the third shot him six times in the face, neck and chest. The *coup de grâce*, probably administered by Frankie Yale, was delivered into his brain while he was on the floor. Mike Genna drove the getaway car. This famous killing became known as the "handshake murder." O'Banion was buried in a casket that cost $10,000, and his funeral cortege was nearly two miles long as it wound its way to Mount Carmel Cemetery. Police didn't look too hard for the killers since they estimated O'Banion had been responsible for over 25 killings. A Polish immigrant, "**Little Hymie**" **Weiss** now assumed leadership of the O'Banion Gang and let everyone know that he held Capone responsible for O'Banion's death. Weiss had less than two years to live. After Weiss was killed, he was succeded by Schemer Drucci, who also ended up on a slab in the morgue.

Dion O'Banion

How did Capone deal with Robert St. John, founder of the Cicero *Tribune,* who wrote anti-Capone editorials?

Capone had his men beat him up, and while he was recovering in the hospital, Capone forged his signature to a document and bought the newspaper. St. John left town when he was released from the hospital.

What prompted Capone to order a specially built Cadillac from General Motors in 1925?

Hymie Weiss and Bugs Moran tried to avenge the murder of Dion O'Banion by raking Capone's car with murderous fire. One of Capone's bodyguards was injured, but Capone escaped unharmed. The new $30,000 car weighed seven tons and had armor plate on the body, half-inch thick bulletproof glass, a protected gas tank, and a gun compartment in the rear to fire at pursuers.

Did Al Capone have life insurance?

He applied for life insurance in 1925 but was turned down by six different companies.

What happened when innocent bystanders were occasionally injured in the gangland wars?

Capone usually made sure they received the finest medical treatment money could buy.

What was Capone's reaction to the charge that he was responsible for the killing of William McSwiggin, an assistant state's attorney known as the "Hanging Prosecutor?"

Capone's reply: "Why should I kill him? I paid McSwiggin, and I paid him plenty, and I got what I was paying for." McSwiggin, age 25, was hit by twenty bullets April 27, 1926, fired from a Capone motorcade. Red Duffy and Jim Doherty were killed with him. Authorities were outraged and "**Who Killed McSwiggin**" headlines were prominent in the daily newspapers. Cook County taxpayers paid the $200,000 for four grand jury investigations in an effort to get at the truth, but no one was successfully prosecuted.

Did any of the Chicago police ever plan to murder Al Capone?

Yes. McSwiggin's father was a policeman, and a plan was developed in which his police buddies would haul Capone in for questioning about the McSwiggin killing and take him to a room where McSwiggin's father waited. The plan was to have the sergeant kill Capone and claim it was self-defense. The plan worked, but when the golden moment arrived, McSwiggin lost his nerve. He later said it wasn't in him to shoot a man in cold blood.

Capone's armour plated Cadillac

What was the *casus belli* for the most lengthy gang war in Chicago's history?

It was the attempted murder of Johnny Torrio in late January of 1925. Torrio and his wife were returning from a shopping trip when he was shot several times in front of his home at 7011 Clyde. One of the shooters was thought to be **Bugs Moran** from the O'Banion gang. Schemer Drucci and Hymie Weiss were the others. One gunman placed a .45 against Torrio's head and pulled the trigger. But there was only a loud click – probably a malfunction. The gunmen fled because they thought Torrio was mortally wounded and neighbors started coming out on their porches to see the commotion.

After Torrio recovered, he was sentenced to nine months in jail at Waukegan for his culpability in an earlier law violation. For his own safety, he decided to stop contesting the conviction and begin serving his term early, starting February 7, 1925. When Torrio got out of jail, he formally retired from the syndicate and turned everything over to Al Capone, who began planning a vendetta to eliminate the other gangs. One of Capone's most valued recruits for the upcoming war was a man named **Jack "machine gun" McGurn.** During the course of his career, some 25 murders were ascribed to him. McGurn, good looking and athletic, became a favorite with journalists and was considered one of the few *colorful* members of the Capone mob.

Little Hymie Weiss, O'Banion's successor

What was the famous incident between entertainer **Joe E. Lewis** and Chicago gangsters?

Lewis was a very successful comedian at the Green Mill, a North Side cabaret. The owner wanted to sign him to a new contract, but Lewis was determined to work for a rival establishment, the New Rendezvous. In November of 1927 three men, under orders from Machine Gun McGurn, beat Lewis up and knifed him in an effort to intimidate him into staying with his original contract. He was horribly disfigured, and it took Lewis nearly ten years to recover. The incident ruined the old claim that "gangsters only kill other gangsters." There was also personal animosity between McGurn and Lewis because of their affection for the same girl. A group led by **Sophie Tucker**, **Tom Mix** and **Al Jolson** staged a benefit performance to help pay his hospital bills. He became known as "**the man the mob couldn't kill**." This story is told in the Frank Sinatra movie, *The Joker is Wild.*

Early in **Milton Berle's** career, he was scheduled to play at Chicago's Palace. But he received a note from Al Capone requesting his presence at the Cotton Club that same night to entertain Capone and Mayor Thompson. Berle declined, saying there wouldn't be enough time for him to play both clubs. But Berle's mother convinced him to play the Cotton Club so she could meet Capone. After it was over, Capone offered Berle $20,000 for his fine performance. Berle declined the money and said perhaps Capone might be able to do him a favor one day. Berle made it back to the other club for his engagement with five minutes to spare.

Milton Berle

What happened to Johnny Torrio after he got out of Lake County Jail in Waukegan in October of 1925?

Torrio developed cold feet and found the gangland wars too tough for him so he decided to get out of machine gun range. He and his wife went to live in Italy. About the only contact Torrio had with the Capones was a $5,000 birthday gift he sent to Sonny every year for his birthday.

What was Capone's secret to being so popular with reporters?

He was an affable man, and when he held interviews he would pass out free drinks and cigars to reporters. He almost never failed to give them a good quote they could use in the papers.

Was Capone adept at golfing?

He liked to play with associates, but he wasn't very good. Since they were all racketeers, there was considerable cheating, and frequent fights often broke out on the links. Al kept a concealed .45 revolver in his golf bag, and one day it accidentally went off and wounded him in the leg.

What were Al Capone's favorite songs in 1928?

"Lover Come Back to Me," "You're the Cream in my Coffee," and "I Can't Give You Anything But Love, Baby," ranked at the top.

What was Capone's favorite sport?

Like many other hoodlums who saw boxing as a metaphor for their own violent ways, Capone spent a lot of time in local gyms. Capone's favorite boxer was Chicagoan **Barney Ross**. He bet on him nearly every time he fought. Jack Dempsey, another Capone favorite, who lost his title to **Gene Tunney**, got a rematch in 1927. The fight was at Soldier Field in Chicago. It was rumored Capone had big bets on Dempsey and had sent him a note warning him not to lose. Capone even met with the referee, Davey Miller, and told him he had bet $50,000 on the Manassa Mauler and that he wanted him to give Dempsey a fair shot. Interestingly, it was the same Davey Miller who had been wounded by Dion O'Banion four years earlier outside the LaSalle Theater.

Shortly before the fight, Miller was replaced as referee. Dempsey knocked Tunney down in the 7th round and would have won the fight had he gone to a neutral corner. Referee Dave (Long Count) Barry had to push Dempsey in the right direction before starting his count. Tunney barely got off the canvas before the count of ten, having been given five extra seconds. Tunney went on to win by a knockout in the 8th round of the controversial fight.

After it was over, Capone threw a large party at the Metropole Hotel that cost about $3,000.

Dempsey later worked for the Capone organization as a fight promoter but quit when he realized the fights were being fixed. The popular Dempsey next went into the hotel business in Miami Beach with a couple of Jewish New York racketeers and lived for 55 years more after the "long count" fight.

What happened when Torrio lost his nerve, quit the rackets, and moved to Italy?

It only lasted about 2½ years because Mussolini's Fascist government stamped him as an undesirable in an effort to rid that country of the Mafia and U.S. gangsters. Torrio returned to the U.S and got back in the business. Sicilians traditionally were a rebellious and anti-authoritarian people. When Mussolini came to power he decided Sicilians were a threat so he persecuted them. Lucky Luciano and Joe Bonanno were two other Sicilians who left their native country and came to America to escape persecution.

What were Italians called wops?

It comes from a corruption of the Italian word "guappo" that loosely translated means *handsome scoundrel.*

Was Capone a moviegoer?

Yes. With the darkened interior, Al could relax and let his guard down a little. He once went to see Al Jolson in *The Singing Fool* with a sixteen-year-old girl friend (Babe Sullivan) and her brother, who happened to be Al's caddy. When the movie ended and the lights came on, they were astounded to see tears streaming down Capone's cheeks.

Car with guns blazing

Al Capone (Famous Photos)

Jack Dempsey (author's collection)

What was the 1926 **Hotel Sherman Treaty**?

It was a big meeting between Capone and his men, and Joe Saltis and his mob, plus some smaller gangs. The purpose was to arrange a truce between the warring factions. No one was allowed to bring guns to the meeting, and reporters and police detectives waiting outside were kept informed about each step of progress that was made. In summary, each side agreed not to steal the other's customers nor encroach on their territory. Each was to be responsible for punishing any of its members who broke the agreement. The only reason Capone agreed to the meeting was that his son had a mastoid infection behind his ear, and he wanted to spend more time at home with him.

Big Bill Thompson (Chicago Historical Society)

What did **Mayor Big Bill Thompson** say he was going to do after losing the 1923 election?

The man who liked to wear big Stetsons said he was going on a south sea expedition to find **a rare fish specimen** that had the ability to live on land and could climb trees. Unbeknownst to Thompson, the Field Museum in Chicago already had a mudskipper on display.

Did Mayor Big Bill Thompson ever return to power after losing to the Democrats in 1923?

Yes. He made a comeback in the spring of 1927, winning a third term. He stooped to his usual demagoguery by criticizing the number of pro-British books in the Chicago Public Library. Thompson blamed the British for dragging us into World War I and thought our country should be isolationist. Capone secretly donated $260,000 to his campaign fund. All of it with strings attached, of course. Capone was to be given a free hand in prostitution, gambling joints, slot machines and booze distribution. Bill won a relatively peaceful election. Only two bombs were thrown, and a mere duo of election officials were beaten and kidnapped. The flamboyant Thompson, who was married but kept several mistresses, bought a $25,000 yacht which he dubbed "Big Bill," and had the front hull rigged with a figurehead that was a likeness of himself rather than the traditional full-busted mermaid. After he won the election, he started driving around Chicago at night in a touring car with a spotlight turned on him so people could see their new mayor.

Schemer Drucci on the coroner's slab (Famous Photos)

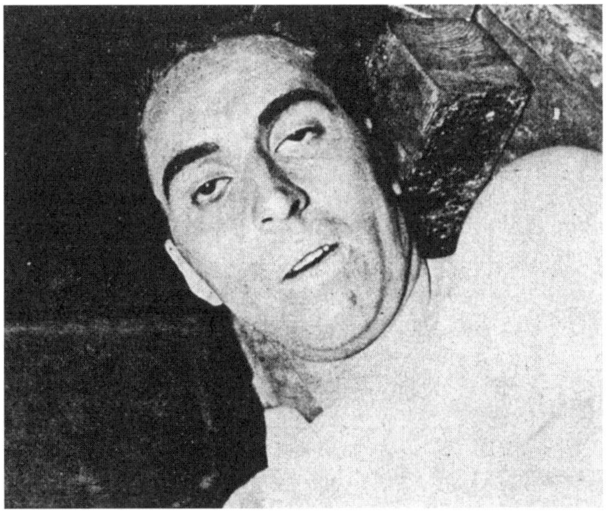

How did **Schemer Drucci** die?

Drucci decided to help Bill Thompson in the mayor's race by kidnapping a key advisor to his Democratic opponent. But he was caught red-handed and arrested by police. Four policemen escorted him in a car to the Criminal Court Building. On the way there, one of the policemen taunted him unmercifully. Drucci flew into a rage, struck the policeman and grabbed hold of him. The cop fired four shots at point blank range, killing him instantly. This was about three years after police had killed Frank Capone on the streets of Chicago.

Joe Aielo (National Archives)

What big event happened in Chicago on May 15, 1927?

Benito Mussolini, the popular dictator of Italy, sent one of his aviators on a world tour as a goodwill ambassador. Francesco de Pinedo landed his hydroplane on Lake Michigan. This event nearly coincided with the May transatlantic flight of Lindbergh. The city had a welcoming committee of bigwig politicians, and even Al Capone was added to the list. Officials explained that Capone was invited because it was hoped his presence would prevent any anti-fascist demonstrations.

How big a gambler was Al Capone?

Capone was compulsive, and when it came to horses he always bet big and to win – not place or show. In a span of about five years, it was said he lost ten million dollars alone on horse races in Chicago.

Who put out a $50,000 contract on Capone in the spring of 1927?

It was Sicilian **Joe Aiello,** who replaced the Gennas as the boss of the alky cooking industry in Chicago's Little Italy. They bribed a restaurant owner to put prussic acid in Capone's soup, but the man became frightened and told Capone about the plot. Two St. Louis torpedoes (hit men), **Tony Russo** and **Vincent Spicuzza** came to try and collect. But Tony and Vince were found shot dead shortly after they arrived. A nickel was found in each of their right hands, reported to be the trademark of **Machine Gun McGurn**. Sociologists think McGurn was a sociopath.

Ex-boxer, Machine Gun McGurn

What Chicagoan made a bid for the Republican U.S. presidential nomination in 1928?

It was Mayor Big Bill Thompson, credited with starting the America First movement. Since the presence of Big Al in Chicago would be an embarrassment to his bid for national office, Capone was pressured to take a vacation. Capone chose to leave for St. Petersburg, Florida, but at the last minute he changed his mind and went to L.A. He found a cold reception there, and the police chief gave him 24 hours to leave. Capone went back to Chicago and was arrested every time he appeared in public, for the sake of appearances. But the pressure was off when Thompson saw he had no chance to win the U.S. presidential nomination and withdrew from the race. At the end of December in 1927, Capone and his family quietly went to Miami and rented a privately owned bungalow. In all, Thompson served three terms as Chicago's mayor.

Why did Big Bill Thompson criticize England's King George V in speech after speech?

Thompson, considered by many to be a blustery buffoon, railed against America becoming entangled in foreign affairs. He was anti-League of Nations, anti-World Court. "Keep out of foreign wars and make the King of England keep his nose out of our affairs," he said. Thompson was an Anglophobe who saw to it that the official language of Illinois was called American – not English. In all likelihood, Thompson was angling for German, Irish, and Polish votes in elections, thinking these workingmen would hate the very mention of a king. A reporter once wisecracked: "**Thompson's for America First and Capone's for America's Thirst**."

Towser is asleep and friendly to crooks (*Chicago Tribune*)

Why are policemen sometimes referred to as coppers?

An early mayor of Chicago, John Haines, invested heavily in copper and was called "Copper Stock" Haines. This, in turn, led to his policemen being called coppers. This author has heard many other explanations, including the fact that early badges were often made of copper.

Did Al Capone ever play any competitive sports?

While he was in Miami, he took up tennis. He performed poorly and frequently threw or smashed his racket.

Did Capone ever go hunting?

In November of 1927 Capone sent some of his men to Marshall Field's department store to spend $5,000 on hunting and camping equipment. Capone decided that he needed a vacation from the gang wars by going to northern Wisconsin. When he got back on December 5, he held a press conference in the **Metropole Hotel** on 2300 South Michigan Avenue. He spouted bits of wisdom to reporters in his suite of rooms (409-10) from his favorite easy chair. He told them he was going to retire and go to St. Petersburg, Florida. Supplying the people of Chicago with liquor was a thankless job, Al told them.

"YOU CAN ALL GO THIRSTY" IS AL CAPONE'S ADIEU

Chicago Tribune – Dec 6, 1927

Did Capone ever own a home in Miami?

Yes. He bought a winter residence on Palm Island that had been built in 1922 by the **St. Louis** brewmeister, **Clarence M. Busch.** His new villa was neo-Spanish in architectural style, bright white, with a green-tiled roof, fourteen enormous rooms, several patios and a large porch. Capone spent over $100,000 renovating the place and improving security. A high wall was built around the garden. Capone also added a swimming pool, a boathouse, and several large fishing boats that were docked off his landing.

When was Mayor **Big Bill Thompson** finally thrown out of office?

There was tremendous violence in the April 1928 Chicago primary elections. There was so much violence (61 bombings) and so many bombs between rival Republican factions (U.S. Senator Deneen and Diamond Joe versus Thompson and Small) that it is sometimes referred to as the **Pineapple (hand grenade) Primary**. The Thompson/Small/Crowe forces had never lost a primary, but this time the excessive violence backfired and voters turned out in record numbers to throw the bums out of office.

One of the men killed in the violence was restauranteer (The Napoli) **Diamond Joe Esposito**. His belt buckle was encrusted with diamonds, and he came to be known as the Mayor of Little Italy (45,000 strong), the King of the Valley. He was in power from 1920 to 1928, and he kept an $80,000 summer home on Bass Lake in Indiana. Jane Addams' Hull House (she would eventually win the Nobel Peace Prize) was in Esposito's district, but she only accepted his donations when sent by an emissary.

Diamond Joe Esposito (author's collection)

It was said that Esposito was apraised of all upcoming Italian nuptials and bedded the more desirable women first. He obviously made many enemies during his reign.

Several days before the primary, Esposito was warned to get out of town or be killed. He refused to leave. Senator Deneen's home was wrecked by a bomb, but the Thompson people claimed Deneen's own thugs probably did it to gain the sympathy vote – an explanation that dumbfounded Chicagoans. Diamond Joe was gunned down on the streets by men in a slow-moving car. His bodyguards, the Varchetti brothers, dropped down to the sidewalk to avoid the gunfire, and they survived.

When did **Big Bill Thompson** suffer his final political defeat?

Thompson defeated Judge Lyle in the 1932 Republican primary, but he lost the general election to **Anton J. Cermak**. Cermak went to Miami in February of 1933 to greet president-elect Franklin D. Roosevelt. He was accidentally shot by gunman **Giuseppe Zangara,** who was trying to kill Franklin Roosevelt. Of course, revisionist historians maintain Zangara actually was hired by Al Capone to kill Cermak for depriving him of his greatest political ally. Others say the hit was ordered by Frank Nitti and Murray Humphreys, Capone's successors, because Cermak had promised in his campaign to run them out of Chicago.

After losing a 4th term bid, did **Big Bill Thompson** give up on trying to become mayor again?

No. He died on March 19, 1944, after suffering a crushing defeat in the Republican primary.

In the summer of 1928, what became Capone's new headquarters in Chicago?

He moved diagonally across the street from the Metropole on on South Michigan Boulevard to the **Lexington Hotel**, his associates occupying all of the fourth floor and much of the third floor.

Who were the Annenbergs?

Max Annenberg was circulation manager for Colonel Robert McCormick's Chicago *Tribune*. He once called Capone to his office and asked him to intercede and prevent a damaging strike by the delivery drivers. For years Capone liked to tell people how he helped solve Chicago's labor problems. Moses (Moe) Annenberg, Max's brother, was the father of Walter Annenberg who owned the Daily Racing Form, a news service for track bettors. Walter was later appointed ambassador to England. Moe was sent to jail in 1940 for tax evasion. It was the Annenberg family who founded **"TV Guide"** magazine and **"Seventeen"** magazine for young women.

What popular number one radio show originated in Chicago around 1928 starring Freeman Godsen and Charles Correll?

Freeman Godsen and **Charles Correll** had a blackface vaudeville act that they brought to Chicago radio. Within a year **Amos 'n Andy** was a hit show on NBC radio. Their program was so popular in the 1930s that movie theaters often stopped the film they were showing and piped the 15-minute radio broadcast over the loudspeakers for the audience. When the radio show ended, the film was resumed.

How can it be said Al Capone saved jazz music as an art form?

Jazz (originally called jass, a Negro euphemism for sex) originated in New Orleans after the turn of the century in the honky-tonk red light district of Storyville. But the U.S. Navy, during World War I, shut the place down because so many military men were contracting venereal diseases. When Chicago became famous for its speakeasies and thirst clinics during Prohibition, the musicians, including **Louis Armstrong**, moved north to ply their trade. Chicago became *the* place for young musicians, black and white, to learn the craft and play their music. Armstrong, incidentally, was an ardent smoker of marijuana, which wasn't made illegal until 1937. (Incredibly, the gravel-voiced Armstrong would become the oldest singer to have a number 1 hit record with "**Hello Dolly**" in the early 1960s.)

Bob Hope (Famous Photos Inc.)

Capone had cabarets and after-hours joints all around town. Capone used to say he loved jazz because "it's got guts, and it don't make you slobber." People like **Bing Crosby**, **Bob Hope**, **Eddie Condon** and **Bix Biderbecke** played these clubs, and it was frequently dangerous. Fights and shootings were not uncommon. Few musicians left their instruments overnight for fear the place might be bombed or burned.

What finally happened to **Frankie Yale**?

Capone had a bootleg deal going with Yale, but he suspected Yale was chiseling. Capone hired Machine Gun McGurn and four other plug-uglies to gun him down. They caught up with Yale in Brooklyn while he was driving his car on July 1 of 1928. They pulled along side and blasted him to kingdom come. Yale had a bulletproof car, but he forgot to do anything about the windows. More people attended his funeral on July 5 than the 20,000 who showed up for Dion O'Banion's funeral. This was the **first tommy gun murder** in New York's history.

What were the circumstances leading up to the **St. Valentine's Day Massacre** on February 14, 1929?

Capone was bedeviled by **Bugs Moran's** Irish gang from the north side of Chicago. They hijacked his liquor, bombed his establishments and tried to murder his associates – notably a near successful killing of Machine Gun McGurn. Moran gave interviews in which he taunted Capone by calling him an *ape* and a *behemoth* who was on dope. He also accused him of selling inferior rotgut. **Machine Gun McGurn** masterminded the plan to lure Moran and his men to an abandoned garage at 2122 North Clark Street. Outside hit men were recruited for the job so if any of the intended victims survived, they would be unable to identify their attackers. **Fred "Killer" Burke** was brought in from St. Louis to head the project. Burke was with the Egan Rats gang. Another Rats member named **James Ray** also participated. McGurn decided to use the ruse of men dressed as Chicago policemen, ostensibly conducting a Prohibition raid, to give the element of surprise. A police car and several uniforms were stolen on the day of the attack. Moran and his men went to the garage, thinking they were going to purchase a shipment of Canadian whiskey. At 10:30, on the morning of the 14th, the police car arrived with its distinctive gong ringing. Four men jumped out, two of them wearing police uniforms. Their guns were wrapped with newspapers to look like packages. The men in the garage were disarmed and then mowed down. One of those killed was an innocent dentist who was there by happenstance because he was a crook buff. As it turned out, **seven men were killed**, but Bugs Moran was not one of them. He was a few minutes late to the meeting and arrived on the scene just in time to see the police car pull up to the garage. Not wanting to get caught in a raid, he kept on walking and unwittingly saved his life. Autopsies revealed each man had been shot about fifteen times. Years later, when Moran's garage was torn down, a large crowd gathered to collect pieces as souvenirs.

Bugs Moran (Famous Photos Inc.)

Capone was back in Florida at his Palm Island villa with his platinum blonde wife (Mae) so he would have a perfect alibi. McGurn kept him informed of what was going on with regular phone calls. The only living being to escape the slaughter that day was a German shepherd dog (Highball) chained to a truck. The dog was making such a fuss, the men wanted to kill it too, but McGurn wouldn't let them. From 1924 to 1928 there were about 38 murders attributed to inter-gang warfare in Chicago. Everyone knew that Capone and his men were behind the massacre, but no one was ever convicted of committing the crime. Fearing a gangland bloodbath of reprisals and counter reprisals was about to occur, about thirty hoodlums and racketeers decided to leave Chicago for good and headed for the sunny climes of Florida.

St. Valentine's Day Massacre (Chicago Historical Society)

There was a persistent rumor that the crime had actually been perpetrated by Chicago police, but there was no equipment available to analyze the bullets. A couple of years later, a forensics lab was established at Northwestern University. All of the Thompson machine guns owned by the Chicago police (at the time of the shootings) were tested by firing rounds into cotton waste material. (Today, such labs fire weapons into containers of water with a mesh tray at the bottom.) The experts were unable to match any of the tested bullets and shells with those recovered after the murders, thus exonerating the Cook County police.

McGurn, the mastermind of the **Crime of the Century**, married his live-in girlfriend, Louise Rolfe, at the Lexington so she couldn't be forced to testify against him in court. She became known as the "**Blonde Alibi**," telling authorities that she and McGurn were in bed all day making love on Valentine's Day.

A coroner's jury decided there wasn't enough evidence to charge anyone, but they were convinced **Fred Burke**, a former member of the **St. Louis Egan Rats**, was one of the triggermen. Burke eventually died in the Michigan state prison, serving a life term for killing a policeman.

The **St. Valentine's Day Massacre** was the biggest story to come out of Prohibition. In 1967 **Jason Robards** and **George Segal** starred in the movie depicting the event.

McGurn & alibi, Louise Rolfe (author's collection)

SAINT VALENTINE'S DAY MASSACRE

Why did Capone give a huge banquet party on May 7, 1929, at a roadhouse near Hammond, Indiana, a small town he controlled?

He did it to lure several Sicilian thugs who were conspiring against him. **Joe Guinta**, **John Scalise** and **Albert Anselmi** were among the dozens of mobsters invited. Late in the evening the three were accused of being traitors and were bound to their chairs. **Capone then beat them to a bloody pulp with a baseball bat**. After that they were shot. The next morning the bodies were found on a road near Wolf Lake, Indiana. It was probably the most grotesque, sadistic act ever committed by Al Capone.

Did Capone attend a national meeting of gangsters in Atlantic City, New Jersey, May 13-15, 1929?

Yes. He told people he was going to a prizefight, but it was to attend the big meeting. This **Who's Who of Racketeers** included New Yorkers **Albert Anastasia**, Lucky Luciano, **Joe Costello**, Dutch Schultz, and Jack Guzik from Chicago. Even Johnny Torrio came out of retirement and was there. There were lesser-known thugs from places such as Cleveland and Detroit. Instead of meeting in a smoke filled room, they discussed matters on the Boardwalk and on the beach. Capone was shunned by most of them because they thought of themselves as respectable businessmen, and Capone was responsible for too much violence. They decided Capone should be forced to retire and his holdings would be parceled out to other members of the group. Johnny Torrio was scheduled to become the new commissioner of this network.

Albert Anselmi and John Scalise (Chicago H.S.)

How did Capone end up at **Holmesburg County Prison** in Pennsylvania in May of 1929?

After the big racketeers' meeting, thinking he would be killed when he went back to Chicago, Capone made sure he was arrested on a concealed weapons charge in Philadelphia. He was then taken before Judge John Walsh, assuming he was going to receive a sentence of a month or two. Walsh gave him a full year. This was the first time Capone had ever been behind bars. Capone sent out word he would give $50,000 to any lawyer who could get him out, but it was no use. Ironically, the prison warden treated Capone like a celebrity, allowing him to furnish his own cell and granting visiting privileges every day of the week. His work detail was clerking in the library. Capone was a model prisoner, and during his tenure a prison surgeon removed his inflamed tonsils. The good behavior led to two months being knocked off his sentence, and he was released on March 17, 1930.

Joe "Hop Toad" Guinta

Was Capone ever allied with the **Egan Rats gang in St. Louis**?

Yes. He had a nation-wide network of alliances that included the Egan Rats, the Jewish Purple Gang in Detroit and the Hoff Gang in Philadelphia.

How dangerous was it to become president of the Italo-American Union in Chicago?

It was deadly. Those who ascended to the presidency and were murdered included: Tony Lombardo, Anthony D'Andrea, Pasquale Lolordo, Peter Rizzito, Agostino Loverdo and **Joe Aiello**.

When Capone began to realize Prohibition would not last, what other field did he move into as a money maker?

He bought interests in pinball machines, nightclubs, and moved into the protection business. Estimates of the annual cost to consumers of racketeering activity ran as high as $36 million in Chicago. A list was compiled in 1928 showing that about 91 unions had fallen under the thumb of racketeers.

Who invented the **mechanical rabbit** that led to dog racing becoming a popular activity?

It was a promoter and greyhound lover **from St. Louis** by the name of **Oliver P. Smith**. He invented the device around 1909 and spent several years testing and perfecting it. He then formed a partnership with an astute Irish lawyer from St. Louis named **Edward J. O'Hare**. O'Hare soon realized dog racing was so profitable he decided to open a track of his own. It was known as the Madison Kennel Club, and it was located just **north of East St. Louis**. O'Hare married at a young age and fathered three children, including a lad named Edward who became known as Butch. O'Hare also built tracks in Chicago and went into partnership with Al Capone. He was gunned down November 8, 1939, while driving his car on Ogden Avenue. This happened shortly after Capone was released from Alcatraz, purportedly a payback for being a snitch in Capone's tax trial.

Bodies of Anselmi, Scalise, Guinta

Whom did Capone hire to "clean up his image?"

It was Chicago writer **Damon Runyon**, who wintered in Florida on an island near Capone's villa. He advised Capone to give the impression that he had quit Chicago and retired from the rackets. Runyon liked Al Capone and cared little about his illegal activities, preferring to use him in his articles and stories.

After **Herbert Hoover** won the 1928 election and took office in March of 1929, what did he plan to do about Al Capone?

Incredibly, Hoover hardly knew who Capone was. He had to be given all the details by **Colonel Robert McCormick**, the publisher of the *Chicago Tribune,* who was a staunch Republican but a foe of Prohibition. It was McCormick who suggested to Hoover that the government nail Capone for failure to pay taxes. Capone was difficult to nab because he endorsed no checks and kept no bank accounts – a trick he learned from Johnny Torrio.

Eliot Ness (Cleveland S. Univ. Archives)

How did **Billy Sunday**, the famous Chicago evangelist, feel about Al Capone?

Sunday, an ardent opponent of Prohibition, rented a theater in the Loop and preached against Capone for seven straight days. "I'm going to do my level best to give Capone and his gang of cutthroats the hot end of a poker," he said. Sunday planned to "preach Capone out of Chicago."

How did Capone get to be **Public Enemy Number 1**?

The first list was actually complied by Frank Loesch, the 78 year-old head of Chicago's Crime Commission. His list, which also included Ralph Capone, Frank Raio, Jack McGurn, "Bugs" Moran and Joe Aiello, was published by the *Chicago Tribune*. The list was reproduced by many other newspapers in the USA.

How did the ***Untouchables*** federal crime unit come into existence?

President Hoover eventually came to see Capone as a national embarrassment. Hoover was the moving force behind the creation of a special squad from the Department of Justice to break up Capone's ability to make money and another squad of Internal Revenue agents to get the goods on him and send him to jail. Ness and his men made life miserable for Capone with raid after raid on his establishments. **Elliot Ness** was the leader of nine specially trained agents who earned the sobriquet "untouchables" because they couldn't be bought.

Capone had been advised by inept lawyers that he didn't need to file tax returns since his income was derived from illegal activities. Capone agreed it didn't make sense for the government to try and collect legal taxes on illegal income. Filing such a return, he figured, would violate the Fifth Amendment right not to incriminate one's self.

Frank "the Enforcer" Nitti

Ralph Capone, Al's brother, was given a three-year sentence for tax evasion. Frank "the enforcer" Nitti received an 18-month sentence. It was more difficult nailing Al because he never opened any bank accounts, signed no checks or receipts, and didn't own property in his name. He kept his stash of money in a large wooden chest at the foot of his bed and paid people in cash. This prompted the agents to compile a list of his expenses for goods and services, such as telephone bills. But to get at his real source of income from speakeasies, gambling houses and brothels, the Feds bribed one of the prostitutes to collect evidence for them.

Ness later claimed to have raided 25 of Capone's breweries and seized 45 of his delivery trucks. Ness loved publicity, and these figures were probably inflated.

The blue-eyed, blondish Ness was born in Chicago in 1903, the son of Norwegian immigrants. He was named for the famed writer, George Eliot. His father ran a bakery, and his older sister married an FBI agent. Ness studied jujitsu for self-defense and never carried a gun. Handsome and personable, he had many love affairs and several marriages.

Italian-Americans took offense at the *Untouchables* TV show in 1959 and protested, claiming they were being stereotyped. Objections by the Federation of Italian-Americans led Chesterfield cigarettes to stop sponsoring the show and it went off the air not long after that. (In later years, when the movie ***The Godfather*** was filmed, these same Italian-Americans forced the director to eliminate the word "Mafia" from the final version.)

Neville Brand as Capone on TV

How many gangland slayings were there in Chicago from the start of Prohibition to its end?

According to one tally, an astounding 530.

How did Miami, Florida, authorities harass Al Capone?

They did not want Capone around and harassed him by arresting him repeatedly on vagrancy charges or by saying he was wanted for questioning. He was arrested on at least three different occasions in 1930, but Al and his lawyers obtained an injunction against these tactics. He was successful, but a later court overturned the prior decision. Authorities tried to close Capone's estate at Palm Island by declaring it a "public nuisance," but the case was dismissed.

What and where is **Chicago's Gold Coast**?

It was a posh section of town near 1100 Lake Shore Drive where many of the city's richest and most powerful people lived. **Samuel Insull**, the founder of Commonwealth Edison, Chicago's utility company, lived there. At one point in the bull market of the Twenties, Insull was worth $170 million. But a combination of bad decisions, the Depression, and House of Morgan manipulators in NYC, brought him crashing down to bankruptcy in 1932, causing banks to fail and thousands who had invested in his company to go bust – much like the 2002 Enron scandal in Texas.

Miami police mug shot of Al Capone

How did Capone try to deal with Ness?

He sent a go-between to his office and offered him a bribe to lay off raiding his breweries – two crisp one thousand dollar bills. Ness turned it down. In all probability, Ness and Capone never had any one-on-one conversations. It is interesting to note that a hundred dollar bill is the largest denomination currently being printed by the U.S. government.

What was a "soft drink parlor?"

This was a euphemism for a speakeasy.

Is it true Capone ran a soup kitchen for the needy and unemployed?

Yes, at the cost of about $10,000 a month. It was the first one in Chicago after the Depression hit. His sign at the kitchen read: Free Food For The Workless. But Capone did not bear the entire financial burden. He "encouraged" local butchers, bakers and coffee roasters to contribute.

Capone's Soup Kitchen (UPI)

Why was Chicago *Tribune* reporter **Jake Lingle** murdered?

Lingle's extravagant lifestyle for a $65-a-week reporter puzzled some people. Jake explained it away by telling friends that part of it was an inheritance and the rest came from smart investments in the bull stock market. Lingle was shot in the head at an Illinois Central train station near Michigan Avenue. (Note**: Ralph Anderson** of Edwardsville says that many books have this fact wrong. He asserts Lingle was shot in a subway that allowed people to walk under busy Michigan Avenue to get to the Illinois Central station. This enabled them to board a streetcar to get to suburban towns east of Chicago. At the time, Lingle was heading for the Washington Park racetrack to gamble some of his ill-gotten bucks.)

Lingle was killed on June 9th in 1929, the 11th Chicago killing in ten days. In an editorial, Robert McCormick's *Tribune* said he was killed because as a police beat reporter he was too good at his job; it was an act of intimidation. It looked as if gangland had stepped over the line. But after huge rewards were offered to bring his killers to justice, the image of Lingle as a First Amendment martyr began to crumble. Under close scrutiny, the image of Lingle the reporter deteriorated to Lingle the racketeer. His inheritance and stock profit claims were exposed as a sham. It soon became clear Lingle consorted with the underworld and earned extra money as a middleman between Chicago politicians and the Capone organization.

Reporter Jake Lingle's impressive funeral (Illinois Historical Society)

In all probability, Lingle was being paid to keep certain facts he came across in his line of work from getting into print. He decided to ask for more, and that's when they decided to kill him. Another possibility is that Capone found out that he had agreed to inform on him to the Treasury Department. Lingle was only 39 when he was shot. Lingle was killed the day before he was to meet with the T-Men, a meeting arranged by Colonel

McCormick, the *Tribune's* owner. The *St. Louis Post-Dispatch* began publishing a series of articles that described Lingle as a "fixer." Investigations showed that in a two-year period, Lingle had deposited $64,000 into his account at the Lake Shore Trust bank. Lingle also wore a diamond studded belt buckle, given to him by Capone.

Jake Lingle's body in the subway (*Chicago Herald*)

Was anyone ever convicted in the Jake Lingle slaying?

Yes. It was a tall blonde man from **St. Louis** named **Leo V. Brothers**, a thirty-something labor slugger. At his trial, half the witnesses identified him as the man fleeing the scene while the other half could not. None identified him as the actual shooter. He was found guilty on April 2 of 1931 and sentenced to fourteen years in prison.

What did Europeans think of Prohibition?

The liquor lovers across the big pond thought it was appallingly stupid and tended to be sympathetic to American gangsters who broke the law.

What kind of a reception did Capone receive when he attended a football game at Northwestern University?

Capone was cheered when he made public appearances at Wrigley Field, Soldier Field or at racetracks. But he and Jake McGurn were roundly booed at Dyche Stadium while attending a football game. This was followed by an article in the student newspaper that said Capone was unwelcome at Northwestern football games. It is interesting to note that Northwestern takes its name from the fact Illinois was once part of the Northwest Territory, created in 1785.

What was **Capone Castle**?

It was what tour bus drivers called Capone's Hawthorne Inn as they passed it.

What was the first movie made about Al Capone?

After **Edward G. Robinson** starred in *Little Caesar* (1930) and **James Cagney** in *Public Enemy* (1931), **Howard Hughes** studio went to work on *Scarface,* starring **Paul Muni**, with screenplay by Chicagoan and former newsman **Ben Hecht**. It was an enormous hit when it was released in 1932. Will Hays' censorship office forced them to tack on the subtitle, *The Shame of the Nation.* **George Raft** played the part of a psychopath gangster who cut out paper dolls in his spare time. When Raft wasn't making movies he loved to chum around with real-life gangsters.

What was the Secret Six?

It was a vigilante group of wealthy Chicago businessmen who dedicated themselves to ridding Chicago of Al Capone. The Six were headed by Colonel Robert McCormick, who once met with Capone at the Lexington Hotel to try and convince him to quit the business. Capone told McCormick he employed 135 men who were gangsters and ex-cons, and if he went out of business, these men would simply prey on the town. Capone also met with journalist **Cornelius Vanderbilt Jr.** Capone upbraided him and claimed people like his dad were just crooks in their own right. The group was accused of vigilantism and bending the law, so the anti-crime group was disbanded in 1933.

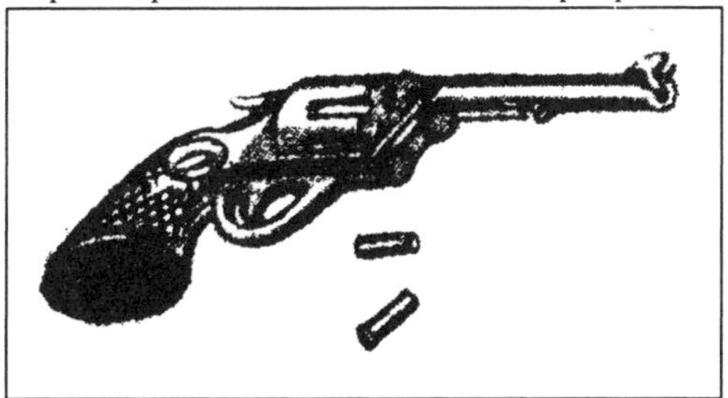

Who was the government's greatest ally in preparing its tax fraud case against Capone?

It was St. Louis lawyer and dog track operator, **Edward O'Hare**. *Post-Dispatch* reporter John Rogers introduced O'Hare to investigators at the **Missouri Athletic Club** on Washington Avenue in St. Louis. O'Hare wanted his son Butch to go to Annapolis, and he hoped that his cooperation would help him get an appointment. On

Saturday, October 24, 1931, Judge **James Wilkerson** imposed a $50,000 fine and eleven years in prison for tax evasion – the toughest penalty ever handed down to date for tax evasion. During the eleven-day trial, Capone wore eleven different suits. The jury deliberated about eight hours. One of his prosecutors, **Dwight Green**, went on to become governor of Illinois in the 1940s. The government also froze Capone's assets so he could not sell or transfer them before paying his fine. Capone arrived at the Cook County Jail on October 24, 1931, where he was treated like a VIP.

Capone: Time's Man of the Year for 1930

Did **Butch O'Hare** ever get his commission to Annapolis?

Yes. He graduated from Annapolis in 1937, and during the war, he received the Congressional Medal of Honor for **shooting down five Japanese medium bombers** in his Grumman Wildcat fighter plane. He was given the Congressional Medal of Honor by FDR. A year later he was killed in aerial combat near Tarawa in the Gilbert Islands. O'Hare's father, the informer, later became president of Sportsman's Park and manager of the Chicago Cardinals pro football team. On November 8, 1939, his dad was blasted by two men with shotguns in a passing car on Ogden Avenue. The killers were never caught. In 1949 Chicago International Airport was **renamed O'Hare Airport**.

Did Al Capone receive a fair trial?

Probably not. The IRS couldn't prove Capone's income, so they called in witness after witness, who described his extravagant lifestyle and reported seeing him carry around huge wads of cash. The government put heavy pressure on the prosecutors and the judge to get a conviction. Incredibly, the prosecution team did a masterful job while Capone's lawyers botched it. Defense put witnesses on the stand who testified Capone didn't have much money because he lost such huge sums betting. But the judge noted, "What you pay out is at least a circumstance to show that you got something in." At the conclusion of the eleven-day trial, the judge even went so far in his instructions to the jury to tell them exactly how they could find Capone guilty, despite the dearth of hard evidence against him. On the other hand, Capone's men tried to bribe or intimidate all of the jurors. After the conviction, Al complained that his blankety-blank dumb lawyers couldn't spring a pickpocket. Poor Al wasn't going to be around for the **Chicago World's Fair** in 1933.

What happened to Capone's brother, Ralph?

Ralph "Bottles" Capone was also indicted for tax evasion in April of 1930. Ralph was married to a woman named Valma and had a fourteen-year-old son, Ralph Jr. Ralph gave his address as 7244 Prairie Ave. Ralph was listed by the Chicago Crime Commission as Public Enemy Number 3. He was found guilty and sentenced to three years in Leavenworth. He was out many months on appeals, but his last stay finally expired.

On his arrival at Leavenworth, he was immediately transferred to McNeil Island in Puget Sound in the state of Washington. While there, he worked on a road repair gang. He got out of prison in February, 1934. Ralph quickly went back to his old racketeering life of bending the rules and breaking the law. It is interesting to note that the recidivism rate for criminals has been at about 60 percent for decades.

CAPONE'S BROTHER LEAVES FLORIDA TO GIVE UP

New York Times – Nov. 4, 1931

What happened to **Jack "Greasy Thumb" Guzik,** Capone's bookkeeper?

He was indicted for failing to file tax returns for 1927, 1928, and 1929. He was found guilty and sent to jail in 1932 after he ran out of appeals.

What comic strip creator got his plot ideas from Chicago newspaper headlines?

Chester Gould's comic strip character **Dick Tracy** began appearing regularly in Chicago newspapers in 1931. Eliot Ness was thought to be the prototype for Dick Tracy. Chicagoan Gould used Capone in his strip but gave him the title **Big Boy**. Ness wanted to become an FBI agent, but somehow the appointment from J. Edgar Hoover never came. He took a job in Cleveland as the public safety director and had a checkered career. He was soundly defeated in a bid to become mayor of Cleveland. The thrice wed, alcoholic Ness died prematurely from a heart attack at the age of 54 in 1957. Two years later, he was immortalized by **Robert Stack** in the television show, *The Untouchables*.

Robert Stack as Eliot Ness

What did Sonny (Al's son) and the rest of the Capone family think of ***The Untouchables*** 1959 television series?

They filed suit to stop it, claiming the network was trying to make money off a dead man, but they lost.

What mobster dignitaries visited Capone while he was in the Cook County Jail?

He was visited by **Johnny Torrio**, **Dutch Schultz** and **Lucky Luciano**. Capone apparently served as an arbiter in a territorial dispute between Luciano and the Dutchman. Capone told Warden Moneypenny he needed privacy for the meeting, so he was allowed to use the **death chamber**. Capone presided over the meeting while **sitting in the electric chair**. When the judge found out Capone was running his business from his jail cell, he used his influence to get him sent to Atlanta as quickly as possible. Capone even offered to let the warden use his $4,500 **16 cylinder Cadillac**.

Herald and Examiner — Chicago — LAST METROPOLITAN

FRIDAY, MARCH 11, 1932 — Telephone Randolph 2121 — PRICE 3 CENTS

'LET ME HUNT LINDY'S BABY!' AL CAPONE PLEADS WITH U. S.

How did Capone offer to help in the **Lindbergh baby kidnapping case**?

Capone was interviewed by a Hearst columnist, and he told him that if released, he would do everything he could to get the baby back. If anyone connected to the mob had anything to do with it, he could find this out, he said. Capone proposed that his brother take his place in jail as a guarantee he would return after it was over. Even **Will Rogers**, the humorist, visited Capone in his cell to get his take on the kidnapping for his weekly column. But government and prison officials weren't interested. Charles Lindbergh was intrigued by Capone's offer but was finally convinced by authorities to nix the idea. Kidnapped on March 1, 1932, the baby's badly deteriorated body was found a couple months later in May. On June 22, 1932, Congress passed the Lindbergh Law, making it a federal crime to take a kidnapped person across state lines.

In a nutty 1981 book, based on the psychic revelations of **Edgar Cayce**, *In Search of the Lindbergh Baby*, Theon Wright asserts the kidnapping was carried out by the Capone mob in a plan to get Capone released from prison. It also claims the dead baby found by authorities wasn't Lindbergh's and that his son was raised by his abductors and grew up in a Michigan town.

"Looks as if we got the old fort rebuilt just in time."

Where was Capone taken after his short stay in the county jail?

He was taken to the federal penitentiary in Atlanta by train, the Dixie Flyer, a regularly scheduled Pullman. His prison number was 40,822. Capone used smuggled-in cash to bribe the guards to make his life easier in the Atlanta pen. He was put to work eight hours a day cobbling shoes.

Capone on the train (Famous Photos)

What was the result of Capone's physical exam, administered by prison doctors?

For the first time his syphilis was officially detected. It was now in the 3rd stage and was incurable. It would eat away at his brain and cause Alzheimer-like behavior. The wonder drug penicillin did not become available until 1942, but even then its use was reserved for military purposes.

What happened to Johnny Torrio after Capone went to jail?

Torrio left Chicago for New York and formed a partnership with Dutch Shultz. Capone wrote him a letter urging him to dissolve the partnership, but Torrio ignored him. **Capone hated Schultz** and never forgave Torrio. He ordered his wife to tear up the bonds Torrio had sent his son every year on his birthday, which were now worth about $80,000.

How did **Alcatraz** come into existence as a maximum-security prison?

U.S. Attorney General Homer Cummings suggested it in a 1933 letter to the director of U.S. prisons. He thought a place in Alaska or an island could be used to lessen prisoner contact with outsiders and to make escapes more difficult. Alcatraz became America's kinder, gentler version of Devil's Island. Authorities decided to remove about 100 men from Atlanta and Leavenworth to Alcatraz. The restored military garrison was located near the Golden Gate Bridge in San Francisco Bay, more than a mile from land. The current there was swift and dangerous. On top of that there was a treacherous riptide. Prisoners were warned that the waters were infested with **ravenous sharks**. Alcatraz was given its name by Spanish explorers, and it means Pelican Island. During the Civil War Union forces imprisoned a few Confederates at "Fort Alcatraz."

Chicago Daily News

Alcatraz is approximately twelve acres in size. Its highest point is about 136 feet above the level of the water. Many new security features were installed, including bars that were casehardened against tools. The cells were single occupancy and were a claustophobic eight feet by four feet. The Hole was a small cell with a steel door that was in total darkness. It had what was called an Oriental toilet – a hole in the floor with a flushing unit operated by one of the guards. In case of a disturbance at the mess hall, a rack of tear gas canisters were located in the ceiling. Prisoners quickly dubbed the room **the gas chamber**.

On August 22, 1934, a six-car train with specially constructed prisoner cars with bars on the windows took Capone and 52 other prisoners to Alcatraz. The floor of the train cars had boilerplate. When the train arrived at the shore near Alcatraz, the cars were loaded onto barges and taken across the water under the watchful eye of an armed Coast Guard cutter. The prisoners wore leg irons and handcuffs. About 85 men were transferred from Atlanta. About a month later, 100 more arrived from Leavenworth, Kansas, and Lewisburg, Pennsylvania.

In the beginning, a strict code of silence was enforced at Alcatraz, "The Rock" was designed to be escape proof. Prisoners were allowed one visit a month from blood relatives and no more than two at a time. Alcatraz was strictly a place for punishment – not rehabilitation.

What did Capone do for a diversion at Alcatraz?

He tried to make the softball team, but he was so clumsy he was relegated to the bench. He also pitched horseshoes. He took up playing the banjo and helped organize a band. **Machine Gun Kelly** played the drums. (Kelly was so good he could write his name on a barn wall with his tommy gun.) But much of the time, with his mind slipping badly, Capone lost himself in nostalgic reveries of his wife and son. Guards and prisoners alike were unaware of his neuro-syphilis, and they assumed he was stir crazy from spending too much time behind bars.

What special considerations did Capone receive from the warden at Alcatraz?

None! Warden Johnston was determined Capone would soon be just another number (85) at his prison. Even talking was forbidden among the prisoners. Nor were they allowed to listen to the radio or read newspapers. Guards practiced their shooting in the yard by using realistic-looking dummies. When finished, they left them there for the prisoners to see. Time in "The Hole" was limited to 19 days as psychologists thought that was the extent of human endurance. Alcatraz had one guard for every three prisoners. In one year alone, fourteen prisoners went insane. Several committed suicide. Five men tried to escape while Capone was there, but they were all shot or drowned.

Alcatraz (San Francisco Maritime Museum)

How much time off for good behavior could a prisoner earn to reduce his prison sentence back then?

Surprisingly, it was as much as ten days a month.

What was Capone's first job at Alcatraz?

He operated an ironing machine called a mangle in the laundry room that rolled and pressed items that it was fed. Not only did prisoners wash the gray denim prison outfits, they washed uniforms of nearby army bases, including **The Presidio**. Capone also mopped the floors and that prompted other prisoners to call him the "**Wop with the mop**." Other notable felons at The Rock were **Arthur Barker** (Ma Barker's last surviving son) and Roy Gardner (a notorious train robber) and **Alvin Karpis,** a new "Public Enemy Number 1," who arrived in 1936).

Capone's villa on Palm Island (Wide World)

Was Capone ever attacked at Alcatraz?

Yes. He was stabbed in the back with a pair of scissors in the prison barbershop. The perpetrator who did it had another twelve years tacked on to his sentence. Another time an inmate jumped him when he was on his way to see the prison dentist. Capone was nearly strangled before he broke his attacker's grip and knocked him unconscious. These incidents were widely reported in the press, and soon condemnation began to be heaped on Alcatraz. Many said it was some kind of unconscionable Devil's Island and an exercise in cruel government sadism.

Capone's villa on Palm Island in Florida (Famous Photos Inc.)

How did Capone try to bribe the new director of the U.S. Bureau of Prisons, James Bennett?

Capone wanted Bennett to transfer him from Alcatraz to a prison on the mainland to serve out the rest of his term. In return, Capone said he would give Bennett all the information he needed to write a biography of himself. Al even said he would throw in the movie rights.

How did the public come to know many of the details about what went on at Alcatraz back in the 1930s?

Alvin Karpis kept a diary of events and goings-on and described them in vivid detail.

How many years in prison did Capone serve?

He was sentenced to ten years but was released after six years and five months for good behavior and work credits. He was released on November 16, 1939, suffering from paresis (minor paralysis after a stroke).

Where did Capone's family take him after he was released?

They took him to Johns Hopkins in Baltimore, hoping for a miracle cure for syphilis. Unfortunately for him, penicillin was not developed for specific medical applications until after World War II. He spent the rest of his life on Palm Island, a near vegetable, fishing, swimming and playing simple card games that his friends and relatives let him win.

Capone and trainer on Palm Is. (S. Florida Hist. Association)

Did Capone's son follow in his dad's footsteps?

No. He first attended Notre Dame using the alias preferred by his dad, Al Brown. When his true identity was discovered, he transferred to the University of Miami, majoring in business administration. Unfortunately, Al didn't consult with a Merrill Lynch financial planner back then, and after his estate was settled, his family had to work for a living. After Al's death, Sonny and mother Mae ran a restaurant named The Grotto in Miami Beach. She worked the cash register and Sonny was headwaiter. The restaurant failed, and he drifted from job to job. He was arrested once for shoplifting several items worth only $3.50. After that he legally changed his name. Sonny was hard of hearing, a legacy of his father's syphilis. Surprisingly, Capone's wife was not infected with the venereal disease.

Where is Al Capone buried?

At the age of 48 Capone died penniless, after living off his family and owing the government money. He died at Palm Island on January 25, 1947, from pneumonia and a stroke. He was first buried in plot 48 at Chicago's Olivet Cemetery. He was later interred at Mount Carmel, but the monument was left at Olivet to throw off the curious. He was basically destitute at the time of his death, owing money on his estate for back taxes.

Jack "Machine Gun" McGurn (author's collection)

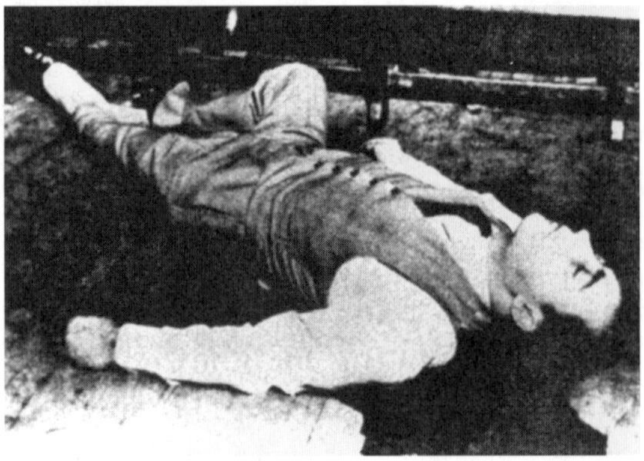

What did **Joseph Bonanno** say Al Capone's last name meant when translated?

Bonanno thought the name was similar to the word "capon" and said Capone stood for "castrated male chicken." Bonanno later became the head of one of the 5 New York families that ran the mafia in that state. They became known as The Commission and met once every five years to discuss situations and make decisions. When Bonanno's son (Bill) got married, no expense was spared. There were 3,000 guests and singer **Tony Bennett** was hired to entertain. The lavish affair was the inspiration for the wedding scene in the first *Godfather* movie. At age 78 Bonanno wrote his memoirs, *A Man of Honor*. **Rudi Gulianni**, a U.S. Attorney, used the information in the book to put away numerous mafia leaders. This helped Guilianni gain recognition that led to his becoming Mayor of New York and Time Magazine's Man of the Year in 2001.

McGurn's valentine: You've lost your job; you've lost your dough; Your jewels and cars and handsome houses! But things could be worse, you know . . . At least you haven't lost your trousas!

How did Jack "**Machine Gun" McGurn die**?

McGurn was killed at a bowling alley in front of a large crowd. Two unknown men blasted him with machine guns. He was shot on the eve of St. Valentine's Day in 1936. In a cruel gesture, the killers left a comic valentine next to the body.

Did **Johnny Torrio** ever go to prison?

Yes. Torrio's partnership with Dutch Schultz was ended when the latter was killed by Luciano's men. Torrio paid taxes but was caught concealing large amounts of income. Torrio was sent to Leavenworth for two and a half years. After serving his time, Torrio had a fatal heart attack at a barbershop on April 16, 1957.

With Al Capone locked up at Alcatraz, what new breed of criminals rose to replace him?

Now that the Depression was in full swing, the next crop of lawbreakers gained notoriety by robbing banks. They became heroes in the eyes of many because it was banks that had failed and cost numerous couples their life savings. And many banks that survived went into the business of foreclosing on delinquent mortgages. The most famous of the newcomers included **Machine Gun Kelly, Pretty Boy Floyd**, **Baby Face Nelson**, **Ma Barker, Bonnie and Clyde** and **John Dillinger**. The enamored public took great satisfaction in living vicariously through the actions of robbers who meted out justice to institutions, such as banks. The public perceived that the robbers were evening the score for having caused countless citizens to lose their life savings.

Bonnie Parker, age 19 (Famous Photos Inc.)

Did Capone ever write his biography?

After reporter Fred Pasley wrote an unauthorized *Al Capone: The Biography of a Self-made Man*, Capone was motivated to write his own story, place himself in a favorable light, and make millions off it. He authorized Howard O'Brien of the *Chicago Daily News* to interview him. They had numerous meetings, and Capone talked endlessly, but O'Brien came to realize that the more he knew about Capone's activities, the greater danger it posed for him because he knew too much. He begged off the project, saying it was taking too much of his time, and published the memoirs only after Capone was dead.

Was Al Capone a big tipper?

Capone was extravagant beyond belief. He carried huge sums of cash in his pockets. When he went out for a night on the town he handed out money like it grew on trees – a thousand dollars to a café singer, a hundred dollar tip to a waiter, fifty to a street panhandler, twenty to a hat-check girl, five dollars to a newsboy. He sometimes bet twenty thousand dollars on a single roll of the dice. From 1920 to 1933 he probably squandered more than fifteen million dollars.

What happened at the crime convention hosted by Al Capone at the Congress Hotel in May of 1932?

Mobsters from all over the country came to the meeting. Salvatore Maranzano was confirmed as the new head of the mob and the victor in the Castellamarese War in NYC. Capone was given the nod as the head of the Chicago Family. Three months later, Maranzano was killed by Lucky Luciano.

"Lucky" Luciano (Wide World)

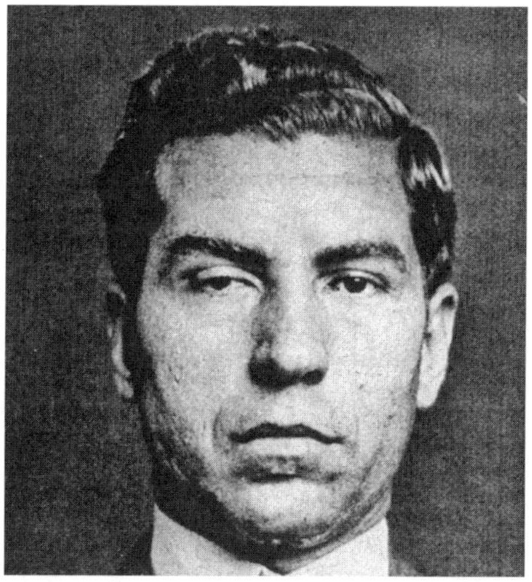

Why did some gangsters **rub garlic on their bullets** before inserting them in their guns?

It was thought this practice would cause infections and increase the deadliness of the wound. Back then, many doctors cauterized bullet wounds to stop infections.

Why did most politicians and pundits like **H.L. Mencken** think Prohibition would never be repealed in their lifetime?

Because it only took 12 dry states, such as Maine and Oklahoma, to block passage of a constitutional amendment to nullify the 18th. Constitutional amendments had to be ratified by ¾ (36) of the 48 states. (Alaska and Hawaii were not yet in the union.) But the Depression changed everything. Prohibition was repealed because: (1) Liquor sales brought needed revenue to the federal government (2) Repeal would help stimulate the farm economy (3) Liquor licenses for taverns brought in municipal revenue (4) Repeal meant fewer police needed to be hired (5) It took away a huge source of income for gangs (6) Less gang money meant less bribery and corruption of public officials.

FDR campaigned in 1932 on the promise to repeal Prohibition and the 21st Amentment became law near the end of 1933.

Did the Chicago mob extend its tentacles as far as Hollywood?

Yes. As early as 1936, Frank Nitti and **Murray Humphreys** obtained a foothold in Hollywood by backing fellow bootlegger **Joe Kennedy's** entry into the movie business. They put two of their men, **George Browne** and **Willie Bioff** in power as the head of the Motion Picture Operators Union. They created one big union, 12,000 members strong (all paid a 2% tax) and assessed the studios a fee for allowing pictures to be made. The move gave the Syndicate absolute power over Hollywood's film industry and the theaters in which films were shown. It also explains why most projectionists made more money than the managers. Rela-tionships with **Jack Warner**, **Samuel Goldwin**, **Columbia's Harry Cohn**, and **Louis B. Mayer** were important to Chicago. Both Browne and Bioff went to jail for labor racketeering.

Murray "the Camel" Humphreys

How did **Frank "the Enforcer" Nitti,** the dapper little man with the mustache, meet his demise?
Nitti was facing another prison term at Leavenworth and decided instead to shoot himself in the head with a pistol.

Who was Capone's successor?
It was Murray "the Camel" Humphreys. According to author John Morgan, it was Humphreys who invented the idea of "laundering" dirty money. He introduced gambling to Nevada; he exerted firm control over Hollywood film unions; he knew Joe Kennedy when he was a rival bootlegger. And it was Humphreys who invented the legal maneuver of saying "I refuse to answer on the grounds that I might incriminate myself." Humphreys was dapper and stylish. Some called him a "gentleman among thugs." Born of Welsh immigrant parents, he was one of the few gangsters of the era who was not Italian or Irish.

How did **Lucky Luciano** come to power in New York?
Luciano was a member of a group of Sicilian Young Turks who led a rebellion against the old, traditional, despotic leaders. They wanted to run things by committee choice rather than having orders being handed down by a dictator. There was a yearlong conflict known as the **Castellamarese War** between two factions that resulted in nearly 60 deaths.
Luciano rose to the top by coup d' état, murdering two top remaining men, **Joe Masseria** and **Salvatore Maranzano**. In the new order, each family head ran things within his district but agreed to defer to the national group when it was necessary to decide what was needed for the common good. **Meyer Lansky** reigned over gambling in Florida and the Bahamas. Luciano took over prostitution and narcotics. **Dutch Schultz** got the numbers racket, **Abner Zwillman** had the New Jersey domain, Abe Reles headed **Murder Incorporated**, the enforcement wing of the mafia, and playboy **Ben "Bugsy" Siegel** was given gambling operations in Las Vegas and California. The mob invested $6 million in the Flamingo, the first casino/hotel in Las Vegas. As profits failed to meet expectations the mob discovered Siegel was skimming. On June 20, 1947, he was shot by five 30-30 slugs through the living-room window of the Beverly Hills mansion of his paramour, **Virginia Hill**. Hill was in Europe at the time. She deposited the stolen money in a Swiss bank account. Virginia was called to testify before the Kefauver Committee, and although the nation was transfixed at the sight of a pretty "gun moll," she claimed to know very little, saying the men she knew and dated didn't talk about their business affairs. Organized crime would not be forced out of Vegas by the FBI until the late 1970s.
There are those who claim that during World War II Luciano worked with Naval Intelligence to help suppress sabotage on the NY waterfront and helped aid the military in the invasion of Sicily. Thomas E. Dewey, the man who earlier was responsible for sending Luciano to prison, became governor of New York and pardoned him in 1946 for service to his country. **Walter Winchell** said Luciano might even receive the Congressional Medal of Honor. The idea of a crook turning patriotic was used in several movies. **Alan Ladd** played that role in *Lucky Jordan,* and in 1942, Bogart uttered the line "I may be a rat, but I'm no traitor" in *All Through the Night*. When Luciano went to Clinton State Penitentiary, Frank Costello took control of NY. Luciano died of a heart attack in Naples, Italy, in 1962.

Who was on the top ten 1930 list of "outstanding personalities" at the Medill School of Journalism in Chicago?
The list included: Benito Mussolini, Charles Lindbergh, Admiral Richard Byrd, George Bernard Shaw, golfer Bobby Jones, Herbert Hoover, Mahatma Gandhi, Albert Einstein, Henry Ford and Alphonse Capone.

What ever happened to **Bugs Moran**?
He served ten years at Leavenworth for bank robbery and died from lung cancer on February 25, 1957.

What happened to **Alberto Capone**, another one of Al's brothers?
He became the head of a gambling and vice ring in the southwest suburbs of Chicago. He died in 1969 at the age of 62.

What happened to **Ralph Capone**?
In 1950 Ralph Capone was summoned to Washington to testify before the Kefauver Committee. He gave them some inside information on the bootlegger trade, but when asked about the Mafia, he said that all he knew about it was what he read in the newspapers. This was probably a true statement. The Kefauver Committee painted the Mafia with a broad brush and failed to distinguish the difference between the Mafia's five families in New York and The Outfit in Chicago. Several months later, his son Ralph Jr, disgraced by his father, committed suicide by consuming a deadly mixture of alcohol and sleeping pills. Ralph died at a rest home in Wisconsin in November 22, 1974.

Who were the Newton boys? Willis and Joe Newton led a gang of Texas robbers who looted banks and trains before being sent to prison for a two million dollar mail robbery near **Rondout, Illinois,** in 1924.

What was probably the biggest bank robbery in East St. Louis?

On May 7, 1920, the **Drovers Bank** at 1st and St. Clair in the **East St. Louis/National City** stock yards was robbed of $19,000. One bandit, James Haywood – a former convict - was killed and another captured. Six men, all wearing black handkerchiefs over their faces and armed with machine pistols, entered the bank at 10:00 a.m. The robbery was foiled when their getaway vehicle, a stolen Cadillac touring car, failed to start. When the car stalled, the cashier, J.L. Dooley and his brother, came out of the bank firing their pistols. The National City police quickly arrived on the scene and captured one man. The others escaped by running across Black Bridge and were last seen headed toward the vicinity of **Brooklyn**.

Did the Chicago mob have any other significant effect on U.S. political affairs?

It has been said that, through vote stealing, they worked in concert with Richard Daley to insure Kennedy carried Illinois in the 1960 election, thus winning the presidency by the narrowest of margins. **Victor Lansky** and the Chicago and Miami Mafia convinced **Fulgencio Batista**, dictator of Cuba, to let them come into his country and make huge profits on casinos and prostitution down there. Batista, of course, received a big cut of the profits. **Albert Anastasia**, the New Yorker, was killed in a barber's chair by **"Crazy Joe" Gallo** after he demanded to be let in on the action. When **Fidel Castro** failed to make the roster (as a pitcher) of an American League baseball team, he turned to revolution instead. His army took control of Cuba January 1, 1959. Castro and the Communists quickly threw the mob out and smashed the slot machines and gaming tables. The mob later supposedly worked with Allen Dulles and the CIA in several failed plots to assassinate Castro (poisoned food and poisoned cigars).

Jack Ruby killing Lee Harvey Oswald (*Dallas Times Herald*)

It is a well-known theory JFK was killed by the mob because brother Bobby Kennedy was putting them in jail in record numbers. The Justice Department bugged **Sam Giancana** with wiretaps and surveillance. Giancana was so frustrated that he filed suit and charged the government with harassment. The mob set Oswald up as a fall guy in this scenario. J.D. Tippett, a patrolman killed by Oswald shortly after the assassination, was one of the actual shooters that day. When Lyndon Johnson became president, Bobby Kennedy resigned as attorney general, and the heat was off. **Jack Ruby**, the man who killed Oswald to shut him up, was the Chicago mob's point man in Dallas. When Bobby ran for president in 1968, the mob **had him killed** and found another patsy in Sirhan Sirhan.

It has been suggested the assassination of Martin Luther King Jr. was also a mob action. The huge amount of cash James Earl Ray had on him when arrested was thought to be mob money. But that could easily be explained since he had robbed a London bank shortly before his capture. King was putting pressure on the government to end a war in Vietnam that was making a lot of people rich. The military-industrial complex was a big money-maker for the mob at the time.

RFK's assassination, June 4, 1968 (Wide World)

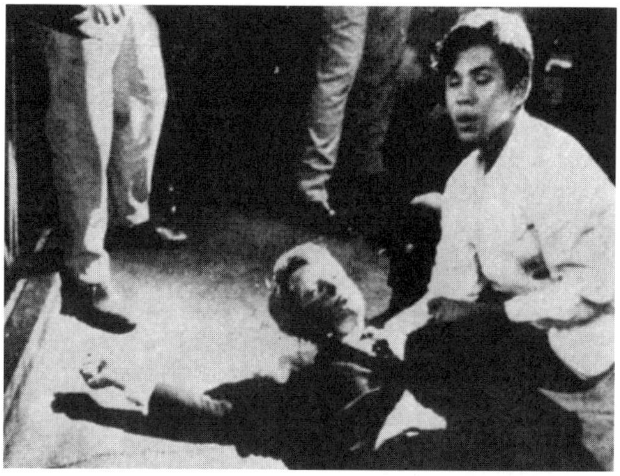

Sam Giancana was killed in the basement of his **Oak Park**, Illinois, home on June 19, 1975. He had been called to testify before the Senate Select Committee on Intelligence. He was shot with a .22 Duramatic target pistol - once in the back of the head, once in his mouth, and five times under his chin – murdered in true gangland style. Some say it was the CIA who killed Giancana, and they merely made it look like a mob hit. They ostensibly feared his disclosure of information regarding the entanglement of the CIA with organized crime. Giancana was in ill health and not any kind of a threat to anybody in Chicago's Outfit.

What was the unusual reason for the **Ottawa**, Illinois, police calling the penitentiary at Joliet on November 10, 1920?

The purpose of the call was to see if prison authorities could lend them a safe cracker who could rescue a teller locked in the vault of the National City Bank due to a robbery.

What happened to the payroll of the Western Coal and Mining Company in **Herrin** on September 29, 1921?
Robbers held the place up and escaped with $25,000.

How much money did the **St. Louis Egan Rats** gang nab in a U.S. mail truck heist on April 2, 1923? They netted a cool $2.4 million in bonds. On April 20th police raided the gang home of **Whitey Doering** and recovered much of the loot.

Baby Face Nelson and wife, Helen Gillis

Who was killed in the **Easter Massacre** of April 20, 1930?
Three Capone mobsters were shot to death by an unknown gunman in a bar at 2900 South Wells Street in Chicago.

Who robbed an **Itaska, Illinois,** bank of $4,600 on October 3, 1930?
It was **Baby Face Nelson** and partners Stanton Randall and Harry Lewis. On November 22, 1930, the trio robbed a bank in **Hillside, Illinois**, of $4,000.

How did **Baby Face Nelson** escape while being taken to the Illinois state prison at Joliet? He had been given a sentence of one to twenty years for a bank robbery at **Wheaton, Illinois**. It is believed his mother slipped him a pistol and he used it to escape from a train en route to the prison on February 17, 1932.

How was **Frank Nitti** almost killed on December 19, 1932? Chicago police, headed by Harry Lang and Harry Miller, conducted a raid on a Capone syndicate office at 221 North LaSalle. Lang claimed he shot Nitti when he resisted arrest. The wound was not fatal. Nitti later alleged that Chicago mayor Anton Cermak conspired with **mobster Ted Newberry** (of the Bugs Moran gang) to kill him. Cermak was also accused of encouraging **Des Plaines bootlegger Roger "the Terrible" Touhy** to conduct warfare on the Capone organization with help from the Chicago police. Less than a month later, Newberry was shot to death near Bailey Town, Indiana. On February 15, 1933, Cermak was shot by **Giuseppe (Joe) Zangara** while riding in an open touring car with president-elect Franklin D. Roosevelt in Miami. The generally accepted notion is that Zangara was trying to assassinate Roosevelt, and shot Cermack by accident. Zangara's trial lasted one day, and he was executed 33 days after he committed his crime.

Edna Murray, (r) the Kissing Bandit

Touhy later wrote a book called *The Stolen Years*, and it touched on his days as a Chicago-area bootlegger in competetion with the Capone mob. **He was gunned down in 1959, shortly after the book came out.** Many thought that Murray Humphreys ordered the hit because the book said too much about Touhy's enemies.

Who was "**the Blonde Tigress**?
She was a female bandit who, along with two male accomplices, robbed James Swock's shoe store at 4050 North Avenue in Chicago on August 4, 1933. Less than an hour later, they robbed a haberdashery shop at 5948 Division, killing the owner. Eleanor Jarman and her cohorts were later captured. The gang leader was executed, and Eleanor and her other partner received a sentence of 199 years.
Another woman named **Edna Murray** became famous as the Kissing Bandit.

JOHN HERBERT DILLINGER - PRINCE OF DESPERADOES

Why was John Dillinger, age 29, released from the Indiana State Prison at Michigan City, Indiana, in May of 1933?
His stepmother was terminally ill, and he had already spent **nine years behind bars**. He arrived a day too late to see her before she died, but he made it in time to attend her funeral. John was angry because he was paroled on May 10 but was not actually released until May 22. Dillinger told everyone he was sick of the life of crime and that he was going straight. But two weeks after his release, he robbed two markets, a drugstore and a small bank.

Was there anything in Dillinger's early life that suggested he might turn out bad?
Dillinger was born in Indianapolis in 1903. His mother died from a stroke when he was only three. He had an older sister who

mothered him for a while, but she soon married and moved away. His father was busy running a grocery store and didn't seem to have much time for his son. Dillinger greatly resented this. He ran around with his only friend, another troubled boy from an unhappy home life. By the time Dillinger was in the 6th grade he was the ringleader of a gang that called themselves The Dirty Dozen. Whippings and lectures only made Dillinger angrier. He quit school at age sixteen and began working at various factory jobs. In an attempt to get his son away from the temptations of city life, his father sold his business and moved to Mooresville, a small town near Indianapolis. He began attending Mooresville High but never studied and received failing grades in nearly every subject. He became interested in stories about the Wild West and read everything he could about **Jesse James**, who quickly became his role model.

John Dillinger's high school picture

Dillinger was a pretty good shot with a rifle, as were many young men in the American heartland in this era. He also was a very good baseball player, and he liked fast cars.

He became sexually active at an early age and was obsessed with making numerous conquests. He fell in love with his uncle's stepdaughter, Frances Thornton, and asked for her hand in marriage. His uncle thought they were too young and talked the girl out of it.

Dillinger got in trouble with the law and joined the navy under a fictitious name. But he hated the regimen of military life and went AWOL. He was thrown in the brig for ten days, and when his ship docked, he fled military life once and for all. He went back home and told everyone he'd been kicked out of the Navy. He then married a 16 year-old girl named Beryl Hovius, but he still didn't settle down.

On September 6, 1924, he tried to rob a grocer of his daily receipts. The man struggled with Dillinger, who was armed, and his shouts for help caused several neighbors to come to his assistance. Dillinger ran away but was later arrested and charged with attempted armed robbery. Dillinger's father and the prosecutor convinced him a lawyer was unnecessary, and that if he confessed, the court would be lenient. Dillinger felt angry and betrayed when a stern judge sentenced him to Pendleton Reformatory for 10 to 20 years. Some think it was this harsh sentence that turned Dillinger into a hardened criminal. As Dillinger once said to a reporter, "They took away nine years of my life, and I decided to do some taking of my own when I got out." He repeatedly tried to escape but was unsuccessful. His wife sued for divorce in 1929, increasing his bitterness.

Who were the worst influences on Dillinger in prison?

Dillinger on a baseball team, 2nd from right (Famous Photos Inc.)

For the first eight years Dillinger was a moody, rebellious prisoner but finally learned how to put on an act to convince prison authorities he was worthy of parole. But his change was outward only, and he fell in with characters like **Homer Van Meter** and **Harry Pierpont** who talked about robbing banks and living the easy life after getting out of the slammer. Pierpont was respected by Dillinger and was generally thought to be the "brains" of the gang. But Pierpont and Van Meter hated each other, both claiming to be the toughest hood, like Duke Mantee, the classic tough-guy character **Humphrey Bogart** played in the movies. Dillinger spent most of his time as mediator between the two rivals. Dillinger kept Van Meter around because he was talented, and he made Dillinger laugh.

Van Meter was killed by authorities in St. Paul, Minnesota, about a month after Dillinger died. He was ambushed in a similar manner, and authorities fired about 50 shots that riddled his body.

Pierpont used the Dillinger trick and carved a gun from a bar of soap to escape from the Ohio state prison. But he was recaptured and on Oct 17, 1934, was strapped in the electric chair.

What was it about the times that led to the 1930s being a decade full of bank robbers and kidnappers?

We started down the road to becoming a nation of scofflaws when many citizens openly flouted the laws against drinking during Prohibition. Public apathy led numerous criminals to believe the citizens were on their side. Banks were hated because many lost their life savings in the financial collapse in 1929 and 1930. As the Depression deepened, banks began to foreclose on homes and farms, causing ever more bitterness. The advent of the tommy gun gave criminals an edge in firepower against law enforcement

Homer Van Meter, Dillinger partner

officials who were loathe to use the weapon for fear shootouts would result in inordinate loss of civilian life. The popularity of the automobile and concrete highways enabled robbers to make get-aways and cross state lines to avoid capture. **Bonnie Parker and Clyde Barrow** were among the first to embark on a series of violent holdups, using heavy artillery, fast cars, and then fleeing from Texas to places like Joplin, Missouri, as a "safe haven." Bonnie and Clyde were gunned down by law officials who set a murderous roadside trap for them at Acadia, Louisiana. Their bodies were riddled with lead; 150 bullets hit the car.

Kate "Ma" Barker and her motley crew (including **Alvin Karpis**) started their crime career in Tulsa, Oklahoma, and St. Paul, Minnesota. On January 17, 1934, the Barker-Karpis gang kidnapped Edward Bremer, a Minneapolis bank president. Fred Barker sapped him and threw him in the car bracketed by Harry Campbell and Alvin Karpis. Fred Barker drove away, and they were followed by a second car driven by Dock Barker with three other men armed with submachine guns. Negotiations stalled because the police found blood in the victim's car and were convinced he was dead. They immediately called in the Feds. The family said they would pay the $200,000 ransom.

However, the gang got so jittery, the planned swap didn't occur. Karpis went to **Chicago** and begged Ma Barker to come in on it and take control. She refused, saying she told them it was a bad idea in the first place. She did tell Karpis how to make the switch. The gang got the money and released the victim unharmed. Fortunately the FBI obtained one of Fred Barker's prints in the process, and the heat was on. Barker and Karpis decided to have facial plastic surgery and fingerprint removal. They were so unhappy with the results, they threatened to kill the doctor.

Kate "Ma" Barker – Mother of Criminals – has no mug shots, she was never arrested

The Barker/Karpis gang split up. Ma and Fred were later killed in Florida. (Interestingly, Ma Barker was never arrested, so there are no mug shots or news photos of her, only family pictures.) Karpis became Public Enemy Number 1 and was the last of the Depression gangsters to be apprehended. Hoover made his capture a top priority when Karpis sent him a threatening letter. They found out Karpis was living in New Orleans with his girl friend on Canal Street. Hoover personally wanted to be in on the arrest. Karpis and a man named Fred Hunter were surprised just as they seated themselves in their car. Karpis reached for a rifle in the back seat, but Hoover grabbed his arm before he reached it. No one remembered to bring cuffs, so the two were tied up with agent's neckties. Hoover called Karpis a hoodlum, which brought a sharp rebuttle: "I'm a thief, not a hoodlum. A thief is anybody who gets out and works for a living. A hoodlum is a lousy sort of scum. He works for gangsters and bumps guys off." Karpis was sentenced to life at Alcatraz.

What did Dillinger do that first caught the fancy of the working press?

When Dillinger robbed a bank in Indiana, he vaulted over a high barrier between customers and tellers. This demonstration of agility was quickly compared to the swashbuckling screen feats of **Douglas Fairbanks Jr**. In another bank holdup, tellers told reporters that Dillinger sat cockily on the high counter with his legs crossed. A straw hat tilted jauntily on his head.

Is it true that a police official purposely ground out Dillinger puff-piece stories for the press for the expressed purpose of inflating his reputation?

Yes. Indiana State Police Captain **Matt Leach** was the one who continuously leaked the colorful stories to the press. Some of the

Ma and Fred Barker on slabs in the county morgue

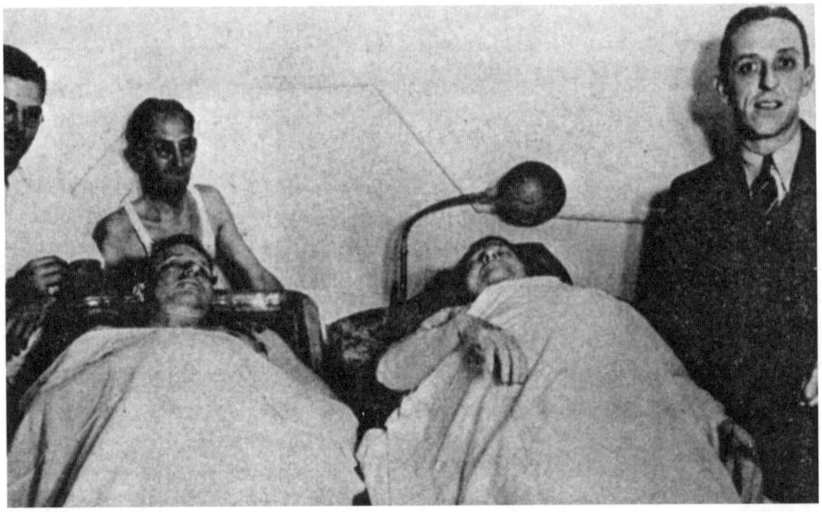

tales he told were outright fabrications. He did this for two reasons. The first was for his self-gratification and publicity; the other was to make Pierpont jealous of Dillinger and break up the gang. Dillinger developed an odd hunter-hunted relationship with Leach by sending him post cards that taunted the nervous man's stuttering. He also insulted Leach by sending him a copy of a book titled *How to be a Detective*.

Leach was bitter at having his publicity mill stolen out from under his nose, and he attacked the bureau for the way it handled the Dillinger case. At the request of J. Edgar Hoover, Leach was fired from his job in 1937. Leach died in an auto accident in 1955.

Publicity seeker and Dillinger nemesis, Matt Leach

Law enforcement officers began the practice of taking **target practice with large photos of Dillinger** instead of the traditional circular target.

In what manner did most people mispronounce John Dillinger's name?

The German name, which became almost as famous as Capone's, was nearly always mispronounced with a soft "g."

How did a Dillinger picture greatly upset J. Edgar Hoover and ruin the career of prosecutor Robert Estill?

Dillinger liked to make clever wisecracks and entertain reporters. Dillinger had been arrested and was about to be sent to jail at Crown Point. A group of reporters had gathered around Dillinger and when he realized one of them was about to snap a picture, he rested a friendly arm on Estill's shoulder. Estill was talking to Lillian Holley, the county jailer at the time, and didn't realize what was happening. When the photo was picked up by wire services and splashed in newspapers all over the country, many were incensed that Estill lacked decorum and seemed to be friendly to a "cold-blooded killer." It was the end of Estill's career.

When Dillinger escaped from the Lake County Jail at Crown Point, Indiana, what trick did he use?

Dillinger and Harry Pierpont were apprehended by the police in Tucson, Arizona, on January 25, 1934. They were then sent back to Indiana. On March 3 he pulled the "**wooden gun**" trick to escape and then stole a car and fled to Chicago. According to the story, Dillinger used a razor blade to carve out a crude gun and blackened it with shoe polish. He then shoved this wooden pistol into the back of a cellblock turnkey. He did the same thing to a guard which allowed him to get his hands on the real thing. Crown Point became the butt of many jokes, and this single act of derring-do transformed Dillinger into a legendary outlaw. In all likelihood, the gun was probably made on the outside and smuggled in to Dillinger. By crossing the state line in a stolen car, he violated the **Dyer Act** and this enabled the Feds to get involved. That was a big mistake – like Napoleon marching on Moscow. Diminutive Melvin Purvis was in charge of the Chicago FBI office, located on the 19th floor of the Bankers' Building.

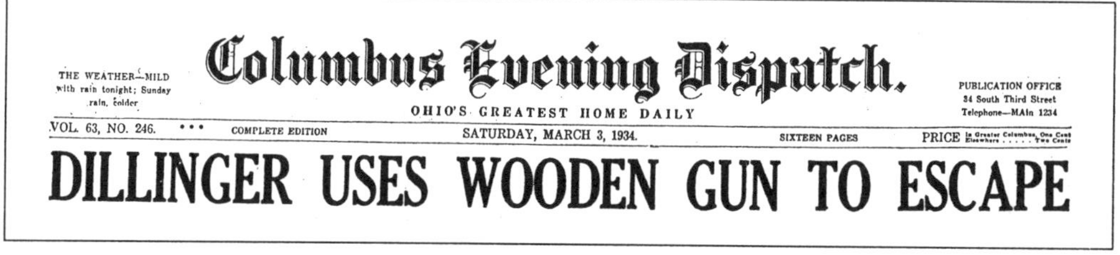

THE WEATHER—MILD with rain tonight; Sunday rain, colder

Columbus Evening Dispatch.

OHIO'S GREATEST HOME DAILY

PUBLICATION OFFICE 34 South Third Street Telephone—MAin 1234

VOL. 63, NO. 246. *** COMPLETE EDITION SATURDAY, MARCH 3, 1934. SIXTEEN PAGES PRICE

DILLINGER USES WOODEN GUN TO ESCAPE

The story about the gun added to the growing Dillinger legend because the judge in Dillinger's trial boasted that 100 men couldn't break Dillinger out of that jail. Police officials conducted an inquiry and claimed the gun was real and probably smuggled to Dillinger by **Billie Frechette** (who claimed to be his wife) when she visited him. Many reject this claim and say authorities concocted the story so the incident wouldn't be so embarrassing.

Dillinger took another man with him when he escaped, Herbert Youngblood, a Gary, Indiana, man awaiting trial on the charge of murder. When Dillinger's escape car neared the outskirts of Chicago, Youngblood was let out of the car. Youngblood, a Negro, was killed in a gun battle with police several weeks later.

Dillinger's carved wooden gun (Dillinger Museum)

Who was in charge of the Chicago special Dillinger Squad?

It was **Captain John Stege** who hated Dillinger with a passion. They were heavily armed and worked in two shifts on round-the-clock duty. "Shoot first, and shoot to kill," were Stege's orders to his men. After escaping from jail, Dillinger formed a new gang (March 6, 1934) and made plans to rob another bank to get spending money. His "torpedo," or main gunman, was Lester Gillis, better known as **Baby Face Nelson**. The stocky five-foot-five man liked two things – violence and women. He had grown up near **Chicago's Union Stockyards** in a neighborhood known as The Patch, served a term in St. Charles Reform School, and was sent to Joliet Prison for robbing a bank. He was also known for killing 3 G-men. The new gang promptly robbed a bank in Sioux Falls, South Dakota. It always bothered Nelson that the press referred to the new gang as Dillinger's instead of Nelson's.

Interestingly, Chicago born and bred Nelson was the **only major Depression era gangster who did not come from a small town.** Baby Face Nelson killed two agents in a spectacular and gutsy shootout (November 27, 1934) but was hit with 17 different slugs and died the next day. His body was found in a ditch near St. Peter's Cemetery in **Niles**, Illinois, stripped naked to prevent immediate identification.

Baby Face Nelson in the morgue with 17 slugs (author's collection)

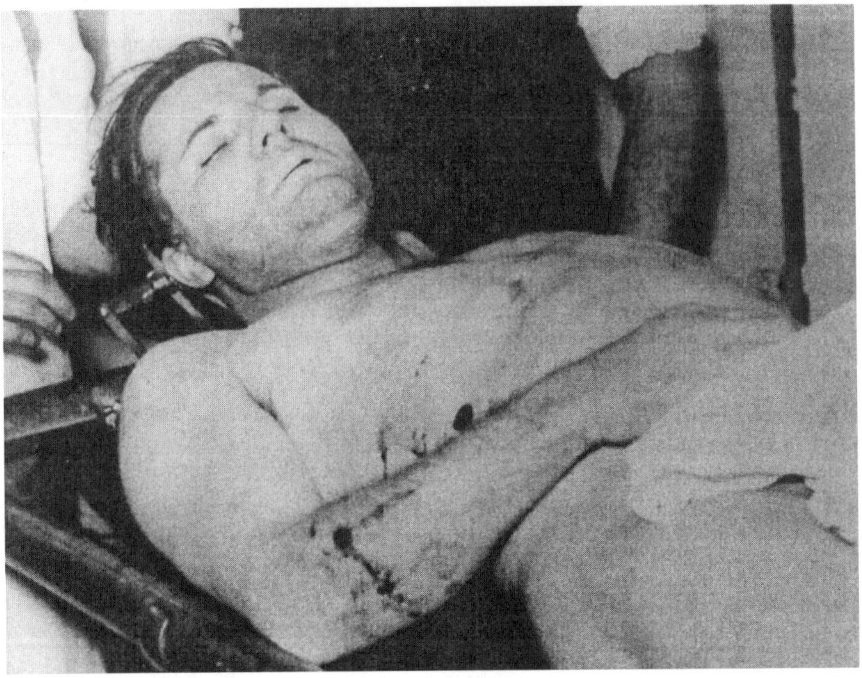

How did a large money tip result in Dillinger being captured?

After Dillinger escaped from the Indiana jail, he and his gang went to Tucson, Arizona, in January of 1934 to let things cool off. While they were there, a fire broke out in their hotel, and one of the gang members gave a huge tip to a fireman who rescued their luggage. Surprised at the size of the tip, the fireman took a good look at the generous man. The next day he was leafing through an issue of "True Detective" magazine, recognized the face and notified authorities.

The police arrested the gang, one at a time when they went out for a pack of cigarettes or some similar errand. Dillinger was flown by special charter on American Airways to Chicago's **Midway Airport**. From there a heavily armed police escort took him to Crown Point, Indiana. "If he would have given the guy an average tip, we never would have been caught," Dillinger lamented.

After Dillinger escaped from the Crown Point jail, how did he nearly get caught by Melvin Purvis on the night of April 9, 1934?

Acting on a tip, Purvis and his men stormed the State & Austin Tavern at 416 **State Street in Chicago**. As luck would have it, they only arrested Dillinger's girl friend, **Evelyn Frechette**. Dillinger was parked outside and drove away when he saw the G-men go inside.

Dillinger at home with wooden gun (Dillinger Museum)

Dillinger was highly sexed and had to constantly be around female companions. Frechette was a French-Indian beauty born on a Chippewa Reservation. The raven haired, slim-waisted looker had a husband, but he was serving time at Leavenworth. She quit her job as a hatcheck girl in a Chicago nightclub and moved in with Dillinger at his Chicago apartment. In Chicago, the gang didn't have to hide out or hole up. They moved freely around town, looking like successful businessmen. They frequented the movies, and Dillinger's favorite was ***Three Little Pigs***. They avoided the Dillinger Squad by moving frequently. There were numerous times when the police made a surprise visit and found they had missed Dillinger by a day or two. Frechette would ultimately serve two years in prison for harboring a fugitive.

What was the big excitement in **Pana, Illinois,** on April 19, 1934? The local bank was robbed of $27,000 by what was believed to be the Dillinger gang.

What happened when the police surrounded Dillinger in a hotel room at **Kankakee**, Illinois?

Several hundred curious onlookers jammed the streets near the hotel when the police, acting on a tip, surrounded it. The man they thought to be Dillinger turned out to be a candy salesman and his "dangerous weapon" was merely a knife for slicing the candy.

Was Dillinger bloodthirsty?

Although he carried a "heater" and posed with weapons in photographs,

Dillinger tried to avoid gunplay. With Dillinger, shooting was a last resort. The only person he killed was Officer William O'Malley while robbing the First National Bank at East Chicago, January 15, 1934.

Did John Dillinger ever visit St. Louis?

Yes. He and Billie Frechette attended the auto show on January 18, 1934, held at the Municipal Auditorium on Market Street. Frechette's Boston terrier got loose and an officer on duty **caught the dog and returned it to Dillinger**.

Did Dillinger wear any protection?

After several bank holdups where police arrived on the scene and gunfire was exchanged, Dillinger and his gang began to wear bulletproof vests. They often slept in their vests and frequently went over what they would do, step by step, if they were surprised by the police in the middle of the night. Dillinger obtained weapons, ammo and vests by robbing police station arsenals.

> **ATTENTION**
>
> **ALL LOCAL AND STATE POLICE, SHERIFFS, NATIONAL GUARDSMEN AND FEDERAL AGENTS**
>
> Be on the lookout for John Dillinger, Public Enemy No. 1.
>
> Wanted for murder, armed robbery, grand theft auto, aggravated assault and racketeering. He is heavily armed, extremely dangerous, and will readily take hostages. Do not attempt to capture alone. National Guard units are on 24-hour duty to assist.
>
> Description: male caucasian; medium build; age 31; height, 5-7; eyes, grey; complexion, medium; weight, 153 pounds; occupation, machinist. Culprit is known to wear flashy clothes and sports a rakish hat.

After Dillinger robbed a bank, how did he discourage police, who chased after him in their squad cars?

He would scatter a box of roofing nails on the road behind his car. Sometimes he took hostages and made them stand on the running board and hold on while making the escape, releasing them later after they had lost their pursuers. The getaway car was usually nondescript so as not to draw undue attention. He had several sets of license plates and changed them when the coast was clear.

John Artery, a police car-driving specialist who unsuccessfully chased Dillinger, paid him tribute when he said, "That bird sure can drive." Dillinger kicked Ed Shouse, a wheelman, out of the gang when he made a play for Evelyn "Billie" Frechette, Dillinger's girl. Dillinger was also upset when he learned Shouse had pulled some jobs independently.

What kind of a reward was out for Dillinger, Public Enemy Number 1?

For a long time it was only $25 for his violating parole. Then Illinois governor Henry Horner convinced four other Midwest governors to each kick in a thousand dollar reward, along with the state of Illinois, upping the reward to $5,000. Back then, you could buy a decent five room house for about $5,000.

How did Dillinger try to make authorities think he was in Detroit instead of Chicago?

He wrote a famous letter to auto maker **Henry Ford**.

Hello Old Pal:

Arrived here at 10 a.m. today. Would like to drop in and see you.

You have a wonderful car. Been driving it for 3 weeks. It's a treat to drive one.

Your slogan should be.

Drive a Ford and watch the other cars fall behind you. I can make any other car take a Ford's dust;

Bye-bye

John Dillinger (note Dillinger's interesting punctuation)

Note Dillinger left on an apartment door in Indiana; he was superstitious about signing his name

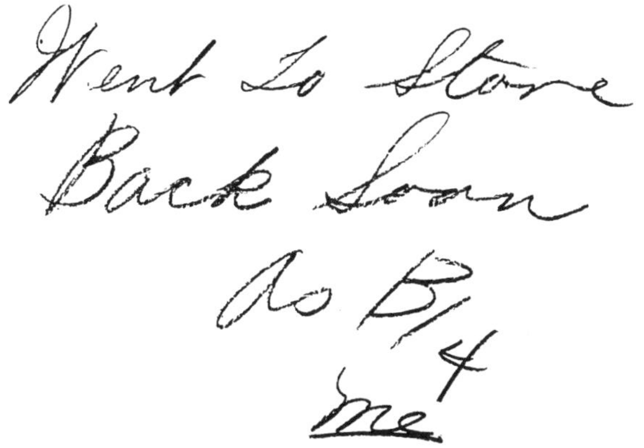
Went To Store
Back Soon
Ro B/4
me

How close did Dillinger come to receiving a pardon on the condition he would surrender peacefully to authorities?

A petition from Mooresville was sent to the Indiana governor by Dillinger's friends, asking him to make such a deal. They cited a precedent, noting this kind of a deal had been made by authorities in Missouri with Frank James, brother of Jesse. Dillinger now had a big fan club that collected articles and pictures and wrote songs and poems about him. The Department of Justice was concerned about this rising tide of Dillinger popularity and convinced President Roosevelt to make a radio address and speak out against the lawlessness.

Indiana authorities chose to ignore the petition.

Where did Dillinger have his plastic surgery operation to alter his looks and to remove his fingerprints?

The surgery was performed May 27, 1934, by a Doctor Wilhelm Loeser in a two-story building on Chicago's north side at 2509 N. Caldwell. The house was owned by a former speakeasy operator, James Probasco. Loeser needed the money. He had been sent to Leavenworth for violating narcotics laws. His assistant accidentally gave Dillinger too much ether and he **swallowed his tongue**, which they extricated with forceps. Doctors had to give him artificial respiration to get him breathing again. They removed a couple of small moles between the eyes and tried to fill in the dimple on his chin. Dillinger was unhappy with the first operation, saying he looked like he had been in a dogfight. But the doctor convinced him the scars would heal, and the swelling would go down. Five days later a second operation was performed. A caustic solution was applied to obliterate the skin on his fingertips. An attempt was also made to remove a tattoo from his right arm.

Where was Dillinger on July 11, 1934?
He and his girl friend, **Mary Longnaker**, brazenly visited the **World's Fair on Chicago's lakefront**.

How many banks in all did Dillinger rob?
He robbed at least 10 different banks in Indiana, Illinois, Iowa, Ohio, Wisconsin and South Dakota.

Dillinger's getaway car with accessories. Ford dealers bragged cops would never catch him as long as he drove a Ford V-8

How did Dillinger's new girl friend, **Polly Hamilton**, lead to his undoing?
Polly was a shapely redhead, and she rented a room from a Romanian woman named **Anna Sage**. Because she had twice been convicted of running a house of prostitution, Anna was about to be deported. Dillinger was convinced most people could not recognize him because of the plastic surgery. Dillinger told the ladies he was a businessman named John Hamilton. Both women guessed his true identity but never brought up the subject. He boldly **attended a Chicago Cub baseball game** against the Dodgers (June 26, 1934), frequented a local ice cream parlor and went to movies at the Biograph Theater.

Anna Sage told authorities that Dillinger and Polly were staying in her apartment and she could help them capture Dillinger if they wouldn't deport her. On the hot evening of Sunday, July 22, 1934, she phoned the police and told them she and Polly were attending a movie with Dillinger. **Melvin Purvis** and five other FBI agents made plans to capture him when he left the theater. Dillinger came out of the Biograph with Polly Hamilton on one side and Anna Sage on the other. They had just seen the movie, ***Manhattan Melodrama,*** with William Powell and **Clark Gable**. In the movie, Gable portrayed a killer who was sent to the electric chair. Purvis lit a cigar as the trio passed him. It was a signal to his men that the man actually was the real Dillinger. Dillinger sensed he was being followed and ran for the alley in a crouched position. He was struck by four bullets. One ripped into his left side, another zipped into the back of his neck and exited below his right eye. Yet another entered his neck. He was dead when he hit the ground. Two female bystanders suffered minor leg injuries from stray bullets. Ironically, the Biograph Theater was only a few blocks away from the garage made notorious by the St. Valentine's Day massacre.

Polly Hamilton – woman who was with Dillinger the last 2 weeks of his life

Dillinger was taken to Alexian Brothers Hospital but was pronounced dead on arrival. He was then transferred to Cook County Morgue. When Sergeant Frank Reynolds of the Dillinger Squad arrived, he was so overjoyed to see the corpse that he shook Dillinger's dead hand. The body was held in the morgue an extra day before releasing it to the mortuary so approximately **15,000 Chicagoans could come and view the body**.

Ironically, the press heavily criticized the FBI for shooting Dillinger instead of arresting him. Anna Sage became famous as the Woman in Red who had fingered Dillinger. Because of the plastic surgery, when people went to see the body during visitation at the E.F. Harvey Funeral Home, they said it didn't look like him. Rumors spread that the FBI had killed the wrong man. Writer Jay Robert Nash, in his *Dillinger Dossier*, puts forth the bizarre theory Dillinger wasn't killed at the Biograph Theater and somehow survived.

Dillinger was buried a few days later at the Crown Point Cemetery in Indiana. Fearful the grave might be robbed, **three feet of concrete** was poured on top of the casket. Some objected to his being buried in the same cemetery as president Benjamin Harrison and writer James Whitcomb Riley.

Dillinger's family received offers from various carnivals offering them large sums of money for Dillinger's body so it could be a sideshow attraction. They indignantly refused. Part of Dillinger's brain was sent to labs to determine if it was diseased or in any way abnormal, in hopes that might somehow account for his criminal behavior.

Many were critical of the FBI, since the only *federal* law Dillinger violated was that of driving a stolen car across state lines – an offense for which one is seldom shot.

Dillinger's career of fame was incredibly brief, lasting only a little more than a year.

Some weeks after Dillinger died, the law also caught up with Pretty Boy Floyd (Melvin Purvis, Oct. 22, 1934 on an Ohio farm), Baby Face Nelson (shootout at Fox River Grove/ Barrington) and Fred and Kate "Ma" Barker (Lake Weir, Florida), all killed in shootouts with the FBI. Fred Barker, his lifeless hands still clutching his Thompson, had been hit 11 times. Next to Ma Barker's body was her Lewis .300 automatic rifle, with 40 of its 94 rounds missing. She had been hit 3 times, once in the heart. On November 27 Nelson was shot 17 times yet managed to escape from police, only to die a few hours later at a house in what is now part of **Skokie, Illinois**. (For Floyd info see Jeffery King's *The Life And Death of Pretty Boy Floyd.*)

Who betrayed Dillinger?

It was an illegal alien named **Anna Sage**. She was dubbed **The Lady in Red**, but it was actually an orangish-colored dress she wore that night to confirm that the man with her was Dillinger. In the marquee lights the dress looked red. After nearly 15,000 people came to see the mangled corpse, his body was shipped home, and he was buried in Crown Hill Cemetery, Indianapolis. The Feds found out **Anna Sage** was an alien and threatened to have her deported unless she cooperated. Anna Sage received a reward of $5,000 from the FBI for her services but was still deported to Romania where she died in 1947. The alley where Dillinger died that fateful evening became a tourist attraction.

Ghosthunters believe an ethereal figure of John can be seen running from the box office to the alley, where he falls, mortally wounded, on each anniversary of his death. When in Chicago, hundreds of people visit Lincoln Avenue and Fullerton and the most famous alley in the world, located due south of the Biograph Theater.

When did **John Dillinger**, the bank robber from Indiana, first come to Chicago?

His first trip to Chicago was in July of 1933 when he and a couple of girl friends visited the Chicago World's Fair known as the **Century of Progress**. The Dillinger gang moved to Chicago October 26, 1933, after the Indiana governor called out the National Guard to deal with him. In December of 1933, eight members of Dillinger's gang were listed on the Chicago police department's **Ten Most Wanted** list.

Pretty Boy Floyd on the autopsy table (author's collection)

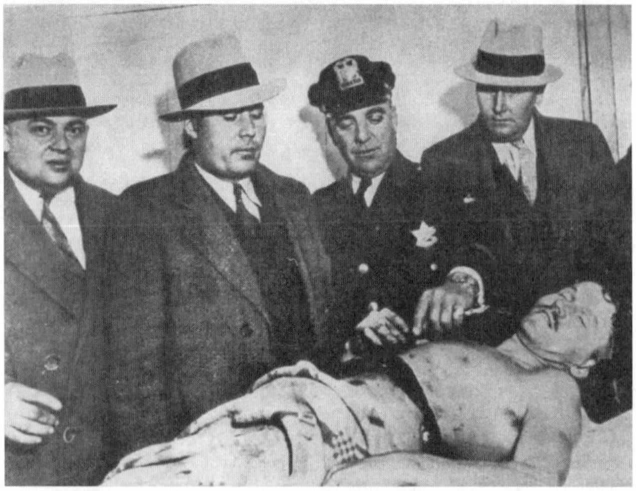

Dillinger was on the lam in May of 1934, pursued by as many as 5,000 agents assigned to his case. He sneaked into Chicago later that summer. He and his gang lived quietly in Chicago apartments and robbed banks in Indiana when the need for money arose.

By now Dillinger was listed as Public Enemy Number One and **Melvin Purvis**, the federal agent in charge of Chicago, was obsessed with his capture. On July 22 he was told Dillinger had gone to the **Biograph Theater** on North Lincoln Avenue with two women. Purvis positioned his men when Dillinger came out of the theater. One of the women, **Polly Hamilton**, told Dillinger they were being followed. Dillinger ran to make his escape and was gunned down as he was hit by four bullets. Curious onlookers ran up and dipped their handkerchiefs in his blood as macabre souvenirs. Some women **dipped the hem of their dresses in the blood**.

For years J. Edgar Hoover kept a replica of Dillinger's death mask hanging in his office in Washington, D.C. The original death mask was sold to a Japanese collector for $100,000. This author purchased one of the 10 copies from an E-Bay auction in June of 2002.

J.Edgar Hoover and Melvin Purvis

Where is the Dillinger museum? (800-ALL-LAKE)

Once located in Nashville, Indiana, it was moved to Hammond.

Why was there a falling out between **G-man Melvin Purvis** and J. Edgar Hoover? Hoover was jealous of the attention Purvis was getting in the press. When the FBI released a diagram showing the shootout with Dillinger at the Biograph Theater, Purvis was left out of it. Hoover then sent Purvis on a series of useless missions and so frustrated him that he resigned from the service. A revengeful Hoover even saw to it that Purvis was unable to get any kind of work related to law enforcement, including private security.

Purvis wrote a best seller about his G-Man days titled *American Agent*. G-Men became so popular that little boys started wearing G-Man underwear and pajamas. Post Toasties featured G-Man badges, certificates and toy gun replicas as cereal prizes. **Purvis later fell into a state of depression, killing himself** in his South Carolina home in 1960.

Who portrayed Dillinger in the movies?

Lawrence Tierney (*Dillinger*, 1945) and Warren Oates (*Dillinger*, 1973) gave the most memorable performances.

FAMOUS PEOPLE & GANGSTER QUOTES

"Tonight John Barleycorn makes his last will and testament. Now for an era of clear thinking and clean living!" - The Anti-Saloon League of New York on the eve of Prohibition

"It wouldn't be healthy to bring in a guilty verdict against these guys. Why I'd have to carry a gun around for the rest of my life." - Potential juror to a Chicago judge

"When Judgment Day comes and them 3 graves are opened, there'll be hell to pay in this cemetery." - Mourner comment noting the proximity of Angelo and Mike Genna near Dion O'Banion's grave in Chicago's Mount Carmel Cemetery

"You can get much farther with a smile, a kind word and a gun, than you can get with a smile and a kind word." - Attributed to Al Capone

"I'm not as black as I've been painted. I'm human. I've got a heart in me." - Capone

"Chicago: first in violence, deepest in dirt, loud, lawless, unlovely, ill-smelling . . . a spectacle for the nation." - Lincoln Steffans

"I've been accused of every death except the casualty list of the World War." - Capone

"There is in the city of Chicago a colony of unnaturalized persons, hostile to our institutions and laws, who have formed a super government of their own – feudists, black handers, members of the Mafia – who levy tribute upon citizens and enforce collections by terrorizing, kidnapping and assassinations." - Chicago banker **Charles G. Dawes** who became vice-president under Calvin Coolidge, referring to Torrio, Capone, the O'Donnells, the McErlanes, Ragens Colts and other gangs. Dawes won the Nobel Peace Prize for his Dawes Plan to help Germany pay reparations for World War I. **He also wrote the song popularized in 1958 by Tommy Edwards, "All in the Game."**

Copyright, 1928, by the Chicago *Tribune*
HE WOULD PLAY WITH MATCHES
—Orr in the Chicago *Tribune*.

"Chicago is a #!*!# crazy place. Nobody's safe in the streets." - Capone's Brooklyn schoolmate turned gangster, **Lucky Luciano**, after a visit to Chicago

"I was never a crumb, and if I have to be a crumb I'd rather be dead." – Lucky Luciano

"If people abuse me and I abuse them back, that ain't abuse." – Lucky Luciano

"The Italian is by nature criminally inclined." - American sociology report, 1914

"Dear Al:
Could you please come over to England and take care of a problem for me. I have money and can pay you well." - A disgruntled Londoner who wanted Capone to kill some neighbors she didn't like

"Vote early and vote often." - Slogan attributed to Republican Chicago Mayor Big Bill Thompson

"I violate the prohibition law, sure. Who doesn't? The only difference is I take more chances than the man who drinks a cocktail before dinner. I could bear all the criticism if it weren't for the hurt it brings to my mother and my family. They hear so much about what a terrible criminal I am." - Al Capone, to reporters in an interview

George "Machine Gun" Kelly

"Maybe the law of self-defense is a little broader than the law books have it." - Al Capone, when reporters asked how he justified killing off his rivals

"Chicago has the smartest way of handling crooks of any city. They get rival gangs to kill off each other, and all the police have to do is just referee and count up the bodies." - Humorist **Will Rogers**

"The worse crime a child can commit is to eat the raisins that Dad brought home for fermenting purposes." - Humorist Will Rogers

"Keep an eye on the storm sewer grates. The alky cookers are stealing them to set their stills on over an open fire." - Chicago police official to his men who walked a beat

"The rockets' red glare, the bombs bursting in air
Gave proof through the night that Chicago's still there." - Newspaper columnist describing the Pineapple Primary

"It would be stretching it a bit far to say that the Fifth Amendment authorizes a criminal to refuse to state the amount of his income from lawless activities." **- Oliver Wendell Holmes** in a Supreme Court opinion that said gangsters like Al Capone had to pay taxes on their ill-gotten wealth.

"I can do 14 years standing on my head." **- Leo Brothers** after being convicted of killing reporter Jake Lingle

"To heck with the Constitution. I'm a damned sight bigger than the Constitution." - **Sam Rubin** to **Morris Becker** in an effort to convince him to agree to "protection" for his cleaning establishment. Becker claimed that having to pay protection would violate his constitutional rights.

Leo Vincent Brothers, Jake Lingle's killer

"I'm a public benefactor . . . you can't cure thirst by law." - Al Capone

"We can't all be saints!" - John Dillinger to a newspaper reporter

"I'm innocent but I'll probably get the works. They got me charged with everything from strangling goldfish to stealing the socks off a blind man." - Dillinger to reporters before his trial at Crown Point, Indiana

"I don't smoke much, and I drink very little. I guess my only bad habit is robbing banks." - Dillinger

"That bird's too fast with the fireworks." - Dillinger's criticism of Pretty Boy Floyd's propensity for gunplay

"Because that's where the money is." - Willie Sutton, when asked why he robbed banks

Bonnie Parker's ventilated body (Famous Photos)

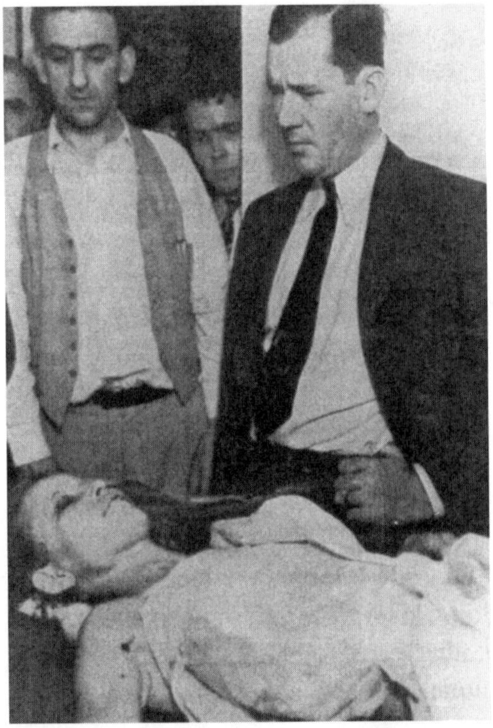

"Only queers wear silk shirts. You can get a good-enough shirt for two bucks." – Arthur Flegenheimer (Dutch Shultz) voicing disdain for other fancy dressing gangsters

"They've hung everything on me but the Chicago fire." - Al Capone to a reporter

"When I sell liquor they call it bootlegging. When they serve it on silver trays on Lake Shore Drive they call it hospitality." - Al Capone

"Bonnie and Clyde are the kind of punks who give armed robbery a bad name." - John Dillinger to reporters

"I don't want to encourage the business, but if somebody has to be killed, it's a good thing the gangsters are murdering themselves off. It saves trouble for the police." - Chicago police chief Collins after the death of Hymie Weiss

"He deserves to die . . . he's a reptile. We'll give him the chair if at all possible." - Judge Lyle, talking about Al Capone

"Here's twenty bucks, kid. Run along home to your mother." Al Capone: to a young newsboy as he bought his remaining supply of 50 papers on a bitterly cold night. Newspapers cost 2 cents each back then.

"Without a pre-dawn explosion to wake them up, many Chicago citizens would be late getting to work." - A prominent Chicago reporter commenting on the bombing wars in the Twenties

Clyde Barrow

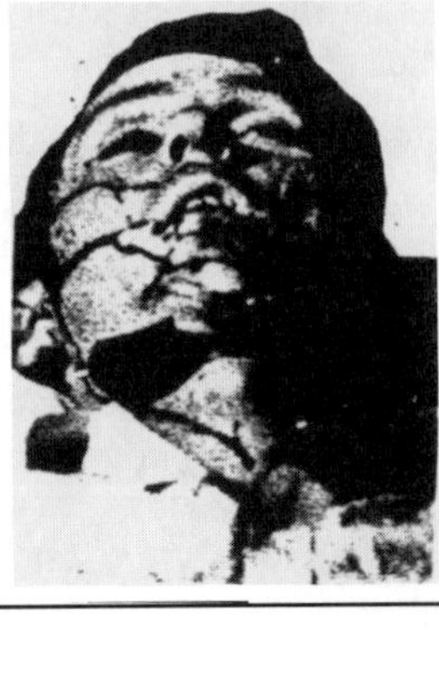

"You don't need to be ordering any fancy duds, you're going to prison." - Frankie Rio, to Capone who was being measured for two Florida suits shortly before the judge sentenced him to jail for tax evasion. Capone thought he would get off with a big fine.

"Jeez, you'd think Mussolini was passin' through." - Al Capone's response to shouts of encouragements from prisoners as he was transferred from Cook County jail to the federal pen in Atlanta.

"My unjust conviction will be an issue in the next presidential election; you'll see." - Capone to reporters in an impromptu press conference on the train going to Atlanta prison

"Imagine, some government creep gets me on a blankety-blank tax rap. Ain't that a helluva deal?" - Capone to one of his prison mates

"How in the heck can a fat Dago like me have a son that good looking?" - Capone, when he showed a picture of his son to Warden Rudensky at the Atlanta prison

"He's Irish; hit him again." - Familiar cry of those who picked on Irish immigrants because they were Catholic

"No Irish need apply." - Sign often displayed in windows of employers

"My God, you don't come back from The Rock." - Capone's last words before being transferred from Atlanta to Alcatraz

"Are you kidding? Al is nutty as a fruitcake." - **Jake Guzik's** reply to a reporter when asked if he thought Capone would resume command of the Chicago mob after he got out of prison

Dillinger Death Mask (Chicago P. Museum)

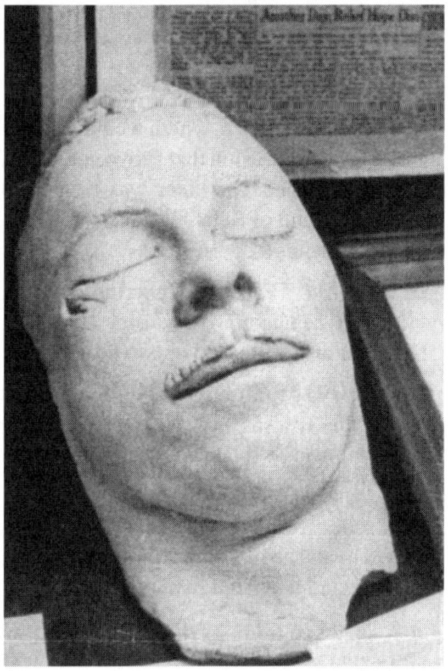

Chicago police mug shot of Al Capone

"God pity **those poor people in East St. Louis** when the police record of that city is kept in the handwriting of a robber." – Prosecutor venting his frustration at defense efforts to show police records indicating that the Sheltons were in an East St. Louis jail at the time the robbery they were accused of took place.

Frank Capone, killed by cops in 1924 shootout

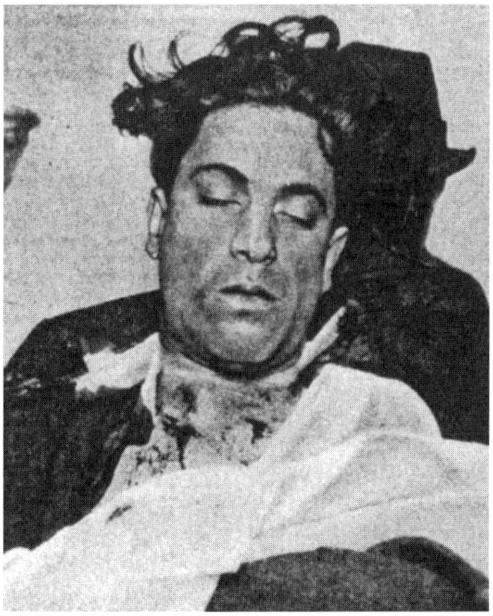

"It truly is a beautiful world." - One of the comments Charlie Birger made on the gallows as he smiled and bantered with authorities before his hanging

"I believe that you are not without character. I am sure that the same amount of energy applied to some legitimate pursuit would be more satisfactory to you, and I know it would be much less dangerous." - Judge Lindley lecturing Carl Shelton in **Danville**

"The secret of success in my business is to buy up old junk, fix it up a little, and unload it upon some other poor fellows." - **Charles Tyson Yerkes**, monopoly titan of Chicago's streetcar system Theodore Dreiser, a Chicago resident, used Yerkes as the basis for his main character, the rapacious Frank Cowperwood in his novel, *The Titan*.

"Buy out or destroy any competitor whose products are better than your own." - Philip Armour, Chicago's meat packing mogul

THE SHELTON GANG: CARL, BERNIE & BIG EARL

Was Carl Shelton musically inclined?

According to **Taylor Pensoneau**, the Shelton brothers' biographer, those who knew him said he once played the organ at the Methodist church in **Merriam**. He was also a great roller skater.

Which Shelton brother spent the most time in jail?

Ironically it wasn't Earl, Carl, or Bernie – the ones who made the most headlines; it was Roy. The other three were charged with an assortment of crimes, including robbery, assault, kidnapping, conspiracy, grand larceny, highway robbery, riot, vagrancy, bigamy, disturbing the peace and murder. Citizens were reluctant to testify so prosecutors had a tough time getting them convicted.

Which Shelton brother was the only one to serve in World War I?

The only Shelton to wear his country's uniform was Earl. But he never saw any combat because the war ended before he could be shipped to France.

Mug shot of Earl Shelton (Bell. *News-Democrat*)

How was S. Glenn Young partially responsible for the Sheltons getting into a life of crime?

According to sheriff George Galligan's retelling of events, all three Shelton brothers were working honestly in a coal mine before Young arrived on the scene. Young and his men raided a place occupied by Earl Shelton and Jack Skelker. They administered a beating to Shelton and burned the place. Earl Shelton swore out warrants against the Klan, and after that he and his family were harassed by Young and his men. The Sheltons left **Herrin** and went to live in **East St. Louis**. Young and his men frequently came to the Shelton home on West Monroe Street and asked their mother where "the boys" were. The harassment of the family (Mom, Dad, two sisters) got so bad they bought a farm near Fairfield, about 70 miles from Herrin. While in East St. Louis, the Sheltons got mixed up with Art and Bess Newman, who financed their foray into bootlegging.

Who became the number one ally of the Sheltons in East St. Louis?

It was Art and Bess Newman, who ran the Arlington Hotel, a sleazy joint not far from City Hall and the Relay Depot. The Sheltons owned a gin joint at 19th and Market and for a while made the Arlington their base of operations. Some say it was Bess Newman, who was also a notorious madam, who first loaned the Shelton boys money to get into the bootlegging racket. But Bess grew tired of the Sheltons' shenanigans, like sitting in the lobby of the hotel and scaring off customers while they cleaned or played with their guns. The Newmans later hooked up with the Birger gang and became foes of the Sheltons.

One of the Shelton's staunch enemies was **S. Glen Young**, the **KKK** leader who was determined to enforce the Prohibition laws. How did they deal with him?

Young said, with typical braggadocio, he was going to clean up East St. Louis the same way he had Williamson County. The Sheltons weren't about to let that happen, so they ambushed his car along the **Okaw Bottoms** on May 23, 1924. With Bernie driving, they pulled along side Young's touring car and blasted away. Mrs. Young was struck in the face with buck shot; S. Glen was hit in the leg with a .45 bullet. Passing motorists rescued Young and his wife and took them to a hospital in Belleville. Mrs. Young lost most of her sight in both eyes as a result of the shooting.

Which of the Sheltons was wounded at the August 30 shootout with the Klan in Herrin?

The southern Illinois version of the gunfight at OK Corral occurred at John Smith's garage, a favorite Klan hangout. Sheriff Galiigan, along with Ora Thomas, a special deputy, and Shelton brothers Carl, Bernie and Earl, went there looking to provoke a fight. When the western-style showdown was over, Carl, Earl and the sheriff were wounded. **Five Klansmen were killed** along with one of the sheriff's deputies.

According to Art Newman, what was a favorite song of the Shelton brothers? They loved a tune titled "That Old Gang of Mine" and sometimes ordered musical groups to play it over and over.

Did the Sheltons ever work with the storied Cuckoo gang from St. Louis?

Yes, especially during their all-out war with the Birger gang. Members of the Cuckoo gang performed various and sundry tasks incidental to large bootlegging operations, such as guarding stills or serving as guards on trucks delivering illegal hooch. After the Birger hanging, the Sheltons dismissed the Cuckoos and told them their services were no longer needed.

What happened in the April 13, 1926, **Herrin shootout**? This one was prompted by a primary election dispute with Klan and anti-Klan forces resorting to gunplay in an effort to prevail at the ballot box. Incredibly, much of the shooting took place at Smith's Garage, the scene of a shootout less than two years earlier. In addition to the Sheltons, **Blackie Armes**, one of their gunmen, was a participant. The National Guard arrived on the scene quelling the gunplay at the garage, but the combatants simply moved their contest to the Masonic Temple. Six Klan supporters died in the "**election day riot**," thus ending once and for all their power in Little Egypt.

How did Carbondale-born **Virginia Marmaduke** run afoul of the Sheltons?

She worked at the ***Herrin Journal***, a newspaper owned and run by her husband's family. Her reports and editorials against illegal gambling caused Shelton gunman Blackie Armes to place her on his enemies list. When her marriage failed, she left Herrin and went to work for the *Chicago Sun* where she earned the nickname Duchess. She told the Chicago paper, "I want to be a police reporter and cover blood, guts and sex."

Virginia Marmaduke (*Chicago Tribune*)

What led to the falling out between the Sheltons and Charlie Birger?

Some say it was due to rivalry for the affections of a Shawneetown babe named **Helen Holbrook**. Charlie Birger was having an affair with her, and when Birger found out she also had a liason with Carl Shelton, their alliance was ended. Others say it was due to the Shelton gang robbery of a Harrisburg man who was a friend of Birgers. A third version claims it was due to Carl Shelton concluding that Charlie Birger was skimming profits from slot machine operations they had previously agreed to split on a 50-50 basis.

What kind of armored vehicle did the Shelton gang decide to construct?

They acquired a gasoline tank truck and modified it for their purposes by mounting a machine gun on the rear and cutting out gun ports on the sides. When Birger and his men found out the Sheltons had a "tank," they converted an old REO truck into an armour-clad war wagon of their own. Although there is no recorded proof the two vehicles ever engaged in combat, Harvey Dungey, a Birger gunman with some basic art skills, drew a sketch that showed them in battle. (See page 19 of this author's *Southern Illinois: An Illustrated History)*

How did Art Newman plan to kill Earl Shelton while he was in St. Mary's hospital in East St. Louis?

Art was sick with malaria and when Newman found out about it, he hatched a plot to kill him. Newman and his buddy Freddie Wooten disguised themselves by **dressing in drag**. Hidden in the folds of Newman's female attire was a hunting knife. They were sidetracked in their first attempt, and their second effort ended in failure when they were stopped by a policeman who questioned them about their strange attire. By the time they planned a third attempt, Earl had been treated with quinine and released.

Mug shot of Bernie Shelton (*Bel. News-Democrat*)

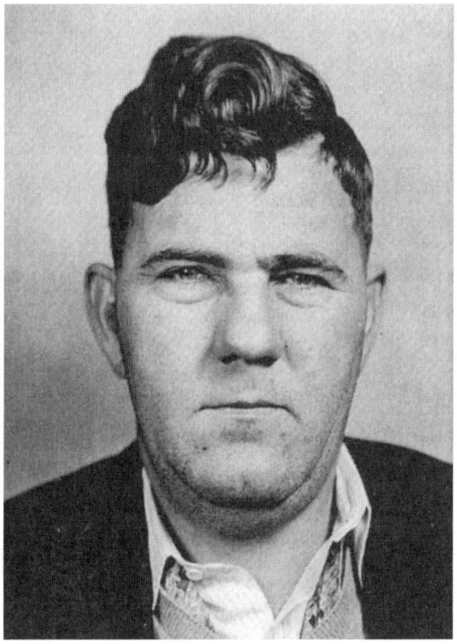

How were the Sheltons involved in the **first aerial bombing attack ever carried out on U.S. soil**?

Two barnstorming pilots in Illinois flew over from **Sparta** to **Benton**. The Sheltons introduced themselves and hired out the plane for the purpose of attacking Birger's lair at Shady Rest, with homemade bombs. The payoff was a thousand dollars plus a car. One of the barnstormers flew the plane, and a Shelton hireling (probably Ray Walker) dropped the bombs. The first bomb (crudely constructed from bottles of nitro strapped to sticks of dynamite) failed to explode. The roar of the plane's engine caused Birger's men to rush outside and begin firing at the Curtiss "Jenny." The second bomb also failed to explode, and the third one missed its target but landed close enough to kill one of Charlie's pet eagles and a favorite dog. The plane then landed at **DuQuoin**. It so happened that the auto the barnstormers were given for partial payment was stolen, and they were caught, fined $100 and given 60 days in jail.

How did the Sheltons get blamed for a mail robbery on January 27, 1925, in **Collinsville**, Illinois? James Mathias, a mail messenger, had just picked up two mail pouches from the Pennsylvania Railroad depot on the south edge of town. One of the pouches contained a $15,000 payroll for the nearby Lumaghi Mine on Lebanon Road. At a trial in **Quincy**, Illinois, Birger, Newman and Harvey Dungey all gave perjured testimony that the heist was masterminded by the Sheltons. The Sheltons were defended by one of their friends, **East St. Louis** attorney, **Joe McGlynn**. Carl, Bernie and Earl were found guilty and sentenced to Leavenworth in Kansas. The Sheltons were released after three months when Harvey Dungey admitted his perfidy to *St. Louis Post-Dispatch* reporter John T. Rogers and said his testimony had been false.

How did the East St. Louis police try to help free the Sheltons from the charge they had participated in a **Kincaid**, Illinois, bank robbery on September 27, 1924?

It looked bad for the Sheltons when Art Newman testified Earl had told him they were going to hit the bank at Kincaid. Worse yet; when the prosecution produced a sawed off shotgun dropped by the robbers, Newman testified it was one that he had sawed off and given to Carl Shelton. The Sheltons were saved when the defense brought in three East St. Louis policemen who testified the Sheltons were in the East St. Louis jail at the time of the robbery. They produced the police blotter that showed Bernie and Earl's names on the arrest record. A lieutenant on the force, Thomas F. O'Brien, testified that he'd seen the Sheltons in jail. What was even more interesting is that the last five names on the blotter all seemed to be in fresh ink and in the same handwriting – last minute forgeries.

The jury came back with a guilty verdict, but the conviction was overturned on appeal by the State Supreme Court. The judges ruled that the Sheltons didn't receive a fair trial. Prosecution declined to retry the case.

Handsome Carl Shelton (Bowen Archives SIUE)

Which of the Shelton brothers was considered the smartest?

All the brothers considered Carl to be the smartest, so naturally he assumed leadership of the gang.

Which of the Shelton brothers was considered the dumbest?

Some opponents of the Sheltons ranked the brothers in order of formidability. Carl was number 1, Bernie was number 2, and Earl lagged behind at number 3.

Which of the Sheltons was the biggest womanizer?

It was said that Carl chased anything in skirts.

Which of the Sheltons had the biggest temper?

Bernie was the pugilist who resorted to using his fists or a gun before the others.

What was probably the biggest gangland slaying in East St. Louis?

It happened on February 2, 1931, and the incident was well chronicled by East St. Louisan **Carl Baldwin**, working for the St. Louis *Post-Dispatch*. Joseph Carroll was a partner with Bernie Shelton in the Red Top Cab Company in East St. Louis. Carl and Bernie were on their way to a business meeting with Joe Carroll and Tommie Hayes at Ralph **"Wide-open" Smith's** establishment at 330A East Broadway, only a couple of blocks from the police station and city hall. Just before they went inside, a cabbie tipped them that there was an ambush waiting inside. The information meshed with a notion Carl had about Hayes, a former gunman for the Cuckoo gang, that was trying to supplant the Sheltons. They burst through the doors with their Thompsons blazing and when the smoke cleared, three men were dead. The bodies of Joe Carroll, Ted Kaminski and David Hoffman were found in a ditch on the outskirts of Madison a day later. Smith left East St. Louis for Florida, never to return. Hayes was machine gunned to death in April of 1932 near Granite City.

On what charge was Bernie Shelton arrested on February 24, 1934, by East St. Louis police?

He was charged with vagrancy. On the back of his mugshot picture he was listed as age 35 and living at 5004 State Street. Vagrancy was a charge police often made against someone they didn't like and wanted to harass. Next to the line that asked, Criminal Specialty? was the word *gangster*. (from **Carla Keller Anderson** of the *Belleville News-Democrat*)

Estimated Income of Shelton Gang Circa 1930

Slot machines	$2 million
Handbooks	$1 million
Dice and Cards	$1 million
Vice	$1 million
Bootlegging	$1 million
Gross	$6 million
Expenses	$4.5 million
Net	$1.5 million

Why were the Sheltons hired by Phillips Petroleum in East St. Louis?

Phillips was in the process of building a $15 million pipeline terminal with storage tanks. The oil company was using some non-union labor and there was trouble with the local unions. Things turned ugly when there were several violent clashes, so the company hired some of the Shelton gang to stand guard in July of 1932 to help put an end to property damage from union thuggery. There were rumors that Carl Shelton had decided to try and get into labor racketeering by taking the boilermakers union away from **Ollie Moore**. Shelton offered him a $30,000 bribe to "get lost," but Moore, who was also head of the powerful Central Trades Union, refused. When Carl Baldwin interviewed Moore, he told him that when he refused the offer, Carl threatened to kill him. A short time later, Moore was gunned down.

Although none of the Sheltons were charged with the murder, the bloody incident marked the beginning of the end of the Sheltons in East St. Louis. A new governor, Henry Horner, was a close friend of labor and was greatly disturbed by the killing of Ollie Moore. Horner set up a special commission. Its essential purpose was to work with Sheriff **Jerome Munie to run the Shelton gang out of East St. Louis**. A tough retired detective teamed up with Munie's forces and began cracking down on the

Sheltons by use of whatever means necessary. Sometimes this meant they fired their guns first and asked questions later. By 1934, the Shelton forces in East St. Louis, frequently harassed and arrested, were so depleted that Carl and the gang decided to retreat to their homestead on Merriam Road near Fairfield in Wayne County.

What secret meeting took place between gambling interests and state officials at the **Broadview Hotel** in East St. Louis in September of 1941?

Dwight Green became the new Republican governor in 1940. Those in the know allege that he quickly spread the word he was ready to do business. At the **Broadview Hotel** meeting, gambling reps were informed that an injunction against illegal gambling would be lifted in return for payoffs. The state was divided into regions, and a designated gambling chief was chosen to make a monthly payoff at a designated time and place. For about eight years after the meeting, Carl Shelton was one of those who regularly met with a state official and handed over $2,000 to keep the card and dice games, slot machines and related enterprises free from police interference. The agreement was terminated when reform-minded Adlai Stevenson became the new governor.

A young Bernie Shelton (*East St. Louis Journal*)

When were the glory years for the Sheltons in **Peoria**?

Their best years were from about 1941 to 1945. Before that time the Sheltons were in alliance with Clyde Garrison, who ran the **Windsor Club**. By 1941 Carl had muscled him out of the rackets and into the wholesale liquor business. It didn't hurt that Mayor Ed Woodruff's philosophy was the belief that Peoria could best prosper as a wide-open town and that the city, like East St. Louis, could be run on profits from illegal gambling and prostitution. Carl's base of operations were at the **Palace Club**, not far from City Hall. The quid pro quo Woodruff extracted from Carl Shelton was that violence would be kept to a minimum. The beginning of the end for the Sheltons in Peoria was marked by the election of a new reform mayor, Carl Triebel, in 1945. Carl Shelton decided to retire and become a gentleman farmer and dabble in the oil business back in Wayne County. But baby brother Bernie stubbornly decided to stick it out. Bernie set up headquarters at the **Parkway Tavern**, a nondescript bar on Farmington Road, just beyond the city limits. Bernie lived royally on a large estate that he called **Golden Rule Farm**.

Mug shot of Earl Shelton (*News-Democrat*)

What accounted for the estrangement between Frank Buster Wortman and the Sheltons?

Buster and **Blackie Armes** were sent to Leavenworth, then Alcatraz, for assaulting federal officers during a raid on an illegal *still* near Collinsville in 1933. (It is interesting to note that Wortman relatives maintain he never served time at Alcatraz. But **Taylor Pensoneau**, in *Brothers Notorious*, says that he did. And the Kefauver Crime Committee, in one of its reports, stated that he did.) Both men expected that the Sheltons would use their influence to make sure their life in prison wasn't as hard as it would have been otherwise. To their surprise and bitter disappointment, the Sheltons forgot about them. Seeing an opportunity, Murray Humphreys and certain factions of the Chicago mob won both men over by doing favors for them while they were in the stir. Both Wortman and Armes decided to throw in their lot with the Chicagoans, who also brought St. Louis gangsters into the fold. With the help of Egan Rats members - **Frank (Cotton) Eppelsheimer** and **David (Chippy) Robinson** - Wortman elbowed his way to the top in East St. Louis after he was released from prison in 1941. The Chicago syndicate tried to make a deal with the Sheltons, but Bernie unwisely turned them down.

Why did Wortman and Eppelsheimer make a visit to Chicago in 1944? By 1944 Wortman was in firm control of East St. Louis. He had muscled his way into the **Hyde Park**, a casino in nearby **Venice**. And he had somehow wrested control of Pioneer News Service (horse racing information) away from **Bev Brown** and **Gully Owen**, a couple of old Cuckooites. When St. Louis authorities put the clamps on racing wire services, Wortman moved the company across the river to the friendly confines of Fairmont City. Wortman and Eppelsheimer went to the ***City of Big Shoulders*** to set up a strategy with the Chicago mob for dealing with the Sheltons. Every time Wortman tried to expand his base beyond the metro east, he ran into Shelton control and Shelton loyalty, dating all the way back to the mid 1920s. It didn't take long for word to get out that there was a $10,000 reward out for both Carl and Bernie – dead or alive.

What happened to **Blackie Armes**, also known as Wortman's *heat*?

Blackie was killed in an argument with Thomas Propes, a **Herrin nightclub** owner, who was a cousin to Ray Walker. Both men were fatally shot in the ensuing exchange of gunfire. A cousin of Armes, Ray Dougherty, is believed to have fired the shots that killed Propes. The loss of Armes prompted Wortman to bolster his forces with henchmen Norman Farr and Harley Grizzell.

Other new recruits were Roy Armes of Herrin (Blackie's brother), a former Sheltonite, and **Charles "Blackie" Harris**, a former chum of the Shelton brothers. Blackie was a neighbor of the Sheltons from the Pond Creek area. Blackie was in the bootlegging business with the Sheltons and ended up in Leavenworth on a counterfeiting charge. Like Wortman, Harris nursed a grudge stemming from lack of Shelton support or favors during his 10 years in prison. Ostensibly, he was called Black Charlie because of his swarthy complexion and dark hair. Harris, a slightly-built, diminuitive man, was a dangerous foe for the Sheltons. He knew their territory inside and out and was credited by the FBI with killing at least 20 men.

Home of Ben and Agnes Shelton near Fairfield (Bowen Archives SIUE)

How did the killing of Ray Daugherty foreshadow the end of the Sheltons?

Daugherty was related to Blackie Armes and had cast his lot with Buster Wortman. Daugherty was shot and his body dumped near the waterline of Crab Orchard Lake in Carbondale. The rumor quickly circulated this was a signal that meant the Sheltons intended on reclaiming their old territory. Obviously this was not going to sit well with Buster Wortman or the Chicago syndicate. To further complicate things for the Sheltons, some of their prized black angus cattle were stolen. In an effort to find the culprits, Carl administered a beating to someone related to Blackie Harris. That same person was later shot and wounded. Blackie Harris was incensed. A short time later, on the morning of October 23, 1947, Carl was shot while riding in a Jeep on his farm. Ray Walker and Little Earl Shelton, who were following in a truck, heard Carl say: "Don't shoot me anymore, Charlie . . . You've killed me already!" The coroner found 17 bullets in Carl's body, from at least three different weapons. Walker and Little Earl said they thought there had been four participants in the ambush.

What happened to Blackie Harris, the accused killer of Carl Shelton?

Harris fled his hometown after the shooting but was apprehended in a bus depot in Tulsa, Oklahoma. Incredibly, a grand jury refused to indict Harris for the murder. The killing of Carl Shelton was never solved. Buster Wortman now had a free hand to expand his empire beyond the realm of Madison and St. Clair Counties.

Mug shot of Bernie Shelton (*News-Democrat*)

What happened to Bernie Shelton after Carl's death?

The Chicago/East St. Louis axis approached Bernie one more time in an effort at reconcilliation. Once again, Bernie stubbornly refused to buckle. The word went out from the combine that Bernie was still on the Peoria hit list.

Bernie was determined to be the sole kingpin of his new territory on the Illinois River. Bernie escaped the first ambush set for him several months later by two carloads of gunmen on a road near **Galesburg**. Bernie was on his way to Iowa to sell some of his palomino horses and cheated death when he inadvertently took a different route. But on the morning of July 26, 1948, a lone gunman saw to it that Bernie met the Grim Reaper. Bernie walked out of his Parkway tavern to his car. Hiding in thick underbrush, near the base of a hill behind the Parkway, was a man with a .351 caliber Winchester automatic. Bernie collapsed from one shot in the chest, then somehow managed to get back on his feet and stumbled back inside the tavern. One of his friends called for an ambulance, and Bernie was taken to St. Francis Hospital where he died from a large chest wound, shortly after arriving at the emergency room. Bernie was buried at Parkview Cemetery in Peoria, not far from his tavern.

What unexpected political development made the syndicate's killing of Bernie a phyrric victory?

The newspapers had a field day with the Shelton killings and offered them as proof for the need to change the political and moral climate in Illinois. This led to an upset victory by underdog Adlai Stevenson over Dwight Green in the governor's race in 1948. After his election, Stevenson waged a vendetta on crooked politicians, corrupt judges and illegal gambling that led to national recognition. This, in turn, led to his nomination for president on the 1952 Democratic ticket in the race against Dwight D. Eisenhower and the Republicans. He was badly defeated in the November election.

Were any of the other Sheltons shot at or killed?

In September of 1949, Little Earl was ambushed at his home on Elm Street and miraculously survived eight gunshot wounds. In May of 1950, Little Earl again received a minor wound as he was riding through the Pond Creek area, inspecting some oil drilling operations. Blackie Harris was charged, but the case was again dismissed for lack of evidence. Then on June 7, 1950, Roy Shelton was out plowing a field when he was struck by two bullets, one in the spine and the other in the groin. He fell from the tractor which then started going in circles, running over him several times. Roy's corpse was a bloody mess when it was found. Big Earl decided that it wasn't safe to stay in Fairfield so in January of 1951, he, his wife and Little Earl left for Florida. Big Earl died in 1986 and is buried in Jacksonville, Florida. Little Earl died in Florida in 1998.

Bernie Shelton's body in St. Francis Hospital (Bowen Archives)

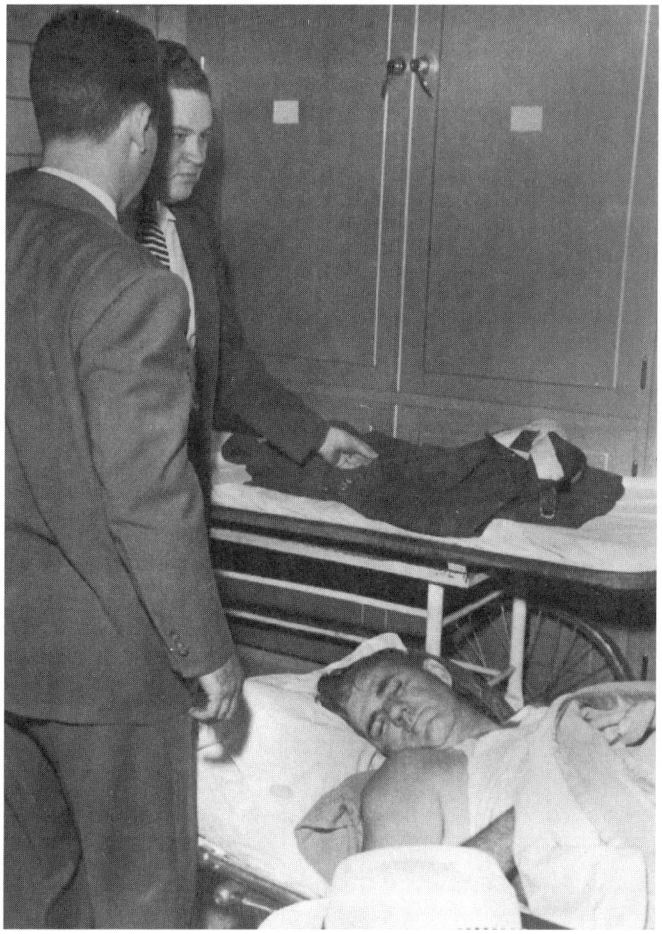

What happened to Blackie Harris in 1963?

He was charged with the murder of a neighbor, H.S. Taylor, who had won a civil suit against him, claiming that part of his crops were destroyed due to pigs from Harris' farm wandering off the property. Again, Harris was acquitted by a Wayne County jury. But in 1964 Harris was charged once more, this time for the murder of two people who were found shot to death in a burned Pond Creek house. One of the victims, Jerry Meritt, had testified against Harris at the Taylor murder trial. This time the 69-year-old Harris was found guilty and in 1965 was sentenced to 75 years at Menard. After spending more than 15 years in jail he was pardoned in 1981.

Did **Buster Wortman** ever serve time again after his release from prison in 1941?

He came close due to IRS investigations into his finances but he never again saw the grim gray walls of a penitentiary. With the elimination of the Sheltons, Wortman became the undisputed boss of southern Illinois. Governor Stevenson's state troopers shut down most of his gambling parlors such as the Hyde Park and the 200 Club. Reporter/historian **Carl Baldwin** said that after the crackdown on gambling, Wortman "dabbled . . . in labor racketeering, trucking, jukeboxes, pinball machines, race horses, real estate, restaurants, night clubs and loan companies."

In the mid-1950s he built a two-story brick fortress of a home and dug a moat around it. It was located in a secluded spot in rural southeast Collinsville on Lemen Settlement Road, accessible only by a bridge.

Carl Shelton's funeral in Fairfield (Bowen Archives)

In 1962 Buster was convicted of Income Tax evasion and sentenced to five years, but the verdict was reversed on appeal and he was found *not guilty* in a subsequent trial.

Wortman's chief lieutenant, **Elmer "Dutch" Dowling**, along with a lesser hood, Melvin Beckman, was found murdered near **Swansea** in 1962. Beckman had been a co-defendant in the income tax trial. Like many others before, these east side killings went unsolved.

In 1964 Wortman was **accidentally shot in the buttock** in a drunken argument, most think by Harry Kelly, owner of the **Gypsy Inn** on Route 3 near Monsanto (now **Sauget**), Illinois. Note: Newspaper accounts of this incident say he was shot in the gut, but every person this author has talked to about it says that he was shot in his backside.

He died in 1968 at Alexian Brothers Hospital in **St. Louis** at age 63, the victim of liver ailments and a lesion on his larynx, probably due to his excessive smoking. His death marked the end of an era of big-time gangsters in southern Illinois.

CHARLIE BIRGER: THE SCOURGE OF LITTLE EGYPT

It was a bright and sunny day in the southern Illinois town of **Benton**, Franklin County, Illinois. For a handsome Jewish man who was 45 years old, it was Friday, April 19th – his last day on earth. His lawyer's final appeal had been turned down the night before by the Illinoios Board of Pardons. Charlie Birger was about to dance at the end of hangman Phil Hanna's rope, expertly tied with 13 traditional knots. There was no way of knowing it then, but Birger would become famous for being the last man publicly hanged in the state. The noose and scaffold were scheduled to be replaced by the more modern and *humane* electric chair.

H. Dungey drawing of shootout between Birger and Shelton "tanks" near Marion (courtesy D. Bain/Anderson-Austin News)

The wooden scaffold, with the unlucky 13 steps, had been built in the courtyard next to the county jail. There were perhaps 100 people who had official tickets in their pockets, granting them access inside the fenced area. Outside the fence were an estimated 5,000 people – the largest crowd anyone in Benton could remember. The curious onlookers included men and women and children. Some boys sat perched on their father's shoulders. They were viewing an object lesson about what might happen to them if they strayed from the path of righteousness and were tempted to venture into lawbreaking. Justice was swift and sure. A few intrepid teens climbed mature trees for a better view. In some cases, men were perched on nearby rooftops to watch the proceedings.

As the time neared 10:00 a.m., the heavy jail door swung open and various officials led Charlie Birger out to keep his rendezvous with destiny. Birger, lean and of medium height, was smartly dressed in a new gray suit with a conservative tie. His hands were cuffed in front of him. Next to Birger in the solemn procession was rabbi Mazur from St. Louis, reading words of comfort from a small black book. Birger exchanged a few pleasantries with acquaintances as he was led past the crowd toward the steps. He obviously had many friends in the gathering. To his left was a large wicker basket that would hold his body after he dropped through the trap door. Witnesses say he spat into it as he ascended the stairs.

Charlie Birger awaiting execution (*Post-Dispatch*)

Outwardly, Birger appeared more calm and relaxed than those in charge of the execution. But close inspection revealed that his hands were slightly shaking. And his jovial appearance belied the fact that the night before he tried to cheat the gallows with an attempted suicide. As Birger reached the platform he briefly glanced up at the noose that swung gently in the breeze as it hung suspended from a large horizontal beam. He chatted amiably with the rabbi and lawmen as final preparations were made. When asked by Hanna if he wanted a white or black hood, he replied saltily: "I'll take the black one. I ain't no Klu Klux."

Reporters from all the local newspapers, and as far away as East St. Louis, Chicago, and Paducah, were busy snapping pictures and anxiously awaiting any memorable last words. There were about ten minutes to go until the fateful hour but Charlie told lawmen he wanted to get it over with. When asked if he had any final thoughts, his comments were brief. He said that he was not bitter and he forgave everybody. Birger surveyed the crowd below one last time. Many of them had tears well up in their eyes. Then he looked up at the sky and said: "It's a beautiful world." Everyone there would remember the pleasant smile on his face.

He stepped onto the trap door and the noose and hood were set in place. Straps were tightened around his arms and legs. The knotted part of the rope was snugged around his neck under his left ear. Sheriff Jim Pritchard took a firm hold on the lever and drew a deep breath. As he yanked the lever back, the trap door fell open and Birger's 170 pound body plummeted downward, snapping his neck at the 5th cervical vertebra. Minutes later, several doctors checked for a pulse or a heartbeat. Finding none, they pronounced Birger dead.

Birger's body would be taken to a Jewish cemetery in University City at St. Louis, and he would be buried next to his father. Shachna Itzik Birger, the granite would read. But the death of this celebrated bootlegger only led to the growth of his legend.

According to biographer **Gary DeNeal**, who wrote *A Knight of Another Sort* in 1981, Charlie Birger was a Lithuanian Russian, born in 1883. His family journeyed to America at the end of the century, part of the wave of Eastern European Jews processed at Ellis Island in New York. The family moved to St. Louis and joined a local synagogue. As a youth, Birger hustled newspapers in a tough neighborhood for the *Post-Dispatch*. When Charlie was old enough, he joined the U.S. Cavalry and served in Montana and South Dakota where he became a skilled bronco buster. After a back injury ended his stint, he returned and started running a grocery store in the Edgemont area of East St. Louis. He had a brother (Sam) who became a successful merchant in the nearby town of **Glen Carbon**.

(Note: to order *A Knight of Another Sort,* send $22.95 to Springhouse, Box 61 Herod, IL 62947)

Rope used to hang Charlie Birger (photo by Bob Rea , Franklin CHS)

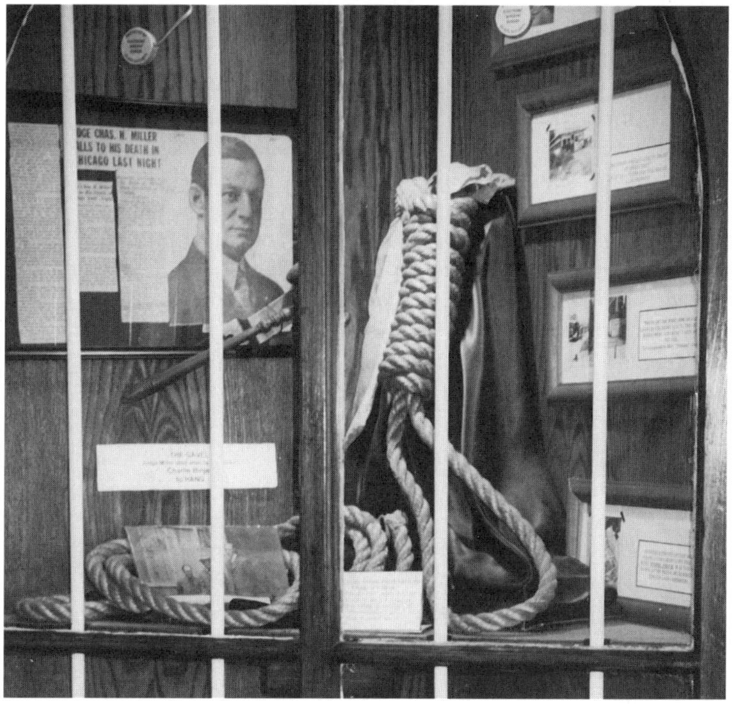

The 5-8 wiry Charlie Birger killed his first man in a barroom quarrel in East St. Louis. He later married for the first time - a tall, blonde local girl named Edna Hastey (around 1909). For nearly 8 years he worked at various odd jobs, including coal mining at the Nigger Hollow mine near **O'Fallon**. He lived for a spell in **Staunton** (1908-10), next **Virden** (1910), followed by **Christopher** (1912) and then he moved to **Ledford** in Saline County. For a while he sold watermelons from the back of a Model-T Roadster with a pickup truck bed. Birger developed a distaste for hard labor but found he could make a fast buck in the gambling, bootlegging, and prostitution rackets. Birger also bought a couple of gin joints in **East St. Louis** near the colored part of town. His favorite spot in that tough place was a raucous place named the Monkey Cage. In 1915 Birger and his wife separated but the divorce was not finalized until 1917. He served time in the **Massac County jail** in 1918 when three stolen cars were found in his barn. That same year he married a second time, to a woman named **Beatrice Bainbridge**. He tried to shield his family from his shady activities as best he could. Charlie was adept at baseball and even played for a while on one of the local teams.

Charlie left Ledford and bought a white frame house on Poplar Street in **Marion**. On the outskirts of town he purchased some property and built a large cabin that he called **Shady Rest**. For the rest of his life he lived in the Marion/Herrin/Harrisburg area. With the advent of Prohibition in 1920 came a golden opportunity for Birger and others of his ilk. They knew drinking alcohol was a centuries-long social habit that would be difficult to legislate into oblivion.

Birger machine guns and wicker basket for body (Bob Rea, Franklin County Hist. Soc.)

Birger's success came due to a combination of personal traits, mirrored by others like Al Capone and John Dillinger. Birger was flamboyant and had a winning personality. He could charm the spots off a leopard. He emulated cowboy movie star Tom Mix in his dress and mannerisms. He loved the acclaim from becoming a public benefactor and bought bags of groceries for destitute widows and threw handfuls of loose change and penny candy to an adoring army of neighborhood children. His largesse made a big impression among locals who called him a modern-day Robin Hood. His other skill was a certain ruthlessness in dealing with those who crossed him or became a business rival. By the early 1920s Birger had killed 3 men but was acquitted on pleas of self-defense in each instance.

Violence in the area was not limited to Charlie Birger and his cohorts. There was a bitter coal mine strike at Herrin that led to an infamous massacre of guards and scabs by striking miners in 1922. Nineteen men were brutally murdered in the notorious incident. Like many southern Illinois mines, the owners were absentee landlords who lived in the ostentatious Gold Coast section of Chicago. When a Klan war broke out, and Charlie Birger became involved in numerous shootouts with his rivals, the area came to be known as Little Hell and what historian Paul Angle called Bloody Williamson.

Southern Illinois, long known as Little Egypt, became a breeding ground for the Klan because it opposed corrupt law-enforcement officials who took bribes and payoffs from the bootleggers. The Klan hammered hard at themes like law and order, distrust of Roman Catholics who paid homage to a foreign Pope, and adopted a nativist mantra, stressing the importance of continued Anglo-Saxon/Protestant dominance – 100 % Americanism. The Klan endeared itself to local Protestant churches by also opposing the teaching of evolution in schools.

Replica of Birger's scaffold (Franklin County Historical Society)

Protestant churchgoers found themselves in an unholy alliance with hooded nightriders. Baptists and Methodists were often at odds with policemen, whom they could not trust to enforce the laws. Into this volatile mix came an odd character by the name of **S. Glenn Young**. Young was bantam-sized, bowlegged crusader, who quickly came to be called Little Napoleon. A discredited Prohibition agent who once killed a Granite City man in a raid, he quickly took leadership of the Klan and led the vigilante fight against lawbreakers, corrupt police, and bootleggers. Young, like Charlie Birger, was flamboyant and sported military clothes festooned with pearl-handled Colt .45s. He posed for pictures with a machine gun cradled in his arms.

Young was both reckless and ruthless with his raids. Stories began to emerge of coarse treatment, robbery, and planted evidence. Those who were abused by the raids quickly became sympathetic with Charlie Birger, who soon became one of Young's main targets.

Birger joined forces with another local gang, the Shelton brothers from the Fairfield area in Wayne County. Young and his wife were ambushed near the **Okaw Bottoms** (Washington County) while driving to East St. Louis for a 1924 Klan meeting in **East St. Louis**. Young's Lincoln touring car was run off the road in a hail of gunfire. Young was wounded and his wife was left legally blind in both eyes from buckshot. Ironically, the anti-Catholic Young was given care by the sister's at St. Elizabeth's hospital in **Belleville**.

Young's crusade came to an end in January of 1925 when he and some of his men were at the European Hotel in Herrin. A bitter enemy, Ora Thomas, a lawman who was friendly with Birger, confronted Young. Both men went down in a blaze of gunshots. Thomas and Young died of their wounds, and two of Young's henchmen were also killed.

E. St. Louisan Bill Jacobus in Charlie Birger's old cell in the Benton Jail

Young's body was viewed by more than 75,000 people, and an estimated 20,000 attended his funeral service at the First Baptist church in Herrin. He was buried in a local cemetery, and a large vault was placed over his grave. Because he made so many enemies, his tomb became a target for vandals. Today it bears the scars of bullet holes from those who used it as target practice.

Despite the loss of their leader, Klan influence remained strong until April of 1926 when an election-day shootout resulted in the death of three more of their ranks. The bloodshed demoralized their ranks, and their power was broken once and for all. Birger, the chief focus of Klan raids, had survived with the help from friends in the area. Birger decided to join forces with the Shelton brothers, who also joined the fight against the Klan. A deal was struck. The two rivals joined forces to enlarge their base of operations and extend their power. Liquor was brought up from Florida and Cuba, and then it would be cut (watered down) at Shady Rest and distributed. A bargain was also struck whereby profits from slot machines and gambling joints would be split. But it didn't take long before there was a falling out among thieves. Carl Shelton became convinced that Birger was skimming from the profits, according to one theory. Others say it was a dame from Shawneetown by the name of Helen Holbrook who caused the problem. It seems that Holbrook was carrying on with Charlie Birger and Carl Shelton simultaneously. (Birger's womanizing caused his wife Beatrice to leave him and file for divorce.) A third theory holds that Birger became angry when Carl Shelton refused to help smuggle in some of Birger's Russian relatives down in Florida.

Whatever the cause for the split, a new chapter in the Bloody Williamson saga began in the summer of 1926. Before it was over, dozens of people on both sides would be killed, Birger's Shady Rest would be burned to the ground, and shootouts between armored cars became commonplace. In one incident, the Sheltons targeted Art and Bess Newman, former associates who had gone over to the enemy. Newman was considered Birger's number two man. The Sheltons constructed a two and 1/2 ton truck with an elongated steel tank on its bed. Protruding through gun ports, cut by torches, was an assortment of weapons that were used to open fire on the couple. Despite a fusillade of 25 shots, Art was unharmed and his wife received only a minor wound.

Earl Shelton died in Florida at age 96

About a month later, the Sheltons rented a Curtiss Jenny barnstorming plane and used it to fly over Shady Rest and drop homemade bombs. There was negligible damage due to the Shelton's lack of experience with speed, distance, and trajectory. Ripley's **Believe It or Not** immortalized the deed by touting it as the first aerial attack ever carried out on American soil.

Birger eventually grew bold and careless during his feud with the Sheltons and their associates. He assured local town folk that he was their protector, and their lives were in no danger since he and his men were gunning for other gangsters, not local citizens. His downfall came when he hatched a plot to kill a Sheltonite, Joe Adams, who also happened to be the mayor of **West City**, located near **Benton**. He even boasted to Joe's wife over the telephone that he planned to kill her husband. In December he paid $50 to Harry and Elmo Thomasson, a couple of teenage gang wannabes, who happened to be orphans. They knocked on Adams' door, and when he answered it, they handed him a note, written by Birger, but ostensibly from Carl Shelton. They boldly shot Adams in the stomach in broad daylight while he was reading the note.

Birger probably would have gotten off with a stiff jail sentence had it not been for some other killings. A few days before he was arrested for the Adams murder, Birger and his men killed a member of the state highway patrol, who was on their payroll. Lory Price and his wife Ethel were abducted from their home. She was taken in a separate car and shot. Her body was then thrown down an abandoned mine shaft. It was a cold-blooded killing because the local schoolteacher was obviously pregnant. Her husband was shot several times, driven to a deserted field, dumped, and shot again. The tide of public opinion turned quickly against Birger as former admirers now saw him for what he really was.

Karl Hassinger pass for execution of Joe Chesnas at Harrisburg, 1927

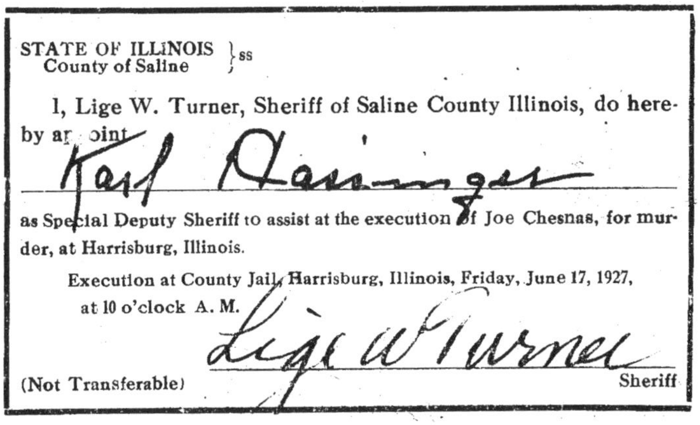

STATE OF ILLINOIS } ss
County of Saline

I, Lige W. Turner, Sheriff of Saline County Illinois, do hereby appoint Karl Hassinger as Special Deputy Sheriff to assist at the execution of Joe Chesnas, for murder, at Harrisburg, Illinois.

Execution at County Jail, Harrisburg, Illinois, Friday, June 17, 1927, at 10 o'clock A. M.

(Not Transferable) Lige W Turner Sheriff

Birger's trial began on July 6, 1927. His lawyers tried to play on the sympathy of the jury by having his third wife, Bernice, and his two pre-teen daughters, attend the trial. But the worm turned when Harry Thommason took the stand and described how Birger planned and paid for the murder of Joe Adams. Art Newman and another Birger hireling were convicted of killing Lory and Ethel Price, but they were given prison terms – not the death penalty. Birger's lawyers tried various appeals and even employed a last-ditch effort to save him with an insanity hearing. But the psychiatrist concluded that while Birger might have been mean, vicious, and mentally deranged, he was legally sane. His date with the hangman was now assured.

In a radio discussion on KMOX radio in December of 2001, this author debated with **Gary DeNeal** and **Taylor Pensoneau** (*Brothers Notorious* author) which of three southern Illinois gang leaders was the most famous – Buster Wortman of East St. Louis, Charlie Birger, or the Sheltons. DeNeal won the argument by pointing out that only Birger has been paid the ultimate tribute – that of having a building in Benton dedicated to preserving his memory. The old jail has been converted to a museum featuring Birger photos, news clippings and assorted memorabilia such as the hangman's noose. Outside, there is also an authentic full-sized replica of the execution platform.

In April of 2002 this author gave a presentation to a history honor society at SIU in Carbondale. In a later conversation with **Marji Morgan**, the chairperson, she told me the Birger topic is so hot with students that all of the professors, weary of reading the same material, have had to forbid them from writing about him as a research paper topic.

Why was Charlie Birger missing his ring finger on his left hand?

According to local historian **Bob Rea** of **Benton**, Charlie got in a barroom fight and was bitten on the finger. The human mouth is full of bacteria and the bite became infected. This was before the discovery of penicillin, so the finger had to be amputated. The missing finger can be seen in photos of Birger taken at the Benton jail.

When the judge sentenced Birger to die on the gallows, why did he say that he would be "hanged by the neck until dead, dead, dead?"

The word "dead" was repeated by the judge three times because after the hanging, three different doctors would listen for a heartbeat before pronouncing him dead. (from **Bob Rea** of Benton)

Did flambouyant **Billy Sunday** ever have a talk with Charlie Birger?
In 1927, while Charlie Birger was in jail, he was visited by the famous Chicago evangelist **Billy Sunday**, who was holding a revival in **West Frankfort**.

Evangelist Billy Sunday

THE 1922 HERRIN MASSACRE

The **Herrin Massacre** took place on June 22. This infamous incident occurred during a bitter coal miners' strike against the **Southern Illinois Coal Company** strip mine at Crenshaw Crossing. The company tried to break the union by firing its unionized workers. Next, the management imported armed guards and replacement workers from Chicago to work the Lester strip mine. There were mine strikes all over the nation at this time, ordered by **John L. Lewis** and the United Mine Workers of America. The millionaire owner of the mine sought to profit by continuing to mine coal that would be sold at a premium price due to shortages.

Map of the Herrin Massacre

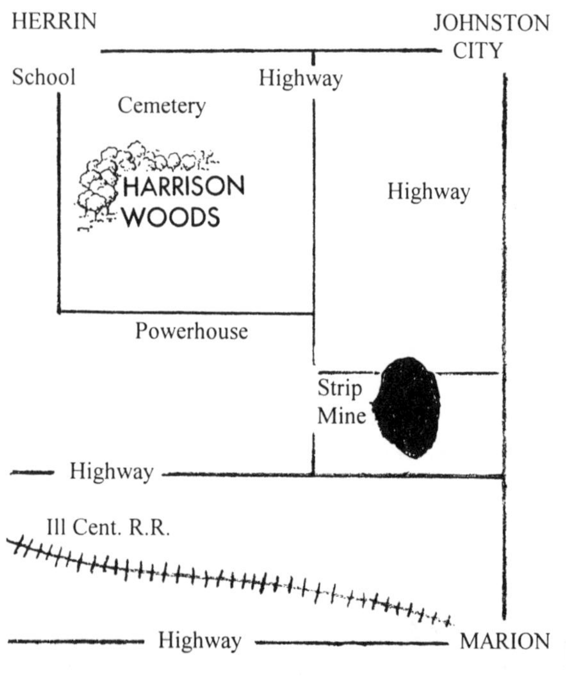

Striking workers attacked the mine, and in the ensuing mayhem, **three union men were killed**. Enraged, the belligerent miners sent for reinforcements and men came in from **Marion, Herrin, Dewmaine, Zeigler, West Frankfort, Harrisburg and Johnston City**. The crowd swelled to about 1,000 and they surrounded the facility, cut power and telephone lines, and lay siege to the place. A big steam shovel was dynamited and coal cars were set on fire.

Terrified, everyone in the besieged strip mine surrendered on the promise that they would leave Williamson County. As the 47 men filed out, the angry mob began striking the scabs, shouting ugly epithets. Then they dragged off the mine superintendent, C.K. McDowell, and shot him two times, killing him. A man in an automobile drove up and told the mob not to kill the captives on the highway where it might be seen by women and children. The captive men were herded into a woodland and told to run as fast as they could back to Chicago. But most of them were shot and killed while trying to flee. One small group was taken captive in the Herrin schoolhouse until the mob of about 200 people worked itself into a frenzy and dragged the men to a cemetery a mile away. The group of six men, pleading for their lives, while yoked together by a large rope, were beaten and shot. Those found still to be alive, bodies broken and bleeding, had their **throats cut** by a man with a pocketknife. One mine boss was hung and then his body was riddled with bullets. When it was over, authorities found a total of **nineteen bodies**. Eight more victims were wounded.

The next day hundreds of people from neighboring towns came to view the dead bodies. A photographer arrived to take pictures but was threatened and changed his mind. W.J. Lester, president of the company, was in Chicago when the trouble began. One other man, a refugee from the coal mine, was killed the next day. He and two others were chased by a mob of men in West Frankfort. Two of the men escaped but the third, a Mexican, ran up to the top of a coal chute of a nearby mine and jumped to his death.

An article in the June 24, 1922, St. Louis *Globe-Democrat* described the massacre as . . . "the most brutal and horrifying crime that has ever stained the garments of organized labor." After the massacre, Williamson County gained a national reputation as **"Little Hell."**

William Allen White, the Kansas newspaper editor, wrote about the emergence of a new doctrine in the conflict. Labor was beginning to believe that ***skill*** had the same status as ***property***. The right of a worker to apply his skill in a place where it would produce value was beginning to be seen as a human right. The right of a laborer to work for profit was gaining equal status with the right of owners to make a profit.

On January 19,1923, five men who were tried for murder in the Herrin Massacre were found not guilty by the jury in the **Williamson County Courthouse**. Illinois miners, in a convention at **Peoria**, pledged one percent of their monthly income to establish a defense fund for the accused. Six other defendants, tried in a separate case, were also found not guilty. The defendants included: **Otis Clark, Bert Grace, P. Hiller, Joseph Carnaghi, Leva Mann, Hugh Willis, Philip Fontanetta, Oscar Howard and James Brown**, a Negro.

In order to put some perspective on the actions of the Herrin mob, it must be remembered that in the long struggle for worker's rights and the effort to unionize, the authority of the law had almost always sided with management. For years mine owners had exploited workers. The mines were dangerous places to work, and safety measures were lacking. Wages were piteously low, and payment was often issued in script that could be exchanged for goods at the company store. At the turn of the century, the 12-hour day and 7-day week were common. When periods of recession came around, wages were slashed and were slow to be restored when prosperity returned. And black lung disease led most miners to an early grave. Author **Jack London** once wrote that a scab strikebreaker was the most vile person on the face of the earth.

It was conditions like these that led **Karl Marx**, who once lived in America, to write the Communist Manifesto and *Das Capital* (Capitalism). Workers of the world unite. You have nothing to lose but your chains. What Marx failed to forsee was the rise of political reformers such as "progressives," who pressured the legislatures into enacting reform. This was coupled with the rise of unions, which slowly wrested power from management, and led to Americans having the highest standard of living in the world.

But in 1922, unions were quite weak. Strikes by miners in Colorado and Idaho had led to small wars. Pinkerton guards and deputy sheriffs, equipped with machine guns and armed cavalry, lined up against armed strikers. Mines were dynamited; men were killed. Local communities were terrorized with soldiers breaking into miner's homes and seizing men on the streets. When writs of habeas corpus were obtained, the soldiers refused to obey the judges' orders. When the practice was challenged in court, one judge remarked: "To hell with the Constitution; we're not following the Constitution."

Whenever miners lost a strike, a familiar routine was followed. Fenced areas were established in which strikers and sympathizers, even women and children, were imprisoned. Along with this went the firing of sympathetic local officials and workers who were blacklisted. Union officials were deported to other states and warned never to return.

This does not excuse the Herrin Massacre, but it makes the "not guilty" verdict of the jurors much more understandable.

For more detailed information on the massacre, read **Paul Angle's *Bloody Williamson*.**

****

From **Lois Zimmerman** of **Wood River/Zeigler**: My grandfather, **Richard Marsden** (English) worked in mines 55 years. He started at age 14. He moved up from Arkansas to Zeigler and worked in Bell and Zollar mine number 1 and 2 at Zeigler. I think mine number 2 was developed around 1921. I lived with them and went to Zeigler grade and high school back then. They had to do away with the old high school because of mine subsidence. Grandpa also attended the **Birger hanging** at Benton in Franklin County. My grandfather helped organize the union down there. The mine ownership often hired scab labor to try and break the unions. The company had a big truck with machine guns mounted on it to pick up the workers and safely take them to work. One time I started off to school and the wives of the scab laborers chased me back home. My grandmother, Ollie, **put a butcher knife under her sweater** and marched me back to school under her protection. My grandparents took the mattresses off the bed and put them on the floor because the scabs sometimes threw bricks through the windows. There was a riot at **Royalton** (about four miles from Zeigler) and my grandfather's best friend, a Mr. Daveys, was killed. **Grandpa was shot** in the knee. The dead man's wife never remarried. She was very pretty and did some small town modeling. Back then some of the stores would have fashion shows at the high schools. **Belle Daveys** was the talk of the town for a while because she dyed her hair blonde, but somehow it turned out lettuce green. Many of the scab workers came down from **Gillespie** and **Mount Olive**. There was a minister named **Roy Baugh** who had a congregation in East St. Louis. And every time the Sheltons or Wortman tried to open a new gambling den, he contacted the state police, and they made a raid. Roy later ministered to a congregation in **Rosewood Heights** in East Alton.

THE UNBELIVABLE LEOPOLD AND LOEB "THRILL KILLING" OF BOBBY FRANKS

Jacob Franks

It was a startling, shocking story. Two brilliant minds, fatally flawed. On May 31, 1924, two wealthy, well-dressed, intellectual youth confessed to the callous slaying of **Bobby Franks**, purely for the thrill and adventure involved. Nathan Leopold, age 19, and Richard Loeb, age 18, were sons of wealthy and prominent Chicago families. They killed a 14-year-old boy who lived in their neighborhood on May 21, without apparent motive.

On July 21, the defendants appeared in court with their lawyers and stunned everyone by changing their plea from "not guilty" to "guilty."

Frank's body was found early in the morning on May 22, 1924, by some workmen who cut across a field on their way to work. They accidentally discovered the body of a naked boy that had been stuffed into a drain culvert. A pair of horn-rimmed reading spectacles were found near the body.

Bobby Frank's parents lived in Hyde Park/Kenwood, a wealthy suburb near the University of Chicago. The Franks family was social outcast among neighboring Jews because they had rejected the Jewish faith to become Christian Scientists, and Jacob Franks made his first big money running a pawnshop. Bobby Franks had last been seen the day before, walking home from Harvard School, a private institution for families who lived in the area.

The Franks were contacted by kidnappers the morning after their son's disappearance. A man called and said his name was Johnson. He told the Franks their son had been kidnapped, and they would receive further news the next day. A special delivery typewritten letter arrived, as expected, demanding the sum of $10,000 in old money for the return of their son. The bills were to be placed in a large cigar box and wrapped in white paper. The father decided to pay the ransom and not contact the police. It was a reasonably small sum of money for Mr. Franks, who had amassed his fortune in real estate. But before he could deliver the money, the police called, saying they had found the body of a young boy. Because of the glasses, they didn't think it was Bobby Franks. When Jacob Franks went to view the corpse, he sadly identified the body as his son.

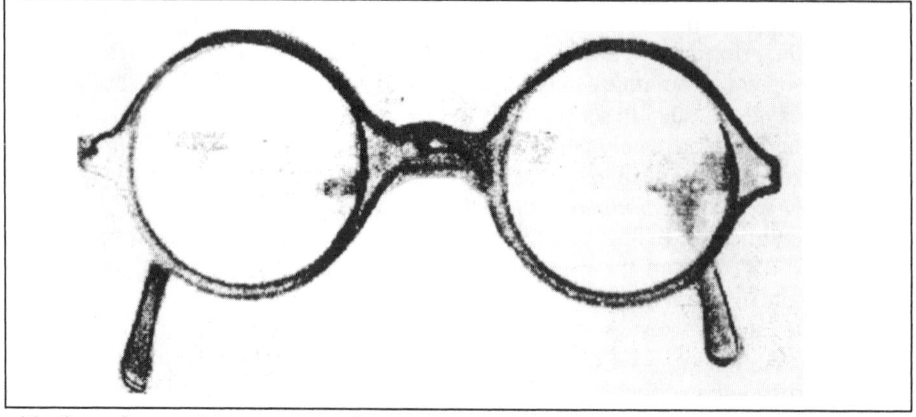

Richard Loeb was the son of the prominent Albert Loeb, who was vice-president of Sears, Roebuck and Co. Son Richard was actually a distant cousin of Bobby Franks. The two had played tennis together on the courts at the Loeb home. Aside from the wealth aspect, Loeb was the opposite of Leopold. Richard was tall, bright and popular, graduating from the University of Michigan at seventeen, **the youngest ever at the school**. Richard had private tutoring and also had attended the nearby Harvard School. Ironically, the first suspects hauled in for questioning were teachers at the Harvard School. Their motive for kidnapping one of their rich charges, police reasoned, was ransom money to supplement their meager salaries.

Bobby Franks

Hegewich prairie, the area where the body was found, was a tract of land popular only to birdwatchers. Leopold was an avid birdwatcher and an expert on the rare Kirtland Warbler. Detectives checked with various oculists in the city and soon discovered, through the prescription, the glasses found at the crime scene belonged to Nathan Leopold. When questioned about this, the young man said the glasses did not belong to him, and thought his spectacles were somewhere in his house. However, he could not produce them. Loeb was at the Leopold home when the detectives arrived, and was also questioned. The ransom note had been typed on an Underwood. When asked what kind Richard used, he replied a Hammond. Detectives found a student who had done some college research with Richard, and he said the report was typed on the machine at Richard's home. Richard had stolen the typewriter from a fraternity house the year before. When the research paper was compared to the ransom note, the letters were identical.

The boys gave an alibi for the day of the murder by saying they had decided to eat at a restaurant, picked up some girls, dropped them off, and then drove around for a while. But the chauffeur said he had been repairing and cleaning the car all that day. When confronted with these facts, Loeb confessed. He said Leopold concocted the scheme that was merely an impulse to see if they could commit **the perfect crime**. Loeb explained he merely went along for the excitement. When questioned, Leopold said the two found their life of the genteel rich rather boring, and they were merely looking for something stimulating. Raised and tutored by governesses, sheltered from contact with other "vulgar" youth of their age, they spent much of their time with the insular world of books. They wanted to put some of their knowledge to practical use. The only difference in their stories was that each accused the other of the actual killing.

Their first target as a victim was a boy named John Levinson, but they lost track of him and then they encountered the Franks boy. Franks, they decided, was a suitable victim because they knew they could get him into the car on a ruse about a tennis racket question. Once in the car, Loeb put his hand over Bobby Franks' mouth and hit him on the head with a chisel. When he did not readily succumb, a gag was placed in his mouth. Franks died from suffocation. Then they drove to the prearranged spot for disposal of the body. To make identification more difficult, they poured hydrochloric acid on the boy's face and naked body. Next the body was disrobed and shoved far into the metal drainpipe near the Pennsylvania Railroad tracks. Richard later noticed that his glasses had fallen from the breast pocket of his "birding suit." But he thought authorities would not be able to trace them to him. Then they made their phone calls and dropped the letter in the telegraph blank box. The rented car (a Willys-Knight) was taken back home for a good cleaning before returning it. The chauffeur who helped them was told the red stains were spilled wine. The

The Franks' Home

murdered boy's clothes were burned in the furnace in the basement at Richard Leopold's house.

The Jewish/German Leopold family originally came to this country around 1820. Leopold was the youngest of the children in his family and was of frail health. He attended an all-girl's facility and was escorted to and from school by a nurse until he was 11. Nathan's father was worth millions.

Nathan Leopold's interest in books and birds gave him a solitary life with few friends.

Nathan Leopold, Clarence Darrow, Richard Loeb

Richard Leob was just the opposite. However, his Jewish/German family, like the Leopolds, also had millions. He was sickly as a youngster, but by the time he reached puberty, he was strong and hardy. Richard's governess made sure he excelled in school, and he was well liked with many friends. He began going with girls at age fourteen, the same year he entered the university. When he switched over to the Harvard School and later entered college at age 14, he was well liked and accepted into the group of older boys. After his arrest, several girls he had dated totally went to pieces. All of his friends voiced the opinion that it was Nathan Leopold who drew the immature "Dickie" into the web of crime. Dickie Loeb was also tenderhearted. Once he crashed into a woman in a carriage with his automobile. He wept and nearly fainted when he learned the woman was injured. He persuaded his mother to take care of all her medical bills and to pay off the mortgage on her home.

The accused seemed to take great delight in telling authorities all the details of the crime. The pair said they took the typewriter after writing the ransom note and threw it into a pond at Jackson Park. A diver recovered the machine. They showed authorities the drugstore where they had purchased the acid. They even took them to the hardware store where they had bought the chisel. By the time the defense attorneys arrived on the scene, the boys had already given the State's Attorney all the information he needed. Sixty-seven year-old **Clarence Darrow** of Chicago, who would argue for the defense in the famous 1925 Scopes "monkey trial," was hired by Jack Loeb, Dick's uncle. Ben Bachrach, another distinguished lawyer, was hired as co-counsel. Incredibly, the two boys were so used to leading a pampered life, they quickly made friends with other prisoners and got along quite well. Huge crowds were drawn to the daily courtroom drama, many of them young girls. The boys, who had known each other for 4 years, put aside their differences and became friends again. During the trial, the boys smiled often and laughed when the gallery laughed. Their smirks and smiles in court further angered an already enraged public. There didn't seem to be any remorse for what they had done.

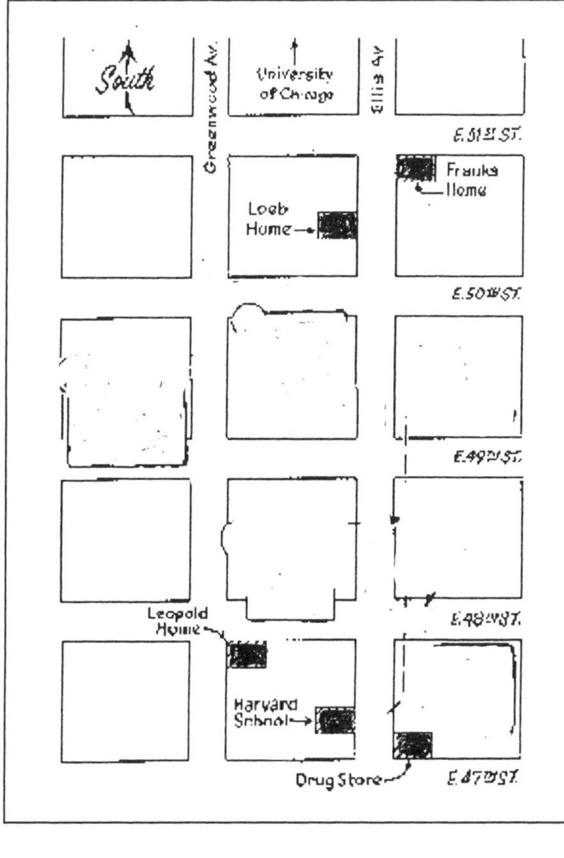

The trial began June 6, 1924. Leopold and Loeb were charged with first-degree murder, and prosecution sought death by hanging as the appropriate punishment. Darrow and Bachrach cobbled together a defense that admitted the boy's guilt, but argued the guilt was mitigated by certain mental defects. In essence, these two spoiled, rich, bored youngsters were social misfits. Both blessed with brilliant minds, they had studied Friedrich Nietzsche's philosophy, especially his notion of the "superman," who was someone above the law. Committing the perfect crime and getting away with it would prove their superiority and validate Nietzsche's thesis. The judge would not let defense use an insanity plea because Illinois law at the time had a rigorous standard – did they know right from wrong? Darrow, the infamous agnostic, was brilliant. He waived a jury trial and put the boys' fate in the hands of Judge John Caverly. By pleading them guilty, he hoped to save them from the hangman's noose.

Mr. Crowe of the prosecution argued strenuously against the "degrees of responsibility" defense scenario. He also hammered at the defense theory that although the boys didn't have an organic brain disorder such as paresis or a tumor, their upbringing had impaired their ability to distinguish right from wrong, the way normal people do. This was the first case ever where psychiatrists examined the boys for hours on end and presented every facet and fantasy of their life before public scrutiny. Every aspect of family history was put under a microscope. It must have been embarrassing for the parents and close relatives.

Nathan Leopold contracted gonorrhea at age 15. A first cousin of the father went insane and was sent to Elgin. At age 12 Nathan stammered. His governess was repressed about sexual matters, so he didn't learn about the birds and bees until age 12. He played a game with people by secretly following them around, pretending to be a detective. He suffered headaches and doctors thought a pair of glasses would eliminate the problem.

Dickie Loeb: He was effeminate until he had his tonsils removed at age 9. Overweight at age 14. Started drinking age 15. Considerable dental work. Prone to hives. Fainted easily without much provocation. One governess exposed herself indecently to him. Some crude boys at school implanted him with some abnormal ideas about sex. Read numerous bizarre ancient books. Drew pictures of hooded figures marked K.K.K. Once stole another boy's stamp collection. Made a chart of attributes for defining the perfect man – gave himself a score of 62 out of 100. Earliest sexual experiences were with his governess. At age 8, believed his father who told him babies were bought at the store. Because of his mental superiority, did not believe that ordinary conventions of right and wrong applied to him. Decided he would never tell his children there was a Santa Claus. Cheated at cards. Stole some meerschaum pipes from a department store in Chicago. Began drinking at age 15.

In an incredibly long summation before the judge, Darrow gave an impassioned plea on behalf of the boys. Some excerpts: There was no malice toward Bobby Franks, and the defendants did not torture him. Killing these two would not bring the victim back. Leopold and Loeb were simply too immature to fully comprehend the consequences of their actions. Their tender age and lack of maturity should disqualify them from the death penalty. Humanity is moving away from the death penalty. We no longer burn witches at the stake. There used to be 200 offenses that called for the death penalty. Europe found that as penalties became more humane, crime decreased. The very principles of Christianity call for love and understanding. If we execute these boys, what next? Do we start killing 13-year-olds? In the entire history of Illinois, not one person under the age of 23, who pleaded guilty, has ever been hanged. Society bears part of the blame for their deed. After the Napoleonic wars, crime in Europe increased. After the Civil War, crime increased. And it has only been a few years since the Great War in Europe took the lives of millions of young men. War tends to cheapen the value of human life. Finally, Darrow asked the judge to consider the unnecessary grief for the families of the two defendants. Executing the two boys would bring them untold misery. Capital punishment, he further argued, does not deter crime.

Orson Welles

Sentencing was handed down on September 10th, 1924. More than 5,000 persons waited outside the building, anxious to hear the decision. Leopold and Loeb were given **life imprisonment** for the murder of Bobby Franks and 99 years for the kidnapping charge. They were taken to Joliet prison the next day.

Afterwards, the rich parents haggled over the attorney fee and ultimately Darrow accepted $30,000.

Although this was billed as the **Crime of the Century**, it was quite amateurish in nearly every aspect. Leopold carelessly lost his glasses at the crime scene. They dumped the body in an area associated with Leopold, who was known to birdwatch there. Their alibi was full of holes. The body was found before they could collect the ransom. And so on.

People would talk about this celebrated case for years. The crime produced hundreds of articles, dozens of books, and inspired two films – ***The Rope***, a Hitchcock film, and ***Compulsion***, starring **Orson Welles** and Bradford Dillman.

Prison officials came under fire for the special treatment that Leopold and Loeb received. They had private cells, special-order meals, filing cabinets, and kept a pet canary. Everyone assumed the families were giving extra money to prison officials in exchange for the pampering. Loeb was killed in a 1936 prison brawl. He had been slashed 56 times. Leopold was turned down for parole numerous times despite becoming a model prisoner. In 1958 poet **Carl Sandburg** pleaded his case for parole, even offering to let Leopold come to live in his house if released. Leopold won release on his 4th parole hearing later that year. He wrote his story, *Life Plus 99 Years* and then moved to Puerto Rico. He died from heart problems in 1971.

TONY (BIG TUNA) ACCARDO

Tony "Big Tuna" Accardo

Tony Accardo died at age 68. How many of those years did he spend in prison?
For years Tony boasted that he never spent a single night behind bars.

Who was responsible for convicting Tony of income tax fraud on November 11, 1960?

Richard Ogilvie was the federal attorney who successfully prosecuted Accardo. It was shown that Accardo was guilty of taking phony tax deductions over a three-year period in the late Fifties. Unfortunately, the sentence of six years in prison was overturned by the U.S. Court of Appeals on grounds of "prejudicial error." He was tried again in 1962, but the jury found him not guilty. Although the outcome was a setback for Ogilvie, the recognition he achieved from the case was a stepping stone that led directly to the Governor's Mansion.

What was Tony's position in Chicago's underworld?

He was head of the old Capone syndicate for about 13 years from about 1944 to 1957. He stepped aside, and Sam Giancana took the reins with Accardo staying on in a highly respected advisory capacity. By this time, Giancana already had 60 arrests on his record. Giancana later made his home in Las Vegas and lived with **Phyllis McGuire**, one of the McGuire Sisters, who performed on the stage. Giancana was murdered in his home in 1975 at the age of 67.

What was Tony Accardo's connection with Capone when Big Al was in his glory years?
Tony grew up in Chicago's Little Italy and dropped out of school when he was in the 6th grade. He became Capone's bodyguard and carried out an assortment of other more sinister tasks with chilling efficiency. Many crime buffs claim that Tony was one of the shooters in the St. Valentine's Day Massacre.

How did Tony rise to the top in the Capone organization?
After Capone went to prison, "the Outfit" was run by Frank Nitti and Paul "The Waiter" Ricca. Nitti committed suicide in 1943, and a year later Ricca went to prison, convicted of attempted extortion. Accardo, who had been their front man, assumed leadership after they were gone.

How did Accardo earn the nickname "Big Tuna?"
Giving gangsters Runyonesque nicknames went all the way back to the advent of Prohibition. Accrado was saddled with the sobriquet Big Tuna for his numerous fishing expeditions.
The American gangster image was so pervasive in Europe that when American flyers were shot down and captured by Germans during World War II, they were paraded through town and derided as "gangsters" who were killing innocent civilians.

THE SHOCKING MURDER OF VALERIE PERCY

Ann Margaret, the female Elvis

Chuck Percy came of age in **Chicago** during the Depression. His father was a night clerk in a hotel and seldom could afford more than five gallons of gas for the family car at a time. The family even received relief checks during those trying times. And it was probably those lean years that drove Chuck Percy to excel in life. He attended **New Trier High School** in Winnetka, the same school where **Ann Margret** would later lead school spirit yells as a cheerleader. The turning point in his life came when he started attending a Christian Science Sunday school class taught by the president of Bell & Howell. Percy attended the University of Chicago. He earned tuition money by being paid $10 for every high school senior he recruited. In high school and college, he was social, outgoing and popular. Percy served in the Navy during World War II, starting in 1943. While in the navy, he married Jeanne Dickerson, a Northwestern coed. After his navy stint, at the age of 29, he became president of Bell & Howell Camera, earning $40,000 a year. By 1967, with 82,000 shares of Bell & Howell, he was worth approximately $6 million. Under his tutelage the company grew from a $13 million dollar company to $160 million. On televison, Bell & Howell sponsored "Cimarron City," "Restless Gun" and "Ellery Queen."
His wife gave birth to three children, including a son, Roger. But she died in 1947 because of a reaction to penicillin after a colitis operation. A few years later, Percy met Lorraine Guyer, a California college girl, on a ski vacation at Sun Valley. They married in 1950 and had two more children, a son and a daughter.

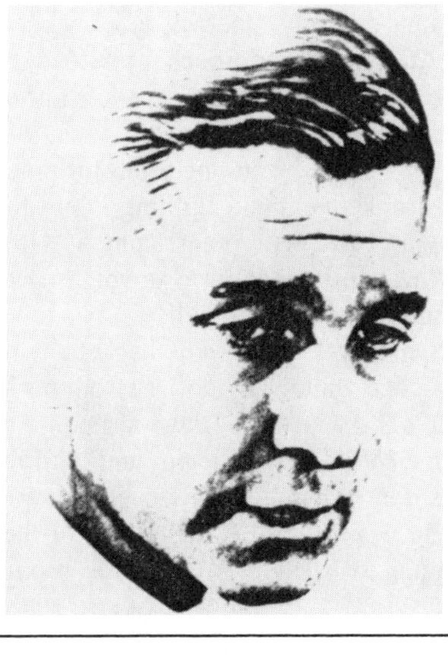
Senator Charles Percy

In 1959 Percy was offered an important post on the Eisenhower Republican Committee and jumped at the chance. He was growing bored with business and became hooked on politics. Percy was with the Nixon wing of the party, and in order to placate **Nelson Rockefeller** for the 1960 Republican Platform, 14 significant concessions were made to the liberal wing of the party. Percy ran for governor of Illinois in 1964 and narrowly lost. He attacked Otto Kerner for the scandals in his administration and for being a tool of **Richard Daley's** political machine in Chicago, but to no avail. Percy was dragged down to defeat as local and state Democrats rode to victory on the coattails of Lyndon Johnson in his landslide over Barry Goldwater. Percy ran for the U.S. Senate in 1966 and took the seat from incumbent Democrat, Paul Douglas.
With less than two months to go before election day, tragedy struck the family around 5:15 a.m. on September 18, 1966. Valerie and Sharon had been active campaigners for their father in the U.S. Senate race. Sharon was Valerie's twin sister. Percy's wife Lorraine was a notoriously light sleeper, and she was awakened early in the morning by a low moan. She drowsily walked to her daughter's room and called her name. She was shocked to see a man wearing a light shirt and dark slacks standing over her daughter's bed. The man whirled and ran past her down the stairs. Mrs. Percy screamed for her

husband, who ran to the room, saw his murdered daughter, and dialed the operator to call the Kenilworth police. He called a doctor, then a practitioner of Christian Science. Next he informed Henry Witting of the murder. He was the family's English butler who lived over the garage. Percy noticed the door to the southeast corner of the house was wide open. He started to go after the killer but then thought of the Speck murders and thought about the possibility that the killer might still be in the house. He gathered the family together to make sure they were all right and then went back to Valerie's room. He turned on the light and saw a ghastly sight. She had been struck over the head with a blunt instrument and then stabbed in the **chest and abdomen fourteen times**.

Family members on both sides were notified. **Paul Douglas**, who was campaigning in **East St. Louis** at the time, sent a telegram of condolence. The killer had apparently gained entrance by cutting through a screen door and a glass panel in a terrace door. Nothing was taken, so robbery was ruled out as a possible motive. Campaign aides were given lie detector tests, but there were few clues and no real suspects; the case would never be solved. Chuck Percy sold the house in 1967.

The funeral was held in a non-denominational church, three blocks from the Percy home named Windward, overlooking Lake Michigan. The Christian Science faith has no liturgy for a funeral.

In immediate years to follow, there was talk of the personable Chuck Percy as a potential vice-presidential running mate, or perhaps the presidency itself. He was the odds-on favorite to win the 1976 Republican nomination for president until Nixon was forced to resign, and Gerald Ford became President. Charles Percy's wife Lorraine did not want any mention of her husband's name connected to presidential politics. The assassination of John F. Kennedy and the murder of her daughter in 1966 were too painful and brought up concerns about family safety.

After three terms in the senate, Percy was upset in 1984 by challenger Paul Simon of Troy/Makanda. He then quit politics and became the head of a trade and technology consulting firm in Washington, D.C.

RICHARD SPECK – BORN TO RAISE HELL

Rich Speck,1965 (Dallas Cnty. Sheriff's Dept.)

This incredible and shocking crime drama began on July 10, 1966, a year of unrest. There was growing turmoil on the college campuses against the widening war in Vietnam. **Martin Luther King Jr**., with only two years left to live, had recently posted a list of 14 demands for racial equality on Mayor **Richard Daley's** office in Chicago's City Hall. Richard Speck, a Dallas native, was visiting his sister and her husband in an apartment at 3966 North Avondale near Wrigley Field, home of the Chicago Cubs.

Speck was a little over six feet tall and weighed 160 pounds with dishwater blonde hair, a heavily pockmarked face and blue eyes. The angular-faced man had already settled into the comfortable lifestyle of a shiftless drifter. He had been at his sister's house for a couple of weeks and talked about getting a job on a freighter and earning enough money to buy a new car. In the back yard, Speck carved his initials, the year 1966 and a gang logo on a tree with a large hunting knife. On Monday Martha and Gene Thornton drove their visitor and his packed suitcase to the maritime union hiring hall. The union hall was only a few doors down from a residence hall for nurses, who worked at the South Chicago Community Hospital. His brother-in-law gave him twenty-five dollars and assured him he would be able to hire out on a ship. Unknown to Thornton, Speck was wanted by police in two states. He had robbed a store back in Dallas, and he was the leading suspect in a murder/rape of a barmaid in **Monmouth**, Illinois, back in April.

Speck and six of his other siblings grew up in Monmouth, Illinois, but after his father died, Speck and a younger sister went to Dallas to live with their mother and a stepfather in Dallas. The stepfather hated Richard and refused to adopt him. Speck dropped out of school at age 16 and worked at various odd jobs. He was quickly becoming the black sheep of the family.

Artist's sketch of Speck

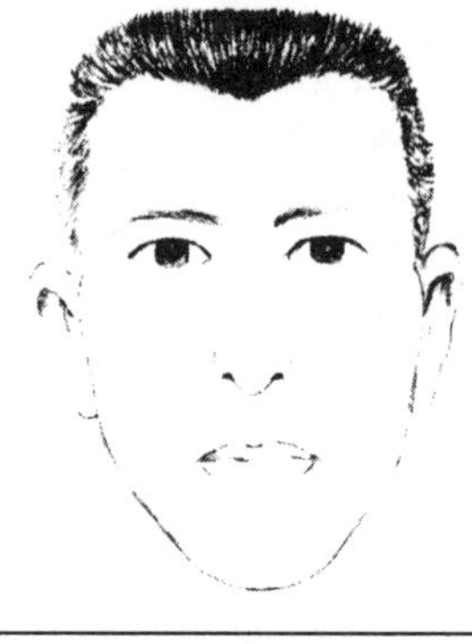

Authorities had Speck's photo and fingerprints on file. He had applied earlier for a job with the Coast Guard at the Calumet Harbor area, and this was required procedure. In May he found work aboard the *Clarence B. Randall*, an ore-carrying ship that plied the Great Lakes. But he was sidelined by an operation for removal of his appendix. He went back to work but was fired for drunkenness and fighting. On Monday, July 11, Speck spent most of the day drinking, and playing cards with other seamen. He slept that night on the enclosed porch of a rooming house that was full. Speck was unable to get an assignment the next day. He slept that night on a park bench near the union hall.

On July 13, he went back to the hall. Gene and Martha Thornton showed up, and he mooched another 25 dollars from his sister. Speck gave up on the hiring hall and went to a bar, Pete's Tap, instead. Several people there noticed his tattoos – the fatefully prophetic *Born to Raise Hell* on his left arm and a knife with a snake entwined about it on the other. The tattoo was done when he was 19. Speck was drunk and couldn't think of what he wanted on his arm, so he went with the suggestion of the tattoo artist. The night of the murders he finally found lodging at a ten dollars a week rooming house. Later that evening he had sex with Ella Mae Hooper, a middle-aged woman he encountered. She had a .22 caliber pistol in her purse, which he stole. After making his decision to invade the nurses' sleeping quarters, it took him 30 minutes to walk there from his rooming house.

The dormitory that houses the student nurses contained a mixture of American and Filipino girls, who were close to graduation. It was on the Southeast side of Chicago. The dorm was run by Josephine Chan, a Filipino. The nurses' town houses were in an area of Chicago known as Jeffery Manor. Speck chose townhouse 2319 because it was more isolated from the others. He pried open a back window and reached inside to unlock the door. It was about 11 p.m. He accosted two nurses with his gun and forced them to take him to the large bedroom where the others were. He forced the six women to sit on the floor in a semicircle facing him. Three were American, and three were Filipino. Another girl, Gloria Davy, came in from a date with her fiancée. When she entered the room, Speck forced her to join the others. It was now around 11:40. Speck tried to reassure them by saying he only wanted their money. He took out a 3-inch long switchblade that he carried and sliced a bed sheet into strips. One by one, he tied each nurse up, while making assurances he wasn't going to kill them.

Prosecution's scale model of the murder scene

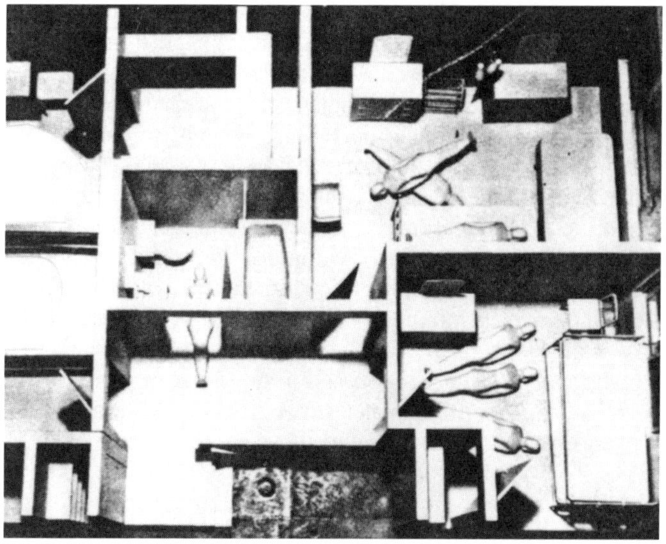

Around midnight another nurse arrived from a date, Kathy Emmons, who lived at 2311. She failed to notice anything unusual. Speck took Pamela Wilkening to a separate bedroom, intent on rape. While he was gone, the remaining girls had a discussion. The Filipinos wanted to fight the intruder, but the American girls thought it best to use psychology on him. At 12:30 two other nurses arrived at the complex, just beating the curfew. Suzanne Farris and Mary Jordon arrived at 12:30 to sleep in Suzanne's room because it had an air-conditioning unit. They walked in on Speck where he was getting ready to attack Pamela and surprised him. When they saw his gun, they resisted, so he brutally stabbed them to death with his switchblade. Farris was stabbed 18 times. He then stabbed Mary Ann three times in the chest. Then he went over to the bound Pamela and stabbed her in the chest. Before returning to the other women, he washed the blood off his hands, so as not to alarm them. Speck came back to the bedroom, and one by one carried them off to another room where he raped them, killed them, and then washed his hands. Each time he returned to the room, he peeked out from the curtained window to make sure everything was OK. Around 2:30, a.m., with just two victims left, Gloria Davy had fallen asleep during the ordeal because she was close to being intoxicated. When she awoke, Speck raped her in the bedroom and then led her to the bathroom where he killed her. The last nurse, Corazon (Cory) Amuraco, managed to crawl under a bed and hide. Speck came back from killing Gloria Davy, turned on the light, and looked around the room, then disappeared into the night. Cory survived because Speck lost track of the number of victims. **Eight nurses were brutally murdered** - Gloria Davy, Suzanne Farris, Mary Jordan, Nina Schmale, Pat Matusek, Pam Wilkening, and two Filipinos, Merlita Gargullo, and Valentina Pasion. The only nurse he mutilated was Gloria Davy. Some thought it was due to her striking resemblance to Speck's wife, Shirley. Speck walked back to his rooming house and along the way threw the switchblade into the Calumet River.

Speck shortly after his arrest
(*Bell. News-Democrat*)

Amuraco would never forget the tattoos on Speck's knuckles: **L-O-V-E** and **H-A-T-E**.

Around 6 a.m. a nurse from another unit saw Cory on an outside ledge crying, "Oh, my God, they're all dead." The nurse and a housemother went inside, saw the carnage and called the police. Officer Dan Kelly was the first to arrive on the scene. Jack Wallenda was the first homicide detective to get there. The police secured samples of Speck's semen and recovered two blood-stained T-shirts. Speck, in anticipation of a bloody night's work, had brought along several changes in a small bag. Most of the nurses were nude and had stockings tied tightly around their throats.

On Thursday morning, Speck awoke, dressed and went back to Pete's Tap to continue his routine of drinking, bragging, telling tall tales, and looking for sex. Chicago still had four daily newspapers and the headlines rocked the city with lurid details. The manhunt was on. Cory Amuraco told police it was a white male, approximately 25 years old, 6 feet tall, short hair, and wearing dark clothes. It wasn't long before police established that their man had a southern accent, was probably a sailor, and lived near the nurse's dorm. The police checked out the union hiring hall, and someone remembered a man with a southern drawl being really upset that someone with more seniority got an assignment ahead of him. He fished through some papers, and Richard Speck's name was on the assignment slip. A real lucky break for the cops. The police learned that Speck had visited his sister's house, so they had the hiring hall call the Thorntons to set a trap by telling them there was an assignment for Richard if he came down to the hall. When Speck got the message and called the hall, the set up failed when a secretary told him his assignment was on a ship that had already sailed. The suspect was a no show.

Speck was drinking and playing pool at the Shipyard when a couple of detectives came in and asked the bartender if he had seen anyone fitting Speck's description. These detectives didn't yet have Speck's name. Incredibly, the bartender said the description didn't ring a bell. Speck, alerted that the police were looking for him, took a cab and was now on the lam. Speck got out of the cab in a mostly black area called Old Town. He walked about six blocks and took a room in the Raleigh Hotel at 648 North Dearborn. He paid nine dollars, one week's rent. He wore a white jacket to mask his tattoos. Most of the evening of July 14 was spent at the Pink Twist Inn on Clark Street. In the midst of the manhunt, Chicago was suffering through racial unrest as city police fought with rioters. Speck went back to his hotel with a black prostitute. When she left a half-hour later, she told the desk clerk that the man called himself Richard and that he had a gun. The next morning the manager called the police. Officers Robert Rutledge and Clarence Shuey soon arrived, and the manager gave them the key to Speck's room. Police found him asleep, and next to his pillow was a gun, which they confiscated. Rutledge awakened a surprised Speck who told him the gun belonged to a Puerto Rican prostitute, and that she had stolen money from him – complete lies. When asked his name he said Richard Speck. Speck was calm, cool, and collected and looked them in the eye. They figured he was harmless, so they left without arresting him. They did, however, confiscate his unlicensed gun.

R. Speck at his trial (*Chicago Tribune*)

Later that Friday morning, Cory identified a picture, furnished by the Coast Guard, as the killer. Authorities now had his name and knew what he looked like. The FBI provided them with Speck's fingerprints from his extensive file when he lived in Dallas. His prints matched two prints lifted from the murder scene. The police placed stakeouts at the home of Speck's sister, the hiring hall and the Shipyard Inn. At 5 p.m. the police learned that Speck had called his sister and told her that he was drinking with a man named Red in a bar on Clark Street. The newspapers had run a sketch of Speck, based on Cory's description, but it wasn't a very good likeness. The police dragnet checked out the Pink Twist later that evening but missed Speck by 15 minutes. They went to the Raleigh Hotel, and when the manager saw his picture, she said they had just missed him.

Speck, meanwhile, had acquired a couple of new drinking buddies, One-eye Lunsford and Shorty Ingram. The three of them now registered at the Starr Hotel, in the middle of Skid Row. Speck was talking about going back to Dallas. Meanwhile, the city was in flames, due to racial unrest. On Saturday morning, Gloria Davey's funeral was held. Speck was now the most wanted man in America. Speck was up and drinking again in a bar next to the hotel. He bought a newspaper and saw his name and picture on the front page. He decided the only way out was suicide. He broke a wine bottle and slashed his left elbow and right wrist. One-eyed Lunsford stumbled into Speck's room and found him bleeding on the bed. When he asked Speck what happened, Speck lied and said he cut himself on the window. The window was glass block, so Lunsford knew it was a lie. Lunsford went downstairs to the lobby and saw the picture of Speck in the newspaper. He phoned the police from a pay phone and told them the man they were looking for was in room 584 of the Starr Hotel. Incredibly, the police never responded to the call because the informant refused to give his name.

Claude One-Eye Lunsford

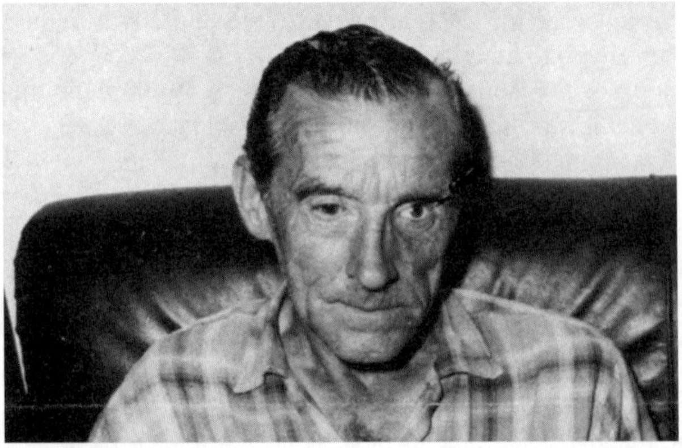

Speck staggered into the room of George Gregrich, dripping blood. The police were called and told a man was bleeding to death in room 584. The police arrived shortly after noon and took a weakened Speck to the Cook County Hospital. The two policemen never bothered to check their dashboard that had a description and photo of Speck. By now Mayor **Richard Daley** had persuaded Governor **Otto Kerner** to bring in the National Guard to quell the riots. Speck was admitted to the emergency room as patient B. Brian. It was now nearly one o'clock, and Speck had a weak pulse and had gone into shock. Speck was attended to by Dr. Leroy Smith, who recognized him from the newspaper photo. He asked the man what his name was, and he whispered Richard Speck. The doctor notified patrolman Alan Schuman, who was guarding another patient. Schuman at first didn't believe it. **Within five minutes nearly 50 police arrived on the scene**. Speck was chained to his gurney and placed in leg irons before being wheeled into surgery. **Speck wanted to know if the doctor was going to get the $10,000 reward**. On Monday, all the remaining victims - Suzanne Farris, Mary Jordan, Pat Matusek, Nina Schmale and Pam Wilkening, had their funerals. On Tuesday, Cory Amuraco was taken with several other attending nurses to Speck's room to surreptitiously identify him. She left the room after three minutes and said the man in the hospital jail was the killer. She also said the gun that had been taken from Speck's room was similar to the one she saw the night of the murders.

The case was presented to the grand jury on Monday, July 25, 1966. Prosecution was terrified of having the case against Speck being overturned because of a technicality. Only recently the **Earl Warren** Supreme Court had set a man named Miranda free because he had not been "advised" of his rights. Speck meanwhile had turned belligerent and spent his time in bed smoking and reading detective magazines. On Monday, August 1, Speck was taken to court by 50 armed guards and arraigned. The indigent Speck was assigned a lawyer, Chicagoan Gerald Getty, and the case was given to Judge Herbert Paschen. On August 2 the newspaper headlines were stolen by **Charles Whitman, who killed 16 people** and wounded 31 from a tower on the campus of Texas University in Austin before he was killed by police. Many wondered if the publicity of the Speck murders had influenced Whitman to commit the mayhem.

R. Speck in 1976 (*News-Democrat*)

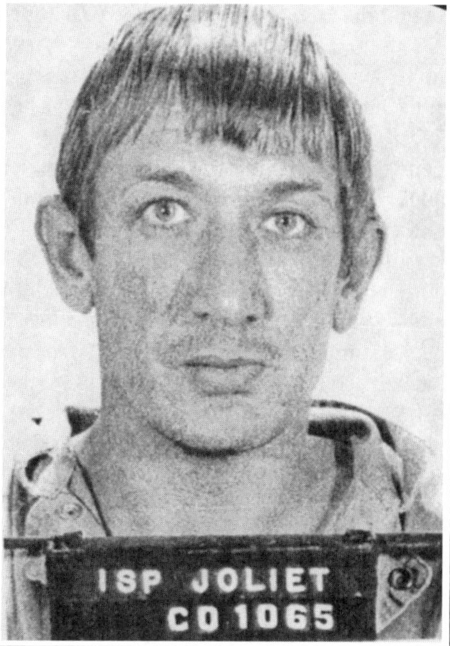

Fortunately for the prosecution, shortly after the incident, Cory had hand-written 22 pages detailing her night of horror, embellished with drawings. Checkbook journalists offered Cory huge sums for her story, but she declined, saying it would taint the memory of her colleagues. On August 7 the 24 surviving members of the senior hospital nursing class graduated. After Speck had sufficiently recovered, he was transferred to Death Row. Another good piece of luck. Two detectives took an aluminum boat and dragged the bottom of the 26 feet deep **Calumet River** near the 100th Street Bridge with a powerful magnet. They almost gave up the search when the magnet brought up Speck's switchblade knife. Various bloodstains were still on the blade but in amounts too minute to categorize as human or animal. Unfortunately, it could not be introduced as evidence.

For the next six months, Speck talked for over 100 hours with his psychiatrist (Dr. Ziporyn), who convinced Speck that he was not responsible for what happened because he had been traumatized psychologically as a youth. Speck told his psychiatrist he harbored no bad feelings toward women, and that he wasn't even sure he had committed the act. Speck's lawyer wanted a panel of psychiatrists to determine if his client was competent to stand trial. But evidence and testimony gathered by police from Dallas, Monmouth, Chicago and Michigan pointed to a hardened criminal – not an insane person.

Ironically, the rest of Speck's family led normal lives. His parents had lived in small farming communities in central/west Illinois. His German father was from **Oquawka** and his Dutch-Irish mother was from **Kirkwood**. They were married in 1921 and there were eight children. His father died in 1947 when Speck was only six. Speck was the 7th child, born December 6, 1941. Speck met a high school senior (Shirley Malone) at the Dallas State Fair, got her pregnant, and married her in 1962. Six months later a baby daughter was born. Richard was continually drunk, in trouble with the law, and abusive toward his wife. They divorced in March of 1966. Speck had a low IQ and poor social skills. In 1965 he served about four months in jail for assaulting and trying to rob a woman. Speck stabbed a man in January of 1966 in a bar fight. The judge gave him three days in jail. By age 24 he had 41 arrests. In March of 1966, he stole over 70 cartons of cigarettes (he smoked Kools) and was selling them from the trunk of his car. When the police started looking for him, he fled Texas and came to Illinois. He went to **Monmouth**, where he had family, and worked at various odd jobs.

Speck after suicide attempt (notice tattoos – *Sun-Times*)

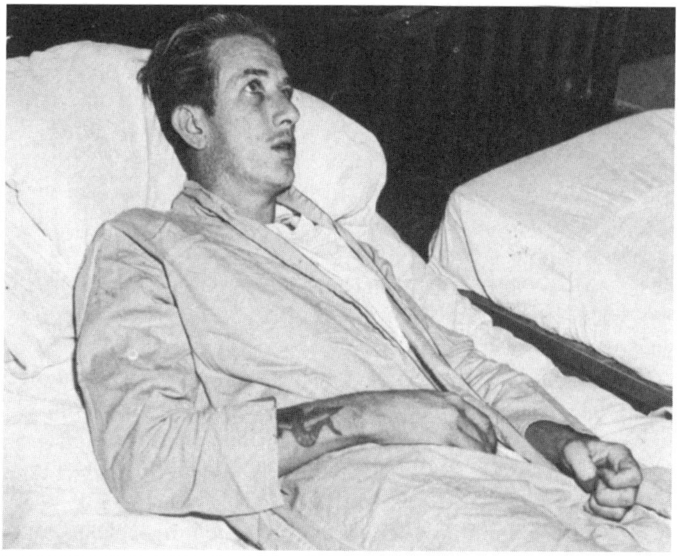

On April 2, he raped a 65-year-old divorcée in her home. Then he became the leading suspect in an April 9th murder of a 32-year-old barmaid. He left Monmouth and went to live with his sister and her husband on April 19. He found work with Inland Steel and went on two Great Lakes voyages. He seemed to like physical work and indulged himself with comic books. Speck met a Scandinavian nurse named Judy Laakaniemi when he had his appendix removed. After his discharge from the hospital, he visited her several times at her place in Michigan. She tried to help him find work in her town, but he didn't follow up on any of her suggestions.

On October 22, 1966, a panel of six psychiatrists gave their findings that Speck was not insane. Speck's court-appointed defense psychiatrist disagreed, saying his brain had been damaged over the years by drugs, alcohol, bar beatings and pistol whippings by cops. Speck claimed he didn't remember killing nurses or anything else from that night because he had been drinking so much.

Pretrial motions were made on November 4. Getty asked for a change of venue, saying Speck couldn't get a fair trial in Chicago. (On November 8, **Charles Percy**, buoyed by a sympathy vote because of the murder of his daughter, defeated Democrat **Paul Douglas** to become the state's new U.S. Senator.) On November 28, seven men and five women were selected to rule on the competency hearing. After listening to various expert opinions, the jury voted Speck competent to stand trial. Prosecution did not object, moving the trial for fear charges of unfairness might cause a conviction to be overturned. And **Sam Shepherd**, the Ohio doctor charged with murdering his wife, was found not guilty when the courts ordered a second trial for him. State's Attorney offices in the Illinois' 101 other counties had mixed reactions when approached about hosting Speck's trial. In **Edwardsville**, the answer was a flat out *no*. Finally, **Peoria** was the site chosen on December 19. Meanwhile, Richard Speck, courtesy of food provided by taxpayers, had gained 25 pounds and took up painting to help him relax. He also liked reading war stories and watching Road Runner cartoons.

Speck's trial was held in a new Peoria courthouse, dedicated in 1965 by **Ladybird Johnson**. He was locked up in a heavily guarded cell in the basement of the building. Jury selection began on February 20. Incredibly, it took six weeks to go through 609 jurors. Judge Paschen had issued gag orders for the trial, and the *Chicago Tribune* filed suit to challenge his ruling. Meanwhile, Speck and his psychiatrist worked out a deal with Hawthorne Books to publish ***Born To Raise Hell***.

Gloria Jean Davey's funeral (AP/Wide World)

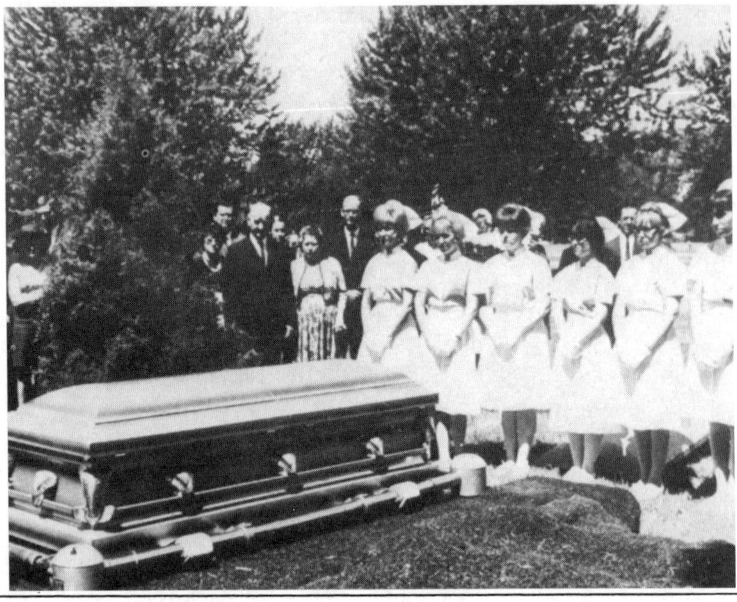

The trial began on Monday, April 3, 1967. Courtroom A had room for only 36 spectators. No one under age 18 was allowed to view the trial. Defense objected to use of an FBI scale model of the murder scene, calling it inflammatory and prejudicial. The judge allowed it. Prosecution also used a large map with red stickers to show relevant locations. People who had encountered Speck before and after the murders were called to the stand by the prosecution. A member of the FBI testified about relevant features of the scale model of the townhouse. The star witness, of course, was Cory Amuraco, who described the events of that terrible night in excruciating detail. Then a lab technician testified about the blood on the two shirts Speck had left at the crime scene. Next came the testimony of Eugenio Tapia, who did the autopsies. Fingerprint experts, who found Speck's fingerprint on the south bedroom door, took the stand. When defense cross-examined, Speck's lawyer asserted that the police were under intense pressure to find the killer, so they framed Speck by transferring his print from a beer can to the door. Either that or they had "developed" fake prints. After 8 days of testimony, Martin and the prosecution rested its case.

Getty began his defense on Wednesday April 12. His first two witnesses were Speck's mother and his youngest sister. Then his sister Martha Thornton and her husband testified. Defense's best witness was a bartender, who claimed that Speck was in his bar (Kay's Pilot House) at the time of the murders. A waitress at the same place also said that Speck was there. On cross, prosecution got them to reluctantly admit the place was very crowded at that time of night. Prosecution then argued it would have been difficult for them to know when Speck was or wasn't there at any given time. The defense rested its case, and both sides gave summations. The judge gave instructions to the jury on Saturday, April 15. When closing arguments were given, prosecution harped on what a vile and cruel person Speck was and that people like him were the reason the death penalty was created. Defense attacked nurse Cory by claiming the sketch that she approved didn't look anything like Richard Speck. Defense also argued that the police and prosecution rushed to judgment to find the killer and assuage public fear.

Speck's picture of Bambi (*Chicago Sun-Times*)

The jury wasn't fooled, reaching a decision in 49 minutes. They found Speck guilty on all counts and recommended the death penalty.

On April 20, Dr. Ziporyn was fired from his job for pursuing private interests (writing a book about Speck) while working as the Cook County jail psychiatrist. On Monday, May 15, 1967, Getty argued for a new trial based on numerous procedural errors by the judge. Request denied. Getty then asked that Speck be given a brain wave test to determine if he had suffered from "epileptic furor" the night of the murders. William Martin countered by saying an EEG had already been given to Speck. Defense motion was denied. Interestingly, Dr. Ziporyn, the man who had spent so much time with Speck, was never called as a witness by the defense.

The judge heard one final witness, a Freudian psychologist went over the details of Speck's troubled life, point by point, and said Speck had a chronic personality disorder. That mental disease was the reason, the doc said, why he was so different from the rest of his family. He recommended that Speck be incarcerated in a mental facility where psychiatry could "study him" in the hope of preventing future Richard Specks. Martin countered by telling the judge that Hitler was evil – not insane. "We know there is evil in the world, and it does not masquerade as insanity."

Speck, the 24-year-old, who had not uttered one word out loud or caused any commotion during the trial, stepped forward for the fateful decision. The judge sentenced him to die in the electric chair on September 1, 1967.

The one thing Speck feared was dying in the elecric chair. Illinois had only three – at the Cook County Jail, at Joliet and Menard. Speck avoided the death penalty when the higher court ruled that potential jurors, who opposed the death penalty should have not been excluded from sitting in judgment. Speck spent the rest of his life in Statevllle Prison at **Joliet**, dying from a massive coronary in 1991. He had ballooned to a paunchy 220 pounds. To the very end he remained a loner and was left alone by other inmates. He ate, painted and slept. Never once did he try to escape. Speck was a loser and a jerk who would be termed a sociopath in today's parlance. On the wall of his jail cell, he displayed photos of the eight nurses he had murdered.

John Wayne Gacy (another mass murderer) was a workaholic while Richard Speck and James Earl Ray drifted aimlessly. We'll probably never know whether the urge to commit murder is imbred or induced, heredity or environment.

JAMES EARL RAY

James Earl Ray's birthplace, March 10, 1928, in Alton, Illinois

James Earl Ray was born March 10, 1928, in the basement of his maternal grandmother's home in **Alton, Illinois**. Mary Maher allowed Ray's parents to live in two rooms in her basement while they waited for their first-born to arrive. Ray's parents lived there about a year before moving to St. Louis. Ray's father (George) got in trouble with the law and went to prison for several years in 1921. His father was arrested again at Alton in 1935 for forgery. While out on bail, his mother-in-law helped the family buy 60 acres of land in Missouri near Ewing. The father skipped bail, and they were now on the lam.

Ray flunked the first grade at Ewing. He was frequently picked on by other boys in school, resulting in numerous fights. He soon started wetting the bed and began to stutter.

Tragedy struck the family in 1937. Ray's sister Marjorie was playing with matches and set her hair and dress on fire. She died a day later. Two more sisters were born in 1938 and 1941, Carol and Melba. The Ray family was so poor that one winter (1940) they were forced to start tearing rooms apart to make kindling for heating the house. The family now lived in a one-room shack, and Ray had to sleep on the floor. Then another misfortune; Ray broke his leg in 1942, at age 14, while playing a game of scrub football.

J.E. Ray's school picture (small boy, face partially hidden)

Ray continued to struggle in school and quit in 1944 when he was 15. In 1943 Ray began to frequently visit his uncle and grandparents, who lived in **Quincy, Illinois,** a rivertown with a population of about 45,000. Ray sometimes went with his uncle Frank, who made the rounds of bars and houses of prostitution to collect money for the mob. Ray began to burglarize houses, and his uncle helped him fence the stolen goods. Sometimes he spent the money earned on various local prostitutes. Ray was crushed the day his uncle was arrested and sent to prison.

As a teenager, Ray was arrested by Alton police for stealing a bundle of newspapers and selling them. He had returned to Alton to live with his grandmother, and she helped him get a job at International Shoe in **Hartford.** It lasted two years, from 1944-45. He worked in the dye department and earned 75 cents an hour, commuting by streetcar. He was laid off because of returning war veterans. So he joined the army. After completing basic training, he was stationed in Germany. Ray showed strong admiratiuon for **Adolf Hitler**, believing that someone like him would rid America of "niggers and Jews." Ray's mother, Ceal, was afraid her son's beliefs might get him killed. Ray was a misfit and subject to much ridicule by his peers. He used the skills taught to him by his uncle in Quincy and became involved in the black market, trading cigarettes for cameras, radios and jewelry. Ray visited the local brothels and was treated by army doctors on several occasions for venereal disease. He served time in the stockade for being drunk and disorderly. He escaped and went AWOL, was captured and court martialed. Ray was demoted from PFC to buck private. He was given a general discharge in 1948, only two days before his regular enlistment ended. It infuriated Ray while he was in the army that many of the Negroes in his unit married white German girls.

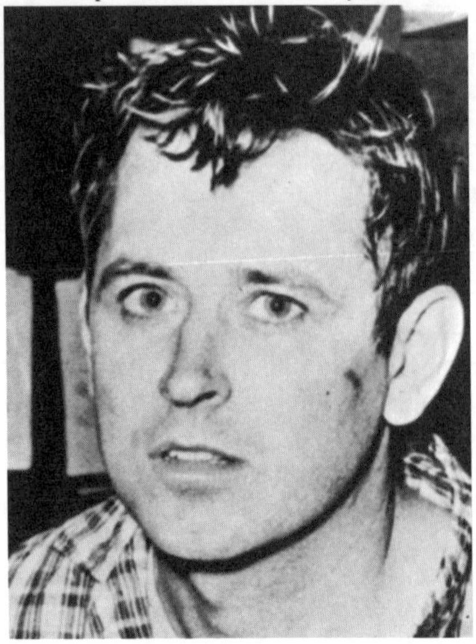
Prison photo of James E. Ray in 1959

When Ray returned to the states, he went to live with his parents, who had moved to Quincy, and had their 8th child, Suzy. By now both his parents were drunks and neglected the children. Quincy authorities visited the family household and found the place filthy, and the young children infected with lice. The parents were warned to improve things under the threat of losing their children to the state.

Ray's uncle Earl was back in prison at **Menard in Chester**, Illinois. It was at this point that Ray began a life of crime in earnest. In 1952 he held up a taxi driver in **Chicago**. It was a botched robbery, and Ray was wounded in the arm during a wild chase scene through the streets of Chi town. He was caught and sentenced to two years at **Joliet.** He was released in 1954. In 1955, at age 27, he was sent to Leavenworth prison for forging money orders.

Alton Police Chief Harold Riggins, who dealt with Ray on several occasions, called him a pathological liar. Ray later was given a 20-year sentence in Missouri after a failed robbery attempt of a Kroger store in **St. Louis** in 1959. It was his fourth major offense. Life behind bars was tough. The 100-year-old prison had twice the number of inmates (2,000) for which it had been built. The place was once described as "square foot for square foot, the bloodiest 47 acres in America."

Ray had two botched escape attempts, in 1961 and 1966. In prison, he had repeatedly made disparaging remarks about **Martin Luther King**, and **H. Rap Brown**. He escaped from Missouri State Penitentiary at Jefferson City in April of 1967. In July he bought a 1962 Plymouth from Bundy Olds in **East St. Louis**. He drifted around, spending time in **Edwardsville**, **St. Louis**, **Chicago**, Indianapolis, Detroit, Toronto, Atlanta, Los Angeles, Mexico, and Birmingham, Alabama, where he began stalking King.

King was murdered around 6:01 p.m. on April 4, 1968. He had gone to Memphis, Tennessee, with Ralph Abernathy, **Andrew Young** and **Jesse Jackson** to lead a civil rights march in support of about 1,300 striking sanitation workers, nearly all of whom were black. Strangely, about a month before shooting King, Ray graduated from bartending school in Los Angeles. He used a Remington 30.06 rifle he had purchased in Birmingham about a week earlier. Ray had stalked King previously when he was in Atlanta but could never find the opportunity to kill him. He fired just one shot from the rear bathroom window of a dingy complex where he had rented a room. The walls were paper-thin, and the tenants next door said they remembered that the man in 5B spent a lot of time in the bathroom but seldom flushed the toilet. The bathroom window gave Ray a good view of the balcony of King's room in the Lorraine Motel in Memphis, 200 feet away.

Fatal shot fired from this bathroom window

Ray pulled the trigger while standing in the cast iron tub. The powerful shot tore a hole in King's jaw about the size of one's fist. The bullet severed his spine and caused severe brain damage. King was rushed to a hospital where doctors worked to save his life, but he died about an hour later. Ray probably killed King because he was a racist and sought recognition by slaying "The Dreamer." About 3,500 FBI agents were immediately assigned to the case. They eventually found Ray's abandoned white Mustang, parked at a housing project in Atlanta.

Many assumed it was a conspiracy from start. It was thought that only a hired killer would have enough money to go to Canada (in Montreal he used the alias Eric Gault), then to London, to Portugal, and back again to London. After Ray was captured, he claimed innocence. Ray said he had been in Memphis with a swarthy man named Raoul and was involved in a deal that went sour, smuggling drugs and guns to South America. Ray said it was this Raoul who probably killed King and set him up. Ray claimed that when the alleged deal went south, and he later heard about King's murder, he got scared and decided to leave the country.

There was much talk about the shooting being a conspiracy and that Ray was probably dead, killed by the other conspirators. Author **Truman Capote** voiced that very opinion on the *Tonight* show. Ray was arrested about two months later on June 8, 1968, at Heathrow Airport near London. He was carrying a loaded .38 revolver at the time. Ray also had an airline ticket for Africa and two Canadian passports with the name Ramon Sneyd, another alias. He had disguised himself by letting his hair grow longer, wearing dark-rimmed shell glasses, and by having plastic surgery performed on the tip of his nose.

"Oh, God, I feel so trapped," was about all Ray had to say when he was apprehended. Ray was extradited from London and flown to Memphis. The 65-day manhunt was over. Ray's two brothers, John and Jerry, set up a defense fund in Memphis on his behalf. Judge W. Preston Battle presided over the trial, and Arthur Hanes was to be his counsel. Shortly before his trial was to begin, Ray changed his mind and asked for famed Houston lawyer Percy Foreman to represent him, thus delaying the trial. Ray wanted to plead *not guilty*, believing that "no southern jury would convict a white man for killing a nigger." In the end, Foreman convinced Ray that the jury would make an example of him and give him the chair.

James Earl Ray letter to Ron Fitzgerald and Robert "Little Tree" Sweeney of East St. Louis, son of police detective Robert Sweeney

30 Nov-1991

Sweeny & Fitzgerald:
Thank's for the card. We are still trying to 'smoke em out. I've been on 5 TV stations & numerous talk-radio about the boo. Geraldo has been the only bummer.

Sincerely,

J. E. Ray

Mr. Sweeny
9844 West Main Street
Belleville, ILL 62223.

7475 Cockrill Bend Ind. Rd.
Nashville, TN 37209.

Publishers Weekly

NONFICTION

WHO KILLED MARTIN LUTHER KING? The True Story by the Convicted Assassin
James Earl Ray. National Press, $21.95 ISBN 0-915765-93-4

800-275-8888

Still serving his 99-year sentence for the slaying of Martin Luther King in Memphis in 1968, Ray offers compelling arguments for reopening the case in this dramatic, spirited chronicle. An escaped con, self-described as a "two-bit career criminal" having no strongly held racial views, Ray tells of smuggling "contraband" between Canada, Mexico and the U.S. for a man known to him only as Raoul, who directed him to Memphis a few days before the shooting. While Raoul's activities are as vague as his identity, serious questions are raised by the apparently frantic desire of the authorities to have Ray, who was captured and charged in England three months later, plead guilty and forgo a trial. If Ray's story is accurate, his lawyer, Percy Foreman, obsessed with money, eagerly orchestrated the guilty pleas. Ray also suggests that the FBI's role in the case bears examination, given J. Edgar Hoover's hatred and persecution of King. Whether readers will be convinced that an injustice has been done or not, many may support Ray's call for vigorous reinvestigation. Photos not seen by *PW*. *(Nov.)*

Foreman cited the following evidence: Ray's weapon was found near the scene of the crime (with his fingerprints on it); his white Mustang was seen on the street next to the rooming house; another boarder at the rooming house said he saw Ray flee after the shots were fired, and that he was carrying something in a blanket, probably a gun. A customer at a store saw a man screech away from the curb in a white Mustang several minutes after the shooting.

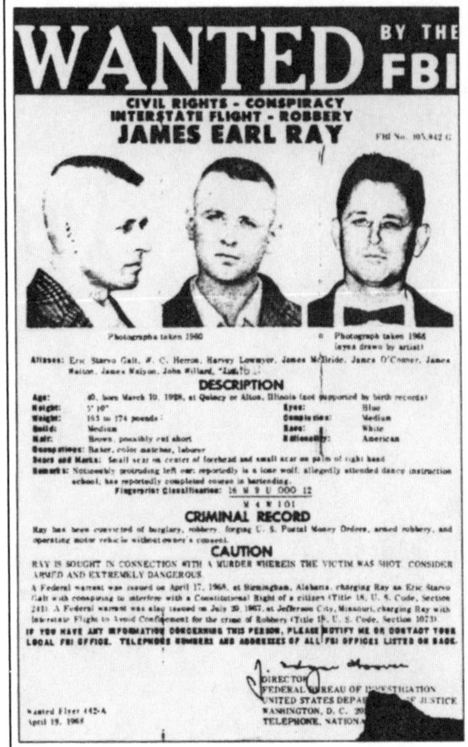

Ray escaped the chair by pleading guilty in exchange for 99 years.

More controversy and turmoil erupted less than a week after the trial when Ray claimed innocence. He said Percy Foreman pressured him into a guilty plea. He now demanded a new trial. Judge W. Preston Battle succumbed to the immense pressure caused by media scrutiny and died of a heart attack just three weeks after Ray was sentenced.

Conspiracy theories were all over the place. Some said it was a mob hit and that Ray, a loner and a misfit, was the perfect patsy. Another theory held that Hanoi had hired Ray to kill King. The killing of King might cause such civil disorder that the U.S. would no longer have the stomach to fight in Vietnam. Some thought the KKK put him up to it, but authorities rejected this because he had no Klan connections and didn't use the word "nigger." Yet another scenario held that it was an inside job – a power struggle within King's own organization, or a hit by black militants who hated his non-violent approach to civil rights problems.

Ray's pleas for a new trial were ultimately rejected. Ray escaped from Brushy Mountain, a Tennessee prison, in 1977 and avoided capture for three days. During a second trial for his escape from prison, **Ray met courtroom artist Anna Sandhu**. They were married, and she campaigned for his freedom, convinced he was innocent. She divorced him in 1990 after a phone argument in which he admitted the murder and slammed down the receiver in anger.

In 1978 Ray appeared before the House Select Committee on Assassinations, represented by conspiracy buff lawyer, **Mark Lane**.

Ray probably killed King for the same reason Oswald shot Kennedy – for the recognition. Conspiracy buffs will, of course, think this author is nuts for holding such a belief. On Thursday, March 27, 1997, MLK's son, Dexter King, met with Ray, who had a terminal illness from a damaged liver (cirrhosis). Ray told King that he did not kill his father. Dexter King believes Ray, and thinks his father was killed by a massive **government conspiracy**.

Anna Sandhu and Jane Pauley on *Today* show

Ray's father was quoted as saying his son wasn't smart enough to pull it off by himself. Oswald's new lawyer, William Pepper, asserted in his book *Orders to Kill*, that King was killed by a covert team of **Green Berets** from the 20th Special Forces Group.

James Earl Ray died on April 23rd, 1998, after being in prison almost 30 years.

JOHN WAYNE GACY: THE KILLER CLOWN

John Wayne Gacy was born in Chicago on St. Patrick's Day, March 7, 1942, of Polish and Danish heritage. His father was a machinist, his mother a housewife. He attended Catholic schools with his two sisters until he was eleven, switching over to tuition-free Carl Schurz Public High School. He suffered from blackouts, due to a playground accident until doctors removed a blood clot. Gacy's appendix was removed at age 15. At age 16 he began taking medication for a heart problem.

Gacy didn't fare well with his strict alcoholic father, who disciplined him with a razor strop. His father hated homosexuals with a vengeance. But Gacy got along well with his sisters and Marion, his mother. He helped with cleanup and repair projects for the church and regularly went to confession. He switched to a vocational school but later dropped out and worked odd jobs.

He left home and went to Las Vegas at age 20. After several months of working cleanup at a mortuary, he decided to go back home. He enrolled in Northwestern Business College and graduated from their yearlong program with a certificate in accounting and business management. Making money soon became an obsession with him. He managed the Nunn-Bush shoe store for several years where he was an exceptional salesman. He was promoted and transferred to one of their branch stores in **Springfield**.

In September of 1964 he married co-worker Marlynn Meyers in a Catholic Church ceremony. Gacy was short and pudgy, but she found him to be a go-getter, personable and generous. When Marlynn's parents bought a Kentucky Fried Chicken business in Iowa and moved to that state, the newlyweds moved into the Springfield home they left behind. Gacy joined the local Jaycees, and through hard work and devotion, won numerous awards plus the recognition for which he desperately longed. His only scrapes with the law were a few traffic tickets.

His father-in-law soon offered him a job in Iowa, which he accepted. He worked 10 hours a day at Kentucky Fried and learned the business from the bottom up. He quickly joined the local chapter of the Jaycees, serving on the board of directors in 1967. Most who knew Gacy in the organization remember him as hard working, overly ambitious, and somewhat of a braggart prone to exaggeration. At this point in life Gacy weighed about 212 pounds and stood five-feet eight-inches tall. His body was like a sack of potatoes. One of the lies he told was that he was an ex-marine. He was fascinated with the authority that went with police work and installed a spotlight, flashing red light and a siren on his station wagon. He used it to go on Merchant Patrol, driving around at night to protect local businesses from burglaries.

John W. Gacy's house in Des Plaines (author's collection)

The fried chicken franchise employed numerous young men and Gacy took to giving them rides home. In May of 1968, at age 26, he was arrested for sodomizing a teenage boy. His reputation and marriage were in shambles. Gacy posted bond, and while out on bail was arrested on a new charge, this time burglary, while he was on Merchant Patrol. Gacy protested and took a lie detector test but failed it miserably. He was examined by a police psychiatrist, who determined Gacy was bi-sexual and a thrill-seeker. His IQ test came out at 118 – bright/normal. Judge Van Metre gave him a stiff 10 years in the Iowa State Reformatory. His wife filed for divorce, was given the home, car, and custody of their two children. Gacy told his wife that henceforth he considered her and the children dead.

While behind bars, Gacy was a model prisoner. He became an avid reader of the *Wall Street Journal*. With his experience, he was assigned the job of cook, which he went about enthusiastically. He was paroled after 18 months.

On his release, Gacy went back to Chicago to live with his mother, his father having died in 1965. He obtained a job as a cook in a restaurant near The Loop. It was where many of the players for the Chicago Blackhawks ate, giving Gacy access to hockey tickets. He soon moved into a house of his own at 8213 West Summerdale in **Des Plains**, a middle-class Chicago suburb. Part of the house had a three-foot deep crawlspace. The house had been built on reclaimed swampland, and the crawl space was frequently plagued with sogginess. Gacy, although not adept at carpentry, was frequently involved in remodeling projects that usually lacked a quality finish. Gacy liked to bowl (185 average), play cards, drink and gamble, but was moderate most of the time.

Wedding photo of Gacy and his 2nd wife, Carol Hoff in June 1972 (*Chicago Tribune*)

In February of 1971, Chicago police charged Gacy with picking up a youth at the Greyhound bus terminal and trying to force him to have sexual relations. Only eight months after his release from prison, neither his neighbors nor Iowa authorities found out about this incident. The case was dismissed when the boy failed to make a court appearance.

Gacy became friendly with his neighbors next door and through them he met his future second wife. He married Carol Hoff, a divorcée with two daughters, and told her his first wife was the daughter of Colonel Harlan Sanders.

John Gacy had already made his first kill, another boy he had picked up at the Greyhound bus station. Gacy prepared the food for his wedding reception that was held at his own home in June of 1972. Many of the guests noticed a strange odor coming from the house. When his wife also complained, he said it was from dampness in the crawl space and brought in lime to take care of the problem.

The Gacys hosted many parties and backyard barbecues. In 1973 Gacy went into the home remodeling business that he named PDM Contractors. He got along well with his two stepdaughters and built a playhouse and an above ground pool for them. But he and his wife divorced after four years. He was a workaholic and spent little time with her. On several occasions there were marital spats, during which he lost his temper. He threw things and broke furniture when he lost control. She also caught him bringing home magazines containing pictures of nude males. The divorce was finalized in March of 1976.

Gacy was a man of several talents. He designed a clown outfit, painted his face and began entertaining the neighbors' children at parties with a character he called Pogo the Clown. He collected accessories such as a rubber chicken, a leash and collar for an invisible dog, juggling balls and a pair of "trick" handcuffs. He also entertained children at local hospitals. He bought clown paintings and hung them on his walls.

Gacy was a good businessman with gross receipts of $200,000 in 1978. But his partner disliked Gacy's habit of hiring very young boys. It was his experience that youth under age 21 usually messed up on the job. It wasn't long until boys all over the neighborhood began disappearing. Nationally, with over 175,000 teenage runaways annually back then, police were overwhelmed and often told distraught parents there was a good chance they would come back home in about eight months. Gacy continued to putter around his house, but he let the hedge around it grow 8-foot tall, drawing complaints from his neighbors. Gacy often placated his neighbors with sudden acts of generosity, such as, shoveling their sidewalks when it snowed. One day he built an odd-looking attachment to his garage that was located at the rear of his narrow lot. Shortly after he built the storage shed, he paved over the dirt floor with concrete. His partner, who helped him with the pour, joked that it would be a **great place to hide dead bodies**. Several of the missing youth had worked part-time for Gacy's construction company. Another neighbor thought it odd that Gacy dug a hole one day in his backyard, filled it in, and then built a barbecue pit over it. About a year later, Gacy had his contractor partner pour a fresh concrete driveway for him. When he ran out of places to bury the bodies, he started dumping them in the Des Plaines River.

Diagram of Gacy's home (author's collection)

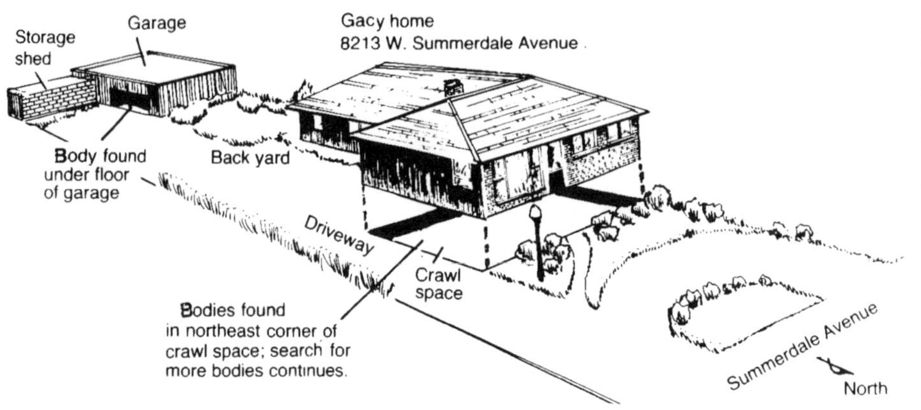

Sometimes Gacy looked for young victims simply by cruising the streets at night in his dark Oldsmobile. One of his choice spots was the Gaytown area of Chicago. Sometimes he enticed them with marijuana or free drugs and then pressed a chloroformed rag over their face to knock them out. There was another youth who lived at Gacy's house for a while but all of a sudden disappeared. When the neighbor next door asked what happened, Gacy claimed the boy was a slob and was drinking all his liquor, so he kicked him out.

In 1978 Gacy went to a hospital and told nurses he needed attending to because he had been mugged. In reality, Gacy made the mistake of propositioning a karate instructor in a gay bar.

Gacy also emersed himself in politics. He became a precinct captain for the local Democratic party. For several years he had been in charge of the annual Polish Day Parade in Chicago, during the month of May. First Lady **Rosalyn Carter** was the featured guest one year, and Gacy managed to have his picture taken with her, one that she autographed for him. Gacy had been checked out by the FBI for the occasion, but somehow they did not learn about his felony conviction and jail time in Iowa.

The whole thing began to unravel for Gacy in March of 1979. A young man named Jeff Rignall was abducted by Gacy, tortured and then raped. Luckily for the youth, Gacy dumped him in a park while he was unconscious, and he lived to tell the tale. When the police were slow to act on the complaint, Rignall took it upon himself to do the detective work. He spent hours daily cruising the area where Gacy had picked him up. All he remembered was Gacy's dark Delta 88 Oldsmobile had spotlights on it. One day his persistence paid off, and he wrote down the license number (PDM 42) and followed Gacy home. He obtained Gacy's name from real estate records at the courthouse and took the name to the police. The police ran a tracer and learned he had a record in Iowa. When they obtained Gacy's picture from that state, Rignall identified the man as his attacker. Police filed a battery charge against Gacy, but he got out of the mess by paying off the young man with a check for $3,000. Rignall dropped the complaint.

Gacy mug shot on British book

Then another boy who had worked for Gacy disappeared – Robert Piest. Piest, the final victim, was last seen with Gacy. Meanwhile, police discovered that yet another youth had accused Gacy of attacking him. When the police questioned Gacy, he told them the Piest kid was probably a runaway. But police were suspicious because Piest was a good kid – two badges shy of an Eagle Scout - and didn't fit the profile of a runaway. They began to piece the puzzle together and obtained a search warrant for Gacy's house. They recovered a hair sample from Gacy's car that was similar to Piest's. A film receipt in Gacy's wastebasket was confirmed by the parents as belonging to their son. They also found an empty bottle that smelled of chloroform, books about gay sex, and a high school ring with the initials JAS. The police put Gacy under 24 hour a day surveillance. He angrily responded by filing a $750,000 harassment suit against them. The police soon discovered that the ring belonged to John A. Szyc, one of the missing boys. Police secured another search warrant, and this time they hit the jackpot when they searched the dank crawl space that smelled sickly sweet - like a morgue. When the graves were uncovered, police were driven from the scene by methane and hydrogen sulfide gas, the result of decay and putrification. They eventually unearthed 29 grave plots on Gacy's property.

Jane and Governor Jim Thompson, George Ryan (*Belleville News-Democrat*)

Gacy quickly waived his Miranda rights after being arrested. He confessed that he had killed about 30 people. Gacy told them one ruse he used for capture was offering to show the victim the trick handcuffs he used in his work as a clown. Bodies were also found in various other places around the house that had been covered with concrete.

Unfortunately for Gacy, **Governor Thompson** had recently signed a new law making Gacy eligible for the death penalty. The toll of bodies from his house, plus those fished out of the river, now reached 32. (Gacy tossed the bodies from the Interstate 55 bridge.) During the search for bodies, so many boards had been cut and partitions torn down that the structural integrity of the house was compromised. There were large numbers of sightseers and authorities feared someone would get hurt. Subsequently, the Gacy house was completely demolished.

Gacy surprised everyone when he changed his mind and told his lawyer to plead him innocent. At one point he claimed to have multiple personalities and the one known as "Jack" killed the boys. Gacy was examined by prison psychiatrists and found competent to stand trial. The trial started on Feb. 6, 1980, in the Cook County Criminal Courts Building. It lasted six weeks. Defense, of course, presented psychiatrists, who testified Gacy, in part due to his dysfunctional relationship with his father, was a paranoid schizophrenic. Prosecution argued that burying the bodies to cover up his crimes was the act of a rational, evil man. The multiple personalities? Clever faking. "And do you really believe it is possible to have 33 separate instances of temporary insanity?" prosecution psychiatrists argued. The evidence against Gacy was overwhelming, and after only two hours of deliberations, the jury rejected the insanity plea, finding him guilty of murdering 33 people. (Robert Piest's body was finally found near the Illinois River.) Because it was feared that innocent men had been executed by the state under the old death penalty, the new law had built in safeguards for delays and appeals. Gacy was sent to **Menard Prison in Chester**. In February of 1983, Henry Brisbon, a black inmate, broke free of his restraints and stabbed Gacy in the arm. Brisbon was known as the I-57 killer, having robbed and murdered two people for a paltry sum. Brisbon's punishment? He lost his radio and TV privileges.

John Gacy on death row (author's collection)

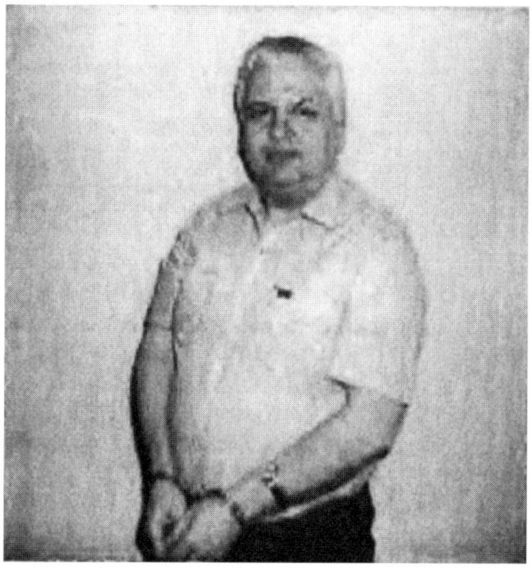

In 1984 the Illinois Supreme Court upheld Gacy's conviction. But so much time elapsed that instead of Gacy being electrocuted, the state had now adopted a more humane method of execution - injection. Gacy was transferred to **Joliet** and administered a lethal injection nearly 15 years after his conviction. Around midnight on May 10, 1994, Gacy was placed on a gurney and given an injection of sodium thiopental to sedate him, a mixture of pancuronium bromide to stop his breathing, and potassium chloride to stop his evil heart. But it takes about eight minutes for the lethal drugs to take effect, and so the brutal killer, who had caused so much pain and suffering for others, died painlessly in his sleep.

THE ORVILLE HODGE SCANDAL

Orville Hodge won the race for state auditor in 1952. Hodge had wanted to be governor but was persuaded by party officials to run for auditor instead. In earlier years, Hodge had been a member of the Board of Review of Madison County. He had previously served three terms in the Illinois General Assembly. In 1947 Hodge helped craft the legislation that forms the basis of the property tax system that exists today in Illinois. It was believed by many that Hodge had been staked for campaign funds by **Buster Wortman** and others on the promise that he would help legalize gambling after the election. It was no secret Hodge had much more money to spend than any other candidate in 1952. **Phil Brown**, state police superintendent, said Hodge came to him and asked if he could ease up on the gambling spots in and around East St. Louis.

Orville Hodge (*Edwards. Intelligencer*)

In 1956 incumbent **Orville Hodge of Granite City** ran against Democrat Michael Howlett for state auditor in November. Hodge used his legislative skills to obtain a budget for his office that was $2.5 million higher than was needed for the previous biennium. He spent the money so freely that he ran short and had to be bailed out with an emergency $525,000 appropriation. George Theim, a reporter for the *Chicago Daily News*, acting on a tip, began to investigate Hodge's extravagant lifestyle. He examined the auditor's payroll and discovered friends and relatives on the list in an apparent effort to broaden his political base. He also found that Hodge had a plush suite of rooms at the St. Nicholas Hotel in **Springfield**. Hodge was a joiner and a member of the **Belleville Country Club** and the **Sunset Hills Country Club** in **Edwardsville**. He had formerly run an insurance agency at 1915 Madison Avenue in **Granite City**. He also owned a hotel in Florida, several Cadillac cars, two airplanes, a summer home on the lake, a new hardware and appliance store, motorboats, and farms stocked with expensive Aberdeen-Angus cows. Theim's investigative trip to **Granite City** made it obvious that Hodge's real estate business hadn't paid for these extravagances.

When asked on the stand about stolen funds, padded expense accounts and forged checks, Hodge tried to lay the blame on his confederates. And he denied using tax money to pay personal hotel, food and liquor bills.

After Hodge's thievery was exposed, U.S. Attorney John W. Stoddart of Springfield subpoenaed **Frank "Buster" Wortman** and **Elmer "Dutch" Dowling**, a close associate, to try and learn what Hodge did with the money he stole. Buster's lawyer was St. Louisan **Morris Shenker**. But Buster said he never lent Hodge any money, nor did he ever have any business dealings with him.

The *Post-Dispatch* ran a story that asserted Wortman at one time was in partnership with Hodge in his half-million dollar Florida motel. Buster met Hodge, the story said, when they considered starting a number of gambling establishments in Florida and in Havana, Cuba. After the Kefauver hearings exposed local vice and corruption, Florida authorities cracked down, and the plans were abandoned. Wortman, Dowling and a slot machine operator named **Tom Berry** bought a Las Vegas casino and ran it through "front men" until Nevada authorities put the squeeze on them. They sold out to a San Fransisco syndicate. The story said Hodge was known to members of the Shelton gang, and when he was a state legislator, he collected gambling payoffs in Madison County during the administration of Governor Green. Hodge supposedly collected the payoffs in return for the privilege of operating dice games, slots, and policy rackets without interference from officials.

Granite City star Whip Wilson with Roy and Dale

Hodge was often seen with **Paul Powell**, a Democrat from **Vienna** (Johnson County) and Speaker of the House. Powell even visited Hodge when he was sent to Menard Prison at Chester. Hodge also chummed with former governor (back in 1940) **John Stelle** of **McLeansboro** at Cahokia Downs in East St. Louis where Stelle was a significant stockholder.

The final audit of Hodge's three and a half years (1953-56) as state auditor listed over a million dollars worth of embezzled state warrants and misappropriation of another half-million of bank funds.

Hodge served six years in prison at **Menard Prison in Chester** and then went back to Granite City to work in his sister's hardware store in the Bellemore Shopping Center on Nameoki Road. He later became an insurance broker. He died in 1987 and was buried at Sunset Hills in **Edwardsville**. **Harold Zeigler** says the cowboy movie star from Granite City, **Whip Wilson**, is also buried there.

Ed Rooney of the *Chicago Daily News* won a Pulitzer Prize in 1957 for his reporting on the Hodge scandal. The *Daily News* folded in 1978.

THE PAUL POWELL SHOEBOX MYSTERY

When did Paul Powell's career in **Springfield**, Illinois, begin?

The **Vienna**, Illinois-born Powell was first elected to the House of Representatives in 1934. He was elected Speaker of the House in 1949, 1959, and again in 1961. He became secretary of state in 1964 and was reelected in 1968.

Paul Powell home in Vienna (courtesy Mike and Joanna Coles of Anna, IL)

What kind of a relationship did Powell have with his wife, Daisy?

She suffered from ill health the last 20 years of her life and was bitter and profane about her husband's womanizing. She remained back home in Vienna when Paul was in Springfield. She died in 1967. Much of Powell's private life we know from a stack of letters Daisy wrote to her husband over a 5-year period. She even threatened to expose his infidelity the night a "This is Your Life" event was held for Powell in the local high school gym. Daisy was his second wife, his first having been tragically killed by the infamous 1925 tornado that swept through southern Illinois, killing over 1,000.

Why was Powell so successful in the state capitol?

Powell was a shrewd politician and built a base of loyal followers among southern Illinois voters and lawmakers by delivering southern Illinois votes for northern (Chicago) projects, but always in exchange for some kind of quid pro quo.

He also knew how to extract support from special interest groups, such as the horse racing industry. Southern Illinoisans loved him because he gave them clout. Powell was known as a man of his word. He was liked for his loyalty to southern Illinois and his homespun humor and folksiness. The Springfield press corps twice voted him the state's outstanding legislator. In addition, Powell was successful in obtaining substantial increases for funding of SIU at Carbondale. And during his tenure, the days of harness racing increased from 90 in 1946 to 235 by 1963. The state of Illinois took in an astounding $20 million in revenue from horse racing for the year 1963.

What was it about the purchase of racetrack stock that raised quite a few eyebrows?

The Chicago Downs Association, at Sportsmans Park in Chicago, offered an elite number of people the chance to buy stock for a measly ten cents a share. Included in this inner circle were several key legislators who had helped shepherd passage of favorable legislation to the racing interests. Paul Powell's wife (Daisy) was allowed to buy 16,900 shares for a mere $1,690. Of course the returns on this investment were considerable. There was a huge public outcry about this being graft and pay-off money. Powell shrugged it off by saying he had also invested in county fair racing at Vienna and **Metropolis**. From 1967-70, Powell received $20,000 annually as a "consultant" for Chicago Downs. This was for serving as Illinois' goodwill horse racing ambassador and for more or less being a lobbyist for the industry in Springfield. Powell also had investments at Cahokia Downs, on the outskirts of **East St. Louis**.

How did Powell get in trouble over a special license plate issued to **Sam Giancana**?

The FBI observed reputed mobster Sam Giancana acting suspiciously in Mexico in a car with the special tag, PG 5000. When the FBI searched the Secretary of State's records, the file for that particular license could not be found. Powell's chief administrative assistant, **Nicholas Ciatto**, wrote Powell a memo saying that he found no office bribery scandal nor any conspiracy to issue plates without fees or appropriate records. But in later years, bribery is exactly what happened during George Ryan's tenure.

What were the circumstances surrounding Powell's death?

Powell died from heart failure in a two-bedroom hotel suite up in Rochester, Minnesota. He had gone to the Mayo Clinic to undergo medical tests for cardiac problems. A few eyebrows were raised when it was discovered the 68-year-old widower was accompanied by his divorced secretary, **Marge Hensey**. Powell had left an envelope with her name on it containing $55,000 cash. In his will, Powell left her shares in the Chicago Downs Racing Association worth $700,000. Powell had told Hensey that if anything ever happened to him, she was to contact John Rendleman, who was a lawyer and executor of Powell's estate, so he could go over his personal effects.

Who discovered Powell's stash of $800,000 in shoeboxes and briefcases?

Three days after Powell's death, **John Rendleman** and several other people went through his personal effects at the St. Nicholas Hotel in Springfield. Rendleman was a friend of Powell's and Chancellor at SIU in Edwardsville. The St. Nicholas Hotel was where Powell stayed while he was in Springfield. It was an astounded Rendleman who found the money. Rendleman later searched Powell's home in Vienna and found additional cash in some closets.

Why did many think John Rendleman **should have resigned** as SIUE's Chancellor?

Because after Rendleman found the money, he did not make disclosure until 81 days later. He chose to release the story through **John Gardner**, editor and publisher of the *Southern Illinoisan*. Governor Richard Ogilvie was especially critical of Rendleman. Despite probes by the IRS and a grand jury, no one was indicted or jailed as a result of the investigations. The only thing the public could do was speculate, which they did with gusto.

SIU Edwardsville Chancellor, John Rendleman (courtesy SIUE)

Who also learned about the shoebox money about three weeks sooner than its public disclosure?

John Rendleman told Lieutenant Governor **Paul Simon of Troy/Makanda** about the money. In an interview with this author (July 2002), Paul Simon said Rendleman asked him to come to his office in Edwardsville to talk about something very important. Rendleman told Simon there were only two other people who knew about the money and swore him to secrecy. Simon had once told Rendleman he thought Powell was a crook. Rendleman, who would die of cancer in 1976, admitted that Simon had probably been right about Powell. Simon's theory is that the money was actually found in Powell's safe in his Springfield office and then taken to the St. Nicholas Hotel. That way it would seem more like money Powell had saved or invested rather than money that belonged to the state, hence a scandal. Simon also believes the amount found was actually about a third larger than reported and that some of it was "lost" during the transfer from the office to the hotel.

Another take on the money is that this large sum was income from dubious sources, and by keeping it as cash, Powell would not have to report it as income to the IRS. William J. Nettles, of the Illinois Attorney General's office, thinks the shoebox money came from kickbacks. Yet despite his wealth, Powell did not live an extravagant lifestyle.

Paul Simon and wife campaigning in the New Hampshire primary, 1988

Why was the shoebox money mystery considered a "time of troubles" for all Illinois public officials?
As reporters dug for answers as to the source of the considerable sum of cash, they revealed other embarrassing facts, casting an unfavorable light on a number of other politicians, especially those linked to the horse racing syndicate.

What were the various speculations about the source of the shoebox money?

Much of the money consisted of $100 bills. Some said Powell somehow skimmed the money from car license fees. Others thought it was money accepted in return for political favors from special interest groups. Or maybe it was just bribe and kickback money, much like the scandal uncovered in the office several years ago when Governor George Ryan was Secretary of State.

The librarian from Vienna, **Margaret Mathis**, said a good number of citizens believe it was for his War Chest to run for governor. One savvy **East St. Louis** politico believes it was simply "walking around money" to be given to county chairmen and their foot soldiers throughout the state to help get out the vote during elections. Relatives said it was money he had saved and invested. The riddle has never been solved.

Rose Mary Orr of Vienna also believes the money was to be used in his campaign for governor. She supports Paul Simon's belief that the money was originally in an office safe - not shoeboxes. She said Powell was a good businessman accustomed to keeping his money in either a safe or a bank, not hidden in closets. Orr told this author Paul Powell was the former owner of

Powell's Café on the square in Vienna. Her parents bought the business after Powell went to Springfield and later changed the name to **Hunt's Café**. She says Powell was well liked and that in his will he left a trust fund so all nursing home patients in Vienna would receive a poinsettia for Christmas.

Paul Powell (Bell *News-Dem.*)

What raised eyebrows again in 1978 when Powell's estate was finally settled?
The size of it. For someone in public life for over 35 years, it was a whopping $4.6 million. The *Wall Street Journal* calculated that his salary for all those public servant years amounted to a paltry $300,000.

How much of the shoebox money did the government get back?
The government filed suit to get all of it, but a compromise with heirs was reached whereby the federal government snatched $1.8 million, the state received $100,000, and an inheritance tax of $222,215 was levied. The rest of the money went to his heirs and various charitable causes.

What hampered government efforts to trace the true source of all the money?
Immediately after Powell's death, his secretary and close friends went to his office in the Statehouse and his hotel suite and removed numerous amounts of documents and papers. Everything should have been inventoried and the serial numbers of the bills recorded, but this was not done.

Is Powell considered a scoundrel or public benefactor in his hometown of Vienna?
His Vienna home is run by Johnson County as a museum. Powell is a local hero and it is their belief that he looked out for southern Illinois' interests, long considered an inferior stepchild by the rest of the state. For the most part, hometowners feel Powell fell victim to the "yellow press," looking to sell newspapers, and unscrupulous muckraking journalists seeking to advance their careers. His tombstone bears several inscriptions: 'Here Lies a Lifelong Democrat,' and the presumptious 'A Great American.'

Who benefited from Powell's largesse in his will?
Marge Hensey was left the $55,000 in an envelope, Powell's Buick, worth about $3,000, and Chicago Downs stock valued at $695,200. Another female friend of Powell's, Lucille Koval received $15,000 in cash and $90,970 worth of shares in Fox Valley Trotting Club. Powell had originally left $50,000 to SIU Carbondale for a trust fund, but a subsequent codicil removed the provision because Powell was upset about the anti-Vietnam War demonstrations by students. Rendleman was given about $21,000 in bank stock and a whopping $200,000 for serving as executor of the estate. (Rendleman told reporter **Pat Gauen** the stress nearly killed him.) Only one Powell relative was in the will, **Lillie Panghorn**, a cousin from **Marion**, who received bank stock worth $105,000. He also left money to the Boy Scouts, various Democratic organizations, the American Legion, Moose Lodge, the Shri-ners Hospital in St. Louis and several churches. $200,000 was set aside to maintain Powell's home in Vienna as a museum. The state contended Powell had stolen from the citizens but was unable to prove criminal wrongdoing. The IRS accused Powell of fraud in the settlement of his wife's estate back in 1968. In all, the IRS claimed Powell owed more than $3 million in unpaid taxes.

What reform legislation was passed after the Powell brouhaha?
A law requiring public disclosure of political campaign contributors was passed. Governor Ogilvie also issued an executive order requiring thousands of state officials to report sources of income and any capital gains of $1,000 or more.

SPRINGFIELD'S FRANK ZITO

Doug Pokorski's Address to the Sangamon County Historical Society, February, 2002 (courtesy Doug Pokorski)

As you all know, we're here tonight to talk about Springfield's Godfather, **Frank Zito**, the man who many believe, with pretty good evidence, ran organized crime in and around the city for roughly half a century.

In many respects, the story of Frank Zito is a classic American success story. A young Italian boy from a poor family comes to this country as an immigrant and, by dint of effort rises to the top in his chosen field, becoming rich and powerful and earning the respect and perhaps even the affection of his neighbors.

True, Frank Zito's chosen field was not medicine, nor the law, nor construction, nor the arts. It was crime. But, before we rush to judgment, remember that President John F. Kennedy's father, Joseph Kennedy, built his fortune in the illegal liquor business during prohibition, and another President Kennedy ancestor had participated successfully in the opium trade with China a century earlier. (Note: **Joe Kennedy**, with the help of New York underworld figures like **Frank Castiglia** (Costello), bought up huge quantities of European Scotch, realizing that enormous profits could be made during Prohibition. He invested heavily in the stock market, made a fortune, then got out before it crashed in 1929. He was a huge contributor to FDR's 1932 campaign, became first head of the newly-created SEC, and was later appointed ambassador to England.)

I've said that Frank Zito became rich and powerful in his chosen trade. Just what do I mean by that? Well, it helps to understand that for most of the 20th century Springfield was a wide-open town as far as illegal activities such as liquor, gambling, and prostitution were concerned. And from at least the 1920s on up to his death in the 1970s, Frank Zito would have had a cut of all that action, in return for providing protection from both law enforcement and from outside competition.

What kind of money are we talking about here? If Zito kept any financial records they were never made public, but we do have some indirect evidence. In the late 1940s the **St. Louis** *Post-Dispatch* ran a series of exposures on organized crime in Illinois. It reported that at the time Zito was making protection payments to city, county and state officials totaling $10,0000 a week. That's $520,000 a year, or more than $3.5 million a year in today's dollars. If that kind of money was just one of the costs of doing business, one can imagine what Zito's actual revenues might have been.

Springfield's Frank Zito (courtesy *Journal-Register*)

As to the extent of Zito's power, nationally syndicated columnist **Drew Pearson** listed Zito among "**Illinois' worst hoodlums**" in 1962.

He said, "Outside of Chicago, the most powerful underworld figure in Illinois is Frank Zito, whose balding, grey-fringed head, conservative clothes and scholarly appearance belie his violent background. He controls gambling, prostitution and bookmaking in Springfield and (the) Sangamon (County) areas."

I first heard of "Springfield's Godfather," though not by name, more than 30 years ago, when I was still a teenager living up the road in **Lincoln**. You may recall that at the time, in the mid-to-late 1960s, the term "Godfather," meaning the head of an organized crime "family," was just becoming a part of the nation's vocabulary as a result of books like "**The Valachi Papers**" and Mario Puzo's "**The Godfather**," which was later made into a very successful movie.

At the time, my dad was operating a plumbing and heating business, and one of his main suppliers was Capitol plumbing and heating supply here in Springfield. The Capitol salesman he dealt with most often was a man named **Paul Gaitens**, and one day, perhaps because this new term was coming into the vocabulary, Mr. Gaitens just happened to mention it to my father that one of his neighbors was Springfield's godfather. Dad later told our family about this comment.

We were all somewhat surprised, since we thought of godfathers and organized crime as being something to be found in places like New York and Chicago. But Springfield? Aw, common. No way! Still, Paul Gaites was a good guy, so maybe there was something to it.

It wasn't until years later, when I came to work for the *State Journal Register*, that I found a little bit more information in our files, just a little, but not much.

I would later learn that one of Zito's trademarks was keeping as low a profile as possible. What I did learn was that he had been picked up at a law enforcement raid of a November 14th, 1957 mobster's convention in the upstate New York town of **Apalachin**.

It would be much later before I began to piece together a more complete picture of Zito's life and activities. That was in 1999, when I wrote a year-long, daily series for the paper called "A Springfield Century." The premise of the series was that on each day of 1999, we would revisit a story that appeared in the *Journal-Register* or one of its predecessors, The Illinois *State Journal* and the *Illinois State Register,* on that same date in a previous year in the century.

The story revisited for April 17 was from 1932. It concerned the murder of **John Picco**, consular agent for the Italian government, who was gunned down by two men with sawed off shotguns, while his young son looked on, near Picco's brother's house in the 400 block of West Monroe Street.

As consular agent, a position that involved his looking out for the welfare of the many Italian immigrants who were working in Illinois mines and factories, Picco was an integral part of the local Italian community. His death, still unsolved, was major news not only here, but in places such as Chicago and St. Louis.

Shortly after my story ran, I heard from a member of the Picco family who still lives in Springfield. He wanted to talk about the murder and see if I had any additional information that wasn't in my story, so I visited him at his office.

It is kind of round about, but it leads to an interesting discovery. As we chatted, he asked if I knew anything about another gangland shooting that took place shortly after Picco's murder in Christian County.

As luck would have it, I had brought news clips on that shooting with me on a hunch that there might be a connection to the Picco shooting.

The second shooting involved a small time bootlegger named **Arthur Cioni**, who lived in **Langley**, near **Taylorville**. Cioni had reported to police that three men had threatened to kill him if he didn't pay them not to. The police set a trap at Cioni's house for the three blackmailers.

When the men arrived, Cioni and his bodyguard, **Henry Alegrucci,** hid in the house. The men pounded on the doors. Most of the police had been called away by a bogus phone call. When the men pounding on the door got no answer, they began shooting at the house and Cioni and Alegrucci began shooting back. Some of the remaining police also appear to have shot at the three thugs.

One of the thugs, **Pete LaRocca** of Springfield, was killed in the shooting, as was Alegrucci. The other two extortionists, later identified as **Jack Scire** and **Vincenzo "Blackie" Mantella**, sped off in their car.

The police caught up with them on Vandeveer Street, in **Taylorville**, and Scire was killed. Mantella, who was believed wounded, escaped.

Now as the Picco family member that I was chatting with read these news clips from 1932, he became very excited. "Those are the names. That's them," he said. He went on to explain that although the Picco murder was officially unsolved, family tradition had maintained that the three men who were ambushed in Christian County had been responsible for the killing of John Picco, apparently as part of some freelance criminal activity not authorized by the local "Godfather."

Picco had been a close friend and associate of Frank Zito, and Zito had acted quickly to identify Picco's killers and bring them his own kind of swift justice.

The three men were said to have boasted of the Picco killing while at a café in **Kincaid**, and news reports said the car they drove in Christian County matched the description of the car used in the Picco killing.

As further evidence, Cioni, the bait for the trap of the three thugs, was a small time criminal of the type who normally wouldn't go to the cops for help in solving his problems. But he was also reportedly a former employee of Picco, and Picco is said to have at one time, used his position on the state parole board to shorten a prison sentence Cioni was serving.

Picco family stories in Italy and this country match the contemporary newspaper descriptions of the Langley incident in great detail, with one interesting difference being that some say that not everybody dressed as a policeman that evening really was one.

If LaRocca, Scire and Mantella really did kill Picco, their fate would also explain something else, why the Picco murder investigation, which at one time involved state, local, federal and even Italian officials, petered out rather quickly.

After all, with LaRocca and Scire dead in Christian County, and Mantella reportedly meeting the same fate at the hands of some of Zito's underworld associates in Chicago, the case was closed.

Learning of Frank Zito's connection to the Picco shooting and the Langley incident gave me a new appreciation for both the extent of his power and the duration of his reign as head of organized crime locally.

Previously, I knew that he was the head guy on the mid-50's, but this moves everything back decades.

As I continued to research "A Springfield Century," I began to turn up cases that pointed to his involvement, even though his name was seldom mentioned.

For example, just a year after the Picco and Langley incidents, a suspected bank robber and extortionist named **Rocco Siciliano**, was found in a ditch south of **Broadwell**, in Logan County, with three bullets in his head and a crushed skull – a classic example of someone who had been "taken for a ride." Siciliano had been charged with a couple bank robberies and with the complicity in the kidnapping of **Jerome Factor**, son of John "Jake the Barber" Factor of Chicago. And, yes, **he was a relative of the Max Factor cosmetics family**.

Siciliano apparently knew a lot about a lot of tough characters and he was awaiting trial for one of the bank robberies, which gave him incentive to share his knowledge with the authorities. It was believed at the time that he was killed to keep him quiet. And it seems plausible, if not likely, that the kind of gangland execution he received would have been done with Zito's knowledge or approval, if not his orders.

Another killing in August, 1948, bore the Zito imprint even more clearly than the Siciliano murder. On August 9 of that year, a hoodlum named **Leonard Giordano** was found in a ditch on Route 66 north of Springfield. He had been knocked out with a blackjack, shot through the neck with a .45 caliber bullet, his jugular vein had been slashed and there was evidence he may have been tortured. And, yes, he was dead.

Giordano was a barber turned professional gambler who was a close friend and associate of one **George "Red" Smith**. Smith had been identified as one of two men who had tried to hold up the Springfield Kresge's store that July. Smith's body had been found a week earlier near Joliet, in a similar condition to Giordano, including the evidence of torture.

Smith was reportedly part of a group of out of town gangsters who were trying to muscle in on the local action, and there was talk that Giordano had helped set up the Kresge job.

While there was a pretty clear consensus that Smith and Giordano had been killed by, or at the behest of local organized crime figures who weren't about to let any outsiders set up shop on their turf – read Frank Zito – local authorities, no doubt mindful of the $10,000 he was providing them each week – insisted on treating the killing as a personal matter.

When Giordano's roommate, **John Jasper Teresi**, was found dead ten days after Giorsdano's body was discovered, authorities were again quick to rule out any organized crime connection to his death. It was, they said, a suicide, caused by Teresi's despondency over his friend's death.

Never mind the fact the coroner had originally reported that the deadly bullet had entered Teresi's head from the left, exiting from the right side, and that there were powder burns on his left hand, while a state police investigator claimed that Teresi had shot himself with his right hand, which did not have powder burns, in the right side of the head.

However, a compliant Sangamon County coroner's jury ruled the death a suicide. That prompted the Illinois *State Journal* to editorialize that the way the Giordano and Teresi cases were handled was "A symbol of all that is wrong with law enforcement in Sangamon County."

"One does not need a blue nose to smell decay in a government which permits such degredations," the *Journal* said.

Another murder in which Frank Zito was not only suspected of involvement, but was actually brought in for questioning, was the 1957 murder of **James DeRosa**, a pinball machine dealer who had been missing two weeks when a pet collie brought DeRosa's skull to his master's home near Andrew. DeRosa's badly decomposed body was soon found in a nearby cornfield,

Now in those days pinball machines were legal only if they didn't pay off in cash. But many tavern owners ignored that distinction, and the machines were an element of the local gambling operation. It was believed DeRosa had been trying to expand his business into somebody else's territory, territory sanctioned by Zito's organization.

The Illinois *State Register* called the DeRosa killing the result of "a powerful, ruthless, underworld vendetta."

In a 1999 interview, **Don Young**, a retired deputy chief of the Springfield Police Department, said that "all the policemen back then knew who killed DeRosa."

"A guy killed him for our local contingent (of) the mob – again read Frank Zito – but he didn't leave any tracks," the policeman said.

In February 1959, Zito was hauled before a U.S. Senate committee investigating organized crime, where senate counsel **Robert F. Kennedy**, yes, *that* Robert F. Kennedy, questioned him about the DeRosa killing. Zito invoked his Fifth Amendment rights. The murder has never been solved.

One aside to that incident. When Zito first tried to plead the Fifth, he said he would refuse to answer the questions. One of the senators on the committee asked him to use the phrase "decline to answer," out of respect for the committee.

Zito's English was not perfect even after 30 or 40 years in the country. Zito started to say "I recline to answer" . . . then he said, "You hafta excuse me. I don't mean I don't wanna said it. I cain't said it right."

There were other murders over the years where it was suggested that Zito and his organization may have been involved. The 1929 killing of **Dominic Tarro**, the **bootleg king of Benld**, whose body was found beaten and shot, his hands tied with wire, in the Sangamon River, was one such case.

Tarro was a close associate of Zito's, but he was also believed to be on the verge of providing evidence against some of his associates to the authorities.

That same year, **Caesar Sansone** was gunned down practically in front of the Abe Lincoln home. Sansone had been a close advisor to John Picco, who may have come to know too much about Zito's affairs through his association with Picco.

Sansone was also alleged to have been a bit too talkative for his own good.

A couple other points concerning Springfield's Godfather deserve mention before we wind up.

First, the notorious **Shelton Gang of East St. Louis** operated during part of the same period and controlled organized crime in much of the same Illinois area outside Chicago that Zito operated in.

The Sheltons – Carl, Earl, Bernie

At one point, an honest sheriff drove the Sheltons out of East St. Louis, and they easily relocated to Peoria where they ran the city through the World War II years and beyond.

They did not, however, ever establish a foothold in Springfield or the surrounding area, though they no doubt would have liked to. It probably can't be proven, but it's probably equally a safe bet, that the reason they never committed a crime in these parts, that we know of, is because Frank Zito and his associates wouldn't have liked it.

And while I am speculating – I would point out that the city of Springfield went more than 100 years between the time it was founded and the time of its first bank robbery by a group of **East St. Louis gangsters** in 1924. Amazing as that seems, the city would go another 42 years until another bank was robbed in 1966. This at a time when bank robberies were flourishing everywhere. Could it be that Springfield has Frank Zito, who was amazingly determined and successful at protecting his turf, to thank for the prolonged security of its banks. I would not be against it.

Despite his many illegal activities, Zito seems to have lived a quiet, peaceful life, out of the spotlight and without the personal risk that brought an early end to the lives of so many of his Mafia associates.

The same retired police officer, Don Young, who said everybody knew that Zito had ordered the DeRosa killing, said that he and his henchmen did not act like mobsters.

"They didn't go out and drink," he said. "There wasn't any of this stuff where they pulled up in a big limo. They just drove ordinary cars."

And while Zito did serve time in a federal penitentiary for bootlegging in the 1930s, and had some trouble with the IRS in the 1950s, as well as with the immigration department, he was mainly a "Teflon Don" as far as the law was concerned.

Springfield's Godfather died of natural causes 64 years after he had come to the United States from his native Sicily, in August of 1974, at St. John's Hospital, at the age of 81.

Neighbors and former neighbors described him as a "quiet gentleman." "He was a model citizen,"one said. "He was a real good neighbor. He didn't bother anybody," said another.

I had a call today from a woman who used to frequent a tavern and restaurant that Zito's wife owned and he sort of managed across from the fair grounds. She said "Did you know Zito?" No I didn't. "Well I knew him." She said, "He was the sweetest, nicest person to talk to you would ever want to know. Folks called him "Uncle Frank." He would come over and visit and sit at your table with you while you were having dinner."

But she also remembered that she asked him a question once. She couldn't remember the exact question, but it was something about his criminal activities. "All he said was 'you shouldn't ask questions like that.' "

A couple of other things that I have picked up about Zito in the last couple of weeks are perhaps trivial, but kind of interesting.

At the Lincoln's birthday symposium at the Old Capitol last week, an acquaintance who is a former Springfield resident came up to me and said he wouldn't be able to attend tonight. He was sorry about that because he once had personal contact with Zito.

Back in the 1950s, when he was attending college, he got a job over Christmas break delivering mail, to help out with the Christmas rush. His route included Zito's Illini Road home. He was curious to see what kind of mail such a notorius criminal was receiving, he said, but he was disappointed to find that it was just like everybody else's mail – Christmas cards, catalogs and bills.

Another caller, a 73-year-old Chatham gentleman, said he had met Zito back in the 1940s, when he was still in his teens. He was working for his father's tree service and was part of a crew, including his father, who were called to do some work at Zito's house. I think this would have been his house on West Wabash.

When they were finished spraying the trees, Zito came out and invited the crew inside. He took them to the basement and produced a large pitcher of wine and some glasses. He began to pour a glass of wine for each of them, but when he came to his seat the father said "None for the boy."

Zito replied "Old enough to work, old enough to drink" and poured the boy a glass anyway.

Another coincidence I suppose occurred back in 1999 when I was working on "A Springfield Century." I had been writing about Frank Zito and his activities for several months when, one Saturday in July, I opened the newspaper and turned to the obituaries. There, much to my surprise, I ran across a death notice for 100-year-old Tony Zito, who had been involved in some of brother Frank's business ventures. I was amazed that he had been alive so recently.

My first thought was "Gee, it's a shame I hadn't known earlier. Maybe I could have talked to him about his brother. Then, after thinking about it for a while and considering some of the possible ramifications, my second thought was "Maybe it's just as well I didn't talk to him."

In looking back at the long, successful career of Frank Zito, it's worthwhile to put that career in perspective. His violent business methods are, of course, deplorable, but he seems to have been one of that generation of gangsters who applied those methods only to business rivals. There is no indication that he ever treated "civilians" with anything other than the civility and kindness we would expect of a good neighbor.

As for the business he was in, Prohibition has long been abandoned as a failed social experiment, and liquor can be legally purchased as nearby as your local supermarket. As a character witness once said of Frank's brother Tony's bootlegging conviction, "It's not against the 10 Commandments."

Gambling, too, has become respectable. Far from trying to eradicate it, the state of Illinois has joined many other states in running the games itself.

And while prostitution is still illegal, it is no longer a crime for adults to have sexual relations outside of matrimony, and what was once sold by Zito's operation is now available for free.

In fact, if Frank were alive today, he might look around him with some perplexity to discover that with the passage of time he had practically become "legit."

Dale Cavaness (St. Louis County Police)

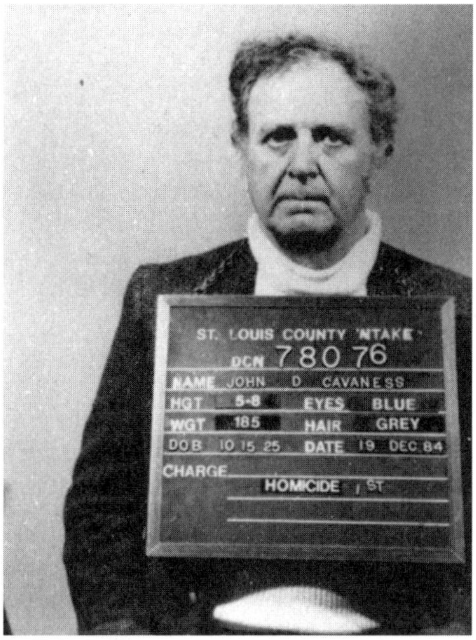

DR. JOHN DALE CAVANESS

In 1984, Dr. John Dale Cavaness, a prominent southern Illinois physician, was arrested in St. Louis. He was charged with the **murder of his son** (Sean) in **St. Louis County**. Detective Dave Barron was one of the chief investigators assigned to the case. **Sam Yarbrough**, the chief polygraph examiner for the county police, administered the "lie detector" test. Cavaness had become an early suspect when the police caught him lying about having just visited his son shortly before the murder took place. Yarbrough reported to the authorities that the test showed Cavaness to be a liar. Police often use the MOM technique for determining probable cause. Cavaness had the (M)eans (a .44 gun, the (O)pportunity, (he had just visited his son, but the (M)otive perplexed them. Prosecutors finally concluded that the doctor, a perfectionist who was heavily into genetic engineering, killed his two sons because they just didn't measure up. It was a rare and shocking case of filicide, a father killing his own offspring.

In his 1985 trial, Cavaness proclaimed his innocence. The trial was held in Clayton at the St. Louis County Courthouse. **Steve Goldman** prosecuted the case but was not allowed by the judge to tell the jury that another son (Mark) had mysteriously been shot to death in the woods of Little Egypt seven years earlier. The jury found Cavaness guilty as charged and recommended the death penalty. The popular Dr.'s southern Illinois supporters thought the trial was a travesty and hoped the conviction would be overturned on appeal. On November 17, 1986, a prison guard found Cavaness hanging in his cell from an electrical cord.

It was a case that had polarized **Eldorado** and **Harrisburg**, between those who were sure he was guilty and those who were just as sure he was innocent. His wife inherited a $198,000 life insurance policy. A clause with the provision that the policy would be invalid in case of suicide **expired the day before Cavaness hanged himself**.

His funeral was held at the First Presbyterian Church in Eldorado, officiated by Reverend Langham.

THE PAULA SIMS CASE, ALTON, ILLINOIS

On April 29, 1989, a woman named Paula Sims called **Alton** police, telling them a masked gunman had kidnapped her baby girl. Paula had made a similar call in June of 1986 when the family lived near **Brighton** in **Jersey County**. The Alton police called Sheriff Frank Yocom of Jersey County in for a consult since he had handled the first case.

Robert Sims, the husband (*Bell. News-Democrat*)

Back in 1986, Paula ran to a neighbor's house shortly after 10 p.m. and hysterically told Don and Minnie Gray that a masked gunman broke into her house, ordered her to lay on the floor and abducted her baby Loralei. She explained that her husband Robert was working at the Jefferson Smurfit plant when it happened. Loralei, the red haired baby, was only 12 days old.

The police were called and deputy sheriff **John Hazelwood** arrived on the scene and found Brighton patrolmen **Chris White** and **Don Stewart** already there. They had heard the broadcast on their radio and immediately went to the Sims house on rural Cotter Road.

Sheriff **Yocum** was notified and arrived around 11 p.m. There was a tear in the screen door and everyone assumed that was how the gunman got in. Minnie and Paula had searched the baby's room upstairs one more time before the police arrived. Minnie thought it strange that the baby's blanket in the bassinette was folded neatly. Shortly after the sheriff arrived, Paula's husband, a bearded man of 35, came home from work. He had to stop at a friend's house on the way home because he was so emotionally distraught he couldn't drive. The state police dogs were called in from Springfield. Paula's parents, Mr. and Mrs. Orville and Nylene Blew of **Cottage Hills**, near **Wood River**, were called and they also came over. The immediate suspect was an unknown man with a green truck who had been told earlier that evening he couldn't fish in the nearby Sims pond. When interviewed, Paula couldn't describe the gun and said the family dog didn't bark to alert her. She did say the invader was white and wore a mask and a dark T-shirt. Paula said they had no enemies and couldn't think of why someone would kidnap her baby. The Simses had been married five years.

Paula Sims /Deputy Jim Neumann (*News-Democrat*)

A dog was brought in to sniff the scene but found no scent of a dead baby or that of the kidnapper. Authorities thought it strange that Paula cried at all the right times, but there were no tears.

When police later questioned her high school boyfriends in rural La Plata, Missouri, where she grew up, they said she was sexually active, smoked marijuana and was not above telling a lie. Paula's 19-year-old brother had been killed in a car crash, in which Paula suffered severe facial injuries at age 16. Her other brother Dennis was mentally challenged and required constant care. The family moved to Illinois and Paula finished her senior year at Civic Memorial in **Bethalto** where she lettered in softball. She attended **Lewis and Clark Junior College** in **Godfrey** but never finished her course work in computer programming. Those who knew her said she was a loner and a bit strange. Paula was 22 when she met and married Robert in 1981. Robert was older than Paula by seven years. Neither of them attended church. Paula was fired from her job at National Food Store on Godfrey Road in 1983. The manager caught her selling groceries at a discount to her friends.

Authorities called in a boat with sonar to check the pond. Nothing! A plane with an infra-red camera flew over the area to check for a body. Nothing! Police thought it strange that neither Robert nor Paula helped in the search of the adjacent woods. They also learned Robert had wanted a boy and that Loralei's room was painted blue.

Paula consented to a lie detector test but she failed it. Robert was given a similar lie detector test, which he also flunked. The police grilled both suspects, telling them that they didn't believe their stories. But neither one cracked. Meanwhile, friends, family and workplace had raised a $14,000 reward for the kidnapper's capture.

Joe Trail bags leaves in front of house where Sims' lived in Alton (*News-Democrat*)

Robert Sims was born in 1952 at **Carbondale**. At the time, the family lived in **Marion**, home to the prison that replaced **Alcatraz** as the maximum security federal prison. His father was a schoolteacher and the family moved to Alton in 1958 so he could teach music in the public school. Robert was a quiet kid with average grades who played tuba and sang in the chorus.

After graduation he went to work as a loan collector for Laclede Steel in the credit union. He started attending classes at **SIU Edwardsville** but dropped out after a year. He enlisted in the navy in 1972 and was stationed in Maine. He married a local girl named Martie and they moved to Alton when his stint in the military was completed. Robert resumed his job at the credit union but resented taking orders from a female superior. He soon quit and took a new position at the credit department in the **Olin** plant in **East Alton**. (This author worked at Olin one summer in 1983.) Once again Robert couldn't get along with co-workers or superiors and quit after less than 2 years. He then began working as a laborer for **Alton Boxboard**, known as Smurfit after it was bought out. He ran afoul of the law and was fined $100 for shoplifting a few tools from Alton's Central Hardware. Martie found her husband too domineering and filed for divorce in 1978.

On June 24, 1986, nearly two months after the reported kidnapping, the police decided to search a wooded hillside, behind the Sims house – opposite the direction Paula said the kidnapper fled. Robert tried to discourage the police by telling them the woods were full of poison ivy. A search dog found the baby's body, badly decomposed in a thicket. The left arm and leg were missing and it was assumed some small animal had eaten the remains. The baby was too mangled to determine its sex, and cause of death could also not be determined. It was believed by authorities, however, that this was the missing baby. Scientific tests later determined that there was a 97 percent probability this was Paula's daughter.

Lee Plummer, the state's attorney, had a difficult decision. Every policeman on the case thought Paula did it, but there wasn't enough evidence to take it to trial. No smoking gun. A grand jury was convened at the courthouse in **Jerseyville** with Paula and Robert being subpoenaed for testimony. Both took the 5th Amendment. No charges were filed and public interest in the case soon faded away.

Sheriff's deputies John Onesky and Jerry Knight escorting Paula Sims (*Belleville News-Democrat*)

When the Simses later bought a two-story home at **1053 Washington in Alton**, a tall chain-link fence plus a wood privacy fence was erected to shield from prying eyes. The couple did most of their shopping in north St. Louis County. A second child was born in February of 1988 – a boy named Randy. Another baby girl named Heather was born about a year later.

When a second alleged abduction took place, Paula told the same story. A white man wearing dark clothes and a mask and carrying a pistol had abducted her daughter. This time Paula said she couldn't tell whether he was white or black. Paula told patrolman **Bob Eichen** that she took out a bag of trash with soiled diapers around 10:30 p.m. and was confronted by the abductor. Husband Robert was again at work. By their odd behavior and hesitations before giving out answers, the police immediately decided the couple was lying. Paula said the man struck her but when examined for injuries, police didn't find a single mark. Paula said it was dark and couldn't give many details about the intruder. But the cops didn't believe her because they noticed a huge night light above the back porch. They also thought it strange that the first thing Robert did after they arrived was to call his lawyer.

Sergeant **Rick McCain** was the detective assigned to the case. His father Clarence had been assistant chief in **Collinsville**. Five dogs were brought in but no scent was found of daughter Heather. When McCain arrived around midnight, the first thing he noticed was neither of the parents were visibly shaken or upset. The authorities were stunned that the Simses had the audacity to do the same thing a second time. When they tried to grill Paula, she feigned sickness and said she needed to go to the hospital. She complained of a headache and a sore neck from a karate chop but a cursory exam by a nurse revealed nothing wrong with her. This threw serious doubt on her claim to being knocked out by the intruder for over half an hour. Another odd statement. "Everything is OK - my little boy is all right," Paula said. About the only thing different this time was that Paula and her mother were now attending the First Baptist Church of **Rosewood Heights**.

Don and Norman Weber, 1984 (*Edwardsville Intelligencer*)

State's Attorney **William Haine** turned the case over to his top felony assistant, **Don Weber** of **Collinsville**. Don's father Norman had served as town mayor for four years in the 1960s. Like his father and grandfather before him, Don was a dyed-in-the-wool Republican.

(Note: Don Weber was in this author's social studies class when he taught at **Collinsville High** in the late 1960s. Don was smart, aggressive, competitive and conservative. He was also a crackerjack tennis player, number one singles on the Kahok team. We somehow struck up a friendship and I remember playing tennis against both Don and his father on several occasions. Despite my being a "hacker," I managed to give Don spirited competition, although he usually won.)

Don was elected State's Attorney by a narrow margin in 1980, defeating his former boss, **Nick Byron**. (Note: Nick's son Andy and this author's son (Steven Nunes) once played together on the same soccer team coached by Bill Nunes.) Weber was one of the few Republican officeholders in blue collar, heavily Democratic Madison County. Weber prosecuted some controversial cases and then narrowly lost the next election to **Dick Allen**, a Democrat. Bill Haine defeated Allen in the following election and soon hired Weber who was an experienced felony prosecutor.

When the police searched the house they noticed there were pictures of the boy on the walls but none of the girls. And Randy's room was extensively decorated while Heather's was plain. When the trash bags were checked, only the one on the bottom had a diaper stained with diarrhea. When Robert was questioned, he said he came home from work and found Paula unconscious. Weber had a hunch that Heather's body would never be found because it was the only mistake the couple made in the first case. But prosecutor **Larry Trent** disagreed and thought Paula would want the body to be found so she could give it a Christian burial and gain sympathy as a grieving mother by the media.

Heather's body was found May 3, five days after the reported abduction by **Charles Saunders**, a fisherman at the old Locks and Dam 26 in St. Charles County, just across the river from **Alton**. The infant had been stuffed in a plastic bag and placed in a trash barrel.

The body was in good condition which likely meant that one or both of the Simses put the baby there after she had been reported abducted. Shortly after the baby was found, the Simses placed their house on the market and sold it a week later. They went to live with Paula's parents. **Mary Case**, the St. Louis County Coroner, did the autopsy. Vertical cuts on the inside of the baby's upper lip convinced Case it was a homicide – she had been smothered. Due to several red splotches, it also looked as if the body had been frozen or refrigerated before disposal. It was Weber's theory that Paula had hidden the dead baby in her parent's freezer when they were out of town. After the cops searched her house, she got the baby and brought it back to her freezer. The police obtained a search warrant for the Simses house and took anything they thought might help them in the case. The police gave Robert Sims a good grilling, thinking he might crack and tell them how Paula had planned the murders. Police even suggested that their son Randy might be in danger. Randy was soon taken into protective custody by Children and Family Services as a precaution.

Police had several theories for motives. Paula did it due to postpartum depression or because of gender preference – she didn't like the girls. One other theory was that Paula was emotionally disturbed because she was in the car wreck that killed her brother.

On July 2, 1989, Paula was arrested and charged. **Don Groshong** was hired to be her attorney. He had gone sailing on **Lake Carlyle** and was upset that Weber had arrested Paula on a holiday weekend. Paula's father posted the $25,000 bond and secured her release. A grand jury handed down an indictment and Paula was arrested again, this time with no bail. From that point on television viewers would remember scenes of Paula in handcuffs wearing the orange jumpsuit issued by the county jail in **Edwardsville**. At this point a macabre recurring joke swept through the courthouse. Instead of SIDS – sudden infant death syndrome, it was SIMS – sudden infant murder syndrome. Weber's best grand jury witness was 46-year-old **Mary Case**. She was authoritative and intimidating – with a list of credentials and achievements a mile long. Because of sensational media coverage, a request for change of venue was asked of Judge **Andy Matoesian**, which was granted. Weber also announced his intention to seek the death penalty.

(Note: For the full story about this sensational case, be sure to read *Precious Victims* by Don Weber and Charles Bosworth of the *St. Louis Post-Dispatch*.)

Another damning piece of evidence against Paula was expert testimony that the bag the baby was found in had the same heat seal as bags found in her home when it was searched. Paula spent about five months in jail while her lawyer engaged in various pre-trial court battles to help her case. He wanted to muddy up the waters by suggesting that the Alton police had ignored other leads, but Matoesian ruled against him, saying there was no evidence to support such a notion. Weber offered Paula a last chance to plead guilty in exchange for a prison sentence, but she turned it down.

Richard Thomas portrayed Don Weber

The trial started Monday, January 8, 1990, in **Peoria**, about 160 miles northeast of Edwardsville. It was the same county courthouse where mass murderer **Richard Speck** had been tried. Matoesian denied a motion by defense to sequester the jury and limit lawyer comments to the media. Prosecution jury selection consultants told Weber he was too harsh and unfriendly with potential jurors. But Weber angrily replied that he had successfully picked death penalty juries before and was more interested in them deciding the case on his hard, cold facts rather than establishing some kind of rapport.

Groshong objected to Weber's continually pointing at Paula when her name came up, but the judge dismissed the objection. The biggest obstacle to picking the jury came when potential jurors learned that they would be dismissed if they had strong opinions about the case. Most citizens don't want their lives placed on hold for three or four weeks. It took three days to pick the jury and **Harold Ryan**, an engineer at Caterpillar, would end up being the foreman.

In his opening statements Weber called Paula's story about an intruder a big fairy tale and said the jury shouldn't believe that on two separate occasions some "roving Rumpelstiltskin" had stolen her baby girls. Paula did not help herself with the jury. Most of the time she sat rigid and looked straight ahead, with a stern look on her face. Her attorney countered by claiming Weber's theory was the real farce in this melodrama. Fourteen witnesses were called the first day, including Sheriff Yocom and several canine unit dog handlers. Hospital nurses were brought in to testify that the Simses were elated when Randy was born and less so when the two girls arrived. Twelve more witnesses were called and examined on Friday, the second day of the trial. Over the weekend Weber played doubles tennis to relax. His team lost! On Tuesday Weber introduced a tape into evidence. The tape showed a reenactment of Paula's version of events, showing them to be highly improbable. Groshong objected to the tape, but he had inadvertently opened the door by referring to it on cross-examination of previous witnesses. Weber's last witness that day was the man who had found Heather's body in the trash barrel. The old man's voice was full of emotion and it had dramatic impact on the jury.

County Coroner, Mary Case (photo by Ken Hoelker)

On Thursday the jury was shown the bassinette Heather had slept in. Then Allen Robillard, the expert, testified about the two trash bags being linked – the one the baby was found in and the others, still unused, at the Sims home.

Weber saved the best for last. Mary Case was called to testify that the baby had been suffocated. There were whispers and chatter when Paula Sims received permission to leave the courtroom so she wouldn't have to listen to the coroner's report. Case's testimony clinched the case for Weber. Groshong spent less than three minutes cross-examining her.

On Friday, defense began to present its case with testimony centered on the death of Loralei, the first child. Ten witnesses were called that day, mostly people who said Paula was a loving, caring mother. On Monday, Jan 22, 18 witnesses were called by defense. **Linda Condray**, Robert's sister, took the stand and she produced pictures taken of the Simses at the hospital with their babies – smiling and happy, and . . . apparently normal, not homicidal.

Donna Ewigman, Orville Blew's sister, was called to the stand. She said they were visiting her brother's house and during that evening she had gone to the freezer to get something to help prepare supper. Ewigman testified she didn't see anything in the freezer that remotely looked like a plastic bag with a baby in it. Defense was unaware Weber had finally guessed the reason why. He figured Paula had *already* gone to her parents' house and **taken the baby back to the freezer in her home.**

On Tuesday Paula's father, **Orville Blew**, was called to testify. Defense tried to scrounge up sympathy for Paula by having her father tell the jury about all the tragedy in her life. Husband Robert then testified. Trying to look like an average guy, Robert trimmed his shaggy beard and wore a shirt and slacks instead of a suit. Robert's slow, soft, and deliberate manner of speech was utterly boring and unconvincing. Fortunately for Weber, Robert testified that Paula had gone to her parents house by herself to get away from the press. In Weber's scenario, this finished the big three – means, motive and opportunity. When Weber cross examined, he brought up for the first time the accusation about Paula going over to the Blew's house to get the dead baby out of the freezer. It was dynamite. Another crusher was when Weber brought to light the fact that Robert and Paula, between the time Heather disappeared and her body was found – a supposed time of great sorrow and stress – told friends that they had the **greatest sex of their life.**

Paula Sims took the stand on Wednesday, January 25. She testified how she had saved her dolls and a favorite dress so one day her little girl, or girls, could have them. But Weber's female assistants told him that the Barbie doll shown to the jury was in poor condition and in a tattered shoebox – hardly the way one would save something for the future. When Weber crossed examined Paula, his hardest job was to ask tough, demanding questions, without badgering and causing her to break down and cry, gaining sympathy from the jury. Paula denied that she went over to the Blews and claimed she only went to her sister-in-law's house. Matoesian dismissed court on Friday because of a huge snowfall. Closing arguments would be given on Monday.

Weber's closing was dramatic and effective. He went over the holes in Paula's testimony point by point. Then he took out three photographs – the Blew's freezer, the Simses' refrigerator freezer, and the Simses' basement freezer. Next he placed three walnut shells on the pictures and played the old shell game, showing how Paula kept switching the dead baby's location. Weber's summation was nearly two hours long.

Robbie Benson portrayed Robert Sims

Defense slamed Weber's photo session with the jury and called it a giant shell game. Groshong also showed the jury pictures – the ones taken by Linda Condray showing a smiling happy family shortly after the birth of the daughters. He blamed the killings on a Charles Manson-type maniac who might have been apprehended if the police had not been so close-minded and jumped to the conclusion that Paula did it. His explanation for the trash bag match was simple. The kidnapper took one of the trash bags to place the baby in before he fled the scene.

When Weber had his chance at rebuttal, he referred to the "Barbie doll defense" shown to impress the jury. "Too bad Paula didn't take as good care of her baby as she did this doll. At least this doll got a shoe box and not a trash bag."

The case was now in the hands of the jury of eight men and four women. They deliberated that afternoon and then retired. The next morning the jury left their hotel room and went back to work. After asking the judge several questions about the law, they arrived at a verdict around 2:00 p.m. As the jurors took their seats, one of them winked at Weber. He knew he had a guilty verdict. Matoesian said the punishment phase would begin at 9 the next morning.

Several area newspapers took 50-cent call-in telephone polls to see if the public supported the death penalty for Paula. One reporter thought it was in poor taste and asked if the number was **1-800-FRY-PAULA**? Most callers thought Paula deserved to die! At this final stage, Weber pulled another dramatic stunt. He reminded the jury how **Mary Case** had testified that it probably took about two minutes for Paula to suffocate her baby. He had the jury pause and watch a clock on the wall to show them how excruciatingly long it took for the baby to die. The jury found Paula's crime was so heinous, it was eligible for the death penalty. Weber looked over at Paula for a reaction and finally saw in her face the look that he had sought but had never before seen. Paula was no longer defiant but totally crushed and defeated. He asked the jury for the death penalty, but without much enthusiasm. When the jury came back from deliberating the penalty, the juror who had winked at him before didn't even look his way. Matoesian followed the jury's recommendation and sentenced her to life imprisonment. Apparently the jurors wanted a life sentence, hoping some day this would help bring out the role of Robert in this sordid affair. Paula was taken back to the jail at Edwardsville and later transferred to the correctional facility in **Dwight**. A jail snitch at Edwardsville disclosed that Paula had broken down and sobbed, saying Robert was as much to blame as she was. Paula and Robert were divorced in 1991, and he regained custody of their son Randy.

The Sims case was made into a television movie, and Don Weber was given a bit part. Richard Thomas played Don Weber, Park Overall portrayed Paula Sims, and **Robbie Benson** was efective as the bearded Robert Sims.

This author recently talked to a **Glen Carbon** policeman who said Robert Sims was working around 1995 as the handyman for a trailor park, known as East 30, on Glen Crossing Road. The last he had heard, Robert had left the area and moved to **Chicago**.

EX-GOVERNORS OTTO KERNER AND DAN WALKER GO TO PRISON

Otto Kerner defeated **William G. Stratton**, the incumbent, in 1960. Paul Powell was elected Speaker of the House. Stratton was indicted four years later for violating tax laws, vis a vis political contributions. A costly trial ended in the former governor's acquittal. Kerner won a second term in 1964, narrowly defeating Republican challenger **Chuck Percy**, as he rode to victory on the coattails of LBJ's landslide victory over Barry Goldwater. Kerner's lieutenant governor, **Sam Shapiro**, became governor when Kerner accepted an appointment to the federal bench. In 1973 Kerner was convicted on several counts of mail fraud, conspiracy, income tax evasion, and making false statements on his tax returns. Most of his problems stemed from his purchase of racetrack stock from Mrs. **Marjorie Lindheimer Everett**, a prominent figure in Illinois racing circles. It was one of those "one hand washes the other, you scratch my back, and I'll scratch yours," sweetheart deals. After receiving stock from Everett, Kerner appointed her associates to racing boards and gave her tracks the prime racing dates she requested.. He also signed into law other favorable legislation she had requested. She, in turn, donated $45,000 to his campaign fund. Kerner profited by as much as $150,000 in one of the stock deals. He won parole due to poor health. Kerner had been indicted for conspiracy, bribery, mail fraud, tax evasion and perjury in connection with racetrack owners in Illinois. In 1975, Otto Kerner, former governor of Illinois, was released from a prison in Lexington, Kentucky, after serving seven months. Kerner died in 1976.

Paul Powell might have been indicted on similar charges, but his death precluded any criminal prosecution.

In 1972 Chicago lawyer **Dan Walker** accomplished the impossible. He bucked Richard Daley's political machine and won the governorship of Illinois. In doing so, he beat the favorite for the Democratic nomination, **Paul Simon of Troy**, who was already Lieutenant Governor of the state, but perceived by voters to be associated with the corrupt machine in Chicago. Following on the heels of the Powell scandal, Walker, an iconoclast independent, promised to put an end to "racetrack politics" in Illinois.

Polls showed Simon had been the overwhelming favorite to defeat incumbent governor, Richard Ogilvie. **Taylor Pensoneau**, Walker's biographer, says the contest was called the Bow Tie vs Red Bandanna Dan. Simon was given his nickname by **Bill Ryan**, a reporter with the ***Alton Telegraph***. Walker's running mate was **Carbondale Mayor Neal Eckert**, a member of the family that operated Eckert Farms in south **Belleville**.

Walker's populist candidacy, a grass roots four month walking trek of 1,197 miles, started in 1971 at **Brookport**. Walker also visited **Golconda, Elizabethtown, Shawneetown** and SIUE at **Edwardsville**. His campaign was managed by **Charles and Sue Kolker**, white liberals who lived in East St. Louis and helped **James Williams**, a political unknown, become the city's first black mayor. After Williams' upset win, Charles became the city's lawyer.

Walker would soon go from the Governor's Mansion, the pinnacle of success, to the nadir of a Minnesota prison. He was defeated for a second term and became involved in some business dealings that caused his ruin. After being noted for an austere lifestyle while governor, he divorced his wife of 30 years, married a younger woman, and began to live life in the fast lane. In the end, Walker pleaded guilty to perjury and fraudulent conduct and was sentenced to **seven years in prison** in 1987.

Dan Walker campaigning for governor

Governor Otto Kerner (*Belleville News-Democrat*)

THOMAS BRIMBERRY SCANDAL

Brimberry was found guilty on May 26 of 1983 at the **Alton** Federal Court building in connection with the theft of $16 million from Stix and Company brokerage, the now defunct firm he worked for in St. Louis.

Brimberry's wife also went to jail concerning this because she had bought jewelry with the embezzled money. All assets were to have been turned over to the government, but the wife held out on the jewelry and was caught when she tried to sell some of it. **Janice Brimberry** gleefully helped her husband spend the $16 million he stole. In a taped interview with the IRS, she admitted they made regular trips to Las Vegas penthouses, gambled $20,000 "at a whack," built a $2 million house in Granite City (in a middle class neighborhood) and went on $10,000 shopping trips. Thomas Brimberry also spent huge sums on $500-a-night prostitutes, arranging lavish orgies in luxury Las Vegas hotels. He would spend $10,000 a night for champagne and caviar and an equal sum on prostitutes.

Janice was tried in U.S. District Court in **East St. Louis** on charges of making false statements to the IRS. Janice denied she had any assets, and tried to evade payment of $19.5 million in taxes, interest and penalties the IRS claimed the Brimberrys owed on the stolen money. Her sentence was 33 months in a federal prison. Janice was caught on videotape trying to sell two diamonds for

$37,000; a few months earler, she had told the IRS she had no assets. After being confronted, she led them to a bag of jewelry worth $69,000 hidden behind a TV in her home.

Janice Brimberry (*News-Democrat*)

Brimberry said the stones came from her necklace that once caught the eye of actress **Ann Margret**, who was staying at the Desert Inn in Las Vegas at the same time as the Brimberrys. She asked her husband, Roger Smith, to get her one.

The smaller diamond had come from a necklace Brimberry said she was given by a wealthy Saudi arms dealer by the name of Khashoggi. She was probably referring to Adnan Khashoggi, a flamboyant businessman, accused of brokering the **Iran-Contra** arms deal. She told agents "**Playboy**" magazine had asked her to pose for pictures after the news broke of the Stix looting by her husband. She refused, saying, "I've had three children. I wouldn't take my clothes off in front of myself." **Len Schere**, former police chief in **Marine**, testified against Brimberry. He was the one who had set up the meeting between Brimberry and an accomplice in a **Collinsville** hotel in March of 1988 for the purpose of buying the purloined diamonds.

The 30 pieces of Brimberry jewelry, worth nearly $70,000, was auctioned off in May of 1992 at the **Collinsville Holiday Inn**. There were 141 registered bidders and the sale (including an $8,000 Rolex) took in $34,000. Leon Streif, who now owned the former Brimberry home, buying it at a bargain price, was one of the successful bidders.

Thomas Brimberry (senior vice-president) and his accomplices stole the money from Stix and Company brokerage, which was declared insolvent and closed in late 1981. He started out as a margin clerk at Stix in 1974. He began stealing on a small scale in 1975 by buying and selling securities in his wife's maiden name, without meeting the 50 percent margin requirement required by the SEC. It grew from there.

Through the use of dummy accounts and money laundering through banks and casinos, a fortune was stolen. **Jerry Maeras** and his wife Sally became jealous of the Brimberrys and blackmailed them for about $400,000. Brimberry anticipated that the house of cards was about to collapse. His **Belleville** lawyer, **Edward Maag**, secured a deal whereby Brimberry would be given leniency in return for his cooperation in bringing others to justice. The government reneged on the deal when it discovered Brimberry was the "hand that wiggled all the fingers."

Thomas Brimberry (*Belleville-News-Democrat*)

Judge **William L. Beatty** tried the case in **Alton**. One witness at the trial testified he saw Brimberry lose $250,000 at blackjack in 30 minutes. Through creative accounting, his confederates made it appear that Stix was worth $49 million in securities, but $36 million of it was bogus. Others convicted in the scam were **Duane Skinner** (12 years), **Leonard Bednar** (5 years) **Jerry Maeras** (4 years) **Arthur E. Miller Jr.** (5 years). Brimberry was given 20 years for his six year spending spree and served about eight. While in prison, he made 11 cents an hour.

Jerry Maeras was the son of **Stephen Maeras**, the first mayor of **Madison**, Illinois. Jerry's uncle, **John Maeras**, served as Madison County sheriff and treasurer before being convicted on federal racketeering charges in 1979 while he was sheriff. He was spared a prison sentence because of illness and died in 1983.

In an interview with a reporter, Brimberry said he feared retaliation by **James Massa**, whose conviction he had helped to bring about. Massa maintained his inncocence all along, and Brimberry feared Massa, whom he believed to have mob connections, would take revenge on him and his family. Massa was a lawyer from **Collinsville,** who received a 20-year sentence. In 1987 a federal judge rejected a request by Massa for a reduction of his sentence. The request was based on a claim that Massa suffered a mental illness that had put him under the influence of Brimberry, the swindle mastermind.

Brimberry donated huge sums to the Catholic Church – St. Margaret Mary on St. Clair in Granite City. When the local parish raffled off a couple of brand new automobiles, Brimberry was the one who bought the autos for the charity. The church gave him a special award called the Knights of Malta. He also paid for some big wrought iron gates for the church. His largesse was so outstanding, he was given special audience with the Pope in Vatican City.

After the scandal broke, Tri-City printing in Granite City began selling 100 share certificates in "Bum-bury and Stux Inc." for $1.25 each. The certificates were numbered 13.

Brimberry was bitter about his conviction. He said flatly: "What I done is common practice in the securities industry – at least the part about buying and selling without putting any money up. Everybody does it, I just got caught." Perhaps Brimberry is right. When **Joe Kennedy** became the first head of the Securities and Exchange Commission in 1934, critics said he was qualified to prosecute wrongdoers because he had engaged in many of the illegal acts he now prosecuted.

Two million dollar Brimberry house in northeast Granite City

Brimberry was the son of a **Carlinville**, Illinois, coal miner and was a high school dropout. He completed his sentence at the Dismas House of St. Louis, a work-release center. He was required to spend each night at the center from 9 p.m. until 6 a.m. He was allowed to spend his days working at his wife's interior decorating business, which she ran from her house at 2700 Washington. Janice's friend, **Sandra Harper** of **Granite City**, bought the house in her name for Brimberry. His wife's trial was held in December of 1989. Janice Brimberry was granted a divorce in 1987, but sources said the couple had later reconciled.

The man who bought Brimberry's house from the government, **Leon Streif**, owned the Vandalia Bus Lines, a **Caseyville** company. Incredibly, **Streif also went to jail**. He had a contract with Amtrak to transport passengers if a train broke down. He got greedy and was charging Amtrack money for passengers he didn't transport. He worked the scam with Kevin Shaughnessy of **Florissant**, an Amtrak supervisor. **Robert H. Rice and Ralph Derango of Belleville** were the lawyers who represented Streif and Brimberry. In March of 1988 Streif was given a 5-year sentence; 5 years probation was handed down to Shaughnessy. Streif was also charged with tax evasion. In addition, he was ordered to pay $100,000 restitution to the Amtrak Company.

Shaughnessy didn't receive any money, but he was given a new car, season tickets to Cardinal baseball games and a Carribbean cruise. It is thought that Streif's wife still lives in the mansion.

Strief, a native and resident of **Lebanon**, died in 1996. The sports teams at Lebanon High are called Greyhounds. In the late 1960s, Streif donated to the school's athletic department a Greyhound bus, painted in the school's purple color, for use in traveling to away games. (Information for this article supplied by **Gregg McGee** and the Granite City library.)

THE 1993 LICHFIELD MURDER

It was on a Saturday night, May 8, 1993, that **Todd Burdell** saw a fire burning at Picnic Area 5 near Lake Yaeger in Litchfield. He rushed to get the campground superintendent, **Paul Stevenson**, and the two of them discovered a headless and nude body of a woman whose torso had been charred by the flames. **Randy Quinn** with the Litchfield police was one of the officers called to the scene. **Paul Schuh** of the ISP Crime Scene Investigators gathered evidence. Some young people told police they had seen an orangish-red van with Missouri plates driving wildly away from the scene. Since the murder happened on prom night, rumors quickly spread that the body belonged to a student. But officials eventually identified their Jane Doe as Lynne Marchem-Thomas, a 35-year-old **St. Louis woman,** who had been reported missing.

Curtis Thomas, an African-American, was arrested for the murder in January of 1995. The woman he killed had been his wife for six years. His trial was held in October. Bond was set at half a million, but he was unable to come up with the minimum ten percent of $50,000.

In an effort to identify the light-skinned African body, the **coroner had to amputate a finger** to get a good fingerprint. When the print was run through the database, there was no match. Detectives **Mike Sheeley** and **Alva Busch** of the state police pursued the case with dogged determination. Busch saw a flyer about a missing St. Louis woman and phoned the mother. He asked her if her daughter was light skinned and had female problems. (The coroner found several benign tumors in an enlarged uterus.)

Through investigation and testimony, it was established that Curtis Thomas was the last person to see her alive. Martin Plummer, the victim's new boyfriend, was looked upon by police as a possible suspect. But Thomas remained the primary suspect because there had been a history of violence ever since they had been married. Lynne had once worked as a private watchman in the city and her fingerprints were on file at police headquarters on Clark Street. When the police informed Thomas that his wife had been murdered, his lack of emotional response enhanced his status as the perpetrator. It turned out the van Thomas used to transport the body from St. Louis to Litchfield was owned by his workplace, a social welfare agency. Most of the evidence against Thomas was circumstantial, but a grand jury indicted him nevertheless. Authorities grew suspicious of Thomas when they learned he cancelled his wife's costly health insurance shortly after she disappeared.

The first big media surprise came when the original murder charge in the Litchfield case was dismissed by the judge, based on the fact that the murder was probably committed in St. Louis, not Litchfield. Lack of jurisdiction. **Kathryn Dobrinic**, a popular lawyer from the state's attorney's office, prosecuted the case. Thomas, a black urbanite, had an all-white country jury. The trial was held at the courthouse in **Hillsboro**, the county seat of **Montgomery County**. Hillsboro was noted for its glass works that manufactured all the brown bottles for Hiram Walker whiskey.

Thomas had been in trouble with the law before. He was once arrested for robbery but fled to Canada. Eventually caught and extradited, he was given a suspended 5-year sentence. Thomas's downfall came when his new girlfriend, Deborah Claybrook, testified that Thomas told her he had killed his wife and hid her body in the basement for two days. Thomas told Claybrook he took the head and placed it in a bucket of concrete. They never found the head.

At the trial, Thomas's lawyer countered Claybrook's testimony by claiming she had been jilted by Thomas and her motive for testifying was therefore suspect.

Nor was any forensic evidence found in the van. Despite the lack of evidence, the strong concealment case against Thomas made the murder charge quite logical. At the trial, three locals - **John Reeves, Nathan Gerl**, and **Josh Hogsett** - testified separately that they had seen the van near the fire.

On the last day of the trial, Thomas took the stand in his own behalf, but the man with a degree in social work from Washington University was unconvincing. After four hours of deliberations, the jury found Thomas guilty on two counts of concealment of a homicide. He could not be charged with murder due to lack of jurisdiction. The murder had been committed in Missouri. Because of the brutal nature of the concealment, the judge gave him ten years, twice the normal amount. Thomas did six months in the Illinois State Penitentiary and then was tried in January of 1997 in St. Louis for the actual murder. After three hours of deliberations, a racially mixed jury returned a guilty verdict.

Thomas was given a life sentence at the Crossroads Corrrectional Facility in Cameron, Missouri. Thomas refused to tell authorities the location of the missing head, saying sarcastically they should ask the person who had committed the crime.

CHARLIE "BLACKIE" HARRIS by Jennifer Dumbris, 1985, courtesy of the *Wayne County Press*

Charlie Harris

On July 26, 1896, a son was born to John M. and Tadiesa Harris, on a farm near **Fairfield**, Wayne County, Illinois. The name they gave their newborn was **Charles Bryan Harris**.

Charlie, as everyone now calls him, is the twentieth child, **out of the 22 born to John and Tadiesa**. Charlie is in the midst of writing an autobiography, which he hopes will be out soon. "I am not writing for publicity," he said. "I just want to set the record straight. Each of your questions will be dealt with because they are a part of my life," he said, "but I'd rather not dwell on them at this time."

"I deny working with the Sheltons as depicted by the news media. What people heard has been magnified so out of proportion."

At the age of 20, Charlie went to Arizona to work as a common laborer. Later, as **James H. Linville** wrote in his article for the *New Harmony Times*, "He went to Detroit, Michigan, where he hired out as an apprentice carpenter."

So began events that eventually landed him in prison for ten years on charges of counterfeiting.

The money he received to buy legal whiskey, allegedly for the Sheltons to run back to the area, was not of legal tender. So may have started the area's long time bitter feud between Charlie Harris and the Shelton brothers.

In 1946 Charlie moved to the farm of **Pond Creek**, **east of Fairfield**. "I wanted to be a good neighbor of the community," he said. "I would love that again, but age and physical conditions are against that."

Charlie's age and physical condition may be against it, but his appearance now looks to be that of a well taken care of 90 year old.

His stature is straight and confident, with eyes that sparkle when he smiles. Not what I was looking for in a 90 year old man, who had spent about 28 years of his life in different prisons.

When asked why he left the business of carpentry, he said, "I left carpentry to go back to my love of the farm." Charlie was a master carpenter.

Charlie was considered a local "Godfather" of sorts to many Pond Creek residents and a friend to many, but would not comment on this.

Even so, a local man known as **"Alley Oop"** did comment. "In a sense, I guess you could say he was kind and generous," said Alley Oop. "I was there. I grew up by Charlie. He'd have given us the shirt off his back if we needed it."

Alley Oop added, "If us kids needed money, Charlie was there to give it to us. He'd help us anyway he could."

The question of what makes a good friend was asked because of Charlie's reference to it throughout our conversation.

Rare, but damaged photo of Carl, Earl and Bernie Shelton on trial (courtesy Bowen archives SIUE)

"A good friend is a person who comes to your rescue no matter what the circumstances," he said. "Not only in person, but with his pocketbook."

In 1947 Charlie was **accused of killing Carl Shelton**, the oldest and leader of the Shelton brothers. The coroner's jury recommended that Charlie should be held for investigation, but the grand jury refused to indict him, citing lack of evidence.

Many was the time Charlie saw the inside of the Fairfield jailhouse, but in 1965 he went for his longest look, after being accused of the murder of **Betty Newton** and **Jerry Merritt**.

"I was convicted of that," he said. "It was then that I learned a conviction by jury does not make one guilty. It only means you were proven so, regardless of by what means."

As to why a married woman and a single man were there at that house," he concluded, "your guess is as good as mine. I doubt that they were there to shingle the roof. Personally, I liked Jerry. He was a good farm hand."

On Sunday morning, August 16, 1964, a fire was reported to the Fairfield fire department. The fire was located at the Courtney Merritt farmhouse, east of Fairfield. By the time firemen arrived at the scene, the house was nearly reduced to ashes. Two bodies were found in the house, presumably the bodies of **Jerry Merritt** and **Betty Newton**. Both were from the Fairfield area. Betty was married to Charles Newton, who at the time was at the St. Louis Veterans hospital. The area citizens began pointing an accusing finger toward Charlie Harris. So began the fires that raged as vengeance became a part of life for the local residents.

The first to burn was Charlie's trailer, in which he resided, but could not be found. Second came the burning of his truck that was parked at a friend's house. Lastly came the burning of Bob Higgins' home near **Burnt Prairie**, where Charlie had found refuge.

Were these burnings coincidence or was a vigilante group behind them to get back at Charlie, became the question of the time.

On November 3, 1965, at the age of 69, Charlie was convicted of the two murders. The conviction came down after 21 days of testimony from various residents of the Fairfield area. These included his former housekeeper, a close neighbor, his nephew, a grand niece and her husband and a niece by marriage.

In the process of testimony, **James Lawder**, one of Charlie's lawyers, insisted that the state had not proven their case against Charlie.

Point one Lawder made was against a witness who had been convicted as a perjurer.

Point two Lawder made was that the state had never positively identified the bodies as those of Jerry Merritt and Betty Newton. The clothes were never identified nor was a dentist ever brought in to identify a set of dentures found on one of the victims.

Point three he made, a belt buckle, supposedly belonging to Jerry, was found not by a crime expert sifting through the rubble, but found by a relative of Jerry Merritt.

Also at Charlie's defense was **John Holland**, who concluded it was hard for him to believe that a man would go around telling everyone he was going to kill someone and then proceed to tell them how he would do it.

The state, on the other hand, brought out witnesses against Charlie who testified to the above. They also brought out the fact about different guns owned by the accused and that he had been arrested on an earlier charge with a loaded rifle. The State's Attorney also concluded that Charlie's alibi would not stand up because he had no one to collaborate it.

After closing statements from both sides, the jury was led out. One hour and thirteen minutes later the six man and six woman jury had reached a decision. "We the jury, find the defendant guilty," came the voice of the foreman of the jury. The verdict was the same for both murders and a charge of arson.

The minimum Charlie could spend in **Menard Prison** (at Chester) before parole from prison was 20 years. In 1981 Charlie was released from prison to reside with his niece.

"I have spent 28 years in prison," he said. "I believe my book will be convincing that I should have never been put to trial." I am proud of my conscience," he went on. "Not the accusations heaped upon me that ill affected and ruined my life. They have dogged me since 1927. My mind-conscience is clear."

I found Charlie to be very much a gentleman and have heard many refer to him as that way. "I don't want to be rude to anyone," he said. I also found, people who know Charlie either love him or think he is the worst man to come out of the area.

But Charlie had a quote for that: "Consider the source and look at what they have accomplished. There are lots of people in Wayne County. Some of the best and some of the lousiest."

Before Charlie left our company he told my children to get their book learning. All that they could. He said he missed the boat many times.

As **John Linville** said, "I do not know the extent of his guilt or innocence, but he has paid his debt to society."

I wish Charlie success with his book and hope to read it soon. (Note: This author checked with the Fairfield public library and no such Harris book exists. They, too, looked forward to the book, but he apparently never published it. Some think the family might have destroyed the manuscript after he died.) **(submitted by Bert and Helen Middeke of Breese)**

HANGED IN 1928, BIRGER STILL DRAWS A CROWD IN BENTON

Springfield Journal-Register Aug 27, 1984

They were buying a little bit of history Saturday – pieces of Franklin County Courthouse and memorabilia from the trial of Charlie Birger, the last man to be hanged for murder in Illinois. About 100 people sweltered in the midday sun at a county garage near **Benton**, waiting for a chance to bid on furnishings and materials removed from the courtroom where Birger was tried in July 1927.

The courtroom is being renovated and supervising engineer **Jack Licata** said that rather than throwing the furnishings away, the county decided to sell "pieces of the Birger trial." Among items sold were the original courtroom railing, 11 jurors' swivel chairs, 23 benches and eight sections of seating for court visitors.

"That's a big drawing card: Birger memorabilia," said **Judi Pearl of Herrin**, who was examining a juror's chair. "The name Charlie Birger still is a dramatic chord to the people who know about him.

Birger, a reputed Prohibition era gangster, was convicted of murder in the shooting death of **West City** mayor Joe Adams. He was hanged outside the county jail in Benton on April 19, 1928. Birger was the last execution by hanging in Illinois, and hundreds of people watched as he was sent to the gallows.

"I was too young to go," recalled **Virginia Jones of Benton**, who bought 38 pieces of courtroom railing.

"I was in grade school at the time," said Jones, 68. "But my grandfather had a card to get in to see the hanging and my father got on top of the Methodist church with his field glasses and watched it."

Along with the curious or those to whom the trial was part of personal history, there were others with specific reasons for bidding.

"I run an antique store," said **Kenny Parkinson of Zeigler**. "My buddy and I each bought two of these jury seats. I'm just going to put them up for exhibit."

In addition to the original courtroom furnishings, more recent additions were removed and sold, such as paneling that covered the jury box. "Did Charlie Birger lean on this?" auctioneer **Dale Bennett** asked, patting the paneling amid laughter. "No, it was added later," he said. "Well, do I hear a dollar? One dollar? A dollar there. Do I hear two? One dollar – once, twice, sold."

(from **Lois Zimmerman of Wood River**)

THE HARP(E) BROTHERS OF CAVE-IN-ROCK: AMERICA'S FIRST SERIAL KILLERS

There is a place in the part of southern Illinois known as Egypt, known as **Cave-In-Rock**. Located in Hardin County, about twenty miles below **Shawneetown** on the Ohio River, the natural limestone formation became a notorious den for riverboat highwaymen in the late 17th century.

The opening of the cave is in a limestone bluff overlooking the Ohio River (near the juncture of the Saline River), not many miles from where the river joins the Mississippi at Cairo. The first written record of its discovery by French explorers is dated 1744. The cave was formed in some remote geological age and was possibly the drainage for one of the many sinkholes in the area. Almost directly in front of the cave is the lower end of Cave-In-Rock Island, which becomes submerged during high water. A stone carving of a sitting man, unearthed in 1918, suggests that prehistoric natives may have used the cave for religious rituals. **Henry Schoolcraft**, the man who gave us the first good topographical description of the East St. Louis site, visited the cave in 1818.

The elliptical opening at the mouth of the cave is about 55 feet wide. The cavern extends to the rear about 160 feet at a uniform width of about 40 feet. The floor and ceiling are smooth and contain no stalagmites or stalactites. There is a gradual incline from the front of the cave to the back.

As flatboats made their way down the river, the pirates had a confederate hail a passing boat, yelling out to occupants that they were stranded. When the boat came ashore for rescue, the crew was attacked and the boat was robbed of its supplies and provisions. Sometimes the crew and boat would be released but often the people were killed and their bodies, weighted down with rocks, were thrown into the river.

One group of cutthroats turned the cave into a pleasant-looking inn and by this deception ensnared weary travelers. Another ingenious band of robbers used the treacherous serpentine river channel at that point to good advantage. They stationed a confederate about ten miles above the cave near Battery Rock. He would pose as an experienced pilot and offer to steer the boat safely past the sandbars for a sum of one dollar. He would then proceed to run the boat aground so it could be attacked by his partners. The fact that the West (as this part of the country was known) was so sparsely settled at this time made these outlaw attacks on the citizenry possible.

Probably the most brutal persons to occupy the cave were the **Harp(e) brothers**. They seemed to have had a lust for blood. They were a couple of backwoodsmen, native to North Carolina, their fathers immigrants from Scotland. According to historian Doris Lane, they passed for brothers, but were cousins. They fought against the Americans on the side of Banastre Tarlton, the British commander at the battle of King's Mountain in North Carolina during the Revolution. They spent much of the war as members of a Tory outlaw gang that pillaged the N.C. countryside.

The oldest, Micajah "Big" Harpe, a big-boned man with huge limbs, curly hair, and a weather-beaten face, claimed two women as his wives, Betsy and Susan. Susan Wood had been kidnapped from her family by Harpe during the forays. His brother/cousin, the red-haired Wiley "Little" Harpe was married to a woman named Sally Rice. They left a trail of murder, arson and thievery in the frontier areas of Tennessee and Kentucky. Big Harpe was known for splitting opponent's skulls open with a big tomahawk that he carried in his belt.

Cave-In-Rock State Park on Route #1 in southern Illinois (courtesy Mike and Joanna Coles of Anna)

The whole clan was once arrested for killing a man named Thomas Langford. While they were in the Danville, Kentucky, jail, all three of their only children were born. But the two brothers eventually escaped from the jail, leaving their wives and babies behind. The court and townsfolk took pity on the abandoned women and released them, thinking they would seek a fresh start in life. But instead they made their way to Cave-In-Rock where they rejoined their murderous husbands. The Harpes killed three men as soon as they crossed into Illinois. The trio were sitting around a campfire at Potts Station near the mouth of the Saline River. There were other outlaws at the cave while the Harpes were there, but most of the men left and went elsewhere, fearing that too many of them would bring the authorities down on them.

One day a flatboat came down the river and stopped about a mile north of the cave to make some repairs. Two passengers, a young man and his sweetheart, decided to go for a walk to the top of the bluff where they sat down to take in the view. The Harpe brothers rushed from the woods and pushed them off the cliff above the cave. The man and woman fell forty feet but miraculously landed on a sandy beach below, and neither was seriously hurt.

There was another time when a boat was captured and passengers were taken prisoner and robbed. They stripped one of their captives naked and tied him to a horse. The Harpes then led the horse to the top of the cliff and placed a blindfold on the animal. They frightened the horse with yells and gunshot, and the horse raced blindly over the cliff and fell 100 feet to the rocky shore below. Both the man and the horse were crushed. The Harpes often **gutted their victims** and placed rocks in their stomach cavities to weight them down when they tossed them in the Ohio River.

The Harpe family left Cave-In-Rock and continued their killing spree in Kentucky and Tennessee. The Harpes even killed several children who came upon them by chance, seemingly for the sport of it. There was one instance where Big Harpe grabbed his own young infant from the arms of his wife and bashed its brains out against a tree. In all, the Harpe cousins committed infanticide on their own flesh and blood on four occasions.

Finally, after the Harpes had been responsible for the brutal murders of more than twenty people, a vigilante group chased them. In a desperate shoot-out, Harpe was mortally wounded but managed to lead his pursuers on a short chase until they finally caught up with him. After giving him a chance to make his peace with God, which he ignored, they shot him again and killed him. Then one of the men named Steigal **cut off his head as a trophy**. The decapitated body was left to be devoured by animals.

Gallows Field, Jefferson County, Miss. where two cave outlaws were hanged

Little Harpe managed to escape and continued his criminal ways in other states. The women, seemingly glad to be free of their polecat husbands, and the recipients of much sympathy, were not charged.

The severed head of Big Harpe was placed in the fork of a tree near a public road in rural Kentucky as a grisly reminder to all monstrous outlaws. Today, it is known as **Harpe's Head Road**.

There was one wily fellow by the name of **Samuel Mason,** who came up with an imaginative scheme. He made Cave-In-Rock his headquarters around 1797 and stayed there for nearly a year. Both Mason and the cave already had nefarious reputations, so he schemed to avert suspicion. He changed his name to Wilson, and he converted the cave into an inn of hospitality. He and his family brought in tables and chairs, and he erected a large sign outside that read: "Wilson's Liquor Vault and House for Entertainment." Thus for a spell, the place was known as **Cave Inn Rock**. But Wilson had nothing but skullduggery, robbery and booty on his mind. After about a year, fearful that authorities would organize an expedition against him, he transferred his activities to **Wolf Island**, near the juncture of the Ohio and Mississippi rivers. After a while, Mason gave that up and continued to make a disreputable living by robbing travelers on the Natchez Trace.

Old map: Cave-In-Rock, Goshen Road and the Natchez Trace
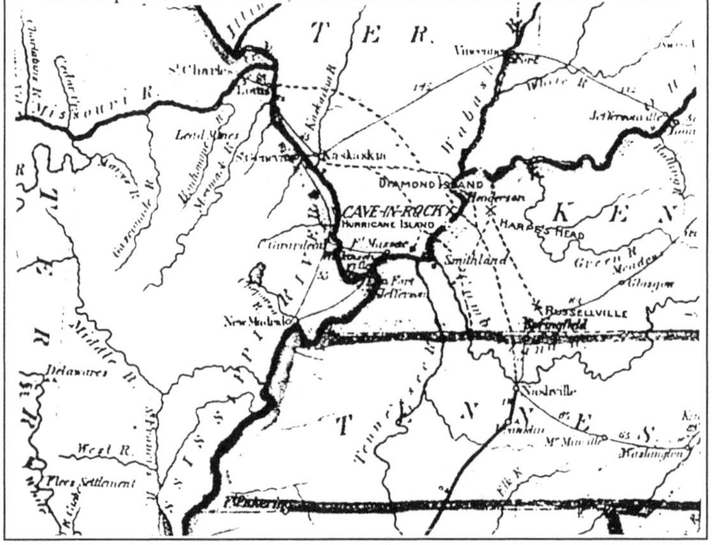

There was a large reward on his head, and that ultimately was the cause of his demise. One night in 1804, by a campfire, he was counting his loot when one of his associates buried a tomahawk in his brain. The head was then taken to the governor of Mississippi by two men, **James May** and **John Setton,** who tried to collect the reward. Someone recognized Setton and claimed that he was really "Little" Harpe. Setton denied that he was Little Harpe, but a mole on his neck and certain body scars, convinced authorities in Greenville, Mississippi, it was Little Harpe. Both men were tried and found guilty of various charges. They were taken to a field where a log was placed horizontally so that it rested in the forks of two different trees. Two nooses were tied to the pole. The men were led from the jail and made to climb ladders to reach their hangman's rope. Then the ladders were kicked out from under them. After their execution, their **heads were placed on poles** on opposite sides of the road along the **Natchez Trace,** as a warning to other outlaws.

The three wives survived. Maria Davidson, also called Betsey Roberts, remarried and raised a family in Illinois. The other two went back to Tennessee and eventually remarried.

ELIJAH LOVEJOY: AMERICA'S # 1 MARTYR FOR FREEDOM OF THE PRESS

In 1836 St. Louis enhanced its reputation for violence in the **Francis McIntosh** affair. McIntosh, a mulatto steward on a steamboat, was arrested after a skirmish down on the levee. He was charged with interfering with the duties of law enforcement officials. McIntosh broke free as they were taking him to jail. He killed **George Hammond** by cutting his throat and then seriously wounded the other officer, **William Mull**.

Historian James N. Primm says McIntosh was captured and sent to jail where an angry crowd of about 2,000 people gathered. They rushed the jail, overpowered the sheriff, and took the prisoner out to hang him. When someone in the crowd suggested that hanging was too good for him, they took him to a tree at 10th and Market and bound him to it. A fire was lit, and he was slowly **roasted alive**. One eyewitness to the event said the flames caused his bowels to fall out of his body. Someone in the crowd asked if he "felt any pain," and he replied with an anguished *yes*. He expired after about eighteen minutes of torture. None of the newspaper accounts of the incident ever identified any specific persons as the ringleaders, and no one was prosecuted for the crime.

The **Alton *Telegraph*** was highly critical of the lack of government initiative in stopping the mob. And **Elijah Lovejoy**, editor of a St. Louis religious weekly, incurred the wrath of locals by keeping the issue alive week after week. Judge **Luke Lawless** (actual name, no kidding) held a grand jury probe that, to no one's surprise, indicted no one.

Lovejoy now stepped up his attacks and lambasted Judge Lawless and the jury. He inferred that Judge Lawless's faulty logic was attributable to his Irish birth and Catholic upbringing. After Lovejoy's editorial attacks, his office was twice broken into and damaged. He opted to move to a safer location in Alton, Illinois, 20 miles north of St. Louis and located in a "free" state.

Owen Lovejoy, his brother, later became a leading abolitionist.

But the people of Alton were also outraged by Lovejoy's incendiary editorials. In 1837, on November 7, an angry mob attacked and killed **Elijah Lovejoy**, the newspaper editor who ironically hated slavery but thought abolitionism was inexpedient. He died in a riverfront warehouse defending his press.

Lovejoy had originally worked in **St. Louis, Missouri**, as editor of *The Observer*, a Presbyterian newspaper. As he grew more critical and outspoken about slavery, threats of violence from pro-slave sentiment in that town was so strong he moved to Alton in 1836.

Lovejoy further angered people when he said the Depression of 1837 might be God's way of punishing the people of Alton. His first press was destroyed and thrown into the river in 1836. A second press and a third were destroyed, so he ordered yet another, and it, too, was destroyed. He was shot and killed as a mob tried to set fire to the warehouse near the riverfront that housed his newest machine.

As the angry mob first began to gather, Alton's mayor, **John Krum**, tried unsuccessfully to try and stop the violence. There were about twenty other defenders inside the building with Lovejoy. A bell from Alton's First Presbyterian Church began to ring out a warning, hoping to enlist aid for the defenders. The crowd started throwing stones, and nearly every window in the place was broken by hurled paving stones. The defenders tossed earthenware pots down from the second story on the attackers. Ladders were then brought and burning torches were prepared to be tossed on the roof of the building. Lovejoy was shot five times while trying to push away one of the ladders.

Lovejoy Monument in Alton by Roscoe Misselhorn

No one was ever convicted of his murder. Prominent townspeople, who had been supporters of Lovejoy, moved away, and the economic and population boom which had marked previous decades, was reversed.

This incident reflected how divided the country was becoming. Martin Van Buren was president at the time, and he was against slavery. He was Andrew Jackson's hand-picked successor; yet Old Hickory was an ardent slave owner. Alton was a microcosm of the national battleground with the Whig *Telegraph* versus the Democratic Alton *Spectator*.

The *Alton Telegraph* currently has part of one of Lovejoy's presses in their newspaper office. In the 1960s, the SIU library at Edwardsville was named in Lovejoy's honor.

The tarnished reputation of St. Louis was further damaged when newspaper reports indicated that St. Louisans were part of the mob that killed Lovejoy. Lovejoy was an important martyr in both the anti-slavery movement and the struggle for freedom of the press.

Joseph Smith

JOSEPH AND HYRUM SMITH MURDERS: AMERICA'S #1 MARTYRS FOR RELIGIOUS FREEDOM

In the early 1820s a devout man named **Joseph Smith** prayed to God and asked him what church he should attend. Smith claims he was visited by an angel named Moroni, who led him to a cave near the family farm at Palmyra, New York. Smith was given a record of God's dealing with former inhabitants of the North American continent. He put on a pair of "magical" spectacles that enabled him to translate the strange writings on golden plates into English. This became the basis for the Book of Mormon and the beginning of a new religion.

Smith founded the Mormon Church in 1830 at Fayette, New York. The movement spread westward, first to Kirtland, Ohio, and then Independence, Missouri. In each instance they met pressure and opposition from their neighbors, causing them to move on. The Mormons left the Independence area in 1833 and moved to an unsettled area in Clay County, which they reorganized into Mormon County. For political, economic, and religious reasons, they once again came into conflict with their neighbors. In 1838 the Missouri governor signed an "Extermination Order," saying that the hated Mormons needed to be driven from the state. The Mormons fled the settlement and left for **Quincy**, Illinois, where they found sympathy from local citizens.

Brigham Young, from a daguerrotype

Joseph Smith (The Prophet), who had been imprisoned in Liberty, Missouri, escaped and joined his flock at Quincy. The Mormon leaders purchased land in nearby Commerce and renamed it **Nauvoo** – Hebrew for "beautiful place of rest." Previously, the land was occupied by Fox and Sac Indians. The new town was located on a unique bend in the Mississippi River across from Iowa. The old Ripley's *Believe It Or Not* claimed it had the **only Main Street in the world with a river at both ends**. About 5,000 believers flocked to the site in 1839. The Mormons were adept at missionary work, and converts migrated to the new city from Canada and Europe. By 1846 Nauvoo, with about 11,000 people, was the largest city in Illinois.

The Mormons established a militia and its "legion" was the largest military force in the state and **second in size only to the U.S. army**. Mormons were also feared for their political activism. They voted as a large bloc and had significant influence in the state. This gave them control over the balance of power between Whigs and Democrats. One prominent writer accused the Mormons of plotting to take over about 5 midwestern states so they could establish a religious oligarchy. This was seen by opponents as a threat to democracy. Other rumors spread like wildfire. One said that women from local communities were being kidnapped, forced to live in sin and serve in polygamous Mormon harems. Local communities, such as **Carthage** and **Warsaw**, feared Mormon manifest destiny and took to mob violence and lynchings against the "Saints." Smith was seen as a fugitive from justice back in Missouri, one who set himself above the law. Perhaps the straw that broke the camel's back was when Smith and his army destroyed an opposition printing press, *The Expositor*, which opposed polygamy. Joseph Smith and his brother Hyrum were arrested for treason and taken to the jail in Carthage.

In 1844 an angry mob stormed the Carthage Jail where Governor Thomas Ford had Joseph Smith and his brother (Hyrum) confined for their protection. Carthage was the county seat of Hancock County. **Both men were killed**. The assailants were probably part of a posse from Warsaw that made pre-arrangements with the jailers to load their guns without balls so none of the intruders would be killed. After a faux show of resistance, they allowed themselves to be subdued.

The Nauvoo Temple 1845

Persecution and mob violence by "gentiles" dropped off after the murders but soon became resurgent. Governor Thomas Ford sent a commission, headed by Stephen Douglas, to persuade the Mormons to leave Illinois. Under the leadership of Brigham Young, the Mormons left Nauvoo and settled in Salt Lake City, Utah. In 1848 their temple back in Nauvoo was burned to the ground by an arsonist. A group of French Icarians, led by Etienne (Steven) Cabet, bought the abandoned Mormon property and tried to establish a socialist/communal society. It fell into disorder and eventually failed.

In 1846 **Brigham Young**, the new leader, led the Mormons from Nauvoo in a westward trek that would end with the establishment of Salt Lake City, Utah.

When Brigam Young died, one enterprising political cartoonist drew a picture of "Bigamy Young's" wives in mourning. Six of them were depicted crowded together in a large bed, wiping their tears with handkerchiefs.

Nauvoo had been unique. It was a carefully planned city with farms located on the perimeter. Many of the houses were constructed of brick. Their Nauvoo House was the largest hotel in the entire area. The Temple, built of bluff limestone, was situated on the highest point in the city. The National Park Service has designated Nauvoo as a National Historic Site. A huge restoration effort was started in 1962, led by **James Kimball**, resulting in the town's becoming a huge tourist attraction.

THE HAYMARKET SQUARE RIOT

The Haymarket Riot started at the Cyrus McCormick Harvester Works in Chicago where a fight between strikers and police officers erupted. On the night of May 4, 1886, a crowd gathered in Haymarket Square, between Halstead and Des Plaines, to protest police violence. As the rally broke up, someone threw a bomb into a group of policemen who had been watching the heretofore peaceful demonstration. The explosion killed one policeman, and the others, panic-stricken, began to fire into the crowd. Four civilians and 6 more officers died in the melee. Many more were injured in what came to be known as the Haymarket Riot. The events in Chicago shocked the nation. Quickly, eight German immigrants were arrested for the crime. These men were anarchists who opposed any form of government on the grounds that it was oppressive. Their radical views, and the fact that many American labor union members were becoming attracted to this "foreign doctrine," made them guilty in the eyes of many Americans even before the trial started. Judge Joseph Gary convicted the anarchists on the basis that they had "incited" the bomb throwing and so were as guilty as those who actually threw the bombs. One of those convicted was August Spies, editor of the *Arbeiter-Zeitung*, a radical newspaper. He was one of the speakers at the rally and had advocated violence in retaliation for the labor troubles at the McCormick plant.

The murder of Joseph Smith

The men were convicted on largely circumstantial evidence, and four of them were hanged, and one committed suicide while in jail. Six years later Illinois Governor John Peter Altgeld created a storm of controversy by pardoning the remaining three. President John F. Kennedy wrote about this incident in his book, *Profiles in Courage*. By his actions, Altgeld committed political suicide. Newspapers all over the country criticized and condemned his action. Altgeld also incurred the wrath of voters by opposing President Grover Cleveland's efforts to end the Pullman Strike in Chicago (1894) by sending in the federal troops. Altgeld, a German liberal, was defeated in his campaign for reelection in 1896. He was never again elected to significant political office.

Poet Vachel Lindsay (1879-1931), of **Springfield**, Illinois, paid tribute to Altgeld's courageous action by writing a poem about him, *The Eagle That is Forgotten.*

Sleep softly. . . . eagle forgotten. . . . under the stone,
Time has its way with you there, and the clay has its own.
Sleep on, O brave-hearted, O wise man, that kindled the flame-
To live in mankind, far, far, more. . . . than to live in a name.
1913
(courtesy Poetry: A Magazine of Verse)

ATTENTION WORKINGMEN!

MASS MEETING

TONIGHT, AT 7:30 O'CLOCK

HAYMARKET, RANDOLPH ST.
BETWEEN DESPLAINES & HALSTEAD

Good speakers will be present to denounce the latest atrocious act of the police, the shooting of our fellow workmen yesterday afternoon.
Arm yourselves and appear in full force!
THE EXECUTIVE COMMITTEE

CHICAGO'S MURDER CASTLE

It was during the Gay Nineties that Chicago hosted the World's Columbian Exposition of 1893-94, commemorating (a year late) the discovery of America by Christopher Columbus. Reproductions of Columbus' three ships were anchored along the lakefront. The event drew an astounding 21 million people to the Windy City. At the same time people were sightseeing at Jackson Park along Chicago's lakefront, a dapper man named Herman W. Mudgett was using a house on the south side of Chicago to conceal bodies of his victims. This would ultimately give him the dubious title of the most prolific murderer in American history. Mudgett had attended a medical school in Michigan, but was expelled for stealing cadavers. He later changed his name to H.H. Holmes. He came to Chicago around 1886 and began working in a drugstore in the Englewood area. In 1887 the owner disappeared and Holmes produced a forged document to show that he had purchased the store from her before she "left for California." He expanded his store and enriched himself through a number of fraudulent insurance schemes. He used the money to build a "castle" at 63rd and Wallace Streets. The 3-story brick and stone structure, with 65 rooms, became known as the **Murder Castle**. Many of the rooms were converted into **torture chambers**. The house was full of sliding walls, trap doors, hidden rooms and secret passageways. The dank basement had a dissecting table, "stretching" table, lime pit and a crematory. It is believed that he might have killed over 100 people but no one knows the exact number. Workmen unearthed numerous bones, skulls and teeth, but many bodies were impossible to identify due to lack of forensic technology.

Mudgett often used the alias Harry Howard Holmes, and he was eventually hanged for murdering his business partner after they had a falling out, quarreling over an insurance fraud scheme. Mudgett confessed to authorities that he killed 27 people. Many of the victims were women who were lured to their deaths through newspaper ads that promised jobs or marriage. He then killed them and took their money and jewelry.

Frank P. Geyer, a Pinkerton detective, began to investigate Holmes and his various connections to insurance claims and mysterious disappearances. In July of 1895 Geyer searched the Holmes castle and found disturbing bits of hair and various human bones. City construction crews were called in to excavate the basement. On August 19 the castle was burned to the ground with arson being suspected. Meanwhile, Holmes was convicted in Philadelphia of committing a murder in that city. He subsequently confessed to killing 28 people, although dozens of people disappeared during the Colombian Exposition in 1893. He was hanged on May 7, 1896. "Don't bungle," he said to the hangman. Although the fall through the trap door and abrupt jerk broke his neck, his heart continued beating for nearly 15 minutes. His body was buried under two tons of concrete.

Bernie Shelton showing off a couple of old stomach bullet wounds

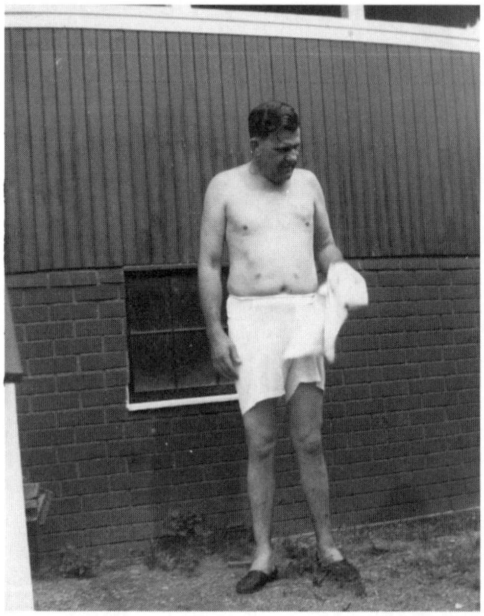

PERSONAL INTERVIEWS ABOUT GANGSTERS

Note: the series of Shelton gang pictures on subsequent pages are courtesy of Mary Webb Rousan of East St. Louis/Freeburg. Her father, Roy Webb, was a close friend and associate of the Sheltons in his early years.

From **Gene T. Dodd** of **Chatham, Illinois**: When I was about 16 years old I worked with my dad who was in the business of spraying trees for bugs. One of our jobs was **Frank Zito's** place at Oak Knolls in southwest Springfield. After we finished, Zito offered us a glass of wine. I told him I wasn't old enough to drink. He said "Nonsense, old enuf ta work, old enuf ta drink." I went to school at Cathedral High with **Sam Zito** who, I think, was his nephew.

Zito was caught up in a big raid on a Sicilian mafia meeting at **Joe Barbara's** 150 acre estate in Apalachin, New York, on November 14, 1957. Barbara was a Magaddino lieutenant. The meeting, attended by about 100 mobsters, was about **Vito Genovese** wanting to come back from Italy to be Don again after being gone 10 years and **Frank Costello** taking over. It turned out to be the mob's biggest blunder because only about 40 of them escaped the state police dragnet.

Roy Webb & Carl Shelton

The incident embarrassed Herbert Hoover because he had said for years there was no such thing as the Mafia. Hoover then invented the term **La Cosa Nostra** — Italian for "Our Thing" — to make it look as if he was informed on the subject. The debacle ruined Genovese's dream of once again being number one. Genovese would eventually be convicted of racketeering and tax evasion and sent to prison for 15 years. It was said that the brotherhood used intermarriage to promote solidarity and unity within the organization.

According to the July 1 report of the **McClellan Committee** in 1958, the most frequent areas of involvement for organized crime included: coin machines, organized labor, construction, trucking, real estate, produce, restaurants and bars, entertainment, horses and tracks, and linens and laundry. Zito's interests were listed as coin machines, olive oil and cheese. It was before the McClellan Committee that **Joseph Valachi** testified and talked about all the inner workings of the Mafia. And both Bobby and Jack Kennedy made names for themselves, grilling Teamster union officials.

From **Mary Newman** of the **Benld** public library: There is a farm on a piece of property on Route 4 south of **Carlinville**, Illinois. The original owner built an earthen incline so farm machinery could be stored on the second level. The place is known as the **Ortic Farm;** that is Citro spelled backwards. According to locals, one of Al Capone's organizations had the name Citro.

When later era Chicago gangsters came down to the area, they knew the man who owned the place and they parked their cars in the second story of the barn so no one would know they were there. Some say they came down from Chicago to meet with representatives of **Frank Zito,** the **Sheltons** or **Buster Wortman** at the **Colosseum**, the big dance hall where big bands played in **Benld**.

From **Beth Kaburick** of the **Carlinville** public library: The original owner of the **Colosseum** was the **Tarro family**. On February 14, 1976, the owner, **Joyce Tarro**, was killed in an ambush in her home by several youths who were later captured in **Decatur**. She had a fairly large sum of money on her – the daily receipts from the Colosseum. The story received national attention when it was written up in "True Detective" magazine. **Dave Hammond** is the current owner of the Colosseum.

There were rumors in the old days that the **Shelton's** threw their victims in the pile of slag near the mine shafts and their bodies would sink into the pile and disappear. Those slag piles always seemed to be smoldering.

(Note: Author John Martin claims the Sheltons were so notorious even Al Capone's gunmen feared them. He also maintains they were responsible for the deaths of at least 35 people.)

Roy Webb's wife Dolores and Bernie Shelton

From **Ed Speer** of **New Athens**: My great, great grandfather homesteaded some land near the town of **Junction**, which was not far from **Shawneetown**. At that time in Illinois history Shawneetown was *the place*.

I have a cousin named Dwane, who was the County Supervisor. He married a girl from **Junction**, and he had an Abe Lincoln room in his house that was full of memorabilia. He was a successful businessman, who ran a general store in town.

My father, John Speer, had a cousin who was married to **Charlie Birger**. This was his wife, mind you, not the "Shawneetown Dame" Birger ran around with. I always heard **Earl Shelton** finked on Charlie Birger and caused him to get hanged because he was also sweet on that Helen Holbrook gal from Shawneetown.

I was born and raised in **Sin City**, also known as **East St. Louis**. I was born in a house on 15th and St. Clair Avenue, not far from the entrance to the Stock Yards, a wild and bawdy area that was known by the term Whiskey Chute. My father was a bootlegger, selling the stuff to all the speakeasies and "soda parlors" in that town. He wasn't with the Sheltons or Egan Rats; he was a loner and did it by himself. But the authorities finally caught up with him, and he went to jail. I can remember going in the saloons with my dad when I was a kid and seeing people pay for stuff with what was called goldbacks. This was oversized currency, backed by gold, which were green on the front and golden in color on the back. The biggest bill in circulation nowadays is a Franklin – a hundred dollar bill. But back then guys were spending five hundred and thousand dollar bills.

Charlie Birger

When my dad got out of jail, we moved back to Junction, but the Depression was on, and so we went to Detroit to find a job. I got a job at the Dodge factory in Hamtramic, Michigan, near Detroit. Back in those days about the only job a black man could get was janitorial. One of my fellow workers was a black guy named **Junior Hatchett**. He wasn't a big guy. He was about 5-10 and weighed around 180 pounds. One day he told me he was going to quit his job and move back to **Colp** in southern Illinois because there was a better opportunity there. Now this sounded strange to me because I was from southern Illinois, and I knew things were pretty bad down there in 1938. I was making 40 cents an hour, which was considered good wages back then.

My father had moved back to Junction and was farming around 500 acres. One day I went back to visit, and I decided to look up Junior Hatchett. He said his mother was putting up the money to open a new tavern, and they were going to call it **Ma Hatchett's Place**. He took me over to see it, and the building was something else. It was a nice place, and it even had lights in the floor. I had never seen anything like it in a night spot. Of course the place later became famous for allegedly being a house of ill repute. I later thought about it and decided Junior had probably gone to Michigan because of some problems and only came back because the heat was off.

I drank a lot in my younger days, and I ran around with **Blackie Harris**. We both had a job out in the woods cutting timber for some lumber outfit. We were near **Fairfield**, Illinois, over by the Little Wabash River. My guess is that Blackie was only about 19 years old at the time. We went into town one weekend and had drinks at some tavern. I was trying to stay away from the liquor at the time, so I ordered a Coke. I owned a

Kalamazoo guitar back then, made by the Gibson Company. It cost me eight bucks, which was a lot of money. Blackie's girl friend started messing with it, and she scratched it all up. I read her the riot act, and I got mad at Blackie because he started defending her. Now Blackie's girl was a prostitute and some guy in town was pimping her. Blackie didn't seem to mind as long as she put out for him on the weekends. I actually saw him give her the money he had earned during the week cutting wood.

Shelton family and friends gathering: Bernie Shelton (front center) Little Earl Shelton (standing 2nd from right), Dolores Webb (standing rear left), Dalta Shelton (standing rear middle)

There was another time we went to a tavern one night and I found out Blackie was bad-mouthing me. I went over to him and called him on it. We started to get into a fight. I didn't want to wreck the saloon so I said, "Let's go out back and settle this."

We went outside but he ran away and sneaked into another tavern and then fled in his pickup truck to some farm. Some friends of mine told me where Blackie had probably gone, so I followed him. This time when I confronted him he was holding on to one of those double-bladed axes used for chopping trees. I was bigger than Blackie and managed to take it away from him before he could hurt me with it. I got him down on the ground and **nearly killed him**, but one of the other guys said I should let him up because he wasn't worth going to jail for. It wasn't long after that incident I resumed my drinking again and Charlie "Blackie" Harris started working for the **Shelton Gang**.

I was working as a welder for Shell Oil in the mid 1960s in the **Wood River/Roxana** area. My fitter was a cocky black guy and I knew he belonged to a gang in **East St. Louis** named the **Warlords**. One day he comes to work and he's all smiles. "What's up?" I said.

Gregg McGee interviews Leon Streif, owner of Brimberry mansion

"Me and some of the boys got an education last night."

"How so?"

"We were having this meeting and a bunch of white guys wearing suits came into the room with machine guns. They said our gang had been intruding on **Buster Wortman's** territory and that if we ever messed with any of his pinballs, jukeboxes or cigarette machines, we would end up dead. They said they knew who we were, where we lived, and even knew who our brothers, sisters and cousins were."

From **Pete Krietemeyer** of **Swansea**: Eliot Ness once led a raid on the **Mounds Club** when the **Sheltons** had it back around 1928-29. My brother Vick helped build **Fairmount** Jockey Club in 1924. The Mounds Club was built shortly thereafter. I got into the bottle collecting business when I was a kid and I worked the ditches along Route 40. I found seltzer bottles that still had the valve on them. I cleaned 'em up and if they weren't chipped I got 25 cents from **Mel Ostle** who owned the drug store on Seminary and Main in **Collinsville**. I seldom bothered with milk bottles or soda bottles; they were only worth a penny. I went down to the dump on South Clinton Street and you could find all kinds of old bottles.

From **Alan Cox** of St. Louis County, a former **East St. Louis policeman**: The Chicago syndicate won over several former Shelton men like **Buster Wortman** and **Blackie Armes** because **Murray "The Camel" Humphreys** had done little favors for them when they were in the penitentiary in the late 1930s. I took Buster Wortman to the police station one time because he was in an accident. He ran into another car at 20th and State and he didn't have his license with him. **George Dowling**, the police chief, said "Let him go or else the press will crucify him. You know that he has a license and you know he'll pay for damages." I let him go.

I was only two blocks away on my motorcycle when that grenade went off at **Helen McCoy's** Tavern on State Street back in the mid-sixties. I was the first cop on beat to arrive on the scene. It was a light-skinned black man named **"Swede" Jefferies** who was head of **Warlords** at the time. Buster found out that the Warlords were responsible for throwing the bomb so one day he and his men paid a surprise visit to one of their meetings. They lined them up against a wall and **threatened to mow 'em down** if they didn't stop messing with his machines and property. Jeffries had one of those Afro haircuts. "And by the way," Buster said, "get yourself a haircut." He got the haircut. **Abe Kaufman** and **Louis Shoulders** were two of the guys with machine guns.

Ray Walker (the man who bombed Birger's Shady Rest) and Roy Webb (wearing tie)

Some think that Wortman didn't get into prostitution but it isn't true. A guy named **Sonny Bridges** took care of the Wortman outfit's prostitutes. Sonny's mother was real nice and worked at a store on 40th and Waverly.

Tom Sanders was one of Busters toughest associates. He later became a lieutenant for **Giardano** - the top mafia guy in **St. Louis**.

I was at a cafeteria one time at 19th and State. I got something to eat and saw **Fred Davis**. I went over and sat down with him. He threw a barbecue for policemen every year. There was another guy with him who I didn't know. After a while there were about 10 guys who walked in the front door with a policeman that I knew. They went into a side room. Then the guy at our table excused himself, got up and went into the room with the other guys. "Who is he?" I asked Fred. "That's Tom Sanders - a mafia guy."

Ed Wondolowski was a nice guy and a real honest cop. He was Adam's brother. Adam worked for Buster, servicing his juke boxes. Ed married **Delores Wurth** of the Wurth Dairy family.

Ed was the jailer one time and **Tex Sanders** brought a guy into station. It was really strange because this guy still had his gun. "You gotta give me the gun before we go in," Tex said. **Frank Kerrigan** was the desk sergeant at the time. Then this tough guy starts to fight everyone and a wild mele breaks out. Ed accidentally got hit in the head with someone's nightstick. This guy started to put a bullet in the chamber of his gun and Kerrigan **shot him in the head and killed him**. He fell behind a railing and no one wanted to poke his head over to see if he was dead. So they threw a tear gas bomb to see if he was really dead. The place stunk badly for days because of the bomb.

Ray Walker and wife (left), Dolores Webb (button dress) and Bernie Shelton with his wife

A guy named **Joe Abernathy** was the head of Laborer's Local 100. Abernathy was accused of killing several people but got out of it. He killed a 7th guy and top officials were paid $3,000 not to prosecute. They took the money but told him enough was enough and that he had to leave the state.

There were some instances in East St. Louis where 16-year-old kids were paid three grand to take the rap for something someone else did. The young boys only got two or three years from the judge whereas someone else would have gotten a life sentence.

Traine Polk was a black policeman in the south end of town. He was a **one-legged cop with a wooden leg**. He called me one time and said to come and get some guy out of cell 4. I was a rookie at the time. I took him into the office and the guy in charge told him to take off his shirt and pants. When he did $400 dropped out of his pants pocket. I was then sent on an errand. Other officers were told to turn him loose and when they gave him his property back, he had only $20.00.

There was a famous incident where detective Robert "Tree" Sweeney dragged **Carl Shelton** (recovering from an operation) out of St. Mary's Hospital and threw him in jail on some trumped up charge. Shelton threatened to sue but nothing ever came from it.

From **George Joseph** of Edwardsville/Oklahoma: I was attending Bradley University in **Peoria**, Illinois, and was with my future wife, **Betty Hunt**, at **Hunt's Drive-in** on Farmington Road. Bernie's Parkway hangout was also on Farmington. We heard an ambulance siren and decided to follow it to St. Francis Hospital. When we got there we were told **Bernie Shelton** had just been shot and that he was dead.

Bernie's funeral/grave site after he was killed in Peoria

From **Tom Powers** of St. Louis: I was a mailman 41 years and remember all the gangsters. Prohibition was the worst thing that happened to our country. It took away millions in liquor taxes. I once sold newspapers near Union Station from 1927-35. I remember seeing Honus Wagner there, a future Hall of Famer for Pittsburgh.

I once won $3,000 shooting craps at the Red Rooster on **Collinsville Road** owned by Charlie and **Minnie Bartsch**. I had no fear of getting rolled because their people escorted you to the parking lot if you were a big winner. They wanted their customers to keep coming back. I went there nearly every night. I was there so often they didn't bother frisking me like they did most of their customers. **Morris Shenker** and Locke Tarleton shot craps at the Ringside next to Bush's Steak House by the Eads Bridge. **Leo Durocher's** first wife (Grace) gambled there also.

The Syndicate came in from Chicago and took over bookmaking. A Jewish gangster named **Sam Londe** bombed one of the cleaning establishments that refused to play ball. A colored guy ratted on him and they took him out and shot him six times in the head, but he miraculously recovered. He was taken to Homer Phillips hospital where somebody finally threw him out of the window to get rid of him.

J. Edgar Hoover was full of baloney when he said there was no Mafia. I grew up with a lot of guys who ended up in the Mafia.

Morris Shenker's favorite game was shooting craps. That's why he went to Vegas all the time. He opened up the Dunes Hotel in Vegas with money he made from representing the Teamsters.

Carl Shelton's Jeep on the farm near Fairfield

In 1924 the **Cuckoo gang** robbed the St. Louis Federal Reserve Bank and they got caught and were sent to prison. **Chippie Robinson** and **Ray Renard** were gangsters in the 20s. Sometimes gangsters paid someone else to assume their identity and do time for them. The gangsters paid them $1,000 a month to do time.

From **Ray Henzell** of Belleville: Blackie Armes once dressed like a woman and sat in a car out on the street in East St. Louis. Someone went inside a tavern and told **Carl Shelton** there was a woman outside who wanted to see him. But Carl was too smart to fall for the trap and didn't bother going outside.

Mule Pole Fritz was kidnapped one time and held for ransom. He was gone for three or four days but somehow got away. He drove a 1940 Olds. **Bros(z) Thomas** was a partner in the handbook operation at 414 Missouri Avenue across from the *Journal*. They called it National Cigar Store.

I worked at **John Kriwanek's** haberdashery at 221 Collinsville Avenue across from Zerwecks Jewelry. All the mobsters and politicians came there. **Adam Charles "Mulepole" Fritz** wore suspenders, smoked fat cigars and wore thick glasses. He had about a 45-inch waist. Fritz ran a real estate office near the Spivey Building. It was called the Fritz Building. He seldom drove because of his poor eyesight and had a black chauffeur. Mrs. Fritz later lived at Our Lady of the Snows retirement apartments. I married Ray Nash's daughter, **Audrey Nash**. My uncle was **Jack Cooper**, and he lived at our house at 1400 north 49th Street near Wilson School. My uncle had dealings with **Carl Shelton**, and he took me with him to Carl's house on Lake Drive near Grand Marais. My uncle was one of their mechanics and drivers. One day they were bringing in illegal booze and they got caught. They had agreed in advance that whoever got caught driving would do the time, and those in the passenger seat would be passed off as hitchhikers. My uncle was one of the "hikers." He had to appear in court at **Danville**, Illinois, but the charges against him were dropped.

A happily retired Big Earl Shelton with wife Earline and Kelly Rousan at 1515 Azalea Terrace in Jacksonville, Florida

From **Bob Tyler** of Fairview Heights: I played piano and performed at the Old English Inn, Broadway Hotel, Colonial Inn near the Stock Yards, and Bush's Steak House. At the Playdium I saw Musial, Schoendienst, Terry Moore. I played at Bush's Steak House on Friday night gigs. I was on the organ in a trio (sax and drums). We started at 11 and went to three in the morning. Hookers from St. Louis came over there after hours to relax and unwind.

Buster and Ted played cards at **Margie Helms' Surrey Club**, previously known as Club Chateau on 4000 Collinsville Road near Fairmont City. Buster always had a bodyguard with him. One Saturday night at the Surrey, after hours, we had finished and were at a table drinking coffee and unwinding. In came four stout guys, and they began to play cards. **Buster Wortman** was with them. They sat down and Margie played cards with the guys. The waitress set some drinks on the table behind Buster. He reached back to get the drinks, showing the biggest gun I had ever seen. It scared me to death. Margie's granddaughter grew up at the club. Her mother, June, was a waitress there.

People forget how things used to be. When entertainers such as Sarah Vaughn and Billy Eckstein played the nightclubs in East St. Louis, they often went to **Buster Wortman's Paddock Lounge** afterward. Buster firmly believed in segregation. Black people like Nat King Cole had to eat and drink in a back room in his establishment, separated from the white customers.

We came in one Saturday to work and our drummer, **Don Stroh**, found his set of King drums and Zylgian cymbals were full of dings and bullet holes. The hoods apparently had a big

Big Earl Shelton in Florida home with Kristin Rousan Jones

party there the night before and decided to use them for target practice.

I remember seeing **George Shearing**, a blind man with a quintet, play the piano at the Terrace Lounge.

At Bush's Steak House musicians from St. Louis came over after hours and we had jam sessions. We also performed at the **Collinsville Ballroom and Lounge** at Collinsville Park.

My first date with my future wife, **Dodie Karr**, was a double date with **Robert L. Belt** and his girlfriend. He was a 1952 East Side grad. He has recently published a novel about old time airplanes called *Flyboy*. Later in my career I met Glen Campbell, Roger Miller, Sammy Davis Jr. and Boxcar Willie.

Earl Shelton & wife Earline in Florida home with Mary Webb Rousan

I played the Surrey for seven years. One time I heard a scuffle to my left. I saw an orange flash as a guy fired at another man with a Derringer from his suit coat. The bullet hit the guy in the breastbone and riccoched off and went into the wall near the bar. The wounded guy was dripping blood all over. He went out to the parking lot and sat down on the tailgate of his Nash Rambler Wagon and waited for the ambulance. The shooter fled out another door. The police came in and made everyone leave except those eating their dinners. Then they closed it all down, but we reopened the next night. I never saw a word about it in the paper. I suspect Margie might have had a friend or two at the *Journal,* and it was kept hush-hush.

From **Bruce and Mary Morgenstern** of **Pinckneyville:** Mary's grandparents, **Bill and Sophie Saunders,** had their car break down one day near Benton. They were amazed when a complete stranger stopped and gave them a lift to town. They immediately recognized the man to be **Charlie Birger,** and they found him to be very friendly. When they later read about his date with the hangman in 1928, they attended the event in Benton.

According to **Janet Flynn** of **Columbia**, who is very much into geneology, Buster Wortman attended grade school in north St. Louis County and later moved to East St. Louis. At a book signing she told this author that Frank "Buster" Wortman was born at Burksville Station, just south of **Waterloo in Monroe County**.

From **Dean Little** of **Granite City**: I was in the oil business and owned a 15-room house on Route 162 on the outskirts of Granite City. I planned to sell my house and buy Buster Wortman's moat home after Buster died in 1968. Buster's second wife Sylvia owned a strip of land next to the house that Buster had thought about making into an airstrip. But Sylvia, who was divorced from Buster, wouldn't sell that part. Susan and Billy said they would hold the house off the market for a year but if my house didn't sell by then, they would list it with a Realtor.

I was given a tour of the house and met Susan and Billy. Billy liked to race cars, and Susan became a beautician. They told me that at one time Buster was going to install an in-ground swimming pool and a landing strip for a private plane, but never got around to it. It was a beautiful place and the foyer had Italian marble on the floor. The rumor going around was that Buster had many union connections and he was

Joie and Laura Beuckman in spacious living room of Wortman's home

charged very little for construction costs. My guess is that Buster's fortress had about a 16-acre moat/lake surrounding it. I remember it having many bedrooms and baths and a commercial grade bar on the lower level. The furnace system was oil heat. There was a big safe next to the bar. The master bedroom was on the lower level. There was also a 3-car garage on the premises.

Unfortunately, my house never sold, so Buster's home was listed with **Glenna-Delker Realty.** They sold it to Fred "Bo" **Beuckman**, the local Ford dealer ("Everybody Knows Bo!")

The meter for the utility company to read was located out on the road so they wouldn't have to come on the property to read the meter. I talked to some state conservation officials who told me the moat lake was the best stocked private lake in Illinois. **Joe Ashman** of Collinsville was Buster's pharmacist, and he frequently let Joe come to the lake and fish.

I knew a guy named "Red" Moore who worked for Buster. The last time I saw him was at the Ground Round in St. Louis. He and two couples were at the bar having a drink, and they talked to Red while he was servicing one of the jukeboxes. When they tried to pay the bartender he said there was no charge, courtesy of Mr. Moore. The Ground Round had to stop letting patrons throw peanut shells on the floor because the inspectors declared them to be a safety hazard.

Wall safe in the Wortman home (*Post-Dispatch*)

I was half-owner of the **Surrey Club** on Collinsville Road near Fairmont City. Margie Helms owned the other half. She was the widow of **James Helms**. They had a big Christmas party at the Surrey for Wortman's associates not long after Buster passed away. In 1966 she owned **Margie's Cocktail Lounge** that was located near 9th and St. Clair. She also owned a cab company.

My oil wells were mostly in **Lawrenceville, Olney, Salem** and **Sandoval**. I remember using the very drill bits invented by **Howard Hughes** that were the source of his fortune. A long time ago there was a big hullabaloo about several oil wells on what is now **Keller's Farm** at Peters Station near Routes 162 and 157. The owners went all over the country selling potential investors on the idea, but the well turned out to be a bust.

I am friends with **Guy Michaels,** who owns the restaurant in **Highland**, and the recently deceased **Walter "Shang" Greathouse** who was supervisor for the Metro-East Sanitation District in **Granite City**. The district was a great source of political patronage. Walter probably knew a lot of interesting stories, but I figured I was better off not pumping him about it. (Note: This author once had a conversation with Walter. Walter said he could tell me things that would curl my toes but opted to remain silent.)

I saw Buster only one time when some friends and I went to the Paddock after a Cardinal baseball game. Buster's bar girls kept a close eye on him, and when his drink started getting low they went over and refilled it. Buster gave them good tips as a reward for being on the ball.

From **Erwin Wein** of **Glen Carbon**: I attended **Vern Hilmer's** funeral in December of 2001. There were two brothers. One was named Bill and the other Vernie. Vernie was an operating engineer out of Granite City. His dad used mules and horses to help build the dog track that operated back in the 1920s on **Choteau Island**. The body of water that separated the island from the Illinois shore was called the Choteau Slough, even thought it was really just part of the Mississippi. There was another greyhound track on Collinsville Road (Route 40) and another near Monsanto/Sauget by Route 3.

A guy named **Harry Murdoch** owned the Mounds Club on Collinsville Road. A guy I went to school with named **Ed Epping** worked at the club as a card dealer. The Mounds Club was later the site of the original Grandpa's Store before it moved closer to Route 157. I was surprised as heck when I found out Epping later went to work in Springfield as **Orville Hodge's** office manager. Orville was a native of Granite City. Hodge, of course, was the State Auditor. He received financial backing from Buster Wortman on the promise that he would use his influence to get gambling legalized in Illinois. Hodge and Epping eventually went to prison after getting caught in a financial scandal. Orville was a personal friend of mine. He married into a family that had money because of their lumber business. It was his wife's money that helped get him started in politics. Hodge was fairly well known in the area because he had worked in real estate.

There was a minister named **Roy Baugh** from East St. Louis, but in the 50s he was pastor of a Methodist church in **Glen Carbon**. Every time Buster would try to open a new gambling joint Baugh notified the state police and they would shut it down.

George McDaniels of **Granite City**, who is still alive, owned a tavern and a filling station near the entrance to the dog track on Choteau Island. I lived on my father's farm that was located near the dog track. We had about 80 acres and raised potatoes, corn, beans and horseradish. We grew clover and rye and then plowed it under to add nitrogen to the soil. No chemicals were used. Today they call that organic farming.

Harry Murdoch also owned a joint near the track. He also had a landing strip on some property he owned out by **Nameoki**. That's where they flew in the illegal booze from Kentucky or Canada during Prohibition.

There was a guy in **Alton** who was in the meat packing business. I think it was called Luer Packing. Some gangsters kidnapped him and held him for ransom. They stuck him in a pit located near a road that went between **Madison** and East St. Louis. I don't remember exactly what happened but somehow he came out of it alive.

Bill Nichols of East St. Louis once owned about half of Horseshoe Lake, and he also owned Lakeside Airport on Route 111. Besides that he also operated a sand pit for construction and sold fish at a market. Because he lived near the lake they were always spraying chemicals to kill mosquitoes. I think repeated exposure to the chemicals sent the whole family to early graves. Their daughter got cancer and they amputated her leg in a futile effort to save her life. She died when she was about 12.

My cousin lived out by Bend Road near the place where they killed some federal agents. These agents were supposed to enforce Prohibition laws but they got into the shakedown business instead. They must have gone too far because the moonshiners killed them and buried the bodies not far from where their alky cooking stuff was located.

I remember another guy named **Adcock** who lived in Washington Park. I once bought a recipe from him for making coalicide. It was supposed to keep hogs from getting sick. As it turned out the coalicide really worked well. Another guy on the Lacomp farm below Peters Station tried to raise hogs. He was called **"Gumbo" Lecomp** because of the bottom land. Several brothers in the family ended up running afoul of the law. Gumbo himself ended up getting killed in East St. Louis. Everyone said the parents were really nice people.

I was a good friend of **Clint Walker**, the guy who ended up starring on the "Cheyenne" TV show. We ran a health food club back then and Clint was a member. His brother-in-law is **Paul Westbrook,** and he runs a health food store in Belleville. Paul's wife died recently. She was Clint Walker's twin sister. She had a great artistic talent. Clint drifted out west and ended up being a bouncer in Las Vegas when a talent scout for Warner Brothers thought he would make a good western star.

My friend **Chas Klug** said there was a 14-bedroom mansion between Routes 3 and 111, built in 1897 by Ben Biszant, known as the **Hartford Castle**. It was a speakeasy during Prohibition. One of the strangest things about my life is that I have six friends who have lost an eye. **Larry Kacer** of Glen Carbon lost his eye in a hunting accident. **John Payne** lost his in a woodworking accident.

From **Wilbert Cordus of Wood River:** In 1933 there was an incident that happened at the dog track. There was a guy who won a considerable sum of money at the track near old Route 66 west of **Mitchell**. He left and headed for home in the Hartford/Wood River area. A bunch of gangsters followed him and opened up with their machine guns as they fled down the highway in pursuit. He reached Main Street in Wood River by the Standard Oil office. The guy in the touring car didn't make one of the turns, and he wiped out the gas pumps at some filling station on Ferguson Avenue. After the incident, the man's car was displayed with the bullet holes at **Carter Brothers Ford** in Wood River. I remember seeing the car. My father-in-law, **Dave Logan**, was a guard at Menard Prison in **Chester**. He remembers attending the Birger hanging.

Dinty Colbeck, an old leader of the **Kerry Patch Gang**, got out in 1942 after 16 years in the slammer. Instead of going straight, as advised by wife and friends, he tried to regain some of the power he thought rightfully belonged to him. The word was that he was trying to get a piece of the action at the **Hyde Park Casino** located in **Venice** at the foot of the **McKinley Bridge**. In 1943, he was shot to death near 9th and Destrehan in **St. Louis** shortly after his car crossed the McKinley Bridge. Dinty was a Polish plumber who was said to be so clumsy he was always "dinging" the pipes, hence the nickname Dinty.

From **Joe Southard of Smithton/East St. Louis**: I had the Olympic Health Club at 3302 Caseyville Ave. in East St. Louis. Senator **Dick Durbin** and **Jerry Costello** worked out there when they were at Assumption High. I normally wasn't open on Sundays, but several of **Buster Wortman's** guys made it worth my while to open up so they could come out to my sauna and sweat the booze out of their system from Saturday night carousing. One time I was at one of Wortman's places by the name of **Ramon's** on 9th Street, near State. **Phil Moody**, the manager, later became head of the Bartender's Union. There was a nightclub in the back with music and dancing going on. The place had only one bathroom and several of us guys tried to use it about the same time. **Merle Taylor** was the floor manager, and he tried to run us off because he said there were too many of us in the hall next to the bathroom and we were creating a fire hazard. I told him I had to go really bad, and he merely opened his coat and showed me a gun. I was plastered and got mad and decided to go outside and get a gun from my car. **George Shedane**, my buddy, talked me out of taking the gun back inside. However, when I went inside, Taylor was sure I had a gun, so he pulled his and stuck it in my belly. I shoved his hand down, and the gun fired. The bullet went through my right thigh. Fortunately it didn't hit any bone or do any serious damage. I retaliated by socking him in the jaw, and I think I fractured it. I went to St. Mary's Hospital for treatment and was out in a few hours. I think he was in the hospital about a day or two.

Joe Southard, East St. Louis bodybuilder

I won the "Mr. St. Louis" contest in 1957. Then I was "Mr. Ohio Valley." I was president of World Yoga Assn. in the late 1960s, only the **2nd American honored** in its 70-year history. I had the **world record** with dumbells, lifting about 80 pounds in each hand in a routine called the crucifix, holding them at arms length with palms up. I also held the cable pulling championship of England when I was in the military in the early

1960s. These were actually steel springs that you stretched horizontally and worked like chest expanders in later years. I currently run a health food/supplement business.

Actor George Raft

How was **Virginia Marmaduke** a thorn in the side of henchman **Blackie Armes**?

Virginia Marmaduke
(*Pinckneyville Democrat*)

Virginia was born in Carbondale, the daughter of an Illinois Central Railroad executive. Her husband's family ran the ***Herrin Daily Journal***. She worked for the newspaper and soon became a crack reporter, writing exposés about the criminal element in the 1930s. It was widely rumored that she was high on Blackie's enemies list and needed to watch her step. She left southern Illinois and headed for Chicago when she divorced her husband. She began working for the *Chicago Sun* in 1943 and was tabbed "The Dutchess" due to her regal beauty and manner. She covered Chi Town's social scene and wrote numerous stories about the town's rich, famous and infamous. She also wrote some noteworthy crime exposés in Chicago. She once attacked a gangster with a spike-heeled shoe. She liked to say her beat was covering "blood, guts and sex – not necessarily in that order." She became the talk of the town when actor **George Raft** began to squire her around town. There was a touch of irony here because Raft, with his dark slicked-back hair, frequently played mobsters on the silver screen. When Raft's film career began to fade, he was hired by a number of mob-owned casinos to greet people as they came in the door.

In 1965 Marmaduke went to the New York World's Fair (visited by this author and his wife) as hostess for Illinois' Land of Lincoln pavilion – the highlight of her career, she said.

In later years she did an SIUC television show with **Irv Copey**. She was a trustee of SIU at Carbondale. She died in a **Pinckneyville** hospital in 2001.

FIVE GUILTY IN WHISKEY CASE

East St. Louis Journal, March, 1972

Five men were found guilty of charges in connection with whiskey stolen from an interstate shipment and a sixth was acquitted Monday in U.S. District Court in East St. Louis. The five were found guilty on two counts, aiding in the possession of stolen whiskey and aiding in receiving and concealing it.

The five are **Kenneth Fults**, president of East St. Louis Teamsters Local 729, **Joseph Alonzo**, Canteen Township highway commissioner; brothers **Daniel and John Zitta** of **Highland**, and **William Phillips**, an East St. Louis painter.

Edward F. Brennan, East St. Louis attorney, was acquitted on one count of aiding in the concealment of the whiskey. Earlier in the trial, Judge **William Jurgens** had acquitted him of another count.

Albert Zitta, brother of the two other Zittas, was also on trial on two counts. When he became ill last week his case was separated from the others and a mistrial was declared. A new trial will be held later.

The case was developed through undercover work following the theft last Dec. 5 of about 840 cases of whiskey from an interstate shipment in St. Louis. Government undercover agents posed as contacts for purchasers of the liquor. Last December 10 quantities of the stolen whiskey were seized at the Canteen Township garage, 6881 Forest Blvd., and at the Fults' home. A fire started before agents moved in, and they were only able to identify 169 of them as stolen from the shipment.

Frank "Buster" Wortman

The government's case against Brennan was based on his being with Fults at Fults' house a short time before the fire and before the liquor was seized. **Rex Carr**, Brennan's attorney, contended Brennan had gone to the Fults home as an attorney to advise a client. (contributed by **Joe Southard**)

From **Clyde Allen:** I worked with Buster Wortman's brother, **John Wortman**. He was an ironworker, and together they worked on repairing the ore bridge at Granite City Steel. Like his brother Ted, John was fond of going to the racetrack at Fairmount and betting on the ponies. John was very respected by his fellow workers.

What was the **Bookie Gang**?

This was a group of ex-cons and hillbillies (people from southern Illinois) who in 1945 decided to start robbing Syndicate bookies. The Chicago police Robbery Detail focused their attention on the West Side, particularly the part of town at the crossroads of West Madison and Paulina Streets – just across the Chicago River. It was a seedy region of pool halls, cigar stores, dance halls, taverns and nightclubs with girlie shows.

The gang's biggest coup was the heist of 19 big bettors at the Syndicate's commission house for big bettors near The Loop. They made the men take off their pants and took them along because they knew all big gamblers kept money in hidden pockets. The gang consisted of ex-cons who became acquainted in prison back around 1938. It included Virgil Summers, Christ Perres, Jim Kelly, Richard Todd, "Red" Smith and Renoto Lolli. They also had connections with Bugs Moran, who had moved his operation downstate. Their big mistake was when they killed a policeman. The manhunt was on. The only gang member who wasn't killed or arrested was Grover Dullard. **George "Bugs" Moran** was arrested for armed robbery in Dayton, Ohio, and sent to prison.

How close did Hollywood ever come to making **a movie about the Shelton Gang**? Frank Sinatra and his "Rat Pack" (**Dean Martin, Peter Lawford, Joey Bishop, Sammy Davis Jr**.) made several "heist" movies in the 1960s, including *Robin and the Seven Hoods* and *Ocean's Eleven*. For a while they toyed with the notion of doing a movie based on the lives of the Sheltons. My guess is they abandoned the idea because the other movies took place in "cool" places like Chicago and Las Vegas. They probably figured towns such as **Marion, Herrin** and **Benton** weren't chic enough to be the setting for a movie that would attract a large audience.

Sinatra, of course, came very close to getting in big trouble because of his friendship with Sam "Mooney" Giancana and other members of the mob. Sinatra and the Chicago mob put a lot of money into John Kennedy's 1960 election. He even built an addition to his Palm Springs estate, hoping it would become a vacation retreat for the Kennedys. In 1959, when JFK was at the Cal-Neva Lodge at Lake Tahoe, Giancana had Sinatra set him up with broads like **Angie Dickinson**, **Marilyn Monroe**, and Judith Campbell (at the Sands) to feed the president's huge libido. Giancana secretly made tapes of Kennedy's trysts and hoped to keep knowledge of his infidelities as an ace in the hole that might come in handy at a later date. The biggest thorn in Giancana's side at this time was sheriff **Richard Ogilvie** of Cook County, a mob buster who would later become governor. Sinatra's song, "High Hopes," from the movie, *A Hole in the Head*, was used as a theme song for Kennedy's election run. But Bobby Kennedy ruined all that when he became attorney general and went on a crusade against organized crime. Bobby gave his brother a thick report that showed Sinatra's connections to the mob. After that, he was declared persona non grata at the White House. Sinatra turned into a Kennedy hater and kicked Peter Lawford out of the Rat Pack because he was married to Patricia Kennedy. Sinatra then became cozy with Richard Nixon, and it was Vice-president Spiro Agnew who spent time at Sinatra's estate instead of JFK.

They did make a film about the **Looney Gang**, an outfit that had a grip on the Quad City area of northwestern Illinois. The Quad Cities are on either side of the Mississippi River and include **Rock Island**, **Moline, Davenport** and **Bettendorf, Iowa**. The gang operated from about the turn of the century into the 1920s. John Looney was arrested and spent time in prison. He died October 6, 1922 and remnants of his gang carried on through the Prohibition era. At the height of their power, the Looney gang even controlled a newspaper. **Max Collins** wrote the graphic book about the Looney gang and Sam Mendes" ***Road To Perdition*** is loosely based on this work. The **Chicago** movie features **Tom Hanks** and **Paul Newman**, although the gangster's name is changed to Rooney.

Giancana invested a quarter of a million in refurbishing **Villa Venice**, a swank nightclub near **Wheeling**, Illinois. Around June of 1963, there was a grand opening. **Eddie Fisher**, Sinatra's Clan, and **Dinah Shore** (a great partier) sang for the club's revelers.

BIBLIOGRAPHY/SOURCES

Newspapers: *Alton Telegraph, Belleville News-Democrat, Benton Evening News, Chicago Tribune and Sun, East St. Louis Journal, Herrin Daily Journal, Marion Daily Republican, Pinckneyville Democrat, Springfield Register, St. Louis Globe and Post-Dispatch.*

Author unknown. *Chicago Gang Wars in Pictures*, Chicago: Spot Publishing, 1930. (British reprint)

Allen, Edward. *Merchants of Menace – The Mafia*, Springfield: Charles Thomas, 1962.

Allen, Troy. *Gang Wars of the Twenties*. Chatsworth, California: Barclay House, 1974.

Allsop, Kenneth. *The Bootleggers and Their Era*. London: Hurchinson, 1974.

Altman, Jack and Ziporyn, Marvin. *Born to Raise Hell*, New York: Grove Press, 1967.

Andrews, Wayne. *Battle for Chicago*, Harcourt, Brace, 1946.

Angle, Paul. *Bloody Williamson*, New York: Alfred A. Knopf, 1952.

Bergreen, Laurence. *Capone: The Man and the Era*. New York: Simon and Schuster, 1994.

Bielski, Ursula. *Chicago Haunts*, Chicago: Lake Claremont Press, 1998.

Boardman, Barrington. *Flappers, Bootleggers*, Harper and Row, 1988.

Brashler, William. *The Don: Sam Giancana*, Harper and Row, 1977.

Breo, Dennis and Martin, William. *The Crime of the Century*. (R. Speck) New York: Bantam Books, 1993.

Bruns, Roger. *The Bandit Kings*, New York: Crown Pub., 1995.

Cahill, Tim and Ewing, Russ. *Buried Dreams* (John Gacy). New York: Bantam Books, 1986.

Casey, Robert, and W.A. Douglas. *The Midwesterner*, Chicago: Wilcox and Follette, 1948.

Churchill, Allen. *A Pictorial History of American Crime*. New York: Holt, Rinehart, Winston, 1964.

Claitor, Diana. *Outlaws, Mobsters and Murderers*. New York: M and M Books, 1991.

Cowdery, Ray. *Capone's Chicago*, Minnesota: Northstar Commemoratives, 1987.

Cromie, Robert and Joseph Pinkston. *Dillinger: A Short and Violent Life*, Evanston: Chicago Historical Bookworks, 1990.

Demaris, Ovid. *Captive City*, Lyle Stuart, 1969.

DeNeal, Gary. *A Knight of Another Sort*. (Charlie Birger), Carbondale: SIU Press, 1998.

Flanders, Robert B. *Nauvoo: Kingdom on the Mississippi*. Urbana: University of Illinois Press, 1965.

Frank, Gerold. *An American Death* (M.L. King). New York: Doubleday Books, 1972.

Fredericks, Dean. *John Dillinger. New York: Pyramid, 1963.*
Fox, Stephen, *Blood and Power*. New York: William Morrow, 1989.
Galligan, George, and Jack Wilkinson. *In Bloody Williamson*, 1927. 1985 reprint by Williamson County Hist. Society.
Giancana, Sam and Chuck. *Doublecross*, New York: Warner Press, 1992.
Godwin, John. *Alcatraz 1868-1963.* New York: Doubleday and Co., 1963.
Goulart, Ron. *Lineup, Tough Guys*. Los Angeles: Sherbourne, 1966.
Gurko, Miriam. *Clarence Darrow*. New York: Thomas Crowell Company, 1963.
Halper, Albert, ed. *The Chicago Crime Book*, Cleveland: World Publishing, 1967.
Halwas, John B. *The Bootlegger*, Urbana: University of Illinois Press, 1998.
Hammer, Richard. *Playboy's Illustrated History of Organized Crime*. Chicago: Playboy Press, 1975.
Hartley, Robert. *Paul Powell of Illinois*, Carbondale: SIU Press, 1999. Also, *Charles H. Percy: A Political Perspective*, 1975.
Helmer, William. *Public Enemies*, New York: Checkmark/Facts, 1998.
Helmer, William. *The Gun That Made the Twenties Roar*, London: Macmillan, 1969.
Higdon, Hal. *Crime of the Century – Leopold and Loeb*. New York: G.P. Putnam's Sons, 1975.
Hirsch, Phil, ed. *The Racketeers*. New York: Pyramid, 1970.
Howard, Robert P., *Illinois: A History of the Prairie State*, 1972.
Johnson, Curt. *Wicked City: Chicago: from Kenna to Capone*, by December Press, Highland Park, IL 1994.
Kefauver, Estes. *Crime in America*. New York: Doubleday and Co, 1951.
Kimball, Stanley, ed. *The Mormons in Early Illinois*, Southern Illinois University at Edwardsville.
Kobler, John. *Capone: His Life and World*. New York: Da Capro Press, 1971. (also: *Ardent Spirits – Prohibition*)
Landesco, John. *Organized Crime in Chicago*, University of Chicago Press, 1968.
Leopold, Nathan. *Life Plus 99 Years*, New York: Doubleday, 1958.
Levell, Mark, and Bill Helmer. *The Quotable Al Capone*, Chicago: Chicago Typewriter, 1990.
Letts, Mary. *Al Capone*. London: Wayland, 1974.
Linedecker, Clifford. *The Man Who Killed Boys*, New York: St. Martin's Press, 1979.
Louderback, Lew. *The Bad Ones*. Greenwich, Connecticut: Fawcett, 1968.
Maas, Peter. *The Valachi Papers*, New York: G.P. Putnam's Sons, 1968.
Martin, John. *Butcher's Dozen and Other Murders*. New York: Harper, 1945, 1950.
McClellan, John L. *Crime Without Punishment*. New York: Duell, Sloan and Pierce, 1962.
McPhaul, Jack. *Johnny Torrio*. New Rochelle, NY: Arlington House, 1970.
Mendenhall, Harlan. *Fall of the House of Gacy*, M & K Enterprises, 1996.
Moore, William. *Dateline Chicago*. New York: Taplinger, 1973.
Morgan, John. *Prince of Crime* (Murray Humphreys), New York: Stein and Day, 1985.
Moss, Jason. *The Last Victim*. New York: Warner Books, 1999.
Murray, David. *Charles Percy of Illinois*, New York: Harper and Row, 1968.
Murray, George. *The Legacy of Al Capone*, New York: Putnam's, 1975.
Nash, Jay Robert. *World Encyclopedia of Organized Crime*, New York: DaCapo Press, 1993.
Nunes, Bill. *Illustrated History of Southern Illinois*, printed by Thomson Shore of Dexter Michigan, 2001.
Oblinger, Carl D. *Divided Kingdom*, Springfield: Illinois State Historical Society, 1991.
Parker, Chatland. *The Herrin Massacre*, Marion: Williamson County Historical Society, 1925.
Pensoneau, Taylor, and Ellis, Bob. *Dan Walker*, Smith-Collins, Evansville, Indiana: 1993.
Pensoneau, Taylor. *Governor Richard Ogilvie*, Carbondale: SIU Press, 1997.
_______________. *Brothers Notorious*: *The Shelton Gang*, New Berlin: Downstate Publishers, 2001.
Pepper, William. *Orders to Kill*, (James Earl Ray Story) New York: Carroll and Craf, 1995.
Posner, Gerald. *Killing the Dream*, (King assassination) New York: Random House, 1998.
Sann, Paul. *The Lawless Decade*. New York: Crown Publishers, 1957.
Sifakis, Carl. *Encyclopedia of American Crime*, 1982.
Simon, Paul. *Elijah Lovejoy, Martyr to Freedom*. St. Louis: Concordia Press, 1964.
__________. *P.S. : A Memoir*, Chicago: Bonus Books, 1999.
Stage, William. *Litchfield*, St. Louis: Floppingfish Publishing, 1998.
Stewart, Charles O. "Tavern and Juke Box Men Asking Vital Question," *East St. Louis Journal*, 27 July 1947.
_______________. "Hoodlums Filter Into Jobs at Cahokia," *East St. Louis Journal*, 22 July, 1962.
Sullivan, Terry, and Maiken, Peter. *Killer Clown*, New York: Pinnacle Books, 1994.
Taylor, Troy. *Haunted Illinois*, Alton: Whitechapel Press, 1999.
Terkle, Studs. *Chicago*. New York: Pantheon Books, 1986.
Theising, Andrew. "Profitable Boundaries: Incorporating the Industrial Suburb" (East St. Louis), Unpublished Doctoral thesis, 1997.
Thiem, George. *The Hodge Scandal*, New York: St Martin's Press, 1963.
Toland, John. *The Dillinger Days*, New York: Random House, 1963.
Wallis, Michael. *Oilman: Frank Phillips*, Garden City, NJ: Doubleday, 1988.
Weber, Don and Bosworth, Charles. *Precious Victims*, New York: Signet books, 1991.
Wendt, Lloyd and Kogan, Herman. *Big Bill of Chicago,* New York: Bobbs-Merrill Co., 1953.
Wilson, Colin. *A Criminal History of America*, New York: Putnam's, 1984.

Roy Shelton's home in the Merriam/ Fairfield area of Wayne County, Illinois: Bowen Archives

Roy Shelton – Courtesy of Bowen Archives SIUE

Bernie Shelton's grieving widow, 2nd from the left, at the funeral parlor :Bowen Archives

Carl Shelton's grieving widow at a church memorial service: Bowen Archives SIUE

The crime of 1920 – Feds pour 130,000 quarts of hard liquor down the drain at Waukegan, Illinois (UPI)

Des Plaines bootlegger, Roger Touhy (Wide World)

Roy Webb at Bernie Shelton's Happy Hollow Ranch (from Mary W. Rousan)

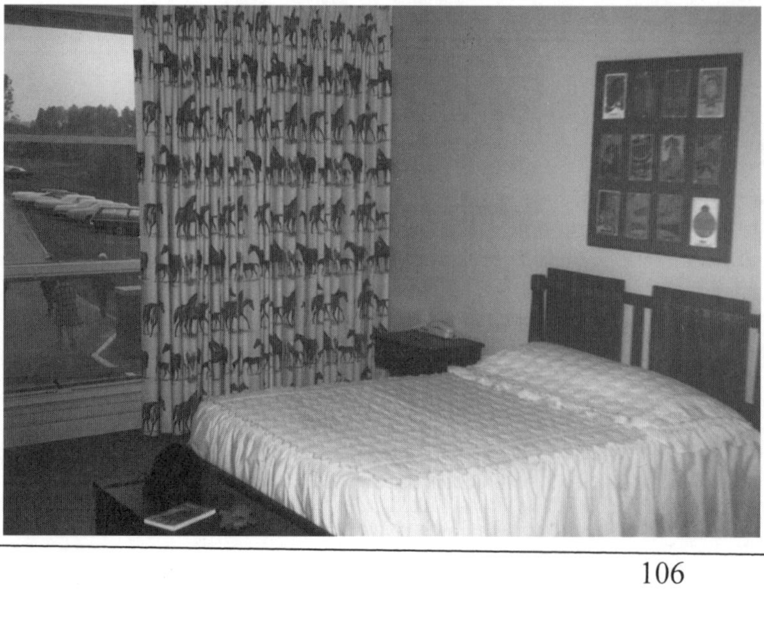

Guest bedroom at Buster Wortman's moat home (courtesy Harry Fiebig)

Photo reenactment of Bernie Shelton's shooting from wooded area at Parkway Tavern in Peoria, Illinois

Photos courtesy of Bowen Archives and the photo service department at SIU Edwardsville

Photo reenactment of Roy Shelton murder scene on his farm near Fairfield/Merriam, Illinois

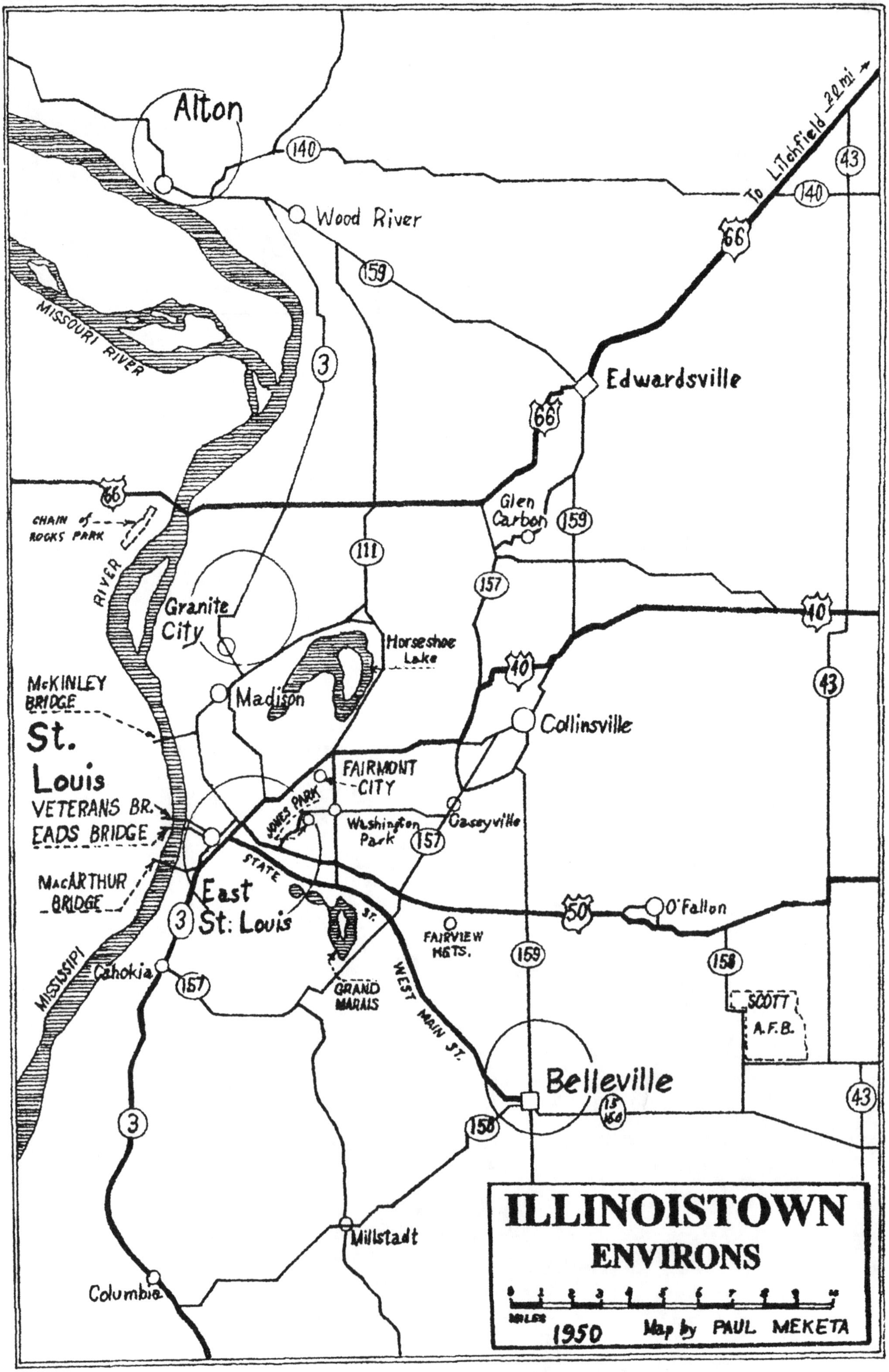

Alton
140
To Litchfield 20 mi
43
140
66
Wood River
159
MISSOURI RIVER
3
Edwardsville
66
66
CHAIN of ROCKS PARK
Glen Carbon
159
111
RIVER
157
Granite City
Horseshoe Lake
10
40
43
McKINLEY BRIDGE
Madison
Collinsville
St. Louis
FAIRMONT CITY
VETERANS BR.
EADS BRIDGE
JONES PARK
Washington Park
Caseyville
157
STATE
MacARTHUR BRIDGE
East St. Louis
3
50
O'Fallon
ST.
FAIRVIEW HGTS.
159
158
MISSISSIPI
Cahokia
157
GRAND MARAIS
WEST MAIN ST.
SCOTT A.F.B.
Belleville
13 160
43
3
158
Millstadt
Columbia
ILLINOISTOWN
ENVIRONS
MILES
1950
Map by PAUL MEKETA

ILLINOISTOWN –

Fiction

Gangster/Romance drama set in 1950's America

Printed in the U.S.A. by Thomson-Shore of Dexter, Michigan

By Bill Nunes
5 Mark Trail
Glen Carbon, IL 62034

Bill Nunes (East Side Class of 1957)
(618) 288-5185 bnunesbook@aol.com
Fax: (618) 288-3417

Acknowledgments

This novel is about a working-class town that was one of the most fascinating cities in America. What seems to bind my biases and prejudices together was the presence of a rare quality that is lacking in most cities: a distinctly recognizable, outrageous, flamboyant, irrepressible texture and personality. It was a city that had much to say, and it did so with a rare swagger and braggadocio. It had soul; it had attitude. The place had a character and quality uniquely its own. It grabbed life by the lapels, looked it square in the eyes, and shook it. East St. Louis was one of those rare cities whose sum was much greater than its parts, and to its denizens, no place was more bewitching or beguiling.

One goal of this book is to help preserve the historical flavor of this unique place before memories fade and everything recedes into sepia-toned myth. Accordingly, I tried to reconstruct a vivid evocation of East St. Louis and America at mid-century.

Except for Robert Sweeney, the Shelton brothers and Charlie Birger, the major characters in this novel are entirely fictional. In order to add realism, the names of numerous actual public figures and businessmen are interspersed throughout the story. Sal Delonzo and his men, Missola and her husband, Montrose, Roland Jones, Lance Troutman, Lloyd "Knucky" Walters and John Rafferty are pure fabrications. Much of the testimony from the reenacted Kefauver hearings closely parallels that actually given in St. Louis, Missouri, though some literary license has been taken. The factual vignettes at the beginning of each chapter are based on the history and lore of East St. Louis. I am grateful to my friends who lent their names for numerous characters in the book. I hope they enjoy their fictitious alter egos. **The story itself is not an exposé and is purely a product of my imagination, meant to entertain. It is fiction. And yet . . .**

Thanks to my support team of about twenty-five people: former residents who now live in surrounding suburbs and who love that old city as much as I do. I am indebted to Walter Boyne for his help with military matters in the Cold War era. And Mark Godwin's incredible knowledge of railroads was particularly useful. Special thanks to Mildred Rongey, Jackie Rader and Casey Selix, who tirelessly corrected my imperfect grammar and syntax; to Mary Barber, Joan Vail Andrew Theising and Dave Heth, who proofread for sense, order, logic and content, and to others like Mike Gillespie who read parts of the manuscript and offered suggestions that helped shape the book's final form. And a special thanks to my loving wife and supportive children who form the center of my universe and gave me motive and inspiration to overcome the tedium involved in editing a manuscript.

I owe a special debt to many other East St. Louisans whose special knowledge of that city helped give me the broad base of information that was necessary to write a period piece of historical fiction. I beg your indulgence in my excesses and unbridled enthusiasm, and your pardon for errors which are wholly my own.

I alone am responsible for any inaccuracies or unlikelyhoods.

For many, this book will be a bittersweet reminder of better times. It is my love letter to the city of East St. Louis.

INTRODUCTION

To say that old East St. Louis was unique is a gross understatement. It was a rough-and-tumble place that grew out of a sandbar in the middle of the Mississippi in 1800 and spent nearly a million dollars in 1888 to pull itself out of the mud by raising its streets by an average of ten feet.

On three separate occasions the entire town was practically washed downstream by Mississippi River floods. A devastating cyclone struck in 1896. It suffered the nation's largest race riot in 1917 but bounced back in 1960 to be named an All-America City by Look Magazine, one of only eleven cities so honored. No city of comparable size could boast of equal commercial and industrial achievements as it acquired the nickname "Pittsburgh of the West." By 1920 it was the second largest city in the state of Illinois and the 86th largest in the nation.

View of the Great Flood of 1903.

It started a severe decline in the mid-1960s and today is a town racked by poverty, crime and neglect. But you needn't feel sorry for it. Better to have reached the pinnacle and fallen back than never to have climbed the mountain. Better to be the once-proud East St. Louis, locus of industrial America, than one of those tepid, faceless burgs that dot the national landscape, lacking even a modicum of social or historical significance. East St. Louis was like an incredible meteor that brightly streaked across the heavens and caused the world to gasp at its brilliance. It may never again recapture that prominence, but for one brief moment in time, it stepped from the shadows of obscurity and tasted glory.

How does one reconcile the two north-south images of East St. Louis that seemingly are oxymoronic? Most outsiders heaped criticism on the place while the majority who lived there in the 40s and 50s wouldn't trade that experience for anything. One teacher from the Catholic high school referred to the place as "heaven on earth." With full employment, safe neighborhoods, moderate taxes, the lowest utility rates in the nation, and good schools, citizen boosterism overcame the cloud of doubt created by gangsterism and civic corruption. Many of these same critics flocked to East St. Louis for shopping, entertainment and employment. For the most part, it was other gangsters—not average citizens—who feared local crime bosses.

There was a multiplicity of organizations that seemed to be the glue that held together the social order of the city and provided the enduring human need for community. This included a kaleidoscope of churches, Jaycees, Knights of Columbus, Shriners, Demolays, benevolent societies, fraternal lodges, ethnic social halls, literary societies and the like. It was far from the Hobbesian jungle that outsiders would have us believe.

While it is true that political, sectarian, racial and class cleavages crossed the community at different angles, the idea that everyone seemed to own stock in the future of the community minimalized these differences.

There are those who maintain that the city began to decline after World War II; but as late as 1961, when the city celebrated its Centennial, almost no one thought along those lines.

How else do you explain Holiday Inn building a million dollar hotel complex in the downtown area, a structure that would be abandoned a little more than a decade later? It is only through hindsight and by examining arcane statistics that one can look back and find warning signs that the city was in trouble. The trucking and airline industries hurt the city's railroads severely. River commerce declined, and East St. Louis lost its geographic advantage. Industries left town and moved to the Sunbelt. Hard times descended on the city as it fell victim to the nexus of historical change and its own contradictions.

The civil rights revolution of the mid-1960s produced a division along a single fault line that had devastating effects. A wave of drug culture, gang turf wars, and mindless violence against Caucasians in unprecedented fury resulted in white flight on a massive scale. Today, no city of comparable size has a greater disparity between blacks and whites. The population has fallen to roughly 31,000, and only about one percent of it is white. In the late 1970s, the U.S. government labeled it as the most distressed small city in America. It was also the murder capital of the U.S.A. back then with the highest per-capita homicide rate in the nation.

Having spent one-third of my life in East St. Louis (1939-1962), I wanted to weave a story that would give readers a good sense of what my home town, with all of its paradoxes and complexities, was all about.

It is an historical curiosity that many of the things the old time gangsters made the newspaper headlines for (gambling), and what they went to prison for (illegally making and selling liquor), are now perfectly legal and sanctioned by the state.

I would like to dedicate this book to World War II veterans who sacrificed so much to make my idyllic boyhood years possible.

ILLINOISTOWN

CAST OF CHARACTERS

EAST ST. LOUIS, ILLINOIS—A lively Mississippi River town that embraces a unique collection of politicians, shady characters and opportunists.

BRAD LOGAN—Neophyte lawyer—has a lot to learn about life and love. His naïveté could get him killed.

LORNA SANDERS—Fresh-out-of-college news reporter, looking for security in a career instead of a husband.

LLOYD WALTERS—An East St. Louis businessman-gangster being hard-pressed to hold on to his empire.

SALVATORE DELONZO—St. Louis, Missouri, crime boss and Walters' archenemy—obsessed with adding East St. Louis to his criminal fiefdom.

GLORIA HORNBACK—Lorna's loyal roommate—more than happy to dispense pearls of wisdom about life and love.

LAURIE MCINTYRE—Happy-go-lucky busybody—works the front desk at the Beulah Club residence hall for women.

LANCE TROUTMAN—Young scion of old money family—his predatory intent, handsome looks and suave manner could spell heartbreak, or worse, for unwary women.

MONTROSE AND ROLAND—Lloyd Walters' loyal, tough-as-nails bodyguards, one black and one white.

MISSOLA—Negro cleaning lady at Brad Logan's law firm—has been chewed on by life but still exudes tenacity.

HARRY FIEBIG—Brad Logan's curmudgeonesque office associate with a weakness for playing the ponies and anything stronger than twenty-proof.

PRISCILLA BARTLETT—Lorna's steamroller nemesis at the office—out for revenge in the worst possible way.

ESTES KEFAUVER—Tennessee senator—used organized crime as a political stepping stone to stardom the way Joe McCarthy rode to fame on a horse named Communism.

ROBERT SWEENEY—"The law" in East St. Louis. A two-fisted cop—Walters' thorn-in-the-side. This hard-boiled detective killed as many men in the line of duty as Jesse and Frank James combined.

VIKTOR AND STEFAN—Two representatives sent by President Tito of Yugoslavia to accompany the YAK-23 Soviet airplane secretly taken to Scott Air Base for inspection. They will ensnare Brad in a dangerous world of Cold War intrigue and espionage.

PROLOGUE

Probably no other city of comparable size has produced so many famous people. This lively Midwest town was home to the likes of Miles Davis, the legendary creator of "cool jazz;" Ike and Tina Turner, who honed their music skills in local nightclubs, tennis star Jimmy Connors, silent screen legend Lillian Gish; New York Yankee baseball stars Bob Turley and Hank Bauer; football Hall of Famer, Kellen Winslow; NBA basketball star LaPhonso Ellis; New England Patriot's outspoken linebacker Bryan Cox; U. S. Senator Dick Durbin; the World's Greatest Female Athlete, Jackie Joyner-Kersee, and Olympic gold medal winner Al Joyner.

Curtiss "Jenny" airplane: courtesy Walter Boyne

Legend has it that when Josephine Baker, the famous dancer of the 1920s, was a little girl, she was smuggled out of the place during the 1917 race riot in a coffin from RMC Green Funeral Home. The Wilde twins (Lee and Lyn) went to Hollywood and made a dozen movies, including ***Girl Trouble*** with Mickey Rooney. Actress Virginia Mayo's great, great, great grandfather, James Piggott, founded the city in 1793. One of the featured singers on the Arthur Godfrey television show in 1950 was Bill Lawrence, also a product of East St. Louis.

Silent screen star – Lillian Gish

Yet if you lived in that urban encampment on the cusp of the 1950s, the most ubiquitous person in town was a colorful and enigmatic hoodlum by the name of Lloyd Walters. Walters was a throwback to the ballyhoo years of the Roaring Twenties. The onset of Prohibition introduced a new factor into the city's complicated equation—gangsters and organized crime. This became a national dilemma, yet the vagaries of the political, social and economic mix that was East St. Louis heightened its impact there. So much money was to be made with illegal booze that politicians and policemen alike were corrupted by what President Hoover naïvely referred to as the "Noble Experiment." Greenbacks and alcohol flowed freely and East St. Louis was well on its way to becoming a wide-open town. Al Capone's Chicago Syndicate ran things in the northern part of the state. From Peoria to Cairo, the crime lords allowed lesser minions to be in charge. They only had to swear allegiance to the chieftains from Cicero and send regular payments of tribute from their ill-gotten wealth.

The Shelton Gang, from the Fairfield area, evolved into the dominant and most notorious mobsters in southern Illinois. The Birger Gang was their chief competition. Birger's hideaway was a place called Shady Rest. It became a national landmark of sorts when Ripley's "Believe it or Not" reported that the first aerial bombing raid on American soil occurred when Carl Shelton's rival gang dropped crude bombs on the place in a tragi-comic effort to destroy the opposition. The bombs, thrown from an old Curtiss Jenny—used mainly for barnstorming—did little damage, except to kill Charlie Birger's favorite pet.

Lloyd Walters started out as one of the low-echelon errand boys for the local mobsters. He quickly became Carl Shelton's ***protégé***. Walters ended up doing time at Joliet for assaulting a Prohibition agent. When the irrepressible gangster arrived on the East St. Louis landscape in 1941, after his stint in the slammer, he found the Shelton empire in disarray. The three brothers had moved the base of their operations to Peoria, Illinois. Surprised to discover that no one else had established hegemony over neglected East St. Louis, Walters moved quickly to consolidate his power and eliminate competitors. In a couple of years he was the city's undisputed crime boss. People whispered that he could make rivals disappear faster than Judge Crater. He became a living legend of sorts—a curious alloy of hauteur, intrigue and aloofness, with a brooding volatile temperament that simultaneously fascinated locals. Yet his dichotomous personality had a soft side. He was generous, polite to women and a father devoted to his family. He owned a popular restaurant on 5th and Missouri Avenue, a block south of the Ainad Temple, home to those secretive Masons and Shriners. Walters called it the Club 501 Lounge. It had been a speakeasy in the old days. He probably had his finger on most vice activities in the area, but nobody, save his closest associates, knew for sure.

This was 1950 East St. Louis, a blue-collar town with hard-scrabble origins. There was no city like it in the history of the planet. It was a tough town whose image was rooted in a brawling, bloody past that was part truth and part fiction. It was a sprawling, rambunctious place of saints and sinners, the sacred and the profane, juxtaposed on a Midwest landscape full of roughneck, kinetic energy. A saloon on every corner and a church on every other corner, so the saying went. It was a place where an unintentional overheard conversation had potentially fatal consequences.

In East St. Louis, nothing was too absurd to be possible. Prosperity, fueled by the economic engines of World War II and the Korean Conflict, had returned. A well-known slogan permeated the metro area: "If you can't find a job in East St. Louis, you won't find work anywhere." East St. Louis was a city of infinite possibilities—a mirror image of the Cold War economic promise that was post-war America.

ILLINOISTOWN

CHAPTER 1

Grand Marais, with well over a thousand acres of ground and lakes in East St. Louis, was the *third largest municipal park in America* when it was built in 1929.

Thursday, August 17, 1950

East St. Louis, Illinois, was home for all twenty-six years of Brad Logan's life. He was a freshly minted lawyer, having recently passed the Bar exam after law school at the University of Illinois, at Champaign-Urbana. St. Louis University had been a consideration—it would have been closer, ergo cheaper—but it was a Jesuit school, and Brad's upbringing was Protestant. Graduation had ejected him from the insular world of books and lectures, contracts, writs and torts, into the harsh world of reality. He joined the team of Ernst and Lancaster, a relatively new firm in East St. Louis that owned a cluster of offices in the Spivey Building. The twelve-story high brick monolith was the tallest building in southern Illinois. A new chapter in his life was just beginning. Anticipation filled his soul. He was one of those young legal eagles hoping to rise to the top someday in the contentious world of laws and contracts. His specialties were criminal and tax law. The expectation that he would become a partner before age thirty-five was being carefully nurtured.

The Spivey Building

He had no idea of what the Fates—those fickle modifiers of human destiny—had in store for him. His world was totally different from that of Lloyd Walters. "The Godson," reputed to be the old Capone gang's notorious representative for downstate Illinois, was often named in the blaring headlines of local papers, but Brad had never personally laid eyes on him. Little did he know that their paths were soon to become entwined.

Lake Park/
Grand Marais

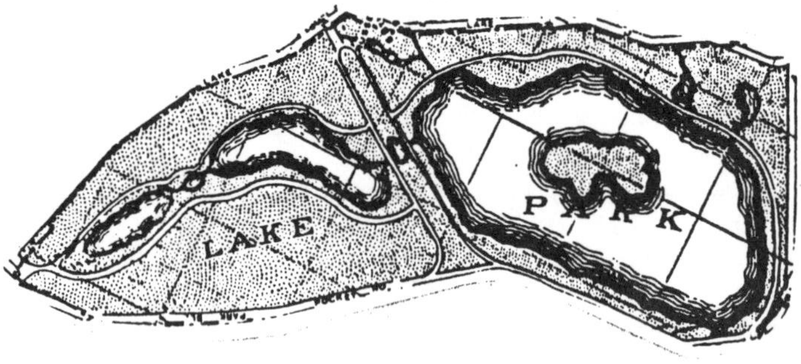

* * *

It had been raining hard that evening—a typical gully-washer that sent torrents of water rushing down from the near-by bluffs to the broad flood plain below called the American Bottom. The rain-swollen Harding Ditch diverted much of the water through the heart of East St. Louis over to Lake Park, better known by its old French name, Grand Marais, meaning "great swamp." It had been one gigantic lake when Native Americans fished its shores, but the city park board had dredged, channeled, and bulldozed it into three separate but connecting entities.

By 11 P.M. the sky had only partially cleared. Filmy clouds were still floating high above. The Milky Way streaked a swatch of light against the dark, starlit sky. It was now 1:30 A.M. New star patterns had emerged in the black canopy. Jupiter was a bright white dot sitting thirty-seven degrees above the horizon.

The mid-point of the night looked foreboding, a dark monochromatic landscape of water. A veil of mist hung over the surface of Lake Number Three. It was a murky place where reptiles, fish and amphibians bred in the dark shadows. Birch branches, laden with foliage, softly rustled their leaves. Cattails, sedge, arrowhead weed and saw grass were dancing rhythmically as waves gently lapped the shore. Queen Anne's lace listed to port in a slight summer breeze.

A hoot owl swooped down and sated its ravenous appetite with an unsuspecting field mouse. Bullfrogs were croaking and tree frogs trilled, competing for air space with other nocturnal creatures that were serenading potential mates. Crickets rubbed their legs together, punctuating the sonnet of sounds emanating from the moonlit darkness. The lake's organic medley swelled to a crescendo of considerable decibels. An occasional thrashing of the water's surface signaled a Darwinian event in the struggle for survival. A ring-tailed raccoon was busily foraging until a discordant noise tensed its muscles.

Beams of light and the whoosh of tires splashing puddles on the gravel road invaded the murky habitat and stilled nature's symphony. The metallic click of an opening car door caused a cottontail rabbit that had been munching tender shoots of clover to prick its ears. It scurried to the safety of underbrush. A new sound, something being dragged from the car to a place on the ground near a picnic table. The swishing of feet on the lush grass and the snap of a small twig kept the night crowd hushed. Then a door slammed, followed ten seconds later by another one. After the intruder had gone, the inhabitants of the riparian community returned to their nightly ritual.

* * *

"**BODY FOUND AT GRAND MARAIS LAKE**" screamed the August 21 headline from the East St. Louis ***Journal.*** Brad scanned the feature column at the right for details. He was working at the office, finishing up some legal briefs when the local newsboy, Johnny Moberly, came in hawking his wares. His thick, straw-like hair bounced in unruly fashion over his freckled forehead. He was a likable kid with hair that was usually bent in several directions and a cowlick that just wouldn't quit. He was partially deaf in one ear, a casualty of an ill-tempered stepfather. Despite the fact that Moberly looked like a street urchin and his fingers were always smudged with newsprint, Brad liked his offbeat verve. The scratchy, squeaky sound of his peppy adolescent voice brightened his day. Brad regularly bought a copy of the afternoon ***Journal*** from him.

The newspaper said the deceased was the owner of Torricelli Construction Company, located along the Southern Railroad tracks at 20th and St. Clair Avenue. Someone had shot him in the back of the head, the occipital lobe of the brain. The police thought it had all the markings of a gangland slaying. Detectives Bob Sweeney and Jerry Sullivan were immediately assigned to the case. Authorities were asking that anyone who might have seen or heard anything to come forward.

According to the article, Vito Torricelli's body was discovered around 7:00 A. M. A preliminary report, pending an autopsy, said it was believed that the time of death was probably between midnight and 2:00 A. M. that same day. The police were yet to determine what the motive might have been. Simple robbery had not been ruled out because his wallet was missing. However, a gold wedding ring and watch were on the deceased when the body was found. It appeared he had been shot with his own gun, a .38 caliber weapon. The forensic lab at the police department was expected to verify the caliber of the bullets in a day or two. There was no evidence or sign of struggle.

The story, by reporter Charles O. Stewart, stated that a Negro male named James Washington, who had gone there to fish, discovered the body. Torricelli was found face down along a side road near a picnic table at Lake Number Three, known as Whispering Lake. The gun, found next to the body, had been wiped clean of prints.

Brad furrowed his brow, somewhat surprised that the gun wasn't rusting away at the bottom of the Mississippi River.

East St. Louis was was famous for its unsolved murders, dating back to 1885 when former Mayor John Bowman was shot in the back by unknown assailants near his home at 10th and College. Brad's newly trained analytical mind began to search for answers.

What did this Torricelli guy do or what did he know or say that would cause those who controlled the dark side of the city to snuff out his life? Brad wondered. ***Why was he shot with his own gun?*** In the back of Brad's brain lurked the notion this might have been a gangland-style copycat slaying to divert attention from the actual perpetrator.

Attention shifted from matters of homicide to the realm of the stomach. Hunger pangs gnawed at Brad's innards, and he marveled at how it felt like his small intestine was being devoured by the big one. "My big gut is eating up my little gut," he often told his mother when he was a blooming teenager. He had grown weary of hamburgers and club

sandwiches at Walgreen's lunch counter. Brad flipped the pages of the ***Journal*** and grazed the ad section. Music lessons at Sunny Shields. Armstrongs that G-R-I-P the road at **Bond Tire.** Dancing and dining on an Admiral riverboat cruise. Scrumptious seafood at the **Oyster Inn.** A small ad, praising the dining experience offered at the Club 501 Lounge, caught his eye. It was worth a try.

There was no way of knowing a snap decision about one meal would set off a chain-reaction of events and change

Brad's life forever. In a stage play its significance might have been anticipated by music that swells to a dramatic crescendo, perhaps the first four notes of Beethoven's ***Fifth Symphony.*** Fate knocking at the door. Da, da, da dum!

But the real world is not like that. Life is full of ephemeral and illusory happenstances whose meanings are often hidden and perplexing. Like the riddle of the Sphinx. The relevancy of simple choices and mundane events often escape us. Unless one's sensory perceptions are fully attuned, most occurrences in life are ambiguous. Ironically, it's the not knowing; it's the mystery of what the Fates have in store for us that transposes dull, day-to-day living from something flaccid and listless into an adventure worth anticipating.

Brad took the elevator down to the street level and briskly walked the two-and-a-half blocks to his destination. He had never before been in the Club 501, and he approached it with some trepidation. It was well known this was Lloyd Walters' bailiwick, a legitimate establishment that gave Walters a veneer of respectability. His brother Lou, who lived in an appealing apartment on Alexander Place, helped run the business. It was common knowledge Lou was big into horse racing and had several nags that ran at the Fairmount racetrack on Collinsville Road. Fairmount, a local monument to the sporting life, was more or less the minor leagues of the horseracing world. Thoroughbreds that did well here moved on to the Big Show at Arlington in Chicago. The name Club 501 was chosen because Walters bought a policy number after he was released from prison, and at 500-1 odds it paid off big and allowed him to get a new start.

Almost directly across the street was the Continental Trailways Bus Depot that also served Trailway Lines. From its unassuming exterior, the average patron would never have guessed the Club 501 was "home base" for someone notorious, such as Lloyd Walters. The two-story building, masoned in brick, was typical of taverns built when Prohibition ended after Roosevelt's election in 1932. The upper level was sometimes rented out, but more often than not, it was the living quarters of a waitress or bartender who worked there. The main entry to Walters' place was on St. Louis Avenue, and there was a side entrance on 5th Street. A green neon sign with the word ***Club 501*** was blinking above the corner entrance. Several small buzzing signs in the windows, outlined with colorful tubes, advertised various suds—Stag, Falstaff and Hyde Park. Brad gingerly pushed open a sturdy oak door with a Cyclops porthole window at eye level.

Simultaneously, his senses were aware of stale air, smoke and pungent alcohol, reminding him of Rick's place in ***Casablanca.*** Brad half expected to be greeted by some barrel-chested bodyguard, perhaps a former linebacker for Central Catholic High, who would pat him down in case he carried a piece. No such imposing figure darkened the doorway. The smell of beef wafted from the grill. T-bone, New York strip and ***filet mignon***, he guessed. Like Pavlov's dog, his mouth began to salivate before his brain fully comprehended food. He was hungry enough to eat the napkins. It was the hunger of anticipation, not real hunger. Not the kind of hunger felt by those starving kids in China, for whom your mother made you clean your plate. He was a product of countless sermons, bellowed from a pulpit that condemned smoking, drinking, gambling—a host of venial transgressions that jeopardized one's soul. Yet he tried not to wear religion on his sleeve. A large Wurlitzer jukebox was playing "The Continental," by pop diva Doris Day. Brad made his way to the nearest empty table and pulled up a chair. A pert, redheaded bar girl in a brief black and white outfit sashayed over and politely asked if he wanted to order a drink. She was concave and convex in all the right places.

Doris Day

"No thanks. I'll just have a Mississippi highball," he said in East St. Louis vernacular. She brought him a glass of water.

Gliding from one customer to another with flirtatious ease, she handled suggestive remarks and come-ons with an aplomb Brad figured earned her extra tips.

Brad surveyed the dimly lit room while he waited for the waitress to take his order. There were about twenty sets of tables and chairs; three-fourths of them were filled with customers. The medium-oak tables were covered with white linen. The place was clearly upscale from your run-of-the-mill taverns that dotted the city's landscape. A highly polished mahogany cocktail bar flanked the right side. Chrome-legged bar stools with black leather seats were lined up along the outside edge of the bar.

A beefy butch-cut bartender with a half-apron was polishing shot glasses and talking with one of the customers. Wet smudges stained the white of his apron. In front of him were three chrome and china draft beer-pump handles. Behind him, between the usual array of liquor bottles and beer glasses, a small sign read: "DON'T SPIT ON THE FLOOR—REMEMBER THE JOHNSTOWN FLOOD." Next to the sign, leaning in an upright position, was a hand-carved shillelagh, crafted from hickory, the size of a baseball bat. Running its length were crudely painted white letters that said "Peacemaker." Brad assumed it was there to discourage barroom brawls. Except for the fearsome looking cudgel, the overall ambiance was pleasant and not at all stodgy or sinister as he had half expected.

Bette Davis

A waitress in her late twenties came over and blocked Brad's view. Expressive Bette Davis eyes shone the color of aquamarine. She gave him a dimpled smile while she regarded his friendly eyes and athletic build.

"Can I take your order, sir?"

She was wearing a white cotton blouse and a coral-colored pinafore. Her chestnut hair was nearly down to her shoulders. She reminded Brad of Margie King, one of his former schoolteachers. A pleasant scent of perfume offered a mild diversion. Her face looked a little tired, but she had an Ipana toothpaste-ad smile. She glanced at her Benrus.

"I've nearly finished my shift. You're my last customer of the day."

Brad ordered a small rib eye steak, a baked potato and a small salad with Thousand Island dressing. "I'll wash it down with a cherry Coke," he volunteered.

"I kind of figured you for the sarsaparilla or chocolate milk type," she said, with hands on hips.

"What is that crack supposed to mean?" he sourly responded.

"Oh, I meant it as a ***compliment.***"

Yeah, a left-handed compliment, Brad thought.

Brad's order was written on a pad of light green forms from the B & P Bookstore on Collinsville Avenue. He had seen similar forms in many of the area's drive-ins and restaurants. She used her own Gregg method of waitress shorthand. R-eye, B-tater, sal. w/1,000 & C-Coke were hastily jotted.

"How do you want your steak?"

"I always order medium well."

She dutifully scribbled m/w on her order form.

Brad knew connoisseurs were adamant that "rare" was the only proper way to order a steak, but he never could handle the sight of blood-red juices oozing out of the meat when he sank his knife and fork into it. It reminded him of headless eviscerated beasts hanging upside down on meat hooks. That gruesome fate met thousands of cattle daily at the stockyards in National City, a mere seven blocks away.

Brad briefly closed his eyes, giving them respite from the busy—no, hectic day. When he opened them again, they began to wander over the other patrons. There was a married-looking gentleman at the bar talking to a leggy blonde, who definitely wasn't his wife. Three banker-types, dressed in pin-stripe suits, monopolized one table. He heard snatches of language couched in the jargon of their professsion—"inflation," "collateral," and "Federal Reserve," but loans and interest rates seemed to dominate the discussion. Rex Carr and Harry Cruncleton, a couple of figures representing the city's power structure, were talking quietly at one table. Harry was an executive of that cathedral of commerce known as First National Bank. Rex, a product of a neighborhood known as Denverside, was a rising star lawyer.

Peering through the smoky haze, Brad noticed a man in the back of the room beckoning to him with his index finger. As Brad walked toward him, he could more easily make out his features. Wearing a gray pin-stripe suit, he appeared to be in his late forties. His hair was dark and coarse and beginning to thin a bit on top. A weak smile tried to replace a slight scowl that seemed to be permanently chiseled on his granite-like features. A plume of smoke from his cigarette made its way toward the ceiling.

"Do ya know who I am, kid?" he asked with the rasp of a heavy smoker's voice.

"Aren't you, uh . . ? "

"Yeah, it's me," he interrupted. "You ain't scared of me, are you?"

"As far as I know, I don't have any reason to be afraid." Brad suppressed a twitch and tried to remain outwardly calm.

"Have a seat." The timbre of his voice eerily resembled Edward G. Robinson's in a generic gangster movie. "I hate to eat alone."

Brad sat directly across from him on the booth's fluted leather cushion. Despite all his training at law school, Brad felt somewhat intimidated.

Edward G. Robinson

"Russ de Greeff, the manager at Sears, usually keeps me company on Friday nights, but he must be sick or somethin'. What's your name?"

Brad tried to hide the slight quiver in his voice. "Brad Logan."

"Yeah? What kind of name is that?"

"It's Scottish."

"So that explains the green and blue tartan tie."

Brad looked at him with a face that bore the imprint of his highland forebears. "Yes. My mother, Edna, was a Holmes —it's English. My dad, Herb, is a foreman at the C. K. Williams plant over on Lynch. I still live with them in Washington Park."

Walters took a sip from his glass. It looked like a Tom Collins. Brad wasn't very good at identifying mixed drinks.

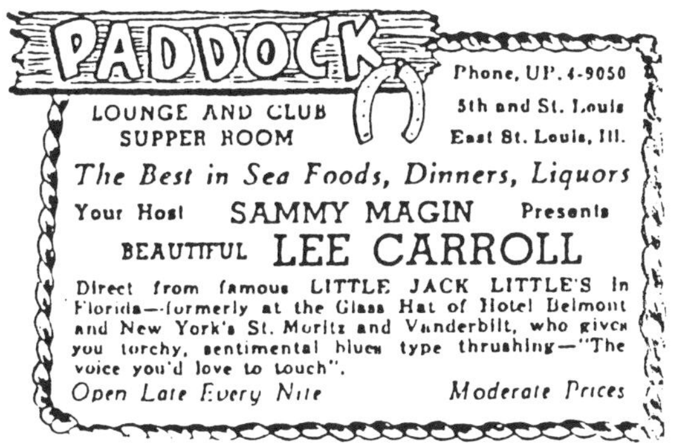

"Tom, my old man, was a fireman," he said in a matter-of-fact tone. "Lives over in Alta Sita. He retired in '39, but he had been a captain at Engine House No. 3. He's like your dad, I guess, a real ham-and-egger. By the way, you don't have to call me sir. My friends and family call me Lloyd."

"Yes, sir . . . er, okay, Mr. Walters."

"Any brothers or sisters?"

"One older sister. I lost a younger brother to diphtheria."

Walters' features softened. "I know how tough that is. Had a cousin who died when I was a kid. From the whooping cough, it was."

"One of my neighbors caught it, and their house was quarantined two weeks by health authorities," Brad said. He figuratively pinched himself. Brad couldn't believe he was actually having a conversation with the leading underworld figure of southern Illinois.

"So your old man is a workin' stiff at the 'paint mill.' Any remote chance we got any mutual acquaintances?"

"I don't know. I have an uncle and a cousin who work at Veteran's Linoleum on Collinsville Avenue."

Walters' eyes widened, and his eyebrows arched a bit. He flicked the gray residue from his cigarette into a nearby ashtray. "That'sa coincidence. They just installed some new tile at my home up in Caseyville. Don't some big Jewish fellow own the place?"

"Uh huh, it's Morris Kaufman. When I was a kid, we called him Big Uncle Morris. He's thinking about opening another store on Collinsville Road near the Mounds Club. How long have you owned the Club 501?"

"A little over a year. I got it from a guy named Pickett. He also owned the Oasis on 22nd Street and needed some quick cash. I figured he either had a cash-flow problem or was being squeezed by the IRS."

The waitress brought the meal Brad had ordered. The steaming juices were still sitting on top of the meat. It looked mouth-watering. The fluffy white potato had been split open and a huge chunk of yellow butter was melting along the fault lines. Brad lightly sprinkled some pepper on it. "Do you have any steak sauce?" he queried.

"Hey, kid—take my advice. You'll ruin the taste if you smother it with that stuff. We've got the best steaks in town. I've got a Polish friend at Circle Packing Company who delivers the best cuts—straight from the slaughterhouse."

Circle Packing at 319 Winstanley

Brad knew what pleased his palate, but he wasn't much of a gourmet, so he followed Knucky Walters' advice. With his fork and knife he sliced off a wedge of tender meat. There was just a slight bit of pink showing in the middle of the steak—exactly the way he liked it. He popped it in his mouth and gulped it down. The first pang subsided. "That's a very good piece of beef," Brad said.

"Go easy on it," Knucky advised. "Food is meant to be enjoyed. Take time to savor what you're eating. A fine steak, like a classy woman, should be handled with patience. Life's pleasures shouldn't be rushed."

"Thanks for the tip."

"You look pretty wet behind the ears, kid—kinda square, like a member of the old Tom Mix straight shooters club. Probably don't even smoke, a real do-gooder Boy Scout type."

"I smoked a catalpa pod in the old shed one time."

"A what?"

"One of those lady cigars from a smoking bean tree."

"When I was a kid, we smoked corn silk and dried grape vines," Knucky said.

He continued his playful game with Brad's naïveté. "Yep! I bet you're the kind that don't step on flowers an' shoos flies out the door instead of swattin' 'em."

"I shot a bird once with a .22 rifle," Brad boasted.

"So it was ***you*** who killed Cock Robin! Shame, shame."

Had anybody else uttered those taunts Brad would have been angry, but he sensed Knucky was only playing with him, and he was enjoying his little game.

"I'll wager my Italian silk tie you've never even bumped uglies with a woman, have you? Bet you're saving it for that one special girl in your life."

"Bumped what?"

"You know, had sex with a girl."

A flush came over Brad's face. "I saw a girl naked once," he said. "That ought to count for something."

"How'd ya get so lucky?" Knucky inquired.

"One time I dropped some change in the bath house at Jones Park pool, and it fell through the floorboards. I went outside and crawled underneath to get it. I found myself under Velma Anderson's dressing stall. She was a half-year ahead of me in school, and she was really stacked—you know—and she undressed as I was crawling past her stall. I watched her disrobe down to her unmentionables. Then she stripped to the buff and put on her bathing suit. Velma was a real dish. My heart was pounding so hard I thought it was going to jump out of my chest. Naturally I was consumed afterwards by Protestant guilt, but I tried to console myself with the notion that guys have been sneaking looks at naked women for eons."

"You're right about men looking at women for centuries," Knucky said. "I'll bet even old Alley Oop peeked in the cave when his girl friend was undressing."

He inexplicably changed the subject. "What's your racket?"

"Pardon?"

"What do ya do for a livin'?"

"I just graduated from the University of Illinois law school. I've been working a couple of months for Ernst and Lancaster. Their office is on the third floor of the Spivey Building. I'm one of the indentured servants who looks up precedents, runs errands over to the Federal Building and helps prepare legal briefs. No telling how long it will be before I get to argue my first case."

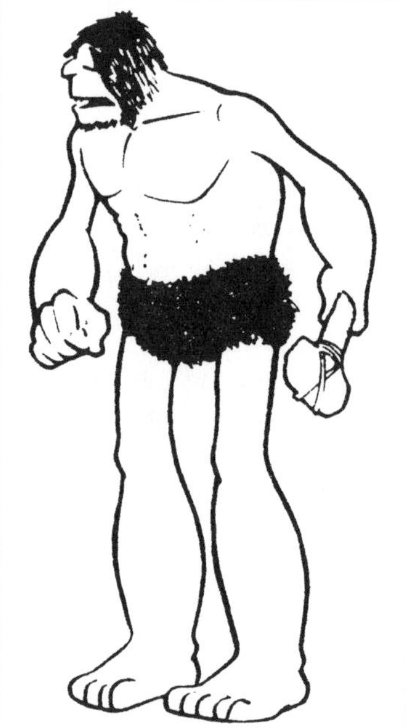

"I dropped outta school when I was fourteen," Knucky dryly remarked.

"I thought you had to be sixteen to quit."

"State law back then read fourteen," he said. "I bet your old man dropped out after the eighth grade, just like me."

"You're right; he did."

Another shift in the conversation. "That's a half-decent set of threads you're wearing, kid."

"What do you mean by 'half-decent?' " Brad asked.

"Let me give ya a bit of advice. I'll bet ya bought that suit off the rack at either Sears or Robert Hall."

"Robert Hall," Brad confessed.

"People judge a man by first impressions, and believe me, a classy suit makes a big difference. Save your money until you can afford a really good set of threads, such as Hart-Shaffner & Marx or Brooks Brothers. My tailor works at Brooks Brothers on Broadway in St. Louis. Buy one gray suit and a dark blue one. Set them off with a nice pair of Florsheims. I get my leathers from Al's Men Shop on Collinsville Avenue. Al Oglander and I have been friends for some time now. You get a perfect fit at his place because they have a newfangled X-ray machine. It looks like a Crosley console radio and you stick your feet in a slot at the bottom. The clerk looks through a window at the top, presses a button, and the floor . . . er, fluoroscope shows your feet inside the shoes."

"I'll try to remember that. I'm much obliged."

"And don't forget, a guy should always wear gold or silver cuff links. By the way, what kind of car are ya drivin'?"

"A Studebaker."

Brad's bullet-nosed Studebaker parked next to a F-86 Sabre Jet

"Interesting car, only they say you can't tell whether you are coming or going with its odd body style."

"I've heard that. But I like it because the front end, with its bullet nose grille and fenders, reminds me of the P-38 Lightning with its twin fuselage configuration. During the war, the Germans had a special name for the plane. They called it the 'fork-tailed devil.' "

"What model?"

"A Champion Regal Deluxe with 85 horses under the hood and 113 inch wheelbase. It has a unique feature known as a 'hill-holder.' "

"Hill-holder?"

"Yes. It helps when you're parked on a hill and keeps you from rolling backwards while you're trying to work three pedals with two feet. You let the clutch out half way, slip your right foot over to the gas pedal, and the brake will still hold until the clutch is out all the way before it moves forward."

"I was a Ford man when I was your age," Knucky recalled.

"Dillinger liked that brand, too," Brad said. "He once wrote a letter to Henry Ford, congratulating him on building a fast reliable car that could be used for getaways following bank robberies. But John Bauer, a friend of mine, hates Fords. He says F-o-r-d stands for 'Found On Roadside, Dead.' "

Officials looking at Dillinger's body (Wide World)

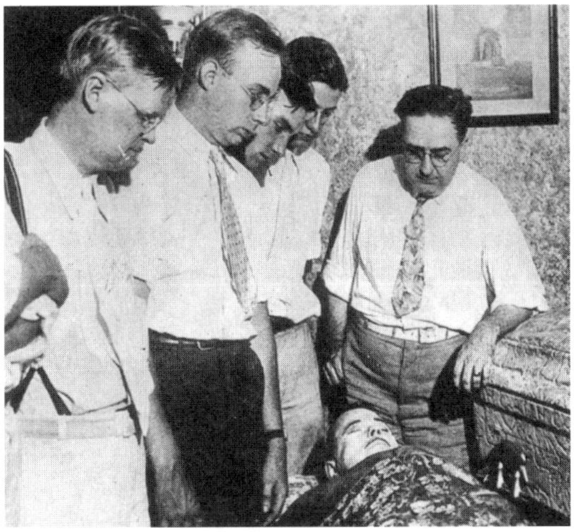

"Dillinger! Now there was a guy who led an exciting life. It's a shame the Feds shot him down in the streets of Chicago like he was a mad dog or some-thin'. "

"He used acid, you know."

"What do ya mean?"

"Some doc put a caustic solution on his fingers in an effort to destroy his prints."

Knucky leaned forward. "Did it work?"

"No, because the scar tissue that formed had its own characteristics, as unique as any normal print."

"Bet that really stuck in his craw."

"Fingerprints are hard to destroy. I read where scientists were able to take prints from mummies when they opened King Tut's tomb."

"Know anything 'bout criminal law?" he asked.

"Not much experience, but my niche is ***that*** plus tax law. I had a few courses in divorce and corporate law, but the pro-fesssors were boring."

"Niche? What's that mean, somethin' you're good at?"

"Exactly."

"You said somethin' about Protestants. Are ya one of those Baptists?" Knucky inquired.

"I've been a member of the Washington Park Church of God since I was in the fifth grade at Charles Manners School. I try to live by the Golden Rule, and I believe God has a purpose for everyone's life."

"Church of God . . . what's that, some kind of Pentecostal, speaking-in-tongues, screamin' an' shoutin' holy-roller group?"

"You're thinking Assembly of God. Our church believes in repentance, salvation and an eternal afterlife. We adhere to the New Testament teachings of Jesus and strive to lead decent lives. Do . . . uh, you have any religious inclination?" Brad asked.

He grinned. "Nah, I'm Catholic."

Brad wasn't quite sure how to respond to his little quip.

"I sometimes attend St. Elizabeth's. I go to confession and recite Hail Marys, but I haven't darkened the doors of a church for some time. Down deep I kinda believe in God, but sometimes I wonder if organized religion is what The Man really wanted. An' by the way, how come you Protestants got it in for us Catholics?"

"There's been bad blood between the two groups ever since the Reformation. A lot of Protestants were tortured and killed in Europe by the Spanish Inquisition and Bloody Mary. Fifty thousand were murdered by French Catholics in the eve of St. Bartholomew's Day Massacre."

"Yeah, but wasn't that hundreds of years ago?"

"Anti-Catholicism in this country also stems from the belief that the Catholic hierarchy keeps their subjects in the dark."

"Why? 'Cause they speak in Latin?"

"That's part of it. There's also the thing about loyalty to a foreign power and objection to the doctrine of infant baptism."

"What's wrong with that? ***I*** was baptized in a Catholic church."

"Most Protestants think a person has to be old enough to comprehend the significance of his decision before he can be baptized. There are no examples of children being baptized in the Bible."

Brad didn't bring up the thing about Catholics being derided as "fisheaters" or "mackerel snappers."

"So you don't think there will be any Catholics in heaven."

"Catholics who lead holy lives should make it."

"What about Jews?"

"Most Protestants don't think Jews, Buddhists or Moslems will be there."

Knucky shot him a look of astonishment. "Why not?"

"Because they don't believe Jesus was the Son of God."

"What if a Jew or Muslim converts to Christianity?"

"Then I guess he's all right. At least, that's what my church teaches."

Knucky sat silently a few moments, sifting through what Brad had just said, as if his mind was gnawing on his words. "Sometimes I think all religion is a lot of hooey, a bunch of rules and regulations to make people feel guilty and donate their money."

Brad waited for him to say more but he didn't.

The whole time the two were engaged in the teté a teté, there was a powerfully built man at another table stoically watching them. His face was a clinched fist with an unchanging expression. A small scar sat above his left eyebrow. A pair of ice blue eyes, the kind you see on an Alaskan husky, sent a slight shiver down Brad's spine. His pate was slightly bald and his hands and forearms were very muscular. An imposing package. One cold-blooded reptile. But the singular quality that impressed Brad the most was his height. He judged him to be at least six foot, five inches tall, and his most immediate comparison was with Robert Wadlow, the Alton (Illinois) Giant.

Wadlow was the tallest person in the world, a huge monolith of a man at eight foot, ten inches tall in his stocking feet. He died in 1940 when a metal brace on his leg caused a blister that led to blood poisoning. But unlike the Gentle Giant, as Wadlow was known, this man at the table looked menacing.

"Mr. Walters," Brad said in lowered tones. "Do you realize there's a fellow over there who's been watching us the whole time I've been here?"

Robert Wadlow – World's tallest man (Madison Cnty. Hist. Soc.)

"Relax kid. That's Roland Jones, my most trusted bodyguard. He can crush walnuts with his bare hands and can shoot the eyes out of a squirrel at fifty paces. We've known each other since we were kids when I lived in north St. Louis. We've gone through a lot together, and there ain't nothin' we wouldn't do for each other."

Brad could feel the tenseness in the back of his neck begin to melt away with that reassurance.

Knucky unconsciously rubbed his forehead with his fingers. Then he consulted an expensive-looking gold watch. "I gotta go now." He stood and pulled the French cuffs out the ends of his suit coat. "Goin' out to the Fairmount race track to see the ponies run. Have ya ever been here at the Club 501 before?"

"This is my first time," Brad said, "but I work late every once in a while, and this is close to my office."

"Why not make it a regular habit? I kinda like ya, kid. Ya seem honest, intelligent an' easy to talk to. Unlike most of the other palookas I associate with, I don't have to watch my P's an' Q's, an' I can tell ya what I really think. That's kind o' refreshing. Whadda ya say? You can teach me a little of your book learnin', an' I'll give it to ya straight an' drop some tips about survivin' in the real world."

"Suits me fine." One of Brad's professors told him the first thing a successful lawyer does is to learn the power structure of the town where he works—both perceived and actual. ***This man is street savvy. I can learn some things from him,*** Brad thought. He wasn't really sure if getting friendly with Knucky was such as great idea, but based on the flow of their conversation that first evening, he reasoned there couldn't be any harm. Besides, Brad knew his sheltered life left him vulnerable. He figured Knucky was a graduate of the School of Hard Knocks and thought life itself was war.

Knucky knew the ins and outs of East St. Louis politics and was savvy at negotiating the bureaucracy at City Hall. He was reputed to have great instincts. Knucky was a street fighter who knew what it took to survive in a world crammed with challenges, disappointments and danger. But Brad also knew Walters was a member of the criminal class and was used to getting his way, even though it meant playing by a different set of rules and bribing or intimidating lawyers, judges, police officials and politicians.

Brad figured it was an unlikely friendship and he would need to be careful. He couldn't understand why Knucky would want to waste his time talking to someone like him. It made no sense. Brad figured Knucky took a liking to him because he knew he didn't want anything: a loan, a favor, or residual power that came from rubbing elbows with him.

Knucky went to the hat rack, grabbed a gray Fedora, and brushed back a lock of hair as he placed it on his head. The big burly man got up from a corner table and preceded him out the door. Brad noticed a slight bulge under his suit coat. He figured it was a shoulder holster, home to a nickel-plated revolver with six .38 slugs which probably had been manufactured at the Winchester/Western plant in nearby East Alton. Brad looked out the window and saw them climb into an expensive-looking Fleetwood Cadillac. Black, of course.

Probably loaded with extras, like bulletproof glass and gun ports, Brad mused. He finished his meal, left a larger than usual tip. He didn't want them to read him as cheap. Then he headed back to the office.

CHAPTER 2

The railroads built East St. Louis. The Illinois & St. Louis, constructed in 1837 to haul coal from the bluffs down to the Mississippi River, was the *first in the state.* In its early years it almost went bankrupt but by 1860 it was the richest dollar-per-mile railroad in America. By 1950, the city had 27 different railroads and was the second largest rail center in the nation. The railroads allowed the city to tap the agricultural hinterland and beat the drums to promote manufacturing and commerce.

Friendly little Litchfield was a quiet, archetypal Midwest village, a little more than fifty-five miles northeast of East St. Louis. It had long been taken for granted that small towns like this in Middle America fostered a healthy moral climate. Much of this was myth, but the people who lived there clung to the notion that life in a small hamlet was conducive to moral responsibility and produced upright qualities.

Midwesterners, particularly people from Illinois, generally thought of themselves as salt-of-the-earth types—honest, hard working, ambitious, self-reliant folk who were the backbone of America. The Land of Lincoln was the breadbasket of America. Prairie state residents took pride in the fact that Illinois (Algonquin for ***superior men***) was the only state in 1950 to rank in the top ten both industrially and agriculturally. And people from the heartland had the audacity to believe they were the only ones in the entire nation who didn't speak with an accent.

Litchfield's population numbered six thousand or so. Employment could be found at Roll-A-Way Skate Company, American Radiator, Brown Shoe, Schutt Athletic Clothing, and the Litchfield Creamery. Much of the population was composed of retired farmers and coal miners that had worked the mines at Gillespie and Farmersville. Their chief source of excitement was to gather every day in barbershops and taverns, or on wooden benches at the park in Town Square, known as Library Park.

One group of old-timers whittled with Barlow knives while arguing national politics or talking about the weather. People watching. Surveying fellow citizens. They were good at telling jokes and tall tales, particularly Grandpa Roy Armistead, a wily old-timer with a thick shock of white hair and a ready wit. Decades of farming under an unforgiving sun had taken their toll. His deeply tanned face was a road map of crevices and his sandy hair had been bleached, transforming him into a celluloid negative.

He spoke with an old-fashioned Midwest drawl. "Hey, Otto, didya' hear Luther Burbank once crossed a milkweed with an eggplant?"

"No, what happened?"

Gramps put his thumbs in the straps of his bib overalls. "He ended up with custard pie."

Otto thought that was a real knee-slapper. He was a few years older than Roy and frequently reminisced about seeing the fire that destroyed the Planet Mill in 1893.

Roy tugged at his suspenders. "Hear 'bout the gentleman farmer over in Livingston who accidentally put his tractor in reverse?"

Otto was loosening the strings on his tobacco pouch, getting ready to roll a cigarette. "Don't believe I have. What on earth happened?"

"Unplowed five acres before he could get the infernal machine stopped. He called me the other day and wanted me to come over and take a look at his prized three-year-old yearling."

Sometimes the oldtimers would spend hours exchanging tall tales and cracker-barrel philosophies about life.

* * *

Litchfield was named for its "first citizen," Electus Bacchus Litchfield, who settled in the area around 1853. The place had an interesting connection to East St. Louis. Cahokia Creek, snaking its way into East St. Louis just north of the Stock Yards, with waters dedicated to the Mississippi River, had its origins in Litchfield. Route 66, that had a bypass route through East St. Louis, cut across Litchfield on the west side of town.

In a place like this, there are restless young people, intrigued by life outside their insular world. The quaint, picturesque life that fascinated Norman Rockwell was suffocating isolation to many of them.

The most popular gathering place of the young folk was the town's largest drug store where they congregated by the soda fountain, or in booths that lined the walls. The soda jerk behind a marble counter was equally adept at manufacturing

root beer floats, strawberry phosphates or hot fudge sundaes. Boys mostly dressed in flannel shirts, letter sweaters and dungarees while the girls were typically decked out in skirts with poodle appliqués, bobby socks and saddle oxfords or penny loafers.

The teens ordered hamburgers and malts and pondered the future. Sometimes they discussed their plans and contemplated what it would be like to be a movie star and leave your mark on the world. They complained endlessly about the most irritating facet of small town life—living in a fishbowl under oppressive communal scrutiny. Everybody knew everybody else's business.

Some were restless. They were anxious to pack their bags and escape the mundane life of Dullsville. They longed to experience life in the big city where unlimited opportunities awaited and exciting careers beckoned. An adventuresome life was there for the taking.

Ayn Rand – author of *The Fountainhead*

"I want to go to New York and become a famous writer like Ayn Rand," said one girl, tossing her strawberry blonde hair.

The girl next to her stopped sipping her phosphate. "I wouldn't mind being a ***Life*** photographer like Margaret Bourke-White, traveling all over the world."

"Getting paid for taking pictures." Her boyfriend was slurping a fountain Coke from a paper cone resting inside a stainless steel container. "Can you believe it?" he said.

Boys had the freedom to pretty well do as they pleased. But girls, constrained by the social order of the day, had to talk their parents into going along with the notion of leaving.

Most, of course, never realized their pubescent dreams and married the boy next door or the girl behind the counter at the local confectionery and went to seed in Litchfield. Many were relatively happy with their lot in life—a loving spouse, two or three kids and a burdensome mortgage. But there were those who led lives of quiet desperation, always nurturing the inner resentment that they had settled for less than life had to offer.

Margaret White on Chrysler Bldg.

The majority of the parents in Litchfield were born and raised in the area, and most all of them came from European stock—Germans, Poles, Czechs and Irish were most prevalent. They were provincial in outlook with a fear of outsiders and a dread of any big city. Most were imbued with strong religious convictions. One could tell by their conversation that they pictured East St. Louis as Sin City, full of temptation and pitfalls for the unwary, and a good place to avoid. Consequently, they stifled the subject when the younger crowd dared to bring it up. The teen set was forced to wait and dream. And wait and dream most of them did, until the idea shriveled and died.

One of the Litchfield dreamers endowed with wanderlust was Lorna Sanders, a country girl whose family was slightly upscale from most in town. Her roots went deep into rock-solid midwestern traditions. Her father, Noel, was a carpenter and Margaret, her mother, was an elementary schoolteacher.

Margaret's lineage was tinged with blue blood, but the subject was almost never broached at home. One of those proud Armisteads, she was a descendant of General George Armistead, the man who defended Old Glory at Fort McHenry during the War of 1812. Francis Scott Key had watched in awe, scribbling furiously on the back of a letter while the British unsuccessfully bombarded the place. Another twig of the family tree could be traced to General Lewis Armistead, who was killed during Pickett's ill-fated charge during the third day of battle at Gettysburg.

Lorna's dad had built them a comfortable three-bedroom bungalow on Monroe Street on the outskirts of town. Lorna's grandpa, Roy Armistead, lived with them, sleeping in the extra bedroom. Her father was somewhat of a leader and authority figure among his peers. He came of sturdy stock, honest, ambitious and God-fearing. His dad had been a dirt farmer near Steelville, Missouri. He grew up watching his father toil from sunup to sunset with not much to show for his efforts. Crop prices always seemed to be abysmally low, and farmers were at the mercy of Mother Nature. The economic wheels seemed out of balance when it came to agriculture. If

Mr. and Mrs. Noel Sanders – Lorna's parents

the weather and rain cooperated, the harvest was bountiful. But high yields only brought lower prices. If insects, hail, drought or fungus took their toll, prices went higher due to scarcity, but one usually had less to sell. Farmers were ongoing victims of processsors, middlemen, retailers and the Chicago Board of Trade.

Noel's bloodline was undistinguished except somewhere he was related to the popular singer Buddy Clark, who hit the top of the charts with "Linda." Clark died in a tragic 1949 California plane crash. Noel's ancestors had come to this country in the post-Civil War era, looking for a new life and economic opportunity. He was the church treasurer and taught an adult Sunday school class—a man to whom many went for advice. His opinions were respected. He was a rugged individualist in the Hoover tradition. The way he saw it, as outlined in the Bible, it was up to each person to make his way in the world through his own initiative and industry.

The family's social life was limited to occasional visits with relatives. After Margaret came home from school, fixed supper, cleaned up the dishes and graded papers, it was nearly time to go to bed and get some sleep to recover for the next day's routine. Noel worked six days a week building spec houses but gave the Lord his due on Sundays, a traditional day of rest. His pet dog, Trixie, was always by his side, but his real joy, and the main soft spot in his heart, was his loving daughter, Lorna.

When their daughter was born, she was named for the Lorna Doone character, the heroine of R. D. Blackmore's novel. The book had been one of her mother's favorites. She grew up in a home with typical midwestern sentiments: family, church, work. As an only child, she received the full scrutiny of her parents, especially her mother. Margaret kept strict control over her life, even to the point of deciding what books she should read. Lorna's bookshelf was stuffed with Bobbsey Twin adventures, ***Black Beauty***, ***The Wizard of Oz***, ***The Yearling***, ***Little Women***, and other literature she deemed appropriate for her daughter. Margaret had even invested in a set of encyclopedias and ten volumes of Collier books containing an anthology of tales and stories for young people.

But a high school English teacher's passion for modern literature rubbed off on Lorna. He seduced her precocious young mind, introducing her to that which was provocative, more daring, more mature. Lorna became incurably fascinated with the type of book that might have been banned in Boston by puritanical prudes. She used her library card to secure copies of Virginia Woolf's ***Mrs. Dalloway, 1984*** by George Orwell, and ***The Little Foxes*** by Lillian Hellman. Convinced her mother would disapprove, she hid them behind other books that were on her shelves.

Lorna's voyeurism through a literary world fashioned by wordsmiths was exposed one day when her mother discovered the contraband while she was dusting shelves. The ensuing confrontation wasn't pretty.

"Look what I found in your room, young lady," Margaret said as she shook the book in her daughter's face.

"Mother, you had no right to invade my privacy."

"Are you trying to tell me what I can or can't do in my own house?"

Lillian Hellman

"It's called snooping, Mother. Don't you have any respect for me as a person?"

"Don't you try to turn me into the bad person here." Margaret held the offending book at arm's length and read the title. "***Ulysses***: I've heard about this book—it's immoral. You should be ashamed of yourself." She tossed the book on Lorna's bed.

Lorna picked it up, walked over, placed the volume on her bookshelf and ran her hand horizontally across the spines of the others. "I've read all of these books, Mother. They've taught me some interesting and important things. But they're written for twelve-year-olds."

Margaret stood firm and resolute; her arms crossed in typical school marm disapproval.

Lorna pulled her Bible from the shelf and clutched it to her chest. "I've read the Good Book from front to back, Genesis to Revelation, three times since it was given to me by my Sunday school teacher."

"But why do you want to read this other trash?" Margaret asked.

"It's not trash. These books have won prizes and are hailed as classics. They're considered ***important***, just like the ones you gave me. I need to be exposed to other ideas that are out in the world I'm going to live in. I need to learn how to weigh and consider those ideas against what I have always been taught. That's the only way truths and principles in the Bible will ever make sense."

Margaret looked disbelievingly at her daughter—her own flesh and blood: the large hazel eyes that were darker than her father's, rounder than her mother's; the long slightly upturned nose she'd inherited from her grandmother; small bow-shaped lips that were smallish; a tall lithe figure that was a genetic imprint from the Sanders side of the family.

Margaret didn't give an inch. "I didn't feel compelled to do that when I was your age," she said. "It's rebellion, pure and simple."

"Don't you see, Mom? I'm me, not you. I've got my own set of ideas and perceptions that need to be explored. You apparently didn't feel the need for that. I do. But it's not rebellion; it's the process of growing up. And are you forgetting that your favorite book was ***Lorna Doone***?"

"That's different. I was older than you when I read that book."

Lorna threw up her hands in exasperation. She and her mother never came to a meeting of minds on that subject. Lorna tried her best to be respectful, but she knew her mother had been hurt by the exchange of words. She could sense the tone of reproof and disappointment in Margaret's voice. It was almost as if she thought Lorna had backslid and lost her religion. An icy silence separated them for nearly two weeks before things got back to half normal.

Margaret would have been even more upset had she found Lorna's copy of Daniel Defoe's ***Moll Flanders***.

There would be no mad, heart-wrenching flings with boyfriends for Lorna. She was popular and dated regularly, but avoided intimacy, knowing that an unexpected pregnancy would ruin her reputation and break her parents' hearts. Whenever a boy became demanding, she broke up with him and moved on to someone new. She earned good grades because she didn't want to disappoint Mom and Dad. Lorna immersed herself in after school activities and earned awards and honors because she knew her mother, in particular, had high hopes for her.

Lorna's only other conflict with authority at home came when she met a boy from Quincy at band camp her junior year in school. Bruce was enamored with her and she with him. Her parents voiced strong disapproval when they discovered he was Catholic. They were determined that their daughter would marry within the confines of Protestantism. The pair exchanged frequent letters during her senior year. He even came to town one weekend and they secretly dated when Lorna told her parents she was staying all night at Alene Vancil's slumber party. Alene was in the band with Lorna at school, and the two had become best friends and confidants.

Near the end of Lorna's senior year, Bruce suggested that they elope and present her parents with a ***fait accompli***—a done deal. She gave it serious consideration but finally said *no* and ended the relationship. Lorna just couldn't do that to her parents. She knew full well it would crush them.

Lorna and her date as Popeye and Olive Oyl

Lorna had one more battle to fight. The expectation of college had been drummed into her ever since she could remember. But now, on the exciting threshold of adulthood, she had grown weary of school and wanted something different for her life—perhaps a career, combined with further education at a business school. In high school, she had developed a talent for grammar, typing and working with numbers. A business teacher in school said that her abilities could be put to use in a good paying job either in St. Louis or East St. Louis.

From that day on, Lorna seemed to change. She hungered for the possibilities of cosmopolitan life and opportunity, but she had difficulty mustering the courage to tell Mom and Dad about her ambitions.

When she finally broached the subject with her mother, Margaret angrily told her that neither she nor Noel ever wanted to hear the subject again. Margaret knew intuitively that at the tender age of eighteen Lorna wasn't ready for life's challenges in the big city. She needed an additional four years of weaning behind the cloistered walls of academia.

"You're going to get a college education, young lady," Margaret said. "That way you'll receive proper instruction and find some eligible young bachelor to marry—perhaps a doctor or lawyer."

"It isn't fair," Lorna protested. "All my life you've been in charge. You've told me what to read, what clubs to join, and with whom to be friends."

"That's what mothers are supposed to do, dear. Everything I've done has always been in your best interests. Someday you'll thank me for it."

"But I want to make my own decisions, make my own mistakes, lead my own life."

"Shirley Smith told her mother the same thing. Like you, she didn't appreciate everything her mother did for her. Remember that Dwayne Bland guy Shirley was infatuated with? Her mother told me he was wrong for her. She did everything possible to break them up, but Shirley wouldn't listen."

"Did you ever stop to think that it was her mother's meddling that pushed Shirley into that disastrous relationship?" Lorna said. "Her mother's good intentions drove her to make that choice. She was so desperate to get away from her mother's smothering influence, she decided the risk was worth it."

"But mothers know more about these things because of experience," Margaret protested. "Look at the heartache Shirley could have avoided if she would have followed her mother's advice."

"You don't understand. The only way young people grow up is to have the freedom to make their own decisions and learn from their mistakes."

"I'll never understand why some daughters don't appreciate what their parents do for them."

"I love both of you with all my heart, but it's time I started living my own life. You can't do that for me."

In the end, Lorna gave in. She promised her mother that she would forget all about the idea. But as much as she tried, she could think of nothing else. She confided her longings to Alene and to her grandfather who lived with them, even winning him over to her side.

A few months later, Lorna graduated from high school with full honors. As a senior, she made All-State Band on the oboe, and naturally her parents were quite proud of her.

Lorna was cognizant of the plans her parents had for her, and the very thought of them upset her. Being stuck with the drudgery of four more years of school when life was just beginning just wasn't for her. She was desperate to have a try at a career. She thought of running away from home but quickly put that thought behind her. Finally, Lorna surrendered to her parents' wishes and went to college that fall at Southern Illinois University in Carbondale, taking mostly general studies courses. But her heart wasn't in it and she merely went through the motions, ending up with a mere B average for the year.

Lorna spent the summer working at the local library but hated the idea of returning to school in the fall. She resolved to have one more talk with her dad to see if perhaps he hadn't softened a little on her pursuing a career. She had always been close to him and knew he was the weak link. If she could win him over first, it just might be the wedge she needed to use against her mother. She brought her grandfather along for moral support.

"Daddy," said Lorna one balmy night after an August storm, "I want to talk to you for a few minutes. I have something important to discuss."

"What in tarnation is this? Are you two ganging up to talk me into buying you that new dress you saw in the Monkey Ward catalogue a while back?" He gave a sly wink at Grandpa Armistead. He hadn't the foggiest that his daughter was going to bring up the career thing again.

"Listen Daddy," Lorna pleaded, "do you want to know why my grades in college weren't nearly as good as those in high school?"

Noel nodded but remained silent. His pulse quickened as it began to dawn on him what this was all about.

"Well, it's because my heart wasn't in it. I tried to do what you and mother wanted but it just didn't work out. I wrote to Summers College of Commerce in East St. Louis. They can train me as a legal secretary in a rigorous two-year curriculum. I can hold down a full-time job and take the classes at night. Their tuition is fifty dollars every four months. I can stay at the Beulah Club, which is a place of residence for single women. They only charge twenty-five dollars a month for room and board. Grandpa said he would help with expenses.

"Did you agree to this?" Noel asked Grandpa Armistead.

"I certainly did," he replied in a high-pitched cantankerous voice. "I think this girl has a lot of spunk, and I'll be more than happy to help whenever I can."

Lorna continued her efforts to persuade. "Since I was fourth in my graduating class at high school, I should be able to secure part-time work with one of the lawyers in town. That sounds very reasonable Daddy, and I know I won't have any trouble with my studies. I'm still young, and two years isn't such a very long time to spend at anything, if, in the end, there is a chance to really make something of myself. There is good money in the legal field and there is no limit to how high a person can go, if she makes up her mind to succeed. If it doesn't work out, then I'll go back to college, just like you and Mom planned."

Noel, reaching down to pet Trixie, sat in stunned silence. He hadn't anticipated the subject being brought up again.

"I'll be well taken care of, Daddy," Lorna was saying softly, "and just think of it, I can take a Greyhound back home to visit you and Mom once a month on a weekend. Won't it make you proud to be able to tell folks you've reared a daughter who can take care of herself, and who really will amount to something some day? I need you to say yes. It's the only way I'll ever convince Mother to let me go."

Noel was still speechless as he tried to absorb everything Lorna was telling him.

"If Mother says yes, will you please go with me and make sure everything goes all right? Can we go, Daddy?"

With a big hug and a kiss, Noel was forced to agree to something very unfavorable from his point of view. After all, how could anybody refuse this beautiful daughter of his anything when she looked and spoke in such a manner?

In order to approach her mother just right, she once again enlisted the aid of her grandfather. The next evening, after supper, Margaret was on the sofa knitting. Her needles bobbed and weaved like a dragonfly. Noel was at his living room desk making out checks to pay bills for the church. He kept one eye riveted on the proceedings. The pair walked in and sat down beside Margaret, one on each side.

"Mother, I need to talk to you."

Margaret had an intuitive gift about these things. She sniffed a conspiracy. "It's about your not wanting to go back to college, isn't it?" she said, keeping her eyes down, her needles working furiously.

"Yes," Lorna said quietly.

"You've always been such a good student. You would just be wasting your life if you forgo college."

"I'm tired of school, Mother. I've lost interest. After thirteen long years I want to try something else."

Margaret placed her knitting on the coffee table so she could direct her full energy to the matter at hand. She looked helplessly at Grandpa Armistead.

"Will you please help me talk some sense into my daughter?"

Grandpa's eyes, dulled somewhat with age, still twinkled. "I can't do that, Margaret. I happen to agree with my granddaughter."

Margaret closed her eyes and shook her head in disbelief. "Pray tell, what do you want to do, child, become a waitress?"

"I want to enroll in a business school in East St. Louis and pursue a career as a legal secretary."

"Have you taken leave of your senses?"

"I've already talked it over with Daddy. He said if that was what I really wanted to do, he would support my decision."

Margaret looked sternly at her husband. "Noel, is it true? Has she already discussed this matter with you?"

Noel's shoulders sagged a bit. "Yes, dear. I don't agree with her choice but I respected her right to make it."

Margaret threw Noel a look of disapproval, and then focused her attention back on her daughter.

Rosie the Riveter's sister

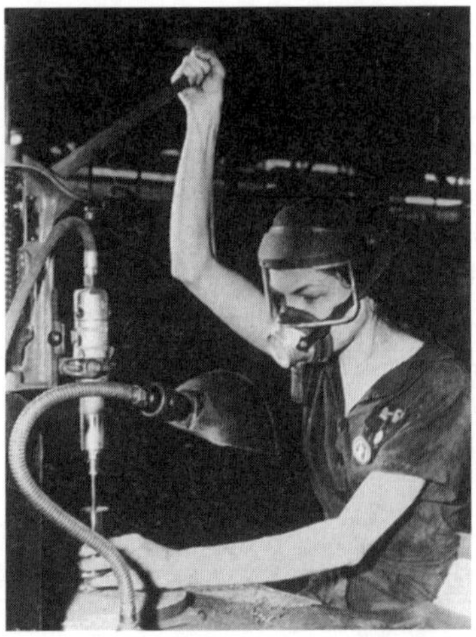

"And what kind of a husband do you think you'll find in East St. Louis?"

"I want to pursue a career," Lorna said. "My primary goal isn't to find a husband. Men have found fulfillment in work for hundreds of years. Now, thanks to women who filled in for men during the war and performed so well, I too have that option."

"Great, we have another 'Rosie the Riveter' in the family," Margaret said.

"You're not being fair, Mother. I want to give myself that chance. I want to see how far my talents can take me."

Margaret, feeling besieged and outnumbered, eventually gave in to Lorna's insistent demands. But not before she let Lorna know how disappointed she was in her, and that she just knew the day would come when she would say, "I told you so."

A few days later, Noel bought two train tickets. It was a great day for Lorna the morning they left. She anticipated excitement, witty and urbane office camaraderie, being able to tell friends back home about her exciting career. Marriage and children would come later . . . maybe. Lorna was ready to defy the canons of prevailing social convention. She was on the threshold of life's big adventure.

* * *

The second time Brad ate supper with Knucky Walters at the Club 501 Lounge, he began pumping him with questions. Roland, his ever-present bodyguard, was incongruently reading a Casper the Ghost comic—watchful yet detached.

"Ya know what, kid? If we're goin' to spend time exchanging pleasantries, there's a thing or two I need your word on."

"What's that?"

Walters' features hardened and his tone became serious. "Everything we talk about is unofficial, off the record an' confidential. Ya don't breathe a word of this to nobody—***not*** your girl friend, ***not*** the police, ***not*** the newspapers, ***not*** your dog. Don't ever ask me anything specific about my business. I want ya to look me straight in the eye an' give me your word."

Brad had a slightly stunned look on his face. He let what Knucky had just said sink in for a few moments. He knew secrecy was the coin of the realm in Walters' world and wondered about the shadows that lived within him. Brad extended his hand: "You can trust my discretion."

Walters' hands were larger than Brad's and his handshake was strong. Brad reciprocated with an equally firm grip. His dad had told him long ago that a man's handshake told a lot about his character.

"I know I can trust ya to keep your word," he said. "I can tell you're one of those principled idealistic types—truth, justice an' the American way. A Joe Citizen who thinks he can make the world a better place by words an' deeds. You mean well kid, but ya sure have a lot to learn."

Brad had done a little research from newspaper articles and court records on Gotham's chief villain. To wit: Knucky, street smart since he was seven, had served about eight years of a 1933 prison sentence for resisting arrest when the Feds raided a Shelton gang still he was guarding near Collinsville, Illinois. While Knucky was in prison, gang wars and the legalization of liquor cut down the ranks of the Sheltons, who were finally run out of the area by local sheriff, Jerome Munie. On his release, Walters moved quickly and soon gained control of slots, pinball machines and jukeboxes. He also consolidated his hold on gambling parlors and loan-sharking.

Between 1947 and 1950, three of the Shelton brothers were murdered—Bernie in Peoria, and Roy and Carl near their homes in Wayne County. Most of the old-timers had faded into the background, and young hoodlums who came along to challenge Walters after the war fought among themselves and ultimately fell victim to unsolved murder or mysterious disappearance.

Walters, a strange agglomeration of talent, moods and temperament, had been arrested over a dozen times since his release from prison, but nothing substantial was ever pinned on him.

His most recent move was into labor racketeering. Knucky learned that if you control a work force, you have an important base of power. The coffers from the union dues were brimming with capital. Union members and their families were an important source of political clout. They tended to vote in lockstep on issues that were perceived to affect their livelyhoods.

Knucky's hegemony was rumored to extend from Litchfield to Cairo, with East St. Louis being the linchpin of his empire. Frank Zito and his brothers held sway over the Springfield area. Knucky's lieutenants were given specific territories, and enforcers did the dirty work. The lieutenants reigned over countless footsoldiers – guys with more brawn than brains – who ran errands and handled the daily street hustlings. He also had a cadre of informants (newsboys, taxi drivers, waiters, bartenders, hotel clerks) on his payroll that passed along information to keep him abreast of political change and possible coups. To put it quite simply, in the metro area Knucky was public domain—news.

"I have a request or two of my own, if you don't mind," Brad said. "I don't feel at ease calling you by your first name. If it's all right with you, I'd just as soon call you ***Mr.*** Walters."

"Fine! If that's what ya want."

"One more thing. Because of my church background, I'm not comfortable being around people who use vulg—uh, rough talk. Could you try to watch your language?" Brad had learned from experience that Walters' patter was often rife with blue words.

"I can respect that," he said. "Me an' my friends cuss like sailors occasionally, but when we're around our wives an' kids, we tone it down. I'll probably slip up once in a while, but I'll do the best I can."

"Thanks, I appreciate it."

Knucky tore away the wrapping and fished a Chesterfield from the cigarette pack. "Brad, you're what they call a well-educated lad, right?"

"No more than anyone else who graduates from college with good grades," Brad grinned.

Knucky pulled a gold-plated cigarette lighter from his breast pocket, flipped it open and flicked his thumb across the roller mechanism; a spark flew from the flint and lit the flame, all in one smooth motion. "But what do they teach ya—anything useful or interesting?"

Usually, that kind of question is meant to be a put-down, but Brad could tell he was sincere and was probably trying to find out if he had missed anything significant by dropping out of school.

"You learn about a wide range of subjects in college," Brad said. "They not only try to prepare you for a profession, their intent is to give you perspective and to broaden your horizons. That's why they require everyone to take courses in literature, art, history, geography, philosophy and science. You're supposed to benefit from learning about the collective wisdom of the ages."

Knucky turned his head and spat a flake of loose tobacco off his tongue. He stared at Brad with his piercing brown eyes. His index finger was lightly tapping on the surface of the table. "Yeah, but what good is all that stuff? Give an example of how it helps ya in real life."

Ever the pragmatist!

"Let me think a minute," Brad said. He frantically searched the inner recesses of his brain to come up with an example that would impress him. "Have you ever heard of a novel called ***Moby Dick*** by Herman Melville?" Brad didn't wait for him to be embarrassed by the silence. "It's about this seaman called Captain Ahab who is trying to find and kill a white whale named Moby Dick. You see, in an earlier encounter, the whale bested him and caused him to lose one of his legs, and he was obsessed with revenge."

"So, what's ***that*** supposed to teach ya?" Knucky wondered out loud.

"It's a tale with a lesson."

"What's the lesson?"

"Well . . . I think it's about controling your passions, and that sometimes hate can be so powerful and consuming, it might be self-destructive if it isn't bridled."

"What do ya mean, teach ya something—is it kind of like one of them Aesop fables?"

"That's pretty good. A valid comparison. Except nowadays Aesop fables are more for children and classic literature is appropriate for adults."

"How does the story come out? Does he find this whale that made him a cripple?"

"Yes, but in the final struggle, Ahab gets tangled in a harpoon line and the whale drags him to the bottom of the ocean and he drowns."

Walters' combative and retaliatory instincts surfaced. "Too bad, but I don't see where this Ahab guy had any choice. If this whale did a bad thing to him, he had to do his best to let him know who was boss. If someone tried to muscle in on my territory or killed one of my boys, I'd have to teach 'em a lesson. It's a dog-eat-dog world. Can't let people push ya around."

"'Cry havoc, and let slip the dogs of war,' " Brad mused.

"What's that mean?" Knucky asked.

"It's a line from a Shakespeare play—he's considered the best you know."

"I heard of him before. Didn't he write some mushy love story about Romano an' Julie?"

"Yes, it was "Romeo and Juliet." They were star-crossed lovers."

"Star-crossed?"

"It means their love was doomed from the very beginning," Brad explained. "The Arabs have a different word for fate—they call it ***kismet.***"

"A-rabs? You mean those guys who ride camels and live in the desert? I was a young man when I saw the movie ***The Sheik*** with that Valentino lover boy character. I always thought he was a Rudie."

"What is a Rudie?"

"You know—a fruit, a queer."

"Oh!"

"How come we never see any of them A-rabs around here?" Walters inquired. "This town is a regular Heinz 57 varieties—full of Wops, Krauts, Bohunks, Micks, Spicks and Polacks."

"They seem to be content with their way of life and stay in North Africa and the Middle East." Brad said. "But their architectural style, with pointed arches, has had an influence on East St. Louis. Both the Majestic Theater and the Ainad Temple are done in Arabesque—that's French for 'in the Arab way.' "

"Hard to believe. Both of those buildings are within hollerin' distance an' I always wondered why they looked different from the others. By the way, how come educated people are always using foreign words? Who do they think they're tryin' to impress?"

"I have to admit, some people believe they are better than everyone else and walk around with their noses in the air. But the use of those words and foreign phrases is supposed to help language and meaning be more exact and make sentences more expressive and interesting to listen to or read. Flowery language helps evoke graphic mental images. Speaking of the Majestic Theater and Valentino, do you like to go to the movies?"

"I liked movies as a kid. How 'bout that Douglas Fairbanks in those swashbuckling pirate movies. An' Ronald Colman was great in ***Beau Geste***. But I don't go no more except to drop my kids off at the Saturday matinees. I always ask the ticket lady what time to pick them up when the show is finished. What else do ya know that's interesting?"

"Let me think . . . you're Catholic, right?"

Ronald Colman

"Yeah, if my policy hasn't lapsed."

"Well, did you know back in the seventeenth century, the church had all-male choirs?"

"So? What's unusual 'bout that?"

"In order for the choir to sound good, they needed high voices to blend with the alto, tenor and bass. So certain boys were castrated before puberty and their pitch stayed soprano. They were called castratos."

Knucky got wide-eyed.

"Holy Toledo! Can you think what it would be like having that done to you? The poor s.o.b.'s couldn't have sex with women. It would be almost as bad as being a fruit."

Brad wanted to hold Walters' interest so he continued his ribald history lesson. "The Roman emperors would castrate their male servants and turn them into eunuchs so they wouldn't mess with their wives. During the Middle Ages, the nobility made their wives wear chastity belts when they were away from the castle. This prevented them from having intercourse with other men because the husband had the only key. In some African countries, young females are held down by the mother while the father circumcises her."

"Crimeny! How do you circumcise a woman? She doesn't have a, uh, a spigot."

"They cut off her you-know-what. It's kind of like a very small spigot. Female circumcision is supposed to prevent them from enjoying sex so they won't seek it before they get married, even though they usually marry in their early teens. It's also done to keep them faithful to their husbands."

"This is unbelievable—do they teach ya that kind of stuff in college?"

"Well . . . you read a lot in school and you pick up some of these things along the way."

Knucky didn't say anything for a moment. He seemed to be letting it all soak in. "You know, talking about private parts reminds me about why I never eat Spam. They fed it regularly to the servicemen during the war. But I never touch the stuff. A friend of mine said that most of the meat in Spam comes from pig peckers mixed in with some better cuts of ham."

"I think he might have been misinformed or pulling your leg. The U.S. Department of Agriculture inspects packing plants and their products. Those things might be in cat food or dog food, but Spam is kind of like bologna—only bologna is beef and Spam is pork. Both are made from cheaper cuts of meat—but not the sex organs."

"Ya might be right, but I dunno. The meat inspectors can be bought off. I keep the heat off me by having a few policemen and some politicians on the dole. The real world works a little different than what you were taught in your civics lessons."

"Do you serve pig snouts here?"

"No way!"

"What about Rocky Mountain Oysters?"

"I never could figure out why people called them by that 'oyster' term. I wouldn't serve testicles at my place for all the tea in China."

"I don't think I could eat them either," Brad confessed. "How do restaurants fix them so they are edible?"

"First they boil them to get rid of the smell and odor. Then they are sliced and breaded and fried in a skillet. Some people actually consider them a delicacy, and others eat the 'oysters' because they think it makes them potent."

"You could offer me a hundred bucks and I still wouldn't touch them with a ten foot pole," Brad replied. "By the way, the term 'Rocky Mountain Oysters' is what is known as a euphemism—a nicer term for something crude or vulgar."

"Like when a hit man says 'You're goin' for a ride,' instead of telling the poor schmuck he's going to drill him full of holes?"

Brad smiled. "I never thought of it that way, but I guess that could qualify as a euphemism." He was a little uncomfortable with the topic, so he shifted gears. "Were you ever in the service?"

"Naw—I got into a fight with a Prohibition agent back in '32 an' he nearly died on the operating table. They sent me to the stir for that one. I did hard time at Alcatraz. Got out shortly after the war started, but Uncle Sam wasn't interested in having ex-cons in the military. Said we were undesirables, or somethin' like that. Guys like me who've done time are good with guns. The war probably would have been over sooner if they'd let us fight."

Brad noticed a picture on the wall in their booth. It was a 1920s era sepia-toned photo of some gang. There were more than a dozen desperadoes posed with their revolvers, rifles and machine guns. "Who are those guys?" he gingerly inquired.

"That's Charlie Birger and his crew. The car is an old Lincoln that he had outfitted with special armor plate. The guy on the end was my second cousin."

"Was?"

"Yeah, he got killed in a gun battle with the local authorities back in '33—just before they ended Prohibition."

Brad's eyes went back and forth across the picture. He couldn't get over how brazen all of them looked. "Which one is Charlie?"

"The cocky one in the middle. He was Lithuanian Jewish, you know. He's buried over in St. Louis."

Two men in nondescript suits barged through the front door as if they owned the place and made a beeline for Walters' booth, abruptly interrupting their conversation. The one in front walked with a John Wayne swagger while the smaller one traipsed along quietly behind. A study in contrasts. Walters' Clinched Fist started to get up, but the second man extended his arm with palm downward, the same way you tell a dog to "stay." Brad's eyes were riveted to the one towering over them. His hair was close cropped and a cigarette dangled from his tight lips. Brad guessed him to be slightly less than six foot tall, but he was built like a Sherman tank. He was fingering a key chain that had a bullet dangling from one end. He looked tough as nails—exactly like the kind of guy you wouldn't want to meet in a dark alley. Brad half expected smoke and fire to come out his nostrils.

"What are ya doin' here, Sweeney?" Knucky asked.

He placed a brace of gnarled hands on the table and leaned into Walters' face. "What can you tell me about the body we found out at Grand Marais?" he boomed.

His coat was open; a pistol hung heavy in his shoulder holster. The ivory grip featured a scrimshawed eagle. Brad found himself thinking: ***We're gonna need a doctor before this is over.***

"Surely you're not dumb enough to think I had anything to do with it," Knucky calmly replied.

"No I don't, but I'm willing to bet this month's salary you could point me in the right direction."

"Now why would I want to do a thing like that? I got a business to run. Why do ya expect me to do your work? Ain't there plenty of doakes out there ya can take back to the station and use a rubber hose on?"

A tight fist pounded the table. "D— it, Knucky, don't get smart-mouthed with me. It would be a cryin' shame if the inspector from the health department came over here and discovered how unsanitary your kitchen is and how many codes you are violating. That would shut you down for at least a month."

Knucky winced slightly.

"Okay, okay. Don't get your Irish bowels in an uproar. I can take a hint. I'll put out the word an' see what I can come up with. Don't expect any miracles. My guess is that this Torricelli guy had diarrhea of the mouth an' was going to spill the beans about somethin'. He certainly wasn't mixed up in any activities I had concerns about. But if it'll get your sorry butt out of my place any quicker, I'll get back with ya in about a week."

"Not good enough. Give me a name or something usable by Friday. My boss is fit to be tied over this one—says this kind of thing ruins the town's image and is bad for business."

Then Sweeney gave Brad a derisive once-over, looked at him with utter contempt and spat out, "Who's this twerp—one of your new drones? He must be a bookkeeper or something because he don't look tough enough to punch his way out of a paper bag."

Harpo Marx

Brad had been watching the verbal fracas as unobtrusively as possible. He was stung by the biting remarks but knew enough to remain as silent as Harpo, that curly blonde-haired Marx brother.

"Leave him outta this Sweeney. He don't work for me so he's not your concern. Why don't you an' your partner go see if you can catch some little old lady jaywalkin' or somethin'? I'll get back to ya in two or three days, now amscray—get lost."

Brad had never seen that much testosterone spilled in his entire life. Sweeney just stood there for a few seconds as though he were trying to think of some smart-alec comeback, but then he wheeled around and stormed out the door with his silent partner following close behind.

"I didn't know King Kong had a relative. Was that really Bob Sweeney, 'the law' in East St. Louis? "

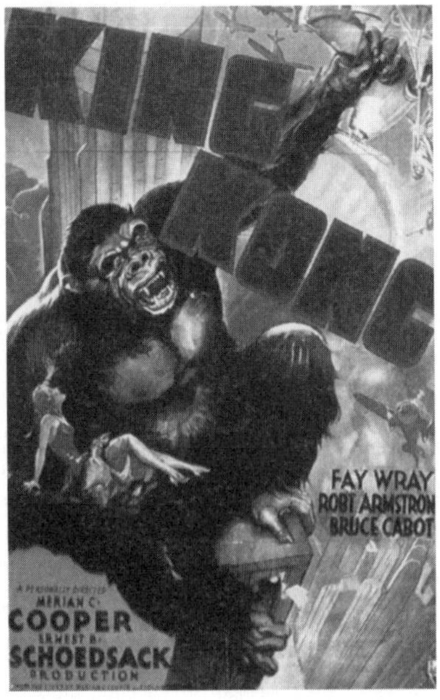

"Yeah, that was him." For punctuation Knucky smashed the lit stub of his cigarette into the ashtray so hard it bent in two like a man with a broken back. "Along with that dopey Jerry Sullivan. Sweeney ain't so tough."

"I couldn't take my eyes off that bullet on his key chain. What is that all about?"

"He tried to arrest a killer one time an' the guy beat him to the draw. Sweeney would have been pushin' up daisies but the man's gun jammed an' Sweeney drilled him full of holes. Sweeney was one lucky flatfoot that day. He took the bullet that jammed to Zerweck's an' had a key chain made for it. Calls it his good luck piece."

"Wow!" Brad said. "Sounds like a story straight out of 'Gang Busters.' "

"Yeah, well, one of these days he's gonna' push me too far an' I'll ... er, he'll be sorry."

"Do you know any other Sweeney war stories?" Brad asked enthusiastically.

"Uh huh, but you've heard enough for one day. I'd hate to have to come over tonight an' sit with ya because you're havin' nightmares."

"I don't believe it. I think Mr. Poker Face just cracked a joke."

A smile almost broke out on Walters' face. Almost.

"I've got to be going back to the office," Brad said. "Here. Nearly forgot. I brought you something I thought you might like to read." He slid a book across the table.

"Hate to disappoint ya kid, but I'm not much of a reader."

"I think you'll like this. It's called ***The Great Gatsby.*** It's a compelling story about this guy who gets mixed up with a bootlegger during Prohibition."

CHAPTER 3

East St. Louis detective Bob "Tree" Sweeney made $95 a month for a six-day week when he began his career in law enforcement in 1926. He killed twelve people in the line of duty (including Ma Barker's nephew). Sweeney knew his gun was his best friend and he spent a half an hour every day cleaning and polishing the chrome-plated Smith & Wesson. Every bullet was eyeballed for defects before being placed in the chambers.

The engineer gave two ear-splitting blasts on the whistle to let people know that the Green Diamond, pride of the Illinois Central Line, was preparing to depart from Litchfield. The IC had been raised to a level of immortality in a song about a legendary engineer named Casey Jones. The conductor yelled "All aboard!" looked for tardy passengers, then picked up the portable step. After about fifteen seconds, the smoke-belching behemoth flexed its steel muscles. The engine's powerful pistons strained to overcome the inertia of a tender, a mail car, and eight passenger cars. As the 200-ton engine slowly crept forward, Lorna felt only a slight jolt when the slack disappeared in the cast-metal knuckle couplers. The cars slowly moved past those on a set of nearby tracks owned by the Wabash Railroad. The Wabash went toward East St. Louis but bypassed the town by crossing the Merchant's Bridge several miles farther north and then proceded on to Union Station in St. Louis. It, too, was nationally famous because of a popular song, **"*The Wabash Cannonball.*"**

Locomotive number 1202, making its last run before being replaced by a sleek diesel, pulling more than one-hundred cars, thundered past on a set of adjacent tracks.

Click, clickety, clack. The rhythmical sound of the train streaking down the ballasted roadbed was music to Lorna's ears. Only now did she realize it was Litchfield's trains that had fomented her rebellion against the mind-numbing boredom of a small town. They became a metaphor for her desire to experience that world beyond the realm of her parent's Eden. The parallel ribbons of steel tempted her to taste the forbidden fruit of the vast expanse of world and beckoned her to leave her finite boundaries. It was the trains and the hum of the rails that pulled her grandiose dreams of escape down tracks that led to a new Utopia. This was her way of giving in to the restlessness that stirred her provincial soul. It was her response to some unnamable call of destiny.

The porter helped them store the luggage. During the train ride, Noel's mood reminded Lorna of the days he gave her piggyback rides and read her bedtime stories. On the surface he was jovial, but underneath his heart was sad at the thought of losing his girl . . . even though it was only to be for a month at a time.

There were no scheduled stops between Litchfield and East St. Louis. The train sped quickly across the flat prairie dominated by fields of corn, wheat and soybeans. Lorna's seat was next to the window, and she quickly became lost in her thoughts. ***Look at that, a brown chicken hawk soaring effortlessly on the thermals. He seems to be going backward . . . probably because he's moving slower than the train. Funny, my thoughts are doing the same: I'm looking forward to this adventure, but I find my mind drifting in reverse. What would it have been like if I had agreed to marry Bruce? Are Catholics really that different? Is religion that important? Hmm, now there are two hawks. Are they hunting as a pair or getting ready to mate? I wish I could have talked Alene into doing this with me. I wonder if I'll regret not going back to college? Look at them . . . so graceful.***

Lorna with Bruce, the Quincy guy she almost married

She loved the soft clickety-clack metallic sound the wheels made when they passed over jointed sections where ribbons of steel rails came together. Their coach swayed gently from side to side as it sped down the metal roadway. For an instant, the memory of her grade school teacher's story about John Henry's race with the steam drill flashed through her mind. It was one of those tall tales about a strong Negro who could hammer spikes into railroad ties faster than any man or machine.

"How fast are we going, Daddy?" she wondered out loud.

"I'm not sure. The old trains weren't equipped with speed gauges, but they have them now because most engineers went too fast. Back then, the engineer had to guess the speed based on how long it took the engine to pass from one point to another. There are mileposts that parallel the tracks and they used their watches to note the time between the markers. They memorized the tables. If it took forty-five seconds to go from one marker to the next, they knew the speed was about eighty miles an hour."

"Why is this train being pulled by an old-fashioned steam engine instead of one of those new diesels?" Lorna asked.

"The ticket agent said a bearing went out on the diesel at Springfield. In order to keep the train on schedule, they switched over to this old 4-6-2 Pacific."

"What is a 4-6-2?"

"Engines are designated by types according to the number of leading wheels, main drivers and trailers. Small switching engines used in rail yards are often 0-4-0s. If the engine is needed to pull big loads, it might be a 2 8 2. Engines are identified by these sets of wheels and are labeled by names such as "Atlantic," "Pacific," "Berkshire" or "Mikado."

The train rounded a curve and Lorna could see sooty columns of emissions, like a black vines reaching for the clouds.

"How do you know all of this stuff?"

"Before I met your mother, I worked a year for the Litchfield and Madison Railroad."

A no-nonsense, smartly dressed conductor came by and collected their tickets. He tore them in two, keeping the top half and returning the lower portion.

"Do you know who the engineer is on this train?" Noel asked the man in uniform.

"A fellow named Mark Godwin. Eldridge Worthhammer is the fireman."

"Well I'll be John Brown. I used to work with both of them."

"What an interesting coincidence," Lorna said. "You know, I like the fact that the diesels are quiet and aren't spewing forth all of that smoke and cinders, but I think the big black steam engines are more picturesque. Will we have to make any stops for water along the way?"

"No. This is a short run, and that won't be necessary. When these passenger trains go long distances, time is important, and they have a unique system to eliminate the need to stop for water. The tender has a special scoop mechanism that picks up water in metal troughs below the tracks at designated points. They are able to secure the water on the fly, eliminating the need for stopping."

"Doesn't picking up water that way make a big splash?" Lorna asked.

"It surely does. One time there was a hobo catching a free ride on a freight train that secured water in this manner. He was drenched to the bone by the spatter. It happened in the dead of winter, and by the time the train arrived at its destination, he was frozen stiff as a board."

"How awful!"

The Illinois Central Panama Limited by Roscoe Misselhorn

The train ate up the miles. In twenty-five minutes it passed through Alhambra, then skirted the edge of Edwardsville and quickly descended the bluffs as it chugged along the flat bottomland. With her face pressed against the expansive window of the day coach, Lorna saw the crops were different now. They were short and leafy green. Workers were bent over the plants, cultivating them by hand.

"What kind of crops are those, Daddy?"

"Horseradish, brought here by German immigrants. The roots are made into a spicy sauce that's often served with roast beef. It's also combined with ketchup to make cocktail sauce for fish and shrimp. Unlike corn or wheat, it's labor intensive. The land down here on the flood plain is perfectly suited for growing it. The locals claim that the soil is so rich you can plant nails and harvest crowbars."

Lorna's pretty face broke out into a broad smile.

"St. Clair and Madison counties grow so much of the stuff, it's referred to as the Horseradish Capital of America," Noel said. "Sometimes you see young teens working in the fields. Since most kids don't like to spend ten hours a day in the field doing backbreaking work, large numbers of migrant workers are hired. Most come from Mexico. The crop is a good moneymaker. It brings four or five times what farmers could get if they planted corn or soybeans."

"I never thought horseradish could be so interesting," Lorna said.

"I'm going back to the next car to talk a while with the conductor. Is that all right with you?" Noel asked.

"Sure, go ahead. I'll be fine."

While Lorna was looking out the window, a man who had been sitting across the aisle moved over and eased into the seat next to her. He was wearing a blue seersucker suit accented by a yellow polka dot tie.

"Excuse me, Miss," the man said in a husky voice.

Lorna was startled by his bold maneuver. "Yes, what is it?" she replied as she turned to face the stranger. He was tall and average looking. She judged him to be about six foot one and weighing near two hundred pounds. His voice was pleasant enough, but he had beady eyes and a certain gruffness of manner that was unnerving.

"My name is Robert Jenkins. I couldn't help but overhear you and your father talking. I'm one of the managers at Call Printing in East St. Louis. I've lived there for ten years now, and I would be more than happy to show you around town."

"It's nice of you to offer, Mr. Jenk—"

"Please, call me Robert."

His manner was making Lorna a little edgy. "Look, Mr. Jenkins, I appreciate your offer, but I can find things by myself. Now if you'll excuse me, I was just getting ready to go look for my father."

"What's the rush?" He leaned closer to Lorna, invading her privacy and making her feel uncomfortable. Then he blocked her path by extending his arm and grabbing hold of the seat in front of them. "I'm just trying to be friendly."

"Mr. Jenkins, I don't know you. We've never been formally introduced. I'm sure you are a nice man but—"

"Gee, doll, I just want to get to know you better. There wouldn't be any harm in that, would there?"

"Listen, Mr. whoever-you-are; if you don't—"

"HEY, buddy, why don't you stop bothering this lady?" Brad Logan, with a stern look on his face, placed his hand firmly on the man's shoulder.

Brad was taking the train home from Chicago. He had just met with clients who owned some freight terminals in East St. Louis and were involved in a dispute with another firm. He had been seated several rows behind Lorna and was reading the paper when he happened to look up and see what was going on.

"And why don't you mind your own business?" the man said as he jerked away from Brad's grasp.

"She happens to be my cousin. That makes it my business," Brad replied.

Lorna's jaw dropped a few inches. She had never seen this fellow in her life, and he certainly wasn't a relative. But she was immediately drawn to his clean good looks and wholesome appearance. She decided to go along with the ruse.

"Er, hello, uh, Tom. I'm sure this gentleman didn't mean to impose himself. I think he was just leaving."

The man, now red about the ears, glanced at Brad's initials on a gold tie clasp and found the letter "T" to be conspicuously absent. "Hey, what is this?" Instead of backing off, he became belligerent. "You don't even know this guy! Are you trying to give me the brush-off?"

A grade school boy in the seat ahead of them turned around and was up on his knees, his curiosity drawn to the commotion. He had just finished a soda and a bag of popcorn and now was chewing on a Switzer's licorice stick. His thoughts were bright with anticipation.

"Please turn around in your seat, Arnold," his mother said as she tried to coax him with her hand.

"But, Mom, I don't want to miss this," he said, with eyes as big as a pair of Moon pies.

"Look fella, can't you take a hint?" Brad said. "The lady isn't interested in your company. Buzz off."

The angry man rose from the seat. "Who asked you to butt in?" he retorted, turning his full wrath on Brad Logan.

Lorna's heart sank as the man flicked out his fist, which landed squarely on Brad's jaw. Taken by surprise, he staggered back slightly. By this time nearly everyone in the car was focusing on the ruckus. Those farthest away were craning their necks to see what was going on. The air hung heavy with the fragrance of the boy's confections—and the exciting smell of a fight. Lorna couldn't believe this was happening and shrank back against the window.

Brad flexed his jaw muscles to see if everything still worked. Undaunted, he got back in the man's face. "I guess you didn't understand me," he said with a look of determination.

The man lunged forward with his fist again, but Brad flung out his arm and caught him by the wrist.

"Wow! Did you see that?" the awestruck youngster said to his mom. "That was fast, really fast."

"Didn't your parents teach you any manners?" Brad said. "Why don't you just quietly walk away, and we'll forget the whole thing."

Jenkins tried to pull free. Now it was a contest of will and strength with two bodies torqued in opposition. Jenkins was bigger and stronger than Brad, but it took a few seconds before he began to gain the upper hand. Realizing he was losing his advantage, Brad whipped the man's arm around his back into a hammerlock, but applied most of the viselike pressure on his thumb, producing excruciating pain.

Lorna, who had been frozen with apprehension, sucked in a breath, and then exhaled slowly.

"Hey, what's going on here?" The uniformed conductor elbowed his way through an aisle full of spectators. Brad's opponent was bent over like the Hunchback of Notre Dame.

"Nothing serious, sir. Merely a little misunderstanding. This guy was just going back to his seat. Isn't that right?" Brad released his grip.

Jenkins stood there with an equal mixture of pain and anger etched on his face. Then his shoulders went into a slouch, and he stared at the floor.

"Yeah, right. I guess . . . I guess I was just getting ready to go to the club car and get a smoke and a drink." He collected himself, then turned and stalked off in a huff towards the door.

Lorna heaved a sigh of relief. With the excitement ended, the passengers turned their attention elsewhere. Those in the aisle returned to their seats.

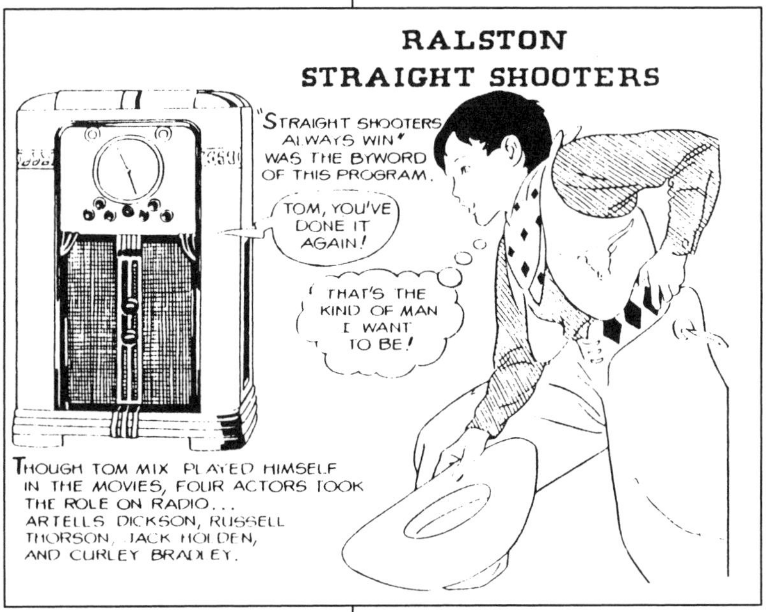

"Hey, mister, how'd ya get lightning-fast hands?" the boy with rollicking blue eyes asked.

Brad crouched down so that he was nearly eye level with the curious youngster. "Hello, tenderfoot."

Then he swiftly made a phantom quick-draw motion with his hand, his index finger extended like the barrel of a gun. "When I was just about your age, I practiced all the time with my Tom Mix cap pistol." He playfully tousled the kid's hair. "I'll be seein' ya, wrangler."

"Gee, Mom, that was really somethin'," the boy said as he flipped around and faced forward in his seat. "Can I have a cowboy outfit for my birthday . . . huh, pleeze, can I?"

"May I," she corrected. "We'll see," she said, throwing an icy stare at Brad. "It all depends on how well you behave the rest of this trip."

Brad turned to Lorna. "I don't think that man will bother you any more, Miss." Brad's composure started to slip. Her natural beauty and svelte waistline caused him to have difficulty with his words.

Lorna was fuming. "What were you trying to do, start a riot? I was handling things just fine until you came along."

Brad was taking inventory: age, early twenties; make-up, light; features, delicately drawn; hair, gorgeous chestnut brown; eyes, incredibly blue-green; skin, exquisitely creamy and flawless; looks, startling; third finger left hand, ringless—angry expression on her fresh-scrubbed, all-American girl face.

"I'm sorry, I—"

"Do you always try to solve everything with your fists?"

She also had a mesmerizing voice despite her present mood.

"But I didn't hit him, I—"

"Here comes my father. I would appreciate it if you just left me alone."

Brad, crushed by her stinging rebuke, dejectedly returned to his seat. Noel sat down next to his daughter.

"What was that all about?"

"Oh, nothing," Lorna said, feeling slightly embarrassed. "What took you so long?"

"I had to stop in the rest room—one of my periodic nosebleeds."

"Are you okay?

"I'm fine."

As the train drew closer to the Mississippi River, Lorna spotted a silver and blue streamlined interurban streetcar headed to St. Louis, by way of Venice. Lorna felt a slight forward pull while the train slowed down a bit as it passed the Litchfield & Madison yards at Granite City. It slowed even more as it approached the outskirts of East St. Louis and began threading its way through the maze of tracks, frogs, crossovers, semaphores, and switches that belonged to the Terminal Railroad.

Lorna looked out the window and noticed the train had reduced its speed. "Why are we slowing down? " she asked.

"It's all about physics. The mass and weight force the engineer to start applying the brakes about a mile away from the depot if he wants to get it stopped in time."

"Yes, I remember that from my high school class," Lorna mused.

The train was going much slower now. It passed over a concrete viaduct at the stockyards and began to come to a complete stop, the air brakes screeching its wheels as it pulled along the side of the passenger relay depot on First Street. The station platform was brimming with people. The Veterans Memorial Bridge, an eleven million dollar ode to concrete and steel and scheduled to open for traffic in four months, dominated the view toward the northwest. The Eads Bridge loomed directly southwest. Industrial outcroppings dotted the South End—smokestack industries. A bituminous haze hung over that part of the city, contesting the brilliant rays of late morning sun.

Noel held on to Lorna's arm as she stepped from the train into the densely packed crowd on the hard deck. She was jostled from all sides. East St. Louis did not disappoint. It was a fascinating mélange of vitality: sights, sounds, and sensations. The engineer's bell was clanging in her ears. Her alertness picked up the harangue of frenzied economic activity in what was known as the old "Island" area. The metallic sounds of dominoed boxcars in the nearby humping yards came crashing down on her with several BOOM! BOOM! BOOMs!

Lorna's attention was drawn to chuffing sounds and the hiss of steam coming out of the cylinder valves of another train departing the station. It reminded her of a hot teakettle spouting off. She couldn't believe how crowded it was. She searched the sea of unfamiliar faces and was intrigued by their collective look of preoccupation, as if they all had important appointments to keep.

A redcap picked up Lorna's luggage. Negroes were almost non-existent in Litchfield. The dusky man, judged by Lorna to be in his late fifties, noticed her astonishment. "It's pretty much like this ev'ry day ma'am," he said. "We average 'bout ninety passenger trains a day, an' over two-hundred an' twenty freight trains wind through the city every twenty-four hours."

A man in a hurry bumped one of Lorna's shoulders, almost knocking her off balance. She was jostled again by a woman who didn't bother to say, "Sorry!" The pinball action made Lorna feel like one of those chaotic characters in a Kafka novel. Like the nearby Mississippi River, the horde of people seemed full of swirls and eddies that moved in various directions. It was a strange yet captivating world where, unlike Litchfield, time seemed important. The briefest of doubts crept through Lorna's inner thoughts for the first time. Was it possible that a small town girl like her would be totally out of her league? Might someone who led such a sheltered life be overwhelmed by fast-paced urban complexities? Lorna pushed the lingering doubt to the farthest recesses of her brain. Such negativity was counterproductive.

They escaped to the fringe of the crowd. Noel tipped the redcap and flagged a ride from the cab lineup. Black & White Cab Co. was stenciled on the side door. In smaller letters below, it said 417 Illinois Ave., UP 4-1104. The driver was a brawny man with the stub of a cheap cigar protruding from his lips. Its gilded band identified it as an El Toro.

"Where to, folks?"

"We're on our way to the Beulah Club on Ninth Street," Noel volunteered.

"That's only about a mile away," the driver said. "The cost will be 20 cents."

"That will be fine."

"My name is Bill Jacobus. There isn't any place I don't know about—lived here all my life. I can get you from point A to point B in this town quicker than any other cabby," he said, giving them a friendly gap toothed smile in the rear-view mirror.

"Just get us there safely," Noel cautioned. It was an admonition that largely went ignored.

The cab, a 1947 Plymouth sedan, merged with other vehicles on Missouri Avenue. The sunlight blinked on windshields as cars moved in congested herds like cattle at the nearby stockyards. The driver chatted amiably as they passed the Two-O-One Tavern, the five-story Savoy Hotel, then the Greyhound Bus Station. Lorna made a mental note of the bus station because that was where she would catch her ride home to visit the family.

When the cabbie found out they were out of towners, he began to narrate the city's past. As the vehicle inched forward through the logjam of traffic, it passed Beckwith Brothers Real Estate, the Youth for Christ building and G&B Sandwich shop.

"What do the letters G&B stand for?" Lorna inquired.

"The natives claim it's "gag and belch," but the letters represent the Greek owner, Gus Boukas. I'm sorry, ma'am. I didn't mean to talk crude and show disrespect for a lady."

"Apology accepted!" Lorna replied, trying to suppress a smile. This throbbing metropolis intrigued Lorna. She found the hustle and bustle of city life fascinating, and soaking up the local color made it even more so.

The cab hit a red light at Collinsville Avenue. The first four blocks of that street were the city's main shopping district. "Here it is—the busiest crossroads in town," the cabby said. "Three banks and the Goldman Building with its distinctive Norman tower. East St. Louis is the only town of real size that didn't have a single bank fail during the Depression. They were backed by funds down at the Stock Yards Bank, which had vaults bulging with money. People always have to eat—in good times and in bad ones."

The city was noisy, crowded, clogged with traffic, throbbing with restless energy. Several buildings looked like gray mountains against the azure blue sky. "This is absolutely ***the most***," Lorna exclaimed.

The cab turned the corner on yellow and an anxious driver on the left leaned on his horn. "Yeah, yeah," Jacobus said, waving his hand in a dismissive gesture. Noel rolled his eyes and shook his head in silent disapproval.

They crawled a few blocks along the most crowded section of downtown. Lorna loved this town, this chaotically vibrant magnet that drew people of all nationalities and promised a glimpse of the future. The cab turned right at Illinois Avenue. The gravelly voice spoke again from the front seat. "Just a few more blocks and we're there."

"I'm curious," Noel said. "Do you own this cab?"

"No sir," Jacobus replied. "I rent it from my boss, Ernie McMullen, for seven dollars and fifty cents a day."

"Who pays for oil and gas?"

"I do." Everyone lurched forward as Jacobus jammed the brakes to keep from hitting a jaywalker.

"And you get to keep fare money and tips?"

"That's right."

"If you don't mind my asking, is it a good living?"

"Well, Monday through Thursday I barely break even. But on the weekend I clear about fifty dollars a night."

"Wow," Lorna exclaimed. "Do they allow female drivers?"

Noel shot a look of disapproval at Lorna, not for asking, but for showing interest in something that clearly was not woman's work.

"No ma'am, they sure don't."

Noel's curiosity got the better of him. "Did you ever have anyone try to get out of paying?"

"There was this big burly fellow who won a bundle out at the race track. Drunk as a skunk. He tried to stiff me."

"What did you do?" Lorna asked in excited anticipation.

"I forcefully put him down on the sidewalk and took his money."

"All of it?" Lorna asked.

"Nope, just what he owed."

The cab negotiated the left turn at the public library on Ninth Street and screeched to a halt in front of the Beulah Club. Catty-cornered was the three-story, Victorian gothic Summers College of Commerce. Its dominating feature was a round turret on one corner, topped by a cone-shaped roof that reminded Lorna of a dunce cap. Its roundish tiles looked like fish scales. Lorna smiled, remembering the time her second grade teacher sat Tommy Barschak in the corner with a conical hat. It was punishment for a little pigtail-tugging repartee during her playground years.

Lorna was a little disappointed. "Summers doesn't look anything like I thought it would."

"That's because it used to be Paul Abt's home. He was one of the town bigwigs around the turn of the century. Later it housed the Niederfeld Undertaking Company," the driver said. "You aren't planning to register for any embalming classes are you?"

"Absolutely not!!"

I couldn't ask for a more convenient location, Lorna silently said to herself.

Noel told the cab driver to wait for him because he would be back just as soon as he made sure his daughter was settled in her room.

Lorna exited the vehicle, placed a hand on top of her hat and spun around with the other arm fully extended. "Daddy, it's wonderful. I never had any idea such a place existed. I know I'm going to love it here."

A few minutes more of standing and gazing, and Noel was beginning to wonder if he hadn't made a mistake in coming. He also wondered about the wisdom of leaving his daughter alone in such a place. All the people, the traffic, the buses, the fast cars. It wasn't a fit place for a defenseless, innocent girl. And if a town like Litchfield was the embodiment of much that was wholesome, then a metropolis such as this must be full of opposites: pettiness, greed, hypocrisy, crime.

Noel carried the bags as they walked to the front desk in the middle of a spacious lobby. Their shoes made clapping sounds against the gleaming marble chip terrazzo floor. A matron was pushing some reddish sweeping compound with a broad dust mop. A pungent, slightly sweet smell hung in the air. The focal point to the left was a large, glass-topped coffee table surrounded on three sides by an overstuffed couch with embroidered covers. Beneath it all lay a luxurious maroon Persian rug with exotic patterns. A telephone booth occupied the far northeast corner. A walnut grandfather's clock ticked loudly in the opposite corner—tick, tick, tock—like the stately clock in Cole Porter's "Night and Day."

The Beulah Club on 9th and Ohio

The girl at the desk, filing her nails, asked for Lorna's full name. "We've been expecting you," she said. "My name is Laurie McIntyre, and I'm more or less the desk clerk at this hotel for females. You're really going to like it here." She was in her mid-twenties but a dusting of freckles on her nose gave her a girlish look. "It's close to downtown, the rooms are immaculate and the people are very friendly." She handed her a room key and a sheet of paper. A list of rules and regulations.

"Read these when you get comfortable, and let me know if you have any questions," she said. "You're on the second floor, first door to your right at the top of the stairs. I need to go first if your father is going to carry your bags."

Lorna couldn't help but notice her hourglass figure. It seemed to have about five extra minutes thrown in for good measure—guaranteed to intrigue red-blooded males.

"Man on the floor!" Laurie bellowed at the top of her lungs.

Noel dutifully followed behind, lugged the bags up the stairs and opened the door to room 221. It was austere but clean and neat as a pin. He heaved a sigh of relief. At least he didn't have to worry about this part of Lorna's living away from home.

"Whew, it's hot in here," Lorna complained.

"I'll fix it," Noel said. He deposited the two suitcases on the highly polished tile floor. Next he opened the two windows and adjusted the transom above the door to circulate the air. "Are you sure you're going to be all right?" he said to Lorna.

"I'll be fine, Daddy."

She gave him a hug and a kiss on the cheek. "Thanks for everything. I know I'm going to enjoy it here. I'll write or call you and Mom to tell you all about my classes. Hopefully, I can find a job to help with expenses."

"We don't consider it any kind of a sacrifice. We're doing this because you're our daughter, and we love you. Study hard, and good luck in finding a job."

Noel's protective instincts tugged at his heart. He wanted to hang around all day to make sure everything went smoothly for his only daughter. He didn't.

"I'd better get back to the cab so I don't miss the next train." He gave her a peck on the cheek and closed the door behind him as he left the room.

Lorna slowly expelled the air from her lungs. She finally felt free from a life that had been fettered and circumscribed by well-meaning adults. ***Freedom, sweet freedom.***

After unpacking her bags and hanging her clothes, she went across the hall to inspect the community facilities. Lorna was fastidious about cleanliness. A mild smell of disinfectant filled her nostrils. It was drab but functional. Institutional gray glazed brick reached half way up the walls. A Kotex dispenser was in the far corner. Six toilet stalls were enclosed in metallic cubicles. A long row of gleaming white porcelain lavatories had large brass taps in the shape of a swan. At the far end were the showers.

Lorna hated the garish glare of the fluorescent lights above the lavatories. They made women look sickly. The glare seemed to cast shadows on her face when she was applying make up. The whole area reminded Lorna of something that was more appropriate for a hospital room, but for health reasons she was glad it had a Spic & Span antiseptic quality.

She went back to her room and took its full measure. The right side of the room was a mirror image of the left. There were two closets on each side of the room near the door; two single beds on opposite walls.

Lorna paused and wondered what her roommate would be like. Then the inspection continued.

Two large windows graced the far end. A beige Formica top, edged with a chrome strip, ran below the windows from wall to wall. There were open storage shelves in the middle. Cutouts on each side were just large enough to accomodate a wooden chair. They were light oak—sturdy but not very comfortable looking, similar to the chair of her favorite Litchfield high school teacher, Miss Anna Rose Miller. The efficient desk and shelving configuration gave access to steam radiators beneath each window.

Lorna had requested a room for two because the monthly fee was much less than a private room. The only stipulation was that her roommate be a non-smoker. She had an accommodating personality and usually had little difficulty getting along with others.

Lorna plopped on the bed to test it out. Covered with a light yellow chenille spread, it looked as if it had been made by an army drill sergeant. She was pleased. Certainly not a Sealy Posturepedic, but it was firm and didn't sag anywhere. A light push or two on a down pillow left her pleasantly surprised. ***That will do just fine***, she thought.

Lorna walked over to the window and looked out. The view wasn't picturesque, but she liked its location on the front of the building looking west. Across the street was Summers College of Commerce. Lorna decided to glance over the Rules and Regulations then freshen up and go across the street to register for classes.

The list of do's and don'ts made it seem as if she were being quartered in a military barracks. A housemother inspected the room every Thursday. Beds were to be made daily. Window blinds and horizontal surfaces were to be cleaned and dusted, clothes were to be either in drawers or closets, with nothing lying around. Lorna was reminded of one of her mother's favorite homilies: "A place for everything and everything in its place." No alcohol was allowed in the building; radios were forbidden to be played after ten o'clock at night, and there was a seventy-five cent charge for lost keys. Housecoats could be worn in the dining room for breakfast only. ***I wonder if these are the same rules they have at a nunnery?*** Lorna bridled at these intrusions on her prerogatives. There were more.

Bed linens were to be changed twice a week, on Tuesdays and Fridays. Gentlemen callers were limited to the front lobby downstairs. There was an eleven-thirty curfew during the week and a two o'clock deadline on weekends.

Lorna went into the bathroom and wiped her face with a cool damp terry cloth. She dug into her purse and pulled out a tube of lipstick—pucker paint, her dad always called it. Crimson Blush by Max Factor. ***Good enough for the movie stars, good enough for me.***

She locked her room, tossed the passkey into her purse and happily skipped down the stairs. The lobby had more people in it than when she had first arrived. Laurie, that perky little chatterbox asked, "Do you have any questions about house rules, Miss Sanders?"

"I looked them over in my room, and they are all perfectly clear," Lorna said as she whizzed by.

Lorna walked outside to the covered entry. Its limestone Ionic pillars led to a couple of steps. A brick path went out to the sidewalk. She spun around one-hundred-and-eighty degrees to see if she could locate her room. That was no problem because it was squarely in line with the covered portico. She decided to get a good look at what she would call home for the next few years or so. The three-story modified Georgian building was simple, yet elegant—like something that might have been in a Currier and Ives print. Brilliant red roses were climbing fan-shaped white trellises on each side of the entrance. A reddish-brown brick veneer enclosed all four sides. Corners were trimmed in a light gray Indiana stone. Three dormered windows, set in green and black slate, enhanced the roof. The window fenestration on the remainder of the building was symmetrical. Those in the main lobby had half-moon arched glass sections above them. A two-foot high black wrought iron fence protected the grass. It wasn't there for security. It was just high enough to discourage dogs and people from cutting across the immaculately manicured grounds. On the south side of the building, literally glowing under the rays of the sun, was a magnificent oak, massive in girth. It looked to be at least fifty years old with its white-washed trunk and gnarled branches, heavy with dark green foliage.

This is incredible. In a little more than a couple of hours I've gone from small town Litchfield to a place fifteen times bigger—from genteel to white-hot intense.

Lorna glanced skyward. A flock of purple martins flew overhead. The position of the searing late August sun confirmed that it was early afternoon. Shielding her eyes with her hand, Lorna's attention was drawn to a bright red biplane flitting around in the sky like a happy butterfly. The plane, a rotary engine Stearman, was built back in the 1930s. The pilot was applying the finishing touches by doing a serpentine zig-zag and forming the letter 'S' with its contrails. DRINK HIRES read the freshly painted sign high above the city. Then banking left, he headed back to the landing strip at Cahokia, a few miles south of East St. Louis. Parks Air College, located there, was one of the nation's first, and in the early jaunty days of flying by the seat of one's pants, had been visited by both Charles Lindbergh and Amelia Earhardt.

Charles A. Lindbergh

The sky was filled with fluffy white clouds that reminded Lorna of cauliflower. For an instant she was drawn back to the inner core of her childhood as she reminisced about lying face up in mid-summer on the lush green grass of her front yard with Alene Vancil, her very best friend. Staring at the cloud formations as the wind pushed them and gently changed their shapes was a happy diversion. They laughed and giggled as they told each other what they thought the shape looked like. Perhaps a circus clown . . . that metamorphosed into a poodle. Sometimes they spent as much as an hour looking upward and flexing their imaginations. Her hopscotch, coloring book, paper doll and bubblegum years had been happy ones.

Between formations they practiced their pig Latin. "Ooday ouyay inkthay athay Aulpay, ethay ewnay oybay inay oolschay isay utecay?" Alene quizzed Lorna.

"Esyay! Ehay ashay ayay eryvay icenay ilesmay," Lorna answered.

Alene frowned. "I didn't quite get that."

"Probably because I added a Bronx accent," Lorna kidded.

Someone honked a horn and brought Lorna back to the present. For the first time she realized that across the street on the north side of Ohio Avenue was a high school. Stone carving above what appeared to be the main entrance read, "East St. Louis Senior High." Cheerleaders were practicing their yells in a small grassy area by the front steps.

"Sittin' in the grandstand-
Beatin' on a tin can-
Who can, we can-
Nobody else can.
Yaay, East Side."

A trio of grade school girls were playing skip-rope on the sidewalk. A redheaded boy on the other side of the street was jambling along, a baseball glove tucked under his arm, eating candy dots from what looked like adding machine paper. In East St. Louis, summer vacation didn't end until after Labor Day.

Summers was one building north of the Beulah Club on the opposite side of Ninth Street, and Lorna carefully looked both ways before attempting to cross. A light blue Plymouth convertible with a squirrel tail fastened to the antenna cruised by. The male driver gave her an admiring wolf whistle as he passed. Lorna was dumbfounded. The boys in Litchfield would never do anything that bold. She felt a slight blush come over her. When the boy looked into the rear-view mirror and saw Lorna staring in disbelief, he lightly tapped his foot on the brake a couple of times. His blue dot taillights winked at her twice as if to say, "you're cute."

Lorna shook her head and rolled her eyes upward. Then she proceeded across the street and sailed through the front doors. She could hardly wait to get registered for her two night classes. As it turned out, one was an advanced typing class, and the other was called Business English. Life was certainly becoming more interesting. Lorna had always done well in school and was confident she would be equal to the challenges that were in store for her.

CHAPTER 4

East St. Louis is one of dozens of towns that owe their existence to the Father of Waters—the mighty Mississippi River (called Mechesebe by the Algonquin tribe). It carries water from the Missouri, Tennessee, Ohio, Illinois, Arkansas, Wabash and Red rivers, in addition to numerous other tributaries coursing through thirty-one states.

"Hey, how'ya doin', Joe," Tony said as he flicked out his fists and bobbed and weaved, landing a couple of imaginary blows to his friend's chin and midsection. Tony had narrow set eyes, a thick head of black hair, and a Fred Astaire triangular face.

"I'm fine, Tony," Joe responded, backpedaling and parrying the blows, then lunging forward with a few of his own after a couple of feints. Joe was Salvatore Delonzo's enforcer when strong-arm tactics were needed. He could be as ruthless as a member of Himmler's SS.

Tony's cheeks were cratered from a bout with adolescent acne. He took the stub of a cigarette out of his mouth and tossed it on the pavement, grinding it out with his foot. "What's the boss want ta see us about, anyway? What's this meetin' for?"

Joe unfastened the top button of an expensive silk shirt. "I dunno, but as soon as Vince gets here, we're gonna find out," he said as he nervously chewed on a toothpick.

Joe playfully threw a phantom gut punch at Tony who reflexively doubled over. Tony and Joe left the parking lot and headed inside Gavanelli's Restaurant, in south St. Louis, and made their way to the back room. They sat down on a Lincoln green leather couch. Vince joined them a few minutes later, pacing back and forth behind the couch while they talked about what might happen at the upcoming Kefauver crime hearings.

"My little finger aches when the weather's about to change," Vince complained.

Joe shook his head. "It's all in your imagination, Vince. Remember, it was bitten off over a year ago in that barroom brawl."

Vince rubbed the stub of flesh at the end of his third joint. "I know it don't make no sense, but I'm tellin' ya, it bothers me."

When Sal Delonzo arrived half an hour later, the room was a haze of blue smoke.

"Sorry I'm late, boys. There was this little misunderstanding I had to straighten out with Sam Jablonski. It seems he was getting a little too big for his britches. It took a little persuading, but he came around. I could use a stiff

drink. How about the rest of you?"

"I'll get the drinks," Tony said.

"Scotch! Bourbon! Griesedieck!" they volunteered. When Tony came back with the drinks, they all gathered around the poker table to talk serious business.

"What's on your mind, boss?" Vince asked.

"Walters, Knucky Walters. His east-side empire is makin' too much money for us to ignore any longer."

Delonzo pictured himself as a consummate entrepreneur and organizational genius. Like Knucky, his pockets were crowded with police and civic officials. He was convinced time had passed Knucky by. The man was of limited vision. Knucky thought retail while Delonzo envisioned wholesale. Knucky was squandering a golden opportunity to triple his earnings. The way Sal figured it, Knucky was trapped in the mindset of the first half of the Twentieth Century. Delonzo was ready to take advantage of the new prosperity and freedom that marked the second half of the century.

"We've tried giving Knucky a few hints, but that hasn't worked out. He's a stubborn old goat," Tony said.

"He's sittin' on top of a gold mine over there and doesn't even realize it. Should be makin' money hand over fist," Sal said.

"Ya talkin' about drugs?" Joe asked.

"Yeah. Cocaine and heroin. Coke from Colombia and Brazil and "H" from Turkey. We're talkin' about extra profits of a million dollars or more."

Tony was overcome by a look of confusion. "Exactly how much is a million, boss?"

Sal thoughtfully took a sip of his bourbon. Then he grabbed three decks of cards and laid a single card face down on the table and tapped it with his finger. "You know what a thousand is?"

"Yeah."

Then he placed a stack of ten next to the singleton. "And ten of these make ten thousand."

"Uh, huh."

Without counting he placed nine more stacks of cards, roughly equal in size next to the first stack. "And ten of these make a hundred thousand G's, right?"

"Right."

Then he combined the ten stacks. "Remember, that's a hundred thou." He took the remaining cards and made nine more stacks. "Well, if there's a hundred thousand in each pile, then ten of them make a million. Got it?"

Tony's brow furrowed then he nodded his head as he tried to absorb what had been said.

"What will Tony Accardo or Sam Giancana in Chicago an' the Gambino group in New York say if we take Knucky out?" Joe asked.

Delonzo took another sip on his bourbon. "New York don't tell the Midwest what to do. An' Accardo an' Giancana might not like it, but as long as they get their cut, the old Capone mob ain't gonna give us no trouble."

"Not even if we clip Knucky?" Joe asked.

"Not even if we clip Knucky," Delonzo answered, his feral eyes shifting back and forth. "The first thing we do is try to scare him off. If that doesn't work, then he has to go."

"Who do we have to replace him, boss?" Joe asked.

"Larry Johnson, one of his young lieutenants has been champing at the bit. He's very ambitious and thinks it's time for him to move up in the organization. He's a little young, but that would just make it easier for us to get his cooperation. I had a secret meeting with him last week, and Johnson said he's ready to come on board. We can do business with this guy."

"Don't we need one of our own men to be on the East Side, just to stay on top of things?" Tony asked.

Sal flicked his cigarette in a tray, turned and looked his cousin straight in the eyes. "That's where you come in, Tony,"

"Why me?"

"Because you're over there all the time visitin' your mother's relatives. Nobody in our organization knows the place as well as you do. And don't you have some friends who hold positions in the Teamsters and electrician unions in East St. Louis?"

"Yeah, and I also know some guys who are ironworkers, steamfitters and plumbers. I met them a few years ago at the race track."

"So who takes Tony's place over here?" Joe asked.

"Ya think Darren Davis is ready to move up a notch?" Sal asked, his eyes scanning his three associates.

They looked at each other, and then one by one started nodding their heads in unison. "Yeah, he's ready for the big time," Vince volunteered.

"So, how do we get rid of Knucky?" Tony asked as he finished his drink.

"It ain't gonna be easy, but I gotta plan," Sal said with a smug smile.

CHAPTER 5

Monks Mound, on the outskirts of East St. Louis, was the largest man-made structure in America when the Pilgrims landed at Plymouth Rock in 1620. Built by ancient native Americans, it stands at one hundred feet tall and has a base more than twice that of the Great Pyramid of Egypt. It was a gold mine of artifacts prompting Buffalo Bill to come to East St. Louis once a year in the 1890s to buy arrowheads for his Wild West Show.

Mound - sketch by Roscoe Misselhorn

Brad was reading the newspaper at the Club 501. He had finished his meal and was hoping Knucky would show up. His molars were busy crunching the ice left in his soft drink.

Fighting between U. N. forces and the Communists around the 38th parallel in Korea dominated the daily headlines. The body found at Grand Marais was still front-page news. The county coroner had ruled it a homicide. Death had been nearly instantaneous from the lead slugs that smashed the skull, tore through the medulla oblogata and gouged a mass of brain tissue in the cerebrum. Brad always wondered about that phrase, "nearly instantaneous." Was it just a sugar pill to assuage the grieving family? He remembered a story about the execution of the Frenchman, Antoine Lavoisier, told in class by a history professor. The man who had discovered oxygen was judged to be one of those traitorous aristocrats during the Reign of Terror in the French Revolution. When sent to the guillotine, he told friends that he would do an experiment to determine if there was life after beheading. "Watch my eyes after they cut off my head and hold it up to the crowd. I will try to blink as many times as I can," he said. According to witnesses, he blinked eleven times.

Knucky came in with his ever-present bodyguard, carefully laid his hat on the rack, and walked over to Brad's booth. Without his asking, a waitress came over with a cup and saucer and filled it to the brim with liquid caffeine.

"Mr. Walters, if I'm going to be a success as a lawyer, I need to know more about how things work in this town. Could you explain things to me in a general way without getting into your private matters?"

"What, for instance?" he countered while lighting a Chesterfield.

"Wel-l-l-l. How is it that you seem to be accepted by so many people in the community? The newspaper refers to you as a gangster, but most people don't fear you, and they say your presence helps keep the riff-raff out of town. They maintain that between you and the police there isn't much petty crime in East St. Louis."

"It's fairly simple," he said, the cigarette dancing between his lips. "My associates tell me that out in Los Angeles there's a special squad of four police detectives. Their chief told them they could operate beyond the law. He gave them permission to use extraordinary means and occasionally bend or break a few rules for two reasons: first, to keep the mob outta the city, and second, to get rid of known criminals who slip through the cracks of the regular justice system. Some called them the God Squad."

Brad leaned forward, drinking it all in.

"In our town it's a little different," Knucky explained. "East St. Louis is what's known as a wide-open town. The only other place remotely like it in the state is Calumet City near the Indiana border, or Storyville, which is in New Orleans. Even Chicago ain't the same anymore since Eliot Ness put Al Capone away for tax evasion. We have guys playing the numbers, poker games in the back rooms of taverns, people betting on the horses at Fairmount, prostitution that is winked at by the authorities and slot machine levers being pulled in taverns and night clubs. Racing is so popular at Fairmount, they're planning on building another track on Route 460, east of the **Aluminum Ore plant.**

He coughed, and some ashes fell on his pants. "D—," he said as he hurriedly brushed off the gray residue.

"Those things can kill you, you know."

"Stop sounding like my wife."

"Sorry!"

"Where was I? . . . oh, yes. People come here from all over southern Illinois. We even get lotsa business from St. Louis because horse racing is illegal in Missouri, and their blue laws forbid the sale of liquor on Sundays. They roll up the sidewalks after their 1:00 A. M. curfew. East St. Louis is an all night town. The only time some of these joints close is between 5 and 7 A. M. —just long enough ta get things straightened out an' cleaned up for another day of business. People come here to have fun an' relax after a hard day's work. They drink our booze, play the one-arm bandits, pay to hear singers and entertainers, and sometimes want some exciting female companionship."

Riotous laughter from the bar briefly interrupted their dialog. Barely within earshot, Brad had heard only bits and pieces but someone was telling a joke about a man with a trained bear.

"But why do the police and politicians let it continue?" he asked.

"A long time ago the city fathers made some decisions. One thing led to another, an' pretty soon we ended up with what we have now."

"What kind of decisions?"

"They purposely kept taxes low as an incentive for big firms like C. K. Williams, Obear-Nester Glass an' Aluminum Ore to locate here. They were given sweetheart deals in order to create growth an' jobs. Politicians discovered people get restless at the polls when their property taxes are high. So the politicians at City Hall made sure property taxes stayed low. This helped 'em stay in office, an' the political machine could pretty much have things its own way."

"So besides cheap property and business taxes where else does the city get the money it needs to run things and pay expenses?"

"You're not gonna' believe this, but it's true. Have ya ever heard people say this town has a saloon on every corner and a church on every other corner?"

"Yep—that's a well-known expression around here."

"East St. Louis has more saloons than any city of its size in the country. Liquor licenses are very expensive—$500 every three months. The tavern owners don't like it, but business is good an' some of the extra expense is merely passed along ta the customer. We basically have a town where anyone can find a job an' housing is affordable. The crime rate is low, streets are safe, our schools are good; we have one of the finest park systems in the country, an' city services are dependable."

"Not bad for one of the most industrialized cities in the country," Brad interjected.

Aluminum Ore plant on Missouri Avenue with airplane marker

"The police in town keep a tight rein on things. They come down hard on muggers, robbers, rapists, pickpockets and other slugs. If they catch ya speeding, the fines are steep."

"What about the ones who slip through the cracks?"

"Me an' my boys take care of the criminals who escape the system."

"How do you 'take care' of them?"

"We beat em' up an' run 'em outta town. Despite the rough an' tumble nature of things, outsiders aren't afraid to come ta town an' drop a few bills for excitement and entertainment. We have an egghead governor, Adlai Stevenson, who is making life difficult by sending state troopers ta raid gambling establishments. He must have macaroni for brains because if they ever shut gambling down in this town, it'll be the death of a fine city. They're tryin' ta kill the goose that lays the golden eggs."

"Where do you fit into the overall scheme of things?" Brad inquired. "Can you tell me in a ***general*** sort of way?"

"Sure—ain't no big secret. My investments an' business dealings are in cigarette vending machines, jukeboxes, pinball machines an' gambling. A lot of guys come see me for loans ta get started in the tavern or the restaurant business. Not only do I get a good return, most agree to place my machines in their establishments. I also get a piece of the action with people playing numbers an' with floating craps games at places like the Green Lantern in Highland."

Brad smiled. "Galloping dominoes, that's what W.C. Fields dubbed a pair of dice. By the way, what is a floating crap game?"

Knucky glanced at his fourteen carat gold watch to check the time. "It's a dice game . . . moves around from one place to another every week to make it harder for the police ta make a raid."

"Why is it called craps?"

"Don't know. Seven an' eleven are good come out roll numbers, an' when you toss snake eyes, you crap out."

"Seven and eleven are significant numbers in the Bible because God created the world in seven days, and there were eleven disciples after Judas committed suicide," Brad noted.

"You a card player?" Knucky asked.

"Never played poker—just rummy and hearts."

"Whew! You sure lead a boring life."

"Not in my book," he answered. "There's lots of symbolism in cards you know."

"Such as . . .

"The queen of spades is the death card. The kings represent actual figures in history."

"Do you know them?"

"Let's see, the king of diamonds is Julius Caesar; clubs, Alexander the Great; hearts, Charlemagne . . ."

"What about Spades?"

"Can't remember for sure—David or Solomon. David, I think."

Just then, a smallish man with a prominent pair of brown and white wing tips came into the club. His cumulus-cloud hairdo dominated his round face. He appeared nervous and fidgety. An expensive looking gold ring encrusted with the initial 'F' in diamonds encircled the ring finger on his right hand. Knucky said, "Excuse me a second," and walked over to him. The man whispered a few things in Walters' ear, and his countenance went south.

"Take care of it," was all that Brad could distinguish from the amalgam of muffled words. Then the man quickly left.

"Who was that?" he asked as Knucky made his way back to the booth.

"Sam Fosterman, my nephew. He does assorted jobs an' errands for me."

Brad decided not to delve any further into the matter and picked up the conversation where they left off.

"Do you have City Hall in your pocket the way they say you do?"

"Lot of people think so, but that politics stuff is boring. I tried to get several of my friends elected a couple years ago, but it didn't work. I couldn't beat the machine. Don't worry about it much anymore. We have a gentleman's agreement. I keep my nose out of their business, make a few donations to the right people on a regular basis, an' grease the right palms under the table. They pretty much leave me alone. The only guy who gives me grief around here is Sweeney, that gung-ho **Dick Tracy** detective."

"So your only interest in politics is to preserve the status quo?"

"That's right, keep everything as it is. Oh, I almost forgot," Knucky added. "Some time ago I set up a racing wire service at Fairmont City called Racing News Agency. It reports the results of other races around the country for people who have placed out of town bets with their bookies. Sam Fosterman manages the operation."

"I thought that was illegal."

"It is in most states, but the Illinois Legislature hasn't outlawed it yet. Got my fingers crossed."

"What about drugs, prostitution, protection and horse racing?"

"You've been reading too many Perry Mason novels, kid. I hate drugs. I let other people like Bess Newman peddle the flesh, an' I don't fix races out at the track. And as for protection, that went out with the Dutch Schultz era. Tavern an' store owners would hate my guts if I tried to lean on 'em for monthly payments. Hey, don't forget, I also make a good profit here at the Club 501."

"Don't you have a brother named Lou?"

"Yeah, he helps me run this place."

"Don't the police ever make raids on the brothels?"

"I have a sneaky suspicion law enforcement tolerates the red light district because they think it keeps rapes to a minimum. By allowing an outlet for pent up sex drive, ya don't have many young men running around preying on women. The workin' girls accept an occasional arrest or fine as a necessary evil. The story of the pinch in the newspaper cools off the religious community and takes pressure off the politicians. Then it's back to business as usual. Occasionally one of the places gets closed down, but the owner merely moves the business elsewhere."

"Have you watched any of the Kefauver Crime Commission hearings on television?" Brad asked, with some hesitation.

Walters' famous scowl crept over his face. "Are you kiddin'? I'd rather have my worst enemy hammer nails through my scrotum!"

Brad couldn't keep himself from chuckling out loud.

"Do ya think that's funny, kid?"

"I'm sorry. It's just that I have never heard anyone use that nails-through-the-scrotum expression to describe something excruciatingly unpleasant."

"I think the SOB is just trying ta make a name for himself so he can get the VP spot on the Democratic ticket in the next election. We'd all be better off if someone in the mob put an end to his circus. Course they won't because of the unwritten code."

"What code?"

"The mob don't like ta go after politicians, policemen or judges. It brings on too much heat."

"Heat?"

"Yeah. Anytime a big shot or a copper is killed, there's lotsa pressure on police to solve the crime. They call in favors, drag people in for questioning an' put the squeeze on small time crooks. Even use the third degree ta get information out of stoolies."

"I thought using the third degree was illegal?"

"Get wise, kid! They go nuts an' do whatever necessary to get what they want. An' God help the poor dope who even thinks about bringin' a lawsuit against 'em. The police also have a code. When it comes to protecting their own or finding out who killed a badge, they close ranks. Besides, if we tick them off, it would be easy for a couple of rogue cops ta declare open season on us an' make the killings look like gangland warfare. And nobody wants their wives an' kids involved. So it's understood family is off-limits."

"That makes sense," Brad said. "I read where the KGB and the CIA have a similar arrangement."

Knucky beckoned a bar girl to their booth and ordered a boilermaker to slake his thirst.

"I read in the paper where the Kefauver commission is coming to St. Louis in a few months to investigate the influence of crime syndicates on local political officials in the metro-area," Brad said. "It's rumored they also plan to check into organized crime connections to anything involving interstate commerce."

Walters' veins in the side of his neck popped out.

"Kefauver made a monkey out of **Frank Costello** an' Joe Adonis in New York—asked 'em all sorts of personal an' embarrassin' questions with millions of people watching on TV. That ain't gonna happen to me, kid."

"What will you do?"

"Make myself scarce as snowballs in Hell. If they can't find me, they can't subpoena me. This just might be a good time to go fishing."

"I didn't know you liked to fish."

"I don't, kid—that's just an expression. By the way, don't breathe a word of nothin' we just said to nobody. Dummy up."

"I already gave you my word."

"I know. It's just that I've taken a likin' to ya, an' I want ta make sure ya don't do anything stupid. By the way, have ya ever mentioned me to your mom or dad?"

"No, sir. I figure the less I talk about you to anyone, the better off I am."

Knucky started patting himself down, looking for his pack of Chesterfields.

"D—, I'm outta ciggies. Hey, Crystal," he yelled. "Bring me over a couple packs of Chesterfields, will ya?"

"Sure thing, Mr. Walters."

The diminutive but shapely blonde went behind the bar and found a set of twin packs.

"An' get me some nuts while you're at it, will ya sweetie?"

"Hold your horses, be there in a jiffy," she yelled back.

After a couple of minutes, she brought him his nuts and smokes. He pulled out a five spot and said, "Keep the change."

"Thank you, Mr. Walters," she smiled.

Knucky lit a cigarette, took a long drag and then helped himself to his drink.

"Know anything about the stock market?" he asked.

"I'm no expert, but I'm fairly well versed along those lines. Lawyers have to know about finance, banking, investments, stock options—things like that."

"If ya ask me, the whole market is a giant shell game. If the president catches a cold, the averages drop. I saw too many families ruined by the '29 crash. They were suckers for believing ya could get something for nothing. I know a lot of people who won't ever again buy stocks or keep their money in a bank—not after all those closings. They hide money under their mattress or bury it in tin cans out in their back yards."

"Have you heard the latest?"

"What?"

"Credit cards. When you buy a radio or eat a fancy meal,

Frank Costello, an unhappy Kefauver witness (UPI)

you show them this plastic card with your name and special number on it. You don't pay anything at the time of purchase, the company just sends you an itemized bill at the end of the month, and you send them a check."

"For the full amount?"

"If you don't want to pay the entire amount, the company lets it ride and charges interest on the unpaid balance."

"Sounds like they're into loan sharking."

"I've heard their interest rates are high."

"Plastic money. What will they think of next? But tell me more about the market. Sometimes I hear 'em say on the radio a certain stock is up six an' three-eighths. What's that all about?"

"The market was established back around 1790 for companies and investors. The most popular coin in the old days was the Spanish 'Pieces of Eight.' It was scored so if you only wanted to spend part of it, you could bite off one of these sections with your teeth. These pieces were called bits and there were eight of them to a coin. Its value became fixed as equal to the dollar. Thus each bit was worth twelve-and-a-half cents."

Walters' eyes lit up. "So that's why we refer to a quarter as two bits . . . "

"Correct."

"An' that's why we say you can get a shave an' a haircut at Dale's barber shop for six bits, meaning seventy-five cents."

"Exactly."

"Hot d—. I can't believe nobody ever explained that to me before. Do you have any money in the stock market?"

"Yes, I have a broker in St. Louis, and I'm in the process of building a portfolio—that's an assorted investment in stocks, bonds, government securities and the like."

"Hey, kid; you're always tossing me little nuggets of wisdom, here's one for you: In the real world, the good guys don't always win. Here's another one—don't take brass knuckles to a gunfight."

"That sounds like something Dutch Schultz would say," Brad said.

"Nope, that's vintage Lloyd K. Walters."

"By the way, do you have a dollar?"

"Sure kid. Did ya forget your wallet?"

"No. It's what they call a retainer. When you give it to me, I'll be your lawyer."

"Hate ta break your heart, but I already have the best lawyer in town, Morris Goldman. Now there is one smart Jew. He's called The Fixer. Besides, you still need some seasoning."

"Don't worry, all this does is invoke the attorney-client privilege. We'll have a fiduciary relationship where I look out for your best interests. If they ever try to pry information out of me on the witness stand, I don't have to say a thing because the content of our conversation is protected by the Constitution."

"Are ya sure all it takes is a dollar?"

"That's all."

"Say, you're beginning to pick up a few street smarts already, kid." Knucky walked behind the bar and got a silver dollar from the cash register. He flipped it to him when he got close to the booth. Brad snared it as easily as he had caught a baseball in his carefree days of youth.

"Nice catch. Now, I've got another one for ya. Guess why those ridges are on the edges of most coins?"

Brad shrugged.

"It's an anti-theft device. Prevents crooks from altering the coin by trimming off the edges an' stealing some of the silver content. Pretty slick, eh?"

"I've never heard that before."

"You don't see them on pennies or nickels do ya?"

"You're right. They have no silver content and ridges aren't on those coins. Well, now that I'm your . . . uh, junior varsity lawyer, things could get interesting."

* * *

After enrolling for her night classes at Summers, Lorna went back to her room at the Beulah Club. As she strolled past the desk clerk, Laurie was chatting on the phone and rearranging a set of index cards with names and numbers on them. Lorna's next task was to find employment, and it dawned on her that Laurie might be able to give her some tips.

James Stewart and Carol Lombard

Laurie hung up the phone and happened to glance up just as Lorna approached the counter. She stopped what she was doing and placed the cap back on her pen. Her mouth was working double time on a piece of chewing gum. An old issue of "True Romances" magazine was under her elbow.

"Can I help you with something, Miss Sanders?" Laurie was one of those effervescent types who always seemed to bubble with enthusiasm. Even her cheerful red and white polka dot dress bubbled. Her short hair sported a Toni perm with tight curls. She proffered an opened pack of Beeman's gum. "Want a stick?"

"No, thanks. I was wondering if you might be able to help me," Lorna responded. "I need to find employment, and I thought you might be able to point me in the right direction. Any suggestions?"

"I might have a couple of leads for you. A lot of businesses keep in touch with us because they know this is one of the main places women stay when they first come to town. A few single women live at the Broadview Hotel, but it's a little expensive. The only other comparable place is the YWCA over on Pennsylvania. Let me check on what's available."

She reached inside a desk drawer and pulled out a battleship gray metal file box. It was interspersed by green file markers that had raised tabs imprinted with black letters of the alphabet. Laurie absentmindedly picked up the pen, placed it in her mouth and wiggled it happily back and forth between a set of Judy Holliday scarlet painted lips.

"Roy Bruder, the manager, is looking for a cocktail waitress over at Johnnie Perkins' Playdium. Now there is a place that's jumpin' with excitement." She gave Lorna a quick once over with her mascara enhanced eyes. "Never mind, it's not you," she observed before Lorna could respond. "Margaret McDermott, the manager of the Avenue Theater downtown, needs someone in the ticket booth. Forget it—too boring," Laurie once again interjected before Lorna could get a word in edgewise.

"James Davis is looking for someone to sell Kelvinator appliances at his store on 20th and State."

"I'll bet he ends up hiring a man for the job," Lorna replied before Laurie could comment. "Stores let women sell notions, clothing and drapes, but men usually get the commission jobs, selling appliances. They think it's a man's job because there is a motor inside. They totally forget it's the women who use refrigerators, washing machines and mixers and that women would do a better job of explaining the various features because they use them everyday in the kitchen."

"Ain't that the truth," Laurie said, nodding her head in agreement. "It's almost like you're a second class citizen in this country if you don't stand up when you go to the bathroom."

"That's going to change one of these days," Lorna said, "and you and I are going to help make it happen."

"Wouldn't that be something," Laurie beamed. She continued thumbing her way through the file, her bright red fingernails dancing back and forth as the cards were pulled forward. "Here . . . I've got just the thing for you. It's a secretarial job at the law firm of Ernst and Lancaster."

"Sounds perfect."

"What time are you available if they want to interview you tomorrow?" Laurie asked.

"Anytime is okay. I have no plans, and my first evening class at Summers doesn't start until next week."

"I'll let you know as soon as I can set up something."

"Thanks for everything!" Lorna leaned over the edge of the desk and gave Laurie a big hug.

"Just one more thing," Laurie exclaimed, wagging her thumb at the second floor. "Your roomie just checked in."

Lorna skipped up the stairs, anxious to meet her new partner. When she opened the door, the girl was hanging up clothes in her closet.

"Hello, you must be my new roommate; I'm Lorna Sanders."

"Gloria Hornback. Nice to meet you."

Gloria was several inches shorter than Lorna. Her brown bobbed hair had a carefree look. Lorna's hair, worn in a pageboy style, was nearly shoulder length. Gloria wore glasses, but they couldn't hide a friendly pair of brown eyes that went perfectly with a pretty smile. She wore a sienna-colored pleated skirt and a peach sweater. A small scarf that had become wildly popular with girls in the last few months surrounded her neck. An amethyst birthstone ring decorated her right hand.

"Where are you from?" Lorna asked.

"Born and raised in East St. Louis, but my parents moved to Caseyville when I started high school. I went to **East St. Louis High** a couple of years then attendance boundaries were changed, and I ended up graduating from Collinsville High."

Brad and Gloria's school – East Side

"Are all the young men around here forward? I just got wolf-whistled out on the street."

"Better get used to it. They sound off at me like a calliope every once in a while, too."

"Do you have any boy friends?" Lorna inquired.

"Yes. I'm going with Bob Von Brock who lives in Edwardsville. How about you?"

"I dated a lot when I was in high school, but I don't think early marriage is in the cards for me. I went with a couple of guys I thought were real dreamboats, but they turned out to be dinghies in an ocean full of luxury liners. They were very good looking, but were still attached to their mother's apron strings."

"I know exactly what you mean." Gloria rubbed a kink out of her shoulder from carrying her suitcases. "Men can be so immature."

"I want to experience what life has to offer and get established in a career first. Marriage and kids are in my plans, but somewhere down the road. I want to start dating again, but I'm not ready for anything serious," Lorna explained.

"I'm starving," Gloria said. "Let's go to the dining room and get a bite to eat. I hear the food isn't all that bad."

"Okay, I'm game."

Immersed in conversation, they left the room and went down to the main level. After exchanging childhood experiences and school memories, they returned to their favorite topic—men.

"I have an appointment for you, Miss Sanders," Laurie relayed as the two of them strolled past the front desk. She handed her a slip of paper, still giving her gum a vigorous workout. "You have an interview tomorrow morning at 9:00 A.M. with Mr. Strohman, a lawyer with the Ernst and Lancaster firm at the Spivey Building. You can't miss the place. It's umpteen stories high sitting at 417 Missouri Avenue."

"I remember the street. It's the one we came in on from the train station—with the busy corner that has all of those banks, right?"

"Yes!"

"East or west of them?"

"Just a building or so east of Union Trust on the opposite side of the street from Walgreens. The ***Journal*** newspaper building is next door."

"What floor and room number?"

"Third floor, suite 306.

"I'll find it. Thanks for everything."

"Good luck."

"Thanks again."

Lorna and Gloria went through the mullioned French doors with lace curtains and glass door handles that led to the caféteria in the north end of the building. The walls were wainscoted Alice blue and the rest was painted eggshell white. A variety of delightful dinner aromas floated from the kitchen and tempted their appetites, but Lorna was already lost in thought about what she would say and how the next day's interview change her life.

* * *

The next morning Lorna got up early, showered, then pondered what she should wear. ***Probably something a little conservative.***

Lorna briefly closed her eyes and mentally pictured herself getting the job. ***Brenda Starr, ace girl reporter.***

She tried on a skirt and blouse and then went to the mirror on her clothes closet to check it out. ***I can't believe they didn't install a full-length mirror in this room. I'll bet the whole place was designed by a bunch of Neanderthals who never once gave it a thought. The rules need to change.***

The blouse looked too informal so she went to a drawer and pulled out a sweater. Too warm for that, she thought, eschewing the cashmere birthday present. She placed it back in the drawer, folded the sleeves and patted it smooth. Moving over to the closet, she just stood there for a couple of minutes. Decisions, decisions. Finally, she put on a conservative light gray suit trimmed with red piping. Then she stepped into a pair of navy and white spectator pumps.

"I guess this will have to do," she said in muffled tones. An eyebrow pencil filled in the thin spots above her eyes. She brushed and combed her hair, put on her lipstick, then dabbed a few drops of toilet water on her neck just below her ears. She pinched her cheeks to bring some color into them. She was never one to overdo it with make-up. Her dad had preached endlessly to her, ever since she reached puberty, that war paint all over a maiden's face only made her look cheap and tawdry.

"God gave you a natural beauty, Kitten," he told her. "Don't hide it with colored grease."

Lorna stood at the mirror and tried to analyze her morning makeover. "I wish I had bigger lips," she mused. "I wish they were like Lana Turner's or Betty Grable's. But I guess I'm just stuck with these." The words echoed off the walls of the empty room.

Then she pirouetted and gave her tall, lithe body a once over. As a child, she had been stricken with jaundice. She missed nearly a year of school, but her mother Margaret, an elementary teacher, tutored her in the evenings. She was able to keep up with her studies but she had remained thin—almost skinny. Now, approaching womanhood, she was beginning to fill out, especially her nicely shaped breasts. Small boobs were a blessing as a teen. Girls with large ones were usually self-conscious about them. Lorna hated the way boys sometimes gawked at girls who were overly endowed and made suggestive comments behind their backs in the halls at school. She didn't want to be flat-chested like the pastor's wife at church but hoped to eventually end up somewhere in the medium range, perhaps a 36-C.

Gloria came into the room having finished her shower. The top of her head was wrapped turban-style with a towel.

Lorna turned her back and glanced over her shoulder. "Are my nylon seams straight?"

"They look fine. Break a leg!"

"I think that's for stage performers, not job interviews," Lorna corrected.

"Oops! Well, then, good luck."

"Thanks." Lorna glanced at her watch. It was nearly time to leave. While clipping on a pair of garnet earrings (ear bobs, her late grandmother called them), she hustled down to the dining room. After gobbling up a cinnamon roll, washing it down with a glass of freshly squeezed orange juice, she hurried out the front door.

It was about six blocks to the Spivey Building. Lorna, responding to a slight rush of adrenalin, moved at a quick pace, feeling invigorated by the exercise. The brisk canter gave her a purposeful sensation of moving, going, doing. Specks of mica glittered on the sidewalk.

Shiny cars passed by, streaking the urban tableau with reflective color. After fifteen minutes, she spotted her destination juxtaposed left of the ***Journal*** newspaper office,

(above: Journal Building)

just as Laurie had described. The Spivey Building was graced with dark reddish-brown brick. The ***Journal*** office had a smooth stucco exterior, done in the Art Deco style popular in the late 1920s.

She entered the mini-skyscraper and walked over to the elevator.

"What floor ma'am?" A Negro man, dressed in a smart maroon and gold uniform, politely touched the bill of his cap.

"Third, please."

When the elevator stopped and the doors slid open the man followed her into the hallway. "It's just two doors down on your right, ma'am," he said gesturing with palm open and right arm extended.

"Thank you very much."

The interview with Mr. Strohman went fine. She fielded all of his questions with poise and did her best to radiate an air of confidence and enthusiasm. When the interview was over he informed her that she did quite well but he planned to hire a girl who had the edge on her when it came to experience. Lorna's spirits, quite naturally, were low as she left his office. She passed a trio of men on her way out. The youngest was wearing an orange and blue-striped tie, the school colors of the University of Illinois, but she was lost in thought and barely noticed.

Crestfallen, she trudged through the double doors of the Beulah Club.

"I guess you didn't get the job," Laurie said in almost apologetic fashion.

"No," Lorna said with a note of dejection, "but Mr. Strohman did say I was his second choice."

"Well, there you are. Coming in second on your first interview in the big city isn't all that bad." Laurie made a determined bid to bolster her confidence.

"I know, but that was the perfect job for me. It's exactly what I had my heart set on." Lorna dropped into an overstuffed chair, uncharacteristically letting her shoulders sag, then tilting her head to the back of the chair while she stared at the ceiling. "I don't suppose you have any more leads for me in that magic box of yours?"

Laurie's face lit up. "As a matter of fact I do."

"You've got to be kidding." Lorna bolted upright and jerked her head in Laurie's direction.

"Nope. There's plenty of jobs around here since the Korean conflict broke out. Men are getting drafted and the economy is booming."

"So what do you have, an opening for a laundry maid at some cleaning establishment?"

"Better than that." Laurie held up a copy of the daily newspaper. "You have a chance to be a reporter. It may not be that dream job you were hoping for with the law firm, but it's a pretty good second best."

Lorna got up from the chair and walked toward Laurie. "Tell me more."

"Maury Mermelstein at the ***Journal*** is looking for a girl with good English and typing skills to cover the social scene—you know, coming-out parties, prominent marriages, meetings of literary societies and so on. Do you think you could handle it?"

Lorna paused for the briefest of seconds. It wasn't that secretarial job at a law firm she had hoped for, but it seemed more interesting than typing and taking dictation.

"It sounds perfect," she said exuberantly. She liked the idea of using something she had learned in school, and the chance to get around town and see some of the social elite interested her. "I earned nearly straight A's in grammar and typing back in high school. And my senior year I worked for the school paper."

"Let me call and set up an interview for you, Lorna. I'm sure Maury will be impressed with your qualifications and enthusiasm. Just be sure that when you're seated, you show him a little leg."

"What do you mean?"

"Believe me, honey, I know this guy. My friend, Barb Edelblute, works for him. He likes to look, but he's harmless. The girls around here have told me he is a very nice man to work for. He gives all the gals a box of Mavrakos chocolates for their birthdays and a bottle of champagne at Christmas."

Two hours later, Lorna had a nine o'clock appointment for the next morning.

* * *

Lorna walked into the ***Journal*** building at 8:55.

"I have an appointment with Mr. Mermelstein," Lorna informed Barb Edelblute, the receptionist. Barb hailed from Harrisburg and still carried a slight southern Illinois accent.

Barb Edelblute

"Please have a seat." The woman's hair was pinned into a chignon covered with brown netting. "Mr. Mermelstein will be with you shortly." Barb's voice tinkled—like wind chimes.

Lorna pulled out her compact and gave herself a once-over. She nervously patted down a loose strand of hair. A couple of dabs with her powder puff removed the shine from her nose. The office windows were open for ventilation and the traffic noise zooming back and forth on Missouri Avenue filtered inside. After a ten-minute wait, an obese man in a French blue rayon and cotton suit approached and extended his hand.

"Miss Sanders, I presume?"

I bet he could kill small dogs with just his shadow.

"Yes," Lorna eagerly responded, lightly grasping his hand and briefly shaking it.

"Let's go where we can talk."

He escorted her through the main office area. A rabbit warren of compartmentalized desks were scattered throughout. The insistent whir of a quartet of paddle fans, hung high from above, stirred the air. The place was a random collage of activity—phones were ringing, typewriters chattering, and people of assorted shapes and sizes were scurrying past her. She followed him into a large office surrounded by wood paneled walls and frosted glass, shutting out most, but not all, of the noise. The arrhythmic beat of a Teletype machine echoed from outside the room as it busily spat out black letters on a roll of paper.

"Please have a seat." He held on to the back of a leather padded chair in front of his twin pedestal oak desk and gestured with an open palm that swept downward toward the chair.

Lorna's eyes darted back and forth, taking in as much as she could as he walked around his desk to be seated. A diploma with beige matte border, framed in expensive cherry wood, hung on the wall to her left. A modernistic print graced the opposite wall. It was as if some kindergartner had dripped paint all over a canvas. The artist was Jackson Pollard or Pollack; she couldn't quite make out the name. His desk was a work of art in itself—a still life of clutter. It was literally covered with file folders, newspaper clippings, pens and pencils and assorted sizes of orphaned paper clips. One of those ubiquitous Southwestern Bell telephones sat on the corner. Available in any color, as long as it was black. Incongruously perched in the middle of the mess was a cobalt blue jar of Noxema cream.

"Do you have any samples of your writing?" he asked.

She handed him a sheet of paper. "Just this essay I did for my freshman English class." She watched for a favorable reaction as he read it, but he handed it back without reaction or comment.

"Tell me about your background, Miss Sanders. Then if I think you are right for the job, I'll give you my standard soliloquy about our operating procedures and principles."

"Fair enough." Lorna offered her most pleasant smile.

"Do you have any work experience?" He propped his elbows on the desk, brought his hands together, and interlaced his fingers.

"I helped open a Helpee Selfee laundry in Litchfield last summer and this summer I worked in the library."

"And how much college?"

"Just one year at Southern Illinois at Carbondale where I carried a B average. I wanted to get started on a career.

"Do you know the five W's of journalism?"

"Who, what, where, when and why. But H. L. Mencken admonished not to forget the sixth question—How?"

"Very Good. What writing experience do you have?"

"My experience is limited to writing for the school newspaper, but all of my English teachers said my grammar and composition skills were exceptional. Plus, I'm registered for classes at Summers Business College to get even better," she volunteered, her responses measured and precise.

"It won't hurt to take a couple of classes, but after that, you'll probably be wasting your time. In this business you either know how to write a story or you don't. A good writer must have a nose for news and a journalist's eye for detail. You either have good instincts and a knack for making it interesting, or you fall flat. Can you tell me what the First Commandment of newspaper writing is, young lady?"

Mark Twain

"Thou Shalt Not Be Boring," came her swift reply.

"Interesting. Do you remember what George Bernard Shaw said was a writer's best friend when revising the first draft?"

"Er . . . perhaps the wastebasket," Lorna hesitatingly answered.

Mermelstein smiled. "No, but that's even better than the original."

"What is your favorite Mark Twain quote?"

"Umm. Let me think . . . oh, yes! 'Humans are the only animals that blush . . . or need to.' "

There was a brief pause in the conversation as he clasped his hands behind his head and rolled his eyes to the ceiling. Then he brought them back down and locked onto hers.

"I'd like to hire you, Miss. You've got moxie. I'm impressed by your plucky enthusiasm. But you seem . . . uh, awfully young for this. How do I know you're up to the job?"

She knew by instinct this was the moment of truth. He was on the verge of hiring her but needed that one little extra incentive, whatever it was, to help him say ***yes***.

Maybe I overdid the demure bit, she thought. All during the interview she had been Miss prim and proper, sitting erect with both knees pressed together, feet on the floor, while looking him straight in the eye.

"Well . . ." she paused briefly and nervously adjusted her skirt. Then she slowly crossed her shapely legs. In doing so, the hem of her skirt retreated almost up to her knee. "I get along well with people, and I'm a quick learner. If you're not happy with my first week's work, you can fire me, and you won't owe me a thing."

She extended her toe downward, the way she'd seen Rita Hayworth do it in the movies.

Rita Hayworth

Her words fell on nearly deaf ears. Mermelstein's eyes were following the gentle curve of her leg all the way down her calf to her delicate ankle.

"Mr. Mermelstein?"

"Uh . . . yes, I heard you. Can you start tomorrow?"

"Absolutely," Lorna eagerly said.

"Your salary will be thirty-five dollars a week, and you get seven days of vacation at the end of a year if you're still around by then." His spiel sounded memorized. "Priscilla Bartlett, the lead secretary, will show you the ropes. She proofs and coordinates articles for several sections of the newspaper. She'll help you get started and fill in missing details. You'll mainly be writing copy for the society page—PTA news, dates for club meetings, prominent weddings and fashion trends. As a writer, people are your grist. But show them respect. Make sure what you write is news and not gossip. William Randolph Hearst practically made up stories about scandal, crime and debauchery. We don't do that. 'Integrity First' is our motto. We're not an exposé rag given to assassinating character or dishing up dirt on people. Any questions?" His magpie eyes were still staring at her legs.

"Is that your wife's picture on your desk?"

"Uh, yes. We've been married for almost a year now."

"She appears to be a lovely person. You must be a very lucky man."

"Yes, I am, thanks."

"Thank *you* very much. I really appreciate your giving me this opportunity. I won't disappoint. I'll be here at a quarter-to-eight tomorrow morning. Good-bye."

Lorna was bursting with excitement and she felt as if her heart was about to explode with anticipation. She quickly left the office and exited the building. She could hardly wait to get back to her room so she could write her mother and father a letter, telling them the good news. The first time Lorna saw her byline on an article she had written, she proudly mailed it to her parents.

* * *

Brad Logan was sitting at his desk, contemplating what he had just written in a legal brief, when Thomas Ernst, one of the senior partners of the law firm walked into his office. Ernst, raised in Benton, Illinois, and educated at Northwestern, ran a tight ship. A Stevenson liberal, he was a very cerebral person, brilliantly incisive. He was a lawyer's lawyer and his colleagues respected him for his grasp of complex issues and his uncanny gift for coming up with solid solutions. A meticulous dresser, he set the in-house fashion trend. If the lapels of men's suits got narrower, or the style went from single to double breasted, he was always the first to jump on the trend wagon. He had rather pleasant features, and an infectious smile that endeared him to most in the office. His fiftyish frame, sturdy and erect, featured a receding hairline, a calm face bisected by a strong nose. His face reminded Brad of radio comedian **Jack Benny**.

Jack Benny

"Brad, I've got some good news. You've been assigned to your first case."

"Who's the client?" Brad asked.

"Actually, you'll be assisting Jim Fishbein on this one. It'll be a good way for you to learn how to swim. So far, you've just been treading water."

Ernst's wit was drier than the Mojave Desert. He walked over to the window and stared down at the cars and pedestrians on Collinsville Avenue. "Fishbein knows how to mentor the inexperienced. You'll be representing Louie Sizemore. He's been arrested for the murder of Mr. Torricelli, that construction mogul who was found shot to death out at the lake. He swears he's innocent as **Moon Mullins**—that he's been framed. He's probably as guilty as sin, but everyone who is accused gets a lawyer. That's the system."

"Working with Jim Fishbein should be interesting," Brad lied, hoping it was one of those minor venial sins. From his limited experience around the office, he found Fishbein to be a braggart and slightly obnoxious. He was good at his craft, but he was quick to let everyone else know that his skills were a level or two above the rest. For many, he was someone to emulate—a prototype of the successful lawyer everyone wanted to be. Brad figured he was the kind of man whose success was built on the backs of other people.

"I'll check with Jim and see what he wants me to do to help out."

"Fine, I'll see you later," Ernst said.

Brad could have done worse. Ernst could have given him to Harold Zeigler—a jockey-sized blowhard who had a vast repertoire of crude jokes. Harold gave most of the secretaries a hard time with touchy-feely hands and suggestive remarks that were superficially innocuous, but had a deeper intent for any girl who was interested. He should have acted better because he was married with two kids, but he didn't let his wedding ring stop him from exploring a workplace full of feminine possibilities.

Brad walked over to the far side of the firm's suite of offices where Fishbein was located. Joan Vail, his vibrant and efficient secretary, was just outside his door at her own desk. Her fingers a blur, she was typing something from a Dictaphone.

"Good morning, Joan, how is the world treating you?"

Joan, a legal secretary for about twelve years, dressed demurely in forties-style fitted suits and always wore her hair pulled back into an Eva Perón bun. Originally with Rathman, Degnan, Goldenhersh and Driscoll, she quit in a huff when they promoted someone with less experience to "lead" executive secretary. She was good at her job, and Brad's group was lucky to have her. Joan was a lawyer's dream—efficient, discreet and loyal to the core. She was as constant as the constellations.

"Oh, I can't complain." She smiled and shuffled some papers. "How about you?"

"I'm hanging in there. You look very chic in that outfit. It's very becoming."

"Thank you."

"Is Jim inside?"

"Sure, just knock on the door and go on in. He's going over some depositions in the Markowitz fraud case."

A light, almost apologetic, tap on the doorjamb.

"It's open," Fishbein called. He was at his desk, soberly puffing on his pipe. He finished blotting the ink dry on his signature, then looked up and waved Brad in. The place had the smell of sweet tobacco and Moroccan leather-bound books. His diploma from Washington University of St. Louis proudly hung behind his desk, framed and matted. A framed picture of David ben-Gurion dominated one corner of his desk.

Probably big into Zionism, Brad thought.

"What can I do for you?" said Fishbein, whose neatness was reflected both in his demeanor and in the appearance of the room.

"Mr. Ernst sent me over here." The entire wall to the right was filled with law books and volumes of Illinois Revised Statutes embossed in gold lettering. The rest of the room was clothed in rich burnished panels of dark, reddish wood. The wall behind Fishbein sported diplomas, citations, and service awards—an ego wall, a billboard of achievement. His massive mahogany desk was a model of orderliness. Brad's was always a couple inches deep in letters, files, and reports.

Indicative of a disheveled mind according to an old proverb, Brad thought.

Some things in life just don't make sense. Brad's office desk was always a mess, but his room at home was neat as a pin. He made his bed every morning with military tucks on the corners. The sheet was stretched so tight you could bounce a quarter off the surface. He was equally fastidious about keeping his car clean and Simonized, and the engine was kept in show-room condition.

"Nice office."

"Thanks. Have a seat." Fishbein placed a letter he had been reading in the bottom section of a three-tiered set of wooden trays. A half-dozen unopened letters were neatly stacked on one corner of the desk. A weak smile reshaped a face that had been etched with a look of pensive contemplation.

"Mr. Ernst told me I've just volunteered to work with you on the Sizemore case." Brad sank deeply into a dark brown leather chair. "I'm sure you have some legwork you'd like me to do. How can I help?"

"Well, Logan, glad to have you aboard. I heard you graduated in the top ten percent of your class at Champaign-Urbana. Your resumé tells me you were a standout in moot court, and that you received the David Lanius award for exemplary performance during mock trial. We're about to find out if you're really worth your salt and can pull your own weight around here. We'll get along just fine if you follow my instructions explicitly, use a little common sense, and have everything that's requested on my desk when it's supposed to be there. Be punctual with your appointments. Remember, if you're on time, you're late."

It took Brad a couple of seconds to figure out what he meant. Fortunately, his face didn't betray him while he sorted out the hidden meaning.

"I understand."

"Our clients pay good money because they expect us to win cases." He was tamping tobacco in his briar pipe bowl. "We do that by being just a little quicker and a little smarter than the opposition. Winning a favorable ruling or verdict is like playing poker and chess at the same time. Sometimes it's smoke and mirrors, style over substance, a bluff or subterfuge that carries the day. Cunning and guile, concede minor defeats . . . the whole process is essentially a giant gameboard where you and your client survive by your wits. You do play chess?"

"I'm familiar with all the pieces and their moves, but I never really got into it. Too sedentary."

Fishbein lit the pipe, sucking the flame down to the packed tobacco from the stem. He exhaled and moved the pipe to the right corner of his mouth. "Too bad," he said, mildly disappointed.

Brad regretted using the word ***sedentary***.

"You'll make mistakes; we all do." He puffed a blue-gray cloud of fragrant smoke. "But there is a big difference between an honest mistake and incompetence. Just be sure you learn from your errors. Don't do anything to embarrass the firm. I know you don't have a lot of experience, so don't be afraid to ask questions. You'll learn a lot just by paying close attention and following my lead. My forte is matching wits in the courtroom. I'm very good at cross-examination. You'll do most of the legwork."

He paused and gave Brad a quick once over—as if he had never really paid much attention to him up to now. Brad could tell he was sizing him up and trying to come to some conclusion about his abilities, the same way lawyers try to make judgments about potential jurors.

"Any questions?"

"No, sir."

"Tell my secretary to give you a duplicate of everything I have on this case. Then get over to see our client at the county jail. He's scheduled for arraignment at one-thirty before Judge Kermit F. Croissant. There isn't any way the judge is going to allow bail in a capital murder case. Louie's going to plead not guilty, so everything is routine at this point. Let me know if the judge sets a trial date. Familiarize yourself with the facts of the case and see if the prosecution has any loose ends we can exploit."

"What is this Judge Croissant like?"

"He can be a bear—like Jeffries, the "hanging judge" of the English Restoration Era. When you run afoul of him, you can hear a buzz saw cutting out the floor beneath your feet."

"Now that's tough."

"He's a crusty old goat who doesn't put up with any nonsense in his courtroom. He's known for imposing onerous penalties. And he's smart. Very smart. He can simultaneously keep track of what's going on in a trial and do a crossword puzzle without missing a beat. A strange bird sometimes. His first name, Kermit, is German—his last, Croissant, is French."

"Weird combination," Brad remarked. "The French and the Germans hate each other, like the Hatfields and McCoys."

"Maybe that explains his occasional schizophrenic behavior. He had a great grandmother on his mother's side who was a madam, and a grandfather on his dad's side who was the last toll booth keeper on the old Rock Road."

"My uncle said the old toll roads were hated by nearly everyone."

"Yes. The goofy politicians even tried to collect tolls on people riding velocipedes."

"Velocipedes?"

"Bicycles."

"Oh."

He relit the pipe.

"Back around 1910 someone set fire to the booth and burned it to the ground."

Brad shook his head in disbelief.

"Well . . . I need to get back to work," Fishbein said. "Any questions?"

"Nope—everything's copacetic."

He seems nice enough, Brad thought. ***Maybe I misjudged him.***

* * *

Brad went back to his office with carbon copies of Sizemore's file, his eyes collecting the pertinent information. The folder contained crime scene information, an autopsy statement, preliminary police investigative reports and photos. Then he left the office and went to the parking lot behind the Spivey Building and climbed into his Bahama blue Studebaker. It was a year-old model bought from L. F. Hutchcraft, a salesman he knew who worked at Mixon Motors on St. Louis Avenue. He weaved through the traffic and made his way over to State Street. From there it was a straight shot to the outskirts of town at Edgemont, about seven miles away. A large banner proclaimed a revival in progress at First Baptist Church next to the Sears store. Brad had vague memories of attending Sunday school there as a young boy when his family lived on Seventh Street. He passed a billboard advertising the latest Buick Roadmaster at Mixon Motors. During the war, that billboard had pictured Uncle Sam with his sleeves rolled up, intoning that production would defeat the Axis.

It was stifling hot, one of those muggy days of late summer when supposedly only mad dogs and Englishmen risked walking in the sun. Brad slipped out of his coat, loosened his diagonally striped tie and rolled down the windows. The light went red at 25th and State. He braked to a stop. His car had a metal visor that extended the roofline about a foot. This helped keep the intense sun off the windshield, but when you came to rest at a stoplight, it was impossible to tell when it changed. Fortunately, some Thomas Edison type invented an ingenious device to overcome the problem. It was like one of those neat ideas you frequently read about in "Popular Science" magazine. For a mere two dollars at Western Auto, Brad had bought a prismatic device whose magnetized base held fast to the metal dash. The mechanism bent rays of light like a periscope and gave him a perfect view of the light, showing him when to proceed. As he approached the bluffs, the large, white frame outline of a church grabbed his attention. Actually, it was their sign:

EDGEMONT BIBLE CHURCH
REV. G. JOSEPH WRIGHT, PASTOR
S.S. 9:30 A.M., MORNING WORSHIP 10:45
"IF YOU THINK IT'S HOT HERE . . . "

Local campaign posters decorated a row of telephone poles. Brad looked up at the wires, wondering about the voices that waltzed through them, and was intrigued by the blue-green insulators that held the message senders apart. As a youth, he had loved shimmying up the scarred trunks and climbing the spikes to the top to touch a cloud, or, failing that, survey his neighborhood. He had also been an avid tree climber and sitter. Tree sitting was a semi-idiotic form of sport that was briefly popular in the early thirties, along with flagpole sitting. He smiled as he passed Eddie Bush's' Standard Station at 60th Street. Someone had mischievously painted "**Kilroy Was Here**" on a fence at the side of his lot.

Twenty minutes later he arrived at the St. Clair County jail in Belleville. A sheriff's deputy arranged for him to meet with his client.

Sizemore sat on a plain chair in the conference room at the jailhouse. The bleak room housed a couple of wooden chairs and a pockmarked table rimmed with numerous cigarette burns. Nervously chain-smoking, he blew smoke rings toward the ceiling. He had reddish-brown hair and a stocky build. A clean white T-shirt with a small tear on the right sleeve clung to his frame. A pack of cigarettes was rolled up in his left sleeve. His pants were a cheap variety of blue denim, courtesy of local taxpayers.

Mr. Kilroy with his cartoon character

"Hello, Mr. Sizemore. I'm Brad Logan, assistant to Mr. Fishbein, your attorney. You have an arraignment in forty-five minutes at the courthouse." It occurred to Brad that Sizemore had the same stuck-out ears as his cousin in Golconda.

Sizemore stroked a prominent Adam's apple. "Well, I'm pleadin' ***not*** guilty." It bobbed when he talked.

"The police have a pretty good circumstantial case against you. Maybe you should think about copping a plea. It might save you from getting the chair."

"No way. I can beat this thing."

"Why do you think the police singled you out for the crime?"

"Knucky fingered me."

"Why would he do that?"

"Because I work for him at Globe Amusement Company.

I deliver hardware and collect the weekly take from his juke boxes, pinball games, and cigarette machines."

Brad leaned forward. "That still doesn't answer my question."

"He did it because he thinks I'm skimming."

"Are you?"

"Absolutely not."

"The last time Mr. Torricelli was known to be alive, he was seen talking to you at Joe and Ted's Brass Rail on 13th and Lynch."

"Yeah, I know."

"The bartender claims he saw the two of you leave the place together. Another guy, who works for the fish hatchery out at the lake, says he saw a gray Plymouth sedan driving through the park late on the night of the murder. He remembered it because it had plastic whitewall rings, and one of the rings was missing on the driver's side. Unfortunately, Louie, you drive a gray Plymouth DeLuxe, and the front tire is missing its fake whitewall."

Louie Sizemore's gray Plymouth

"What can I say? There are probably hundreds of gray sedans in this town."

"There's more. The police had a moulage made of the footprints, a plaster of Paris cast."

He remained resolute. "So what! There's a million guys out there who wear a size eight."

"Don't be stupid, Louie. No jury is going to believe you. Give me something Fishbein can take to the D.A. My partner and I will get you the best deal we can."

A look of dejection and hopelessness settled over Louie's face. His shoulders sagged.

"Okay. Here's what really happened." He had finished his cigarette and began shaking the last two out of the pack. He placed one behind his ear and lit the other one.

"I got a contract to kill this Torricelli guy for $3,000. There was this call on the phone from a man who said his name was Al. I'm sure that wasn't his real name. He said I'd get half the dough up front if I agreed to do it and the rest after the job was done." Blue smoke escaped his nostrils.

"Go on."

"Said it needed to happen before the grand jury met to begin an inquiry into vice and corruption in St. Clair County. That gave me about a week. He must have known I was going to say yes. After I agreed to do it, he told me to go look outside in my tool shed, and I would find the money in a Folger's coffee tin. He told me to leave the can there after I got the dough, and the rest of it would show up within a week after the hit."

"Nothing I have heard so far is going to save your skin," Brad said.

"There's more. Before I killed the guy I asked him if he knew why anyone would pay me $3,000 to get him planted. He said it was because he could prove there was collusion in public construction contracts. Some pretty big fish in the City Hall pond were in trouble because they were awarding contracts to companies that knew how to 'play ball.' After the contract was awarded, there would be cash payments under the table. You know—kickbacks. Torricelli was going to squeal because he had been the low bidder on some public housing projects but didn't get the contract when he didn't 'scratch' the right backs. He begged me to let him go. Said he'd pay me $3,000 plus another $1,500 on top of that. But I couldn't welsh on a deal I had already agreed to. It would ruin my reputation."

"So you can name names and give the State's Attorney something he's been looking for—proof of public corruption."

"Well, not exactly."

"What do you mean, ***not exactly***?"

"He rattled off some names, but didn't have the proof. He said it was in a file somewhere in his home. After I shot him, I didn't give much thought to the list after that. Figured I was better off letting a sleeping dog lie."

"Where does Knucky fit into all of this?"

"He didn't know nothin' about it. I was strictly on my own, moonlightin' to earn some extra cash. My mistake was I started spending the money on booze an' dames. I also placed some big bets with my bookie."

"What's his name?"

"John Cleveland. He doubles as a bellhop at the Broadview Hotel."

"We need names and specifics to take to the D.A. before he's going to be willing to reduce the charges. Was Torricelli married?"

"Yes. He lived somewhere in the French Village area."

"Okay. I'll go see his wife as soon as I can," Brad told him.

CHAPTER 6

Thanks to the riverfront area known as Bloody Island, once a no-man's land in the middle of North America's mightiest river, East St. Louis always had an unsavory reputation. Its name came from the numerous duels, cock fights and bare knuckle brawls held on the island in the early 1800s. It was perceived as a violent place—a repository for miscreants and other do-badders in the "Kentuckyan" image. Bloody Island became a part of East St. Louis in the 1830s when Robert E. Lee and the U.S. Army Corps of Engineers built a series of dikes that caused it to become attached to the Illinois shoreline.

Judge Croissant was everything Fishbein said he was. And more. He stood about six foot tall and was thin, but not

1950 Hudson Convertible

gaunt. He looked more German than French and ran his court like a Prussian drillmaster. Brad could almost envision a spiked helmet on his head. He had a commanding presence from his elevated position on the dais.

"People versus Louis Sizemore, docket number 50733," he thundered, peering over his half-rim glasses. "Mr. uh, Fish–"

"It's Brad Logan, your Honor. I'm Mr. Fishbein's assistant. He couldn't be here today."

"Yeah, yeah—spare me the details . . . Your client is charged with one count of first degree murder; how does he plead?"

Sizemore, in cuffs, was standing next to Brad. Directly behind him was a uniformed officer.

"Not guilty, your Honor," Sizemore said defiantly.

"Defense suggests bail in the amount of $10,000."

"The state ob–"

"I'm way ahead of you counselor," Judge Croissant said to Gary Barber, the new hot shot out of the prosecutor's office.

"And I'd like a new Hudson for my birthday," the judge responded sarcastically to Brad. "This is a capital case. The D.A.'s office has filed a motion asking that the accused be remanded to the county jail for the duration of the trial. So ordered. Trial date is set eight weeks from today. Either of you esteemed gentleman have a problem with that?"

"No, sir," they said in chorus.

Brad figured Sizemore was just a pawn in some kind of deadly game. And there were other unknowns who were rooks, knights and bishops. But who were the grand masters moving them around? Walters? Municipal power brokers? Rival gangsters? What he failed to consider was that another chess piece was now in play—him.

A few days later, Brad went to see Torricelli's widow and they searched the desk and filing cabinet in her husband's office but found nothing to substantiate Sizemore's story.

* * *

Brad was working late at the office, preparing for the Sizemore trial, when he noticed the cleaning lady across the hall vacuuming the carpet. She was a woman of indeterminate years. Age lines were deeply etched across her forehead. Her skin was dark like cowhide, and she seemed prematurely old, but the lines in her face gave her character. She was humming a tune he didn't recognize. Her preoccupation with work kept her from being aware of his presence.

"Hello there," he shouted.

She glanced up from her chores, slightly startled by the sound of his voice.

"I'm Brad Logan."

"Hello, suh. Didn't hear ya steppin' up behind me. Watcha want, young man? Cain't talk now . . . gotta get these rooms clean an' time's a-wastin'."

She turned off the Rexair sweeper, emptied the wastebasket, and began dusting with a soft cotton rag. Curious, he left his desk and walked over to the room where she was working. A yellow floral cotton print hung limp around her body. An askew brown kerchief, tied Aunt Jemima fashion, covered her short coarse hair. Her ebony eyes had a hurried but friendly look to them.

"I don't believe we've met," he offered in an awkward effort to make conversation.

"Now ya pos'tively ***know*** we ain't never met, Mista." She shot him a look of disbelief. "Ain't never seen ya' round' here. Whatcha' tryin' ta do gettin' in way o' my work? Cain't ya see I got rooms to clean?"

Brad stepped back into the hall and put two nickels into the soda machine. He pulled out a pair of Dr. Peppers and went back to her room.

"You look like you could use a break." He winked. "They say you're supposed to drink three of these a day—at ten, two and four to keep up your energy level."

She stared silently for a few seconds at the proffered soft drink.

"Nothin' wrong with my energy level." Her long thin arm reached out and her bony fingers took it from his hand. "Thank ya' just the same. Why'sa rich white boy wastin' his time, an' mine, wantin' to talk for?"

"I try to make it a point to be friendly to everyone. Sorry, I didn't catch your name."

She took a sip and then rolled the cool bottle back and forth a couple of times across her forehead. The back of her hand had the look and texture of a dried leaf of Kentucky Burley tobacco.

"Didn't throw it, but if'n ya really wants to know, it be Missola."

"Missola what?"

"Folks just calls me Missola. Not my real name, but friends an' fam'ly call me that for years. Suppose it's 'cause I be from Me'sippi, like most other cullud folk in this here town."

Her bottle was half drained now.

"Did you ever live anywhere else?"

"Lived for 'while in Colp."

"Where's that?"

"Down by Metropolis an' Mound City." She gave him a curious look. "New 'round here, ain't you?"

"Yep. Only been here 'bout three weeks," he replied, in a vernacular that he hoped might make her feel more comfortable. "What does your husband do for a livin'?"

"My first one's daid. Useda' work at the cre'sote plant down by Route 3. Got killed a couple years back when a chain with a load o' railroad ties went an' broke. Was plumb crushed under that mass o' heavy timber."

"I'm very sorry to hear it, ma'am."

"Preciate that. I do b'lieve you be the first white man ever call me ma'am. Ya' musn't know much 'bout how the way things is between the white folk an' black folk."

"No, ma'am, I don't believe I do."

"My second husband, George, runs the elevator here."

"I know George, he's a fine man. Do you have any children?"

"Three young uns. Big strappin' boy at Lincoln High School an' two sweet girls at Dunbar. My boy play trumpet in the school band. Miles Davis went to Lincoln. My boy

Miles Davis: born in Alton, but his family moved to East St. Louis at age one

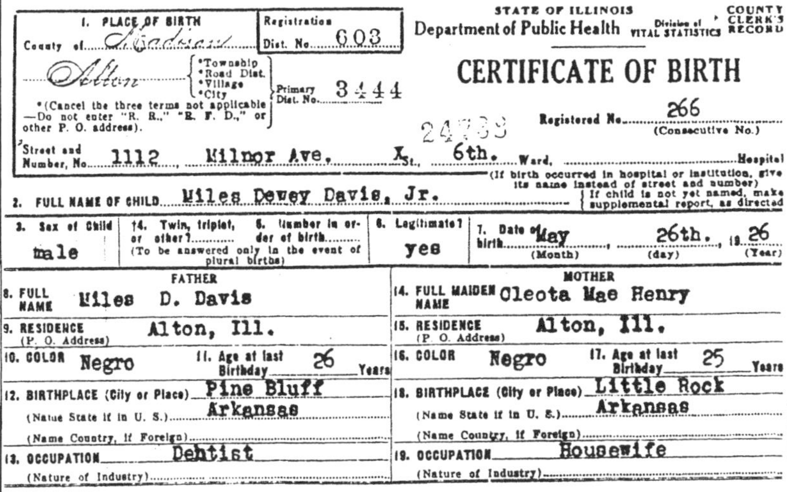
STATE OF ILLINOIS
Department of Public Health — Division of Vital Statistics — County Clerk's Record

CERTIFICATE OF BIRTH

1. PLACE OF BIRTH — County of Madison — Registration Dist. No. 603
Alton — *Township *Road Dist. *Village *City — Primary Dist. No. 3444
*(Cancel the three terms not applicable—Do not enter "R. R.," "R. F. D.," or other P. O. address).
24739 — Registered No. 266 (Consecutive No.)
Street and Number, No. 1112, Milnor Ave. St., 6th. Ward, ... Hospital
(If birth occurred in hospital or institution, give its name instead of street and number)

2. FULL NAME OF CHILD Miles Dewey Davis, Jr. (If child is not yet named, make supplemental report, as directed)

3. Sex of Child	†4. Twin, triplet, or other?	5. Number in order of birth (To be answered only in the event of plural births)	6. Legitimate?	7. Date of birth
male			yes	May (Month), 26th. (day), 1926 (Year)

FATHER		MOTHER	
8. FULL NAME	Miles D. Davis	14. FULL MAIDEN NAME	Cleota Mae Henry
9. RESIDENCE (P. O. Address)	Alton, Ill.	15. RESIDENCE (P. O. Address)	Alton, Ill.
10. COLOR	Negro — 11. Age at last Birthday 26 Years	16. COLOR	Negro — 17. Age at last Birthday 25 Years
12. BIRTHPLACE (City or Place)	Pine Bluff	18. BIRTHPLACE (City or Place)	Little Rock
(Name State if in U. S.)	Arkansas	(Name State if in U. S.)	Arkansas
(Name Country, if Foreign)		(Name Country, if Foreign)	
13. OCCUPATION (Nature of Industry)	Dentist	19. OCCUPATION (Nature of Industry)	Housewife

wants to join him an' his group some day."

"I can tell you're real proud of him."

"Yessuh'. Bet ya' don't never listen to *jazz* music, do ya'?"

"Not really," Brad replied, slightly embarrassed by his narrow taste. "I do like Nat King Cole though."

"Heard o' Duke Ellington?"

"Oh yes, I know the name, but I wouldn't recognize his music."

"East St. Looie be justa 'bout his fav'rite place. Come here all the time an' play night clubs on both sides o' the river. His fav'rite spot be the Terrace Lounge, right here in this ol' town. Wrote a good peppy tune 'round '28 called 'East St. Louis Toodle-O.' 'Came one o' his best theme songs."

"Maybe I'll hear it on WTMV radio some time," he said.

"How 'bout Cab Calloway, famous for his show at the Cotton Club in Harlem?"

"Isn't he noted for his 'Hi de hi de ho' line?"

"That be right, heh, heh," she chuckled. "D'ja know them words is 'bout having a good ol' time in the Valley?"

"Never knew that."

They finished their drinks about the same time. He took her empty bottle. "Let me put these back in the empty case."

"Land sakes! An' a gentleman too. You sho is diff'rent from any white man I ever knowed," she exclaimed. "You've wasted 'nough o' my time. Needs to get back to work before ya gets me fired. Thank ya for the bottle o' pop."

"You're welcome. See you again, sometime."

"I takes care o' ya real nice when I gets 'round ta cleaning your office."

"Thanks, but that isn't necessary."

"I'ze gonna polish that' desk o' yours so bright, ya can use it to comb your hair."

"That's very thoughtful," he said.

She turned and hurried out the door and down the hall to clean another room.

* * *

One of Knucky Walters' warehouses was located just off Route 40, several blocks from **Kassly's Funeral Home.** The old two-story frame had once been a storage facility for Eagle-Picher Lead Company. A clutter of old slot machines, jukeboxes and pinball games occupied most of the first floor. Cigarette machines lined the south wall. The ones on the left were refurbished and waiting to be delivered to customers, some as far north as Madison and Brooklyn. Others needed repairs—a broken knob, faulty wiring, or an internal lever mechanism that required a new spring. One had a broken faceplate, victim of a drunken customer whose quarter had been eaten by the metal monster. Glass shards still lay inside the metal frame.

The fire began shortly after 1:00 A. M. Petroleum distillate had been poured on top of a heap of cardboard boxes, old newspapers and a clump of oily rags piled at the foot of the stairs that led to the second level. It was almost a certainty someone was going to die. A shadowy figure moved stealthily inside and opened a window to ensure an adequate oxygen supply for the flames. After setting fire to the pile, the arsonist doused the wall near the door with liquid and tossed a lighted match in that direction. Then he disappeared into the night.

Kassly's Funeral Home

Most firemen consider each fire different, and they talk about the flames as if they can take on a life and personality of their own—a breathing animal, a living, consuming dragon. The men with axes and hoses dubbed this one Grendel because its scorching breath devoured nearly everything it touched. Yet all fires merely conform to the laws of physics. This time the superheated air, dense smoke and hungry flames rushed like red-hot lava into every vacant space. The temperature inside the building reached nearly twelve hundred degrees Fahrenheit as the fire hungrily searched for more combustibles to satiate its appetite. Plastic wilted and bubbled like hot cakes in an iron skillet. Metal legs buckled. Timbers burned like matchsticks.

Jake Smedly, Walters' manager, awakened with a start. He had been in deep sleep and did not know what caused his eyelids to flutter open. The sour smell of acrid smoke was beginning to assault his nostrils. Ravenous flames had raced up the stairs and were licking at his bedroom door. An eerie groaning and whooshing sound awakened him. The very soul of evil had escaped from Hell. He arose from his Murphy bed and opened the door ever so slightly.

It was his last act on Earth. For a few agonizing seconds he stared death in the face. Then the demon swarmed all over him devouring and roaring, sending him straight to perdition, ending his life on earth in the cruelest manner possible.

His blood-curdling cries and shrieks were heard by firefighters from engine house number two as they arrived on the scene. They responded to an anonymous phone tip that a fire was raging a block or so from the Pennsylvania Railroad overpass on Collinsville Road.

Several half-empty bottles of whiskey on a shelf exploded with a pop! pop! pop! like a carnival shooting gallery. When the intense heat and flames met a five-gallon can of cleaning solvent in a closet, the resulting explosion blew out the building's windows, helping to equalize the pressure. Several walls collapsed. The fire had reached the flashover point and was now fully developed. Scarlet sparks churned skyward.

Black smoke billowed forth, nearly blotting out a three-quarter moon. The fire's distinctive smell of burnt charcoal permeated air that was full of grit. The firemen, withstanding the onslaught of heat the equivalent of a blast furnace, quickly hooked up their hoses. They knew the fire had claimed a life and was too advanced to save the building, but they were determined not to let it spread. The first truck, using its five hundred gallon internal tank, sprayed a steady stream on the roof of a house next door to prevent burning embers from taking hold.

Onlookers watched in morbid fascination as the firemen went about their work. One of those who watched had different feelings. Erik Meade, the man who had set the fire, was ablaze with a mixture of awe and admiration.

"That's the most spectacular fire we've had around here for some time," he said to a thin elderly man next to him.

"Worst I've seen since the grain elevator fire three years ago," the man said.

Meade quietly chatted with those around him, making conversation about what a terrible tragedy it was and speculating about the fire's origins. The fire had sparked his emotions and fully engaged his senses. He stood at the crowd's forefront, wanting to feel the excitement of the fire's heat radiating on his cheeks. In his mind, the visual and symbolic power of fire was spectacular. To him there was visceral magic in watching burning embers being pushed skyward by the updraft of heat, their glow finally diminishing and then slowly floating back to earth.

The second pumper hooked up a four-inch line from the nearby hydrant to the truck. Then three hoses, an inch-and-a-half in diameter, were clamped onto the brass fittings of the trucks' pumping system, and a trio of arched streams of water, gushing out at eight hundred gallons a minute, were directed into the windows. The sounds emanating from the conflagration reminded onlookers of death rattles. A few minutes later, the composition shingles, tarpaper, and rafters imploded in final agony as the building gave up the ghost. When it was over, two hours later, the fire had spared little except for some porcelain bathroom fixtures, a cast iron furnace, and the concrete foundation. A couple of charred walls maintained a wobbly existence until the firemen pulled them down for safety's sake. Fortunately, the fire had been contained.

When the horribly disfigured body was recovered from a pile of rubble, a call was made to the homicide division of the East St. Louis PD.

* * *

Knucky was sitting at his usual booth at the Club 501 when Brad came in the day after the fire. He was hunched forward, and his left elbow was on the table while his hand supported his brow. He looked morose, as if the weight of the world was on his shoulders.

The story about the fire had made the front page of the ***Journal*** and the ***East St. Louis Press.*** On the same page was a story about a fledgling pilot-in-training from Parks Air College flying under the Eads Bridge. The dangerous stunt broke a cardinal rule at the college, but draconian penalties would probably never be applied in this case because no one reported the "buzz" number. Rules against underflying the bridges were broken with abandon because it was said one didn't get to be a "hot shot" pilot without doing this at least once.

Knucky sat up as Brad took a seat across from him. That famous scowl was etched across his face.

"They're out to get me, kid. Those goons think they can just waltz in here and grab everything for themselves. Well . . . I'll show 'em this old dog has a few tricks left. They're gonna be sorry they started this."

"Who are ***they***?"

"Dunno for sure, but I got some ideas. They sent me this penny postcard. Here, take a look." He shoved the buff card stock forward. It had a canceled green picture of Ben Franklin in the upper corner.

"Postmark's from Marion, Illinois, a couple of days ago," Brad noted."Yeah. Well, I'll bet you six ways from Sunday this message came from St. Louis—not southern Illinois."

"Why?"

"Gut instinct."

Brad flipped the card over and read the cryptic message. It contained a thinly veiled threatening rhyme:

Humptey-Dumpty sat on a wall
Humptey-Dumpty had a great fall
All the king's horses
And all the king's men
Couldn't put Knuck—uh, Humptey
Back together again.

It was signed "A friend!"

"They misspelled Humpty," Brad said. "What are you going to do?"

"This isn't anything new. Some gang in St. Louis has been trying to muscle in on East St. Louis ever since the start of Prohibition."

"I remember something in the newspaper about the Cuckoo Gang; was that one of them?"

"Yeah. They tried to take over when I was working for the Shelton brothers, but we taught them a lesson."

"I'm curious. Were you with the Sheltons during their feud with the Birger Gang?"

"Uh, huh. Bernie Shelton an' me ran around together. We were at Charlie Birger's hanging at Benton in 1928."

"So, what are you going to do about the postcard?"

"Think I'll have armor plate put on this building."

"Not a good idea, Mr. Walters. That will scare off your business."

"Yeah, I guess you're right."

"Well, at the very least, I'm going to move so I can sleep at night knowing that my wife an' kids are safe."

"What's wrong with where you live now?"

"It's at the top of the bluff in Caseyville, a half mile north of Bunkum Road. Several of my good friends an' relatives live nearby. Some smart-alec newspaper reporter nicknamed it Hoodlum Haven. The house ain't big enough for me, my family, and my bodyguards. An since it's so close to the road, it would be easy for thugs ta drive by in a car an' blast away at the place with Tommy guns." A smile of self-satisfaction appeared on Walters' face. "I got even with that reporter though."

East St. Louis businessman Lloyd 'Knucky' Walters' home in Caseyville

"Mr. Walters, you didn't—"

"Take it easy, kid. He came in here one day nosin' around for some big exposé he was plannin' to write. Said it was going to win him a pullet, or something like that."

"I think you probably mean a Pulitzer."

"Yeah, that's it—Pughlitzer." His eyes grew bright as he relished the thought of retelling the story.

"The reporter barged in here an' began askin' around about licenses, health inspections an' other stuff. I told him to leave, but he said this place was open to the public an' I had no right to ask. Threatened to bring in a whole slew of reporters, crawlin' around like snakes with forked tongues, asking patrons questions, designed to make them uncomfortable."

"What happened next?" Brad asked. "You didn't hit him with a black jack, did you?"

"Better than that. I told my bartender to put some KO drops in his drink."

"Chloral hydrate—you didn't."

"Yep! Slipped him a Mickey Finn. Carl Shelton once told me that the term came from a famous 19th century Chicago gangster."

"People can die if too much is placed in their drink," Brad warned.

"My bartender, Larry Williamson, is an expert. His dose is anywhere from five to ten grains, depending on a person's size an' weight. The reporter started feeling listless an' decided to leave. It was late at night an' raining to beat the band. When he slipped off into dreamland, his car missed a curve an' he wrapped it around a tree. Put him in the hospital for a couple of weeks with a broken wrist, a fractured rib an' a concussion."

"Why didn't he sue or prosecute?"

"He didn't wake up for a couple of days. By then it was all out of his system. The evidence went in one end an' out the other—so to speak."

All of a sudden, one of those incandescent light bulbs lit up Brad's brain.

"Mr. Walters, I just might have the solution to your problem."

"How's that, kid?"

"Your security problem. My uncle, Frank Gabrial, a coal dealer in Washington Park, owns a farm in rural Edwardsville he wants to sell—at least part of it. It was unseasonably warm last winter, and he did a poor business."

"I'm not ready to be put out to pasture yet, pal."

"You don't understand. It's out by old Poag Road, in the northwest part of an unincorporated area."

"So?"

"It has a small lake with an island in the middle."

"I still don't get it."

"You could build your new house out on the island. It would be like one of those old castles in medieval times—a fortress surrounded by a moat. The old time castles had a causeway—ingress and egress—controlled access. A single road that extended from the surrounding land and crossed the moat. There isn't any reason why that couldn't be done."

"It would take a heck of a lot of dirt," he said.

"Haven't you heard the expression 'dirt cheap'? Dirt only costs two dollars a truckload."

"But I'd want the water ta flow all the way around the house."

"No problem. You could either place culverts in the causeway or build a stone bridge with arches."

"I'm beginning to like it. Do ya think I could have a drawbridge?"

"Now that might be expensive."

"How about crocodiles in the moat?" He was beginning to get giddy, like a kid receiving a sled for Christmas.

"Crocs are mostly in Africa. Alligators are indigenous to the U.S., but this is too far north."

"Yeah, besides, they might come crawlin' up to the house and eat Bruno, my German shepherd. Let's drive out there sometime an' take a look."

"How about now? I don't have to be back at the office for a couple of hours yet. My next appointment isn't until two."

"Okay," Knucky said. "Let's vamoose."

They went out the side door followed by Roland, Walters' hulking bodyguard. When they got to Knucky's car in the parking lot, Brad was surprised to see another man, smartly dressed and dark of skin, was the chauffeur.

"This is Montrose, my driver," Knucky said. "Montrose, meet Brad Logan."

He pumped Brad's hand in a crushing grip. ***Montrose isn't just a driver, he's another bodyguard.***

He flashed a wide toothy grin, exposing a gold bicuspid. Montrose was a handsome man, built like a Mack truck, with dark hair, processed with Kunk. He was, in East St. Louis vernacular, black as the ace of spades.

Knucky and Brad scooted into the rich leather backseat. Knucky sat on the passenger side. Walters' car, like Gatsby's, was the ***ne plus ultra*** of automobiles. It was a 1938

Knucky's 1938 "Spirit of Motion" Supercharger Custom Graham – original cost $1,320

"sharknose" Graham, but it looked brand new.

"I always stay over here," he explained. "That way if someone comes along side of us in a car full of guns, I have a better chance of not getting hit."

"You're not expecting any trouble today, I hope."

Montrose slipped behind the wheel, and Roland rode shotgun. The radio was turned way down low, and it was playing what Brad discerned to be jazz music. It seemed a profane mix of drums, piano, trumpet and saxophones.

Brad looked at Knucky. "Is that what you listen to—jazz?"

"Not necessarily, but it's what Montrose likes, an' in this car he's the cock of the walk. I let him listen to it as long as he keeps it low."

When it came to matters of his car, Knucky apparently gave Montrose ***carte blanche.***

Brad leaned toward the driver. "Hey, Montrose, is that Miles Davis' sky-splitting trumpet?"

Montrose was tapping a syncopated rhythm on the steering wheel with his fingers.

"Sure is. And John Coltrane is on the sax. Man, I dig that stuff."

Brad's feet thunked against what looked to be a violin case on the floorboard. Knucky caught him staring at it.

Knucky gave a sly smile. "Got any idea what's inside?"

"I doubt if it's a musical instrument."

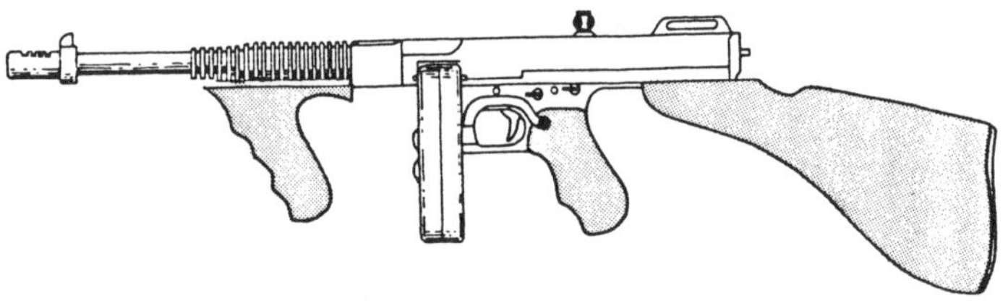

"Ever heard of John Thompson?"

"Sure. Invented the Tommy gun."

"How'd ya know?

"My parents took my sister and me on a trip to Washington, D. C., one summer. In the FBI building they had one mounted on a wall as part of a display."

Knucky unfastened the hinge locks and took it out of the case. He cradled it in his arms like a baby. "Ain't she a beaut?" He handed Brad the weapon. "Fits in your hands almost as good as a woman's body. Whadda ya think?"

"Looks like an antique to me. Thirty-eight caliber?"

"Forty-five."

"Fifty rounds in the drum?"

"It's the deluxe model—one hundred."

"What kind of wood is the stock and front grip?"

"Hand carved rosewood."

"I don't see any notches on it."

"Haven't had to use it on anybody . . . yet."

"Here." Brad gingerly handed it back. "Go ahead and put it back in the case. It makes me a little nervous."

"Sure, no problem."

"What kind of piece do you carry?" Brad asked.

"I don't."

"Really?"

"Really. All I have on me is a sap."

"A sap?"

"Yeah, a blackjack."

"By the way, have you had a chance to read any of that book I gave you?"

"Brad, you're not gonna believe this."

"I know, you've been too busy and haven't even opened it."

Gatsby author F. Scott Fitzgerald/wife Zelda

"You've got it wrong, kid—I'm halfway finished."

"I'll be a son-of-a-gun. Well, what do you think?"

"About what?"

"Who do you think is the hero?"

"Gatsby," Knucky replied, as he flicked a cigarette out the window.

"Some people pick the narrator, Nick Carraway. What female character do you like?"

"Jordan . . . what's-her-name—the golfer."

"Jordan Baker."

"Yeah, she's the one."

"What do you like about her?"

"I've always wondered what it would be like ta hit the sack with a good lookin' athletic woman."

Brad was more than a little pleased that Knucky found interest in one of the great sages of American letters.

As the sedan passed the intersection of Collinsville and Illinois Avenues, the newsboy, Johnny Moberly, stood on the corner holding up a paper.

"**Extra, extra, read all about it. Man killed in fire that destroys Walters warehouse! *Post*, *Globe* and *Journal*,**" he yelled as he named the three area "rags," as Knucky called them, that he was hawking.

No one in the car made a comment.

"By the way, kid, how's your love life?" Knucky inquired.

"It's still on hold."

"At the rate you're going, you're gonna die a virgin. Hey, Roland, do ya think we could find someone to introduce Brad to the ways of the world?"

Roland waggled his eyebrows up and down several times. They seemed to be saying "hubba hubba." He turned his head slightly towards the back seat. He smirked, out of the left corner of his mouth. "Whats about Shirley Stock, dat new cocktail waitress over at Candy Andy's?" It was as if he was speaking English sideways.

"He'd like her all right," Montrose said. "But he'd probably ruin the evening trying to talk her into going to church with him."

The muscled pair in front guffawed.

"Come ta think of it, that might save his life. If they had sex, she'd probably be too much woman for him and give him a heart attack." Knucky grinned, "I can see the headline now . . . LAWYER DIES WITH SMILE ON FACE."

"Never mind, you guys," Brad said. "When it comes to picking apples, I like to make the selection myself." He turned to Knucky. "Getting back to the book, let me tell you something to keep an eye on as you get closer to finishing. Look for a lot of symbolism in the story and see what you think the author is trying to convey by using the colors gold, silver and green. I'd also like to know what you think about the way criminal activity is depicted."

"You're not going ta give me a test at the end of this, are you, College Man?" Knucky was joshing him again.

Brad looked at him with a slightly mystical smile and said, "I just might do that."

* * *

Montrose had taken them through the downtown area, and they were on Collinsville Road approaching the Mounds Drive-in Theater. Historic Monks Mound, the ancient Indian site and largest man-made structure in America when the Pilgrims arrived, was on the opposite side of the highway. Some school children were having a picnic on one of the lesser mounds nearby. Several of them were lying on the ground parallel to the slope. They started rolling to the bottom of the hill, giggling all the way down. The girls were careful to keep their arms straight down the whole time so their dresses would stay close to their bodies and not fly up. That wonderful gift from God called memory transported Brad back to the winsome days of his youth when he strode the land in high-top U.S. Keds. He had rolled down the hill the same way on a Columbus Day picnic.

"Ever do that as a kid?" Knucky asked.

"Yes, several times. What a simple pleasure. How about you?"

"Nope, I was sick the day my class went there."

"I did," volunteered Roland. "Miss Schuetze, my elementary teacher at Hawthorne, took our class one time."

"I never got to do it," Montrose muttered in a sullen voice. "I went to Dunbar School. Colored folk weren't allowed at the Mounds. We had to be satisfied with places like Franklin Park and Lincoln Park, down in the south end.

"The winds of change are sweeping across the land, Montrose," Brad said. "The elementary schools were integrated last year, and the high school is scheduled for integration this year. Jim Crowism is on the way out."

"Well, I haven't seen much change in my lifetime. What we need is a cyclone," Montrose complained. "I graduated ninth in my class at Lincoln, but my family had no money to send me to college. Just about every job I applied for was menial or lowpaying—work that white folk didn't want to do. Colored people aren't even allowed in the A F of L."

Brad nodded in agreement. "That's a shame about the job situation, but there haven't been any lynchings in this country in over thirty years."

"Yeah, but we had some race riots in Detroit and Chicago during World War II."

Right, but Negroes aren't intimidated at the polls the way they were in the past," Brad said.

"Try this one on for size. Nearly thirty percent of the East St. Louis population is colored, yet the town has never had a Negro commissioner or mayor," Montrose lamented. "Council members used to be elected by wards, but when the whites in power saw that the South End would eventually be represented by a person of color, they changed the system so that members were elected from the city as a whole."

"True enough," Brad said, "but I still say that is going to change. By the way, how on earth did Negroes get the city to integrate the elementary schools last year?"

"Wasn't easy." Montrose pinched his lower lip together with his thumb and forefinger. "It was the result of a ton of letters to the newspaper, pressure from the local NAACP, and a flood of phone calls to civic leaders from lawyer Billy Jones. And the colored churches sent memos to all the white churches asking for their support."

"I heard there was also a protest march," Brad said.

"Yeah, it started at St. Augustine's, the colored Catholic church on Broadway, went down Collinsville Avenue past all the main stores and shops, then turned east on Illinois Avenue and ended at the Board of Education office on Eighth Street. They gave the president of the school board a petition with five thousand names on it."

"Any trouble along the way?"

"There was some name calling, nigger and jigaboo stuff, and I got hit in the back by a rotten tomato. We marched four abreast. No horns or drums were allowed. The organizers wanted it to be dignified and somber."

"You were in the march?"

"Sure was. I was right between a couple of younger guys from my neighborhood, Waddell Brooks and Rich Taylor."

"I'm impressed. That took some guts. The NAACP is gaining in clout and that lawyer, Billy Jones, isn't going to stop with just integrating the schools. And there are about seven Negroes on the police force."

"But they're only allowed to arrest colored people," Montrose countered.

"Okay, enough talk about politics," Knucky huffed. "I get tired of listening to that stuff."

Everyone sat silently for a few minutes. Brad thought about some of the things Montrose had said. Down deep, he knew the problem of race had flummoxed government on all levels. America was supposed to be the land of freedom and opportunity—that was our credo. But he knew of a country club in Belleville that was for whites and gentiles only. He heard Harold Zeigler at the office say it was an unwritten rule that real estate agents wouldn't sell property to Negroes north of Broadway. And he had seen the deed restriction to his parent's property that flat-out said the house could never be sold to a person of color.

They crossed the bridge over the Harding Ditch, dug by the Levee District after the turn of the century to help with flood control. Looming on the left was Fairmount Park, the racetrack. Workers were getting the grounds ready for the races that evening. The crowd usually numbered close to ten thousand people on weekends.

The man famous for writing "The Christmas Song" was pounding out one of his up-tempo jazz improvisations on the radio. "***A bop a do bop, a wobbody do dah, . . . de de dabba do wah, a diddley dum de. . .***"

Mel, Candy – married 1949 in Chicago (courtesy Candy Tockstein)

Brad's eyes lit up. "That's Mel Torme, the Velvet Fog. He married Candy Tockstein who's from East St. Louis."

Montrose, his head bobbing to the razzmatazz beat, reached over and cranked up the volume a notch.

"Hey, Montrose. Pull over on the side of the road when we get to the Collinsville water treatment plant," Brad said.

"Go ahead," Knucky reiterated.

The facility had a water fountain along the side of the road that ran continuously, twenty-four hours a day.

"Everybody out of the car," Brad urged. "This is like drinking from Ponce de Leon's fountain of youth."

Brad went first and gulped down mouthfuls of the cool water. It came from an artesian well. The iron content was so high it gave the water a unique metallic taste and stained the concrete a dark reddish brown.

"That was refreshing . . . okay, Roland and Montrose, you two are next."

They each took their turn, first Roland, then Montrose, gingerly—almost apprehensively.

"Well . . . what do you two think?"

They shrugged their shoulders, staring at Brad with a look of indecision.

"Ain't never tasted anything like it," Roland said.

"Hey, Montrose, don't forget. If you had been down in Golconda, Illinois, there isn't any way you'd have been able to drink out of the same faucet with whites," Brad said.

"Yeah, yeah."

Brad smiled. "Now, Mr. Walters, it's your turn."

He walked over to the fountain but just stood there.

"They say if you drink this elixir once a month you won't die of cancer. Go ahead, give it a try."

"You're beginning to sound like a shyster snake oil salesman." Knucky tossed his cigarette next to his feet and ground it into the gravel. He leaned over and took a small sip with his hand on the bottom of his tie so it wouldn't drag in the fountain's drain. Knucky squinched his eyes and his lips curved downward. "What the h—, I swear this stuff tastes like battery acid."

"But isn't it worthwhile if it keeps you from an early grave?" Brad said.

"This water has so much iron in it, I'm afraid my insides will start rusting out if I drink any more."

Everyone laughed at that one, and even Knucky chuckled slightly when he saw how his remark cracked up the others.

"Hey, Knucky." Roland placed a hand on his shoulder. "Are you sure you're okay? You're beginning to look a little green around the gills."

"All right, you guys, knock it off. I'm fine."

Everyone climbed back in the car, and they proceeded to their destination. As they approached the bluffs, Evergreen Gardens, a popular nightclub and restaurant loomed on the left. It was a mish-mash of 19th century Spanish architecture done in a white stucco motif with terra cotta clay tile roof.

"Hey, kid, see the tower on top?" Knucky excitedly extended his index finger.

"I see it."

"Back in the old days they had a guy up there with a machine gun keeping an eye on things. I got into a fight with a guy named Danny Jakle one time. I was shootin' craps in the gambling parlor, and he made some smart remark. I didn't like anything about Danny—his face, that damned smirk, his actions, his ugly girl friend. He even had a sissy toy poodle in his car all the time—never stopped yappin'."

"Stop holding back, Knucky. Why don't you tell us how you ***really*** felt about this guy?" Brad goaded.

The guys in front really broke up over that one. Knucky, unfazed, continued.

"I hit him so hard I broke his nose. Blood all over his shirt. Geez! Must have been years ago, somewhere around 1931."

The dark Graham turned left on Route 157 and made its way north towards Edwardsville.

"That's Hillcrest." Knucky pointed to his right. "Dutch Metzger an' Dave Stricklan, a couple of my associates, live in a wooded area up there."

"What about Roy Magson? Didn't he formerly manage the Club 501?" Brad asked.

"Yep, but now he's at the federal pen in Terre Haute. They drug him in front of a grand jury last year and asked him all kinds of questions about my taxes an' finances. He didn't give them squat. They nailed him on a perjury charge, an' now he's doin' three-to-five."

"They'll cut him loose in two if he does good time," Brad said.

"Roy knows how to do time." Knucky was staring out the window. "He's not like me. When I was at Joliet, my temper was always gettin' me into trouble. It was tough doin' hard time. Capone went goofy in the head at the Rock. While Roy is in, we're taking good care of his family."

Brad didn't say anything for fear it would keep an unpleasant subject alive. For the first time, he became aware of a scar on Roland's cheek. ***Probably from a dram-shop brawl***, he surmised. He also had cauliflower ears.

"Hey, Roland, were you a wrestler in school?"

"Yeah, 'til I dropped out in the tenth grade. I also wrestled at the Social Center a few times."

Montrose passed Belt-Line Route 40 in west Collinsville, signaling his turns by extending his arm out the window in the required fashion. A young kid nearly cut them off by abruptly pulling in front of their car from a side street. The tires on his customized '35 Ford five-window coupe squealed as his car fishtailed in front of them. It was painted purple and white, the high school colors of the Collinsville Kahoks. Montrose just shook his head but kept his cool.

They passed Peters' Station and went over a rough Nickel Plate grade crossing, and soon were on the north side of Edwardsville. They crossed a rickety wooden bridge and snaked up a winding road that took them to his uncle's farm.

"It's at the top of that grassy knoll on the left, Montrose," Brad directed.

He stopped the car on the side of the road, and they all got out and stretched their rubbery legs.

"Just over this small rise," Brad said.

They crossed the road and walked up the slight incline. Everyone stood there and stared in wonder at the serene view before them.

The water surrounding the two-and-a-half acre grassy island was calm and peaceful. It reflected the bright blue of the sky like a mirror. Chipmunks chattered, voicing displeasure at the intrusion. A bobwhite whistled to his mate in his distinctive two-note aria, accompanied by other indigenous twittering sounds of various birds and woodland animals. A squirrel dashed up a tree, scampered along a thin branch, causing the leaves to rustle under its weight. A raccoon, with face markings that reminded Brad of The Phantom's mask, foraged near the shore. Rustic tranquility.

"How many acres do we have here?" Knucky asked.

"Uncle Frank has a hundred fifty-five acres altogether. If he sells you the lake and the island, I think we're probably talking ninety acres."

"Hey, look," Montrose said. "There's a turtle sunning himself on a log,"

Knucky looked around. "Where's the access road?"

"There isn't any now," Brad explained, "but there is a side road up ahead on the left. You would have to put in a road about a quarter of a mile long to get to the lake."

Montrose began trimming his nails with a pocketknife. Roland picked up a flat rock and threw it side-armed. After four skip marks that sent out a series of ever-widening concentric circles, it sank. The turtle's head recoiled inside its shell with the first splash.

"Hey, cut that out!" Knucky yelled. "I don't want my moat to get filled up with rocks and tin cans and other garbage."

"Sorry," Roland apologized sheepishly.

"I ought to make you swim out there and find that damn rock, Roland. Get back to the car and make sure nobody steals it." Walters' famous temper bested him once again. His face was about the same color of red you see on someone just before they are hit by apoplexy.

Roland stared at the ground, then hitched up his trousers and meekly complied.

"I love this place," Knucky gushed. The blush on his neck and forehead began to subside.

Brad pointed to the land in the middle of the water. "Jay Gatsby lived on an island, you know."

"I thought he lived in New York."

"He did, but it was on Long Island."

Knucky rubbed at his chin whiskers. "Oh, yeah." It was mid-afternoon but he already had a five o'clock shadow. "I bet I could build a fortress that would hold off an army for a month," Knucky said, his sentence reaching Brad's ears in fragments due to a woodpecker battering a nearby tree while foraging for insects.

"While you're at it, you can put in an A-bomb shelter just in case Uncle Joe Stalin decides to drop the big one. And you might want to throw in a few hidden passageways and hiding places for good measure," Brad added. "Make it impregnable by using concrete, brick and stone, reinforced with steel I-beams."

"Tell your uncle I'll give him $10,000 for the lake and the access land needed for the road. But don't tell him I'm the one who wants it, or else he'll jack up the price."

"I've known Uncle Frank all of my life. He isn't that kind of man. Besides, you're probably offering him more money than what the whole thing cost originally. My guess is he can use the money to pay off what he owes, bank the rest, and he'll still have a small farm left for retirement."

"Maybe I should only offer him $8,000," Knucky said.

Brad stiffened at the suggestion. "Can't."

"Why not?"

"Because I won't let you. That would be unethical. You would only be offering him less because of what I just told you."

The tri-colored woodpecker left the tree and flew to the lake's edge in a quest for water, flapping its wings in an undulating manner.

"The way I see it, it's just like getting a hot tip from a jockey on a race at Fairmount," Knucky retorted.

"You're going to pay the man what you thought was a fair amount. Don't worry, I'll more than make it up to you somewhere down the line."

"Like what?"

"I don't know. I said I would, and I will. You know you can count on it. You've got to start living by some principles, Mr. Walters."

"I do, kid. They just happen to be slightly different from yours."

"You know what I mean."

"Yeah, I know." He took out another one of his cigarettes and lit up. Knucky drew the first puff deep into his lungs before he exhaled through his nose—like a junkie getting a fix. "Tell you what. I bet when I croak I have more people show up at my funeral than you do."

Brad had no idea where that came from. "I'm not a betting man."

"This'll be a friendly wager."

"How will we know who wins?"

"Yeah. That's gonna be a problem."

He thought a while and then let out with . . . "Hot diggety!"

"What?"

"I'm probably going to die before you, right?"

"You will if the insurance actuary tables are correct. You might even outlive me if you give up drinking, smoking and wild women."

"I'd rather die a few years early," he chuckled, with a gleam in his eye.

Brad shrugged. "It's your life."

"How many people do you estimate will be at your funeral—tops?" Knucky thrust his hands deep into his pockets.

"How should I know? Let's see. Maybe ninety people from church, twenty or thirty relatives . . . and throw in ten to thirty co-workers, depending on how many friends I have left after they find out you and I have been pals on the sneak."

"Very funny," he said with a ***faux*** frown. "What does that come to, about one hundred an' sixty?"

"Wait a minute. Throw in another thirty. I joined Rotary last week."

"Okay, one ninety, tops."

Brad beamed. "I would be pleased if that many people showed up."

"I'll wager that I have well over three hundred," Knucky said, with a tone of braggadocio in his voice.

"You're on. But I'm not sure God is going to look favorably on this wager."

"Maybe not, but I bet the devil will have fun with it."

"Careful," Brad said. "If that grin gets much bigger your face is going to crack. So, what are the stakes?"

"Dunno . . . let me think." Knucky stood there, scratching his head. "I know. If you die first and break two hundred, I'll donate $1,000 to your church."

"How about giving it to the Salvation Army instead?"

"Sure. That church of yours might not want ill-gotten gains from the Walters empire, as they would say in "The Great Gatsby." If I go first and break two hundred, then you have to come and visit me once a year at my grave on my birthday."

"I think I can live with those terms," Brad said, stroking his chin.

CHAPTER 7

East St. Louis seemed to be forever in the shadow of its older, larger and more famous sibling, struggling for recognition and identity in its own right. There had long been undercurrents of animosity between St. Louisans and their ruffian shirttail relatives across the river. But St. Louisans generally looked across the Mississippi with a certain sneer at this upstart stepchild. St. Louisans called their Illinois neighbors "suckers," after a type of plentiful fish caught in their lakes. East St. Louisans retaliated by labeling them "Missouri Pukes," when large numbers of their St. Louis neighbors reportedly threw up after gluttonous consumption of the local fish.

September 27, 1950

Summer slowly gave way to fall. Midwest autumns were like a Grandma Moses print—so beautiful they almost broke your heart. Mother Nature strutted her stuff and laid out a canopy of brilliant reds, oranges, and yellows that were so breathtaking, preachers said it caused God to look down from heaven and do a double take. Outlying farms near East St. Louis were busy yielding their treasures of grain and fruit. October brought Indian summer, that period of about three weeks after the first frost when the days were still warm, but there was a slight nip in the air. The tree-banked hillside along Route 157 became splashed with earthtone splendor. Purple ironweed and stag sumac grew wild along the roadway. By the middle of the month, homeowners were dedicated to raking and leaf burning on Saturdays.

There were times when Lorna would look out her window at the Beulah Club and become mesmerized by dancing shadows from the incredible autumn foliage outside. She got off to a flying start on her new job at the ***Journal.*** Her write-ups about the social scene of East St. Louis were witty and surprisingly urbane. Unlike most beginning newspaper writers, she avoided sounding obscure, verbose and bureaucratic. Barb Edelblute, who worked at the front counter, quickly became her best friend at the office.

"Did Mr. Mermelstein practically undress you with his eyes when you got hired?" Lorna asked Barb one day.

"He sure did."

"Does he do that to everybody? Lorna asked"

"No—just the women." Lorna smiled at Barbara's quick wit. "He claims there's no harm in looking. Says he's just appreciating nature."

The new worker from Litchfield quickly endeared herself to her co-workers. All except Priscilla Bartlett, the lead secretary who teased Lorna by calling her Brenda Starr, junior varsity reporter.

Lorna couldn't figure it out. She had followed Priscilla's instructions to the letter and had turned everything in on time—save one particular story on the Pearl S. Buck Literary Society annual awards tea. It was held one Wednesday afternoon at the Scottish Rite Temple. She was an hour late on that one because she had written down the wrong time and nearly missed the event.

"Sorry. Better late than never," Lorna jocularly apologized when she rushed Priscilla her hastily prepared final draft.

"Better, never late," Priscilla tartly sneered. "You hick town girls don't seem to have a sense of urgency about anything." She flung her snippy words in cruel fashion.

Lorna was so taken back by the remark she just stood there and said nothing. That proved to be a mistake.

"You know, I would just hate it if my mother had given me a name like Lorna," Priscilla said.

A dumbfounded Lorna was still at a loss for words.

"I was joking," Priscilla said. "But you have to admit, it is an unusual name."

Lorna bit her tongue, turned and walked away. But she made up her mind that if Priscilla ever tried that again, she wouldn't just stand there and take it.

Catfight ***redux*** came several weeks later when all the girls at the office went to lunch at the Liberty Cafe. They were comparing notes on husbands, boyfriends and juicy details about their first romantic kiss.

"It's been harder to get dates at the office ever since Lorna started working," Priscilla complained. "The men are all just dying to go out with her, especially Lance." She glanced around the table for reactions.

Lorna's eyes glazed over but she said nothing. Barb Edelblute turned pale, looked down at her plate, and nervously began shoving food into her mouth.

"Now, I wonder why that is? Do they know something we don't know?" Priscilla sighed.

Lorna retaliated by dramatically sighing back. Louder. "Tsk-tsk. Careful, Priscilla, your forked tongue is showing," she said in an uncharacteristically catty manner.

The acerbic banter escalated.

"Lorna has most of the men at work walking around in a daze." Priscilla's fork speared the last French fry on her plate with a vengeance. "Could you tell us what your secret is, dear?"

"Well, first of all, unlike ***some*** people I know, ***my*** hair color is natural. Another secret to my success is feminine hygiene. You could improve your status with the men, Priscilla, if you'd try shaving your legs once in a while," Lorna counterpunched. "And if I were you, I'd start using Lifebuoy; it really stops B.O. Then you wouldn't need so much of that imitation designer perfume you drench yourself with every morning."

Priscilla had been fooled by Lorna's personality. She had guessed her the type to sit there and take it. Instead, Lorna was responding in-kind, tit for tat, catching the stinging barbs and hurling them back in her direction. She decided to turn the heat up a notch.

"I'll bet Lorna can tell us a thing or two about experience with men. I heard she's from Litchfield, that quaint little ol' town between here and Springfield. I hear girls in that place date their second cousins. Is that true?"

Lorna blanched. She was weary of Priscilla's carping and crystalline bits of sarcasm. It took her a second or two to regain her composure.

"I wouldn't know about that," she shot back. "But I did read in the newspaper last year where someone in Murphysboro, where ***YOU'RE*** from, ran off to Arkansas and illegally married her first cousin. They say the whole town is full of retards due to people down there marrying their kin."

The lunch group was agog as the room throbbed with a palpable migraine from the tension. If looks could kill, Lorna would have been laid out at the morgue with forty-eleven stab wounds.

"That's a spurious lie, and you know it. Take it back!" Priscilla demanded.

"Hah! I will not." Lorna's dander was up. "You're the one who started the snide remark campaign."

Lorna and Priscilla had been sitting at opposing ends of two tables the waiter had pushed together to make room for eight. The other girls had been watching the verbal sparring match with disbelieving eyes that zoomed back and forth from one end to the other, as if they were sitting at mid-court watching the ball being smashed back and forth in a hotly contested tennis match. Serve and volley.

"Girls! Girls!" Alva Cox, the manager, rushed over shushing them with a finger pressed to his lips. "Please stop this bickering. Everyone is staring. You two look madder than wet hens. If you can't behave like ladies, I'll have to ask you to leave."

Roughly fifteen seconds of tense silence passed in what seemed like an eternity.

"I will if you will." Lorna broke the spell first.

"Will what?"

"Apologize."

Another embarrassingly long period of nothingness.

"I'm sorry," Lorna said slowly. "I didn't really read that in the newspaper . . ."

A look of triumphant relief crept over Priscilla's face.

". . . I read it in ***Confidential*** magazine."

"Well, I never . . !" Priscilla sputtered. She took a few dollars out of her purse, slammed them on the table, and stormed out of the restaurant.

La guerre des femmes was over.

Barb Edelblute was sitting to Lorna's immediate left. She leaned over: "That was some three-alarm cat fight. For a second I thought you were going to scratch her eyes out. The next time I go to lunch with you two, remind me to bring something along to mop up the blood."

"She deserved it."

"Don't you think you were a little hard on her?"

"She's been riding me for weeks . . . takes these little digs every chance she gets, no matter how trivial. This time she went too far."

Lorna paused and stared intently at her empty bottle of I.B.C. root beer, nervously turning it back and forth with her fingers. "I guess my Sunday school teacher wouldn't be very proud of me about now, would she?"

"I don't think so," Barb said.

"Okay, I'll let Priscilla, with her pithy little comments and Jekyll-Hyde personality, stew a while and then I'll apologize for real."

Barbara, with raised eyebrows, shook her head.

"Okay, you win. I'll tell her I'm sorry as soon as we get back. But first, let me stop in the Salle Ann shop on the way back. I saw this delightful looking aqua colored blouse with a Peter Pan collar. It's been teasing my purse ever since I first saw it while window-shopping the other day."

After Lorna got back to the office, she went over to Priscilla's desk.

"Listen, Priscilla. I don't know exactly what happened or how we have arrived at this point, but I am very sorry that you and I haven't been able to get along very well. It doesn't make sense for us to bicker since we are going to be working together for who knows how long."

Priscilla was steamed. "What you said today in front of the other girls was unforgivable."

"But, Priscilla, don't you remember? You were the one who started it by making disparaging remarks about Litchfield."

"Anyone with a modicum of common sense knew what I said was in jest," she said. "I may have made some teasing remarks, but you got vicious and ran it into the ground."

"Something has been eating at you ever since my first day at the office. What is it?"

Priscilla stared at a seam in the floor, gathering her thoughts. Then she looked up.

"It took me two years of hard work and effort to get where I am today. I started out as a gofer—a Girl Friday. I typed the obituaries. Then you come along, roll your eyes at the boss, and you get a first-rate job right out of high school. You haven't paid your dues; it isn't fair. That really galls me. You just waltz in here with your devil-may-care attitude and think you have the world by the tail."

Lorna's high school picture

"Are you sure there isn't more to this than professional jealousy?"

Priscilla glared at Lorna. "You bet there is! Before *you* arrived, Lance Troutman and I were an item, dating fairly regularly. Now he's thrown me over. He hasn't asked me out since you started working here."

Lorna had spotted Lance Troutman at the office on her first day of work and hoped that he would ask her out sometime. They ended up sitting next to each other several weeks later at a staff meeting, and she found herself immediately drawn to his rugged masculine features and compelling personality. He was just under six foot tall, dark complected and handsone—straight out of a Thomas Costain novel. He had taken her out to lunch on several occasions but had yet to ask her out on an evening date.

Lorna looked at her in disbelief. ***So that's it, Priscilla is carrying a torch for Lance.*** Priscilla had gall, she thought, trying to make her the villain. But she decided it would be better all the way around if she just gave in to her and went the conciliatory route.

"Look, I didn't do anything to encourage Lance, but who he wants to date is up to him. Please don't blame me. I apologize if I overreacted today and said things I shouldn't have. Let's bury the hatchet and try to get along."

Priscilla smiled grimly and didn't respond immediately. Her demeanor slowly metamorphosed from that of anger to resignation. "Agreed," she said in a rather non-compliant tone, but she was thinking ***bury the hatchet in Lorna's back***, if given the chance.

Lorna quickly forgot about the fight. She was not the type to carry grudges. But Priscilla tucked away the memory in a corner of her brain. One day Lorna would receive her just desserts. There would be pay back. Oh, yes!

* * *

Brad had grown weary of the complexities of life at the office. Weather and work were co-conspirators in a plot to make his day doleful. It had been some time since Brad had taken in a movie, and he figured some celluloid fiction would be just the thing to help him unwind. Brad loved the movies. Magic time. He checked out the ads in the paper. There was an Errol Flynn B-movie at the Avenue, but he had never heard of Patrice Wymore, his co-star. Brad was hoping to catch a rerun of ***This Gun for Hire***, with Veronica Lake as the sultry, pouty-lipped, femme fatale. It was one of his favorites, bringing instant stardom to Alan Ladd. He decided on a John Wayne flick co-starring that lovely Irish redhead, Maureen O'Hara. The blandishments trumpeted by the ad promised an action-packed adventure filled with romance. The Duke had long been his hero, even though he had read something in Police Gazette about his failing to enlist in 1942 to fight the Axis Powers, because of a budding film career.

Alan Ladd

The brightly lit Majestic marquee, with its three thousand festive blinking bulbs, was cantilevered nearly ten feet over the sidewalk. The lavish palace had been built in 1928 by Harry Redmon and refurbished in 1948. Adorned with plush crimson carpet, gold tasseled curtains and gilded chandeliers, the largest theater south of Springfield had cost a cool million to build.

Brad paid twenty-five cents for his ticket and ducked inside to the welcome promise of escapism. A box of popcorn and a soda sounded appealing, so he walked over to the counter and placed his fifteen-cent order. He turned and started to walk from the lobby to the inside of the theater. In his haste, he had not noticed another person behind him in line. He was holding his popcorn and soda high against his chest as they crashed into each other. Golden kernels of buttered corn spilled from the box and bounced against their torsos before tumbling to the floor. The soda sloshed back and forth in the cup and then leaped across the slight separation of their startled bodies onto a puffy-sleeved blouse. An astonished "umph" and an equally astounded "oops" escaped two pair of lips.

"Oh, my goodness," the girl said with eyes as big as saucers.

"Please excuse me, Miss; I'm terribly sorry."

The soda had stained her blouse high on her chest. Brad's left hand steadied his drink while the other forced the popcorn box up under his chin. With his free hand, he took a handkerchief from his back pocket. He began to lightly press the white cotton against her fabric in an effort to absorb the wetness.

"Would you please take your hands off me, young man?" she demanded. All of a sudden it hit her. "Oh, my gosh, it's you, that . . . guy from the train."

"I'm sorry, I didn't mean to . . ."

"I can do it," she said in exasperation as she took his batiste cotton fabric and began blotting herself.

"It was clumsy of me," he apologized. "I should have been looking where I was going."

At that moment Brad realized what a rapturous piece of womanhood fate had sent him crashing into. Statuesque, with classic good looks, her chestnut hair dazzled him with its luster. It was long and turned under at the edges. Her gold-flecked hazel eyes lit up a face of high cheekbones and classic features. It was a face that could have been painted by a High Renaissance artist.

She went over to the drinking fountain and wet the end of his handkerchief and rubbed it against her blouse to dilute the stain. Then she came over and handed it back to him. "Thank you for your assistance," she said curtly.

"I'll be glad to buy you another blouse if that stain doesn't come out."

"You can hardly see it now. Soda stains usually wash out easily unless it's on satin. This is just Egyptian cotton."

"Once again, my sincerest regrets for being so clumsy. If there's anything I can do . . . ?"

"Look, Mr., uh—"

For a moment, Brad forgot his name. "Brad, it's Brad Logan."

"I'm Lorna Sanders. I'd like to apologize for what I said to you on the train."

"That isn't necessary."

"No, I insist. I'm truly sorry. I behaved badly. You were just trying to help."

"Apology accepted. I didn't mean to act like a bull in a china shop. Hey, I think the movie has just started. Shall we sit together? It wouldn't be a date or anything, but maybe we could have a cup of coffee afterwards."

"Sorry, I don't drink coffee, especially with semi-strangers . . ."

Brad's heart sank.

"Look, it's not you. I've had a very busy day, and I wouldn't be good company. I just want to relax."

Instead of lighting up with a schoolboy grin, Brad was forced to alter his demeanor and accept stalemate. "I understand, Miss Sanders. Maybe another time."

"Perhaps."

"Have Bill Newbold, that tall uniformed usher over there, show you a seat, and I'll buy your snacks." Newbold was smartly dressed in a spiffy maroon uniform with enough epaulets, tassels, and gold braid to outrank MacArthur.

"Thanks, but that isn't necessary."

"I insist. What would you like?"

"A Seven-Up and a small box of plain popcorn."

"Coming right up."

Brad was taken by the sparkle and vitality of her personality. He could tell by Lorna's carriage and manner of speech that she was strong and sure of herself. He liked that in a woman. ***Maybe I should call her in a day or two if I find out where she is staying.***

He gave the soda and popcorn to Newbold while he found a seat on the front row of the balcony. John Wayne was his usual heroic self, and in the end he won the hand of that lovely lady with the red hair. Ben Johnson played the bad guy, and Chill Wills provided a few laughs. That was all Brad remembered about the movie. He was lost in a world of contemplation, wondering what it would have been like enjoying every second of sitting next to a fascinating, utterly feminine creature.

←Maureen O'Hara/John Wayne↓

As the crowd noisily filed out of the theater, Lorna spotted Brad hunched over at the drinking fountain. She paused for a moment, assessing his merits. ***He's neat as a pin and quite handsome.*** Then she walked over to him.

"Say, don't you work at the Spivey Building?"

He finished his drink and looked up in surprise. "Why, yes. How did you know?"

"I saw you coming out of there a few days ago with a couple of other guys. I'm a reporter of sorts for the ***Journal***, next door."

"Small world. That was probably Harry Fiebig and Charlie Oliver, a couple of my co-workers at the firm."

"Firm?"

"Yes, I'm a first-year lawyer."

"An attorney . . . any exciting cases?"

"Well, I am helping to defend a man in the Torricelli murder case."

"I read about the murder in the paper."

There was an awkward moment of silence.

"Well, I guess I'll run along. Maybe we'll see each other again some time." Brad turned and headed for the main lobby exit.

"W-wait," Lorna yelled, just as he was pushing on the door's brass crossbar.

Brad stopped and pivoted. Lorna walked purposely toward him, eyes vibrant, hair dancing on her shoulders, a slight smile on her red lips. Her movements were fluid and graceful, often lacking in women of her stature.

"Are you still interested in going somewhere? I have about an hour before I turn into a pumpkin."

"Sure, you bet!" A friendly grin showed even white teeth.

"I've heard the banana splits at Jimmy's Malt Shop are out of this world."

"You must have read my mind. That's exactly the place I was going to suggest."

They walked to Brad's car parked across the street behind Pete Lurie's store. Then they drove to 30th and State where Warren Jones ran Jimmy's Malt Bar. A light rain began to fall. Nature was toying with the city before drenching it in a black deluge. Brad found a parking spot just ahead of a fireplug. He got out and opened the door for Lorna; then they sauntered inside and went to the counter to place their ice cream orders.

Bing Crosby

"What can I get you folks?" The square-jawed owner wiped the counter while waiting for an answer.

"A banana split and a chocolate marshmallow malt, please."

"Coming right up." He smiled and wiped his hands on an apron that was an artist's palette of ice cream colors.

A couple of nickels in a Wurlitzer jukebox caused a bakelite disk to begin dizzily spinning at 78 rpm's. Its stylus fell into the groove and played a mellow Bing Crosby tune.

"I saw you get on the train at Litchfield. Is that your home town?" Brad asked.

"Yes, I've lived there all my life."

"Sanders, that's English, isn't it?"

"Yes. And I presume Logan is Scottish. Any interesting history?"

"I'm not much into clans and genealogy. All I know is I supposedly had some ancestors who fought on the losing side with William Wallace against the British."

The initial awkwardness faded as they found out more about each other. They proceeded to exchange information about their private lives. It was a nice surprise for Brad to discover they both had strong church backgrounds. They shared childhood memories and discussed the differences between high school in a large town and a small town. Lorna was easy to converse with and had an uncanny knack for putting him at ease. Brad didn't have much experience talking to the opposite sex. Inordinately shy in high school, his only date was with Jackie Peeples for the senior prom. In college he became immersed in his studies.

Lorna spooned a bite of banana covered with rich chocolate into her mouth. She caught Brad lost in wonderment, drinking in her sparkling eyes, her nose, her forehead, her hair with that velvety sheen. "It's impolite to stare."

"I'm sorry. I didn't mean to. I hope you don't think I'm a cad. I haven't had many dates."

"Well, it's embarrassing." She smiled and nervously flipped the underside of her gorgeous head of hair.

"I just think you look terrific in that outfit. And the stain is practically gone."

She straightened her flared skirt and then pressed a hand to the top of her chest and looked down at the faded stain.

"Thanks for the compliment." Lorna absently toyed with the black bow on her collar. "It's the Gibson Girl look. By the way, how's your jaw?" She ran her fingers lightly over the side of his face. "It looks like the redness from that incident on the train has gone away."

Charles Dana's Gibson Girl

"It was a little sore for a while, but it's fine now." The softness of her skin on Brad's cheek sent a strange sensation through his body.

"That guy was bigger than you. Weren't you afraid?"

"Nope. I'm just glad it ended peacefully."

"Well, thanks for coming to my . . . rescue."

"You're welcome," he replied. ***Calm down, old boy. Don't let her supple feminine softness cause you to hyperventilate.***

Perry Como started singing "Some Enchanted Evening," from ***South Pacific***, the new Broadway musical.

"Any brothers or sisters?" Brad asked.

She shook her head. "I'm a spoiled only child. My mother was seriously injured in a car accident a scant week after she and Dad were married. She suffered internal injuries, a broken rib, and her left kneecap had been crushed. My birth in 1932 was a difficult one. The doctor warned them not to have any more children. What about you?"

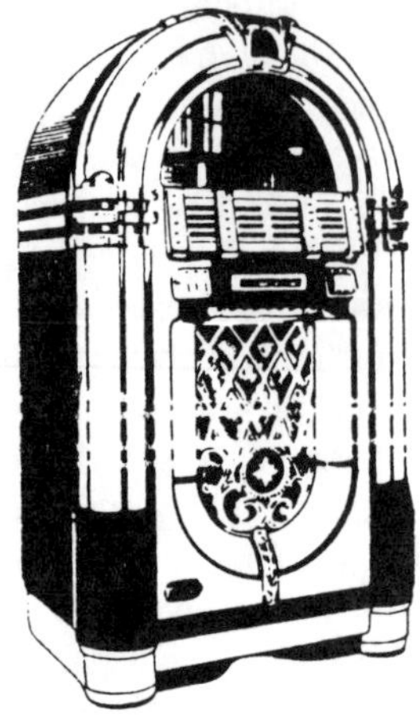

"Just a sister; she's four years older."

"I always wondered what it would be like," she said. "Did you get along?"

"Pretty much. We teased each other a lot and argued over who got to lick the bowl when Mom made a batch of cookies. Nothing serious. I wish I would have had more brothers and sisters."

Lorna's eyes grew bright and mischievous. "I'll bet you're holding back because we've just met. Tell me about something she did that really bugged you. Everyone I know with an older brother or sister has at least one or two horror stories."

"I don't think I should be telling family secrets," Brad said.

"Ah, c'mon! This is when you were a kid—don't be a stick-in-the-mud."

"Let me think. Uh—"

"Make it something juicy."

"Well, being four years older, she often had to baby-sit—be responsible for me when Mom went grocery shopping, and Dad was at work."

"I'll bet you were a handful."

"She took it seriously and liked to boss me around a lot. Naturally, I resented it." Brad paused and shook his head. "I can't believe I'm talking about this on our first date."

Lorna's eyebrows arched. "You said this wasn't a date."

"That makes it even worse."

"Go on," she implored. "It sounds as though you're just getting to the good part."

Brad sighed and then continued. "Jackie outweighed me by twenty pounds and was several inches taller, making me easy prey. She seemed to like bossing me around, and I retaliated by taunting her with names she didn't like."

"Such as . . . "

" 'Gargantua' and 'Miss Prissy'. There was this one time when I got angry at her telling me what to do, and I shot back: "You're not my boss, Freckle Face."

"What did she do?"

"She grabbed me, threw me to the floor, sat on my stomach and pinned my arms."

Lorna shook her head sympathetically. "What happened next?"

"I tried flinging my legs up to get her in a scissors hold but it was no use. Then she lowered her face directly over mine and let a string of spit come down from her tongue until it was an inch from my eyeballs. She swung it back and forth like a slimy Sword of Damocles."

"Now that's diabolical."

"I turned my head to avoid the spittle, and at the last agonizing second, she sucked it back up."

"Wow! Did you tell your parents?"

"No, because she threatened to snitch on me and tell them I called her a name. Besides, I figured they'd think I just made it all up."

Pause.

Lorna started laughing hysterically.

Brad gestured with his right palm face up. "What?"

"That is the funniest, most outrageous story I have ever heard."

"I shouldn't have told you."

"I'm sorry." She reached out and touched his hand. "It took a lot of guts to tell me a story so personal. You must be very secure with who you are. Not many men I know would have ventured telling me something like that. I'll bet you're one of those sensitive types, like Montgomery Clift, aren't you?"

"Stop, now you're embarrassing me."

"Okay, as my aunt Olive would say, it's time to move on to something else."

"Did you know there's a bit of history connected to the Majestic Theater?" Brad asked.

Montgomery Clift

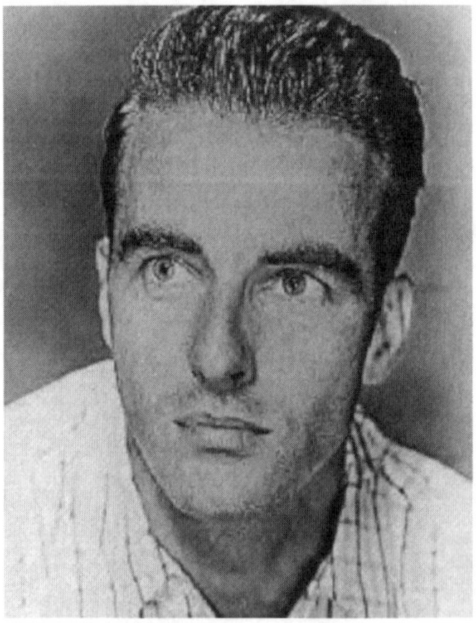

"Really, what?"

"Well, it was the old Majestic, mostly vaudeville, but in the same location. Dorothy and Lillian helped their mother sell confections in an adjacent store she owned—the Majestic Candy Kitchen."

"You don't mean the famous silent screen stars?"

"Yes, the same Lillian Gish who was in D.W. Griffith's ***Birth of a Nation.*** Anyway, it was there that they watched their first motion picture. The sisters were dumbfounded when they saw a grade school chum, Mary Pickford, in the movie. About a year later the theater and the Kitchen burned. There was no insurance to rebuild so the family moved back to New York. The girls looked up their friend, and she introduced them to D.W. Griffith. The rest is history."

Lorna shook her head. "What an amazing story. By the way, when did you decide to become a lawyer?"

"History was my first interest. I loved the stories, the human drama. But after my sophomore year I decided it was too hard to make money by teaching. I still do my recreational reading in history and biography."

"My history teachers in high school were boring," Lorna said. "All they did was make us memorize facts."

"I had three courses in college from Dr. Patrick Riddleberger. He was inspiring. He knew how to make the past come alive. What about you? Did you go to work right out of high school?"

"Oh, no. I made excellent grades in high school and went to SIU at Carbondale for a year, but I was anxious to become a working girl and be on my own . . . mmm." Lorna licked her lips. "This split is really good."

Brad's chocolate malt was so thick his paper straw collapsed, and he was forced to discard it in favor of a long spoon. "This sure beats the chow I had in the navy."

"You've been in the military?"

"Yes." He was literally staring at her again, his eyes a deep, intense blue. "As a kid I had this Walter Mittish desire to become a fighter pilot. I loved Smilin' Jack, Speed Gibson, the Air Adventures of Jimmy Allen, and Jack Armstrong's uncle's plane, the ***Silver Albatross.*** I was a Leatherneck—a World War Two marine fighter jock . . . almost," he said ruefully.

"Almost?"

"I signed up on the anniversary of Pearl Harbor, December 7, 1942."

"Where did you go for training?"

"I didn't get called up until September of '43, after I had completed a year of college."

"What took the military so long?"

"I'm not sure, but it was a little embarrassing because friends and neighbors thought maybe I was four-F or something. My basic training was at Murray State in Kentucky, and then it was on to flight school at Conley, Arkansas. I learned how to fly in a Maytag Messerschmitt."

"A what?"

"That's the affectionate moniker we gave to our Piper Cub trainer."

"Didn't you finish your flight training?"

Curtiss Helldiver

"Oh, yes. When I was at Athens, Georgia, for more schooling, the top brass decided there were too many air cadets so only the upper fifty percent of the class was allowed to continue.

"Don't tell me, you didn't make the cut," she said in a quiet sotto voice.

"I made it. I was part of the group passed on to Memphis for more training in a Stearman bi-wing. Then I was sent to Corpus Christi for instruction in a Douglas Dauntless dive bomber and from there to Jacksonville, Florida, where I flew a Helldiver. I graduated in July of 1945 and was all set to be shipped out for carrier duty in the Pacific when we dropped the A-bomb on Hiroshima. The war was over and due to some paperwork snafu I received an early discharge as part of our demobilization."

"What was your rank?"

"I was a second lieutenant."

"Do you still fly?"

"After the war, I stayed in the reserves for five years and finished college on the GI Bill."

"Why didn't you get called up for Korea?"

"Once I passed the bar exam I figured it was time to give up the military. I quit the reserves two weeks before war broke out in Korea."

"You mean if you hadn't quit Uncle Sam would have called you up for active duty?"

"That's right."

"So a couple of extraordinary circumstances may have saved your life."

"That's one way of looking at it." ***Cheating death without honor***. Brad thought about what she said. He sometimes felt guilty—like some low-life, amoebic slacker—because two of his best friends in high school didn't come back from World War II. One was killed at Saipan and the other at Anzio.

Nat King Cole began his smooth version of "Mona Lisa," the hit song from an Alan Ladd movie.

"Hey, enough about me. How do you like your job at the ***Journal***?" he asked, changing the subject.

"It's interesting. The place has a lively mix of people, and covering the social scene is fun. It's mostly snippets of gossip about the patrician class. Eventually, I'd like to cover the City Hall scene or write a column like David Felts."

"Do you think they'll ever let a woman cover politics?"

"I don't know. Right now things are parceled out

according to sex. Men cover sports and politics while women answer the phones, type the obituaries, and write about schools, churches and weddings."

"It's the same way at my office," he said. "All the lawyers are men and the women are adjuncts—support personnel. It's almost as if women exist for the sole purpose of waiting on men."

"Are there any female doctors in this town?" She took the last bite of her ice cream treat.

"I don't know of any."

"Do you play a musical instrument?" Lorna could see that Brad, his eyes dancing and his head weaving, was really into Cole's song from ***Captain Carey, U.S.A.***

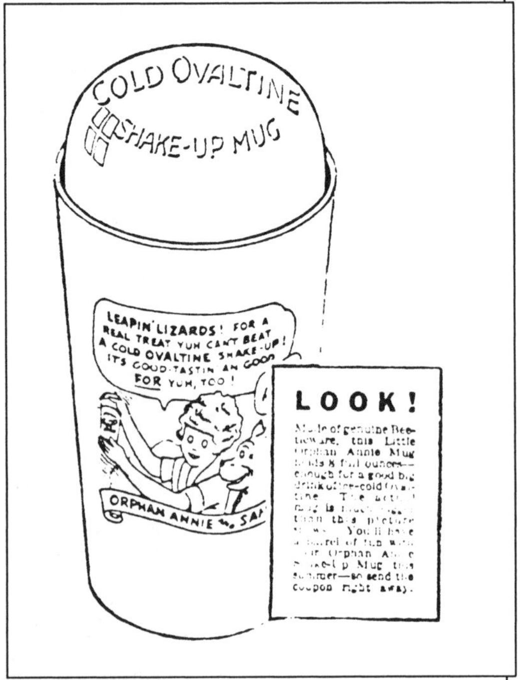

"No. I tried the clarinet in the 8th grade for about a month but I gave it up."

A thunderclap startled both of them.

"Gad zooks," Lorna exclaimed, Orphan Annie style as she looked at her watch. "I've got to get back to the Beulah Club in fifteen minutes or I'll miss my curfew."

The rain had been intermittent before they arrived at the malt shop. Now there was a cloudburst, and it was coming down in buckets. Booming thunder accompanied several forked flashes of lightning. Zeus was hurling thunderbolts across the sky again. East St. Louis was to enjoy no amnesty from the Midwest's fury. As they scurried out the door, the pungent smell of ozone tweaked their noses as it permeated the drenched night air.

"Do you want to make a run for it?" he shouted.

"I'm game."

Brad sacrificed his suit coat, holding it over Lorna's head as they huddled together and ran to the car. Brad got soaked, but he didn't mind one bit. He thought it must have been the same feeling Sir Walter Raleigh had when he draped his cape over a mud puddle for Queen Elizabeth.

The pouring rain limited visibility. They were roughly twenty blocks from their destination. A lumbering freight train loomed ahead at 20th Street, but fortunately there was an underpass. About six inches of standing water forced them to crawl through the low spot. The matron was getting ready to lock the doors at the Beulah Club when they rushed to the covered entrance laughing joyously.

"May I see you again sometime?" he asked.

"Probably. Call me at the ***Journal.*** I've got to go now. Thanks for a nice evening." Lorna waved good-bye as she turned and walked away.

An orchestra of stringed instruments vibrated inside Brad's chest. Cheerful sounds reverberated inside his spinning head: plink, zing, ping—as if Aphrodite was plucking at his heart's chords ♫ ♫ ♫.

Now there goes a gal with a thoroughbred pedigree, he thought. ***I've got you under my skin; and I like you under my skin.*** Brad hummed a few lines from Gershwin.

George Gershwin

As he pulled away from the curb, he didn't notice that a dark sedan began following him.

* * *

"What did you do, stay and see the movie twice?" Gloria asked as her roommate came in and closed the door. She had been reading a book in bed.

"No, smarty-pants, I bumped into this guy at the concession stand, and we went out for a treat afterwards."

"You look bedraggled; it must really be raining out there."

"Yes—cats and dogs. I know because I stepped in a poodle."

"You're a scream," Gloria said, sarcastically. "A thousand comedians out of work and here you are using up all of their bad jokes."

"You're just going to have to develop a better sense of humor, young lady, if we two are going to get along," Lorna teased.

Gloria was dressed in her striped flannel pajamas. "Tell me all the juicy details—did you hold hands? Kiss? Make out in the back seat ♥ ♥ ♥?" She tossed the book aside and bolted upright, with her legs jack-knifed sideways.

"You know me better than that, Miss Grand Inquisitor. He was a perfect gentleman, and all we did was talk."

"No makin' whoopee? How boring." Gloria used both hands to form a letter and a number. "He's not an L-7 is he?"

"No, he's not a square ■ ■ ■."

"By the way, what's his name? Is he good-looking? What's he do for a living?"

"Whoa, girl, slow down a bit. His name is Brad Logan, and he is a rookie lawyer."

"I don't think they're called rookies."

"Well . . . whatever."

"You left out his looks. Wait, don't tell me. Slightly above average, he dresses like Jack Benny but has an out-of-this-world personality that literally sweeps a country girl right off her feet."

"I kept both feet on the ground, thank you," Lorna said.

"Are you telling me he's ***average*** on all three counts?"

"No, he's charming . . . and amusing . . ."

"What else, out with it—jumpin' Jehosephat—trying to get something out of you is like pulling teeth."

"He's about six foot tall, medium complexion, slim build —but he seems strong, dark hair—"

"Curly, wavy, or straight?"

"Not much curl. Quite good looking. He was very nice and—"

"Are you going to date him again?"

"Uh, yes, I think I'd like that."

"But you can't picture him fathering all five of your kids."

"Gloria, you know I'm trying to nurture my career. Marriage is somewhere a lot farther down the road. And I plan to only have two kids—a boy and a girl."

"Yes, Miss Ice Queen of 1950. Whatever you say. It would be just tragic if some fellow found your defrost button."

A big fluffy pillow from Lorna's bed hit Gloria flush in the face.

* * *

After Brad dropped Lorna off, he drove down Ninth Street, planning to take the back road home to where he and his parents lived in Washington Park on the northeast end of town. Washington Park's only major industry was the Emerson Electric plant over by the B&O tracks. Brad had worked at the Emerson plant for five straight summers to help pay for his schooling at the University of Illinois. His parents remortgaged their home to get a loan to pay for the rest of his studies.

The back route split off from Route 40 and paralleled the south side of the B&O tracks. Then it merged with North Park Drive, crossed Forest Boulevard, and ran directly behind his house at 49th and Lincoln. Route 40 angled slightly off to the left and ran along the north side of Fairmont City, home to a large Mexican population, many of which worked at its American Zinc plant.

Brad found himself humming fragments of popular romance tunes as he cautiously drove home. He hadn't felt this way since being smitten with Judy Finkeldey, a strawberry blonde angel, at Lansdowne Junior High. The rain continued to pelt his car. Sheets of blinding droplets made driving dangerous. His windshield wipers were frantically whipping back and forth to maintain visibility in the inky blackness. He glanced at his foggy rearview mirror. A car behind him followed much too close, its headlights swelling in the silvered glass, as if the driver wanted to pass. He thought this rather odd and couldn't believe that anyone could be in that much of a hurry.

"Easy, buddy," he said under his breath.

All of a sudden his Studebaker lurched as the malevolent car smacked his bumper. The jolt rocked him backwards. They hit bumpers again, and this time the driver behind maintained contact. There was a distinct sound of chromed steel groaning in pain.

"I don't believe this—he's trying to run me off the road," Brad muttered. He stole a squinted look into the rearview mirror in an effort to make out the driver. It was like trying to see through pea soup with blinding circus searchlights directly in your face. All he could barely see were two dark profiles.

Brad's knuckles turned white as they gripped the steering wheel in a frantic effort to maintain control.

Bam! . . . scrrunnchhh!

He heard the clinking sound of breaking glass and the metallic clash of front fender hitting rear fender.

"There goes one of my tail lights," Brad moaned.

All he could think about was his car hydroplaning in the slick downpour, skidding off the road, and crashing into a tree. He leaned forward, trying to see through the dark wetness. His sealed beam headlights strained to illuminate the roadway.

Do you turn into a skid or is it the other way around? Brad asked himself.

His pulse was racing and his chest felt tight. He passed a parked car on a curved part of the road, and it was all he could do to keep from ramming the side of it. The beleagured car, like a punch-drunk fighter, fishtailed and the rear came dangerously close to skidding out.

This is like an enhanced version of Dodge 'Em Cars for keeps at the Forest Park Highlands amusement park, he thought. Sweat began to form in the small of his back. Brad flinched instinctively as his side mirror splintered in tune with the sharp bark of a revolver. The fear within him ratcheted up several notches. He slouched down in his seat and tried to gather his wits. Several scenarios that might allow him to escape with his life were rapidly formulated. He furiously began honking his horn, hoping his attacker would not welcome the extra attention that it might bring.

1951 Packard Patrician 400, 4115 pounds, $3,662

Suddenly, it was over. The mystery car careened off to a side road and was swallowed up in the darkness. All Brad could tell was that it was a dark, late model, Packard sedan. A glint of light off the winged woman hood ornament was the giveaway. Since shots had been fired, he didn't feel like pushing his luck trying to chase down the license number.

Brad was shaking like a leaf, and his lungs were wheezing off-key notes like an old pump organ. His nerves were still jumpy five minutes later when he pulled into the driveway behind his dad's Chevy. He sat there nearly a minute before he remembered to cut the ignition. Safe. Home turf, sacred soil where in knicker-clad boy-hood he shot hoops, played mumblety-peg, wore a Lone Ranger bandana, yelled like Tarzan on a tree swing . . .

He sat there a few moments staring blankly through the windshield. ***Who in blazes was that?*** The wheels began spinning. He figured that it was either (a) someone trying to scare him off the Torricelli case, or (b) a thug from the St. Louis mob who had mistaken him for one of Walters' hirelings.

Brad Logan, age 7, wearing his Lone Ranger bandana

Herb, his dad, had just finished working the second shift at the C. K. Williams paint mill where he was foreman. He preferred working the three to eleven slot because production dropped to a slower pace and there were fewer employees. But the main reason Herb chose those hours was so he wouldn't have to rub elbows with those "college educated idiots," as he called them.

"No offense, son," he once told Brad, "but those Ivy Leaguers don't have the sense God gave a goose. He cocked his head and quirked his lips. "When you go off to college, don't forget to use the common sense I taught you."

Brad gave Edna, his mom, a kiss on the cheek. She was forty-six years old and for the first time he noticed the streaks of gray in her hair and wrinkles on her face. She was standing at the sink doing dishes. A box of Ivory dish detergent sat precariously on the nearby windowsill. A pot of something on the stove smelled rich and meaty. Tomorrow's supper was silently simmering on a back burner. Fresh coffee was brewing on one of the stove's front burners. Blue and yellow gas flames caressed the bottom of an all-glass Pyrex coffee pot Brad had given his mom for her birthday. Bubbly, grumbling water was shooting up the stem, cascading over the top, and then percolating through the freshly roasted grounds. The coffee was nearly done.

"Is Jackie already in bed?"

"Yes, your sister called it quits a half-hour ago," his mom said, a dishtowel in hand. "She wanted you to taste her stew to see if it needed anything."

Brad dipped out some tasty victuals with a large table-spoon. He waved it under his nose and savored its rich aroma before cautiously taking a sample. "It needs one more ingredient."

She turned, her deep blue eyes settling on him. "Namely?"

"Alka-Seltzer."

Edna folded her arms, threw back her shoulders and flashed a look of stern motherly disapproval.

"Just kidding. Tell Jackie it's delicious."

His dad, clad in his blue chambray work shirt, came up from the basement, having just checked out the furnace in anticipation of colder weather. His mother had baked an apple pie, and she served him a generous slice, along with a steaming cup of A&P Eight O' Clock coffee.

"Do you want a piece, Brad?" she asked.

"No thanks, I just had a malt about an hour ago. I'm still full."

"Are you sure you're feeling all right? I can't remember the last time you turned down a piece of pie."

"I'm not hungry, Mom."

"You look white as a ghost. Are you sure you're okay?"

"Someone ran into the back of my car and drove off without stopping. It's probably going to cost big bucks to get it fixed."

Brad didn't want to tell his parents any further details, knowing it would upset them. He had concluded whoever did it was just trying to scare him.

This must have been about the Torricelli case. If so, he figured, his tormentors had no way of knowing their actions would have just the opposite of the intended effect. Brad was firm and resolute about finishing what he had started. Not easily cowed, he certainly wasn't about to run a white flag up a pole. Now it was the ***who*** and ***why*** that he was turning over in his brain.

His dad ran his hand through thinning hair. "Don't forget to file a report with the police tomorrow."

"I won't."

"And call John Pazdera at the insurance office."

"Sure thing, Dad."

"How was your movie?" his mom asked.

"Decent—with the usual connect-the-dots John Wayne plot."

"What took you so long to get home?"

"I met a girl and we stopped at a malt shop."

"Protestant? With a good church upbringing, I hope."

"She's a B-girl at the Blue Flame nightclub on Broadway."

"She's what!"

"Don't blow a gasket. You know I'm just kidding."

"Is she nice?"

"Yes."

"Local girl?"

"Just moved here from Litchfield. She's staying at the Beulah Club. Works at the ***Journal.*** Good Christian background. Can we stop now with the questions? I feel as if I'm being interrogated by the KGB. I'm going to bed. See you two in the morning."

"Goodnight," they chirped.

The fender-bender ordeal had totally exhausted Brad. He swagged a cold washcloth over his face and brushed his teeth. On the way to his room he noticed a dress that his mom was making from a store-bought Simplicity pattern laying on the dining room table. Several pieces of a mint green fabric were already cut. Tissue paper, pinking shears and a cushion of straight pins were perched on top of the material. He went into the bedroom and stripped down to his skivvies, set his alarm, pulled back the covers and collapsed on the bed. He was faintly aware that Hobo, their black cocker spaniel, had joined him and was resting his chin on his leg.

"How are you doing, old fella?" Brad reached down and scratched one of his floppy ears.

Brad had found Hobo wandering around in their alley eight years ago. He had the mange and was half starved to death. Jackie and he slowly nursed him back to health. Their dad didn't want to keep him. He said dogs were too much trouble. Herb changed his tune after Hobo inexplicably decided he was his favorite human in the entire world, following him around wherever he went.

Brad slipped between a fresh pair of percale sheets and sunk his face into a goose down pillow. He glanced at the phosphorescent green hands of the alarm clock that registered a quarter past the witching hour. Exhausted, he fell asleep quickly, enshrouded in a black void that was later replaced by a kaleidoscope of colors.

The Sandman must have been short on magic dust that night. No deep and dreamless sleep for Brad. His troubled unconsciousness was plagued by a frenetic stage play filled with menacing characters and animals. A lion from Kipling's ***Jungle Book*** came within a whisker of devouring him. A filmy cloud coalesced into a hysterical Lorna who was pointing at him and laughing uncontrollably. His high school math teacher scolded him for not doing his homework. A car with short, stubby legs chased him up twelve flights of stairs inside the Spivey building. Playing a cat and mouse game, it cornered him on the edge of the roof. Brad lost his balance and fell when it lunged at him. Tumbling. Grabbing at air. Screaming silent screams.

He awoke in a cold sweat a millisecond before hitting the pavement. For an instant, his mind lingered on the peripheries of his dream, not quite knowing on which side of reality to settle on. He sat up and blinked away the sleep from his eyes. The waking skies of sunrise sent brilliant rays streaming in the window and the household's bantam rooster out back greeted the advent of another day with a cock-a-doodle-do reveille. The windup clock on the dresser next to his hairbrush showed it was six thirty.

He went to the basement and did his daily ten-minute calisthenics regimen—jumping jacks, push-ups, toe touching, knee bends, etcetera, taught to him by Lou Wappel, his high school P.E. teacher. Next he lifted weights for ten minutes. His mind briefly drifted back to that time in the eighth grade when the class bully picked on him. While showering and getting dressed, he whistled Sinatra's 1939 hit tune,"All, or Nothing at All."

In the kitchen, he fortified himself with a bowl of Kellogg's Pep and a cup of warmed-over java. Hobo came bounding in and let loose with a loud ***arff!*** as he gave Brad's hand an enthusiastic licking. Begging. While patting him on the back, Brad encountered a prickly cocklebur holding tight. He tugged it loose and tossed it in a wastebasket.

"Have a morsel of crust, old friend."

Hobo caught the large crumb in mid-air and gulped it down. A pair of large dark eyes looked at Brad in happy expectation. Doggie talk for ***more.*** His mom hated it when he fed Hobo table scraps. Brad figured it was a great diversion from his daily regimen of Strongheart canned dog food.

Brad ran his hand over a sandpaper-textured face. ***Uh oh, forgot to shave.*** He hurried into the bathroom and slipped a blue blade into his Gillette. ***What's worse, needing to shave daily or having the monthly blues—the curse, as his grandmother called it—every twenty-eight days?*** Like most things in life, he decided men had the easier path. Scraping his cheeks, by far, was the lesser of two evils. He made a face at the scruffy caricature that stared back at him from the mirror. His throat was a little sore so he swabbed it with tincture of Merthiolate.

Whew, Logan, you look as if you've been run over by a Mack truck. What on earth were those dream fragments about? Meaningless, or perhaps an ominous augury? Oops, cut myself. Where's that darned styptic pencil? A patch of toilet paper became glued to his face as a crimson rose blossomed.

How would neo-Freudians or Jung analyze it? Lorna laughing. Simple: My shyness and insecurity. The scolding. Obvious: Fear of doing something really stupid in front of Jim Fishbein. The car chase. Hmm . . . Am I in real danger? Brad dabbed on some of his dad's Old Spice. It stung like crazy.

He finished dressing and drove to the office. The dream sequence was quickly forgotten as he tabulated a plethora of errands needing to be done sometime in the coming week. His mind read the list like the message bulletin at Times Square: A trip to the cleaners. Oil change. Dental check-up. Haircut. Paint the living room. Mend the porch screen.

CHAPTER 8

Illinois attained statehood in 1818 thanks, in part, to people in Illinoistown who bribed census takers to count them twice to ensure that the required figure of 40,000 was reached. In its early years, the village across the river from St. Louis was called Illinoistown. When it came time to incorporate in 1861, there was another competing municipality in the area—East St. Louis. The two communities merged and the names were placed on a referendum for voters. East St. Louis prevailed because several railroads already had terminals in East St. Louis and did not want a name change. They bribed their workers with a bonus to vote against Illinoistown.

September 30th, 1950

Chain of Rocks Amusement Park: a thrill-a-minute carnival with an assortment of rides that promised plenty of "chills and spills." Located in rural north St. Louis on Route 66, it sat high on the bluff overlooking the Mississippi River. Not as big as its city counterpart, the Forest Park Highlands, it, nevertheless, had plenty of its own charm and appeal.

"How about some cotton candy, Lorna?"

"That sounds fine."

Lorna and Brad watched in fascination as the vendor took a long cone of paper and held it down in the spinning metal bowl. It magically converted sugar and food coloring into spider-like strands that were adeptly wound into a fluffy ball. Pink angel hair.

"Here, try some," Brad said, after paying the man a dime. They were finally on their first real date.

"I haven't had one of these in a coon's age." She held the cone to her mouth and closed her lips around the sweet fleecy fibers. "Ummm . . . good stuff; it literally melts in your mouth."

"And, unfortunately, on your face. You have some in the left corner of your mouth."

She flicked her tongue sideways then frowned in puzzlement. "I mean your other left," he corrected. Because he was facing her, he had told her the wrong side. "Here, it works better when you pick it off the cone with your fingers." He plucked a sticky morsel and playfully dangled it close to her mouth. She leaned her face forward and took it with her tongue.

"Over the lips and past the gums, look out stomach, here it comes!" she puckishly rhymed.

Brad smiled while licking his fingers. "Are you up to riding the Century?"

"What?"

"The roller coaster?"

"Oh, of course," she said. "I love exciting challenges. Why is it called the Century?"

"Pure psychology. It seems as if you are going a hundred miles an hour."

"Let's do it," she said with an impish smile.

They finished the cotton candy then headed toward the ride.

"I just love the clinking sound of the chain as it tows the string of cars up the incline," he said.

A rush of adrenaline pulsed in their ears in fearful anticipation of plummeting down the back of an ancient writhing sea monster. The cars nearly came to a complete stop as they reached the apex of the wood and steel labyrinth, slowly negotiating the turn at the top.

"The brink of impending doom," she said, placing her hands over her eyes.

Then they began to fall, like a car going over a cliff—headlong into the abyss. Faster. Faster. Four hands moved quickly to the steel safety bar and maintained a vise-like grip as they held on for their lives, looking straight ahead, too terrorized to glance at each other. A gale force wind from the breakneck speed pulled Lorna's ponytail backwards. The harsh sounds of alloyed wheels, groaning on metal rails, and the whoosh of rushing air were nearly drowned out in a rising crescendo of screams and yells from passengers.

They hit bottom, caught their breaths, and zoomed up the next hill. As the train of cars careened around the first turn, passengers mouthed oohs and aahs of excitement. The centrifugal force threw Lorna's body against him; she squealed and clamped her hand on top of his. The metal monster squirmed and thrashed as if it were trying to dislodge its offending tormentors. Brad and Lorna trembled through the harrowing final stretch, their limp bodies slumping forward as the brake mechanism brought the ride to a screeching halt. The terror was over. They had survived.

"We're still alive. Thank God," she said.

Two exhausted bodies were gasping for air after the ninety-second exhilarating adventure. Lorna modestly slipped her hand away from his. He had been surprised that the casual, incidental touch of their bodies caused his nerve endings to jangle. Her touch left him feeling uneasy, as if his heart was wandering into uncharted territory.

"Let's go again," she said, with excitement in her eyes. "I felt like we were riding a blazing comet, zooming through the cosmos in frenzied search of a distant galaxy."

"Spoken like a true writer. That's very poetic," he chided.

They rode the roller coaster four more times before moving on to other pleasures.

"Have some hot roasted peanuts," he said, offering the newly purchased bag.

She daintily selected a few shell-covered morsels.

"See the swimming pool over there?" he pointed. "It's sitting smack dab in the middle of the boundary line between St. Louis and St. Louis County."

"How do you know?" Lorna challenged, as if he had made it up to impress her.

"A good friend of mine, Ed Wood, a St. Louis policeman, told me."

Their next stop was the Ferris wheel—a giant Erector set circle with swinging gondolas. It sat near the edge of the bluff, perpendicular to the river.

"When we get to the top look out over the Mississippi," he said. "It's a breathtaking sight—almost as good as the view from an airplane."

Lorna surveyed the picture-perfect view below. "It's absolutely magnificent," she gasped, as the air rushed from her lungs.

Brad loved everything about the amusement park—its carnival atmosphere, the happy sounds, the mixture of smells—Cracker Jack, popcorn, sawdust, crackling electricity—the revelry, the crowds, the energy of it all. They took in as much as they could. A derby-topped barker in a red-checkered vest was persuasive as he described fantastic human anomalies. Side shows—a man completely covered with tattoos, a female contortionist, a sword swallower, the alligator boy, the petrified body of a male dredged from the Ohio River. Brad figured it must have been plaster of Paris.

His marksmanship earned a small fuzzy Teddy bear at the shooting gallery. Lorna jumped up and down and squealed with excitement whenever his small caliber bullet knocked down one of the moving animal targets. A brass casing plopped down on the counter each time he squeezed off a shot.

"Are those real bullets?" Lorna asked.

"Yes and no."

"Meaning?"

"It's what they call a .22 B-B. Twenty-two caliber bullets are made in regular, long, and short lengths. This shell fires a B-B pellet, similar to an air rifle. The pellets are strong enough to knock over the targets without damaging them. Most .22 rifles throw their shells off to the right, but the ejection port on these is on the bottom so they won't hit anyone standing nearby. The gun is mounted on a swivel for reasons of safety."

"Could I try it? I've never shot a gun before."

"Sure—there's practically no kick to these things. You know what Raymond Chandler says?"

"What?"

"There's nothing more dangerous than a beautiful dame with a gun."

"Yeah, that's probably why they fasten them down." Lorna gave him a sly smile and then cradled the weapon against her right shoulder.

He leaned over from behind and showed her the proper grip. The intoxicating smell of her hair momentarily caused him to lose concentration.

"Don't squint like you see it done in Western movies. When both eyes stay open you have better depth perception. Keep your breathing controlled. Line up the target in your sights and squeeze off a round."

Lorna excitedly began pulling the trigger. She let out little joyous squeals each time her B-B found its mark. She kept pulling until the gun made only a metallic clicking sound.

"You're a natural," he said. "One more bull's-eye and you would have won a prize. A regular Annie Oakley, that's what you are."

The Tilt-A-Whirl spun them dizzy; then they rode side-by-side on spirited merry-go-round horses while the machine's happy calliope cranked out several peppy tunes. Lorna won a Kewpie doll at a ring toss game. Then they gorged themselves on plump roasted hot dogs smothered with mustard and pickle relish.

"You have a yellow glob on your chin," she teased.

He playfully thrust his angled feature toward her and she dabbed it with a paper napkin.

"There, that's better. You need someone to take care of you."

"Thank you, Miss," he playfully mocked. "That's exactly what my mother says."

They screamed and hollered on the Whip, an oblong-shaped seated ride that hurled its occupants around the ends with the same cracking motion made by the snap of Lash La-Rue's bull whip. They scampered their way through the fun house—a winding maze of slanted floors. Distorting mirrors brought smiles of mirth. Goofy images—thin, fat, spindly legs, squished body, misshapen faces. Harmless obstacles mixed with unexpected sounds and noises. They recoiled at a clown face when it popped out. The floor below began rocking as if the entire building were about to be consumed by a massive earthquake spawned by the New Madrid fault. Lorna grabbed his shoulder in a futile effort to maintain her balance. She couldn't help but notice the firmness of his muscle tone. ***Masculine yet gentle in spirit***, she thought. One final surprise at the exit—a sudden blast of air went up her dress, eliciting a startled, indignant yell.

Brad mildly protested when Lorna grabbed his arm and dragged him past a tall man wearing a painted sandwich board. The advertising promised bedazzlement from dark-eyed dancing beauties clad in veils and flimsy Turkish pantaloons.

Later, they stood in amazement and listened in fascination as a mustachioed organ grinder, dressed like a gypsy in old-world clothes, turned the crank on his hurdy-gurdy. There was a patch on the sleeve of his shirt. His clothes were worn but clean. They were transfixed by the playful antics of his small monkey, dressed in a red and yellow bellhop uniform, ceaselessly chattering. It darted back and forth on the wooden top of the music machine. A few coins were dropped in his tin cup at the end of the entertaining routine.

"***Hvala lijepo***" (Thank you nicely), the man said in perfect Croatian.

"Hey, there's a gypsy lady. Let's go in and have her read

your fortune." Brad dragged Lorna into the small booth before she could answer.

"Have a seat and show me your hand," the old world woman said to her.

"But, this is silly – I don't believe in palm reading."

"Please, give me your hand—it's a spiritual roadmap."

Reluctantly, Lorna let the gypsy woman take her hand.

She studied the lines. "You're a Cancer, aren't you?"

Lorna nodded. ***Lucky guess.***

"And you're an only child."

A soft *yes* escaped Lorna's lips. ***Next she'll be telling me that I'm going to inherit a very large sum of money.***

"You should treasure that which you have recently found."

More mumbo-jumbo.

A difficult period of great sorrow will soon come into your life, and if you have the strength and will to survive, a long spell of much happiness will follow."

"I don't suppose you'd care to elaborate?"

The gypsy lady shrugged. "I'm sorry, that is all your hand tells me; I can say no more."

Lorna gave Brad a skeptical look as they left the fortune teller's booth. He smiled. "I thought the old woman's predictions were very interesting."

Lorna rolled her eyes.

Brad changed the subject. "Let's go through the Tunnel of Love." They neared the end of a perfect day and Brad saved the best for last.

Lorna was caught off guard. She hadn't expected such a request and a look of confusion spread across her face.

"I'll behave," he promised. "I'll be a perfect gentleman." He had carefully watched her body language all day long, and even though she was clearly having the time of her life, she had offered no romantic encouragement. They hadn't even progressed to the hand holding stage of a male-female relationship.

"Okay . . . but only if you swear."

"Scout's honor," he said, giving a two-fingers over his heart mock salute.

"Isn't it supposed to be three fingers against your brow?" she skeptically asked.

"Oops, sorry. You found me out. I was never a Scout."

"Gee! A poet and doesn't know it. Do you know their motto?"

"Sure. 'Be Prepared.' "

"Very good. How about that of the Girl Scouts?"

"Uh, no."

"Look Out For The Boys!"

He enjoyed her sense of humor. They gingerly climbed into a boat in front of a darkened entrance that featured a big flashing red heart at the top. An attendant held the ride steady to keep it from wildly rocking. All of the couples in front were sitting close together. The guy directly ahead of them had a friendly arm around his girl. They pretended not to notice. A hidden mechanism slowly pulled the boat through a meandering stream of shallow water, artificially colored by a blue dye. The murky interior was decorated in the style of a lush tropical paradise with soft Hawaiian music playing in the background. Electronically reproduced sounds of assorted exotic birds occasionally interrupted.

"That's a toucan calling to his mate," he whispered, hoping she would at least give him a peck on the cheek. An invisible bundling board separated them.

"Yes . . . well, don't let that get you all hot and bothered. I'd hate to see you come down with jungle fever."

She spoke in a manner that was defensively mild, a libido-deflating device. His ego had sent up a trial balloon, and her pointed words pricked it and made it go "pop."

They sat for the rest of the ride in uncomfortable stillness. The enormity of what had just transpired hit her. She had intended to make him keep his distance—not to wound or emasculate. But it ended the date on a sour note.

They drove home in stilted silence. As the car crossed the **Chain of Rocks Bridge,** Lorna finally spoke. "I've had a wonderful time today," she said as she leaned over and tenderly allowed her lips to brush his cheek. "I'm sorry if I bruised your enthusiasm. I like you a lot, but . . ."

"But what?" he frowned.

"It's just . . . I'm not ready for a steady relationship with a man. I'm only going on twenty and I want to experience what life has to offer before I get serious with anyone."

"What about the fellow at your office I hear you're dating—Lance . . . Mackerel?"

"It's Troutman, and that better have been a Freudian slip. He's taken me to lunch a few times, but I feel the same way about him. I don't want an exclusive relationship. I'm not ready for courtship. At this point I would like to continue going out with both of you. And, who knows, someone else could come along I might want to date."

"You do want to eventually get married and have children?"

"Of course, some day. But how will I know what kind of a man I want as a life-long companion, and what personality traits to look for, unless I have a variety of first-hand experiences with men of all makes and models. Er, excuse the car-buying metaphor."

"It makes sense, I guess—quite logical. But the process doesn't seem to allow for the unknown part of the equation that brings most men and women together in mar-riage. Two hearts beating as one in three-quarter time."

"And what exactly is that, pray tell?"

"I don't know if I can explain."

"Please try."

"Uh, did you see the movie ***Pinocchio?*** "

"Yes."

"Remember the scene where Pinocchio has drowned after his encounter with Monstro, the whale? Then an angel comes down from a bright star in the heavens and brings him back to life. Before you kissed me on the cheek back there, I felt like that dead little wooden puppet. I probably shouldn't be telling you this, but I find you magical, a lovely person who has the power to make me truly feel alive."

"I wish I could tell you I tingle all over when I am with you, but I don't. And I don't feel it with Lance either. I have seen other women follow the dictates of their hearts. Sometimes it works, and sometimes it doesn't," she explained. "I am not sure I'm ready to entrust my heart to a man. That's a very scary proposition for me. And I've got my career to think about. A serious relationship would only complicate my life."

"I think I grasp what you're saying," he said. "I wish you felt otherwise, but I'm certainly willing to follow your ground rules if that's what it takes to continue seeing you."

"Thanks for understanding. You're not upset, are you?"

"Totally crushed, but I'm resilient—I'll bounce back . . . You know what?"

Lorna shook her head. "Tell me."

"Maybe your heart is so filled with the other things life has to offer, they're crowding out the trust needed to make any kind of commitment to a relationship. You have to keep your heart soft, you know."

"Why?"

"Cupid's arrow will never penetrate if you build a hard shell around his target."

"I don't think I'm ready to feel the sting of his barb just yet."

"I'm not sure it's something you plan for—it just happens."

"You sound like an incurable romantic."

He turned his head toward her. "I'm sor–"

She pushed her hand softly against his lips and covered them with her fingers. "Hush! It's okay—probably what I like about you the most. That, and your wonderful offbeat sense of humor." She looked him straight in the eyes. "I honestly don't know what is my problem." Her hand moved to his cheek and lingered there. "And I don't know how long it will take to find out. I'm happy with our relationship, just the way it is. Please be patient with me; don't become possessive. And don't rush it." She retreated to the far side of the seat.

"I'll try," he said. "Thanks for being square with me. All I know is I like being with you, and at this point I'm willing to accept you on those terms."

They parked by the curb at the Beulah Club.

"Say, don't we have this dating routine backwards?" he asked.

"What do you mean?"

"Isn't it the woman who is supposed to push things to a serious state of affairs while the man dawdles and hesitates? I'm a bit confused by this modern woman-in-pursuit-of-a-career thing. Do you think perhaps I was born in the wrong century? Maybe I should have been a dashing knight in King Arthur's court."

"You know, I really do have fun when I'm with you." She sat there looking down at her lap as her face broke out in a pretty smile. "I hope you stick around awhile."

He got out of the car, went to her side, and opened the door.

"Thank you, Sir Lancelot."

"The pleasure was mine, my Lady . . . "

". . . Guinevere," she reminded.

"Ah, yes—Guinevere."

Lorna glanced up. "Look," she said as he closed the door. "A shooting star—quick, make a wish!"

Brad looked up at infinity. "Okay, I wish—"

"No." She was waving her hand in front of his face. "If you say it out loud it won't come true."

"It already has."

"What?"

"We're here, together, aren't we?"

"That's very sweet." She leaned forward and gave him a quick kiss on his lips. When they reached the front door, he gently took her hand and said, "I cheated and made two wishes."

"And what was the second one?"

"Can I have a hug?"

"A hug? I've never had a guy ask me for a ***hug*** at the end of a date."

Brad gave her a boyish smile. "Well, get used to it because I come from a long line of great huggers. In my family, it's tradition. Think of it as a safe way to start becoming involved with someone emotionally."

"You're a real schemer, aren't you? I think—"

Brad stopped

her in mid-sentence and pulled her toward him. As he lightly kissed her hair she melted in his arms and took comfort in his reassuring strength. She loved his smell, a manly scent of body oils, soap and aftershave.

He released her as she pushed away. "What's wrong, don't you like it?"

"Au contraire. I ***loved*** it; that's the problem. Goodnight, sweet prince," she whispered, as she turned and disappeared inside.

Brad blew her a kiss that she did not see, then turned and loped back to his car. Whistling a happy tune, he playfully leap-frogged over a fireplug in his path.

She likes me.

Briefly overcome by a touch of melancholy, he pondered their future. Totally enthralled by this angel, he was ready for a serious relationship. He couldn't explain it. For the first time in his life he felt the magnetism, the tugging on his heart strings he'd heard described so many times in his favorite songs. Yet he also felt frustration. ***Don't get close***, she said. No exclusive relationship. Don't become possessive! What she asked for was unnatural - emotional paralysis. A platonic twosome. He would have to coax and woo her in the old-fashioned manner, earning her trust by degrees, loosening that impersonal psyche of hers knot by knot.

I think I'm going to love you, Lorna Sanders.

CHAPTER 9

October 5, 1950

After the great 1903 flood, a strip of houses along Third Street, a mere block away from City Hall, became abandoned by disillusioned owners who grew weary of the endless struggle with Ol' Man River. An enterprising group of women moved in and became "madams," operating a string of brothels. The area became known as the "Valley" because of deep ruts formed in the road by "tin lizzies" and wagon wheels that squished the mud out of their path. When World War I broke out and patriotic young men from town went abroad to Europe, they were surprised to find Englishmen, Belgians, Dutch, and French who knew of a place called the Valley in East St. Louis.

Brad was just about ready to leave the office and head for the Club 501 when his phone rang.

"Hello, Brad Logan speaking."

A gruff voice on the other end. "Yeah, is this Logan, the guy defending Louie Sizemore?"

"Yes, it is. What can I do for you?"

"I have some important information for ya; stuff that could blow the Torricelli case wide open."

"Who are you?"

"Sorry, can't say."

"Then tell me what you know."

"Can't do that either, not over the phone. Someone might be listening on another line."

"What do you suggest?"

"I'll call ya back again, ten o'clock this evening at the Greyhound Bus Station. I'll call the number at the public phone booth. The one on the left."

"Why so late?"

"Because it's the only time I can make it. Ya interested, or not?"

"I, uh, yes, I'll be there."

* * *

"It could be a trap," Knucky said in a grave tone.

"I know, but it just might be the break I need in this case."

Knucky frowned and looked down at his drink. "Hey, Roland, come over here a minute."

Roland ambled over to their table. "What's up, boss?"

"Let's all go into my office a minute."

They went inside a small room, off to the side, near the main entrance. Knucky shut the door to ensure privacy. "Give Logan your ankle holster and your Chief's Special revolver," Knucky instructed Roland.

"I can't take that, Mr. Walters." Brad extended his right arm and pushed at the air with his palm. "I don't have a permit."

"So, who's gonna know?"

"I don't want to do something illegal that might cost me my license."

"Better than getting yourself killed," Roland counseled.

"I'm a grown man. I can take care of myself. Besides, I don't think anyone out there is trying to kill me. When's the last time you heard of a lawyer getting killed in this town?"

"Ex-mayor John Bowman was representing a client in a suit against the Wiggins Ferry monopoly when he got shot in the back," Knucky noted.

"That was a long time ago; before the turn of the century. Law and order has made considerable progress since then."

"Ollie Moore got gunned down in front of the Labor Hall not far from here in 1932," Knucky countered.

"Yeah, but that was during a contentious strike," Brad said. "And he was a union leader, not a lawyer."

"And Leo Quick was shot to death in his back yard in, in uh . . . what year was that Roland?"

"That was 1938, the same year a mini-tornado blew the roof off Clark Junior High," Roland said.

Richard Widmark

"Another labor leader in a strike dispute," Brad reminded.

"But all three of those killings had one thing in common," Knucky said.

"Namely . . . ?"

"There was a lot at stake, just like this construction kick-back thing you're involved in. My boys tell me you've got some people at City Hall kinda nervous."

"I'll be careful."

"Here's a piece of advice. Don't go into a building unless you know how to get back out fast, just in case something goes down."

"Okay, thanks for the

tip."

"And try to keep your back to a wall. The one time Wild Bill Hickok didn't, he got shot."

"Aces and eights."

"What?" Knucky said.

"He was playing cards and holding two pair. Ever since then it's been unlucky—they call it the Dead Man's Hand."

"Another thing: Stay alert at all times. Bad guys, like most gamblers, have a 'tell.' "

"What's a tell?"

"A quirk of some kind." Knucky pointed to his face. "Read the eyes, they're usually a dead giveaway. Whenever someone tries to pull a fast one, you can see it in his eyes. Sometimes it's a blink, a twitch, a sideways glance—or they do something with their body. Maybe a nervous tick, or they scratch their nose. There's always a tip-off if you're watching for it."

Brad listened carefully to what Knucky said because he knew he was the master at surviving. Knucky studied the habits and nuances of other people like a pickpocket. That's what made him an astute judge of character and intent.

"And if somethin' doesn't look right or feel right, run like a bat out of h—an' get outta there," Roland added in his muddled vernacular.

"You want Roland to go with ya?" Knucky asked.

"No. The voice on the phone said I had to come alone."

"Why didn't you insist on meeting him at the public library—someplace where there would be people around?"

"He said I had to meet him alone. Besides, the library closes at six P.M. He's supposed to call me at ten o'clock and give final instructions for the rendezvous site," Brad said.

"I don't like it. I don't like it at all," Knucky mumbled.

Brad knew Knucky had given him some valuable advice. Anticipate . . . plan . . . weigh your options. Knucky was adept at reading his enemies and potential enemies. He studied them, analyzed them, assessed their strengths, exploited their weaknesses. He knew when to act or bide his time. That innate and unerring ability to judge people accounted for his survival.

Laurence Olivier as Hamlet – 1948

Brad was getting ready to leave when he noticed a parchment-colored human skull sitting on a shelf behind Knucky's desk. Its cold unblinking eye sockets stared back at him. ***Alas, poor Yorik . . .*** Brad found himself musing à la Hamlet. Just looking at it evoked flashbacks of youthful explorations where arrowheads, broken relics and ancient mounds whispered of past native-American cultures.

"Knucky, the skull on the shelf behind you—is that some macabre trophy to remind you of a triumph over one of your enemies?"

"You never cease to amaze me, kid. Ya really think I'm some kind of monster?"

"Sorry. So what's the story behind it?"

Knucky was stroking his chin. "That skull goes all the way back to the days of my youth, back when Wilson was president. It was my last year in school, just before I quit."

"So it's a real skull?"

"Of course, but it's Indian, probably hundreds or thousands of years old."

"Indian? I found pottery shards and arrowheads as a kid, but never a skull. Why don't you donate it to the museum at Monks Mound?"

"I keep it as a reminder."

"I don't understand," Brad said.

"I was born in Monroe County but I grew up and went to school here in East St. Louis. There were Indian burial mounds all over the city back in those days. Most of them were eventually bulldozed to make room for progress. The kids I knew carried the skulls to school with them. They were kind of a status symbol. The one with the biggest skull was acknowledged as the leader."

Dagwood Bumstead and Daisey

"What if someone else found a bigger skull? Did that make other boys look up to him?"

"Maybe yes, maybe no."

"Explain."

"The kid with the new skull remained the leader only if he was tough enough to keep it."

"You mean there were turf fights over the biggest skull?"

"Uh huh."

"So you keep this skull because it reminds you of when all the other guys looked up to you?"

"Not exactly."

"Meaning . . . "

"Meaning it isn't the one I originally found. Another kid challenged me and we settled it outside in an alley. He beat me up, took mine, and tossed me this one as he walked away with a stupid grin."

"Did you give him a good fight?"

Knucky leaned toward him, the hint of a smile replacing his scowl. "Yep. He's got a scar on his cheek and he left me with this scar above my left eye," Knucky said as he dabbed at a streak of bare skin that slashed diagonally through his eyebrow.

"Do you still remember the boy's name?" Brad asked.

The smile disappeared. "Delonzo . . . Sal Delonzo."

* * *

Brad left the Club 501 and went back home. His dad was still at work, and his mother was at the kitchen table reading her Sunday school lesson. An Absorene can was on its side next to her elbow and Brad turned it upright so it wouldn't roll off. ***It must be time to clean the wallpaper again with that pink dough.*** His sister, Jackie, who worked as an executive secretary for Dick Fox at Emerson Electric, was in the bathroom getting ready to go out on a date. Brad greeted his mom with a peck on the cheek.

"You can make yourself a **Dagwood sand-wich**, or there's leftover chicken if you want," she said.

"Okay, thanks. I'm home, sis," Brad yelled. "I hope you're not going to be in there for hours, primping endlessly in front of the mirror."

Though both were in their twenties, Brad and Jackie were typical brother and sister. They teased each other and sometimes fought, but there was never any acute rancor. They knew down deep that the bond of family made their relationship special.

"Is that my obnoxious brother out there?" she yelled back.

"All that primping in front of the mirror isn't going to do you any good, you know. Haven't you heard? Ugly is clear to the bone."

The bathroom door opened and a peeved Jackie stepped into the hall. Brad ducked as a hair curler whizzed by his head. "It must run in the family because you received a double dose," she shouted.

Brad only half forgave his older sister for taking him on a snipe hunt when he was a budding adolescent. Jackie had received a double promotion in grade school and graduated from East Side High at the tender age of sixteen. She worked for a year as a secretary at the Bank of St. Louis, and then off she went to Anderson College in Anderson, Indiana. Dad was reluctant to help with expenses. He said college was a waste of time for young girls and claimed she only went there to meet some eligible bachelor to get her MRS degree. Edna, their mother, secretly sent Jackie money on the sly to help with expenses. Her dad's words proved to be prophetic. She married a preacher's son from Alliance, Ohio. The marriage lasted a little over a year, ending in divorce. Now she was back home again, trying to rebuild her life.

Lana Turner and John Garfield

"Who's your hot date for tonight?" Brad asked, while skimming the front page of the ***Journal.***

"Don Rogier of Highland, if you must know." She came into the kitchen, practicing her newly acquired **Lana Turner** walk.

"I bet Dad won't like him."

"He doesn't like any of my boyfriends," Jackie said.

"Isn't he that guy who looks like Frank Buck of 'Bring 'Em Back Alive' fame?"

"Yes. He's ruggedly handsome."

"I remember seeing him in the electronics department the last summer I worked at Emerson Electric."

Brad walked over to raid the gleaming white Norge refrigerator his mom had just bought to replace their old icebox. It was in a generous mood, yielding a leftover wing, a drumstick and a couple of buttermilk biscuits.

Jackie finished dressing and came into the kitchen. "Well, how do I look?"

She was decked out in a red form-fitting dress that flattered her hourglass figure.

"You look fine, honey," her mom said in admiration.

Brad gestured with his drumstick and gave her a mock wolf whistle. "Your outfit is really hot. That shade of red has been outlawed in five states. Wow, once you get all of those freckles camouflaged, you look pretty good, sis."

"Mom told me those freckles are places where I was kissed by an angel when I was a baby. At least I wasn't born defective, like you."

Brad licked some crumbs from his fingers. "How so?"

"Haven't you noticed how the outside of the heel on your right shoe always wears down fast?"

"Yeah, meaning what?"

"Meaning your body is misshapen, out of kilter, defective. You'll probably need an operation to correct the problem in a couple of years."

"All right, you two," their mom intervened. "Stop the fussing." She was shaking her head. "Two grown children who behave like a couple of five-year-olds. Why do you fight like cats and dogs?"

"It's just growing pains, Ma! I'm sorry, sis; you know I was just kidding. Have a great time tonight."

"Me too, brother dearest," she said, flashing him a fingers-crossed sign their mother didn't see. "I don't mean to say all those horrible things about you. Somehow you manage to irritate me to no end at times."

"Yeah, remember how we used to bicker in the car when we went to visit relatives in Paducah?"

"Yes, and when Mom and Dad made us stop, we played word games and searched for Burma Shave signs along the road near

Chester."

"Remember our favorite?" he said.

"Yes, uh, let me think, uh . . . IT GAVE/ McDONALD/ THAT NEEDED CHARM/ HELLO HOLLYWOOD/ . . . GOOD-BYE FARM/. "**Burma Shave**," they screamed, trying to outdo each other.

"Those were good times, sis."

"Perhaps it was the boredom of the trip that caused us to quarrel."

"Remember how you sometimes gave me the evil eye stare, just to aggravate me?"

Jackie laughed. "Yes, and like a brat you'd tattle: M-o-m, D-a-d, Jackie is staring at me again.' "

Brad joined the levity. "And then you'd retaliate by saying: 'mo-THER, fa-THER, Brad is breathing my air and sticking his tongue out at me.' "

Their mother sighed and folded her arms in front of her chest, her face assuming the mask of a long-suffering soul. It was the same sigh she'd used when they were kids, the one that signaled that her patience was wearing thin and it was time to stop fussing. "Aren't we all fortunate both of you act so much more mature now?"

* * *

Brad left the house at nine-thirty and arrived at the bus station around nine-fifty. He went inside and sat down on a long wooden bench that wasn't much different from a church pew. He looked over at the bank of telephone booths. As luck would have it, someone was inside using the phone on the left. ***What am I going to do if he's still there at ten o'clock?***

He sat and waited, drumming his fingers on the back of the bench, glancing at his watch almost every thirty seconds. Nervous energy. It was a minute after ten and the man was still talking. Brad walked over to the booth and stood there, hoping he'd get the message. He didn't. Brad held up his watch and pointed to it. He looked at Brad as though he was nuts and pointed to the next booth. Brad just shook his head and stared. The man finally hung up the phone with a look of annoyance, opened the bi-fold doors and glanced at the empty booth next to his.

"Hey, pal, you got a screw loose?" He looked at Brad the way people do at lunatics.

Brad merely shrugged his shoulders and said, "Sorry."

"Sorry doesn't cut it. I ought to slug you one."

Brad flinched, bracing himself for a blast of foul language—or worse.

Instead he came back with: "I was talking to my wife in the hospital."

Now Brad really felt bad about his behavior. ***What would Knucky do in this situation?***

He pulled out his wallet and handed him a fiver. "I'm sorry! Here, maybe this will help." He stared at Brad in astonishment, scratched the top of his head, and walked away with a smile on his face.

Ten seconds later the phone rang. "H-hello," Brad nervously answered.

"Meet me inside the old McMahon freight terminal at a quarter past ten." His baritone voice sounded synthetic, disguised. "Make sure ya come alone."

"The one on West Broadway?"

"No, the one in the middle of Winter Avenue, west of C Street."

"I don't remember a building in that location."

"It's an old warehouse McMahon Transfer abandoned three years ago."

"Where should I go? How will I find you?"

"Just come on in; I'll be there."

"All right, I'm leaving now," Brad said.

The Greyhound station, in the 300 block of Missouri Avenue, wasn't far from Brad's destination. Brad got in his car and continued down Missouri Avenue and made a right on C Street. He followed C Street to Winter Avenue, a few blocks away. He remembered what Knucky had said about knowing where the building exits were in this type of situation. The place was a derelict. Dark. Brooding. Empty. The nearest street lamp, its ineffectual light encased in a halo of river fog, was a block away. The landscape before him looked vague and murky. He slowly drove around the building, as if looking for a place to park. His eyes flicked back and forth, reconnoitering. There was a dim light in one small window. A side door on the upper level led to a decrepit landing, and a set of metal stairs ended at ground level. Another small door in back led to a narrow alley.

Brad parked a half-block away near a quadruple set of GM&O railroad tracks. A slight breeze carried the smell of the river to him as he began walking toward the warehouse. Searchlights from a Coast Guard cutter were sweeping back and forth across the Mississippi. An assortment of dissonant sounds punctuated the blackness: a tugboat's piercing horn as it pushed some barges up the river; clanging metal from a nearby railroad roundhouse; the groaning and crashing of railroad cars being "humped" in nearby yards. He detoured around a string of tank cars that were on a spur line.

Occasional clouds, dancing past a gothic quarter moon, formed troubling and ominous shadows. An odd feeling came over Brad. It was as if he were on the set of a James Cagney or Humphrey Bogart movie. Dark alleys, detectives in trench-coats, desperate men with guns, treachery and intrigue—a tense drama played out on a chiaroscuro landscape with stark light and plenty of shadows. He had watched enough film noir to know that this was the scene where somebody usually got shot.

James Cagney

He barely heard the soft click-clack of something in the distant somewhere, but it was nearly drowned out by a polyglot of insistent industrial sounds. The riverfront air was so burdened with moisture its dampness further blurred the edges of everything and diminished what the ear heard. Brad looked down at another set of tracks before he crossed them to make sure he didn't trip over a rail or get his foot caught in a frog or switch. A car horn honked and he looked up to catch a glimpse of the traffic on the recently opened Veterans Bridge. It was almost the last thing that ever registered on his brain.

The lumbering colossus was right on him. He had lifted his foot to cross the last set of tracks when something tweaked his self-preservation synapses, causing him to freeze in place. He must have caught a glimpse of it out of the corner of his eye. A big yellow boxcar came highballing down the track and he was directly in its path. Brad had already started to move forward and every muscle in his body strained to reverse his forward progress, enabling him to lean backward slightly. It whooshed in front of him, passing inches from his face. He closed his eyes and grimaced in the second or two it took the car to flash by. It seemed like an eternity. In railroad parlance the car had been "kicked" about a quarter of a mile away and sent to its destination at the other end of the yards. Brad took a deep breath and rubbed his chest, trying to restart his heart. He wondered if he owed his life to divine providence or to sharp reflexes from his Judo training.

Whew, that was close, Logan. You almost became a grease spot.

He looked both ways, crossed the last set of tracks, and made his way to the front entrance of the building. A rusty padlock lay on the ground. The words 'McMahon Freight,' once painted in bright blue, had faded to a whisper. The siding was corrugated tin that had been galvanized. The zinc coating had given way to terminal rust cancer. There were several small windows, but they had been boarded up. The place looked like a cliché in a **Sam Spade** movie. Childhood fears of the dark rushed through his memory. Brad tugged on a heavy bolt that had already been pulled from its hasps. Beating back a sense of dread, the heavy door, which screamed on its rusty hinges, was shunted aside. A cavernous expanse of stygian blackness. ***Where's the room with the light?***

Bogart (Sam Spade)/ Maltese Falcon

Deep into that darkness peering,
long I stood there wondering, fearing . . .

Bah! Just a scary line, courtesy of Edgar Allan Poe, Brad decided.

Nevertheless, it took every ounce of courage he could muster to cross the threshold and enter the room. Brad could feel broken glass and unidentifiable metal offal under foot. A few shafts of dull light streamed down from a couple of broken skylights. A faint whiff of paint and turpentine ran up his nostrils. Brad's fertile mind imagined all sort of terrors. He nearly stumbled over a wooden pallet. His courage fled as his body froze at the unexpected sound of flapping wings above his head. As he looked up, a glob of vague darkness coalesced into a startled barn owl making a dash for an opening in one of the skylights, two stories high up on the roof.

"Hello, anybody there?" he said, hoping his vision would adjust to the shadowy darkness that enveloped him. Another terror. Brad felt what he surmised to be a rat scurry across the instep of his left foot.

He thought: ***Leave! Get out of here, now***, as he turned to vacate the building. All his caution went for naught. It happened so fast. He could do nothing about it. Whatever small amount of light there was went out, and he felt a heavy stab of pain in the rear of his skull. Brad collapsed in a heap like a puppet whose strings had broken.

He sluggishly awoke with a dull, throbbing pain, slightly nauseated, with a roiling headache. ***Great. Probably a concussion.*** He was slouched in an old chair with his chin on his chest. The noxious smell told him he was still in the same building. As he raised his head, someone shined a flashlight in his eyes. There wasn't any way Brad was going to be able to make out any features behind the blazing light. But he could distinguish the muzzle of a very large caliber gun pointed at his heart.

Thoughts of what he should have done (like listening to Knucky), fruitless as they were, tormented him.

"Well, well, welcome back from dreamland, Mr. Logan."

It was the same voice he had heard on the phone, only rough as sandpaper and more sinister. Brad lightly massaged the egg on the back of his head while squinting at the light. He tried to get his bearings, guessing that he was probably in a small office on the ground floor of the warehouse.

Trying to unscramble his scrambled brain, Brad managed to say, "Are you going to kill me?"

"Nah, I just want some information. If ya tell me what I want to know, I'll let you go."

"What information?"

"That folder, that ledger, whatever you got from Torricelli's widow; what's in it?"

"I didn't get anything from her. We went through her husband's things in his office, but the cupboard was bare."

"You're lying. I don't like it when people give me nursery rhymes instead of the truth."

"I'm telling you the truth." The fog in Brad's mind was beginning to lift. He mentally sharpened his senses.

"You'll tell me what I want to know. In the end . . . they always do. Tell me, Mr. Logan, do you have a low threshold? A low tolerance for pain?"

"I, I don't know, but I'm giving it to you straight." Brad began weighing his options, calculating risks for each possible action.

"Whether or not you're lying remains to be seen, but we'll soon find out. For the last time, what about the information on Torricelli's list?"

"I don't have any list or folder, I swear."

"I have some very important clients who want to know. I'm afraid I'm going to have to punish you for lying to me," he said.

Watch their eyes, Knucky had said. But in the dark shadows they were inscrutable. Brad anticipated his captor scooting the chair away from the table so he could stand up. Brad drew a deep breath as his muscles tensed for combat and prepared for the fury he was about to unleash.

It's now or never.

Impelled by adrenaline, Brad grabbed the edge of the desk and shoved it hard, knocking the man backwards. His gun fired a wild shot that whizzed above Brad's head and smashed into the wall behind him. The man yelled a string of curse words loudly and fluently as the chair slid out from under him and he crashed to the floor. The hand with the flashlight struck a small filing cabinet on the way down, knocking it from his grasp. The flashlight made a loud clatter as it hit the floor. The filament broke from the impact. Somehow he managed to hold on to the gun. It was pitch black again, somewhat leveling the playing field.

"Where are you?" The man lay on the floor a few seconds, holding his wrist and moaning. "I'm gonna blow your head off when I find you, unless you tell me what I want to know."

Brad's survival instinct, passed down from one of his Neolithic ancestors, kicked in, raising his blood pressure and causing his heart rate to increase exponentially. He crawled on his hands and knees toward the door, flinging it open. The concrete floor felt gritty, fouled by nature after years of abandonment. Brad scrambled to his feet and lurched blindly ahead. He caromed off a wooden crate and several cardboard cartons went flying.

A couple of sporadic shots rang out. The first splattered against a wall. The other splintered the door molding.

"Where are you, Logan? It won't do you any good to hide," he heard him say as he pushed his way through the door. "You can't get outside. I always hedge my bets. I piled some fifty-five gallon drums in front of the entrance, just in case you pulled something like this. I did the same thing to the alley access door."

Thanks for the info, pea brain. Think, Logan, think. What next? Wait a minute, maybe he doesn't know about the upper level door.

Brad kept low and inched his way along a wall, circumventing an old crate filled with packing excelsior. His hands and the front of his clothes were covered with dust and cobwebs.

Where are the stairs leading to that second story exit door?

He bumped against a table with some glass jars on it. Two more errant shots zipped through the air. One of the bullets struck a container, sending splinters of glass flying in all directions. A warm trickle of blood ran down Brad's right hand.

Miraculously, Brad felt a metal railing. He scrambled up the stairs, tripping and falling several times. Another shot rang out. The bullet ricocheted off the railing and embedded itself in a wooden barrel. It made the distinctive pinging sound one often heard in a Green Hornet radio drama.

Brit Reed a.k.a. as the Green Hornet

Is he out of bullets? Was that six or seven shots?

His hope fled as he heard the disheartening click of another clip being shoved into the gun butt. It was still nearly impossible to see. He stopped at a place where he guessed the door to be. Brad ran his hand along the wall, his blind fingers groping desperately for a handle. Nothing. He crawled another few feet moving his hand back and forth, up and down, seeking escape from his relentless pursuer. Finally, that round knob of blessed redemption. He carefully twisted to the right and pulled. No luck. He tried turning to the left. It was locked.

I'm too young to die. I've never made love to a woman nor fathered a child.

Brad frantically tried twisting both ways while first pushing the door in, and then out. It still didn't budge. His fingers searched frantically for a keyhole. Nada, zip. Then he felt it. The door had one of those locks with the escutcheon mounted flush on the edge of the door and fastened into a large keeper screwed next to it on the doorjamb. He twisted the knob and heard the latch snap back into its assembly. Unfortunately, his assailant also heard the distinctive ***click***.

"I've got you now," he yelled.

His stumbling sounds were getting closer. A yank on the door. It grudgingly moved about an inch. A couple of more shots zinged in Brad's general direction. He pressed his foot against the jamb for leverage and yanked as hard as he could. The door creaked and groaned, scraping the floor and opening about a foot. Brad squeezed through and stumbled outside into the damp night air. He tripped and nearly pitched forward headlong down the rickety stairs. He caught himself on the railing and regained his balance.

Brad could hear him coming. He wasn't far behind. Brad scurried down the wrought-iron stairs two at a time and hit the ground running. His years of track practice were paying off. The slick cobblestones on the street almost caused another fall. He was nearing his car when he found out the hard way you can't outrun a bullet. The slug dug into Brad's thigh and brought him down, landing prone between a set of tracks. He grabbed his leg. More blood.

The man caught up with Brad and hovered over him, looking down, like a vulture getting ready to pick some bones clean. That gun with the big muzzle was pointing at him again.

"Okay, wise guy. You've got about five seconds to tell me what I want to know before I blast your kneecap and make you a permanent cripple. If that doesn't convince you, I'm going to splatter your brains all over these tracks."

Brad could almost see the man's threatening words, as if written in one of those white cartoon balloons above his head.

Click, clickety clack.

"Who do you work for, Sal Delonzo or somebody in East St. Louis?" Brad asked.

It was very uncomfortable, lying there on the railroad ties with ballast rock mashing against Brad's head, his back, his legs.

"That's none of your business."

Click, clickety clack.

"I'll give you what you want if you tell me who you're working for," Brad said.

"Time's up, Lawyerman. Better say good-bye to your left knee." He raised the gun and brought it forward, preparing to fire.

Brad's eyes grew wide as he looked past him and saw his rescuer lumbering toward them.

"What are you lookin' at? I'm not dumb enough to fall for another of your tricks." But then he noticed the abject terror on Brad's face and realized he wasn't acting.

"Oh, my God!" Brad said.

The man twisted his torso and began to turn his head to look behind him. There was a muffled scream and a dull thud as a monstrous flatcar plowed into his body, tossing it like a rag doll about twenty feet away in a weed-choked lot.

Tough noogies, fella.

Remembering what the Bible said about God's love, Brad bit his lip as soon as he said it. He couldn't suppress his imagination: excruciating pain for the briefest of seconds, then nothing. Mashed to a pulp by seven tons of shadowy iron and steel. ***Ashes to ashes, dust to dust. Gone. Finito. Aaughh!***

Brad held his arms against his sides and closed his eyes, pressing his body close to the ground as the car whooshed above him. When it passed, he grabbed hold of a rail and twisted his way across it, just in case another piece of rolling stock came down the pike.

Was he in the wrong place at the wrong time or was that the Lord working in one of His mysterious ways?

By sheer dint of will Brad stumbled to his feet and dragged his aching, bleeding carcass to the car. He fumbled for the door handle and felt himself sinking into unconsciousness.

*   *   *

Groggy and disoriented, Brad awoke in room that smelled antiseptic. Everything looked pastel and blurry, like a typical Monet painting. He was in a metal bed with medicinal sheets, unlike the white ones at home his Mom washed with Fels Naptha that smelled sunshine fresh. An IV was dripping clear liquid into the vein in his left arm, its staccato rhythm miming the cadence of the pulse thundering in his temples. Big Ben's bell was clanging insistently in his brain. A stern-faced nurse in a crisp uniform was strangling his other arm, checking his pulse. Her hips were broader than a battleship. Brad sighed, wishing to slip back into the blackness from which he'd just emerged. ***"That which does not kill you only makes you stronger." Whoever said that was an idiot.***

As the cobwebs cleared, he heard his mother's voice.

"They said you were lucky. The bullet nicked your femoral artery, and you almost bled to death. Dr. Eisele operated on you, removed the bullet and stitched you up. You lost a bucket of blood, and they had to replace it. Your father and sister are downstairs donating. I'm going when they get back."

He didn't say anything, his head nodding in affirmation. Atropos, that Greek Fate of human destiny, apparently had changed her mind about snipping Brad's life cord.

"How are you feeling, Mr. Logan?" the nurse asked. She looked like Aldo Ray's sister and had a starchy voice to match.

"Okay, I guess. A little weak and groggy."

"I almost never got that IV in you." Her hands rested on those big hips beneath her stiffly starched whites. "I must have had to stick you a dozen times. You have those collapsing veins that make life difficult for people like me."

Brad looked down at his arm. It had purplish bruises.

"You were fortunate. Dr. Eisele had just finished operating on Mr. Walters and was getting ready to leave when you came in and bled all over the place."

Her angular words hurt his brain. "Knucky, he . . . something happened to Mr. Walters? Is he all right?"

"He's doing fine, resting comfortably just four rooms down from yours," she said. "By the way, detective Robert Sweeney wanted me to tell you he'll be here in about an hour to get your version of last night's events."

"Great," Brad mumbled out of the corner of his mouth.

She grabbed the palm of his right hand.

Walters' nemesis, Detective Robert "Tree" Sweeney by Lamont Irons

"See that? It's a puncture wound. You'll need a tetanus shot so you don't get an infection and die. That's what you get for playing around railroad tracks."

"I don't think I need—"

"Hush! I've got the shot right here on my tray. You don't have an irrational fear of needles, do you?"

She didn't give him time to answer, but he thought ***yes.***

"Calvin Coolidge's son died from an infected tennis blister, you know. We can't have you kicking the bucket and getting sued by your heirs."

"But . . ."

"Roll over and pull up your gown. I have to give it to you in your backside."

"But that's not where the injury is."

"Shush!" She clucked her tongue. "Nurse Crabtree knows best."

She held the syringe high and looked up, as if admiring the gleaming point. "You're not going to be difficult, are you?"

Brad meekly rolled over. "Could you pull the curtain please?"

Her glasses slid down her nose as she lowered her head and glowered. "My, we're persnickety, aren't we?" she said as she gave a yank on the muslin cloth.

He closed his eyes, bracing himself for the assault about to impinge on his body. "Um," he winced as she jammed in the needle.

She edged closer, her perfume smelling more like disinfectant. "Don't move! We wouldn't want to get an air bubble in the bloodstream. Instant death!"

Brad held his breath and did his best to stifle a sigh of relief when she yanked the needle out. She roughly slapped a

Band-Aid over the puncture wound.

"Looks like you'll live," she said while restoring the curtain to its position against the wall. "I'll be back in about an hour to check your temperature."

"Thanks." ***Oral or rectal*** he wondered.

"How did I get here, Mom? The last thing I remember was trying to get in my car to drive to the hospital."

"I was told a couple of Knucky Walters' gangsters brought you to St. Mary's. They said you would have bled to death if they had taken the longer trip to Christian Welfare Hospital."

"How does my thigh look?" Brad asked as he raised the sheet. His gaze fell upon sutures and angry red marks, looking like the lacings on a Rawlings football.

"How long do I get to stay here at the Ritz?"

"The doctor estimated about five days. He said there was minimal nerve damage," his mother assured him.

He swiped a hand across his forehead to scratch a maddening itch. ***Oww, that hurts.*** He fingered a sore spot. ***Probably the brake rigging from the flat car. And that's why I have this rip-snorting headache.***

His mom was glowering at him with hands on hips.

"You talk about Knucky as though the two of you are friends," she said, flushed with a look of astonishment.

"Yeah, we are, Mom."

She blanched. "How on earth . . . ?"

"I met him one night when I ate supper at the Club 501."

"I know what kind of a place that is. Your Aunt Ludy worked there briefly as a cocktail waitress. That's where she met her husband, your uncle Morris Maltzman."

"Mom, he's not such a bad guy, really."

"Have you lost your marbles? He's a hoodlum. Your father will skin you alive when he finds out you two are friends."

Despite Brad's age, his mom occasionally reverted to her parenting mode.

"Mom, I'm a lawyer. Lawyers deal with people who have problems and people who get in trouble with the law. It's the nature of the job."

"I raised you better than that."

"Mom, don't you remember? Jesus associated with all kinds of people."

"But that's different," she said with a look of indignation. "It wouldn't surprise me if fooling around with Knucky was the reason you got shot. What on earth were you doing gallivanting all over town in the dead of night?"

"Boy, am I hungry," he said, ignoring his mother's question. "I could sure go for a Kingsway Inn hamburger."

She rolled her eyes and threw up her hands in a fit of pique. "Here you are, like Lazarus knocking on death's door, and all you can think about is food."

"I want to get well before that nurse comes back."

Roland popped his head in the room and gave a cheery "***Hello.***"

"What happened to Knucky? Did one of the St. Louis thugs get him?" Brad asked.

"No, he was accidentally shot."

"Is he all right?"

"Don't worry, he's too ornery to croak."

"Where was he shot?"

"In the right butt."

Brad's hospital – St. Mary's in East St. Louis

"No, I mean where was he when it happened?"

"At Harry Kelly's Gypsy Inn."

"Ahem," Brad's mother uttered as she purposely cleared her throat.

"Excuse me for being so impolite. Roland, this is my mother; Mom, Roland Jones, a, uh, friend of Walters'. I vaguely remember. . . He's one of the men who brought me here."

"Thank you for saving my son's life."

"I was glad to be of service. He's a good man."

"If you're one of Walters' men, you need to have a talk with the Lord," she admonished.

Brad looked around the room for a place to disappear.

"Excuse me," she abruptly said. "Brad, I think I'll run home and get your robe and house slippers. I should be back in about an hour."

"Okay, Mom." She leaned over and kissed her son's cheek before turning to leave.

"Nice meetin' you, ma'am."

"Likewise," she replied as she hurried out the door.

"As my grandfather would say, how in the Sam Hill did you and Montrose find me?" Brad asked.

"We had just driven Knucky to the Gypsy Inn. He got worried and sent us looking for you. We figured the meeting was probably somewhere on the Island. We just about gave up hope when we spotted your car."

"Roland, did you say Knucky was shot in the rear?"

"Yeah."

"How did it happen?"

"I'm not at liberty to say. I can tell you there are going to be two different versions floatin' around."

"And they would be . . . "

"Some people are gonna say Knucky an' Harry got into a friendly argument, an' Harry accidentally shot him."

"What's the other version?"

"Walters' ex-wife, Dora, was there and flew off the handle. She plugged him."

Brad thought a moment. "Hmmm. Life imitating art."

"Whatcha mean?"

"Remember that Gatsby fellow in the book that Knucky and I are always talking about?"

"Uh, yeah."

"Gatsby's downfall is due to woman troubles." Brad licked his lips. "Can you pour me a glass of water? My throat's as parched as a desert."

"Sure." He poured a drink, and Brad took several refreshing sips.

"What's the real story?"

"Knucky said it was so embarrassing, he wants to keep people guessing. That's the way he wants it, so that's the way it's gonna be." Roland crossed his arms under his chest and gave a sheepish grin. "I will let you in on something though."

"What's that?"

"He was bleedin' like a stuck hog, an' they got a Kotex from the ladies room to press on the wound until they got him to the hospital."

Brad winced with pain from his bruises as his chest undulated with laughter.

Roland was smiling, but then he got serious. "I hear ya almost bought the farm."

"Yeah, I guess I had a pretty close call."

"I'm glad you're still among the living. I hear the other guy, Ralph Mancuso—one of Sal Delonzo's men, wasn't so lucky. The police figure he had an argument with a railroad car, an' the car won. Being crushed like that must be the worst way possible to die."

"I don't think so," Brad said.

"What's worse?"

"I had an uncle named Eugene who lived over in Alta Sita on a small farm back around 1932."

"Somethin' happen to him?"

"It was a cool day in early December, after the first killing frost of the season. He decided that it was time to butcher a hog. Eugene shot the boar in the head and cut his throat to drain the blood. Then he rigged a singletree and a block and tackle to hoist the hog over a large iron kettle filled to the brim with boiling water. The plan, of course, was to dip the hog in the water and then use a corn knife to shave the bristles. As the hog was lowered into the scalding water he suddenly came back to life. His frantic kicking knocked the kettle over, spilling most of it on Uncle Eugene, with much of the water going inside a pair of high boots he was wearing."

Airmail comes to East St. Louis - Nov 6, 1950

Roland scrunched up his face. "Good grief—that must have hurt like blazes."

"I can't imagine anything worse. He died from shock before they could get him to the hospital. When they pulled his boots off, great gobs of cooked flesh fell from the bone like a stewed chicken."

"Holy moley! You're right. That is a worse way to die."

There was a moment of silence, as if both of them were contemplating matters of the hereafter.

Roland changed the subject. "Hey, did you know you're in a very famous bed?"

"No, what do you mean?"

"Carl Shelton was staying in this very room a few years ago, recovering from malaria or some unknown illness. Then 'Tree' Sweeney found out he was here."

"What did Sweeney do?"

"It's unbelievable, but true. Sweeney barged into the room, cuffed him, dragged him out of bed an' took him down to the city jail. Arrested him on some trumped-up charge like vagrancy."

"I bet Shelton had a fit."

"Oh yeah, threatened to sue the city for twenty thousand dollars."

"What happened?"

"It's really strange. For some reason or another he never sued."

"Maybe he was afraid Sweeney would kill him," Brad said.

"Yeah, Sweeney's tough. I hear he pries the cap off beer bottles with his teeth."

"Really?"

Roland frowned. "No kiddin'. I tried it once an' chipped a tooth."

"Sweeney apparently dislikes the Sheltons as much as he hates Knucky."

"Yeah, Sweeney acts like this is his town. I don't know how he gets away with it, but he does."

Visitors trooped in regularly all that week—aunts, uncles, cousins and colleagues from the office. But no youngsters under sixteen. Like most hospitals, there was a strict rule against children. Within a couple of days, Brad, much like a juvenile, found himself sticking his tongue out and making faces at Nurse Crabtree when she left the room. After half a fortnight's stay, ten pounds lighter and minus ninety dollars and seventy-eight cents, Brad was released.

CHAPTER 10

The nationally televised Kefauver Hearings were conducted in Miami, Tampa, New Orleans, Kansas City, Cleveland, St. Louis, Detroit, Los Angeles, San Francisco, Las Vegas, Philadelphia, Washington, Chicago and New York. Testimony was taken from nearly eight hundred witnesses. It was the first television event ever that kept viewers riveted to their tiny screens. The chairman captured the public's imagination and Kefauver-for-President clubs sprang up all over the country. He lost the nomination to Adlai Stevenson, governor of Illinois, but was placed on the ticket as the V. P. nominee. They suffered a crushing defeat in 1952 against Eisenhower and Nixon.

January 31, 1951

Brad and Lorna had occasional dates for the next few months without any substantial change in their relationship. Then the big event finally arrived. The Kefauver senate crime committee would officially begin hearings at nine o'clock in the morning in the courtroom of United States District Judge, George H. Moore. The inquiry was scheduled to be televised nationally from the third floor of the new federal courthouse in St. Louis at 12th and Market.

Brad got up early and drove over to the office to meet Harry Fiebig. He had been retained to advise Wayne Littlefeather, a Cherokee Indian, who had been subpoenaed to testify about the southern Illinois link to illegal bootleg operations in Oklahoma, which was a "dry" state. Ernst thought it would be a good idea for Brad to go along to soak up some experience in these kinds of proceedings.

As soon as Brad arrived, he called Lorna at the ***Journal.***

"May I please speak with Miss Sanders?" he asked the operator.

"Just a second please," replied the friendly voice.

Pause.

"This is Lorna."

"Hello, Lorna, it's Brad Logan."

"Oh, hello."

"Did you get the flowers I sent you?"

"Yes . . . they're very . . . unusual . . . and pretty too. It's the first time I ever received a jar of blackberry preserves with flowers."

"They're home made. The wildflowers remind me of you—a circus of color and excitement."

"The flowers, interlaced with baby's breath and stalks of asparagus ferns, are stunning, but what kind of flowers are they? All I recognize are daisies and goldenrod."

"They're fairly common garden flowers," he replied. "I asked Mirring Florist to include a bright splash of larkspur, delphinium, and lisianthus."

"They are truly beautiful. How does a lawyer know so much about flowers?"

"I collected them in a scrapbook once for a freshman biology class."

Silence at the other end.

"Listen, the Ice Capades are coming to the Arena in St. Louis next weekend, and I was wondering if you would go with me? I have a friend who works at the ticket office over there, and I could get really good seats."

"It sounds like fun, but I can't go. That's the weekend I take the bus to Litchfield to visit my parents. I try to get back there about once a month, you know."

"Darn, I'm sorry that isn't going to work out."

"Brad, I've got to run now or I'll be late for an appointment. I was just getting ready to walk out the door when you called. Keep in touch. Bye, bye."

"Good-bye," he cheerfully said, masking his true disappointment.

Click!

Brad hung up the phone and moseyed over to Harry's office. He was sitting serenely at his desk, finishing up a cup of caffeine-free Postum and a sweet roll.

"Good morning, Harry." Brad watched as he flung crumbs off his shirt and tie with his hand.

"Same to you, Brad," he responded, licking the sugar from his fingers. "This is going to be some circus. That courtroom will be packed with reporters, lawyers, marshals, gamblers, preachers, politicians, and every conceivable type of hoodlum known to mankind."

"Why are preachers going to be there?"

"Reverends Charles Kamm and Don Mitten of the Metropolitan Church Federation have agreed to give their perspectives. Time's a wastin'. Let's get going so we can get a good seat."

They went out to the parking lot behind the Spivey building and hopped into Harry's car—a three-month old Pontiac Chieftan with a V-8 engine. The hood ornament was a metal and plastic replica of the head of a famous Ottawa Indian leader who had fomented a rebellion against whites in the area before Revolutionary War times.

Harry was proud of the car and turned the lights on to show him how the amber Indian head lit up.

"Isn't she a beaut?" he said.

"Yes, and these leather seats are sharp. But how's your gas mileage?"

"I get about eighteen miles to the gallon. Not bad for a boat like this."

They turned right on Broadway when the car reached Southern Illinois Bank. Then they passed the Chicago Restaurant, Bowman's Restaurant, and the Southern Hotel before dipping beneath a railroad overpass.

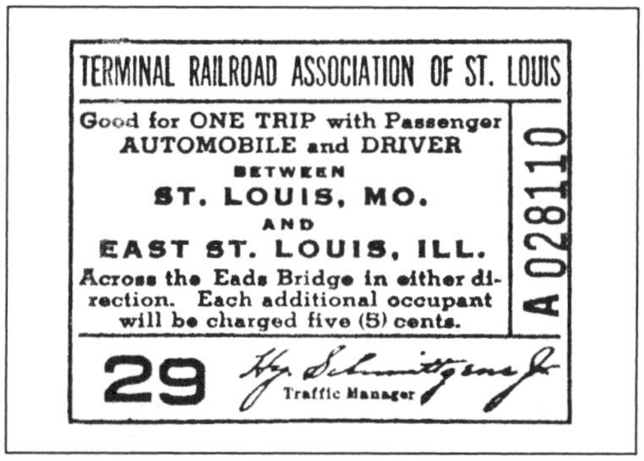
TERMINAL RAILROAD ASSOCIATION OF ST. LOUIS

Good for ONE TRIP with Passenger AUTOMOBILE and DRIVER BETWEEN ST. LOUIS, MO. AND EAST ST. LOUIS, ILL. Across the Eads Bridge in either direction. Each additional occupant will be charged five (5) cents.

A 028110

29 Traffic Manager

Harry looked at his fuel gauge. "I need to get some gas."

"Ever go over the 90 m.p.h. highway speed limit in this car?" Brad asked.

Harry had that Peck's Bad Boy look on his face. "I did 105 m.p.h. a month ago on a straight stretch of Route 15."

Brad shot Harry a look of disbelief. "I didn't think this car could go that fast."

"Normally it doesn't. Some mothballs and aviation fuel in the gas tank did the trick."

Before reaching the Eads Bridge approach, Harry pulled over at Deem Oil Company.

"Regular or ethyl?" shouted the attendant.

"Make it ethyl," Harry replied.

"Want me to check under the hood?"

"Sure, why not."

"I like to put some high

Harry Fiebig's 1951 Pontiac

octane stuff in this buggy every once in a while. A little zip in the gas tank keeps her purring like a kitten. Once a month I take it out in the country and run it at high speed to blow the carbon out of the cylinders."

"I know what you mean," Brad said. "I occasionally do the same thing. It looks as if the gas war is over. The prices have jumped from sixteen cents to twenty-one cents a gallon."

"Keep an eye on things. I'm going over to buy some bridge tickets at that booth over there."

While Harry was gone, an attendant with the name Rodney stitched on his oil-stained twill shirt cleaned the windshield. The wind kicked up, and he edged his cap down over his hairline. After checking the water and oil, he brought the dipstick over to Brad's window.

"It's right on the full mark, exactly where it should be."

"That's fine. Thanks a lot."

Harry came back, paid the man two dollars and forty-two cents, and climbed back in the car.

The recalcitrant engine wouldn't start.

"It's starter lock," Harry said sheepishly, as he put the car in gear.

They got out of the car and began rocking it sideways to disengage the Bendix drive gear stuck in the teeth of the flywheel. That did the trick. The engine turned over and they were merrily on their way again. Bush's Steak House was on the left as they pulled out. Cardinal baseball players and notables such as wrestler Lou Thesz and promoter Sam Muchnik often frequented the popular food and entertainment spot.

Lou Thesz at East St. L. Social Center

"Did you ever hear the Wilde twins sing there before they trekked off to Hollywood?" Brad asked.

"Yes . . . and they were really good. Too bad their careers fizzled after a few movies with Mickey Rooney."

"I hear they ended up marrying a couple of guys in a band out there."

"Yeah, the Cathcart brothers, or something like that."

They went under a railroad trestle and then turned left up the approach ramp to the bridge.

"I've always been a little afraid of bridges," Brad said.

The metal webbing of the roadbed set the tires to singing. A string of coal barges were moving slowly downstream.

"Bridge-o-phobia. How did you catch that disease?"

"Well, Mr. Freud, when I was in grade school, I had an uncle who held me up by the side rail one time while we were walking across. My mother saw him and threw a fit. Really yelled at him."

Harry took out a pocket flask and took a nip. "Remember the bridge at Chester that fell into the river during the war?"

"Wasn't that something? People said a tornado blew it down."

"Maybe it was lousy engineering. Do you want some of this 'hi-test' scotch?" he offered. "It'll put some starch in your legs.""No thanks." Brad's tie clip was off kilter so he straightened it out. "Have you ever been across the Irvin S. Cobb Bridge that spans the river near Paducah?"

"Nope."

"I've got relatives in the Paducah-Mayfield area, and we had to cross that narrow rickety old thing every time we went to visit them when I was a kid. The approaches are very steep, and it's like driving a car on a roller coaster."

"How did you cope?"

"I usually closed my eyes."

Brad glanced at the river as they reached the Eads' midpoint. The wind was forming whitecaps on the brown water below. They approached the tollbooth at the Missouri end of the bridge, and Harry handed the man a paper-thin blue ticket printed by the Terminal Railroad, owner of the bridge. The Eads Bridge was old and stately, having been completed in 1874. It was the first major span across the Mississippi and its structure had been inspected by President Grant—a one-time St. Louisan—himself. The radical, controversial design called for only two river piers and the longest arched tube-truss in the world.

"They had an elephant cross the Eads Bridge, you know," Brad said.

"How come?" Harry frowned.

"When it first opened people claimed it would fall in the river, so the first thing they tested it with was a man leading an elephant. Then they parked four locomotives on the lower railroad deck to determine its strength."

"When it was inspected last year, engineers claimed it was strong enough to survive an atomic blast," Harry said.

"Probably a bit of hyperbole on their part."

"You know," Harry said, "there were fourteen lives lost from the bends during construction."

"The bends? Isn't that what the divers got when they went under the water to work on the piers?"

Harry nodded. "Decompression sickness. They didn't know about coming up slowly to allow the nitrogen in their blood to dissipate."

As they neared the exit, the aromatic smell of the multi-storied Old Judge Coffee warehouse greeted them. Simultaneously, the distinct pungency of black licorice from the Switzer's plant teased their noses.

Harry breathed deeply. "Those two intoxicating smells make every trip across the bridge worth it."

"You said it."

"I pity poor St. Louisans who come to our town from the opposite direction."

"Why?"

"Because the first thing that assaults them is the odoriferous smell coming from our Stock Yards."

"But breathing East St. Louis air is actually good for them," Brad argued.

"Come again?"

"It's true. They should inhale deeply because there're vitamins a'plenty in that organic mixture."

They hooted at that one.

"What's the most unusual idea you ever heard from the mouth of a college professor?" Harry asked.

"That's easy. There was this sociology professor who said men should marry three times during their three score and ten."

Pause.

"Go ahead, I'm listening."

"He said a man in his twenties should tie the knot with a woman of forty."

"The reason being . . . "

"Claimed it was when each member of the species reached their sexual peak. Then when the man attained forty, he should divorce and marry a girl in her twenties."

"Why?"

"Said it would relieve the boredom, reinvigorate, and spur the man to greater accomplishment."

"So what happens when the man reaches sixty? I assume that's the next level?"

"Correct. At that point, according to his thesis, he should marry a woman his age since the pair would ostensibly be equally mature both sexually and mentally."

A blue-uniformed policeman waved them through the intersection at Broadway and Olive.

"So what happens to the kids under his plan?"

"He thought kids would be better off raised by the state in an institutionalized environment."

He shot Brad a look of disbelief. "Now that's strange."

"You asked."

Brad was planning to have Harry reciprocate with one of his professors, but they had arrived at their destination. He parallel parked in a spot on Chestnut Street near the Kiel Auditorium and Opera House. They walked to the Federal Building.

Kiel was home to the St. Louis Symphony and to professsional grapplers such as Lou Thesz, Killer Kowalski, Ed "Strangler" Lewis and Gorgeous George, who demonstrated their skills before twelve thousand screaming fans on weekends. Sam Muchnik had shrewdly parlayed his promoting talent to make St. Louis the wrestling capital of the world. Thesz, the local boy and reigning champion, regularly thrilled crowds with demonstrations of his "scientific" wrestling technique.

Federal Building at 12th & Market - built at a cost of $4 million

As they approached the Federal Building, a contingent of city policemen milled around the entrance. Brad paused as Harry stooped to retie a shoe.

"Hey, Harry, look . . . there's Sweeney and Sullivan, our East Side detectives caucusing with a couple of policeman over there."

He looked up. "Yeah, I see them. You know that Sweeney is one tough son-of-a gun."

"Don't I know it?"

Harry stood up again. "Back in '46, Bugsy Siegel was in East St. Louis trying to get some financial backing from some of his Jewish friends for a gambling empire he was trying to build in Las Vegas. He ran into Sweeney at the Ill-Mo Bar on Missouri Avenue. Siegel caught Sweeney giving him the evil eye and whispered to Ray Doyle, the owner, 'Is that him?' 'Yeah, that's Sweeney,' he replied. Sweeney strode up to Siegel and got in his face. 'You've got exactly five minutes to get outta here and cross the bridge back to St. Louis you blankety-blank cur.' Siegel meekly tucked his tail between his legs and walked out the door."

"Wow! That's an incredible story," Brad said.

"Anything new on the Torricelli murder?" Fiebig inquired.

Brad shrugged. "Postponed indefinitely; several judges had operations and there's a huge backlog."

They walked up the stone stairs that were flanked by large concrete statues of Lady Justice, stoically holding her scales. She didn't seem to mind the cold. As they entered the building, Brad's right shoe skidded slightly on the highly polished marble floor.

"Whoa, careful Harry. I almost went down."

The first thing they did was rendezvous with their client, Wayne Littlefeather. They met him in the first floor lobby and took a seat on a bench to go over final strategy. He was wearing a Western style shirt, pointed snakeskin boots, and a clean pair of Wrangler jeans. Thick black hair framed a face that featured high Mongolian cheekbones and coppery skin. The nose was an exact replica of the Indian depicted on the nickel. Bereft of facial stubble, he possessed all of the characteristics of his ancestors. Brad judged him to be about two hundred pounds and strong as an ox.

"This is my associate, Brad Logan," Harry told Littlefeather.

They nodded and shook hands.

He was wearing a leather string festooned with what appeared to be several bear claws.

"That's an interesting decoration around your neck," Brad said.

"It's a 'natawah,'a talisman—a good luck charm—given to me by an old Chippewa medicine man whose life I once saved. I'm never without it."

"Don't forget the instructions I gave you at the office last week," Harry reminded him. "Speak clearly into the microphone and look the panel straight in the eye. They're not seeking to prosecute you. All they are looking for is a detailed description of how liquor is making its way from southern Illinois to Oklahoma. Tell them the truth, as you know it. They are not after people like you who do the grunt work. They've got bigger fish to fry.

Don't forget, this isn't a jury—it's a government hearing. And I'll be right here to help guide you. If I tap you on the leg that means I want to tell you something before you answer. Any questions?"

"No, sir."

"Fine, let's go find the courtroom."

A blue-uniformed St. Louis policeman strolled by.

"Excuse me, sir," Brad said. "Can you tell us on which floor the hearings are being held?"

"Patrolman Ken Hoelker, at your service." A friendly smile lit up the officer's cherubic, lightly freckled face. "The hearing is on the third floor. You can either take the elevator directly in front of you, or the stairs over in the corner. Enjoy your stay in our fine city."

"He must be getting a kickback from the Chamber of Commerce," Brad said.

The trio huffed and puffed up the stairs to the courtroom that was beginning to fill with people. The television crews were in the process of making final checks on their equipment. Workmen were placing wooden chairs at large oak tables where witnesses and their lawyers were to sit as they faced the committee. They hung their outer garments in the coatroom, and then found seats in a front section reserved for witnesses and their lawyers. The place was loaded with U. S. marshals, and FBI, and Treasury agents. The paneled room had a twenty-foot ceiling and a middle aisle with gallery seating on either side.

Brad spotted Russ Maxwell, ***Journal*** photographer. He had met him three weeks ago at the Federal courthouse in East St. Louis.

"Hello, Russ. Got plenty of flashbulbs?"

He waved and smiled. "Yeah, I have three rolls of film and dozens of bulbs in my bag."

Brad turned to Harry. "Is East St. Louis police commissioner J.T. English going to be here?"

"I don't think so. He's in Barnes Hospital, supposedly with a bad ticker. The police chief is taking his place."

"Fortuitous timing for him. Who are those three guys just now arriving? They look familiar."

"The tall one is Dallas Harrell, ex-sheriff of Madison County. The other two are ex-St. Clair County sheriffs, George Gruenewald and 'Dolph' Fisher. I can't wait to hear what they have to say," Harry whispered. Then he leaned over and asked, "Are you okay, Wayne?"

"I'm fine." He was nervously cracking his knuckles.

As more people filed in and the room began to fill, Brad craned his neck, looking to see if Knucky would show. He spotted his chief legal counsel, Morris Goldman, engaged in serious conversation with a contingent of unsavory-looking clients. A low-pitched hum of buzzing conversation filled the room.

"I don't see Knucky Walters. Do you think he'll show?" Brad asked.

"I doubt it. Not only is he not here, neither are his brother Lou, nor nephew, Gordon Foster."

"I'll bet the committee will really be upset if he doesn't comply with their subpoena."

"They'll probably blow a fuse."

Their Indian friend continued playing the silent stoic. He had a finger in his mouth, chewing on a hangnail.

About five minutes before the hearing was to begin, Senator Kefauver and his four associates marched in and took their seats up front. Kefauver's rangy frame towered over the others and he was easily distinguishable in his black horn-rimmed glasses, worsted gray pinstriped suit, and a pair of black wingtips. Several microphones were scattered about on the committee table. A single mike decorated the one reserved for witnesses. A crush of people were standing in back and along the walls in semi-circle fashion.

"Pay attention, Brad. You're a witness to history today."

"You can say that again." Brad was idly staring at a bronze replica of the Great Seal of the United States behind the dais.

"I've been told many crooks and politicians are suffering from an attack of 'Kefauveritis,' " Harry said.

"Kefauveritis?"

Harry winked. "It's a mysterious ailment that hits potential witnesses just before they are supposed to appear on the stand."

"Yes, I hear it's becoming a much discussed national malady, a sudden outbreak of heart trouble, gall bladder attacks, laryngitis and nervous breakdowns."

"That, plus an acute attack of agoraphobia—an urgent need for privacy," Harry added.

"The committee will come to order," Kefauver said with a rap of the gavel.

Jerry Mizell of Belleville and Delmar Coalby, educational director for Winstanley Baptist Church in East St. Louis, were the first on the "docket." Each had prepared statements he planned to read to the committee. The duo had been members of a grand jury back in 1946 that had indicted the entire East St. Louis City Council and various county officials for failing to enforce gambling laws. A judge later threw out the charges.

The clerk began the proceedings by introducing the committee and stating its purpose. Mizell was called and was sworn in by one of Kefauver's assistants with the right-hand-in-the-air and left-hand-on-the-Bible routine. A woman, seated alone at a small table, dressed very business-like in a taupe jacket and matching skirt, dexterously pushed the keys on her stenotype machine. Mizell described a litany of sins committed by city and county officials dating all the way back to 1927.

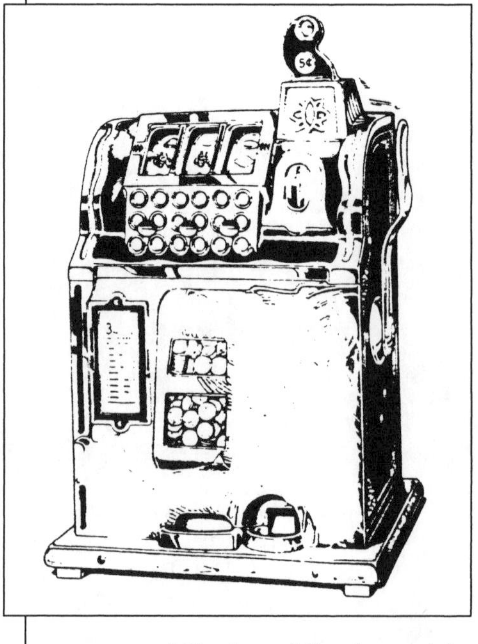

"There has been very little time since the Prohibition era that wide open commercialized gambling has not been tolerated by elected officials of St. Clair County, particularly in East St. Louis,"

he said. "According to numerous witnesses who were called to testify before us, slot machines have been, and are now prevalent in various locations throughout the county. These slot machines exist in filling stations, taverns, nightclubs and other establishments. Several parents came before us and complained that children were playing slot machines in confectioneries with their lunch money."

Everyone in the room was listening intently.

"Bookies are permitted to operate without much interference," Mizell continued. "And the East St. Louis police chief has been quoted as saying, 'As long as pari-mutuel betting is allowed at Fairmount race track, I won't do anything to close the bookie joints.' " He also stated that taking action would throw a lot of people out of work.

"Is this testimony going to hurt the incumbents in the upcoming election?" Brad whispered to Harry.

"It won't change a thing. Mark my words."

"Any chance these hearings could be a crucible for reform in East St. Louis?"

"Don't hold your breath," Harry said.

Mizell droned on. "The nationally known 'Valley' vice area operated freely for years, and frequent underworld murders go unsolved in ongoing gang wars for control of the lucrative 'East Side.' When our grand jury met during a term of the circuit court, newspaper reporters were 'invited' to come and testify instead of being subpoenaed. The witnesses did not respond. Out of fear and respect, most bookie joints closed down while we were in session, but after we were through, it was business as usual."

"When the indictments were forthcoming, the State's Attorney asked the judge to quash the individual indictments on the grounds that he had a group indictment which would be sufficient.

Later, the group indictment was thrown out because it did not directly name the individual or individuals responsible for enforcement of the state gaming laws. He claimed there were also glaring faults in the wording of the document. A subsequent grand jury indicted the state's attorney and his assistants, but that got thrown out also."

Kefauver and his associates

Kefauver sat attentively during Mizell's entire testimony with his long fingers pensively steepled, pyramid fashion.

Delmar Coalby followed with a statement supplementing what Mizell had just said. Then the two ministers, Mitten and Kamm, gave statements. The gist of their testimony could be summed up in a single phrase. Because of gambling and mobsterism, the whole area was "going to Hell in a hand-basket." Next up on the stand was Wayne Littlefeather. There was still no indication Walters and his associates were going to show.

"Mr. Littlefeather, now that you have been sworn in, please state your name and address."

"Wayne R. Littlefeather, 427-A Walnut Street, Cairo, Illinois."

"Please describe the nature of your work," one of the committee members directed.

"I used to drive a truck for a man named Hyman Rousch, operator of Tri-State Liquor Company in Cairo, Illinois."

"And what three states did the firm service?"

"Illinois, Missouri and Kentucky—but we sometimes did business in Tennessee and Arkansas."

"Did you ever engage in illegal bootleg operations by delivering liquor to dry states, such as Oklahoma?"

"Yes, sir. I frequently made deliveries to establishments in the Tulsa area."

"Did you ever have occasion to do business in St. Louis or East St. Louis?"

Wayne was doing fine, but the hot glare of the television lights caused beads of sweat to form on his brow.

"There were several times when our regular sources of liquor dried up, and my boss sent me to East St. Louis for supplies."

"To what establishment?"

"Valley Distributing Company."

"So named because it was in the notorious Valley area?"

"No, this was over on Seventh Street. I think the name has a connection to the Mississippi Valley," Wayne replied.

There was a small ripple of laughter from an audience who found the inquisitor's one-track train of thought amusing.

"Who was the owner or manager of Valley Distributing?"

"A very nice man named Sol Alexander. I think he lived in St. Louis."

"Do you know of any connections between your boss in Cairo and Knucky Walters?"

"Mr. Rousch talked like they were old pals—said they knew each other from the old Shelton Gang era."

"Did you ever see Mr. Walters at Valley Distributing?"

"Yes, many times. My boss said Mr. Walters was a silent partner in several Cairo liquor firms."

"And what did you take that to mean?"

"I guess it meant he was a man of few words. But he always had plenty to say when I was around him."

The gallery let loose with an outburst of guffaws at Wayne's naïveté. He looked hurt and confused by the laughter.

Kefauver banged the gavel and called the general babble to order. "Don't mind the audience," he interjected. "You're doing just fine."

Brad had Kefauver pegged for an egocentric but that didn't seem to be the case. His impressive forbearance and aura of assuredness commanded immediate respect from the crowd. Their disruptiveness receded into oblivion.

"Did anyone ever mention the Cairo places in which Mr. Walters had interests?"

"No, sir. Specific places were never named."

"What kind of money are we talking about in some of these transactions, Mr. Littlefeather?"

"I'm not sure. But my boss once cashed a check from Valley Distributing for over $5,000."

At that point, another assistant with salt and pepper hair in a medium brown suit introduced several canceled checks into evidence. They averaged about $5,000 each and were endorsed by Eugene B. Palmerston of the Valley firm. Also introduced into evidence were copies of court records that showed Sol Alexander paid a $1,000 fine in 1941 after being charged with violating federal liquor laws.

"How big were the loads you carried from Cairo to Oklahoma, Mr. Littlefeather?"

"My trucks were loaded with cases of liquor that brought about $13,000 on delivery."

"Wasn't there an incident where you were arrested one time at Sparta, Illinois?"

"Yes."

"Please tell us about it."

"There was a highway patrolman who found out what I was doing, and he tried to get money from me. Said he would let me alone if I paid him $500."

"So he was trying to shake you down?"

"Yes."

"Then what happened?"

Wayne leaned over and listened to something Harry was telling him. "I told him 'no dice,' and then he arrested me on a concealed weapons charge. I always carry a gun for protection. I was taken to jail where I placed a call to Mr. Rubin. He told me to sit tight and that he would have a lawyer there within the hour. The lawyer came, my bond was set at $2,000, and two hours later I was back driving my truck."

"What happened when your case came up in court?"

"The judge threw it out."

"On what grounds?"

"What do you mean?" Wayne asked.

"Why was the case dismissed?"

"Someone told me the lawyer and the judge were close friends."

"Did the policeman continue to make trouble for you?"

"No, sir. He was transferred so he couldn't make no more trouble."

Once again, gales of laughter erupted from members of the audience, and they began making comments among themselves.

"This hearing will come to order immediately," Kefauver thundered. He directed a stern look of disapproval at the unruly crowd and rapped his gavel. "Anyone who continues to disrupt these proceedings will be escorted from the room by one of the marshals."

His words were oil on troubled waters. Voices drained to a whisper. Commotion and chitchat ceased.

"Did you or your bosses ever make payoffs to any law enforcement personnel?"

"I once went to a club in Cairo with Mr. Rubin's brother, Jake. He took out several envelopes containing money and with special markings on the outside. One of them said 'POLICE.' "

"Do you have any idea how much money was in those envelopes?"

"No, sir. All I know is the envelopes were bulging with dough."

"Do you have anything else to say that might be of use to the committee?"

"I, uh, think I've told you everything."

"Does any one else on the committee have a question for Mr. Littlefeather?" The man in the pinstripe suit looked to his left, then to his right. No one responded.

"Thank you very much, Mr. Littlefeather. We appreciate your cooperation."

The committee adjourned for an hour and a half lunch break, and the trio went to a small bar and grill on Locust Street. After they ate, Wayne Littlefeather thanked Harry and said he needed to leave because he had an appointment with a man in Madison, Illinois, about a job in a warehouse.

"It was nice meeting you, Mr. Logan," he said politely.

"Same here," Brad replied, as he shook his big hand.

Harry eyeballed Brad. "We could just return to the office."

"Go back to the salt mines and miss all the excitement? No way. Besides, Knucky might still get here."

They went back to the courthouse to get ready for the afternoon session. A myriad of journalists with press badges were congregating in the lobby. Brad was surprised to see Lorna, wearing a stunning magenta outfit, amidst the group, chatting with a reporter from the ***Journal.*** She spotted him and waved. Brad reciprocated with a hand gesture of his own, a sweeping arc resembling the swipe of a windshield wiper. Then she disappeared into the jumble of people, discussing the morning's events.

Lorna's 3-button $24.95 suit

"Who was that ***looker***?" Harry asked.

"Oh, just some girl I bumped into at the Majestic."

"Well it appears you've got competition. The guy she was with seemed all bright-eyed and bushy-tailed. And she was enjoying his company as though it were something special."

"We've only dated a few times."

Harry shook his head, his eyes glowing with doubt. "So why did I detect a look of disappointment on your face when you spotted her with him?"

"I didn't think it showed."

"I can read you like a book, Brad. Your face is flushed

with the look of someone who has lost his soul to that little green monster Shakespeare mentions in Othello."

"Well, who knows," he said hopefully, "she may just be playing the field right now."

"Yeah, right. You'd better be careful, she looks like a heartbreaker to me."

* * *

On returning to the courtroom, they found their original seats occupied, so they sat one row farther back. Brad spotted St. Louis Mayor Darst and Paul Simon, the crusading editor of the newspaper in Troy, Illinois, wearing his trademark bow tie. He was exchanging banter with a gaggle of colleagues.

"Kefauver wasn't bombastic or anything like I thought he would be," Harry said.

"I know. I half expected him to come to the hearing wearing the goofy coonskin hat that was his campaign trademark. Who is scheduled to testify at the afternoon session?"

Senator Estes Kefauver

"There are a couple of ex-county sheriffs, a noted bookmaker, and John Rafferty, the East St. Louis police chief."

"Should be interesting," Brad said.

"Hey, look! Your girlfriend and her new beau took seats in the last row of the press section," Harry teased.

"Yeah, I see them. I wonder what she is doing here? Lorna's assignment is the society page."

"So it's Lorna, is it? What an unusual tag. She is only the second girl I've run across with that name."

"My first and only." Brad's throat felt scratchy so he tossed a Red Cross brand cough drop in his mouth.

"Too bad the room is so crowded," Harry observed.

"Why do you say that?"

"I can't tell if they are holding hands."

"Cut it out, Harry." Brad threw an elbow into his ribs. Hard. Harry winced and let out a muffled 'Umhh.' "

The Kefauver Committee solemnly trouped into the room, took their seats, and the Gray Suit gaveled the session to order.

"We are extremely disappointed Mr. Lloyd Walters and several of his associates have willfully chosen to ignore our subpoenas," John Burling, associate counsel for the committee, announced. "If Mr. Walters or any other person under subpoena fails to appear before this committee, they will be required to produce a statement from an attending physician attesting to an illness preventing them from complying with the law. Since there have been no affidavits similar to the one submitted by Mr. J.T. English, who is in a St. Louis hospital, it is probably safe to assume that is not the case with others. The committee warns those who would scoff at the law that such action will not be tolerated. Warrants will be sent out for their arrest, and they will suffer the full extent of penalties allowed."

"The committee calls Dan McGlynn to the stand," Kefauver drawled.

A hushed silence fell over the crowd, and people twisted and turned in their seats to see the new witness.

"If Mr. Dan McGlynn is present, will he please come forth?"

No one stepped forward.

"Was this witness given a subpoena?" Kefauver asked in a calm voice.

"No, sir," said the man with the salt and pepper hair, his face twisted with a slight look of frustration. "He isn't a current officeholder. It was our understanding he was a friendly witness. When we talked to him on the phone, he said he would be glad to testify."

"Perhaps we need to send more subpoenas and make fewer phone calls," Kefauver replied in an irritated tone, shuffling his papers.

The crowd was murmuring again over the failed presence of the noted Republican leader of East St. Louis. The dark oak gavel came crashing down again, bringing the unruly into silent compliance.

"The committee calls James J. Carroll to the stand."

Carroll and his lawyer made their way from the back of the room to the small table in front of the committee. A dark shirt and a light gray tie made Carroll look like a caricature of the hoodlum species. Carroll was the top banana among the bookies. He was known as the area betting commissioner—a bookie's bookie. He had flown to Lambert Field in St. Louis from Miami. He cupped his hand over his eyes, trying to peer through the bright glare of television lights. Then he flailed his arms and hands at the cameras, like a movie director signaling a technician to douse the lights.

"Mr. Carroll, the committee would like to ask you a few questions regarding gambling operations in St. Louis and East St. Louis."

"I ain't gonna tell this group nothin' unless those d— lights an' cameras are turned off." Carroll reinforced his stereotype with a peculiar vernacular that resembled Pidgin English.

"Please watch your language, Mr. Carroll," the man in the horn-rimmed glasses warned.

"Those cameras are an invasion of my privacy. Unless they are turned off, I'm gonna follow the advice of my lawyer an' claim the Fifth Commandment, which says I don't have to testify if my rights are being violated."

Even Brad softly chuckled out loud at that one. The crowd, knowing any outburst would draw the ire of the chairman, tried unsuccessfully to control its amusement. Broad smiles led to audible laughs, which in turn evolved into raucous, hysterical laughter, echoing around the room. Several committee members placed their hands over their brows and stared down in a futile effort to conceal their mirth at the unintended malapropism.

The unflustered Chairman allowed some time to pass so everyone could regain their composure. Then wood met wood, three successive times. Meanwhile, Jimmy Carroll was hunched over in a conference with his attorney, Morris Goldman.

"That is the Fifth Amendment, not the Fifth Commandment, Mr. Carroll," Kefauver said. The former is in the Constitution, and the latter in the Good Book."

"I know that, Your Honor, I misspoke," Carroll angrily answered.

The senator with the determined jaw decided to overlook Carroll's second gaffe of calling him "Your Honor."

"In any event, Mr. Carroll, we can't turn the cameras off because of the need for the viewing audience to be informed on this subject. The public interest supersedes your right to privacy."

"That's a lot of malarkey, an' you know it." Carroll once again conferred with his attorney.

"I'll bet he's explaining what supersede means," Brad said.

"I won't take that bet," Harry replied. "At least not in ***this*** courtroom."

"Well, even if you are a lawyer, I say you're wrong, an' if you don't turn them cameras off, I'm gonna walk outta here in about ten seconds. You can take the matter up with my attorney."

The crowd, stunned by Carroll's audacity, sat glued to their seats, and waited to see who would be wounded in the next verbal volley.

"Mr. Carroll, I warn you to think long and hard about your proposed course of action. It could incur dire consequences."

"I'm outta here." Carroll stood up, the vein on his right temple puffed out and appeared to be ready to burst. He shook his fist at the committee and began using his hands to punctuate sentences. "If you think the whole country is gonna see me perform like a trained monkey, you've got another think comin'. An' you can take those ***dear*** conesquences you were threatening me with an' stick 'em . . . well, you know what you can do with 'em."

A collective gasp of disbelief escaped from the onlookers' lungs as Carroll slammed his fist on the table, turned around, and stormed out of the room.

"That is the most surprising turn of events I have ever witnessed in a courtroom," Harry said.

"Not bad for free entertainment," Brad said.

The chairman called a ten-minute recess to give the committee members time to regain their composure. They announced John S. Rafferty would be the next witness to testify.

"Excuse me, Harry," Brad said. "I need to go to make a phone call."

He went to a booth in the hall, stepped inside, and closed the bifold metal doors. He dropped in a nickel and dialed the operator. He clicked the dial in a circular motion to the stop mechanism, and it sprang back to its original position, rotating counter-clockwise when released.

"This is the operator. May I help you?"

"Yes, I'd like to place a long distance call to Caseyville, Illinois."

"Thank you. Would you please insert twenty cents for the first three minutes?"

"Yes, ma'am," Brad said as he gave her the number and inserted a couple of Mercury-head dimes.

The line at the other end rang four times. A woman answered.

"Mrs. Walters?"

"Yes."

"This is Brad Logan; I'm one of your husband's attorneys."

He could hear a radio in the background.

"I've never heard of you. Besides, I haven't seen my husband for almost a week. I'm afraid he might have been kidnapped."

"Mrs. Walters, I know your husband is there, holed up, trying to avoid facing the Kefauver Committee in St. Louis. I can prove I'm one of his friends and I'm not trying to trick you."

The awkward silence in the air between St. Louis and Collinsville seemed like an eternity.

What can I say to convince her? "Tell him I gave you the word 'cas-tra-to.' "

"Cas- what?"

"Castrato: c-a-s-t-r-a-t-o."

"Excuse me for a minute, please. I have a cake in the oven, and my timer just started ringing. I'll be back in a minute."

The line about the cake was an obvious falsehood. He waited for nearly two minutes. Finally, he heard a gruff voice at the other end.

"H-hello. That you Brad?"

"Yes, Knucky, it's me. I'm here at the Kefauver hearing, and they are very upset you didn't come today."

"I told Morris Goldman I wasn't going to show."

"Have you heard from him today?"

"No. He knows I'm not going to change my mind."

"Knucky, they plan to issue a citation and hold you in contempt of Congress. That could be a very serious charge. You'll probably be fined and sent to jail again."

"Morris can tap-dance around the legal issues for me. He's pretty good at that."

"Unless you have a doctor's statement saying you were physically unable to be at the hearings, you're going to be in big trouble. Morris isn't going to be able to find any loopholes because there aren't any. This is all cut and dried. The courts have repeatedly ruled in favor of the government on this issue."

"Maybe I could show up and then pull a walking act, like Jimmy Carroll."

"I thought you told me you weren't going to watch the hearings."

"I got a little curious when I heard my buddy, Carroll, was going to be there."

"Yes, he has a short fuse—just like you. He became totally unglued; now he's in ***big*** trouble."

"Please deposit another ten cents if you want to continue your call," a high-pitched female voice interrupted.

Brad inserted the requisite coins, their clanging sounds telling the operator the correct amount had been deposited.

"What is the most time I could do if the court ruling goes against me?"

"They'll probably throw the book at you to set an example. My guess would be a thousand dollar fine and a year in jail."

Brad held the phone at arm's length as Knucky let out a string of expletives.

"Pardon my French, kid. It's just that I get so mad because the government is always hounding guys like me. And all I am trying to do is raise a family and earn a decent living."

"Well, losing your cool isn't going to help anything. You must remember these are only hearings. It's good publicity for politicians such as Kefauver. You can probably answer most of their questions without it having any negative effect on your business activities. After they leave town, people will continue to patronize taverns and nightclubs and gamble with their money. The government will pass a few laws, and then all will be quickly forgotten."

"What kind of laws?"

"Probably some kind of racketeering laws that make it easier for the Feds to intervene in the activities of organized crime. And you'll likely see a national law prohibiting the publication or use of out-of-state racing results for the purpose of betting. In all likelihood, your news agency in Fairmont City will be history."

"D—." Knucky paused as he realized the appalling implications of everything Brad had just told him. "Tell you what," he instructed, "have Goldman give me a call."

"I'll do that as soon as I get back inside. Your subpoena was probably ***duces tecum***, meaning they want you to bring some records with you. Check it out and see what they are specifically requesting. Well . . . I need to get back to the hearings. Take care of yourself."

Operator Emily Kobzina

"Yeah, you too. Goodbye!"

Brad returned to the courtroom, went over to Morris Goldman and gave him Walters' message to call. He seemed surprised someone like him had spoken to Knucky. Morris didn't even know who he was. Brad glanced over at Lorna who was busily engaged in conversation with her escort. As much as he hated to admit it, Harry was right. Lorna had an unmistakable look in her eye. This was more than two newspaper co-workers out covering a story.

He made his way back to where Harry was sitting, and they waited for the next witness.

"That might have been my girlfriend, Emily Kobzina, who put your call through. She's in St. Louis for two weeks of special operator training."

"I have no idea who it was," Brad said. "She didn't say her name."

The committee filed back into the room.

"Would Mr. John S. Rafferty please come forward to testify?" that familiar deep voice rang out.

The portly East St. Louis police chief was handsomely dressed in a dark blue suit. Three peaks of a white handkerchief jutted above his left breast pocket. A touch of gray on his temples and a pair of wire-rimmed glasses gave him a rather distinguished look. He was seated next to R. E. Costello, attorney for the city of East St. Louis. Russ Maxwell of the ***Journal*** snapped his picture as he held up his hand and swore to tell the whole truth.

"Mr. Rafferty, it is our understanding that as police chief, you are charged with the responsibility of making sure the laws of the city of East St. Louis are enforced. Is that correct?"

"At City Hall the mayor and commissioners like to think of themselves as a team, but I guess it would be accurate to say that is my main responsibility." John nervously stroked the wattle under his chin.

"When did you become chief of police in East St. Louis?"

"The former chief died in March of 1942, and I was appointed to take his place."

"You're saying that for a period of at least eight years, you have been in charge of law enforcement."

"Yes."

"And how successful have you been at fighting organized crime in your good city?"

Rafferty tilted his head back and gazed at the ceiling, as if the answer might be printed on the alabaster plaster. Then he slowly brought his gaze downward and looked the source of his discomfort directly in the eyes.

"There is no such thing as organized crime, per se, in East St. Louis."

A stunned silence descended on the room and everyone looked to Kefauver for his riposte.

"Mr. Rafferty, I find your statement totally incredible."

Kefauver's biting retort piqued the crowd's interest.

"But it's true. This thing about organized crime is a ploy used by the national and local media to attract viewers, listeners, and to sell newspapers."

"What about the Irish gang in St. Louis?"

"Around here they're known as Egan Rats, but they're just a bunch of hoodlums."

"What about the Lebanese gang in St. Louis, and a fellow named Weber?"

"That's not my jurisdiction," Rafferty replied. "I think they have some connection with the Mayfair and Claridge Hotels in St. Louis, but anything I know about it would just be hearsay."

"What about the alleged underworld connections of John Vitale and Tony Lopiparo? And what about the biggest name of all, kingpin Sal Delonzo?"

John Vitale

"Same thing. I've heard their names before, but they aren't my concern."

"Well, then, let's move right into your back yard. What about 'Knucky' Walters?"

"What about him?"

"Wouldn't you agree he is the Chicago

representative of the old Capone gang in this area?"

Rafferty cleared his throat. "Not at all. That too is something concocted by the newspapers."

"So it is a figment of our imagination—like fairies and pixies?"

"I suppose it's fair to say fairies and pixies are related," Rafferty replied.

The audience once again stirred in bemusement.

"It is your contention there is no connection between Mr. Walters and Chicago hoodlums?"

"They probably know each other and exchange greeting cards and phone calls, but there is no sinister connection that links the so-called Egan Rats Gang of St. Louis, Mr. Walters, and Chicago gangsters in a vast conspiracy network. The picture you are trying to paint for the public is flawed. As far as I know, Mr. Walters runs an establishment in East St. Louis called the Club 501 and bets money on the ponies at Fairmount, but there is nothing illegal about those operations."

"Mr. Rafferty, didn't a grand jury indict you and other officials for dereliction of duty?"

The chief fidgeted with a pen in his hand. "Yes, but it was later proved the indictment was bogus, and a judge dismissed the charges."

"Isn't it true the charges were dismissed on a mere technicality?"

"No, sir. The charges were dismissed because they were totally groundless—without foundation."

"My committee has been informed that at this very moment, there is a handbook operation going on almost directly across the street from City Hall, at 318-A on Missouri Avenue."

"We are handicapped in our efforts by antiquated statutes that need to be changed. Also, we only have a force of sixty-four policemen trying to enforce the laws and protect a population of eighty-two thousand. They can't be everywhere, but to the best of my knowledge, there is no bookie operation at the address you just quoted."

"So you deny there is gambling in East St. Louis."

"What I am saying is that we have a very effective police force, and nearly all major crimes have been solved." Rafferty shifted uncomfortably in his chair. "Our community is practically free of significant crime—illegal gambling included."

Kefauver's jaw dropped. Rarely had Brad seen such disbelief in a human face. He exchanged a mute look of shock with Harry.

"I find your statement incredulous, Mr. Rafferty. I stopped believing in fairy tales when I was in the third grade," said the chairman.

"I'm sorry, but that's the truth as I see it," countered Rafferty. "Mr. Chairman, my throat is parched. I would like to remind the committee I have agreed to appear here against the advice of my doctor. Would it be possible for someone to bring me a glass of water?"

"Of course, Mr. Rafferty."

The proceedings were held up a few minutes while a gum-chewing bailiff named Don DeWitt left the room and came back with a glass and a pitcher of water. The microphone picked up the cool trickling sound of water being poured. Mr. Rafferty took a big gulp, let out a long breath of air, and steeled himself for the next round of questions.

"Are you ready to resume?"

"Yes, I'm ready."

"Have you ever arrested Mr. Carroll or otherwise disturbed his operations?"

"No, sir."

"Did you not know he was practically the biggest bookmaker in the country, and he was operating right under your nose?"

"No, sir."

"You did not know that?"

"All I know is that he's an oddsmaker."

"What about Vic Doyle's place, the Ringside? Hasn't the operation had a wire service and crap tables since 1946?"

"I don't know about that either, sir."

"What do you know about Teel and Stevens of 735 North 16th Street?"

"They say that's a sneak book operation."

"What have you done about it?"

"Every time we send somebody over there, we can't find anything illegal going on. If we ever find evidence of someone breaking the law, we arrest them, and they are fined."

"Do you know anything about Premier News Service?"

"Yes, it's St. Louis-based and it publishes data and information—kind of a bible for racing fans—odds and stuff like that."

"When you discovered the attorney general of Missouri was trying to close Premier News Service, did it not occur to you to ask him to what extent Premier was operating in ***your*** city?"

"No, sir. It did not because I didn't know about his efforts."

"It had been in the papers for over four years. Don't you think keeping up with news is part of your job as police chief?"

"I saw it in the papers, but that was only about eight months ago."

"Let's move on to another subject," said Kefauver, with a slight look of disgust on his face.

Brad bumped shoulders with Harry. "I think Rafferty just gave him the 'Hear no evil, see no evil, speak no evil' routine."

Teacher: Now which of you knows what that sign means? Bobby: I know teacher. It marks the spot where the body was found. (Life Mag.)

"I bet he gets ripped in an editorial for this performance," he replied.

"Mr. Rafferty, you have heard testimony that Jimmy Carroll is reputed to have offices with Premier News Agency, offices at the betting parlor at 318-A Missouri Avenue, and is affiliated with Racing News in Fairmont City."

"Yes, I have, but the only place out of the three under my jurisdiction is the place on Missouri Avenue. My men cannot find evidence of illegal activity at this time. Remember, Mr. Fisher, the former sheriff of St. Clair County, testified he sent a couple of his men to that address and they found nothing."

"Yes, but he was the same person who didn't even know the name of Jack Vickery, the police chief in Fairmont City. Mr. Rafferty, are you aware people in East St. Louis are making bets via the Western Union Telegraph services?"

"I've heard something to that effect, but when I checked with our city attorney on this matter, he told me it wasn't against state law in Illinois."

"Where are the Western Union offices in your city, Mr. Rafferty?"

"There are two offices—one at 338 Missouri Avenue, the Goldman Building, and another in the Exchange Building at the Stock Yards. You realize, of course, the Stock Yards are in National City, which is not a part of East St. Louis."

"Isn't it reasonable to assume there is a gambling connection between the proximity of the Western Union office to the 318-A Missouri Avenue address?"

"Like I said before, sir," Rafferty professed, "I am unaware of any illegal activity at the 318-A address."

Murphy Building in E. St. Louis by Lamont Irons

Kefauver forged ahead. "Mr. Rafferty, we have been told you have a large country estate in O'Fallon, Illinois. We were wondering how it was possible for someone on a public official's salary to maintain such a high standard of living?"

"I have done quite well with several investments."

"What was your annual salary as police chief in 1942?"

"Approximately four thousand dollars."

The lanky senator Kefauver was listening intently to the testimony while fingering an unlit cigarette. He picked up some bits of tobacco with a damp forefinger, which he then inserted into his mouth.

"Do you recall reporting your personal income for 1943 as thirty-four thousand dollars?"

"I object," Mr. Costello, Rafferty's attorney, interjected. "I would like to interpose an objection to any questions regarding Mr. Rafferty's taxes on the grounds they are confidential."

"Objection overruled," said Kefauver. "We are talking about tens of thousands of dollars from political contributions. To raise an objection of this kind is extraordinary."

Costello looked down at his legal pad, shaking his head in silent disagreement.

"What about the money, Mr. Rafferty?"

"I've done well in several real estate investments and I've been very fortunate with stocks and bonds."

"Let's move on to another subject."

"Fine."

"Could you please explain what a lug is, Mr. Rafferty?"

"A lug is a slang expression for a percentage of a city employee's salary donated to help with election campaign expenses."

"Is this donation mandatory?"

"A lug might be mandatory at the county level, but in our city all contributions are purely voluntary."

"Are you saying there is no kind of pressure, overt or subtle, brought to bear on these employees?"

"None whatsoever."

"If you really believe lugs are voluntary then I have a bridge in New York I'd like to sell you."

The audience thought the sarcasm was fitfully funny, but Rafferty sat there phlegmatically.

"Isn't it the purpose of these lugs to perpetuate machine politics in East St. Louis?"

"No, sir. It's not a machine. It's what we call non-partisan elections. I don't think you and other outsiders realize most residents perceive East St. Louis as a city that works. They essentially support the patronage system because it means jobs and contracts. Our town has over one hundred churches and nearly as many civic organizations. We have good schools. We have strong unions. We have a fine Chamber of Commerce. We have the second oldest Jaycee group in the country. Jobs are plentiful; taxes are low; crime is negligible; utility rates are the cheapest in the nation. How many other towns can say that?"

"How much money are we talking about with these lugs?" Kefauver asked, unfazed by Rafferty's soliloquy.

"I don't know."

"What I mean is, how much money is each municipal employee expected to donate?"

"Again, this is purely voluntary, but the suggested amount is two percent of one's annual salary."

"Net or gross?"

"Gross."

"Does anyone else on the committee have any questions for Mr. Rafferty?" Senator Kefauver looked left, then right. "If there are no more questions, then you are dismissed, Mr. Rafferty. Thank you for taking time from your busy schedule to answer our questions."

Kefauver consulted his watch. "Since it is nearly four-thirty, the committee will adjourn and continue our final day of hearings tomorrow at nine o'clock."

CHAPTER 11

The English writer Charles Dickens crossed the breadth of East St. Louis in 1842 on his way to Lebanon, Illinois, to get a glimpse of the famed Illinois prairie. He heaped condemnation on the place, complaining of "pestiferous" Cahokia Creek and moaning about the muck and mire of roads engorged with rain from the night before. Black Hollow (as he called it) was a place "one had to endure."

Five minutes before the next day's morning session was scheduled to begin, Knucky quietly walked in with his attorney, Morris Goldman, setting off ripples of expectation. The entire courtroom was a-buzz, wondering if Knucky was going to complain about the television cameras then walk out à la Jimmy Carroll. Brad and Harry had been there since eight-forty. Brad turned around to see if he could spot Roland and Montrose, Walters' Praetorian Guard. They were standing in the back of the room with uneasy and disgruntled looks on their faces. The source of their unhappiness, Brad figured, was undoubtedly due to not being allowed to carry their usual weapons. ***Probably left them in the car.***

The meeting was called to order, and Knucky was sworn. Lorna and her Lance friend were sitting in just about the same spot as the day before. Glancing Brad's way, she saw him looking in her direction and waved. He waved back just as the inquiry process began.

"Please state your name and address for the record."

"Lloyd Walters, an'—"

"We can't hear you. Could you move closer to the microphone, please?"

Knucky pulled the mike and its short stand closer to him. "Lloyd Walters, an' I live on Missouri Avenue."

"Isn't that in East St. Louis? According to our records you live on Bunkum in Caseyville."

"If ya already have my address, why d'ja ask me?"

"It's as we said. This is just for the record of the proceedings. Could you tell us your occupation?"

"I'm a businessman. The Club 501 in East St. Louis is my lounge an' restaurant."

"What other sources of income do you have, Mr. Walters?"

"I suppose ya already have this information, too. Ya just want the whole world to know my personal business."

"Please, Mr. Walters, just answer the question."

Knucky leaned over and conferred with Goldman before giving a reply. "I have interests in Globe Amusement Company, Racing News Agency an' C&W Loan Company."

"What do the initials C&W stand for, Carroll and Walters?"

"Yes."

"Is that Jimmy Carroll, the betting commissioner from Florida?"

"I don't know 'bout the betting commissioner part, but yeah, it's ***the*** Jimmy Carroll."

"What service is provided by Globe Amusement Company?"

"We distribute pinball games, juke boxes an' cigarette machines."

"What about slot machines?"

"No, them are illegal."

"Didn't authorities find some slot machines in the aftermath of a fire a few months ago at one of your warehouses?"

"Those were old machines that had been sittin' there for years."

"Are you the sole owner of Globe Amusement?"

"No, I own about a third of the stock, my brother Lou has another third. Carl 'Red' Smith an' Sam 'Dutch' Metzger have the rest." Knucky kneaded his temples. "Dave Lloyd, an accountant here in St. Louis, keeps track of all this stuff."

"How many shares are there, and what is the par value of the stock?"

"I dunno for sure, a little over a thousand shares, maybe worth somewhere 'round a hundred dollars a share."

"Wayne Littlefeather testified yesterday that he thought you were a silent partner in several Cairo, Illinois, liquor firms."

"Well, Mr. Littlefeather is only a truck driver, an' he don't know diddly squat."

"So you deny being a silent partner."

"I deny being any kind of a partner."

The committee tried a different tack.

"How much influence do you have on local elections?"

"Not very much, I'm afraid. I usually don't even bother to vote."

The response brought a ripple of laughter from the audience.

"So you are not part of the bipartisan effort over there where everyone gets together and decides in adLance who is going to get elected?"

"Certainly not."

"Do you spread money around to influence the outcome of East St. Louis elections?"

"You guys are gettin' awful personal," Knucky exploded. "Don't the Constitution mean anything anymore? How come you guys get to ask all these things that are none of your business?" Walters' chameleon personality changed colors, and he failed to subdue the turbulence churning within him. Knucky placed his palms on the table and rose from his chair. "Sure, I donate money to politicians, but so do a lot of other people in East St. Louis. Since when is giving a hundred bucks to the Democrats illegal?" he demanded, stabbing his finger

Flash Gordon

at the committee.

Russ Maxwell snapped a dramatic picture of Knucky in action. He shot a look of disapproval at the photographer and blinked a couple of times before resuming.

"If it'll make you guys any happier, I also dropped a five spot in the red kettle for the Salvation Army; I gave a buck to a kid who came knockin' at my door for the March of Dimes. I bought a poppy from the American Legion an' purchased a raffle ticket to help support the Knights of Columbus' annual picnic. Is any of that a crime?"

"Oh, I almost forgot," he added, not waiting for an answer. "I also recently took a chance on one of those fifty-cent punch boards. My brother, Lou, bet on a nag at Fairmount last week, an' my sister-in-law won a blanket at a church bingo game. Do we all hafta go to jail or pay a fine for that? How deep do you guys get to snoop?" Goldman, chewing on a fat unlit cigar, tugged repeatedly on Walters' coattail.

George "Stormy" Harvill

"Hey, I can even rat on some of my friends if ya like. My buddy 'Stormy' Harvill won fifteen bucks in a friendly poker game at the Spot Tavern, an' another cousin won a sawbuck from his buddy on last year's Billiken-Kentucky basketball game. I bet you can find guys playing golf for a dollar a hole at Grand Marais. An' I have a stepsister who saves the blue labels from cans of condensed milk to trade in for **Eagle stamps.** If ya dig deep enough, ya can probably catch kids out there flipping baseball cards an' betting pennies on the outcome of hop scotch an' jacks."

Breathing hard, Knucky was completely unraveled. Anger, like steam, almost seemed to come out the top of his head. He straightened his tie and sat back down. Goldman, head down, had his face in his hands.

Kefauver, remaining calm during the outburst, paused a few seconds to recoup his equilibrium and sense of decorum. "Mr. Walters, would you please try to control yourself? Getting angry isn't going to solve anything. It will only extend the amount of time you are here. Now, could you tell us who runs the C&W Loan Company?"

Knucky took a deep breath. "My brother, Lou."

"What kind of loans does the company make?"

"We make loans to customers of Premier News, Racing News, Globe Amusement an' various other business interests."

"Are Gregory 'Red' Geiger and a couple of gentlemen whose names are Bartlet and Eckelsheimer associates of yours?"

"Yes."

"Is Geiger the same man who runs Geiger's Grill on Missouri Avenue and has the contract to feed prisoners at the city jail?"

"No, sir. That's Bill Geiger you're talking about. 'Red' Geiger an' the other two men originally had shares in Globe Amusement, formed in 1946, but they later sold them back to me."

"We have your ledgers from the Club 501 and Racing News Agency. The bookkeeping appears to be very sloppy. There are numerous times where entries have been erased or changed. According to these records, it is extremely difficult to tell how much money is being made. Is this a conscious effort to conceal the true nature and amount of income from the government?"

"Ted has his own way of keeping books," Knucky said. "He don't have no accounting degree, an' ya probably just don't understand his system. Running a loan company ain't the same thing as operatin' a steel mill."

"How are you able to make accurate payments on your earnings to the IRS?"

"My associates get together with my accountant an' they figure things out. I don't keep track of all that stuff. I hated math when I was in school."

"Isn't it true that the books are being 'cooked' to defraud the government, and the IRS has launched a probe into this matter?"

"There ya go again, gettin' personal. Whatever misunderstandin' there is with the IRS will be straightened out to their satisfaction. They're not about to get me on some stupid tax technicality the way they got Capone."

"Are you suggesting you are into illegal activities in the same manner as Mr. Capone?"

"Not at all. Drugs are illegal, an' prostitution is illegal. I don't have nothin' to do with those things."

"Didn't you serve time in Alcatraz for beating up a Prohibition agent?"

"I paid my debt to society for that. Look, people for centuries have liked to drink an' gamble. The Bible talks about people drinking wine an' having a good time. Wine is served every week by the Catholic church at communion. The government took away the right of the people to drink with the Volstead Act. I was just a part of an effort to give the people back what you'd taken from them. If ya ask me, Prohibition was illegal. I think I was proved right because Roosevelt brought liquor back after he got elected. If the people 'round here want to gamble, what right does the government have to tell 'em they can't? You should come over to Fairmount Park some evenin'. I'll bet ya half of the cars in the parking lot are from Missouri. An' why is that? They have to come to Illinois because a bunch of bluenosed busybodies passed some stupid law over here. I'm in the entertainment business. I provide people with a service for something they like to do."

"So you would have us believe you're a respectable businessman who is merely supplying a service that is in demand?"

"Gambling is a biological necessity for certain types of people—always has been, always will be. Gambling is an exciting activity that gives substance to their daydreams," Walters said.

Brad leaned over toward Harry. "Gee, Knucky as Plato. That's pretty deep stuff."

Harry just nodded and smiled.

"Mr. Walters, we are not here to discuss the morality of

drinking and gambling," Kefauver said in his commanding baritone. "This is a nation of laws, and we are here in an effort to try and determine whether some of these activities are undermining law and order in this country."

Knucky rambled on. "Here's another Carroll story. Back in 1942, when California lived in fear of an attack by the Japanese, an important telegraph circuit, which served part of the state plus an Air Force field, was knocked out by a plane crash. Continental Press, which supplied race and sports results, managed to get its wire service for gamblers resumed in fifteen minutes. It took the Fourth Army, responsible for the defense of the entire West Coast, 'bout three hours. So ya see, you guys are going against human nature."

"The way this committee sees it, people like you are exploiting human weaknesses," Kefauver shot back. "As far as I am concerned, these wire services are Public Enemy Number One, and we will urge Congress to shut them down. Just a few more questions, Mr. Walters, and we will be finished."

Kefauver fiddled with his glasses. "It has been very difficult for us to contact some individuals we would like to have questioned. It's been rumored you told certain people to ***quote*** 'get lost' before our committee came to town."

"Well, that's the thing about rumors," Knucky said. "If ya check 'em out, ya find that's all they are—rumors. I didn't tell nobody to make themselves scarce. They have their own lives to lead."

"You didn't tell Bob Hunter, a jockey at Fairmount, to take a vacation?"

"No, sir."

"You didn't tell Sam Fosterman, or your brother Lou to ignore our subpoenas?"

Knucky threw up his hands. "Not me."

"Why weren't you here for the first day of testimony?"

"Just a mix-up in dates. My wife keeps the social calendar. I guess she just forgot to tell me."

"Do you really expect us to believe that?"

"I showed up today, didn't I?"

"One final question. Yesterday, Chief John Rafferty testified East St. Louis is practically free of crime and illegal gambling. Do you agree with his statement?"

Knucky nodded emphatically. "The people of East St. Louis are happy with the way things are. If they didn't like the way the place was being run, they would throw the bums out. Guys like Connors, Fields, Rafferty, Foley, Beebe an' English are respected members of the community. They've been around forever because voters think they're doing a pretty decent job. Nobody asked you guys to come to town. It was something ya started on your own. Ya might have disrupted things for a few days an' stuck your nose where it don't belong, but everything will get back to normal after you're gone. An' ya can take that to the bank."

The deceptively folksy Tennessean stayed calm during Walters' subdued tirade. If it bothered him, he didn't let it show.

"I realize we don't see eye to eye on a lot of issues, Mr. Walters, but the committee does appreciate your candor and the information you have given us. Sorry to have inconvenienced you." Kefauver looked to his right. "Have you anything else, Mr. Burling?"

"I do not believe so, Mr. Chairman."

"You are hereby dismissed, Mr. Walters."

Harry and Brad looked at each other with disbelieving eyes as they left the courtroom.

"These last two days have been memorable," Harry said. "Wasn't that the weirdest ensemble of evasive, truth-mangling characters ever assembled in one room?"

"Yes. That certainly was a Runyonesque collection of ne'er-do-wells, thrown in with public servants, who seemed to be experts at the old proverbial shell game. Did you ever see so many people feign ignorance about what goes on in our city?"

"That inquiry probably set the record for oblique answers and cock-and-bull stories." Harry began sipping on his flask again.

They spent the entire time on their way back to the office rehashing the events of the past two days.

"Life without the Kefauver Commission is probably going to be a little boring," Brad reflected.

"A little flat, but not totally without excitement," Harry said. "I'm still on the edge of my seat waiting to see how this thing you have for Lois Lane is going to turn out," he teased.

"How many times do I have to tell you, Harry? I've only known her a few months. Sometimes I think you've got necrosis of the brain."

CHAPTER 12

East St. Louisan Sam Jethroe played for the Boston Braves and led the National League in stolen bases in 1950 and 1951.

Brad was working late in his office on a petition that was going to be filed in a personal injury case. It was around nine-thirty, and once again he spotted Missola, the cleaning lady. She was across the hall in Charlie Oliver's office. She methodically dumped an ashtray into a large wastebasket, wiped it clean, and returned it to his desk.

"Hello, again, Missola," he said, in a friendly voice. "Can I offer you another soda while you take a break from your chores?"

"Oh, it you again—Mista Logan." Her voice was mellow and warm, like a well-tuned viola. "I'll have an' RC Cola, if you please."

"You have been doing an excellent job around here. The place really looks good."

He went down the hall and bought a couple of RCs then inserted each one under the bottle cap remover. There was a whoosh of carbonated air as the caps came off, and a dull clink as each cork-lined top dropped into the holder below.

"Here, this ought to wet your whistle."

"Thank ya much. So, what you wantin' to talk 'bout tonight?"

"Who says I want to talk?" he shot back with a grin.

"You sho nuf got that look on your face that says: 'Mrs. Missola, I'se just dyin' to find out more 'bout cullud folk.' "

She reached into a sack and brought out a spoon and a small bowl covered with waxed paper that was held in place by a rubber band.

"Ever eaten any soul food, Mista Logan?"

"Not that I can remember."

"Try some o' this. It called Hoppin' John."

Brad pushed a pile of clutter to one side and set the bowl on his desk. Then he cautiously spooned a portion into his mouth, chewed and swallowed.

"Delicious! What's in it?"

"Black-eyed peas, rice, beans, pork knuckles an' red pepper."

He took a big gulp of his soda. "Red pepper, so that's what's burning out the lining of my esophagus."

"Also brought ya a sprig o' cherries. I've a small grove of trees in my backyard. I sells 'em for extra income at the Cal'fornya Fruit Market."

"Thanks again."

"This dish o' Hoppin' John is s'posed to bring ya good luck for a month."

"I could use some luck. Any chance you know how to cast a spell to make someone fall in love with you?"

"We call it conjuring," she replied.

"Forget it," he said. "I was thinking out loud." He continued to savor the flavorful cuisine of the South.

"Ya see, Mistuh Logan, the white folk an' black folk don't even eat the same food."

"For instance?"

"Your kind gen'raly eat lettuce, taters, corn on the cob, roast beef, bacon n' eggs, n' such. Cullud folk thrive on collard greens, chitlins, turnips, pickled pig's feet, deep-fried tripe, scrapple, an' spoon bread or mock apple pie."

"I know what that is—soda crackers, doused with cinnamon, baked in a pie crust. Had it a few times during the Depression. We certainly live in parallel worlds."

Her lips parted in a friendly smile. "Last time we talked ya' says ya' knows most nothin' 'bout Duke Ellington or Cab Calloway. Ever hear of Langston Hughes, Le Roi Jones, Phyllis Wheatley or Richard Wright?"

"I don't know any of them," he confessed.

"They all be writers an' poets. My people have read their words an' lis'ened to their voices. They is mostly unbenown in the white commun'ty."

"You're probably right."

"How many famous Negras can ya name, not takin' into 'count writers or en'tainers?"

"I read where Crispus Attucks, a mulatto, was the first patriot to be killed in the Boston Massacre. But . . . I can't think of any others."

"That be 'cause white people, who controls pract'ly every-thin', either ignores our successes or run 'em down. Ever hear tell of Charles Drew?"

"No, ma'am."

"Saved thousands of lives durin' the war by makin' blood plasma."

"Amazing."

"Matt Henson?"

"Nope."

"Him with that Perry feller' who 'scovered the North Pole. Woulda' gone plum by it hadn't been for Henson. Did'ja know a black man dezined the city of Washin'ton D.C?"

Matt Henson & Peary at North Pole

"I never heard that."

"The gov'ment paid some Frenchy fella to lay out the city, but then he gets mad an' go back to where he come from when they don't pay 'im what he think he be worth."

"So how did our Capitol get built?"

"His a'sistant were a black man who mem'rized evrythin' up here," she said, with a gleam in her eye, tapping a finger on the top of her skull.

"What was his name?"

"Cain't 'member right now, s'pose it come later. . . Ben somethin' . . . Ever hear of the Buffalo Soldiers or the 'Tusgee' air fellas?"

"No, but I just remembered, I do know about Harriet Tubmann, George Washington Carver and Booker T. Washington."

"Land sakes, boy, you be jus' full of s'prises. Tell ya what. When I thinks of 'nother im'potant Negra, I write the name an' what they be famous for at the bottom o' that ever'day calendar sittin' on your desk. Then ev'ry mornin' you looks an' sees if'n I done left ya' note before ya tears it off an' throw it away."

"I'll look forward to that," he said.

"You keeps bribin' me with these here soda pops, no tellin' what all you is gonna learn from these m'hogany lips of mine."

"You're a fascinating woman, Missola." Brad shook his head in amazement.

* * *

The next day Mrs. Torricelli contacted Brad and wanted to set up an appointment to meet with him that afternoon. He thought about calling Lorna but was reluctant to do so, having just been turned down by her several days before. He anguished over her reason for not going with him to the Ice Capades. ***Was it legitimate or just an excuse?*** He convinced himself that it was probably bona fide because she had told him about monthly visits back home. ***Was she really in a hurry when I called her the other day, or was she just trying to give me the brush off?*** Brad detected a certain tone of urgency and, after all, she did encourage him to try again, he reasoned. ***But what about that Troutman fellow she was with at the Kefauver hearings? What was that all about?***

At two o'clock, Brad left his office for an appointment with Mrs. Torricelli. His mouth was dry, so when he reached the lobby, he fished in his pockets for a penny and tossed it into a machine for a stick of gum. She lived in French Village out near the bluffs on Route 159. It was one of the oldest settlements in the area and it had its own volunteer fire department. People with religious inclinations were serviced by St. Philip's Catholic Church, a beautiful brick structure with a tall gothic tower. The parish had been formed back in 1841 by French families who moved there from Cahokia. They introduced the area to the practice of making wine from the flower of that otherwise useless weed known as the dandelion.

Brad put on his hat and overcoat before leaving. The transition from fall had been abrupt. Only seven weeks ago winter's vanguard had arrived to reconnoiter, borne on a blustery wind out of the desolate plains of Kansas, sweeping across the raw sky to test the city's mettle. Now they were in the dead of winter, and the full fury of its icy wrath had the city in its grip. A trough of frigid Canadian air had slid down from the north—an Alberta Clipper, the ***Post-Dispatch*** weatherbird called it. Swirling billows of pristine snow greeted him as he left the office and trudged through five inches of white powder. A blind man was panhandling. Not exactly. He was playing ***Oh Susannah*** on a harmonica and selling pencils out of a tin cup. His wool overcoat looked as if it had belonged to a displaced refugee from World War II. Brad dropped a quarter into his container and took a pencil.

This way it won't seem so much like charity, he thought.

"Thank you," the man rasped.

"You're welcome."

Gov. Stevenson greets Henry Fuller, a former slave, in E. St. Louis (Mayor Alvin Fields and Ben Day of East St. Louis Democratic Committee on right)

An icy blast of air stung Brad's cheeks. It was about twenty-five degrees outside, and the twenty-eight degree mark was the determining factor as to whether it would be wet or dry. If the snow came down at temperatures below that benchmark, it was dry. If it fell at temperatures above, it was heavy and damp. He reached down and tried to compress a handful into a snowball, but the flakes would not compact. He hopped inside the car, keyed the ignition and pressed the starter. The car coughed and sputtered. He pulled the choke knob out a half-inch and tried again while pumping the gas pedal a couple times. The engine started, but it was running rough, so he let it idle while he got out and began brushing the snow from his windows.

He had a set of chains in the trunk but challenged the roads without them. East St. Louis was one of the flattest cities in America, and that was a blessing for winter travel. The heater in the black box on the passenger side was still struggling to warm the inside. Brad was fortunate. There were many older cars on the road without them. The owners had tried to save a few bucks and hadn't bothered to pay extra for a heater, which was considered optional equipment. Those poor souls had to be content with opening a vent that allowed heat from the manifold to come inside the passenger compartment. He pushed the choke back in and made his way down Collinsville Avenue, turning east when he reached St. Clair. The street and the county had been named for Arthur St. Clair, the first governor of the famed Northwest Territory, which had included the future state of Illinois. Brad hung a right and turned his back on the Stock Yards. Around the turn of the century a series of gin joints, nightclubs and bawdy houses had developed in the vicinity near the entrance, and it subsequently acquired the name Whiskey Chute.

Now it was a straight shot, about eighty-five blocks out to French Village. St. Clair Avenue was an extension of Route 50, which had been known as the Great Western Mail Route back in the old days. As he approached 20th Street, the traffic began to back up because of a train crossing the Terminal Railroad tracks at a snail's pace, so he pulled into Uncle Andy's donut shop. He flipped the collar of his winter coat, just recently rescued from mothballs. Entering the sugar-scented warmth, he perused the scrumptious offerings inside the glass display case. Cinnamon twist, cream and jelly-filled, chocolate-covered, glazed and powdered delights. He bought a dozen mixed donuts. Three for him and the rest for Mom, Dad, and Sis.

A blue-uniformed policeman was sitting at the counter dunking a donut in black coffee.

"Hey, officer! The weather out there is a crime. Can't you do something about it?" Brad teased.

"Yeah—I can arrest the weatherman." The officer wiped his mouth with a napkin and got up to leave. "See ya later, Andy," he said, waving to the owner as he headed for the door.

"Have a nice day," Andy cheerfully replied.

"Didn't he forget to pay you, Andy?" Brad stood there with a quizzical look on his face.

"You don't understand. That's patrolman Matt Mueller. It's his beat. His money is no good here. He looks out for me, and I take care of him."

"But isn't that part of his job?" Brad protested.

"Look, the more he randomly drops in here, the less likely someone will try to rob the place. It's a very small perk that goes with being a police officer."

Brad wondered what other kind of perks he was tempted to cash in on with his uniform.

He bumped into Bob Hrasky, an old boyhood chum on his way out. He had one of those colorful Eastern European names which typically had too many consonants and misplaced vowels. One of his favorite jokes was about a certain Czech fellow who went to the optometrist to have his eyes tested.

The specialist asked, "Can you see the fifth line on the chart?"

"Not only can I see it, I work with that guy down at the Obear-Nester glass plant."

"Hello, Bob. Good to see you," Brad said. "Still working at Armour Packing?"

"Hi, Brad. Yeah, I'm still punching a clock down there as assistant foreman. I just put in for a new job as a government inspector. It would mean a twenty-dollar a month raise."

"Hope you get it. By the way, I ran into our old patrol boy pal Jerry Gruber a while back. He said to tell you hello."

Bob was smiling. "Yeah, remember how the three of us used to eat the white library paste back in second grade art?"

"Uh, huh. I never told you this before, but we used to pretend to eat it just to watch you."

Pause.

"Very funny."

"Hey, give my regards to your mom and dad and sisters for me. I've got to run. See you later," Brad said as he left the store.

Brad had played church league basketball with Bob, who was their center. Bob was only a half-inch taller, but his Eastern European body rested on a big-boned frame, and Bob outweighed him by about twenty pounds. Bob was their mainstay—the best player on the team. And a good friend.

The white flakes were still coming down, but the storm was rapidly losing strength. After four hours of intense snow, Mother Nature granted the city clemency. Brad brushed the accumulation off both windshields, got back in the car, and continued down the highway. The train had passed, and the mild traffic jam had dissipated. There were a couple of pre-school tots playing in their back yard at 23rd Street. They were laughing and talking as they fell backwards; then they moved their arms and legs to make snow angels. They were so bundled up with layers of clothing their arms were nearly perpendicular to their bodies when they stood up. Watching the kids at play sent Brad drifting back to memory lane. He fondly recalled those carefree days of making snowmen, building snow forts and having snowball fights with the Rudd brothers. A honk of someone's horn rudely jolted him back to reality.

Momentarily disoriented from his brief rendezvous with the past, Brad continued toward the outskirts of the city. He drove by several commercial sites: Westerheide Sheet Metal, Rudolph and Herbert coal yards. As he crossed 25th Street, he thought about Jones Park swimming lagoon, several blocks to his left, now covered with a white skin of ice. He continued past American Asphalt and East St. Louis Castings. Back in the 1920s, the city had led the nation in the production of roofing materials. The highway doglegged south and then crossed Kingshighway. Some of the property was now distinctly rural. He passed the Schuette farm, with yellowish-brown cornstalks, left standing after the harvest, rippling in the wind. A hardy pair of bluejays ignored a frozen scarecrow and were foraging the field for food. He gingerly went around a slow-moving, oil-burner car that needed a ring job, crossing the bridge over the Harding ditch in the process. The water was flowing swiftly in the drainage canal, built by the Levee Board for flood control back in 1919. The system covered a two-county area and was a great source of patronage for the political machine. A little farther on the same side sat the recently completed East St. Louis/French Village drive-in theater. **CLOSED FOR THE SEA ON** read the big sign. The wind had blown one of the letters off the rack.

Brad wolfed down two cinnamon twists and was busy brushing sugar crumbs off his tweed overcoat when he pulled into the Torricelli driveway. It was 2:35 P.M. A white picket fence demarcated her property. The house was a light blue, two-story Dutch colonial. A dark blue-shingled roof was barely discernible since most of it was covered with snow. Glistening stalactites hung from seams in her guttering. A couple of mature maple trees in the front yard thrust their dormant branches toward the sky. Four snow-laden poplar trees stood along the driveway like gigantic arctic exclamation points. There were several mounds in the yard where the snow had gracefully drifted into white dunes. He parked his car, switched off the ignition, and crunched his way through the white crystals to her front door. The neighborhood was well to do, but not quite as cheerfully opulent as Signal Hill. He thunked the metal knocker several times on the paneled door. It was a brass ring through the mouth of a roaring lion.

A stiff wind nipped at his cheeks and sent a chill up his spine just before Mrs. Torricelli pulled the door slightly ajar.

"Yes, what is it?"

"Hello, It's me, Brad Logan. We have an appointment."

"Oh, yes, won't you please come in," she said as a weak smile crinkled the corners of her mouth.

"Thank you." He stamped his feet to shed them of ice and snow before crossing the threshold.

She had fierce red hair, slightly stringy—like Raggedy Ann. Her makeup nearly hid the dark circles under her eyes.

"May I take your hat and coat?"

"Thank you."

She hung the coat in a mahogany armoire and set the hat on an antique credenza. The hollow cheeks on her pale face reflected the look of a tired and sad woman still in the throes of the grieving process. Signs of her

bereavement looked genuine. She wore a pink floral dress and a pair of felt house shoes that were so loose they flopped as she walked.

"Won't you please be seated?" She pointed to an overstuffed lounge chair in the living room. The place was tastefully decorated. There was a beige fainting couch in the far corner of the room. Ostensibly for women with the vapors. Brad hadn't seen one of those for years.

She had been cleaning. A triad of odors lingered in the air: beeswax, pine scent and lemon oil. While Brad eased into the confines of lush upholstery, she turned off the television set then went over and stood against the wall, straddling a floor register. The upcoming draft of warm air agitated the hem of her skirt.

Outside, the raw wind picked up and rattled the storm windows.

"Are you cold? Can I help build a fire?"

"I'll be all right. Just a nervous ch-ch-chill. I've been under a terrible strain." Her head tilted back, and she closed her eyes for a brief moment. "Why are you defending the man who shot my husband?"

The first thing Brad did was offer condolences. Next, he proffered an explanation. "Mrs. Torricelli, I'm still trying to find out who might have hired a hit man to kill your husband, and more importantly, for what reason."

"Why don't they just give him the chair?" Her tortured eyes focused on his. "He deserves to die for what he did."

"They abolished mob justice a long time ago, ma'am. Everyone is entitled to a defense under our adversarial system. If he's guilty, he'll probably get convicted."

Obviously she wasn't impressed with his lofty reasonings. Her cat, a hefty looking orange tabby, strolled nonchalantly by, arched his back, and rubbed against his leg.

"Simba, leave the man alone; get away from him."

"He isn't bothering me. I like animals." Brad reached down and stroked his back.

"Would you care for a drink—scotch, bourbon or brandy?"

"No thanks, I just had coffee and donuts."

"Excuse me just a minute while I make myself a pick-me-up."

"Of course."

She went into the kitchen. The tinkling of ice cubes and glass clinking on glass reached Brad's ears. He glanced to his right. A telephone sat on the taboret next to his chair. A saffron book of matches, resting on Lloyd Yerby's ***Pride's Castle***, attracted his attention. It featured a cement truck on the front with the name Torricelli Construction near the striker. He flipped it over. The company phone number and address were embossed on the back. But what really caught his eye was the name ***Jack*** next to two numbers written in blue ink, UPton 4-7100 and UPton 5-2000. He knew the numbers belonged to the police station and City Hall. The amount of $15,140, written below the numbers, he committed to memory.

Mrs. Torricelli glided back into the room, clutching a drink. A pair of black flats had replaced her slippers. She walked over to the window and adjusted the slats on the Venetian blinds.

"Since I last talked to you, have you thought of anyone who might have wanted your husband dead?"

"No. I still have no idea why this happened."

"I still think his death might have had something to do with a squabble over construction contracts."

"We never talked business," she said as she perched on the edge of a muted red club chair.

"Did he seem upset during the weeks preceding his death?"

"Yes."

"And why was that?"

She took a big gulp of her drink. "Don't know." She licked her lips. "Said he didn't want to talk about it."

"Did you hear any phone conversations here at the house that caused him to get agitated?"

"Let me think . . . uh, yes." Her drink sloshed around in the glass as she waved the hand it was in expressively. "There was a call about a week before he was killed."

Simba, purring joyously, gave up on Brad's leg and strolled over to curl up on a small rug in front of a corner fireplace layered in gray ash. The oval needlepoint rug, resting on a highly polished hardwood floor, was marred by a burn spot in the upper corner. He smiled as the cat's expressive tail swished back and forth as it licked a paw.

"Did you hear any of the conversation?"

"Not really . . . Wait, I do remember; he was yelling at a man named Arnold."

"He didn't say his last name?"

"No, I don't think so."

Brad glanced at Simba. His yellow eyes had that smug, distant, independent look he had seen many a time before on other cats. "Do you remember anything else?"

"Uh, . . . no, nothing."

"We already looked through his things at the office."

"Wait, I remember that he kept some things in boxes, and there's an old file cabinet in the basement. I totally forgot about it the first time we met."

"Mind if I look through his things? There might be something—a ledger or some papers—that would help us catch the person responsible for his death."

"Fine, but you'll have to come back later. My mother called just before you arrived. She's a semi-invalid and she wants me to run some errands for her. I'm sorry, it can't be helped," she said apologetically.

"I understand. What time is convenient?"

"It will have to be after eight o'clock."

"That will be fine."

"I'm sorry you have to make another trip."

"No problem. I'll be back a little after eight. If you think of anything else . . . anything, please let me know when I come back."

"Will do."

"Thank you very much, Mrs. Torricelli. I think you'll sleep better when we know the ***whole*** truth about what happened to your husband."

A thickening night enveloped Brad's car as he drove the return trip. Mrs. Torricelli had thoughtfully turned on the porch light. She answered the door after the second knock. Another mixed drink of some kind was glued to her fingers. The radio and television were silent, and Brad began to wonder what she was going to do with her time in the evenings now that her husband was gone. Out of the corner of his eye, he saw Simba dart into the kitchen, batting a catnip mouse around.

"The basement steps are on the other side of the kitchen," she said, leading the way. After opening the door, she flipped the switch at the top of the stairs.

A naked 75-watt light bulb, dangling from a cord, cast garish rays of light on them. The musty smell of a Midwest basement raced up the stairs and greeted his nose—the undiscernable cross-scented mixture of damp concrete and things that were old, mildewed and dank. Typically, the musky odor could be traced to dust motes collecting on canvas awnings, cushioned rattan chairs, and window screens in storage.

"Careful, don't trip on the metal edging my husband tacked around the treads when he covered them with tile," she warned.

He gingerly followed her down the steps. Something organic tweaked his senses. "Is that furnace coal in the bin I smell?"

"Yes, my husband converted the furnace by adding a stoker last year. It's nice having that hopper feed bits of coal automatically. I hired the boy next door to come over every Saturday and shovel coal from the bin and refill the hopper," she explained. "He also takes out the clinkers. My husband was a regular handyman. I still don't know what I'm going to do without him."

Three-fourths of the way down they reached a landing where three more steps, turning left at a ninety-degree angle, led to the concrete floor. Brad eyed several rows of Ball jars, sitting on wooden shelves full of preserves.

"We have a small garden in the backyard," she explained.

He noticed that five months after her husband's death she used the term "we" instead of the personal pronoun "I."

"Did you hear a noise?" she asked, as she paused on the landing.

"Yes, but I assumed it was the furnace ducts groaning from heat expansion. Ours does it all the time."

He should have been more wary, but nothing really registered until a shot rang out, exploding the bare light bulb, spraying them with tiny glass particles and returning the basement to its previous state of darkness. Mrs. Torricelli screamed and fell backwards knocking Brad to a sitting position on one of the steps. An intruder was running pell mell, knocking over boxes and cursing as he bumped into things in a frantic effort to find the storm cellar doors.

"Stop! Who's there?" Brad yelled.

The man paid him no heed. There was a loud clatter of wood and metal as he flung back both cellar hatch doors and continued his mad dash up the concrete stairs to freedom. Mrs. Torricelli and Brad quickly backtracked up the other stairs. He left her in the kitchen as he raced out the back door in a desperate attempt to catch the intruder. Brad barely caught a glimpse of him as he crossed the alley and cut through the yard of a house directly behind the Torricelli home. Brad raced through the yard but in the darkness he tripped over a small wire garden fence, sprawling headlong, landing in deep snow on several frozen mounds of rich soil.

Brad was back on his feet in an instant. As he neared the neighbor's front yard he heard the ***whump*** of a car door, an engine roaring to life, the grinding of gears and the squeal of rubber on the slick street. The distinctive whine of an engine responding to different gearshifts at high speed faded in the distance and disappeared into the night. Only now were Brad's eyes beginning to adjust to the blue-black darkness. There was a gap where the intruder cut through the neighbor's waist-high privet hedge. Strangely, Brad had felt no fear, but his heart was still pounding from the dose of adrenaline called up by his brain. A barking dog in someone's back yard was the only thing that disturbed the cocooning stillness of the falling snow.

He found Mrs. Torricelli, still shaking with fright, sitting with Simba on her lap.

"Are you all right?"

She nodded and mouthed a barely audible, "I'll be fine. Did he get away?"

"Yes, but at least I saw part of his license number. That fellow is probably looking for the same thing I am."

"You've got dirt on you." She brushed her hand across his jacket. "Did you fall?"

"I'm okay. Maybe you ought to stay up here while I check out downstairs."

"Fine." She went into the kitchen pantry and found him a new bulb and a flashlight. "Sorry. A forty-watt bulb is all I have."

Simba scampered past Brad and vanished into the blackness. He played the flashlight beam on the stairs, followed them to the landing and changed the bulb. Then he loped down the final three steps. He turned slowly and with the flashlight did a three-hundred-and-sixty-degree survey of the room. A rotund pewter-colored furnace dominated the middle of the basement. Its adLance into age gave its breath a certain indescribable smell. Huge tentacles reached from the plenum, sprawling upward, like a metal octopus trying to latch on to a meal.

He spotted the file cabinet in the corner. On the floor, next to it, his roundish beam found a small grayish mouse. It was pinned with a broken neck on the flat surface of a wooden trap. A small piece of cheese was still in its mouth. Lifeless eyes eerily reminded him of something he had once seen on a surrealistic Dali canvas.

Three of the file cabinet's four drawers had been emptied on the floor. Several cardboard boxes were torn open, their contents emptied and strewn about in haste. He waded through the flood of papers, moved a roll of hardware cloth, and pulled the remaining drawer open. He flipped through the tabs on the folders but failed to find anything significant. There were several small boxes at the rear of the drawer. When he removed the lids of the first two, he found them to be full of red and green plastic St. Louis sales tax mills. The red ones were worth a tenth of a penny, and the green were worth half a cent. Some people collected the mills and used them for chips in friendly poker games. As he pulled the lid off the third box, a huge brown spider ran across his hand. "Ugh!" He yelled and stumbled backward, flinging it off in a fit of terror. It scurried across the floor to the safety of some dark recess on the other side of the basement.

Easy, Logan old boy. It was just as scared as you were. Spiders don't think of human beings as food.

Brad's heart was thumping against his ribs. He took a deep breath and pulled himself together. When it came to creepy-crawlies, he was a real scaredy-cat. There was this deep visceral fear of anything with more than four legs.

Just a childish misapprehension. Probably a common wolf spider; but what if it had been a brown recluse?

Brad went back to the cabinet and peered into the last box. There was a deck of cards inside and several pairs of dice. Whoever it was might have found what he was looking for, but Brad considered that unlikely since he was still there when they surprised him. He went over and sat on the first step of the landing, collecting his thoughts and looking about, trying to guess the hiding place of Torricelli's file folder or ledger.

It wouldn't be near or on the floor because a sewer back-up or flooding from heavy rains could damage or destroy it. What about a corner of the coal bin, under a pile of black diamonds? Nope. Too messy. He wouldn't keep it near the canned fruits and vegetables. The Mrs. might accidentally find it.

He found himself staring at an old Monopoly game sitting on top of the file cabinet. The dog-eared game looked as if it might have been one of the originals, first produced in the '30s to escape the financial duress of the Depression. Mo-no-po-ly, Brad thought, chewing the word over in his brain. ***Of course, you numbskull***, he reproached himself. All at once it hit him—the figure of $15,140 from the matchbook cover suddenly had meaning. ***What if . . .***

Brad scrambled to his feet and rushed to open the lid. ***The $15,140 figure is the total amount of money in a Monopoly game.*** His elation quickly turned to dross. There was nothing inside except play money and game components. He stared at the pieces in mild disappointment. He started to place the lid back on, but Simba came bounding by from the ledge, knocking some of the components on the floor. As Brad stooped to retrieve them, he realized there were ***two*** sets of property cards, each wrapped with a rubber band. There should be only twenty-eight cards, and it looked as if there were almost twice that amount. He slipped the rubber band off one set and fanned the cards. Nothing. Illinois Avenue, that shiny red property, was lying on top of the second pile. He removed the band and worked the cards apart with his fingers. Beneath Illinois Avenue was a set of fake properties, cut from index cards. There were names, dates, and dollar amounts written on them. ***Advance to GO! Collect $200! Jackpot, Logan!***

He turned around and saw Mrs. Torricelli creeping timidly down the stairs. Simba ran to meet her, but she clapped her hands and yelled "scat." The startled feline bounded up the stairs and disappeared into the kitchen.

"Did you find anything?" she hesitatingly asked.

"I'm not sure." He was tempted to skirt the truth and slip the cards into his coat pocket, not wanting to upset her or give her more stress. "Do you mind if I take these cards home with me where I can examine them more closely? They might have important information on them."

"I—I guess it will be all right." She nervously tugged at her watchband.

"If you have some screws and a screwdriver, I think I can fix the thingamajig, uh, er, the hasp on the cellar doors."

"Oh, you needn't go to all that trouble."

"It's no bother. Glad to help."

"My husband kept some tools and fasteners on that ledge by the file cabinet."

"When the intruder thrust his shoulder against it, the old assembly pulled loose. I think I can fix the problem by simply repositioning it. Can you get me the key to unfasten this lock?"

"It should be right above your head, hanging on a nail in that floor joist."

Brad tilted the flashlight upward and the nickel-silvered key gleamed in its illumination. He gingerly reached up, avoiding a cobweb. "Got it."

"Hold on," she said. "If the lock is still fastened, how did he get in?"

"Is there another door?"

"No."

"Then I have no . . . wait a minute." Brad's eyes widened. "I bet he climbed in through the coal chute door."

"Unbelievable," she sighed, her eyes gleaming in approval of his conclusion.

He found some new screws, moved the latch assembly down about three inches, and secured the lock.

"Done," he said.

"Thank you, I'll sleep much better now. You don't think he'll come back . . . ?"

"I have a hunch he knows who I am now. If anything, he'll eventually come looking for me," Brad reassured her.

She helped him gather the disastrous piles of paper into a couple of boxes.

"I'll bring all of this back as soon as I've had a chance to go through it," he said.

"There's no hurry."

"Thanks for everything. Here's my card. Call me if you need anything." Then he told her to notify the police. "If you want, they'll send a squad car around the neighborhood for several days, just to make sure everything is all right."

CHAPTER 13

East St. Louis High grad Johnny Wyrostek played for the Cincinnati Reds and made the All-Star team in 1950 and 1951. As a youth, Pete Rose used to sneak into Crosley Field just to see his idol practice in the outfield.

Lorna dropped out of her two classes at Summers Business College. Mermelstein had been right when he expressed doubt as to their usefulness. She was doing extremely well with her coverage of social events and had even received a ten-cent an hour raise. She dreaded telling her parents about the change and prayed that the subject wouldn't come up for a few months. By then, she figured, her budding career would make the issue moot.

In addition to her raise, Lorna received a promotion of sorts. A step up in the reporting firmament. She had been anxious to prove to Mermelstein that women could cover news events with substance. She found writing about the social scene only slightly more interesting than writing about proms and football queens at Litchfield High School.

After attending the Kefauver hearings with Lance, she was motivated to write a commentary piece on the state of affairs in St. Clair County.

LORNA'S EDITORIAL - February 12, 1951

Now that the Kefauver Crime Commission has left town, there is a significant question the community needs to ask itself. What are we going to do about the stinking mess? Apparently our prosperous river town is awash in illegal gambling. We strongly urge that the mayor and commissioners give serious consideration to the formation of a Citizen Crime Commission to make recommendations for turning the spotlight on the deplorable conditions in our city and cleaning up the crime and corruption. Normally, the citizenry doesn't think much about the existence of organized crime. We know vaguely it is there and let it go at that. The affable Tennessee senator with the size twelve shoes has aptly defined the problem. Now it's up to each community to do something about it.

Woodrow Wilson once wrote: "Very few men are unequal to a danger which they see and understand."

Thanks to the senator who made the coonskin cap famous, the problem is now obvious. Pressure should be brought to bear on illegal activities of any kind in our city so these problems can be eradicated. Bookie joints ought to be closed. Prostitution should be eliminated. Illegal gambling of any kind must be terminated. The very idea that these shenanigans are occurring right under the nose of City Hall officials is a disgrace. Penalties for any of these illegal activities should be increased substantially. If it is found that our police force is of insufficient size to effectively deal with the problem, additional personnel must be hired. The time is at hand for an all-out effort against criminal activities at all levels of government—federal, state and local. Our county grand jury should delve into the matter and keep the crusade rolling.

In the past twenty years there have been sixty-four unsolved gang murders in the St. Louis-southwest Illinois area. We must make it clear, without equivocation, this is intolerable. It is obvious these murders constitute a studied plan to control large-scale gambling and vice. It's time to put hoodlums and crooked politicians on notice that these activities will no longer be tolerated. The Kefauver Committee aptly demonstrated that members of both groups have vested interests in the status quo. Let's let them know the image of East St. Louis as a "wide-open" town is no longer acceptable. Let's make the vermin who glibly flout the law fear our efforts and force them to crawl back under their rocks. It's time we do our part to help strangle the national crime syndicate and put their foul leaders where they belong.

The nation's crime hub may revolve around the Chicago/New York axis, but Mr. Kefauver has shown East St. Louis is an important cog in the wheel. We urge each citizen to get involved. Form committees at your churches and fraternal organizations. Write letters to City Hall. Telephone your precinct committeeman. Let's make East St. Louis a place we can be proud of by restoring a sense of decency to our community.

Mermelstein was impressed and ran the piece the next day. Lorna's job description didn't change, but he told her she would receive a ten-dollar bonus every time the paper ran one of her editorials. She took her new position as a quasi member of the fourth-estate seriously. Mermelstein praised her work on the Kefauver hearings, calling it incisive, provocative and timely.

* * *

True to her dating modus operandi, Lorna continued playing the field when it came to men. She had gone on a double date with Barb Edelblute at the office. Barb was with an acquaintance from high school and fixed Lorna up with her cousin. But Lorna dropped him after a few dates when she decided that he was too opinionated and too arrogant.

Lance Troutman and Brad Logan continued to be her other interests. When Lance did pop the question for a formal evening date, it was for a night of dining and dancing at the famed Starlight Room at the Chase Park Plaza Hotel in St. Louis. Good-looking as all-get-out, perfectly groomed, and known to splurge extravagantly on dates, Lorna eagerly told him *yes* and decided that if she was going to rub elbows with the hoity-toity elite across the river, a new dress was needed.

"Can you go with me to shop for a new outfit?" Lorna asked her roommate.

"Sure," said Gloria, who was still going strong with Bob Von Brock. "Where are you planning to look?" Still in a housecoat, Lorna headed to the bathroom to shower. Gloria grabbed a towel and followed her.

Lorna, clowning with Barb Edelblute's cousin

"I want to start at Seidel's and Stanley's. If I can't find anything there, we can go over to Stix or Scruggs in St. Louis."

"What ever happened to that Logan guy you met at the Majestic?" Gloria called out over the spray of the water. She soaped and scrubbed to rid herself of a menthol smell from the Vicks salve she had used the night before to clear up chest congestion.

"He's still in the picture, I think," she replied from the adjacent stall. "He asked me for a date last weekend, but that was when I visited my parents back home. I ran into him at the Kefauver hearings a few days ago, but I was with Lance at the time. I hope that didn't scare him off because I like dating more than one man at a time. It makes it easier to keep the relationships from getting too serious. Besides, men treat you better if they think they are up against stiff competition."

"You haven't had any more knock-down, drag-outs with Priscilla at the office, have you?"

"No, but only because she hasn't had any insane outbursts lately. Priscilla is so jealous of me she can't stand it. There isn't much I can do. I feel as if I'm walking on eggshells when I'm around her. She is the most exasperating, manipulative person I have ever known."

"That's a shame," Gloria sympathized. "She sounds like a scheming little vixen. It might be wise not to cross swords with her again."

"How are things going with Bob?" Lorna asked, toweling her body. "I haven't heard you talk about anyone else."

"I think he might be ***the*** one. Bob said that I was his one true love."

"Really?"

"Well, besides Betty Grable." Draped with towels, they walked back to the room. "I'm very much in love with him, and I'm hoping to get an engagement ring this Christmas."

Lorna slipped into her foundation garments, went to the closet, selected a yellow sweater and black skirt and finished dressing. "If that's what you truly want, I'm very happy for you."

"If it happens, will you consider being my maid of honor?" Gloria asked.

Lorna walked over to look out the windows while she brushed her hair. Jack Frost, that angular-faced sprite, had visited the city during the night and blew his breath on the panes. "Don't you have a sister or a close friend? We've only known each other six months." The cast iron radiator with clawed feet was hissing from its valve.

"No, there are four boys but I'm the only girl in my family. And right now, you are my closest friend."

Lorna glanced down at the fluffy snow that had accumulated in a powdery drift on the outside sill. "I'll be delighted to be your 'maid of ornery,' " she kidded, beaming enthusiastically as she put the final touches on her hair.

Bundled up for their winter foray, they headed downstairs. Both waved to Laurie at the front desk. Her attention seemed to be divided between an animated phone conversation and an effort to keep an eye on people coming and going.

"I hear the groundhog saw his shadow a few weeks ago." Lorna placed a knitted, multi-colored tam-o'-shanter on her head.

"Brrr. That means four more weeks of winter left doesn't it?" Gloria said, as she slipped on a pair of white rabbit fur earmuffs. She topped off her outfit with a sort of Brooks tangy ketchup-colored beret, which sat on her head at a cocky angle.

"Yes, something like that." Lorna pushed the front door open.

They emerged into the blustery white world of Old Man Winter and quickly immersed themselves deep in girl talk.

"Have you ever wondered what it would be like to live in a place that's warm all the time, perhaps somewhere in Florida?" Gloria sighed, tugging the back of her navy wool coat collar up around her neck.

"Sometimes I get a little tired of the winter, but I like the change of seasons. And I can't imagine celebrating Christmas in a place where palm trees are swaying in a balmy eighty degrees," Lorna said. "Think about it. Nearly all of the visions you can conjure up about the season are connected to snow and cold weather—Rudolph the reindeer, Santa in a sleigh—you know, all that winter wonderland stuff."

Columbia Records' Jo Stafford

"Dashing through the snow, in a one horse open sleigh," Gloria sang as she mimicked Jo Stafford.

"Chestnuts roasting on an open fire, Jack Frost nipping at your nose," Lorna chimed.

"I'm dreaming of a white Christmas . . ." Gloria crooned, in lowered Crosbyesque tones.

"Just like the ones I used to know," they both warbled, and then let out an embarrassed giggle when they re-alized that a passerby was staring, as if measuring them for straight jackets at the Alton mental hospital.

"Tell me about this Troutman fellow you're going out with," Gloria said. "Is he ***really*** good looking?"

"Very! He's masculine—gorgeous hair, Cary Grant looks, with a deeply cleft chin."

"More, more—tell me more." They passed a couple of snow-laden Austrian pines that were sagging like fatigued old men.

"He's reputed to have a Svengali-like charisma with women."

"Sounds exciting . . . bordering on dangerous."

"Oh, and he's rich!"

"You mean rich as in ***loaded*?**" Gloria swooned. "You know what my grandmother always told me?"

"No, what?"

"It's just as easy to fall in love with a rich guy as it is a poor one."

"Gloria, you're shameless."

"So, does his old man own an oil well, or what?"

"I'm told his family lives in a posh section of town on Pennsylvania Avenue. Old money. Their name has been held in high esteem around here for nearly one hundred years. They made a bundle in real estate. It seems that great, great grandfather Troutman owned a huge strip of land he bought from John Jacob Astor after he grew bored with his East St. Louis holdings."

"Didn't Astor get rich as a fur trader out West and go down with the Titanic?" Gloria asked.

"Yes, except it was his grandson who went down on the 'unsinkable' luxury liner."

They momentarily paused while an exuberant chocolate Labrador retriever playfully bounded in front of them. He trotted by their side for half a block and then took off in a different direction.

"I still don't understand how the Troutman family became rich."

"Keep your underwear on, I was just getting to that." Lorna gave Gloria a look of frustration. "Astor bought a huge strip of land in the South End that ran from the river to the bluffs. He grew impatient with his investment and sold off a big section of it to Sam Troutman. Three years later Troutman sold it to a group of Colorado investors, who turned it into the industrial park that became known as Denverside. That one sale resulted in ***beaucoup*** bucks; the family fortune was made."

"So, Astor made a huge mistake in timing?"

"Well, he still came out smelling like a rose because he later sold the rest of it to the Pittsburg Reduction Company, which built the Aluminum Ore plant, employer of over two thousand people."

"Wow!" Gloria whistled.

"Lance's family wasn't very happy about his decision to become a reporter instead of following in the footsteps of dear old Dad. They reluctantly accepted it, but his father cut Lance's allowance to convince him to come to his senses. His father must have given him some money in a trust or something because he wears expensive clothes and drives a fancy Lincoln Cosmopolitan convertible."

"Who told you all this inside stuff on the Troutmans?"

"According to Barb Edelblute at the office, it's common knowledge."

The first stop for them along shopping's Appian Way was Stanley's, a two-story upscale store on the corner of Collinsville and St. Louis avenues. It had once been Fellner & Crow general merchandise store but now was devoted strictly to women's apparel. They ducked inside and stamped their feet on a large rubber-backed mat.

"Are you looking for any particular color?" Gloria removed her beret and muffs.

"I think I'd like some kind of taffeta cocktail dress in either flamingo pink or crimson."

"Hello. My name is Glenda. May I help the two of you?" a petite saleslady tweeted in a melodic singsong. She looked neat as a pin and sported a fashionable hairdo from a local salon.

"Yes," said Lorna. "I'm looking for a dress that would be appropriate for dining and dancing at the Chase."

"We just got a new shipment in and I'm sure we'll have something in your size you'll just love. Come with me, please."

The saleslady took them to the back of the store toward a rack of clothes built into the wall. They walked past a bored gentleman who was sitting on a maroon Victorian chair, holding his hat in his lap while his wife looked for off-season bargains.

Glenda gave Lorna an appraising once over. "Size ten?"

"Bingo."

"The tens are from here . . . to here," she said, while adeptly pushing other sizes away on both sides. She pulled one off the rack. "Here is a peacock blue V-neck that is quite fashionable these days." She grabbed another one. "Or you might like something a little more sedate, like this two-tiered lavender number with a scoop neck. This one is also

Lance Troutman's 1951 Lincoln Cosmopolitan that weighed a hefty 4,614 pounds

available in pink. And if you want something a little more formal, we have this bouncy little number here in fuchsia that has spaghetti straps. Several interlining layers of crinolines make this an exquisite addition to your wardrobe. Of course, you would need a fur cape or a shawl to go with it for this time of the year."

Pause.

Lorna silently looked at each proffered piece, trying to analyze what would go best with her existing accessories—shoes, purse, earrings and necklaces.

Gloria absentmindedly adjusted the wide contour belt around her petite waist. "Where is your dressing room?"

"It's over in that corner," Glenda indicated with a wagging finger. "Excuse me, there's another customer over there who needs help. I'll be right back."

Lorna took the first two garments and Gloria accompanied her to the dressing area. It was discreetly located in a corner, away from the main part of the store where others were shopping. The floor was completely covered with plush carpeting. Gloria unbuttoned her coat and waited on a thickly upholstered bench seat while Lorna changed into the V-neck.

"Well, what do you think?" Lorna said as she came out, extending the side of the dress pinched between her thumb and forefinger.

"Turn around," Gloria commanded while pensively contemplating the fit.

She did a slow twirl with her right arm thrust upward, emulating a ballet move.

"It's a pretty color, but I don't like the cut. It bunches up in the wrong places in the back."

Lorna went over and appraised herself in a three-sided mirror. She turned her head to the left to get a better view. "I think you're right," she frowned. "You don't think it's because my butt's too big?"

"Oh, ***of course not***," Gloria teased, with splayed fingers on top of her chest.

"You're a scream!" Lorna had a forced look of disgust. "What do you like most about your boyfriend, Bob?" she inquired, while still eyeing the fit of the dress.

"Well . . . he's kind and gentle—very polite, good-looking. I just love the slight wave in his light brown hair. He makes me laugh, and my skin feels all prickly when he comes near me. I think it's love."

"Love? It sounds more like psoriasis to me," Lorna teased.

"Very funny," Gloria shot back.

"You know I'm just kidding."

"Thanks."

"I wonder if love will hit me like a bolt out of the blue, or if I'll have to make some sort of cold rational decision between several men, as if I were buying an insurance policy."

"You know that's one of life's little ironies."

"Ironies?" Lorna asked.

"Yep! Part of the human condition. You don't get to pick who you fall in love with. It just happens."

"I don't want to sound sacrilegious, but maybe that was one of God's mistakes."

"It's the not knowing that makes this thing between men and women interesting. You have to go with your heart. When you're possessed by love you forget yourself," Gloria rhapsodized. "Love is passionate, irrational, reckless abandon. You only get one life, and it should be with someone who makes your heart start racing when you hear his voice."

"Is it like that with you and your Romeo?"

"Yeah, pretty much," Gloria said. "Bob still gives me goose bumps."

"I think I'll try the other dress on," Lorna announced. She began unzipping the back of her dress as she returned to her dressing stall. "I'm not sure I totally agree with you about your heart going pitter-patter and bells ringing when you're with a man. I saw too many girls in high school get carried away with their feelings. Some of them dated safe, well-mannered, nice-looking boys who were predictable but boring. Then along came one of those smooth-talking, dangerous-looking, rebellious types with slicked-down hair. They literally swept the girls off their feet. Why is it females seem to fall for those hell-on-wheels loverboy types so often?"

"I don't know," Gloria responded. "Probably the thrill of something new, unique, exciting."

"A girl from our church, Shirley Smith, ran off with one of those slick talking, break-all-the-rules boys and got married in Arkansas where the legal age is sixteen."

"How did it turn out?"

Lorna emerged in her new outfit. "Ta daa," she said, with both hands in the air.

"What happened?" Gloria begged.

"It lasted a little over a year," she said. "Shirley came back home to stay with her parents, brokenhearted and humiliated because they had done everything possible to stop her from going with the guy. She was four months with child. Divorce, pregnancy and broken heart, all in one sad package."

"Wouldn't that be the gumps, having to go back home to live with your parents after having flown the coop?" Gloria lamented.

Lorna nodded in affirmation. "That's why I think I'll probably be a virgin, or almost, when I finally walk down the aisle."

"There's no such thing as ***almost***," Gloria reminded.

"You know what I mean. I want men to realize that my modesty, my standoffishness, is a lively signal of self worth. I want to send them a message that I think I'm worth the wait. I plan to do this marriage thing only once, and I want that certain man, when he finally comes along, to feel that discovering my womanhood on our wedding night is something very special. And until then it's not you, or you, or you. I don't want to lose my virginity in the back seat of a Chevy at the East St Louis drive-in theater or Falling Springs Park."

"Would you settle for a Packard?" Gloria said in mock coquettish overtones.

"G-L-O-R-I-A! You can be ***so*** exasperating at times."

"Sorry, just trying to clarify things."

"Well, what do you think of this one?"

"Hmmmmmm!" Gloria stroked her chin.

"Could you please expand a little bit on 'hmmmmmm?' "

"The bodice is spectacular; it pushes everything up and over at the top."

Lorna waved her right hand in an up and over manner as she spoke. "I don't think I want everything tumbling out up there."

"Maybe we better go see what they have at the next store," Gloria sourly replied. "A good fitting dress is supposed to flow exquisitely across your hips with smooth symmetry. This one just, uh, sits there. You could get arrested by the fashion inspector for wearing that outfit."

"Gloria, you are so diplomatic. I'm surprised you don't help Emily Post with her column on etiquette."

As they left the store, Lorna thanked the saleslady who was still engaged with her other customer. They braved winter's wrath again as they went across the street into Seidel's which sat directly opposite the Majestic Theater.

"You know," Lorna said to her friend, "those dresses at Stanley's were beautiful, but I'm not sure I could have afforded them."

"Did you see the price tag on that peacock-blue dress?" Gloria gasped.

"Almost as much as Harry Truman spent on the Berlin Airlift."

Gloria threw her hands up in the air and nodded.

"Laurie, our Betty Boop-voiced friend at the Beulah Club, told me Seidel's has a basement section that's a little cheaper than their clothes on the main floor."

"Kind of like buying a Bobbi Brooks outfit at Sears, but with a designer label?" Gloria asked.

"Something like that," Lorna said.

"She's one of life's great big mysteries, you know."

"Who?"

"Laurie, Miss Vitality Plus."

"Why?"

"She can eat three square meals and snack all day long. Doesn't gain a single pound."

"Not me. All I have to do is look at a candy wrapper and I gain five pounds."

"Me too," Gloria sighed.

* * *

As it turned out, Lorna ended up buying her dress from Labelle's Fashion Shop, located a couple of blocks farther south on Collinsville Avenue. The dress was a deep purplish red and had a high bodice with puffy sleeves. Gloria said she looked just like the Queen of Diamonds. It sounded like a compliment. The cost was $29.95, and it was exactly what Lorna had wanted. It may have come from a store in East St. Louis, but to Lorna, it glimmered as if it were a chic avant-garde Oleg Cassini from Sachs on Fifth Avenue.

"I bet Lance will love that outfit when he sees it," Gloria said. They were back at their room now. "You might have to beat him off with a stick." Gloria rolled her eyes. "On the other hand, it might be more interesting if you didn't."

"When I go out with a guy," Lorna explained, "I don't do anything to encourage that kind of behavior. A date buys a man female companionship, engaging conversation, and, hopefully, fun and laughter—nothing more."

"How do you manage to keep them at arm's length?"

"It's all in the eyes and your demeanor. I never flirt."

"Never? That's half the fun of being a girl," Gloria said.

"When I'm in the car with a man," she replied, ignoring Gloria's remark, "I sit next to the passenger door, not in the middle. I keep it lighthearted and avoid serious talk that might lead to something physical."

"But you've been dating since . . . ***kindergarten***," Gloria emphasized. "Haven't any of them tried to get fresh with you?"

"Ralph Malekovic!"

"Who?"

"Ralph Malekovic. He was the star shortstop on our base-ball team. Thought I owed him something because of what it cost to take me to the senior prom."

"What happened?"

"He leaned over and gave me a good night kiss, only he didn't want to stop there."

Gloria nodded in anticipation, eyes glowing with excitement. "Yes, go on."

"He had his arms on my shoulders and he casually slid one to the front of my dress."

"Did you slap his face?"

"Thought about it, but I tried something different."

"Such as . . . "

"I said if he didn't stop, I was going to tell his mother. She was my Sunday School teacher."

"What did he say, or do?"

"Nothing, he just pulled back with a look of total dejection. It was as if I had punctured an inner tube—he just wilted."

Gloria began shrieking with laughter.

"What's so funny?"

"I can just picture the look on that guy's face. He probably thought all night about how he was going to put a move on you and then you put him down for trying to cop a feel. I've gone out with athletes. They think that dating a girl is a sports metaphor. Getting her to say ***yes*** is making it to first base. You know how guys are, they want to tell their buddies they did more than just hit a single."

"They want to brag about scoring," Lorna interposed.

"Right! They accidentally-on-purpose let their hands wander into forbidden territory."

"Like on your knee," Lorna added. "And if a girl doesn't resist too emphatically, it's like stealing second base."

"So when you announced you were planning to tell Ralph's mother, he was thrown out at third base. Poor Ralphie, I bet he was dragging his chin all the way home. Probably felt as if he had just lost the World Series, or like a poor little puppy that had been scolded for wetting on a throw rug."

"Yes." Lorna heaved a long sigh. "I almost felt sorry for him."

"What is it with men, anyway?" Gloria, who had been sitting on the edge of her bed, went to a prone position and propped her head with a bent elbow.

Lorna and Ralph at the Prom

"What do you mean?"

"I think maybe God made a mistake by giving them raging libidos. I know that's supposed to perpetuate the human race, but come on, why is everything with men sex, sex, sex? If you believe the Kinsey Report, men think about ***it*** every fifteen minutes.

"I can believe it," Lorna said. "No wonder they can't diagram a sentence at the blackboard in school. The animal kingdom is the same way you know. We learned in biology class that female black widow spiders often kill and eat the male after mating."

"Yeah," Gloria took a deep breath and exhaled, "but that doesn't deter the horny little critters does it?"

"It sure doesn't. And did you know the male deerfly can attain speeds of eighty miles an hour?"

"Let me guess," Gloria said. "He attains that speed when he's chasing the female of the species."

"Right."

"Unbelievable."

"What ever happened to good old fashioned romance—hugging, cuddling, emotional intimacy, tenderness, sharing innermost secrets? Why can't men learn to be best friends, the big oafs?" Lorna groused.

Gloria continued the gripe session. "Everything we have been taught in church tells us that sex is supposed to take place within the confines of marriage. Anything else is sinful. Men seem to have the same sex drive as women . . . only it's cubed."

Lorna nodded. "And there are plenty of Biblical examples to buttress the notion. Take Samson and Delilah."

"Don't forget David and Bathsheba."

"Salome wiggled her hips for Herod, and it cost John the Baptist his head," Lorna noted. "Have you noticed ministers never preach sermons from the Song of Solomon?"

"Yes, I wonder why?"

"He was definitely oversexed—must have had hundreds of wives and concubines." Lorna brushed a stray hair off her shoulder.

"Yeah, back in the good old biblical times women were treated like cattle," Gloria moaned.

"I once read the book in its entirety and it's lyrically erotic poetry. It contains vivid imagery about different parts of a woman's body. I hear it almost didn't get included in the Bible because it was thought unsuitable for sacred literature."

"Those out-of-control hormones young men have are why a lot of churches don't allow mixed swimming at youth activities," Lorna said.

Gloria adjusted her glasses. "Probably the reason physical education is segregated according to sex. I heard it's why schools stress physical education and sports for boys. All of that hyperactivity is supposed to keep their sex drive sublimated."

"That and cold showers," Lorna added.

They both fell backward on their beds, giggling uproariously like schoolgirls.

CHAPTER 14

East St. Louisan Florence (Candy) Tockstein became a St. Louis model and then went to Hollywood in the mid 1940s and was in four films, including *Knock On Any Door* with Humphrey Bogart and John Derek. She married singer Mel Torme, divorced him, then married Hal March, the game show host.

Lorna's big date with Lance was the next evening. Popular with all the girls in the office, he had an animal magnetism. She was flattered that he had focused his attention on her. The fact that he had a dubious reputation didn't trouble her in the least. She had handled his kind before. The notion that she might have been one of those moths attracted to a dangerous flame never crossed her mind. Nor the possibility that she was walking on the edge of a precipice.

Candy Tockstein

Lorna's new dress was tastefully sexy. It scooped just low enough at the bodice that its edge, slightly swelled by her breasts, gently rose and fell with each breath. Gloria helped her get ready, making sure everything was in place. Lorna curled her eyelashes and applied the Maybelline.

"Wow! So much for the virginal look. Those are the most curvaceous, flirtatious lashes I've ever seen," Gloria complimented. "You look dangerous. Might have to get a special permit to walk around the streets dolled-up that way."

"Are these shoes okay with this outfit?"

"Don't worry. Lance won't be looking at your feet," she chided.

"I hope I don't commit some stupid ***faux pas*** and have him think I'm a country hayseed."

"Just be yourself, you'll do fine," Gloria reassured.

The evening was everything Lorna had hoped it would be. Lance arrived fashionably late, handsomely dressed in sartorial splendor: black slacks, a boutonniered maroon dinner-jacket and black bow tie. He swept her off her feet with a long white box tied with a red satin ribbon. The dozen ruby-red, velvet-petaled, long-stemmed roses inside nearly took her breath away. He then presented her with a gardenia that she fastened in her hair.

Singer Dick Haymes

"I'll put these in a vase until you get back," Laurie offered, from the vantage of her desk.

Lance moved with confidence and maturity, escorting her to a shiny Lincoln Cosmopolitan. He was cool and sophisticated, a man of flawless taste.

"You look absolutely stunning in that dress," he said. His words were soft and low as if Dick Haymes were speaking the smooth lyrics of a Johnny Mercer love song.

"Thank you for the compliment." She gazed admiringly on his perfectly handsome face, marred only by a small chicken-pox scar above his right eye. "You're quite dashing yourself."

Lance failed to acknowledge her compliment. He knew with smug satisfaction his dress was irreproachable. He fully subscribed to the old proverb about clothes making the man. His wardrobe was part of his insignia, his heraldry—his way of fashioning a bold statement.

They drove to the swank Chase Park Plaza in St. Louis, on the edge of Forest Park, where a uniformed valet took the wheel.

"Take good care of this," Lance said, handing him a two-dollar bill, "and you'll get another one when we come back."

Lorna took one look at the posh setting, pursed her lips, and blew a silent whistle in admiration of its elegance. The exclusive Starlight Room at the top was resplendent with Louis XIV armchairs, deep-pile carpeting and velvet drapes. It was a playground for the area's aristocracy. Elegant doors with fancy moldings and an exquisite crystal and brass chandelier accentuated the massive room. Gold leaf on the ceiling and baroque flourishes on the French Renaissance walls lent an air of refinement. The room was an absolute gem. They were met by an impeccably dressed maître d' in a crisp tuxedo. He pulled two leather-bound menus from under the podium. Lance politely slipped him a ten-dollar bill.

"This way, please."

They followed him to a private table in the corner of the room. Thick burgundy carpet muffled their footfalls. He placed the menus on the table—in a refined just-so manner—then graciously pulled a chair back for Lorna. She sat down and the maître d' pushed her to the table.

"Thank you."

"The waiter will be with you shortly." He made a polite bow and retreated.

The band finished playing "All The Things You Are" and moved on to "These Foolish Things."

The highbacked chairs were covered with a rich, textured silk brocade fabric. White on white damask cloth draped the table. Sterling silverware glimmered in the candlelight next to hand-painted china from Luxembourg. Fine linen and stemware graced each place setting.

Lorna gracefully removed her three-quarter length gloves. The waiter politely handed her the ***carte du jour*** which listed a tempting variety of entrées. He recited the "specials" of the evening in the manner of a Lord Byron poem. She indicated her preferences to Lance and then he, with a tinge of ***noblesse oblige***, ordered for both of them. Hers was beef Wellington, potatoes ***au gratin*** and broccoli with boulè cream sauce. The sumptuous meal started with tasty ***hors d' oeuvres.*** The food was rolled out on a fancy cart and the dishes were kept warm with sterling silver covers.

"This is my favorite place to dine," Lance said. He paused as the waiter adroitly set the appetizer in front of them. It consisted of several succulent Belgian truffles stuffed with spinach and a wonderfully delicious sauce Lorna couldn't come close to pronouncing.

"How do you like the atmosphere?" he asked.

"It's magical. I'm having a wonderful time." She felt like Cinderella.

Park Plaza and Hotel Chase overlooking beautiful Forest Park in St. Louis

Lance was one of those men who intuitively knew setting was a prelude to seduction. He understood that surrounding a beautiful woman with the trappings of romance accomplished

wonders.

As expected, the entreé pleased her taste buds. For dessert, the waiter brought out a mouth-watering dish of cherries jubilee, bright with fire, before he deftly smothered the flames with a cover. Then a dollop of whipped cream was added.

"This must be ambrosia—food of the gods." Lorna dabbed the corner of her mouth with a napkin.

"I knew you would like it," Lance confidently replied.

He taught her how to swirl the wine in a goblet, how to inhale and savor its rich bouquet. A sip of vintage chardonnay from a goblet of Italian crystal teased her delicate taste buds. It was demonically seductive.

"And this must be their sweet nectar," she added.

"See the couple over there?" he said.

"Yes."

"That's Raymond Tucker and his wife. Politically savvy people are predicting he'll be the next mayor of St. Louis. And that gentleman near the corner in the gray pinstripe suit . . ."

"I see him."

"John Roedel, the television news broadcaster."

Lorna turned her head and searched the other side of the room. "Look, there's that Goldman fellow we saw at the Kefauver hearings."

"That's right. He's with his beautiful wife. He and another fellow named Kaplar are investors in this hotel. Attorney Morris Goldman married his daughter."

Russ David and his orchestra had been playing soft dinner music throughout the evening. After the tables were cleared and another round of wine was poured in the flutes, the band segued to dance music, and couples began to glide across the wooden parquet floor. The 18th century crystal chandelier bounced a panoply of light patterns off the walls.

Russ David (courtesy of Lonnie Tettaton)

When the after-dinner music started, Lance whisked her onto the gleaming hardwood. He was an accomplished dancer, as equally comfortable with a fox trot as with a slow dance. They glided cheek-to-cheek to a bevy of **Cole Porter** tunes. She gracefully followed his lead, and they nimbly circled the dance floor in romantic ecstasy.

"Enjoying yourself?" he asked, almost rhetorically, as he boldly dipped her toward the floor.

Songs by Cole Porter

Anything Goes, Begin The Beguine, Easy To Love, From This Moment On, I Concentrate On You, I Get A Kick Out Of You, I Love Paris, Just One Of Those Things, Let's Fall In Love, My Heart Belongs to Daddy, Night And Day, True Love

"Absolutely!"

Other female eyes in the room followed them with envy. Lorna berated herself for acting as she knew dozens of Lance's other dates had done before. And she was furious for allowing herself to become infatuated with him, despite his rakish reputation. But it was a heady evening and she liked being the center of attention. She melted into his arms becoming oblivious to her surroundings and completely swept up in the moment. All in all, it was the most dazzling, romantic night in her life.

"Did you enjoy yourself tonight?" he asked, as they reached the portico of the Beulah Club.

"The music and dancing were divine; the food was sinfully delicious and I savored every morsel."

She suspected Lance was over sixty dollars poorer by the end of their date. Chicken feed for him.

"And the atmosphere?"

"Positively decadent. I couldn't get over how elegantly everyone was dressed. The waiters . . . they, they were so crisp and mannered. Everything was just heavenly," she gushed.

Lorna had one more surprise that evening. Before Lance left, he impulsively took her into his arms and embraced her with a passionate kiss that left her gasping for air. The blood in her veins pushed and shoved her emotions the way rising sap forces open the buds of a tree in spring.

She breathlessly said good-bye, then rushed to her room, closed the door and leaned back against the doorjamb. She closed her eyes as if it were the only thing that would stop her universe from spinning in disordered vertigo.

"Are you feeling okay?" Gloria was slathering cold cream all over her face.

"I'm fine."

"My, my, that date must have really been something. You look as if you're about to have a heart attack."

"No, I'll be all right." Her pulse pounded in her temple.

"Did you actually let him kiss you?"

"Yes, and it was wonderful."

"You seem pretty keen on him. You didn't let him go exploring, did you?"

"Of course not. It was just a plain, simple kiss."

"Judging from the way you look, it must have been passionnate. Phew. I can hear your motor roaring all the way over here."

Lorna plunked herself on the edge of her bed, twisted, and then fell back on her pillow. She had difficulty comprehending the rapturous feeling inside her. The first stirrings of womanhood. It was a new sensation. Her skin was moist with perspiration. Exhausted. Spent. She felt as if she had been washed ashore, a survivor from a capsized ship on a storm-tossed sea.

* * *

True to her word, Missola added to Brad's knowledge of the alleged dusky descendants of Ham. She regularly scribbled little tidbits of information at the bottom of his daily calendar. His favorite was about a colorful cowboy back in the days of the old West. According to legend, when Deadwood Dick went to a bar, he always ordered two drinks—one for him, and the other for his horse. Through Brad's various interactions with Missola, he began to wonder if the insidious institution of Jim Crow was undermining and compromising the ideals of our great republic.

But the thing that piqued his curiosity the most, the singular aspect of the city's history haunting the void of his memory, was the race riot during World War I. That one ugly event connected the present with the past because it spun a taut thread that ran from 1917 to 1951.

The tectonic plates of America's race relations converged in the city of East St. Louis. In July of 1917 labor problems caused them to shift, and the ensuing friction resulted in a quake of unthinkable magnitude. The essential facts of the city's darkest chapter Brad knew. Organized labor was in its infancy, struggling for recognition, wages and benefits for its members who were often exploited by the capitalist class. There had been a bitter strike at the Aluminum Ore plant, one of the city's largest employers. The town's vigorous wartime economy had already stimulated a substantial Negro exodus from the South. As their numbers swelled, they began to organize politically to challenge discriminatory practices and the notion of white supremacy. Like other ethnic groups in the city, they discovered patronage politics was a major industry in East St. Louis, and they sought to be participants in the game of exchanging votes for money and power. Management replaced the striking workers with dark-skinned migrants who had been imported from Mississippi by labor agents dispatched by local industrialists. Naturally, the defeated white unionists were bitter. The place became a potential powder keg.

Shaded = riot area (courtesy Meridian Books)

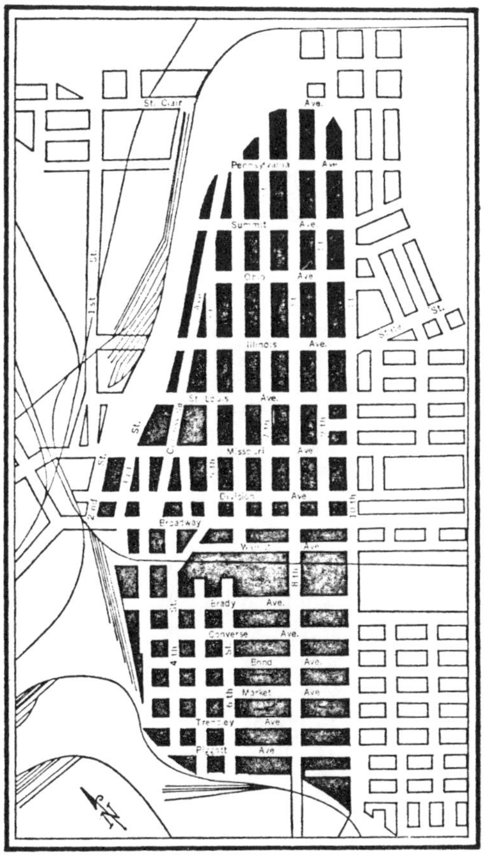

The highly charged atmosphere worsened when the newspaper alleged that newly arriving Negroes were responsible for a local crime wave. Whites began to arm themselves and Negroes responded in kind by securing weapons of their own from friends and relatives in St. Louis. On May 26, there was a clash of about fifty Negroes and whites at 10th & Piggott. Although the outnumbered Negroes were routed, they had fired more than a dozen shots. Rumors quickly spread that "gun-totin" Negroes were planning an armed insurrection to massacre whites on the 4th of July. On the night of July 1, an auto with white occupants drove along 17th and Market and fired several shots into Negro homes. When the residents returned the fire, police received a report that the coloreds were on the rampage.

The fuse was lit when a squad car was dispatched to 10th and Bond where a large con-tingent of Negroes, armed with guns, knives, and clubs, had gathered. The crowd riddled it with bullets, killing two officers. White laborers, on their way to work the next morning, saw the blood-stained car, punctured with holes, in a parking lot near the police station. To them this was proof-positive of an impending race riot, and they angrily talked about getting revenge. The next morning, a protest meeting was held at the Labor Temple on Collinsville Avenue. As the meeting disbanded, the riled-up mob spilled out onto the streets and attacked every black person they could find with little regard to age or sex. Maiming and killing Negroes became blood sport, and the streets ran crimson with the life force of those whose only "sin" was the color of their skin.

The painful dissonance between the two races was costly. The two-day riot caused millions of dollars in damages and the lives of nine whites and thirty-nine Negroes. As of 1951 it remained the largest riot, in terms of lives lost, in U.S. history.

"Missola, I would like to talk about something that might be somewhat painful for you."

"What that be, Mistuh Logan?"

"I know about the race riot from the white perspective, but I'm sure some of the facts and details have been glossed over or distorted by the power structure which wrote the reports. Would you be willing to tell me about that awful event from the viewpoint of your people?"

"Yessuh, you is right 'bout that. It be plenty painful to talk 'bout." She looked at him with melancholy eyes. The pathos of a people's tragic history.

"I really would like to hear what you have to say. I think it would help me better understand Negro resentment."

"It mostly be 'bout sadness, not anger, Mistuh Logan. Sadness that come from knowin' the white man done bring us to this country in chains. Ain't nothin' worse than bein' a slave. Does ya understand that?"

"Not really, but thanks to you, I'm beginning to."

"A slave got no rights, no freedom—jus work all day long an' mind the Massa. Mistuh Lincoln freed the slaves, but lotsa nothin' did change. Jim Crow come 'long an' make sure the white boss gonna stay the Massa. Sharecroppin'! My, oh my—justa 'nother word for slav'ry."

She spoke with that unique rhythm of black oral history. "Then 'long come the big war, an kinfolk tell us, 'Come to East St. Louis.' Work aplenty. It be good place to make a livin'. The white boss man come down to Me'sippi an says he got Negra jobs at the ore plant, railroads, an' packin' houses."

"Did those who came find a better life in East St. Louis?" he asked.

"Yessuh an' nossuh. Has ya ever been to my part o' town in the South End?"

"No ma'am, I can't say I have."

"Places my people live in be like shacks. Not so much better than what we lived in as slaves. Some got dirt floors an' toilets outside. An' this be right now, not years ago. Ya' knows for sure, it hadda be worse back in the old days."

"That's hard to comprehend. The country with the world's highest standard of living, yet many of its citizens live in houses without wood floors," he said.

"They thought mebbe the white man in North don't hate the cullud man like the South'rn crackers. But it a-l-l the same. Negroes belong in the jungle. Can see it in their eyes. Like they thinks cullud folk are a curse; that dark skin be some kind o' di-sease. Somethin' like leprosy.

"Were the whites lying about the jobs?"

"No, suh. Jobs were here an' the life was hard, but they be better than in the South 'cause the menfolk be paid ev'ry Friday. No more sharecropin'. But the black man, he be workin' right next to the white man, doin' same work, but the black man always get paid less. How ya think that make him feel?"

"I would imagine they thought it was grossly unfair. I guess I would feel the same way."

"All that talk 'bout freedom n' opp'tunity—for most all folk, 'cept the black man. Black man hafta ride in back o' the bus, stay outta white ter'tory, not 'lowed in white movie places, hafta go sep'rate schools an' churches. An' if'n the black man look at white woman pecul'ar, he be lynched. Black man learn not to look whites in the eyes, walk with eyes lookin' at the ground. An' we got no say what-so-ever in politik matters."

"When black man bring his fam'ly here befo' the riot, he find out he be takin' the place o' white man who be walkin' picket line. That make white man angry, so he starts lookin' for reason to blame all his troubles on the black folk." Missola's eyelids slowly closed and then fluttered as she shook her head.

"And, naturally, the whites blamed the Negroes for destroying the efforts of the union to gain concessions from the employers for higher wages and better working conditions."

"That be right."

"Go on, then what?"

"The peckerheads soon blame the black man for all that go wrong. Believe that if'n they treat us bad 'nough, mebbe we leave town an' go somewheres else. Bad time. Was season of pure meanness."

Rare night photo of riot flames in East St. Louis

"So the anger just sat there and festered, like a boil that needed to be lanced."

"Uh huh." She stopped and drew in a long breath, as if she were expending part of her very life force in telling the story.

"Night befo' the riot there wuz a car full o' white men. Drove thru the South End, firin' shots at homes. Then a big crowd come t'gether after the inc'dent, mostly make sure their homes not be hit in a'nuther a'tack. When the po-lice car come, the streets be dark. To cullud, it look like the same car that jus' fired the shots. Some people from the crowd start ta shootin', an' two po-lice men gets killed. Paper make it soun' like the men get killed plum dead in cold blood. Next day, the whites get to meet each other at the Hall of Labor to make say what they gonna' do 'bout what happen day 'fore to these po-lice men."

"I think it's safe to assume those who spoke whipped the crowd into a maddening frenzy by saying things like 'Let's kill the niggers,' " he added.

She nodded and spoke slower now, dredging each word from some unfathomable anguish within. "When that crowd went from the hall an' go out in the streets, they be mad as hornets—took it out on any an' all black folk they see. They block the path o' streetcars an' drag all the Negras off, hittin' 'em, beatin' 'em. White folk with guns start shootin' ev'ry black soul they saw. Them who did the killin' was part o' just a small group people, 'haps it only be twenty."

"Let me guess. They were strongly encouraged by the large crowds in the streets. And those whites who wanted or tried to interfere, were threatened by the mob. Sociologists call it mob psychology. People do things in groups they would never think of doing as individuals."

Once again, Missola just nodded. Her eyes were beginning to tear, her face suffused with pain. "I was bar'ly sixteen when it happen'd. In the e'rly af'noon the riotin' jus' be confined to the downtown part of East St. Louis, from Ill'nois Av'nue to Broadway. Then it move to the South End—my neighb'rhood."

"Oh, my. Were you or your family ever in danger?"

"Lucky to 'scape with our lives. Negra homes in that part get s'ronded an' set fire to. As inn'cent black folk run away from the burnin' homes, they be shot an' killed. My neighbor, Sam, was lynched coming home from work to check on his family."

"Was your house burned?"

"Uh-huh. We were the only house on the block with a basement. Me an' my fam'ly stay there b'low as long as we could. Was so much smoke in my lungs I thought I was gonna die. Then we ran out the back an' fled. Bullets was wizzin' past our heads."

"Were you hurt?"

Missola showed him an ugly patch of scar tissue on her left arm. "A burnin' timber fell on me. Hurt like blazes. An' some buckshot hit me in the back, but I kept runnin'."

Brad's face scrunched at the thought of that agony.

"My daddy dug it out with his pocket knife."

"Where did your family go after you escaped the mob?"

"To a thick clump o' bushes on the river bank. Was 'fraid to go back."

"How long were you there?"

" 'Bout a week. Hid durin' the day. Nearly starved 'cept my daddy snared a couple of rabbits. An' he also went out to a slough an' catched some fish with a sharp stick."

"Didn't the police or state militia do anything to stop the riot?" "The mayor had sent for militia the night before it started."

"Militia-man be just young 'ens—white kids too scared to do nothin'. They prob'ly save some lives, but they nevah di-rectly make the mob stop. Some police do same stuff as the people who riotin'."

"How bad did it get?"

"One Negra woman got breasts cut off an' pitched to hungry dogs. Then she got hit in the head with brickbat. Her blood 'n brains come out on the sidewalk. Oh, the crowd cheered an' hand-clapped when they saw it. They take bay'net gun way from one o' them young militia-man. Somebody snatch'd a poor little baby from his pleadin' an cryin' mom-ma's arms, tossed him in the air, an' that poor baby was stuck dead on the end of the bay'net.

Horace Adams, early black activist for Negro rights in East St. Louis

Then the crowd grab hold o' 'nother Negra man, tie a rope 'round his neck, an' drug 'em to one o' them tel'phone poles. They throw the other rope end over the cross-arm of the pole. 'Get hold an' pull for East St. Louis,' someone yell from the crowd. The body was just left there—hangin' for hours. The square block o' 8th 'n Broadway get burned to an ash heap. Then there be sev'ral Negras who go hide in the 'Casland Opery House. Cries o' 'Burn 'em out! Kill all the Negras!' could be heard. This made the rioters more bold an' they set fire to it an' burn it to the ground." Tears were running down Missola's cheeks.

"I apologize, Missola," he said, offering her his handkerchief, his heart going out to her. Her sorrow made him regret picking at the scab of East St. Louis history. "I wish I hadn't brought up the subject."

"No, Mistuh Logan. It better that ya know what really happen'd. I gonna be okay."

He was holding Missola in his arms now, gently stroking her hair, trying in his own awkward way to console her. When the room grew blurry, he knew he was crying. For the first time he realized what was merely a sordid event for most whites, was an insufferable tragedy branded on the very souls of the black folk.

"I didn't know humans could be so cruel," he said. "I'm amazed you can tell the story with such imagery and passion—almost as if someone in your family was killed."

Missola slumped her shoulders and closed her eyes, took a slow, deep breath, swelling her bony chest. Then she opened her sad eyes. They had the hollow look of a Dachau survivor.

"I did lose someone, Mistuh Logan." She struggled to finish, pouring out her demijohn of pain and sorrow. 'Member that woman who breasts be cut off by the mob an' git killed?"

"Yes."

"That poor woman . . . the one who beg for her life . . . she be my gran'mother!"

CHAPTER 15

East St. Louis mirrored the bright lights and levity of an earlier era. It was as if the Jazz Age of the 1920s had been preserved in a jar, unwaxed, and then served up to a population that chafed at dullness and wanted to let off steam after eight long hours of factory drudgery. It took a hundred and sixty-one taverns to quench the thirst of the toiling masses of this workaday city that labored hard and wanted to play hard.

April 20, 1951

Brad's firm was a diverse group, nearly mirroring the polyglot composition of the local community. Except for Negroes, of course. The parents and grandparents of his fellow workers had come to East St. Louis, fleeing the Old World's troubles with the belief that life could only get better. Once here, they banded together in ethnic enclaves and wrote back to their cousins and uncles telling them in glowing terms about the city's jobs, freedom, and opportunity. The place became a living history and geography lesson. Ethnicity with a capital E. French Protestant Huguenots came to avoid persecution by Catholic regimes. Hungarian supporters of Louis Kossuth fled after the failed revolution in 1848. The Irish came after Oliver Cromwell confiscated their lands and again due to the 1851 potato famine. Jim Fishbein's grandfather came to escape Russian pogroms. The Jewish community had its kosher butcher shops, bakeries, and synagogue. Armenians left to evade the oppression of the Turk majority in the World War I era. Many seemed to prosper in the dry cleaning business. The Pazderas, Hraskys, Forhetzes, and Symanskis came in large numbers every time invading armies crossed their country's borders.

The thing Brad enjoyed most at the office was the morning discussions and joke telling around the coffee pot before everyone became immersed in their work. The kibitzing built friendships and established ***esprit de corps***. Sometimes it was wry and witty, like an imagined dialogue with humorous zingers between Dorothy Parker and Robert Benchley from the irreverent Algonquin Round Table. Innocuous chatter about judges' rulings or topsy-turvy jury decisions was often the topic of conversation. The sometimes-stormy banter about political ideology such as the guilt or innocence of

Ethel and Julius Rosenberg, convicted spies executed for espionage

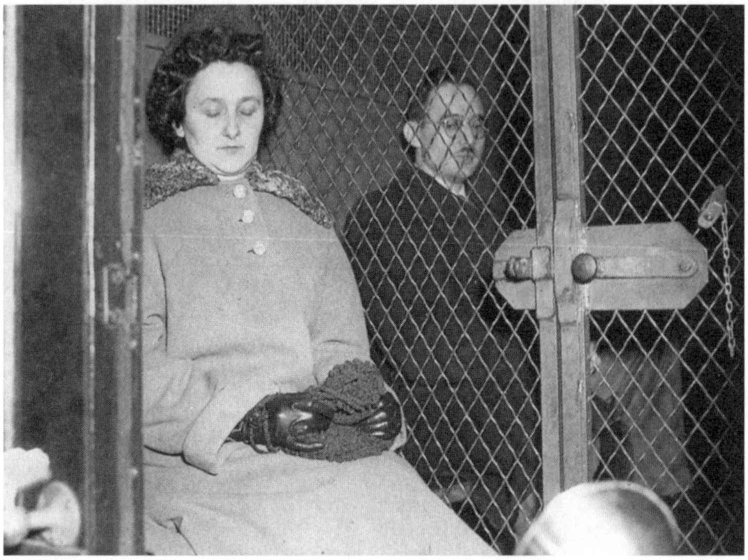

Judith Coplon or Alger Hiss frequently took center stage.

"The Rosenbergs were victims of a witch hunt," Fishbein staunchly ranted one morning.

Brad wrinkled his nose. "Not according to Judge Kaufman."

"The same Red Scare hysteria victimized Sacco and Vanzetti back in the '20s," Fishbein countered.

"If you read Herb Philbrick's ***I Led Three Lives***, you'll be convinced communist subversion is for real," Charlie Oliver groused. "Thanks to communist duplicity in this country, the Russians have the bomb." Charlie was tall and lanky - the Mutt in the Mutt and Jeff of the office. Harold Zeigler was the short half of the duo. Charlie was the most politically active person in the office. Four years earlier he bucked the political machine and ran as a gambling table-smashing independent Democrat for a spot on the city council. He never made it past the primaries.

The group hotly debated the wisdom of Truman's "Police Action" in Korea.

"We have no business sending young men to Korea," Harold Zeigler maintained. "I have a cousin who just got drafted. If anything happens to him, I pity his poor mother."

"Harold, the Communists have got to be stopped," Brad said. "First they took Eastern Europe, then China, and now they want South Korea."

"You're wrong, Brad," Zeigler blurted with mild reproach. He had been the youngest of four boys in his Catholic family—the runt of the litter—used to scrapping for everything. "I can see holding the line in Europe. The formation of NATO was necessary and prudent, but Asians don't have any democratic traditions. It's so far away . . . we don't belong there in an alien culture."

They discussed a wide range of other subjects: the Supreme Court's search ruling in the Rabinowitz case, the Yankees sweeping the Phillies in the World Series, the formation of NATO. Weighty issues: Ezra Pound winning a major poetry prize after making pro-fascist radio broadcasts, MacArthur's daring invasion at Inchon, blame for the communist takeover of China, the meaning of David Riesman's thesis in ***The Lonely Crowd.*** Even the more mundane rehashing of news stories, TV programs and sporting events was stimulating. They sometimes drifted into topics such as the bikini, the length of women's skirts, or an outspoken Eleanor Roosevelt.

"Wouldn't it be great if some television station started showing old movie classics like ***Casablanca***," Brad said.

Rita Hayworth

"It'll never happen," Fiebig responded. "Hollywood and television are at war with each other."

Occasionally, the dialog drifted to subjects of earth-shattering consequence: Who was the most beautiful and sexy—Marilyn Monroe, Lana Turner, Jane Russell or Rita Hayworth? The banter and discussions were political, economic and social snapshots of a nation at mid-century.

"Hey, Logan. Have you seen the latest in the paper?" Charlie Oliver asked one morning.

"No, I didn't get around to reading it yesterday."

"Remember Geronimo, the Indian Harry advised at the Kefauver inquiry?"

"Yes, Wayne Littlefeather, what about him?"

"He bit the dust—went to that big hunting ground up in the sky. They found his body, stuffed in the trunk of his Ford over in Eagle Park near Madison."

Littlefeather's 1951 Ford Crestliner $1,595

"Oh, my! That's a shame. He seemed like a decent fellow."

"Bullet in the back of the head and his front teeth knocked out," Charlie said.

"That's a mob hit, isn't it? A warning to others to keep their mouths shut?" Brad asked.

"Probably," Harry Fiebig said.

Charlie Oliver was chewing on a toothpick. "Do you think Walters' men did it?"

"I don't think so." Brad shook his head. "He wasn't a direct threat to Walters."

"Boy are you naïve, Brad," Marion Strohman chided. Strohman was an excellent artist and devoted much of his spare time doing pen and ink drawings which he used to decorate his office. He had the bushiest, most out-of-control eyebrows this side of **Groucho Marx**. But everyone liked him because there wasn't anything he wouldn't do to help a colleague.

Groucho Marx

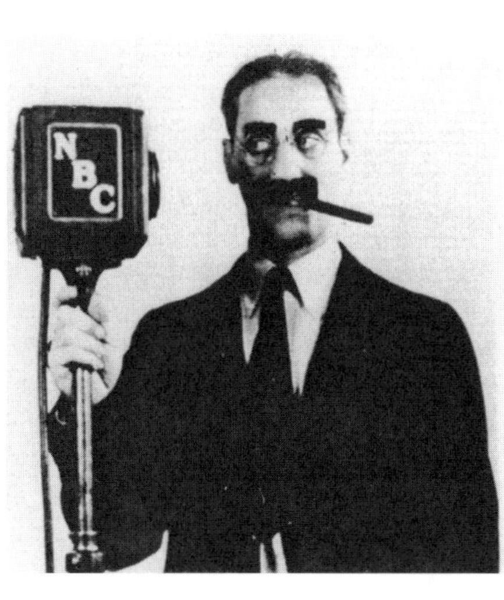

"Not really. I honestly don't think Knucky did it," Brad said.

The shaggy eyebrows went south in disagreement.

"Bad news always comes in double doses," Charlie said. "Has Jim Fishbein told you the latest?"

"About what," Brad asked.

"Louie Sizemore, that weasel-faced slug you two are defending. Got himself stabbed last night."

"Stabbed! How did it happen?" he asked.

"There was a fight among inmates at the county jail caféteria. It seems he walked into an unfriendly four-inch shiv fashioned from a spoon."

"Is he dead?"

"No, but he was stabbed in the back of the head and he's in a coma," Charlie added. "The fight was probably staged. The crowd was so big the guards never saw who did it."

Brad shook his head in disbelief. "What a stunning turn of events. First Wayne and now Louie."

Later in the day, Brad was in the middle of a staff meeting when Margie Noones, a secretary whom he shared with Charlie Oliver and Harold Fiebig, discreetly came into the room and handed him a note.

"It's from Walter Boyne," she whispered. "He wants you to call him as soon as possible."

He silently nodded to let her know that he would call. It was one of those weekly meetings Ernst held to discuss the status of each case or litigation on which they were working. Charlie was handling a dispute between the Terminal Railroad and the Chicago, Burlington & Quincy line about mechanical charges and switching fees. The matter had been complicated by an accident on the TRRA tracks, and the TRRA was pointing the blame at CB&Q that, ironically, was one of its proprietary companies. Charlie was representing the plaintiff, CB&Q, which was contesting the excessive fees and denying responsibility.

"Tom, what are you and Brad going to do now that Sizemore is in limbo?"

"Sizemore was going to plead not guilty," Fishbein replied. "When I explained that the police didn't have a ***prima facie*** case against him, he decided to take his chances with a jury trial. I guess none of that matters now."

"Have the police been able to substantiate his claim that some big politicos were behind the hit?"

"I'm afraid the authorities are dragging their feet on this one. I think they're afraid it might hit too close to home and they don't want to bite the hand that feeds them," Brad volunteered. "I talked to Torricelli's widow and she gave me a couple of ideas."

Ernst took off his glasses, massaged the bridge of his nose, and then sagely looked at Jim and Brad. "Maybe we should drop the whole thing. We're talking about some big names here; you had better be very careful. We don't want to get our tit in the wringer with this one. Besides, I'm not comfortable with you doing investigative work that more properly should be done by the police."

"The doctors don't think Sizemore will come out of his coma," Fishbein said.

"Marion, what's the latest with you?" Ernst asked.

Strohman informed everyone about a new case he was handling for William Shive of Sterling Steel Casting Company. Shive's firm had made some castings as a subcontractor for a Chicago company that was doing work for the U.S. Navy.

"The Navy metallurgists rejected the pieces," Marion explained, "claiming the metal failed to pass the Brinnel hardness test."

"What is going to be your defense in the case?" Brad inquired.

Someone cracked a joke that he missed.

"We think the Chicago company improperly reheated the pieces to make them easier to machine. Their annealing process changed the molecular structure, causing the metal to lose its original tensile strength."

Finally, Charlie Oliver brought them up to date on the progress of a contract dispute between the downtown merchants and Retail Clerks local No. 100. The contract called for a ninety-day period in which new employees were not required to join the union. It seemed the de facto head of the group, Ester Rasch, was being overly aggressive, signing the workers up early and collecting dues from them.

When they finished, Brad went to his office and called Walter Boyne. They had known each other since grade school. Walter had this amazing ability to gross out the girls by turning his eyelids inside out, giving him the appearance of a zombie. They were basketball teammates in one of Pick Dehner's physical education classes in high school. Walter was a year ahead of him in school, but they hit it off well and became best friends.

Walter joined the military almost immediately after graduation. The world was his oyster, and he figured an Air Force career as a pilot was the fastest, cheapest way to explore that world which lay beyond the finite boundaries of East St. Louis. Brad recognized the ADams 3-9647 number on the slip of paper as the main number of Scott Air Field.

"Hello, Walter, this is Brad. Good to talk to you again; it's been at least three years."

"Hi, Brad. It's good to hear your voice too. I'd like to rehash the good ol' Civil Air Patrol days with you, but I'm calling because I need a favor. Can't talk about it over the phone. Is there any chance you could drive out here and meet me? This is a very important matter."

"Sure thing." He could sense the urgency in his friend's voice. "I have a couple of depositions to take, and a letter that needs to be dictated to my secretary, but I could get there at, say . . . three this afternoon. Is that soon enough?"

"Fine. I'll meet you at the guard gate, and we'll go to my apartment to talk. I'm sorry to spring this on you, but it really is important. That's all I can say for now; you know the military is meticulous about secrecy."

"Yeah, I know. 'Loose lips sink ships.' What do you think, is that about a forty minute drive?"

"Yes, forty or forty-five minutes, that should do it," he said.

"See you at fifteen hundred hours. 'Bye."

Brad finished his work then headed out of town along Route 50 toward Scott Air Base. After passing the drive-in theater and then the State Police Headquarters on Highway 161, he continued up the bluff toward Route 159. Brad drank in the ethereal beauty of a roadway bordered with emerging Queen Anne's lace, blue chicory and day lilies. This part of Highway 50 was known as Lincoln Trail. The road worked its way east, past Fairview Heights and O'Fallon. He headed south on Route 158 through terrain that was now distinctly rural. Red barns and silos nuzzled the road. A couple of Shooting Star jets streaked overhead, apparently on their way back to the base. As he rounded a large graceful curve, the military complex loomed before him.

East St. Louis Drive-in at Routes 50 and 157

Walter, dressed in a crisp blue uniform, met him at the gate. He hadn't changed much, still slim and trim. Brad judged him to be roughly five-ten and about one hundred and seventy-five pounds. He was wearing captain's bars.

"Say, you're moving up in the world, you old dog. At this rate, you'll be head of the Air Force one of these days."

"I'm doing okay, and you're not looking bad for someone stuck in an office all day long. All you need is a little more sunshine on that lily-white skin of yours."

"Either that, or a good vacation in Florida," Brad kidded.

He followed Walter with his car past the BX and several Quonset huts. Then they parked in front of his base apartment and went inside.

"Can I offer you a stiff drink?"

"No thanks. A soda will be fine."

"Pepsi or orange Nehi?"

"I'll have a Nehi."

"I need a big favor," Walter said, as he made himself a highball.

"Can't say yes until I know what it is."

"I need you to chaperone a couple of foreign government officials, take them around East St. Louis—show them a good time. It has to be a civilian, someone not connected to the Air Force, someone I can totally trust."

"When?"

"This Saturday afternoon and evening. These guys have been here at the base, cooped up in a room all week. They insist on a little R & R, and I can't say I blame them."

"I had some plans for Saturday, but they are nothing that can't be postponed until next week. I'll be glad to do it if it will help you out."

"Thanks a million. They, uh, they'll need girls."

"I'm not fixing them up with prostitutes," Brad said emphatically.

"That's not necessary. Just get them a couple of dames who want to have a little fun, and won't mind a couple of nice guys spending a wad of money on them. I figure an afternoon at the race track, a meal at a decent restaurant, and maybe bowling afterwards."

"What about dancing?"

"These guys don't know how to dance. By the way, you do know how to find a couple of dames?"

"No, but I have a friend who, I'm sure, can come up with somebody."

"There's one more thing."

"Uh, oh, knowing you—I should have known there was a catch. What is it?"

"This is a top secret mission."

"***Top secret?***"

"You are not to tell anyone these guys are from the base. If the subject comes up or you run into some friends, we need a cover story. I'm not kidding. This really is a matter of national security."

Walter Boyne

"That's not a problem. Mum's the word. I can just say that, uh . . . Stefan and, uh . . . Viktor are in town, checking out a business deal on which I am advising them."

"Good! That's very good; I like it. Another problem. These guys speak limited English. You need to say they are from Austria or Czechoslovakia."

"Yes—Czechoslovakia, but they escaped to West Germany before the Iron Curtain fell."

Walter's eyes shone with a happy glint at the impromptu scenario they had constructed.

"I'm not sure I'm comfortable with all this cloak and dagger stuff. Is there something you're not telling me?"

"Yes, but if I did then I would have to kill you."

"Walter, you're downright creepy sometimes. Do you want me to pick them up here around noon on Saturday?"

"Twelve hundred hours. That will be fine."

Brad rolled his eyes as Walter playfully gave him a military hand salute.

* * *

Brad wouldn't find out the astounding truth behind Walter's secrecy until nearly forty years later. Only after the fall of the Soviet empire was the information declassified. Even now, the real names of Stefan and Viktor remain top secret for fear the information could get them killed. The incredible true story of the Alpha Project went something like this:

In the spring of 1951 the country was smack dab in the middle of the Korean Conflict, and Cold War tensions between America and the Soviet Union were running high. Russian-built MIGs and YAKs were challenging U.S. superiority in the air, established by our F-86 Saber jets.

The U.S. embassy in Yugoslavia was stunned when a couple of diplomats, sent by Yugoslavian President, Marshal Tito, offered to allow U.S. intelligence to secretly take a Soviet YAK 23 to the states for inspection and flight testing. The four-year-old plane was in a wooden crate, part of a Romanian railroad shipment that had been on its way to Albania via Yugoslavia. In return, Tito received a promise from the U.S. government to help him secure low-interest rate loans from a group of British financiers to jump-start his sagging economy.

Military intelligence originally planned to assemble, test and disassemble the plane at Wright-Patterson base in Dayton, Ohio. But F-86 pilots were stationed there, and it was feared they would recognize the plane, compromising the secrecy of the project. If news of this highly classified mission got out, it would cause an international incident. The CIA station chief's plan was to fly the plane to the U. S. in a C-124 Globemaster, accompanied by a diplomat and an aeronautical engineer from Yugoslavia.

Scott Air Base, located about twenty-five miles from East St. Louis, was chosen as the new site for what came to be known as Project Alpha. It was one of the oldest Air Force installations in the country, opening in the year 1917. During the prohibition era the government used dirigibles from the base to detect illegal stills and bootleg operations. It was now a communications school. The military decided that several days of closed hangar inspection, plus three days of aerial testing, with the plane's foreign markings removed and replaced by standard American emblems, would draw less attention at Scott Field.

The Globemaster landed in the early darkness at 0200 hours at Scott Air Base on March 21, 1951. The crate was taken to hangar number two and kept under twenty-four-hour security. Only the base commander, Colonel George Pardy, was informed about the clandestine mission. Other personnel were kept in the dark.

As each part was removed from the crate and carefully reassembled, photographs were taken so the plane could be repacked exactly the way it had been received. Designed and built by the Alexander Yakovlev Company, the Soviet plane yielded its secrets, one by one, to air tech intelligence. It

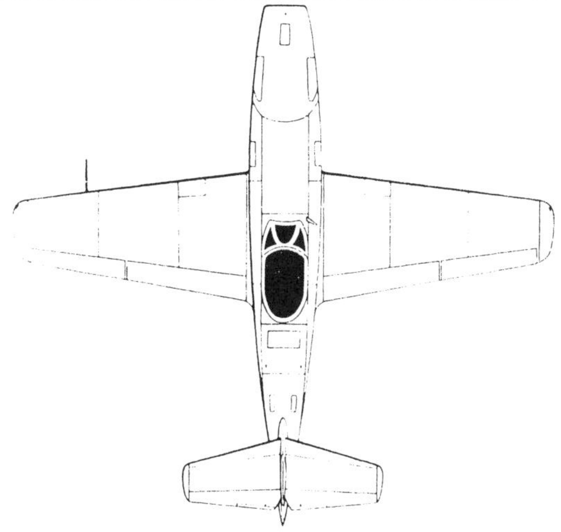

weighed six thousand, six hundred pounds, five hundred pounds lighter than the more famous MIG 15. The cockpit was small and cramped, but it was easy to fly, making it a favorite among eastern European pilots. It was equipped with two nose-mounted 23 milimeter guns. Engineers discovered the R-D 500 engine had a faulty fuel pump. It was feared this would interfere with flight-testing. Then a specialist remembered the engine had been copied from a British Rolls Royce, one of fifty turbo jets that had been sold to the Soviets in 1947. This was just before it became apparent that their erstwhile ally was now the enemy. Fortunately, it was compatible with a fuel pump from a Rolls Royce engine on hand for comparison. A Russian interpreter was used to translate markings imprinted on various parts of the plane.

Three days after the plane's arrival, it was ready to be flight-tested. Everything would be filmed, of course. Pilot Walter Boyne would be the one to put the aircraft through its paces. He and Chuck Yeager had performed similar tests just a month before on a MIG 15 in Okinawa. It had been delivered to one of our air bases by a North Korean pilot who chose economic security over ideology and had collected the $100,000 reward. The tempting offer had been made known to the communists through Operation Moola, during which a million leaflets were dropped north of the 38th parallel.

Chuck Yeager (L) and other flight Premiers beside the rocket plane X-1

Another problem cropped up at the last minute. It was feared the YAK's test flight would have to be canceled because the threadbare tires on the landing gear were worn to the point of making them dangerous. Fortunately, a specialist determined that Goodyear's tire for the F-94 was almost an exact replica. There would be three test flights, done in the early daylight hours when they would attract less attention. Capt. Boyne taxied down the main runway. The YAK 23 had great speed, accelerating quickly then taking off in a blurred thunderous roar.

Boyne sent mid-flight analysis reports by sending signals to a radio truck parked near the runway, manned by Lt. Frank Cumberland. He reported a ceiling limitation of 48,000 feet. Pilot side visibility was limited by placement of the cockpit almost directly over the wings. The YAK, with an old-fashioned straight wing, could not match the air speed of the MIG 15 with its swept wing design. Nevertheless, its top speed was .8 Mach, roughly 574 miles per hour, slightly less than the speed of sound at sea level. The plane had no speed brakes, and Boyne reported the aileron "buzz" to be severe at speeds faster than 500 miles per hour.

While the aging YAK 23 was no match for the newer MIG 15 or the F-86 Saber, it was a workhorse and could be a formidable foe. There were large numbers of these planes in Eastern bloc countries, and if the Cold War deteriorated into a shooting match in Europe, this newly acquired information could prove to be invaluable.

After a week of photographing, testing and analyzing, the plane was carefully taken apart and placed back in its crate. The Globemaster flew back to Europe, and it was surreptitiously returned to Yugoslavia. The plane was then sent on its way to Albania ***without the Russians ever knowing it had been "borrowed" by Tito.***

* * *

The first thing Brad did after talking to Walter was to call Lorna.

"Hello, this is the East St. Louis ***Journal***," Barb Edelblute answered. "May I help you?"

"Yes, this is Brad Logan, may I please speak to Lorna Sanders?"

"I think you're in luck. She just came in from an assignment. One moment please."

Placed on hold.

After about thirty seconds, Lorna picked up the phone. "Hello, Brad, is that you?"

"Yes. How would you like to go out on a triple date?"

"Depends. With whom would I be going?"

"Very funny. With me, of course. I have a couple of European businessmen who are in town for the weekend, and I wanted to show them a good time this coming Saturday. I thought maybe we could go to the Fairmount race track, bowl a couple of games, and then eat a late dinner at a nice restaurant."

"I have a date with Lance Sunday evening, but I am free on Saturday. Who are their dates, anybody I know?"

"Well, there's the rub."

"What do you mean?"

"I don't have dates for them yet."

"Oh, I see. You, in your infinite wisdom, were hoping I might be running an escort service on the side."

"No, no, it's nothing like that. This is strictly on the up and up. These are merely a couple of lonely men looking for some female company and entertainment. The six of us will be together, so it should be harmless fun."

"How old are these men?"

"One is in his late twenties and the other is about thirty or thirty-one."

"Let me ask around, and I'll see what I can do. I'll try to get back with you in a few hours. Will you be at the office?"

"Yes."

"I'll call you as soon as I know something."

"Fine. Thanks a lot."

Lorna called him back about two hours later and told him it was a "go." She had a couple of friends lined up, and they would be waiting in the lobby of the Beulah Club. He told her they would meet them between 12:45 and one o'clock on Saturday.

When the weekend arrived, Brad drove to the base and picked up his comrades-for-a-day. Their shoes were a little dated, but otherwise they looked fine. The one he had dubbed Stefan had on a pair of slate blue gabardine slacks and a cream windowpane plaid jacket. He guessed him to be about twenty-eight years old. Stefan was stockily built and had a slightly receding hairline, but he possessed a pleasant smile and winning personality. Viktor was older than what Brad had told Lorna, but he was handsomely dressed and positively reeked of Old-World charm. His friendly eyes foreshadowed a gregarious personality. He looked sophisticated in a dark brown tick-weave sports coat and tan pants. Both were sans neckties and had their spread-collars over the top of their jackets. From what Walter had told him he expected to hear indistinct sentences with jumbled consonants and blurred vowels. But their English was better than he had anticipated, and they were able to converse with little difficulty. Brad briefed them on their cover story.

On the way back to East St. Louis, all they wanted to talk about was business and industry. Brad quickly realized they might be pumping him for information that somehow might not be in the national interest to divulge. He remembered Senator Joe McCarthy's bombshell speech at Wheeling, West Virginia about a year earlier. He had waved a list of 205 subversives and maintained that communist agents and sympathizers had infiltrated some of the highest levels of government, stealthily working to undermine our way of life. He warned that people with whom the average citizen rubbed elbows—businessmen, co-workers, and neighbors, might really be Soviet agents or their operatives. When Brad read excerpts from his diatribe, he thought McCarthy had used too broad a brush to paint his picture of communist subversion. Brad felt McCarthy was probably right about our country being too blasé about communist perfidy, but his unsubstantiated accusations and Redbaiting tactics were reckless. McCarthy came to be perceived as a demagogue and a mudslinger. Nevertheless, Brad figured discretion was in order, and he could sense his companions' disappointment with his tight-lipped answers.

The three of them pushed through the double doors of the Beulah Club. Brad's charges were champing at the bit in nervous anticipation of meeting their dates. He was anxious and hopeful. Anxious about what the two women Lorna had lined up would be like and hopeful there would be a good personality fit with the three couples.

"These are my two friends, Laurie and Barbara," Lorna said, by way of introduction.

Laurie could see the look of surprise on Brad's face. "I switched days with the part time girl who's at the desk now," she explained, her lids heavy with vampish eye shadow. Laurie was wearing a bright yellow sundress. It almost equaled her personality. A matching ribbon in her hair added a nice touch.

"Nice to see you again, Laurie, and nice to meet you, Barb," he offered.

"I've talked to you on the phone," Barb informed him. "Glad to finally meet you in person."

"Let me introduce Viktor and Stefan," he said, gesturing toward each man. "They will be here only for a few more days, and then they'll be flying back to West Germany."

He was amazed at how nature takes its course. Barb, whose twenty-seventh birthday was two months away, wore a ruffled, scoop-necked, off-the-shoulder dress that gave her the flair of a Spanish señorita. She gravitated to Viktor who was closer to her age. He seemed enamored with her south-of-the-border motif, complete with voluminous skirt, woven leather huaraches on her feet and a rose accenting her hair. Hoop earrings completed the Latin motif. Laurie, with her peroxide blond hair in a French twist, sidled up to Stefan. You would have thought they were made for each other. He couldn't seem to get enough of this fascinating "Amerikan" girl who talked non-stop. The pitch and rhythm of her melodic voice was an obvious delight to his ear.

Brad complimented Lorna's cream-colored linen dress and she responded with a shy "Thank you." It dawned on him that it was the same color as Jay Gatsby's Rolls Royce.

"Let's get going," he said.

"Twenty three-skidoo," Laurie bubbled through her Cupid's bow red lips.

All six of them piled into Brad's car. Off they went to Fairmount for a day at the track. Johnny Ray, the nation's hottest new sex symbol, was belting out a tune through the radio speaker about a tortured soul who had been jilted by his lover. Brad could picture him, Sinatra's successor as the King of Swoon, crooning to a mob of hysterical bobby soxers.

"What impresses you the most about America?" Lorna asked the men in back.

Frankie

"Your te-le-vision programs," Viktor responded.

"The size of your gar-bage cans," Stefan added.

Lorna and Brad looked at each other and smiled.

"Who do you think will win the Cold War?" Brad asked, without directing the question to anyone specifically.

After a brief silence, Stefan volunteered an answer: "Svitzer-land."

"Why do you say that?" Lorna asked.

"The Sovyets und the Amerikans seem determined to blow each other up. Svitzer-land has big banks und is always neutral."

Laurie giggled and fluttered eyes that were coquettishly rimmed with dark lashes. "I just love Stefan's accent. Isn't it just adorable?"

Stefan tugged at the brim of his Panama hat in his lap and returned the compliment. "And you are very sweet, my little

Fräulein," he said in a buoyant accent.

Lorna and Brad were interested in finding out about European folkways and mores, but the two men dominated the conversation with talk about American culture. Brad was thankful everyone seemed to be thoroughly enjoying the venture. They pulled into the parking lot at Fairmount and headed for the grandstand.

"Back in 1922, during Prohibition, this land was merely a level field," Brad explained. "Charles Lindbergh was just getting into flying and ran around with another fellow who was wild and reckless. Flying was expensive, and one day they needed money to buy a new engine. According to old-timers, Lindbergh's buddy talked him into going up to Canada and flying illegal hooch into this country under cover of darkness for a quick and tidy profit. Legend has it they landed their plane on the very ground on which we are standing."

"Five years later, in the ***Spirit of St. Louis***, he became the first to solo the Atlantic," Lorna added.

"What do you think happened to Amelia Earhart?" Laurie asked.

The group tossed out a variety of pet theories.

"The Japs shot her down."

"She and co-pilot Noonan are living on a deserted island with their six kids."

"She crash landed on an uncharted isle. The cannibals ate her."

"She's living like Sheena, Queen of the Jungle, somewhere."

The men paid the fifty-cent per person admission fee, and they went inside, making their way through the large crowd.

"Who are those suits standing around keeping an eye on things? They look as if they were weaned on a pickle," Lorna said. Everyone laughed at that remark.

"They're state regulators, making sure everyone goes through the turnstiles. That way the Illinois treasury receives its proper cut," Brad said. "Hey, let's get a picture of our little outing to preserve for posterity." He had brought his box Brownie along for such an occasion. Barbara took one of Lorna and him together. Lorna, in a chipper mood, put her arm around his neck and her cheek next to his for the shot. Then he took one of Laurie and Stefan, all cozied up, and another of Barb and Viktor. Barb struck a saucy beauty contestant pose while Viktor held her extended hand. Brad found an usher who accommodated them by taking a group shot.

Brad was surprised with the diversity of the racetrack. It was a place he had generally held in low regard, described in sermons as a den of iniquity, a minefield of moral traps. In his mind's eye he had pigeonholed it as an unsavory place for coarser men. But there were people dressed in every mode and manner, and from all walks of life. Downtown office dwellers intermingled with blue collar. They could not be corralled into any discernible demographic.

The men bought some racing forms and found good seats in the grandstand. The horses were in the parade ring and the first race was due to start in twenty minutes.

"We're going to get something to eat and place a few bets. Do you girls want anything?" Brad asked.

Laurie used her peach-tipped fingers to lightly comb her hair. "A beer and a hot dog," she said. "No, make that two hot dogs."

"A beer and a dog for me also," Barb yelled.

Lorna looked a little sheepish. "A hot dog and a soda, if you please."

The three men went to the ticket area. "You can buy tickets for two dollars, five dollars and ten dollars," Brad explained. Viktor and Stefan chose the five-dollar pay window. Brad bought a two-dollar ticket on a horse named Jersey Lightning. It had nothing to do with the info on the scratch sheet. He liked the name.

"Are you two fellows enjoying yourselves?" he asked, as they rejoined at the concession stand.

Stefan could hardly contain himself. "Amerika is wonderful country. We enjoy ourselves much."

"Yes, me too," Viktor seconded.

Surprisingly, Brad spotted Knucky and his two bodyguards. Knucky had just bought a ticket, and Montrose and Roland were at the window purchasing theirs. Knucky saw someone he apparently knew and pushed through the crowd to say a few words. The man was well dressed but he had a paunch and a pendulous lower lip. Roland and Montrose momentarily lost track of their boss. After Walters' friend left, another man put a hand on his shoulder and whispered something in his ear. Brad was near panic when he saw the man motion with his head for Knucky to start moving toward an exit. His other hand was menacingly hidden under his suit coat, but Brad could tell it concealed something pointed. The crowd was so involved with their own agenda, that they were oblivious to what was happening.

Roland and Montrose were beside themselves. Montrose was going in the opposite direction, craning his head and frantically rising up on his toes every few seconds to catch a glimpse of his boss lost in an ocean of heads. Roland wormed his way back to the box seats, hoping Knucky had gone there.

Brad quickly sized up the situation and said, "excuse me" to Viktor and Stefan. Briskly moving at an angle to intercept, Brad jitterbugged his way through a thicket of racing fans.

"Hey, Walters! Knucky Walters," he shouted over the din. His arms waved: an incomprehensible semaphore. "It's me, Mugsy!"

Knucky rotated his head twenty-five degrees and caught a peripheral glimpse of him. An incredulous look crept over his face. The man who had a hold on his arm turned almost simultaneously. Brad's bold gambit took the assailant by surprise.

"The fuzz are outside lookin' for ya Knucky. They want ya for questioning 'bout a moider last night," he said in his best New Jersey accent.

Walters' ham-fisted host abruptly let go of his arm and fled toward an exit. He quickly melted into the crowd.

"Hey, Knucky, are you okay?" Brad asked, as he caught up with him.

"That was pretty stupid, kid. Don't ya realize ya could have gotten yourself shot?"

"I don't think so, Knucky, not with all of these people around. What did he say to you?"

"The oldest cliché in the book—'You're goin' for a ride.' "

"Did you recognize him?"

"Never saw the man before in my life."

"I only got a glimpse. Was he jug-eared with a thin mustache?"

"Yeah, and he had a mole on his cheek."

"I saw him over at the Kefauver hearings. He was talking to a curly haired fellow with a big scar on his cheek."

"Delonzo!"

Knucky mumbled some epithets when he said his name. "That would be Sal Delonzo, the head of the old Egan Rats gang in St. Louis. The man who tried to drag me outta here was probably Joe Rostopovich, Delonzo's ***heat***."

The future is going to be interesting, but perhaps somewhat perilous, Brad thought.

"Who was that snappy dresser you were talking to just before that guy tried to whisk you away?"

"That was Mickey Cohen, top dog out in the Los Angeles scene. He's the commission bookie out on the West Coast. Strange guy. They say he has a thing about washin' his hands all the time."

"Yeah, probably trying to wash all the blood off them," Brad said.

"No, he swears germs kill more people than bullets do."

"By the way; what's a commission bookie?"

Knucky shifted his rolled up racing form to his left hand so he could gesture with his right. "He handles all the really big bets comin' in that can't be covered by the regular bookies."

"How big is big?"

"You'd be surprised, sometimes as much as fifteen thousand dollars. He was the winner in the gangland wars that took place after Bugsy Siegel was shot-gunned to death back in '47."

Siegel was killed in Virginia Hill's Beverly Hills home

"What on earth is he doing here at this track?"

"He has a very large network of friends and contacts. In his line of work you can never tell when you might need a favor from someone. He gets around the country once in awhile just to maintain relationships."

By this time Montrose had backtracked and finally caught up with them.

"Hello, Brad." He turned to Walters. "Hey, boss, you all right?"

"Yeah, I'm okay. Let's get back to our seats. The first race starts in about ten minutes."

Knucky slowly turned and fixed his eyes on Brad.

"Guess I owe ya one, kid."

"You're not indebted to me for anything, Mr. Walters."

"I know ya don't expect anything in return, but ya did real good, an' I won't forget it. Here, take this ticket on the daily double I bought—Christmas in July," he smiled.

"You don't have to—"

"Take it," he said, stuffing it into Brad's shirt pocket.

"Okay, thanks."

"First time at the track?"

"Right."

"This may look like Podunkville to you but this track goes all the way back to 1924 when it was called the Fairmount Jockey Club. In 1947 it became the first track in the world to install lights for night racing."

"The ***first*** in the world?"

"The first! Do ya know how to watch a race?"

"Not really."

"Ya probably think people come here purely for betting purposes."

"What else?" Brad shrugged.

"These fans appreciate the absolute beauty of horses. They watch the Sport of Kings to feed their interest in seeing thousand pound beasts, scientifically bred over centuries for speed an' endurance, competin' on the track."

"So what do I need to look for?"

"There's a certain artistry to a well-run race. Watch for and learn the strengths an' weaknesses of each horse. Some are 'mudders;' they run better on a wet track. Others perform well on a dry fast one. One horse might excel at the stretch run, while another can beat the others getting out of the gate. On top of everything else, there's pacing."

"I thought it was a mad dash to the wire from start to finish."

"Nope. No horse can stay in high gear that long. That's where strategy on the part of the jockey comes in. Some stay back an' then make their move at the half-way mark. Others try to stay near the lead until the stretch run an' then let it all out."

"What difference does a good jockey make in the mix of things?"

"A good jockey, like Eddy Arcaro or Bob Hunter, knows his mount's temprament and looks to get the most out of him. A smart jockey don't let him-self get boxed in. He paces his horse just enough to avoid burnout before the finish line."

"So knowing when to throttle back is all important."

"Exactly. Ya know how you're goofy about baseball?"

"Uh, yes."

"People here feel the same way about racing. A good race can be compared to the way people handle competition an' challenges in life."

"I get it. That's called a metaphor."

"A meta—what?"

"Met-a-phor. It's another word for similarity. People say baseball is a metaphor for life because you set goals, train, overcome setbacks, and work with others as a team."

"So you've got baseball an' I've got racing." Knucky took out a cigarette and lit up. "Let me know what ya think of mine."

"Sure thing. By the way, are these races on the up and up?"

Knucky scratched the top of his head and gave him a curious look. "Most are," he said. "Yeah, ***most*** of them."

"Thanks for the lesson."

Trumpet fanfare announcing the first race interrupted their conversation. "We'd better get going or we'll miss the start. See you two around. Tell Roland hello for me," Brad said, as he headed to the grandstand to rejoin his group.

Brad didn't know it at the time, but the attempted heist of Knucky that day was a catalyst—steeling his determination to go to war rather than to sue for peace. The king was determined to defend his crown against a palace coup. The battle royale for identity, empire, and power was about to begin in earnest. Knucky, the ferocious lion, the shrewd fox, would invoke the ancient code of retribution—an eye for an eye—with dispatch. He knew from instinct how to go for the jugular. And it would be no war of attrition.

After Walters' brush with danger, everything else that happened at the track was anticlimactic. Brad tried the strategy of picking broad-chested horses that were favorites to "show," and just about broke even. Lorna, Laurie and Barb thought the two dollar bills, with Jefferson's picture on them and quite common at the track, were cute. Each decided to keep one in her purse as a souvenir.

The women looked the horses over and made their bets, based on the appearance of the jockey, his harlequin-printed silks, or the coloration and mannerisms of the horse. They particularly liked a certain spirited sorrel sporting a distinctive white blaze on his forehead. Viktor and Stefan, with Brad's assistance, tried to decipher the mass of statistical information in the racing forms and place bets in the manner of professional gamblers. Like many others in the crowd, they poured over the mass of names, dates and numbers, trying to mine useful nuggets of information from a bramble of arcane statistics. Barb was the only one who came close to winning anything significant. She picked a filly named Beauteous Barbra to win the fifth race, interpreting the name coincidence as an augury of good fortune.

"I just know the horse is going to win," she exclaimed. "I'm a Pisces and my daily horoscope advised: 'Be cautiously aggressive in matters of risk today!' "

"You don't really believe in those 'one size fits all,' mumbo jumbo predictions, do you?" Brad asked.

"You'd be surprised how often they are accurate," Barb saucily replied.

"I read my horoscope daily," Laurie volunteered, shifting her wad of gum. "Our future is in the stars. I read where Hitler had his own personal astrologer."

"Yes, and he lost the war," Brad countered. Laurie's lower lip formed a mocking pout and she scrunched her nose dismisssively.

The horses impatiently pranced and snorted before entering into their metal stalls. One skittish stallion neighed, reared up on his hind legs, and nearly threw the jockey to the ground.

Barb's horse took the lead out of the gate, fell back at the first turn, but regained the lead at the three-quarter mile mark. It was a nip and tuck exciting race.

"C'mon you beauteous piece of horse flesh," Barb screamed at the top of her lungs.

Going into the final turn, Beauteous Barbra held a two-length lead over Runnemede, a long shot. Thundering hoof beats echoed in their ears as the two lead horses dashed toward the finish line, straining every muscle to respond to the frantic urgings of their colorful silk-clad riders. Brad was transfixed by the sight of the lead horse, coal-black, eyes ablaze, nostrils flared, white froth dripping from its mouth, charging ahead as if to escape the sting of the whip.

"Go! Go! Go!" Barb exhorted, as she jumped out of her seat and bounced up and down with unbridled enthusiasm.

She disconsolately fell back into her seat as Beauteous Barbra faded and finished in third place.

"My horse died in the home stretch," Barb wailed.

No, I think that was one of those instances where the ending was contrived to enable Runnemede's owner to pay off a feed bill, Brad thought.

It turned out that the ticket Knucky gave Brad was a winner. A long shot, Privateer, won one of the races and the ticket paid a handsome $74.25. He didn't tell anyone else about the money which he donated to the Salvation Army.

After the races, they went bowling for a couple of games at Bowl-A-Way Lanes. Everyone was impressed with Laurie's ability with the light blue ball. In the second game she had a turkey—three strikes in a row. Everything else was uneventful except the frame where Stefan threw his second ball too quickly and almost nailed the pin boy.

After bowling they went to the dining room of the Stock Yards Inn and ate a delicious meal. Everyone ordered the specialty of the night: one-inch thick porterhouse steaks, baked potatoes and crisp green dinner salads. The waiter talked everyone into a portion of their house specialty dessert of bread pudding with whiskey sauce. Lorna and Brad tried to order theirs without the sauce but the waiter insisted they try it with the special flavoring.

"You're gonna love this. I personally guarantee it," he promised.

They reluctantly gave in. It proved to be out-of-this-world fabulous.

Then they went to the Terrace Lounge for entertainment. Not a large place, it was what some would call cozy. Pictures of prominent entertainers who had performed there were displayed on one wall. The floor plan was long and narrow. A well-stocked bar was off to the right. There was a small, elevated stage behind the bar. The left wall was lined with raised booths, on approximately the same level as the stage. Between the booths and the stage were several long rows of tables, each level being one step down from the next to facilitate viewing, hence the name Terrace Lounge.

"Hey, look, here's a Bob Hope picture from when he played here back in 1934," Brad said.

"And here's Sarah Vaughan, Billy Eckstine, the Four Freshmen, Les Paul, Nat King Cole, and Gene Krupa," Barb added, pointing to other framed and autographed black and white glossies.

Davy "The Nose" Bold was the featured comedian at the club that night. He had an Idaho potato schnoz, making his nickname quite appropriate.

"This rubber-faced comic is quite popular in the St. Louis area," Laurie noted.

"Really," Brad said.

"Yeah, I heard he's even planning to open his own club in St. Louis. Somewhere in the vicinity of Union and Delmar. Someone said he plans to call it the Celebrity Club."

Stefan and Viktor insisted on buying everyone at the table a couple rounds of mixed drinks. True to form, Lorna and Brad stuck with Pepsi Colas.

The crowd cheered and clapped wildly when "The Nose" came up on the stage. Besides having a big nose, Davy was large-framed with a swarthy complexion. Brad's first instinct was that he might be Egyptian, but Laurie said she was pretty sure he was Lebanese. He was quite good at mixing it up with the crowd and making them laugh. Like Henny Youngman, he had a vast repertoire of one-liners—most of them aimed at stereotyped foibles of various ethnic groups. A rotund whirly-gig of slurs, insults and taunts. He even tossed in a self-deprecating joke.

"Ya see this schnoz?" he said, turning his body and showing profile. "This beak is what General Motors used as the model for the Indian on the Pontiac hood ornament."

If one of his jokes fell flat he merely harrumphed and went on. The gregarious comedian did a take-off on Sam Spade, the intrepid detective hero in Dashiell Hammett's ***Maltese Falcon***. He performed his routine while sitting at an old upright Everett piano. He would play a few bars from an old standard and then start making wisecracks or telling jokes to loosen up the audience. Davy's parody of Sam Spade was tailored to the bar crowd. He twisted the name into "Sam Shovel, private nose." He vividly described how a beautiful woman walked into his office one day, wanting him to shadow her husband to see if he was cheating on her. He painted a sexy portrait, describing her physical attributes in glowing terms, like someone who stepped out of an erotic dream. She was "voluptuous with hungry lips and eager eyes." Her "silken blonde hair gave her the 'come hither' look of Gene Tierney." Then he set the audience up for the punch line.

Gene Tierney (author's collection)

"Yes, her silken hair hung all the way down to her waist . . ."

He paused, widened his Groucho Marx eyes for effect, and looked the audience over from one side of the room to the other.

"Yes, . . . all the way down to her waist . . . FROM HER ARMPITS," he said with a comical flair.

Brad had never seen a nightclub act before. He looked over at Lorna and shrugged his shoulders. She responded with a both palms-up gesture as if to say, "That doesn't tickle my funny bone either." But the other four in the party, like the rest of the audience, were practically rolling in the aisles. In nightclubs, where booze flowed freely, people refused to be constrained by petty rules of social convention.

Davy next delivered a quick, one-liner ethnic joke.

"Do you know why most Jewish men die before their wives?" he asked, rhetorically.

"Because they want to."

Another quickie. "Do you know what the hypochondriac put on his tombstone? 'See, I told you I was sick.' "

The girls allowed slight smiles to turn the corner of their mouths upward while Viktor and Stefan thought the joke was fitfully funny.

One thing they didn't know about this character was his penchant for poking fun at the audience, especially anyone who had the audacity to leave, for any reason, during his routine. Barb made the mistake of excusing herself to go to the ladies room. When she stood up, he immediately stopped his monologue and singled her out. "Hey, lady. When you get to where you're going, tell them you know me and you'll get a good seat." Barb turned fifteen different shades of red. When she came back, he used her as a foil once more. "Hey, lady, could you hear my act all right while you were in the rest room? I hope so because we sure heard yours." Davy had numerous loyal fans in the audience who had grown accustomed to his style of humor. The place broke up in hysterics at Barb's expense. Surprisingly, Barb seemed to take the ribbing in stride.

* * *

It was 12:45 A.M. when they dropped Barb off at her house on Veronica Avenue. Ten minutes later, Laurie and Lorna said their good-byes to Stefan and Brad at the Beulah Club. Then Brad and the other two men began their journey back to Scott Air Base.

"We had very good time," Stefan said to Brad.

"Yes, thank you for enjoyable evening," Viktor seconded. "That Barbara, she's a—how do you say?—real dish with a swell shape."

"It was my pleasure. I'm glad you liked her," Brad replied.

"I need to go bathroom," Viktor announced.

Brad glanced at his gas gauge. "Uh, oh. I need to buy some gasoline . . . uh, petrol. There's a station out on State Street that's still open. You can use their rest room, Viktor, while I fill up."

Viktor nodded ***okay.***

Brad pulled onto an asphalt island that smelled of oil, kerosene, grease and rubber. The station had a flying red horse on its sign. He thought, ***an appropriate color since Pegasus was born of the blood of the slain Medusa.***

Stefan went inside to buy cigarettes and Viktor went to the rest room. Stefan was standing by the car, puffing away on a cigarette, when Brad returned from paying for the gas.

"Isn't Viktor back yet?" Brad asked.

Stefan smiled. "He must be doing the number two, as you Amerikans put it." His smile quickly changed to a blank stare, and that in turn gave way to a look of apprehension. "I'd better go check on Viktor," he said in a full-blown state of panic.

"Fine." Brad had a confused look on his face.

A minute later, Stefan burst out the rest room door with a wild look in his eyes, screaming "Viktor, Viktor, where are you?" Then he began cursing in Yugoslav.

Brad ran toward him with a look of concern. "What's wrong?"

"Viktor, he . . . he fled out back through the bathroom window."

"I don't understand. What do you mean, ***fled***?"

"He's defecting, you id-i-ot!" Stefan shouted at him.

"Defecting?"

"Yes, come on, you must help me find him." Stefan pulled on his arm. "We've got to go back to Yugoslavia tomorrow."

Brad held back. "Wait a minute, Stefan. This is a free country. I'm not going to help you find Viktor so you can force him to go back."

"The police, the police, we must call police."

"Stefan, you don't understand. He's committed no crime. The police aren't going to help you either."

"D— it, you no understand. I responsible for him, just as he was responsible for me."

"You're on American soil. There aren't any authorities who are going to help you drag Viktor away."

"Hurry, get me back to the base. I'll call our embassy. They'll tell me what to do."

Nothing was said during the entire trip to Scott Air Base. Stefan's veneer of friendliness was gone. When they reached his apartment, he got out of the car and slammed the door without saying another word.

Brad called Walter the next day. Walter told him that Yugoslavian authorities angrily demanded Viktor's return, claiming that he had been kidnapped by the FBI, but to no avail. The base commander explained to them that at this point, no one even knew where Viktor was. That afternoon Stefan and the purloined Yak, disassembled and carefully returned to its crate, flew back to Rhine-Main in Frankfurt, West Germany, and from there, on to Belgrade, Yugoslavia.

Viktor had hidden a few hours in someone's garage, several blocks from the station. Then he hitchhiked to Barb Edelblute's house, and she arranged for him to sleep on a cot in her basement. The next day, they drove to the Federal Building in St. Louis where he requested political asylum. His request was granted, but only after the FBI grilled him for several weeks. Barb helped him find a one-room apartment in East St. Louis and worked tirelessly to improve his broken English. Brad pitched in and found him a janitorial job with Hunter Packing Company.

* * *

August 10, 1951

It was a sweltering day in midsummer. Brad decided to stop at the California Market after work to pick up a watermelon to take home. The store was at 10th Street, directly across from Sears. He filled up with gas at the nearby Standard station, located on a wedge of ground at the confluence of State Street and Illinois Avenue. After he paid the owner, he parked his car at the edge of the filling station lot and walked across the street to the market. The front of the building was rounded. There was roughly a hundred feet of produce bins filled with sweet corn, bananas in various ripened stages, succulent red tomatoes, juicy cantaloupes and a veritable cornucopia of other delicious fruits and vegetables. There were great ice-filled tubs of watermelons. You would select a melon; then they would plug it so you could sample it. Brad couldn't remember ever tasting a bad one.

The blistering sun beat down on him, placing everything in slow motion, like an invisible hand. The market was less than a block away, and from his vantage point he could see that a noisy crowd had gathered in front of the open-air, tin-roofed part of the building. Many were shouting and waving their fists.

Brad spotted Missola in the mass and quickened his pace. She looked concerned. Raised voices and the sounds of an angry mob reached out and switched on Brad's adrenaline system. He closed the distance with a quick sprint. The air was pungent with the organic fragrances of recent harvest.

"What's going on, Missola?" Brad asked excitedly.

"Trouble, big trouble," she said with a frown.

Many in the crowd seemed to be in an ugly mood, shaking their fists under a feverish sun. Some stood watching with disapproving expressions, yet did nothing to interfere. Others had excited looks on their faces but remained passive, clearly content to experience vicariously the intrigue of the moment. Then there were those who were yelling, egging on and encouraging whatever was happening in the center of the crowd.

"My, husband, George," Missola said fearfully, pointing. "I'm afraid he's in a peck of trouble."

Brad pushed and wedged his way through the spectators who were four or five deep. Several grumbled angrily as he forced his way to the inner edge of the crowd. He reached the part of the market that housed countless stalls of appealingly arranged produce. He stopped, his mouth hanging open in disbelief. There was Walters' driver and aide-de-camp, Montrose—of all people, and Missola's husband, back to back, shoulder to shoulder, slowly turning as three men circled them like predatory wolves with cornered prey. There was a youngster on the other side of the crowd, and he was pulling on his dad's arm, pointing at one man lying on the ground, bleeding and out cold.

"Hey," one of the troublemakers yelled, his protuberant eyes ablaze, "Why don't you sell your nigger cherries on your side of town? You don't belong here."

"Yeah," his buddy seconded, his face as red as his hair and his light eyes fierce with hatred. "Now that you've forced your way into our schools, I guess you jungle bunnies think you can go anywhere you want in this town."

Without hesitation, Brad rushed forward and joined the beleaguered pair.

"Hey, nigger lover," someone yelled from the crowd. "What do you think you're doing?"

"Brad, what in the devil are you doing here?" Montrose said with a look of astonishment.

Brad had a cocky smile on his face. "I think with three of us, that should even the odds."

Montrose scowled. "Are you nuts? Get out of here; this isn't your fight. These people have blood in their eyes."

"I'm staying." Brad, keeping a wary eye on the hostiles, slightly turned his head toward Montrose and talked out of the corner of his mouth. "What about you? Why are you here?"

"We ran out of lettuce and onions at the Club 501. Knucky sent me here on an errand. When I saw what these men were doing, I had to get involved."

The trio stood back-to-back and formed a protective triangle.

Two of the angry men made a rush at Montrose and George. Brad was astonished to hear several in the crowd make bets as they egged the combatants on. Montrose grabbed the one with red hair, spun him around, and wrapped his huge arms behind his neck in a full Nelson. The man was flailing at the air with his hands so Montrose subdued him by modifying his grip, wrapping an arm around his neck and applying a chokehold. Then he rapped his attacker hard on the top of his skull with his knuckles and tossed him, rag doll fashion, back to the stunned crowd that let out an astonished swooning sound.

George had his old walking stick from a persimmon branch and brandished it like a weapon. The other redneck made a move toward him. He was swinging wildly, but the cudgel skillfully parried each thrust. Whack! Whack! The man grimaced and rubbed his wrists where red welts began to form. More exclamations from onlookers.

"You're gonna get yours, nigger." He lunged again, and there was a loud ***thwack*** as the thick piece of wood came crashing down on his shoulder. The redneck, fire and hatred burning in his eyes, stumbled back to the edge of the crowd.

A third man saw a flicker of inattention and rushed forward in bull-like fashion at Brad. Missola flinched as the man's fist connected with his chin. Brad, who had been distracted by the other action, staggered and then regained his footing. He shook his head and braced himself for round two. The man swung at him again, but this time Brad was ready and caught his wrist in midair. In one fluid motion he whipped it into a hammerlock. Then he tripped the man and took him down to the ground with a judo move called ***Osotogari.*** Brad extended the man's arm and applied pressure to the thumb, keeping him down with a heavy foot on his back. The man cursed and writhed in pain.

Several other men made ready to rush the trio but Montrose, with eyes ablaze and neck veins popping, stared them down, backing them up with a withering look. His right arm was cocked and his fist balled as if ready to deliver another kayo punch.

The crowd was stunned by the turn of events, and a fearful quiet washed over the scene. There was a simultaneous swallow in the crowd, followed by a nervous gulp.

Ernie Lombardi, owner of the market, arrived on the

scene carrying a baseball bat. "All right, break it up, the party's over," he announced sternly. He was huge and had arms that were bigger than Montrose's.

Brad took his foot off his opponent's ribs and released his grip. The man coughed, stumbled to his feet and stood there, looking at Brad with a murderous glare. Fist cocked, he took a halting step toward him.

"I said, ***it's over***," Lombardi reiterated, moving toward the scene of action. The man stopped, turned and looked at the owner's war club, collected himself then whirled and stalked off.

With the excitement over, the crowd began to disperse, slowly moving away in small groups, making muttering noises.

It was the closest thing to combat Brad had ever experienced. He liked the taste of victory.

Missola marched past the three surprised men, still standing shoulder to shoulder, gave them a disgusted look, and walked over to the stall containing her cherries. Only one quart of cherries was left and it was tipped over on its side. Much of the red fruit was scattered like dark rubies on the sawdust floor. Missola bent down and began picking up the undamaged ones. "***Men***," she said shaking her head. She turned her body, trying to ignore the unspoken question in the victors' eyes.

As the last bully picked himself up off the ground and started to leave, the owner grabbed him by the back of his collar. "Just a minute, Bub. My cashier said you're the one who started this. That's gonna cost you ten bucks." He forcibly took the man's wallet, despite his sputtering protests. "Nine seems to be all you have. Good enough!" He turned the man around, placed his foot on his rear and gave a mighty shove. "Now git." The man stumbled forward and would have fallen flat on his face had it not been for someone catching him by his arm just as he was about to go down. He rubbed his backside, grumbled an angry ***harrumph***, then pivoted and stomped away.

Brad went over to where Missola was and helped her finish picking up the fruit.

"I'm not mad at ya, Mistuh Logan. Jus' hate ta see all that fightin'."

"Because of what happened to your grandmother?"

"Yes, suh, I guess that probably be the reason."

"I understand what you're saying. But, don't you see? Sometimes what you're fighting for is so important, the violence is worth it."

"That's what George says, but I jus' don't know."

"After all, Jesus lost his temper with the money changers at the temple."

"Yeah, but these were jus' cherries, Mistuh Logan."

Brad placed a gentle hand on her shoulder and looked her in the eye. "Missola, it was more than just cherries. Human dignity was at stake here. That's why we fought the Axis Powers; it's why we're in Korea."

A smile that began to slowly form on Missola's face broadened into a huge grin and ended with a boisterous chuckle.

"I don't get it." Brad shrugged. "What's so funny?"

"You men sure gave those crackers a good whuppin'."

Brad joined her in raucous laughter. "We sure did, didn't we?"

Montrose and George, who had been trading viewpoints about the fight, walked over to them. "Mistuh Logan, my husband, George and I, want to thank ya for what ya did. And you too Mr. —"

"It's Montrose. Glad to be of service," he replied. "I can't remember the last time I had that much fun."

"Your gratitude isn't necessary," Brad said. "I was only standing up for what's right. This is a free country. Those bullies had no business trying to run you off."

"Some of your friends may not appreciate what you did today," Montrose said.

"Well, I feel pretty good about what I did, so I think I can live with it."

"Well, thanks from me, too." Montrose shook Brad's hand.

"What kind of timber is that you're leaning on, George?" Brad looked at him in awe. "That was really something, the way you maneuvered it."

"It's called a Bo stick. The technique is known as Kobudo. Picked it up in the orient when I was in the Navy about a thousand years ago."

"That was quite impressive. Hey, I almost forgot. I came here to buy a watermelon. And I think I'll buy some of those damaged cherries. No need for them to go to waste. My mother makes the best cherry preserves you've ever tasted."

Chapter 16

The St. Louis Cardinals have the richest baseball tradition of any National League team. They have played in fifteen World Series since 1926, winning nine times. They beat the mighty 1926 Babe Ruth-led Yankees in seven games. Then they crushed Joe DiMaggio and his mates four games to one in 1942. And the Lou Brock/Bob Gibson Redbirds were destined to defeat the Mickey Mantle-led Yankees in 1964, four games to three. The Cards are the only National League team to have a World Series edge on the Yankees (3-2).

Don Block of Collinsville

May 21, 1951

Lorna and Brad continued dating all through the summer. He knew she was still seeing Lance, and occasionally she went out with a mailman from Collinsville by the name of Don Block. He figured she kept this Block in the picture just to keep the dating scene from deteriorating into a tug of war between Lance and him. She never talked about what she and Lance did on dates, but he found out from a friend of his that he was an aficionado of art and classical music. The two of them frequented the St. Louis Symphony, ranked with Cleveland and Chicago as the best in the Midwest. He also heard they went a couple of times to the St. Louis Municipal Opera in Forest Park, which was the largest outdoor theater of its type in the country. On one visit they saw East St. Louisan William Dollar as the featured ballet performer in ***Transcendence***, choreographed especially for him by George Ballanchine.

St. Louis Muny Opera – world's largest outdoor theater – seating capacity 12,000

Brad and Lorna's dates consisted of sampling the simpler pleasures of life: horseback riding at Grand Marais, bowling at the Playdium, an occasional picnic. But the date Lorna enjoyed the most was their foray into the world of baseball—a hard-fought game between the hated Giants and Brad's beloved Cardinals. He couldn't help it; he bled Cardinal red.

It happened on a beautiful Sunday afternoon; the rubber game of a three-part set between the team from the Polo Grounds and the Cards. They drove in his Studebaker, which inappropriately stalled on Grand Avenue about eight blocks from that magical baseball Mecca, Sportsman's Park. The rear end had just been repaired and painted by Kasson's Auto Body.

"What do you think is the problem?" Lorna asked.

"Vapor lock," he answered in exasperation.

"What's vapor lock?"

"Sometimes the copper fuel line carrying gas from the fuel pump to the carburetor gets so hot it vaporizes the high octane gasoline. When that happens, the engine dies."

A couple of horns behind them honked indignantly in a duet of frustration. He popped the hood release then retrieved a small bottle of water from his trunk and lifted the hood. He slowly poured the liquid over the fuel line to cool it. Ssss. The pump made a hissing noise until it cooled down. They waited for about a minute after he slid back inside the car. Mercifully, the engine roared back to life.

"I think my dad had that happen once," Lorna said. "He clamped a piece of tinfoil on his fuel line with a spring-loaded clothespin. Said it dissipated the heat and solved the problem."

"Sounds ingenious. I'll have to remember that little trick."

"Have you seen Viktor lately?"

"Yes. I helped him buy a used car at Waverly Motors about a week ago."

They parked near St. Louis Avenue and walked about four blocks to the ballpark. Lorna looked fresh and perky in a white cotton blouse and blue-checked pedal pushers. Her ponytail bounced merrily as they walked along. At the ticket window, he bought a couple of grandstand seats, directly behind third base.

"Scorecards, scorecards! Ya can't tell the players without scorecards!" yelled a vendor. Fifteen cents bought a sharpened Red Bird pencil and a scorecard. An usher helped them find their seats. The Cardinals were just finishing fielding practice.

"Have you ever been to a professional baseball game?" he asked.

"Not in person. My dad is a Cardinal fan. He attends many games courtesy of the hyperbolic Harry Caray on KXOK radio while he is sitting in his favorite easy chair," she said. "Me? I find them boring on the radio."

"It's a lot different sitting in the stands and rubbing elbows with a group of Red Bird fans who are linked by a common bond of tradition. St. Louis baseball lore is legendary," he unabashedly bragged. "Their predecessors go all the way back to 1876. The St. Louis Maroons were playing that hot day in June when General Custer got killed at the Little Bighorn. That same year, Anheuser-Busch started brewing Budweiser down on Pestalozzi Street."

"How on earth did they come up with a name like Budweiser?"

"I think it's named for a small town in Czechoslovakia." He ordered a couple of sodas and two boxes of Cracker Jack.

"What are all of these little squares for on the scorecard?"

"Here, look," he pointed. "By using a combination of numbers, letters and symbols—a kind of baseball shorthand—you can tell what has happened over the course of the game. Suppose a batter hits a fly ball to right field and makes an out . . . "

"Right field—that's over there?" she asked, nodding her head toward the screened pavilion.

"Correct. Then you mark the number nine in the box."

"Why is he number nine?"

"Each position on the field is numbered, one through nine, starting with the pitcher and ending with the right fielder."

"What if a batter strikes out?"

"That's a K."

"And I suppose a walk is a Z?"

"No, it's a W. You can keep score and I'll help out."

"You said the Cardinals are a great team. Where are they in the standings?"

"I said they had a great tradition. The Birds are in a talent drought right now and are only in third place. The Dodgers and Giants are ahead of them."

"Tell me, what makes them so special?"

"They own seven National League championships and ***five world titles***—more than any other team in baseball, except the Bronx Bombers—the New York Yankees."

"There are two leagues?"

"Yes."

"When is the last time the Cards won?"

"***We*** defeated the St. Louis Browns from the American League in 1944 and the Red Sox in '46."

"Where do the Browns play?"

"They play right here when the Cardinals go out of town."

Brad's prize inside the box depicting a boy and his dog (Bingo) was a ring with a plastic ruby.

"Hey, look! What's inside yours?"

After scrounging around a while, she came up with a miniature whistle. Lorna puckered her lips and blew. ***Toot, toot.***

"Let's trade. You give me the whistle in exchange for this exquisite piece of jewelry."

"Sure."

"Hold out you're left hand," he commanded. She hesitatingly complied.

"Now . . . it's official," he said, as he gently pushed it onto her ring finger. "From this day, henceforth, you and I, the two of us, are semi-regular dating partners."

She let her hand linger for a while in his as she shook her head in mock dismay.

"You know the ancient Egyptians believed a special vein linked the third finger of the left hand directly to the heart. Their mystics said a person was inseparably connected forever to another who placed a ring on that finger. Someday, somehow, you could end up being my wife, Lorna Sanders."

"I know about the myth. According to legend, the ring has to be made of gold. This one is pretty but it seems to be about twenty-four carats short of being the real McCoy."

"Just my misfortune to be dating Miss Know-It-All."

"Back to important matters, Lancelot. What else makes the Cardinals special?" Lorna continued her semi-journalistic interview.

"During the 1930s they had a motley crew known as the 'Gas House Gang.' They were the most colorful and eccentric collection of oddballs ever assembled. They played the game with a flair and zest that has never been matched—before or since."

The game between the Cards and those dastardly Giants started out as a much heralded pitching duel between the crafty veteran Harry "The Cat" Brecheen and Sal "The Barber" Maglie. Harry was near the end of his career.

The Giants were retired in order in the first inning.

"One of the outfielders left his glove on the field," Lorna said, with a look of astonishment.

"That's because back in the old days the gloves were shared by both teams. It's an anachronism, an old custom that will probably change one of these days when a fielder trips on somebody's glove, and it affects the outcome of a game."

After three innings, the only Cardinal base runner was Enos Slaughter on a single to left.

Future Hall of Famer, Enos "Country" Slaughter

"How do you score the hit?" Lorna asked.

"Draw a diamond inside the box by his name in the first inning. It may not be according to Hoyle, but that's the way I do it."

"Done."

"Okay, now each leg of that diamond represents a single, double, triple, or home run."

"So I should erase three-fourths of this to indicate a single."

"Correct. You're very good at this," he complimented.

Maglie inexplicably lost his control in the fourth, and the Cardinals scored two runs when Red Schoendienst tripled into right center with two men on base.

"Yes, yes!" Brad said, jumping to his feet and clapping enthusiastically.

"Go, you Red Birds!!!" Lorna bubbled unabashedly.

Their good fortune was short-lived as the Giants scored three in the next inning on a home run by Bobby Thompson. The Cards nearly tied it the next inning when first baseman Steve Bilko lined a double off the right field screen. Wally Westlake brought everyone to his feet with a deep drive to center, but Willy Mays made a patented circus catch in dead center to snuff-out the threat.

The Cardinals took the lead in the sixth inning when Eddie

Kazak walked, and Joe Garagiola hit a two run homer.

"See anything unusual about Kazak's name?" he quizzed.

"Umm . . . yes! It's a palindrome—the same thing backward and forward."

"Very astute."

The good-sized crowd of about 30,000 rabid fans infected Lorna with their enthusiasm. Maglie threw a bean ball at the next batter, left fielder Enos Slaughter, and a bench-clearing brouhaha ensued.

Lorna's reaction betrayed her immersion into the heat of the moment. "Sock him one, Schoendienst," she hoarsely yelled at the lanky second baseman.

Hemus was wrestling on the ground with Alvin Dark. "Give him a lickin' Solly," Brad shouted.

Order was soon restored, and the exciting drama continued. Slaughter stole both second and third, but was thrown out at home on an infield grounder.

The Giants scored two in the seventh on a pair of walks, a sacrifice and a two-out single by Don Mueller.

"Why do they call it a sacrifice?" Lorna asked.

"Because the batter intentionally made an out in order to move runners into scoring position. Mark that SF on the scorecard."

Each team scored a run in the eighth inning, the Giants' coming on a home run by Willie Mays. Going into the bottom of the ninth, the Cards were trailing by a run. Manager Marty "Slats" Marion sent in Chuck Diering to pinch-hit for reliever Al Brazel. He struck out on three pitches. Hemus, the batter at the top of the lineup, flied out to Monte Irvin.

"Do you want to leave and beat the crowd?" he asked.

"Are you kidding? We're going to win this game."

"How do you figure?"

"If Schoendienst gets on, that will bring up Musial. The scorecard says he was batting .339 going into the game. According to my chicken scratching, he is 0 for 2 with a walk. The law of averages is in our favor. He's due."

Brad crossed his fingers and flashed them to Lorna who followed suit.

With two men out, the crowd slowly began a rhythmic beat with foot stomping and handclaps, trying to generate a last-ditch rally. Like those African natives chanting and dancing around the fire in a Lex Barker "Tarzan" movie, they somehow believed their actions would appease the baseball gods and turn the game around—snatch victory from the jaws of defeat.

Schoendienst coaxed a walk on a borderline 3-2 pitch. The fans collectively held their breath for fear "Shags" Crawford would call it a strike. The fever-pitch noise became deafening as Musial confidently strode to the batter's box.

"Here comes The Man," Brad said, hopefully.

"I just love the way he stands at the plate," Lorna gushed.

"It's very unorthodox," he said. "Some inventive baseball writer called it a 'peek-a-boo stance.'"

"How did he get that nickname?"

"Back in '48 he had a spectacular day against the Dodgers at Ebbets Field in Brooklyn. After four consecutive hits, the next time he came to the plate the crowd collectively moaned 'Oh no, here comes The Man again.' "

Two deft fingers inserted into Lorna's mouth produced a shrill whistle. "Let's go, Stan."

Brad flashed her a look of admiration. ***How did she do that?***

The count went to two balls and two strikes. Stan barely avoided a strikeout by fouling off a wicked curve on the outside corner of the plate.

"Come on Stan . . . you can do it," Lorna pleaded, with hands folded in prayer-like fashion. Her eyes were almost closed. She could hardly bear to watch the unfolding drama.

A blistering four-seam fastball raced toward the low inside corner of the strike zone.

KER-POW!

The Man hit it on the sweet part of the bat. Everyone heard that joyous sound of ash wood greeting stitched cowhide. A towering drive rocketed toward the right field pavilion. The leather sphere, held together by two hundred and sixteen red cotton stitches, zoomed like a comet streaking through the heavens. Gravity defied. Parabolic poetry. The flight of the ball pulled the hopeful fans to their feet.

Future Hall of Famer, Stan "The Man" Musial

Brad couldn't help himself. It was a rare magical moment of sheer competitive ecstasy. He knew exactly what Harry Caray was saying in the broadcast booth, and he began to emulate his excited voice. "Swung on . . . it's a long drive . . . way, way, back . . . it might be, it could be, it . . . ***is*** . . . a home run! The Cardinals win! The Cardinals win! Holy cow! There's joy in Mudville today, baseball fans."

The crowd let loose with tumultuous applause. ***Yaayyy Cardinals!*** Everyone was jumping up and down. Lorna grabbed Brad and gave him a hug. The guy behind him was happily shaking his shoulders. Several fans threw their hats onto the field. A phalanx of team mates mobbed Musial at home plate.

"Careful, don't spike him boys; he's the franchise," Brad said.

Lorna even hugged a grandfatherly gentleman standing next to her. It was the perfect ending to an exciting game.

Thanks Stosh, I'll keep the memory locked in a small corner of my brain forever, Brad thought.

"Know why people at games are called fans?" Brad asked, as they left the stadium.

"Tell me," she said, not noticing they were holding hands.

"In St. Louis, baseball is the moral equivalent of war. It's an abbreviation for ***fanatic.***"

A mischievous smile crept over Lorna's face that was shadowed by a newly purchased baseball cap he had given her. "Based on the fervor I've seen today, I wouldn't call these people fans—they're more like rowdy disciples of a new religious order."

* * *

Brad and Lorna walked several blocks to the car after the ball game. He was parked in a wide alley off a dead-end street. Though it was late afternoon, it was still steamy-hot. It was one of those typical Midwest summer days when the fiery sun almost groaned in its struggle to climb above the horizon. The prehensile rays from that molten disc caused the city streets to quiver like a mirage.

Brad helped Lorna into the car. He had just slid behind the wheel when two men approached his car from behind and opened his door.

"Not so fast, buddy, we want to talk to you," the muscular one with a mottled, acne-scarred face said menacingly. His beige pork pie hat didn't quite conceal heavy brow ridges.

Homo erectus—the "missing link," Brad thought.

"Just stay where you are, lady," the man on the passenger side said as he leaned against the car with hands on the roof. In doing so, he exposed a revolver strapped to his side beneath his Prussian blue serge suit. He was a cookie cutter replica—a bad-guy parody straight out of a Gary Cooper movie. He even had shifty eyes.

Gary Cooper

"Who are you guys?" Brad was furious.

"We'll ask the questions, if you don't mind," the man said as he opened the door and pulled Brad out by his arm. His partner came around the front of the car, the two of them trapping Brad against the front fender.

"Yes, I do mind," he snapped as he jerked away from a vise-like grip. "Haven't you guys heard? Kidnapping is a federal offense."

"Relax, we ***are*** the Feds." The grim-faced men flashed phony-looking badges.

"Don't get so testy. All we wanna do is have a palaver about your boss."

The one with the bad skin was doing all the talking while the other one kept his hand inside his coat pocket to remind Brad he was armed. Lorna remained in her seat, frozen by fear.

"Now what interest could you two jailhouse refugees have in Mr. Ernst?"

The man with the gun smacked him hard in the gut. His knees buckled. ***Not very intelligent, Logan,*** he chided himself.

"Leave him alone, you bullies!" Lorna shouted. Her plea was ignored.

The other man spoke: "Don't get smart with us, wise guy, or ya might regret it."

Brad remembered having to deal with a bully back in grade school. His dad had always told him most bullies are cowards. If you stand up to them, they generally stop bothering you and look for easier pickings elsewhere. When Roger Dudley tried to strongarm Brad out of his lunch money at Manners grade school, he popped him in the face and bloodied his nose. "There's plenty more where that came from," he threatened. In an all-out fight, Roger probably could have knocked his block off, but Brad's tough demeanor and aggressive physical reaction caught him completely by surprise. He pretty well left him alone after that incident. But Brad figured his dad's truism didn't apply to adult delinquents with guns.

"We're not interested in nobody named Ernst. We want ya to give a message to Knucky Walters."

"I think you've got the wrong man. I don't work for Walters."

"This wiseacre needs a change in attitude."

The big one grabbed hold of his shoulders and bent him over the hood with the side of his face pressed hard against the metal. Brad's teeth cut into his lips and he could taste warm blood. ***Great. Bluto is reshaping my face and Popeye can't find his can of spinach!***

Courtesy King Features

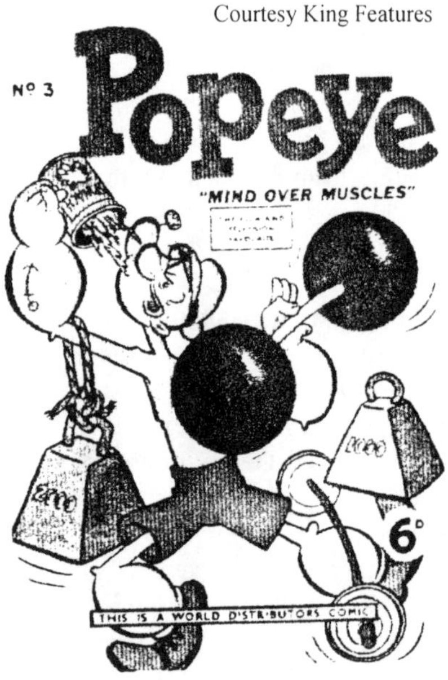

"Walters' not my boss," he groaned.

"Yeah, well . . . maybe, maybe not—but you know him."

"Okay, so I know him."

"Our boss is real upset about Knucky ignoring his messages."

"Messages! What messages?"

"About how it would be wise for him to begin thinking about early retirement."

"So your boss here in St. Louis is the one trying to muscle in on Walters—burned down his warehouse, and sent him a post card?"

They didn't respond to his question. He assumed a non-denial meant they were guilty.

"I thought you said you didn't work for Walters," the thug crushing his skull said.

"I'm just a friend. I don't have anything to do with his business activities."

"Never mind, Mister Smart Guy. We saw you with him on several occasions. Tell your man that if he don't wise up, things are gonna get hotter than the fire at his warehouse."

"So, it ***was*** you two."

"Shut up. We read about it in the papers. Tell Walters it's time to get outta Dodge. Tell him if he wants to die peacefully in bed from old age, he'd better take our advice."

"Do ya think you can tell him that, hot shot?" the other one said as he pushed Brad's left arm toward his shoulder blade and beyond in a painful hammer lock.

"I can pass it along." His muscles burned from being twisted like a pretzel. "Your boss might be in luck. Knucky told me he was thinking of retiring down in Florida—somewhere in Miami," he lied. Brad figured anything he could say to throw Walters' enemies off guard would be better for him in the long run.

Lorna couldn't take it any longer; she flew out of the car and rallied to Brad's defense. "Stop it! Stop hurting him," she screamed as she pounded the big one in the back with her fists. He effortlessly pushed her away.

"Hey, if you hurt her I'll—"

"You'll what? Just make sure Walters gets the message. And here's a little something to help ya remember."

The man wearing the hat gave him a vicious kidney punch. The air went out of him, and he clutched at the car as they released their grip and backed off. ***Someday you two punks might be sorry you ever met me***, he fiercely thought, still prostrate on the car.

"Don't even try to get a gander at our license plate, or we'll come back and give you another dose."

He tried to make out the plate as they drove off. It was smeared with dried mud. He could make out a J and an M. After a space a two-seven-seven something. Only later did it dawn on him that the car was a dark blue Packard.

Lorna moved quickly to Brad's side and placed a hand on his shoulder. "Are you okay?"

"Yeah, I think, I guess I'm all right." Brad held his side and slowly took a deep breath.

"What on earth was that all about? Are you really friends with that Walters gangster?"

"Yes, but it's not what you think. I've only known him a little less than a year. We met one night when I ate dinner at the Club 501 Lounge, which he owns."

"Are you crazy? Don't you know it's foolhardy to dance with the devil?"

"He's not the devil. And I only see him about once a week when I go to his place to eat," Brad protested.

"Well, he might get your soul. If you have any sense, you'll forget you ever met Walters and stop seeing him. You're smack in the middle of a gang war."

"Those two were just trying to scare me, rough me up a little and send a message to Knucky. I know it could be dangerous, but I wonder if this strong-arming has anything to do with the Torricelli murder."

"That's exactly what I am saying." Lorna drew her brows together. "These guys kill people. And if they think you're getting too close to the truth, you could be next on their list."

"I don't think so. They generally don't like to kill civilians. It causes them too much grief. They know people who live in the area don't get too concerned about shootings as long as the gangsters are killing each other off and leave them alone."

Her large angry eyes locked on his. "But don't you see?" she countered, "that's the problem. It's time the taxpayers stopped looking the other way."

"We should start heading back." Brad wasn't interested in continuing a discussion that was so polarized.

"Are you able to drive?"

"Sure . . . just a little sore. I'll be fine."

"I'm not sure, but I think we just had our first argument," Brad said as they drove from the ball game.

Lorna hadn't said a word on the way home. Her mind was going in circles, thinking about the fact that she was dating someone who was friends with a local mobster.

"You're not angry with me, are you?" He looked at her with pleading eyes.

"I don't know what I'm feeling right now. Maybe we shouldn't see each other for a while."

Brad couldn't believe his ears. "You're not serious. We're good for each other. I'm at my happiest when I'm with you and I can tell the feeling is mutual."

"Oh, and since when did you become an expert on ***my*** feelings?"

Brad turned his head. "You know what I think this is all about?"

"I don't think I care to be psychoanalyzed . . . CAREFUL!" She threw a hand toward the metal dash.

Brad hit the brakes and barely avoided hitting a 1950 Olds

1950 Olds Holiday hardtop $2,641

that had stopped to turn left. "You okay?"

She let out a sigh of relief. "I'm fine. I had time to brace myself."

"I believe you're falling in love with me and pushing me away is the easiest way to deal with it."

"That is outrageous and very presumptuous on you're part."

"Is it? I think you're keeping Lance on the string just so you won't have to deal with your feelings for me." Brad knew that he was taking a calculated risk by being blunt, but he was tired of keeping his emotions on a shelf.

"That is the most insane, egotistical, arrogant thing I've ever heard. And why are you putting pressure on me?" Lorna nervously patted down her hair to put several loose strands back in place. "You promised you wouldn't."

He stole a quick glance, and their eyes briefly met, his vulnerable, hers unsettled. "Because we're meant for each other. Can't you see that?"

"I already told you, I'm not going to let foolish notions about romantic love complicate my life." Lorna was so confused emotionally she could hardly think straight. She closed her eyes and tried to calm down. She didn't want to discuss this with Brad. Not here, not now. Normally shy and reserved, it wasn't like him.

"I'm tired of this fraternal relationship you concocted for us. Would getting married to me and becoming a regular housewife be so bad? Millions of other young women make that choice every year."

Lorna turned up her nose. "You must really have a high opinion of yourself. Offer a girl marriage, and out of desperation, or gratitude, you think she'll throw herself at your feet."

"You're twisting my words. I'm just scared to death that Lance or someone else will steal you from under my nose."

Brad's worst nightmare . . .

Brad's hint of marriage was flattering, but Lorna decided to be equally blunt. "I'm as resolute as ever about pursuing my goals. I want to feel the satisfaction of a career: stimulating work, challenges, accomplishment, professional triumphs. At this point and time neither you nor Lance are going to talk me into a serious relationship. And if you can't accept it, maybe we should stop seeing each other."

"You know I want to keep dating you. I just don't want to wait until I'm thirty years old to start a family."

"I told you before I'm not ready to be a nanny and scullery maid. This is the time in my life when I want to discover Lorna Sanders, who she is—what she's capable of—all the ideas, hopes and ambitions that she's had on hold since she was a grade-schooler. And nothing you say is going to change my mind."

Brad braked to a stop as they arrived at the Beulah Club. They were silent as he walked her to the front door.

"Can I call you tomorrow?" Brad asked.

"Not if all you want to do is bring this up again."

"All right, have it your way." Brad tried not to let his disappointment show. "Mum's the word."

She went up on her toes and gave him a peck on the cheek. "Promise?"

"Promise."

She placed a soft hand on his cheek. "Brad, I'm really flattered that you want to marry me, but I have to be honest with you. I might not be ready for six or seven years, depending on how things go at the office. It would be unfair to ask you to wait that long."

He gave her a wink. "You're right, it would be unfair. I guess I'll just have to hang around and hope you change your mind."

* * *

Salvatore Delonzo's career closely paralleled that of Knucky Walters' except his operations were on the St. Louis side of the river. For a while he ran with the Birger Gang, but he quickly grew bored with small town life in southern Illinois. In the late 1920s, he had spent a couple of years in the state pen at Jefferson City, Missouri, for beating a member of the rival Cuckoo gang nearly to death with a baseball bat. Like Knucky, his violent temper flared often. He had slowly risen to the top spot in the Egan Rats gang and had done pretty well for himself. To his thinking, East St. Louis was uncouth, having no real class, and for many years Delonzo was content to dominate the St. Louis crime world. But he would get greedy. Unlike Knucky, he was into extortion.

If someone started construction on a new tavern or nightclub, he and his men paid an unexpected visit. They would "strongly suggest" the plumbing, wiring and lighting be done by local businesses that were legitimate fronts for Delonzo's shady activities. The owners, often young and inexperienced entrepreneurs, usually went along with the suggestion, placing only mild protests. In the end they were convinced this was the way business was conducted in the city and by playing ball now, they would reap other benefits hinted at during the course of the conversation. After the new business opened and got on its feet, the gang paid another visit. They were told what linen service they were to use, from what wholesaler they should buy their liquor, and with what meat distributor to do business. Protests were stronger now as the owners came to the realization with whom they were dealing. And it was the significant moment of knowing who was putting the squeeze on them that caused near panic.

Delonzo and his associates also had an uncanny ability to strike fear into the hearts of the men with whom they were dealing. They dropped not-so-subtle hints that establishments outside the realm of their affiliation had an unfortunate habit of going up in flames. Larceny by extortion. Uncooperative proprietors were framed for concocting an arson-for-profit scheme, doing four to six years in the penitentiary. Many owners reluctantly went along with the new way of doing business because they saw it as the only reasonable way of staying in business and pursuing their entrepreneurial dream. Only now they were under the thumb

Jimmy Hoffa and Morris, his attorney

of Delonzo and his henchmen.

It was an insidious scheme, but Delonzo and his men had just enough politicians, policemen and judges on the payroll to make it work.

Because of Walters' connection with organized labor, he knew **Jimmy Hoffa**. Hoffa had a saying: "If some vicious cur out there is giving you trouble, simply cut off its head." Knucky had little trouble concluding that Delonzo was the source of all his troubles the last seven months. He knew that if something happened to Delonzo, someone else would rise to the top of the St. Louis crime ladder. But if word got around that Delonzo's demise had been due to a combination of greed and messing with the wrong guy, namely Lloyd Walters, the St. Louis mob would leave him alone. At least in the short run. And for now, that was all Knucky wanted.

Delonzo was a cocky character who never bothered to learn the subtle tricks of the trade that enabled Knucky to stay on top of his empire. His was a fertile mind on the racketeering landscape, but he never learned to perceive people's real intentions by reading between the lines. He never learned the art of compromise or subterfuge, of backing down temporarily from a no-win situation rather than pushing ahead like a bull in the proverbial china shop. He never bothered cultivating friendships, at least on a superficial level, which from time to time come in handy when temporary alliances are needed.

Unlike Knucky, Delonzo carried a weapon. It was a pearl-handled .45 automatic that could blow holes in people the size of a half-dollar. He had only one bodyguard and bragged freely to others that he knew how to take care of himself by packing his own "heat."

He had always loved cars. He was an enthusiast from the first time he drove a Model-T to when he bought a sporty yellow Cord, continuing to the present with his souped up '49 Lincoln. His Cord was a sentimental favorite. The unique coffin-nosed, front-wheel-drive car was almost an exact replica of the one **Tom Mix**, the cowboy radio and movie star, was driving the day he plowed into a concrete abutment.

Tom Mix

Delonzo loved his 1937 Cord. It had been meticulously maintained at Lindbergh Cadillac. One of the salesmen there had sold him the car when the company was also handling Cords back in the 1930s. He had the oil changed every 2,000 miles. It was waxed to a mirror finish every time the seasons changed. When he took the car in, the service crew chief was instructed to inspect it with a fine-tooth comb for a possible bomb.

Delonzo was paranoid about getting killed by a car bomb. It was the worst way to die as far as he was concerned. The funerals that he had attended, resulting from such mayhem, were usually closed-casket affairs. The bombs were connected to the starter mechanism by an ignition contact and were placed either directly under the car beneath the driver's seat or behind the firewall near the steering column. It was a bloody, ghastly way to die. Not only did Delonzo abhor the idea of being killed in such a wretched manner, he also loathed the notion his beloved automobile would meet a similar fate and end up a twisted wreck in a local junkyard—a rather ignominious demise for a mechanical ***object d' art.***

Unlike many gangsters, Delonzo enjoyed the thrill of being behind the wheel, feeling the surge of horsepower at his command when he pressed the pedal to the floor. He loved speed. Zooming down the highway in his beloved Cord was a pleasure in life that, for him, was a close second to having sex. He flouted the law in many ways. His glove box was crammed with an accumulation of speeding tickets and parking tickets. He had the serious ones fixed; the penny ante ones he simply ignored.

Delonzo never fully realized the dangerous game he was playing when he decided to make a grab for Walters' empire. He considered Knucky an anachronism, a spent force, an old duffer whose time was long past and was ready to be replaced and eased out of the picture. Delonzo was part of the new breed that had little or no respect for the old ways and its traditions and allegiances. He knew the Chicago mob cared little about the petty rivalries and on again, off again gangland struggles for control of the area. All they cared about was if whoever happened to be at the top of the heap in the "southern region" paid their monthly assessment for the privilege of being a part of the larger crime organization.

Delonzo had just finished a meeting with labor leaders, getting certain procedures and protocol straightened out. He told his bodyguard to wait a few minutes because he needed to use the can before they left. Delonzo sent his driver ahead to bring the car from the parking lot to the front of the building. When Al twisted the key in the ignition, he didn't hear the usual throaty roar of two hundred horses coming to life. The car erupted in a deafening explosion followed by a reddish-orange fireball of flame. Ka-boom! Whoosh! All hell broke loose. It was as though that pale horse from the Apocalypse was running wild. Heat, fire, and metal shot upward and outward from the force of the explosion.

Windows in nearby houses rattled like agates in a tin can. Several people who were standing near the street were hurled to the ground by the concussion. Some bystanders, who were a little farther away, flung themselves to a prone position to escape the flying debris.

One man had been out walking with his two small sons. He threw himself on top of them, trying to protect his seed with his body. The fierce heat singed his hair. He could hear the terrifying rush of superheated air and fire zoom by them. Something whizzed past his ear. "Cover your head," he yelled as globs of fire and chunks of metal rained from the sky, striking the sidewalk and cement road with discordant clanging and scraping sounds. The hood, front doors and other wreckage were strewn over a hundred-foot radius.

Delonzo and his bodyguard were just exiting the building when the deafening roar of metal and shrapnel occurred. They stood there with their mouths open, instinctively bringing their arms up to shield their faces from the orange and black geyser. Part of what had been the rear seat, full of smoke and flames, landed several feet from them. Delonzo looked up and saw a razor sharp piece of metal embedded in the door only two feet away. Neither of them spoke. It was as if the explosion had pulverized the ability to speak. After what seemed like an eternity, the bright red flames slowly gave way to ugly clouds of thick, black smoke. Bits and pieces of cloth and rubber that were still on fire were scattered everywhere. The bright yellow Cord was a derelict of smoldering steel, with missing doors and fenders. The few places where the bright paint didn't bubble-up and curl off the metal were splotched with ugly carbon smears. The front tire on the driver's side was still burning. Liquid rubber ran down the rim like melted wax.

Finally, Delonzo's mouth unleashed a venomous stream of bitter invective. "It's Walters," he said, shaking his fist; "it's that d— Knucky Walters! This is payback for that fire we set at his warehouse," Delonzo fumed. He was wound tight, like a spring that was about to uncoil. "No more warnings. No more fires or kidnappings. It's time to put an end to the Walters era once and for all," he said, his eyes burning from the smoke and heat of the explosion. "Bet on it!"

A gaper's block quickly developed as the street became crowded. The classy car was a burned out hulk, a ghost of its former self. Its grotesque metal carcass would be sent to an auto graveyard. But not before what was left of Sal Delonzo's driver would be pieced back together, like a broken and charred marionette, and sent to a stainless steel slab in the rear of the coroner's office in the St. Louis morgue at 1300 Clark. Both car and driver were incinerated beyond recognition. "Big" Al was dead as a dodo bird. It would take dental records to make a positive identification of the body.

The event created a news vacuum that police and citizens alike rushed to fill with speculative theories. Police and reporters listened in rapt fascination to Delonzo's story about how an accident of fate had allowed him to live. But it was one of those crimes in which evidence would be hard to come by. And it was a case the police weren't particularly motivated in trying to solve. Good riddance to another low-life piece of scum. The deceased became a dull statistic with an asterisk next to it, one more unsolved enigma of the city. The incident made sensational headlines for a day or two, but little or no pressure was applied by City Hall. The murder would never be solved. But not a single detective would ever lose an hour of sleep over it.

CHAPTER 17

Charlie Birger often visited his brother, who was a prominent merchant in Glen Carbon, Illinois. Authorities named a street after Charlie's nephew who donated land for a school. As an adult, Charlie lived in the Marion/Harrisburg area and supplied bootleg liquor to local farmers and miners. He had shootouts with the Klan and the notorious Shelton brothers, and became one of those outlaw folk heroes noted for their local generosity. In 1928 Charlie earned the distinction of being the last man publicly hanged in the state of Illinois. With the death of Birger, the Shelton gang inherited his territory by default but broadened the empire by expanding northward to East St. Louis. It was with the Shelton gang that Knucky Walters got his first real taste of organized crime and making a living by flouting the law.

June 1951

Dating Lorna and playing by her rules was one of the most difficult things Brad had ever encountered. ***Date me, but don't fall in love with me.*** Especially since he knew in his heart she was the girl he wanted to marry.

Mom, Dad: I want you to meet Lorna Sanders, the girl of my dreams. Beauty, grace, intelligence—all rolled into one. She loves God and she loves me. Somehow, somewhere, sometime, we're getting married. The two of us are going to make you some wonderful grandchildren. I just know you'll love her like a daughter.

But, of course, he couldn't do that. She wanted a carefree platonic relationship. He was forced to play the game of courtship behind the facade of a brother-sister act. ***What if you're too tentative, Logan? What if one of your rivals breaks the rules and wins her through boldness, daring to opt for decisiveness over timidity?***

Hemingway catches a swordfish

Conversely, he realized pressuring her by making demands could be just as costly. He was haunted by the no-win situation. He felt like Sisyphus of Greek antiquity, pushing that boulder up the hill, with the realization it could be an exercise in abject futility. That rock might roll all the way down to the bottom. Despite the mind-numbing possibility heartbreak could be just at the crest of the mountain, it was still worth it. He knew philosophers claimed the triumph was in the struggle. Like Santiago catching that magnificent fish in the serialized Hemingway story in "The Saturday Evening Post," only to lose it to a hungry shark. He could only hope it would be more than that. He prayed God was not testing him the way he did Job.

It was a beautiful Sunday afternoon, two turns of the Earth after schools were dismissed for summer vacation. The sky was a deep blue and puffs of wind blew the clouds merrily along. They seemed to be chasing each other.

It was one of those last-minute dates, made possible only by unexpected changes in both of their busy schedules.

"Where are we going dressed so casually?" Lorna demanded as they approached his car.

"Jones Park, my favorite spot in the whole world," he replied.

"Where did you get this old jalopy?" she asked, casting an unappreciative eye at a prized 1927 Stutz Bearcat Brad had driven.

"It's my only hobby. I'm restoring it."

Lorna remembered how important cars were to men and quickly perked up. "I love this color." She slowly walked around the car, nodding approvingly.

"Fire engine red." Brad followed closely behind. "I spotted it a few months ago sitting in an old barn near Edwardsville."

"I adore convertibles. Are you sure this will get us where we're going?"

"Absolutely. I've already overhauled the engine and now I have to restore the body."

Brad loved that old roadster. He memorized every single part, right down to the lug nuts and could take it apart and put it back together, nut by bolt. He caressed the nickel-plated trim around one of the headlights, ran his fingers over the grille like it was a stringed instrument, patted the hood, and fondled the tire in the wheel well.

"Lorna, you look absolutely great," he said.

"Thanks."

Lorna was outfitted in a pair of blue Capri pants that flattered her willowy figure. Red tennis shoes, as bright as neon lights, white socks, and a light blue tattersall shirt, tied at the waist, completed her ensemble. The Cardinal's baseball cap Brad had bought at the game snugged her hair.

"What are we going to do there?" she asked.

"Where?"

"Jones Park."

"Oh, uh, have a picnic." He was wearing navy poplins and an awning stripe shirt, with sleeves turned back to his elbows.

"But I didn't prepare a picnic basket," she said with a mild look of panic.

"Not to worry. I have one of those woven peck baskets full of food in the back seat."

"You, a man, know how to prepare a picnic basket?"

"Well . . . I had some help from my mother and sister."

"It sounds like a group plot to get the black sheep of the family married off."

"My mother says it's not normal for a man my age to be single." Brad shook his head. "She means well," he said as he opened her door.

"Do you mind if I try driving?"

"Dare I trust you?" he asked with a mock look of concern.

"My cousin, Carl, taught me how to drive out on rural roads near Pinckneyville."

He flipped her the keys and then slid into the passenger seat, stretching his legs out to the firewall. She ambled to the driver's side, exhuberantly hopped in, threw him a wiley smile and started the car. The big engine came to life with a mighty roar, and she adeptly shifted the three-speed gearbox into first. She popped the clutch and the car leapt forward, rear tires screeching and smoking on the pavement. They zoomed down the road, the throaty roar of the exhaust trailing behind them. With the cap in her lap, Lorna's hair flailed in the wind while her heavy foot mashed down on the accelerator. It gave her face a fresh radiance that Brad found irresistible.

"Don't you think this is a little fast for a respected member of the fourth estate?" he said, holding on for dear life.

"Who's to know?" she laughed. "The car is registered in your name."

Several times during the frenetic ride, Lorna nearly swept the tachometer into the red. Brad didn't want her to think he didn't have confidence in her driving, so he relaxed as best he could and inhaled the brisk air that rushed over and around the twin windscreens mounted on the car's cowling. Spring, the second movement in nature's symphony, with its sweet and light air, was reaching its climax.

"So what's on the menu?" Lorna gave a quick backward glance at the red and white checked kitchen cloth on the basket.

"There are a couple of ham sandwiches wrapped in waxed paper, tomato wedges, Golden Delicious apples, extra pieces of bread, and two slices of German chocolate cake."

"Umm, yummy, looks gourmetish." She tossed him a questioning look. "Is that a real word?"

"I don't think so. Hey, I also brought a thermos of iced tea."

"It sounds as if you thought of everything. What about a blanket?"

"Underneath the basket."

"Napkins?"

"Basket—top right."

"Salt and pepper?"

"Below the napkins."

"Eating utensils?"

"Oops. I guess we'll have to use our fingers."

"Why are there extra slices of bread?"

"To feed the fish," he said.

The car screeched to a halt as they arrived at Jones Park, over one hundred and thirty sprawling acres of spectacular beauty. An island of whimsical serenity— sanctuary from the frenzied urban activity on its periphery. Peace and solitude with clusters of brilliant flowers; a veritable forest of oak, sweet gum and hard maple trees. The dappled light on the ground waxed and waned with the fluttering breeze. The emerald grass rivaled that found on golf fairways at posh country clubs. Scattered throughout the scenic wonderland were four hundred green park benches. There was a large lagoon at the northeast end that had been stocked with goldfish, sunfish and catfish. Brad had participated in the annual Jaycee Fishing Rodeo there when he was a kid.

Brad selected a shaded spot near some lilac bushes, not far from the baseball field known as Diamond Number One. It was where East Side, his high school alma mater, played its home baseball games. He shook out and spread the billowing blanket on the green carpet. That's when he spotted them.

"Look," he pointed upward, "a cloud of monarch butterflies."

"I've never seen so many before. There must be hundreds of them."

"Aren't they a sight to behold?"

"They certainly are. Their brown, black, and orange markings are spectacular," Lorna said in wide-eyed wonder.

They munched their way through the sandwiches, tomatoes and cake. A pair of robins warbled in a nearby tree, and the smell of flowers lightly scented the crisp air. The happy pair decided to eat the apples later.

Jones Park, largest inland beach in America – guard tower and bathhouses

A small patch of light filtered through the canopy of trees, highlighting Lorna's face, reminding him once again of her natural beauty.

When the last bite of cake was consumed, they washed their hands in a nearby drinking fountain. Then the couple walked along a path towards the concrete bridge that crossed the lagoon. A half dozen mottled gray pigeons were nervously pacing a few yards away on their reddish legs, hoping for a handout. He tore some bits of bread and tossed them in their direction, causing considerable squabbling, scattered feathers, and a brief rush of frenzied feeding.

"When we toss bread to the fish, look out for Goliath," Brad said

"Who's Goliath?"

"He's a twenty-five pound catfish that has never been caught."

"Is that big?"

"Trust me, he's big."

"Have you ever seen him?"

"No, I think he's just a myth or legend."

When they got to the middle of the bridge, they ripped their bread into bite-sized chunks and tossed them below. Several large shiny goldfish came to the surface and eagerly gobbled the morsels. On the other side of the shore, three teenage girls sat on the edge and dangled their feet in the water.

Giggling.

"I can't believe how beautiful those goldfish are. And those clumps of red canna on the bridge island are the prettiest I've ever seen," Lorna said.

"There are some others equally as impressive over at the Sunken Garden on 13th and Summit."

"Oh, yes, I think I've seen them. Isn't that the small, triangular-shaped park only about a block long?"

"Yes. That's it, near Longfellow School."

"Can we go boating?" she asked.

"Do you know how to swim?"

"No," she sourly replied.

"Don't worry, it's not necessary. The lagoon is only about four feet deep."

"Really?"

"Yes."

"What keeps it from drying up in the summer?"

"The swimming pool at the other end has an artesian well. It pumps fresh water into the lagoon and pretty well keeps up with the evaporation rate. The sand-bottomed pool was the largest inland beach in America when the Park Board built it back in the 1920s."

They strolled hand-in-hand over to the boat dock. The upper level was a covered concrete and brick pavilion where the city band gave free concerts. Beneath it was the protected storage area for the boats. Rental was thirty cents for one hour. They picked out a boat tied up next to a flat section of concrete along the edge of the lagoon. He held the boat steady for Lorna as she climbed aboard.

"Hey, let me get a picture of you in this rustic boat." Lorna doffed her cap, tousled her hair and preened for the camera with a smirky grin.

"Perfect," he said as he clicked the shutter and captured her effervescent spirit.

He climbed aboard and sat facing her on the prow seat. Bending to the oars with sure strokes, he smoothly pulled them from one end to the other, following the lazy fishhook pattern of the water.

"Look," he said, as they neared the end by the sand-bottomed swimming pool. "See the boys and girls on the swim platform in the deep part?"

"Yes, they seem to be having the time of their life."

"Notice the one over by the rope that marks the end of shallow water. She looks as if she wants to venture out, but she seems afraid. She keeps holding back. Unless she decides to act, she runs the risk of always being alone, isolated, on the sidelines."

"I know what you're thinking," Lorna said. "It's that allegory about the timidity of my psyche when it comes to personal relationships. But the girl's fear might be rational. You have to allow for that. When I was seven my family was vacationing at Turkey Run Park in Indiana, and I nearly drowned. We were at a lake, and I inadvertently stepped into a deep spot and was literally going down for the third time when my mother swam out and rescued me."

"Lucky for you your mother was alert," Brad said.

"Life isn't fair," she continued. "The queer notion of a woman having to wait to be stricken with love spasms before choosing a mate seems outdated. I don't think God made the process of finding a lifelong companion such a whim of the heart, a random act tied to senseless hormonal emotion. It's an artificial creation of poets, novelists and lyricists. They picture women as all pinched and puckered, like a tulip bulb in early spring, waiting for a man's vernal warmth to cause her to blossom."

Lorna wouldn't admit it, but the frightening prospect of letting go loomed large in her mind.

"So you blame it all on the likes of Browning, Keats, Byron, Gershwin, Oscar Hammerstein and Lorenz Hart?" he asked.

"Yes! Why do poets make it seem as if love is that indefinable force holding the cosmos together? Why are song writers driven by the universal theme of woman needing man; man needing woman; condemned to living only half a life without that perfect other?"

"I don't think I would want to live in a world without ***All or Nothing at All, Someone To Watch Over Me, I'll Be Seeing You, How Deep Is The Ocean?*** or ***All The Things You Are***," he said.

"I'm not cynical. I'm just trying to be a realist."

He could see by Lorna's countenance his words had troubled her.

"Sorry, I didn't mean to get metaphysical." He polished an apple on the front of his shirt and tossed it to her. "An apple a day . . ."

". . . keeps the doctor away," she finished.

"See the edges of the lagoon?"

"Yes, what about them?"

"They used to be lined with headstones from the old city cemetery."

"Why would a cemetery have extra tombstones?" She stared at him, munching on a juicy bite from her apple.

"The cemetery was condemned. The water table here is too high, and during heavy rains, the coffins started popping out of the ground."

"Doesn't the same thing happen in New Orleans?"

"Yes. All the people down there are buried above ground in vaults."

"That still doesn't explain the extra tombstones."

"The bodies that were claimed in the old cemetery were moved up the hill and buried at Mount Hope or Mount Carmel in Belleville. Bodies not taken by relatives were placed in a mass grave. Their tombstones were used to line the lagoon."

"What happened to them?"

"After a while, people who came to the park thought it was rather ghoulish and demanded they be removed. I have no idea what they did with them after that."

A look of astonishment burst on her face. "I think I see him!" Lorna yelled.

"Who?"

"Goliath! Look . . . over there, near the clump of cattails under that weeping willow hanging over the bank."

He cupped his hand over his eyes trying to block the glimmering sun as it bounced off the iridescent blue water. "I don't see anything."

"It was a monster fish, with big whiskers," she said excitedly.

"You didn't see anything. Catfish are bottom feeders."

"I did, I swear."

"You know what they did to Army Air Corps pilots who claimed to see UFOs in 1945, don't you?"

"No."

"They were grounded. Army brass figured it was too much stress from combat fatigue."

"I know it was him. Maybe he only shows himself to outsiders . . . from Litchfield."

Brad looked at her and smiled disingenuously. A cool breeze caught Lorna's hair and blew it across her face. She brushed it back with her hand.

"Have I ever told you how good you look in sport clothes?" he said.

"Thanks for the compliment, but there isn't anything special about this outfit."

"You don't understand. It's you that gives substance to cloth and fiber. I've always thought it's the woman who makes the clothes, not the other way around. I just like looking at you and talking with you. You're easy to be with as a companion."

She leaned forward a bit in her seat. "You've been a good sport about not putting any pressure on me. One of the things I like is your vulnerability and gentleness, the softness in your heart. You seem to have respect for a lot of things—women, people's feelings, nature . . . Yet you have a good masculine quality because you seem to know who you are and where you are going."

"I think a lot of that comes from listening to things my mother and father taught me. Plus the fact that I try to do what God would have me do with my life. By the way, have you been to church since you moved here from Litchfield?"

"I hate to admit it, but since I've been making my own decisions, I haven't been to church."

"Do you miss it?"

A boating scene at Jones Park Lagoon with red canna blooming on the bridge island

"At first I didn't. I enjoyed the freedom of being able to do what I wanted on Sunday mornings. Sleep late if I wanted to. No more boring sermons."

"I know what you mean. I felt the same way when I went away to college. But when I came home for holidays and the summer, I kept attending church with my parents. Since I'm still living with them, I go just about every Sunday."

"I guess it's a good habit to get into," she said. "One of these days I'd like to get back in the saddle again."

"I'd love to take you with me. My church isn't big and impressive, but the folks there are good people, very friendly. And we have a young minister who does a good job with his sermons. One usually comes away from them with a feeling that he can be a little bit better person by applying some of the things he just heard."

"Maybe . . . sometime," she said.

After the boat outing they feasted on a couple of vanilla Dixie cups, purchased from a vendor pushing an insulated cart that was packed with dry ice. Then they walked back to the car and drove over to a stretch of ground that was next to Argonne Drive, named for the World War One battle in France. The median at the western end of Argonne contained the spectacular flag floral, a large horticultural bed of red, white, and blue, forming the proud ensign of the United States. A stone monolith, not far away on Caseyville Avenue, listed the names of the city's sons who were killed in the Great War. A bronze eagle proudly topped the obelisk.

Lorna noticed three boys playing ball. "How can you play a ball game with only three people?" she asked.

"They're playing corkball. As far as I know, the metro area is the only part of the country where it's popular. All you need is a pitcher, batter, and catcher. They rotate positions and keep score for themselves."

"How did the game originate?"

"It's a city game, first played by men in the area who frequented taverns after clocking a hard day's work at the factory. A lot of watering holes around here have wire cages out back where the game is played."

Bird's-eye view of Jones Park – Diamond 1, boathouse, lagoon, diving platform

Lorna shrugged her shoulders and looked puzzled. "They don't run the bases?"

"No. There are only two outs to an inning. A swing and a miss constitute an out. So do foul tips."

"How do you score?"

"Anything hit fair is a single. Four hits in one inning produce a run."

"No doubles or triples?"

"Correct. If you play in a large field, like these kids, any ball that goes a designated distance on the fly is a home run."

"They seem to be throwing something that looks like a miniature baseball."

"That's right. The Rawlings Company in St. Louis makes the ball. And the bat is like a replica of what they use in the major leagues, except it's only about half the diameter."

She turned with her tongue in her lopsided cheek and looked at him. "Then why is it called corkball?"

"When it was originally played at the taverns in the 1890's, they used a sawed off broomstick for a bat and the cork from the bung hole of a beer keg for the ball."

They reached Brad's car and walked around to the rear.

"Wait until you see what's in the trunk," he said.

"Knowing you, it could be almost anything."

"Have a look for yourself."

He unlocked the trunk and raised the lid, keeping a watchful eye on Lorna to gauge her reaction.

Her hand was on her hip—akimbo fashion. "Kites! We're going to fly kites!"

"Don't knock yourself out with enthusiasm. Remember how much fun that used to be?"

"I haven't flown a kite since I was about thirteen years old."

"We're not just going to fly them."

"What else is there?"

"A dogfight."

"Dogfight?"

"Yes, we do battle in the sky. How long has it been since your competitive juices flowed?"

"Not since I won the ping pong championship at Litchfield's teentown."

"Really, you beat all the girls?"

Her eyes danced. "Beat the boys too."

"Touché!"

"There were only three girls who entered the tournament."

"How did you get so good?"

She tucked her thumbs in her belt loops. "My dad made me a table when I was ten, and we played every Sunday afternoon. He wouldn't work on Sunday but ping pong and croquet were among his favorite pastimes allowed on the Lord's Day."

"So you also swing a pretty mean mallet?"

"That's one way of putting it."

"I bought these kites at Gruber's Drug Store—Hi Fliers, one red and one yellow, plus two balls of string.

She asked, "What are we going to use for tails?"

"I brought an old sheet that we can tear into strips and tie together."

"That should work."

Carrying their kites, they sauntered over to the south end

of the well-manicured park and spread them on the ground. Lorna chose the yellow kite. Said it reminded her of Danny Boy, a pet canary she once had. They sat on the grass cross-legged, fashioning the flat sticks into a cross, and then slipping the stringed corners of the kite into the slotted ends.

"Next thing we do is make a bendy-bow."

"I know," Lorna said, "I've done this plenty of times."

He rolled up his sleeves. Then he took his pocketknife and used it to cut the edges of the sheet so it could be easily torn into strips.

"Careful, **Jack Armstrong**, don't stab your self," she teased.

He tossed her some strips and she began fashioning them into a dragon's tail that extended a little over three feet from the bottom of her yellow diamond. He did the same thing with his. Then he tossed her a ball of string.

"Nice catch," he said, as she cradled it in her hands and then brought it close to her body.

"Good throw. I used to play second base on our church softball team."

"Is there anything this talented modern woman can't do?" he teased.

"Certainly," she shot back. "I'm a terrible cook."

They stretched their kites on the ground and straightened the tail sections out behind.

"A kite is merely an airfoil—"

". . . Which we control by playing out the string and tugging on it." Lorna saucily finished the sentence.

He gave her a look of admiration. "Wow! Not just pretty, but smart, too."

She acknowledged the compliment with a wink.

Then Brad playfully licked his finger and held it up to check atmospheric conditions. "Wind out of the west-northwest at twelve knots," he said. "Ready for takeoff?"

Lorna made a sound that was somewhere between a giggle and a cackle. "Steady as she goes, captain." He could tell Lorna was really getting into it. A look of competitive excitement crept across her face.

"We take off into the wind, just as Lindbergh did in 1927 at Roosevelt Field in New York."

"Jackie Cochran, world-famous female pilot, at your service," Lorna replied. "My bird is ready to go as soon as you give the word, Charlie my boy."

He flashed her a grin and she responded with a wave and a smile of her own. It was the best smile he'd ever seen on her face. She looked vibrant and full of life. ***This is the girl with whom I want to spend the rest of my life,*** Brad thought.

He held a hand up in the air the way it was done on aircraft carriers. He quickly brought his hand down to his side, and they took off running in parallel fashion. Lush green grass was scuffed and trampled under foot.

Lorna moved with a gazelle's supple grace. "Up, up and away," she yelled.

"We're airborne, keep your rudder steady," he replied with gusto.

The cheery blue sky sucked both kites to a level above the trees. They loosely held the balls of string on cardboard spools in their hands, letting them play out as the kites reached onward and upward.

"You're very good at this, Miss Cochran."

"Not bad yourself, Lindy."

As they neared Caseyville Avenue, they stopped running and turned to take full control of their flying marvels.

"Let's see you make that thing swing," he challenged.

"Just try to keep up with me, fly boy. If you do, they just might name a dance in your honor."

"Yeah, the lindy hop. He watched out of the corner of his eye as Lorna adeptly moved her hands and wrists, putting the kite through a stunning routine as it turned and twisted, dipped and did a tango in the sky.

He stood there with his mouth open. "You're a regular **Ginger Rogers**. That's quite a performance."

"She's the talented one, you know. She mimics everything Fred Astair does, only backwards, and wearing high heels."

Ginger Rogers (author's collection)

"Very astute. You won't get any argument from me."

"Now what?" she asked.

"We go to war."

"War?"

"Our kites engage in battle, as in 'dogfight'."

"So it's combat you want, is it? Well hold on to your shorts, you're in for the fight of your life."

She jerked the string on her kite and it sharply angled to the right, crashing into his, making a slight tear in the paper fabric.

"Oh, that was a dastardly little sneak attack, Miss Yamamoto. An act of infamy." He yanked his red dragon away from danger and sidestepped a few more feet away from Lorna's wide-stanced position. "You won't catch me napping again. ***En garde.***"

Their kites were sparring now, bobbing and weaving, like Joe Louis and Ezzard Charles in the boxing ring. Probing. Weaving. Ducking. Dancing. Looking for an opening.

"Women should be allowed to fly combat planes," Lorna challenged. Her voice held a rich vibrancy that stirred him.

"How do you figure?"

"Because women have better reflexes."

"Oh, that cut to the quick. So you think women are the superior sex, eh? We'll see about that."

He had subtly and slowly maneuvered his kite below hers. Now he quickly let his string unravel to take advantage of a gust of wind. His kite rose quickly and the two became engaged. Her tail was entangled in the nose of his kite. He gave an adept yank and two small sections of her tail pulled loose.

"Gotcha" he yelled. "You're done for now. It's just a matter of time."

"Oh, yeah," she boldly replied. "I have not yet begun to fight."

Too late did he realize the full meaning of her haughty challenge. A flip of her wrist and a tug on the string brought her kite crashing into his. They became hopelessly entangled, losing their aerodynamic buoyancy. The bright triangles dipped crazily back and forth, slipping sideways and plummeting earthward before plowing into the ground a hundred feet away.

"Crash and burn," he yelled. "The old John Paul Jones trick. Your vessel is going down so catch your ship's rigging in the enemy's. Only in this instance, we both lost our lives."

"Didn't Patton say the object of war was to make the other poor fellow die for his country?"

"Yes, but I don't think he said ***fellow***. It was something much more descriptive beginning with the letter 'B.' "

"I know; I read his speech," Lorna replied.

He dropped his ball of string and made a lunge at Lorna. "You little vixen, I'll get you for this."

She let out a squeal of excitement, dropped her string and dodged his initial lunge.

"Catch me if you can," she said, tossing her beautiful hair to the wind and running a zigzag pattern in a determined attempt to escape his clutches. He dogged Lorna's steps, caught up, but she nimbly danced out of his reach with the aplomb of a gymnast.

"You missed," she taunted.

He lunged again, but like Goliath avoiding the fisherman's hook, she managed to evade his grasp. Lorna's eyes were bright with a mischievous look. He dove and grabbed her by the waist, gently tackling her. As they fell to the soft, grassy park surface, he adroitly maneuvered their bodies so he would be the first to hit the ground. She fell on top of him, full of mirth and laughter.

"Now you're in ***real*** trouble," Lorna said, her body pressing on his. She teasingly pinned his wrists to the ground. "I told you women had quicker reflexes," she bragged, with a triumphant gleam in her eye.

Brad pulled one hand free and used it to tickle her bare midriff. He noticed she had a small birthmark, burnt umber—like one of those exotic colors in a big Crayola box. Giggling, she lost control.

"No fair!"

He twisted and shifted his position, the way he'd seen Lou Thesz do it dozens of times in wrestling matches. After adeptly rolling her over, their positions were reversed.

"Now who's top dog, Miss Feisty Pants? How's that for reversal of fortune?"

They were both breathing hard, warily eyeing each other. He firmly but gently kept her pinned to the ground despite her serious efforts to escape through a series of convoluted wiggles. He felt her body go limp as she finally ended resistance. Then Lorna stared at him, giving him a once over—assessing his looks and physical qualities. She was attracted to his friendly eyes, his tousled hair and the lean, graceful strength of his body. Brad returned the compliment and drank in her wholesome beauty.

"You're quite fetching in the tomboy mode."

She pulled a hand free and ran it up and down his arm. "And you're stronger than I would have guessed."

"Don't let my slim build fool you. I ran track in high school and college. And I've been lifting weights since I was sixteen."

"**Charles Atlas**?"

"Yes, that's where I got the idea. From an ad in a magazine. It also helps relieve stress and tension. I got away from it a bit when I went to college, but I've been trying to stay fit ever since my stint in the military."

"Aren't you afraid you'll get muscle-bound?"

"Oh, no, I do just enough to tone my one hundred-eighty pound body and stay in shape. I go to a judo class once a week to stay flexible."

"Are you any good?"

"The first thing they do is teach you how to fall so you don't injure yourself."

"You didn't answer my question."

"I can hold my own."

"So, I'm messing with a good looking guy whose hands are lethal weapons?"

"Well . . . I wouldn't quite put it that way." He looked deep into her eyes trying to decipher hidden meanings behind her words and probe her labyrinthine thoughts. ***She said I was good looking.***

"Well, are you going to get off me, or what, Lancelot?" she teased.

For the first time since they met he sensed vulnerability in her. She looked so . . . kissable. It must have been an unguarded moment for Lorna—a rare lapse in her defensive shield. He was quick to take advantage. He removed her cap, ran his fingers through her hair.

"No, I kind of like having the upper hand for a change."

A sparrow chitted noisily from a nearby maple, and leaves rustled above them.

Brad's head drifted lower and he kissed her gently on the lips. Her body tensed and there was a subtle, ever so slight, hesitation as she momentarily held back, as if by instinct. But she slowly relaxed and gave in, and the two of them enjoyed a rare moment of bliss between man and woman, the pursuer and the pursued. They kissed again. Longer, passionately. Then she pulled away.

"You taste better than a banana split," he said.

"You rogue. Didn't they teach you any chivalry at knight school? What do you think you're doing, pray tell?"

"I'd say I just stole a kiss from a fair princess. And if I am any judge of a woman's emotions, I'd say you seemed to enjoy it as much as I did, my liege."

He wanted to tell her that he loved her. That his heart ached when they were apart. But he was afraid it might spoil what they had, so he held his tongue. He stuck to his plan to win her over inch by inch.

"You assume too much! Let me up before a park policeman comes along and arrests you for assaulting a female of the species."

"How about one more kiss?"

"When pigs fly!"

They got back on their feet and dusted the grass off their clothes. Then they walked back to the car.

"You're not mad at me are you?"

"I was just teasing," she said as she clasped her hand in his. Dimples dug into her cheeks as she smiled. "I'm happy as a lark."

Like the indefatigable Arturo Toscaninni, enthralled with his New York orchestra, Brad's heart was beating a happy allegro. "That makes two of us," he said with a broad grin.

Arturo Toscaninni

CHAPTER 18

During the mid-1800s, relations between the two river cities became strained when bureaucrats in St. Louis made its sister city a dumping ground, a Botany Bay of sorts for lawbreakers and undesirables. Fines and jail sentences for scoundrels were often suspended if they promised to leave the city and never return. Many of them simply crossed the river and continued their lawless ways in East St. Louis. When the police in that city caught them involved in more skulduggery, they were publicly whipped, confined in the stocks or jailed. Sometimes they were placed on a skiff in the middle of the river and sent on their way to some poor unsuspecting town downstream.

June 30, 1951

It was one of those rare dreary summer days—an aberration—the result of a warm front from the Gulf of Mexico meeting a cold one from Canada. It was unseasonably cold, wet and windy. Brad was on his way home from working late at the office, still feeling elated after his picnic with Lorna. Harold Zeigler, his office co-worker, was with him. Harold's car was getting a ring job, and he had asked Brad to give him a ride home for three or four days while it was in the shop.

"My next door neighbor on North Park Drive is building the first atomic bomb shelter in East St. Louis," Harold said.

"Really, I can't wait to see it," Brad replied.

The new global villains and their nuclear threat was the dominant topic as they drove home.

"Can you believe in a few years the U.S. and Russia will have enough bombers and intercontinental missiles to practically destroy mankind?"

"Yes, we've got the B-50 and they have the Tupelov TU-4, but the next generation will be bigger and with better range," Brad said. "Fortunately, we're ahead of them in technology. Their Tupelov is a poor copy of our B-29."

Harold raised an eyebrow. "Radiation and fallout alone would wreak massive destruction ending in a nuclear holocaust. The new weapons are many times more powerful than the bombs dropped on Hiroshima and Nagasaki."

"As long as we have the edge on them, I don't think there will be a nuclear war." Brad was shaking his head. "Bombers on both sides don't have the range to return to base—it would be a one-way suicide trip."

Harold's demeanor became serious. "I hope you're right. The military is already talking about using ***the*** bomb in Korea."

"Look," Brad pointed to the side of the road. "The city is installing utility poles with civil defense warning sirens on them."

"Yes, and the mayor and city commissioners are meeting to decide which buildings will be designated as air raid shelters." Harold was skeptical. "Do you really think there will be survivors in a nuclear war?"

"Sure, if it's a limited war," Brad said. "You know, all this nuclear stuff is hard on youngsters. My nephew, Morrie Maltzman, told me about the terror of going through duck-and-cover drills at his junior high school. He said that he was even having nightmares about mushroom clouds."

"Duck and cover. Are the school officials nuts? Do they really think hiding under a desk top is going to protect the kids from a six-megaton blast?"

Brad shrugged and gave him a palms up gesture. "A recent news article I read announced that a team of scientists are working on a new 'device' that has been dubbed the hydrogen bomb."

"And it won't be long before the Russkies have their own version. Were getting into an arms race that is insane."

"Do you know the difference between an A-bomb an and H-bomb?" Brad asked.

"I only know bits and pieces from reading 'Popular Science,' " Harold replied. "The atomic bomb works with fission, i.e. splitting the atom. The hydrogen bomb is thermonuclear and uses the principle of fusion."

"Why the term thermonuclear?"

Harold took a deep breath and paused a few reflective seconds before responding. "I think because it takes a great deal of heat to start a fusion reaction."

"Then why call it a hydrogen bomb?"

"Because heavy hydrogen is one of the things used to make the bomb. With the H-bomb, a fission bomb is used as the trigger to generate the enormous heat that is needed."

They arrived at Harold's house, pulled into his driveway, exited the car, and walked around to his back yard to get a better view.

"My neighbor is Doy Freeland—he's a doctor."

All of a sudden, there it was. Instead of a well-manicured lawn that matched the front, there was a big hole in the ground where fruit trees and a rose garden once existed. A white arched arbor, on which ivy and honeysuckle vines climbed each spring, lay on its side. A big pile of dirt was next to the hole. A bulldozer had leveled a couple of trees and ruined a flowerbed of phlox and petunias.

Each day thereafter, when Brad drove Harold home from work, they would get out of the car and inspect the progress on a room that was approximately eighteen feet square. A well was dug. (No need for water witching with a willow twig in East St. Louis; H2O was eighteen feet below the surface, nearly everywhere.) The walls and floor and ceiling were formed from reinforced slabs of eight-inch-thick concrete. A generator and ventilation system was installed. Inside, there was a shower and a toilet in one corner. Plenty of shelving for canned and dried food. One wall had six sleeping compartments, two sets stacked three high, in military fashion.

"The top will be lined with lead," Harold pointed out. "Dr. Freeland told me that six feet of dirt is to be placed on the roof. A set of concrete steps will lead directly from the back of the house to a massive door also sheathed with lead." Brad smiled when he remembered lead was the only thing that could protect **Superman** from Kryptonite.

On the fourth day, after they had checked out the shelter's progress, Harold insisted that Brad stay for supper.

Harold lowered his head and peered at Brad across the table. "Did you know there's a more immediate threat to the area than nuclear Armageddon?"

Brad finished chewing a bite of meatloaf. "No. What would that be?"

"An earthquake, caused by the New Madrid fault." Harold's face had a serious demeanor.

"But isn't it located down in the bootheel of Missouri, over 100 miles away?"

"One hundred and forty-five to be more exact."

"So the destruction here would be minimal, right? In the Frisco quake of 1905, I thought there wasn't much serious damage 100 miles from the epicenter."

"True, but the geological formations at New Madrid are older and harder than the San Andreas fault, which means the shock waves will probably travel much farther. And I think the San Francisco disaster was in 1906."

"My relatives in Paducah said the last big quake in the New Madrid seismic zone hit the region in 1811. They're closer to ground zero than we are."

Harold's wife, a pleasant looking woman in a print housedress, listened intently.

Harold took a sip of coffee. "Actually, there were several major quakes from 1811 to 1812. One of them was so bad it caused the Mississippi River to temporarily flow backward, and the upheaval formed Reelfoot Lake in Tennessee."

Brad nodded to Mrs. Zeigler. "This food is delicious, ma'am. You're every bit as good a cook as my mother."

A broad smile broke out on her face. "Thanks. That's very kind of you."

Brad looked back at Harold. "So how bad do they figure the quake was back then?"

"One of the worst. Fortunately, this part of the country had few buildings of significant size and was sparsely settled. It purportedly rattled windows as far away as Pittsburgh, Pennsylvania."

Brad wagged his head in amazement. "Wasn't there some frontier village in Illinois gobbled up by the river?" he asked.

"You're probably thinking of Kaskaskia. It's the only part of Illinois west of the Mississippi River, but that was caused much later by a big flood that caused the river to change its course."

"Oh, yeah. Now I remember. So if a big one hits, the Spivey Building and our offices would be reduced to a pile of rubble?"

Harold nodded pensively. "Probably. Scientists estimate that a quake of 8.0 in magnitude on the Richter scale would cause more than eighty thousand deaths in a six state area."

"Wow! That would make it the biggest natural disaster to ever hit the United States."

"For goodness sakes. Can't you two men talk about something else beside death and destruction," Harold's wife complained with a look of exasperation. They shrugged and switched topics.

Later, Brad thanked Harold and the Mrs. for the fine meal, excused himself, and went to his car, preparing to head for home. The sun had fallen eighteen degrees below the horizon and dusk was settling in. He backed out of Harold's driveway and sat there with disbelieving eyes. Several car lengths ahead of him, and parked on the side of the street next to the baseball diamond, was a bright turquoise Kaiser.

What the . . . that's Viktor's car.

Viktor's used 1949 Kaiser sedan

Brad had helped him pick it out after he quit work at the packing house and took a job as a Fuller Brush salesman.

What a surprise. I haven't seen him for weeks.

Brad wondered what Viktor was doing at the park. He decided to see if he could find his partner from the triple-date episode. He walked across the ball diamond, his eyes searching right and left for his friend. No sign of him. The park lights came on with an incandescent yellowish radiance.

What on earth would he be doing in the park?

He passed the concrete stadium that had been built in 1934 by WPA workers and then walked over to the boathouse pavilion. Nothing. Brad pulled the brim of his hat down as a chilly, drisly wind swept through the park. A second gust caused his suit coat to billow out, like the spinnaker sail on an America's Cup racing boat. Then he crossed the lagoon bridge and checked the west side of Jones Park. He shook his head and shrugged his shoulders in mild frustration. ***It's getting late. I'd better head for home.***

Brad stopped by the rest room under the baseball pavilion on his way back. He had just finished washing his hands at the lavatory when he caught the sound of low, muted talking just outside. Brad recognized one of the voices as that belonging to Viktor. He was on the verge of walking out and saying hello, but he heard just enough of the conversation to stop him dead in his tracks.

"The ten thousand dollars you promised me isn't nearly enough, Viktor." The other man's voice grew strong and insistent.

The two were standing beside the stadium wall. Brad moved near a high open window and was close enough to hear Viktor exhale smoke after a satisfying drag on his cigarette. "My superiors in the Soviet Union will be pleased to get their hands on this. I'm sure they will be willing to pay you big bonus if you promise to keep working for us in the future."

Brad heard a bird singing. An ill omen after dark unless you're in England and it's a nightingale.

"It had better be a good bonus because I'm taking a big risk. Do you realize the significance of getting inside information on this plane's capabilities? Its importance to America's defense is mind boggling."

"I think I have fair idea—probably some kind of plane with vertical takeoff capability."

"No, that's not it." The sandy haired engineer shook his head. "This prototype that McDonnell Aircraft is building will be able to fly at 73,000 feet." He was still wearing his photo identification badge on his shirt beneath his jacket. The name said Scot Kampmann. "With its huge wingspan, it will be able to soar high above the Soviet Union and gather intelligence. The plane doesn't carry any armament, just the best Edwin Land camera in the world with Kodak Mylar-based film. You don't have anything to match that. You can't even shoot it down. If your country claims your airspace is being violated, the U.S. will simply deny it or claim it was a weather plane that strayed off course. You won't have any proof. This aircraft could tip the Cold War balance in America's favor."

"A spy plane? You mean it will be able to take photographs of our nuclear test site at Semipalatinsk?"

"That and a lot more."

Brad couldn't believe his ears. Viktor was obviously a Soviet agent, and this other man was selling out his country. He began mulling over possible courses of action.

"If this plane can do what you say, Moscow will see that you get more money. Here's the ten thousand I promised." Viktor's English had improved dramatically since Brad had last seen him.

Brad could hear the man open the envelope then a faint ruffling as he thumbed through the bills.

"It looks like all the money is here." He handed Viktor a ten-by-fourteen inch manila envelope bulging with documents. "These are the drawings and specifications of the plane. Contact me when you get my bonus."

"I'm not going to bother checking inside." Viktor said. He tucked it under his left arm. "If you're lying, you'll never live to spend any of the money."

"Don't worry: I know better than to try and pull a double-cross."

Brad's heart was pounding. It felt as though a giant vise was squeezing his ribcage. He had to act before Viktor left with the plans. Brad knew Viktor would be armed. As he turned to look for a club or some kind of weapon, he accidentally bumped a wire mesh trash barrel, and a disgorged soda bottle clattered loudly on the concrete floor.

A spy plane similar to the McDonnell Aircraft prototype

"Uh, oh, I'm sunk," he said under his breath.

Viktor tossed his cigarette and drew his 9 mm Makarov. "All right, I have a weapon. Whoever is in there, come out with your hands up."

Brad let out a huge sigh of disappointment. He raised his hands over his head and walked out.

"What the . . . Brad, Brad Logan. I'm so sorry it had to be you."

The diffused park lighting was sufficient for Brad to see that Viktor's usual friendly smile was gone. "You won't get away with this, Viktor. Barb told me she had suspicions about you," Brad lied. "The FBI and CIA are probably after you right now."

"I don't think so," Viktor said confidently. Viktor gave the other man a sideways glance and motioned with his gun. "Get out of here, I'll take care of this little problem myself." The nervous man hesitated, then turned and walked briskly toward his car, disappearing into the darkness.

Maybe I'll get lucky and a park policeman will come along on his motorcycle, Brad thought, hopefully.

"You know I don't have any choice, Brad." Viktor stood with his legs slightly spread, his weight evenly distributed on the balls of his feet. It was the Balishnakov technique, taught to all agents at the Lubyanka in Moscow. "I'm going to have to kill you. Too bad you had to stick your nose in this. I really liked you." He spoke in the past tense, as if Brad were already dead.

Viktor's inflection changed. Brad sensed his time was running out. "It's not too late, Viktor. Change your mind, now. Stay in this country. Choose freedom. You can hand over the plans to the FBI and give them the name of that engineer from McDonnell Aircraft."

"Save your bourgeois sentimentality." He purged his voice of emotion. "You Amerikans . . . you have too much freedom. Your system is corrupt. Capitalism is dying. Soviet socialism is winning the battle for the hearts and minds of the world's working class. Destiny is on our side."

"You've been in this country long enough to know that isn't true. Besides, you have no real freedom in your country."

"Political freedom will come later, after we achieve our goals. Discipline and willingness to obey our leadership is what's important now."

Brad tried to hide a crestfallen look. He could tell Viktor was blindly following the Stalinist party line, just like gullible Germans who fell for Hitler's twisted Aryan supremacy gibberish.

"Enough talk." Viktor's mouth flattened into a grave line. "Turn around, Brad. That way you won't see it coming. It will be over quickly."

Brad whispered a prayer as he turned and prepared to face eternity. He steeled himself, wondering what it was going to feel like, getting a bullet in the brain. Viktor moved closer and his steps were like hoof beats from that pale horse with a dark hooded rider swinging the big scythe. Brad tried to calm his racing heart while he cudgeled his brains, searching for a solution—a way out. A sick feeling fell into the pit of his stomach.

"HOLD IT! Drop that gun!" A stern voice rang out from the darkness.

Brad slumped with infinite relief, but the feeling lasted only a fleeting moment. Viktor grabbed Brad by the shoulder and spun him around, using him as a shield. The folder was still in his left hand, pressed against Brad's chest. "Not so fast, my friend." Brad could feel cold steel pressed against his temple.

"Put the gun down, Viktor. My gun is aimed right at you. I never miss at this range."

Brad and Viktor were equally surprised. It was Walter Boyne from Scott Air Base.

"I had a suspicion your defection was phony," Walter said matter-of-factly. "I'm with Air Force Intelligence, and I've been waiting for you to show your hand."

Viktor was undeterred. "Drop your gun or I'm going to blow your friend's brains out."

Walter didn't give an inch. "If you shoot him, I'll drop you in your tracks. Throw your gun down. It's your only chance to get out of this alive."

Brad decided not to wait while these two were dickering with his life. Viktor had one arm pinned at his side, but Brad's other hand was free. Almost in a blur, he slammed his fist up, knocking Viktor's gun hand skyward. His finger squeezed the trigger but the bullet went harmlessly into the air. Walter instantly fired his Colt .45 semi-automatic twice. The first shot only grazed Viktor's skull but the second hit him squarely in the forehead, sending forth a crimson blood burst. His body was thrown backward against the concrete wall. A pained expression from disbelieving eyes faded, then disappeared altogether as he fell sideways in slow motion until his head hit the ground. A ribbon of blood gushed from the wound and streaked his temple. For several seconds the blood continued pulsing rhythmically through a mangled hole. The smell of burnt cordite hung heavy in the air.

"Thanks, Walter." Brad stared numbly at Viktor's body.

"That was close." Brad swiped at the sweat on his brow. "A few seconds later and I'd have been a goner. And here I thought this Viktor guy was my friend."

"We've had our eye on this Commie for some time now. And we also know who the other guy is. We'll wait until he gets back home and then we'll arrest him for violating the Espionage Act."

"Were you really going to let him shoot me?"

"I was hoping it wouldn't come to that, but . . . yes, when it comes to national security, nothing else matters." He smiled. "Don't worry, I'd have seen to it that you'd been given a posthumous citation."

"Gee, thanks." Brad shook his head in disbelief. "What about Stefan?" Brad furrowed his brow. "Was he also KGB?"

"I don't know for sure, but probably. They usually work in pairs. My guess is that he and Viktor were also on Tito's payroll."

Brad's eyes widened. "Double agents! Boy, you just never know, do you?"

"Brad, about this experimental plane," Walter said without preamble.

"Plane? I don't know anything about a plane," Brad said with a mercurial grin, unable to resist the gibe.

Brad's Junior High mascot – the Lansdowne Tiger

"Good man, Brad." Walter flashed him a Churchill V for victory sign. "I saw a police call box over by Lansdowne Jr. High at 40th and Caseyville Avenue. Could you phone this in and notify the police. I need to stay here with Viktor and these pilfered documents."

"Sure thing, Walter. Thanks again for saving my life." Brad gave him a firm handshake. "I don't know how I'm ever going to repay you." He started walking back toward his car.

"Invite me to your wedding . . . if and when . . ."

Brad looked back over his shoulder. "I've been dating this girl for nearly a year. She seems more interested in a career than marriage. But I hope to change her mind someday soon. When we decide to tie the knot, you can be my best man."

"I'd be honored," Walter said with a broad smile.

When the authorities searched Viktor's apartment, they made another startling discovery. He had a map of the metro area with the names of several key industries printed on it in red Cyrillic letters. They included Monsanto Chemical, McDonnell Aircraft, Mallinckrodt Chemical, Emerson Electric, the Cahokia power plant, Aluminum Ore and Granite City Steel. If the Cold War suddenly turned into a shooting war, the plan was to give a signal and have members of the local Communist party blow up these companies to cripple America's war effort.

CHAPTER 19

East St. Louis and its surrounding environs at mid-century was a microcosm of Middle America, with all its ethnic diversity, traditions, values, religious beliefs and prejudices. From 1890 to 1920 it had been the fastest growing city in America, doubling its size every ten years. By 1920 it was the 86th largest city in America and *second* only to Chicago in Illinois.

August 14, 1951

Lorna was alone in her room waiting for Barb Edelblute to arrive. They were going to see a Clark Gable movie at the Majestic. She was thinking about Brad and Lance, pondering the complexities and ambiguities of relationships. She catalogued their strengths and weaknesses, weighing the things she liked about each of them. It was obvious that Lance, with his hot-blooded good looks, was trying to charm her into bed. But no man had yet accomplished the feat. Despite her church's teaching against premarital sex, she had to admit there was a certain appeal to making passionate love with a handsome man. With Lance's experience with women, no doubt he'd make a good lover.

There was an abrupt knock on her door.

"Is that you, Barb? Come in."

Barb trudged into the room. "I know I'm early. I didn't have anything else to do so I thought I'd come on over."

Lorna glanced at her watch. "That's okay, we don't have to leave for another half hour. We can just talk until it's time to leave."

"Viktor and I were planning on seeing this movie, you know." Barb's eyes grew muddy with sadness.

Lorna gave Barb a comforting hug. "Viktor—a spy . . . who would have guessed. Are you all right?"

"I'll be okay." She silently decried his deception. "Where's Gloria?"

"She's downstairs in the lobby, talking on the phone with her beau."

"You have a faraway look in your eyes, like you're off in another world. A penny for your thoughts," she said with an impish smile.

"I was just thinking about the two men in my life."

"Don't tell me you're trying to choose one over the other?"

"No. Just idle speculation about which would make a better husband."

"I thought you said you're not ready for anything like that."

"I'm not. It's just something I'm having fun with, uh, day-dreaming."

"Any conclusions?"

"I haven't progressed to that point yet."

"Ever tried the Ben Franklin method?"

Lorna shook her head and prompted Barb to elaborate.

"When you're undecided about something, old Ben recommended making a list of pros and cons."

"Really?"

"Uh-huh." Barb walked over to Lorna's desk and picked up a pencil and a note pad.

"Here," she said, handing them to Lorna. "I'll help you out. Kinda curious myself."

"I don't know—"

"C'mon, that's what best friends are for. It'll be interesting. Hedda Hopper says Shelly Winters made a pro and con list before she decided not to marry Farley Granger."

"Interesting. She's St. Louis Jewish," you know. "Lived somewhere on Newstead, wherever that is, before her family moved to New York." Lorna sat on the edge of the bed while Barb dragged a desk chair over and sat across from her.

"Well, okay." Lorna flashed a look of resignation tinged with expectancy. "How do we start?"

"I'll give you some buzz words—you choose one guy over the other and write down his name."

"Such as . . ."

"Looks!"

Lorna thought a few seconds. "Lance is devilishly handsome while Brad's good looks are accentuated by his demeanor. They're both good-looking, each in their own way."

"Lorna, you have to choose."

"I don't think I like this."

"Do it!"

"Okay, okay." Looks—Lance, she wrote. "But Brad is a ***very*** close second."

"Personality."

"Oh, gosh . . . uh, charm is Lance's forte. He's interesting, but sometimes he can be a little too glib—thinks the world revolves around him. Brad is sincere, thoughtful, easy to talk with . . . he gets the nod."

Jeff Chandler

"Good provider."

"Lance seems to be loaded, my guess is family money, but Brad has potential . . . Lance, I guess."

"Best ***kisser*** – you know, like **Jeff Chandler**." Barb's eyes grew big with anticipation.

"Let's see, uh, Lance makes my knees weak but Brad is very tender, so . . ."

"Choose! This only works if you don't get too analytical."

"All right already, Lance."

"Protector."

"That's easy. Brad really knows how to take care of himself."

"Sometimes those kind turn into wife beaters."

"Not Brad, it's not in him . . . I can tell. He's a Teddy bear—so gentle with me."

"Best dancer."

"No contest. Lance is accomplished—smooth; Brad can't even two-step.

"Integrity."

"Brad, in a cakewalk."

"Are you sure? What about that Walters guy he hangs around with?"

"I know, it's a little strange, but Brad has loads of integrity."

Barb toyed with a hairpin. "Father to your children."

Lorna suppressed a laugh. "Funny, I can't picture Lance even wanting children."

"***Lover.***" Barb gave her an ooh, la-la look.

"Barb!!!" Lorna shook her head despairingly.

Her co-worker allowed herself a bit of a smirk. "Well . . . you know, pretend you're on your honeymoon."

"I'm not sure Brad has ever been with a woman. I guess Lance would be the lover boy."

Litchfield High School

"It's been rumored at the office that he's gotten a couple of women in trouble."

Lorna leaned forward. "You mean p-pregnant?"

"Exactly."

Lorna had heard Lance was, by reputation, a womanizer. Though she tried not to, Lorna couldn't help thinking about a girl in her senior class at Litchfield who suddenly dropped out of school and, according to talk, went to a home for unwed mothers.

"Don't worry about me. I'm cautious, and I have no intention of getting intimate with him."

Barb stretched her neck to see Lorna's list. "Who's winning?"

"Don't you think this is silly? Maybe I should go to one of those gypsy palm readers for advice?"

"This is much more scientific and logical," Barb said. "How about trainability?"

"What do you mean?"

"You know men are incomplete—just overgrown boys with big egos. They need firm guidance from a woman before they make suitable husbands."

Lorna scribbled Brad's name. "Are we finished?"

Lorna's eyes were glazed in mock frustration.

"Yes . . . uh, no—wait, let me think." Barb knitted her brows. "How about religion? Won't your parents disown you if you marry an agnostic?"

"Yeah. Brad wins hands down on that one too."

"I can't think of anything else. Who won?"

Lorna threw up a hand. "Wait, I just remembered another one. When I'm with Brad, I'm really, really happy. He makes my heart sing. I laugh and feel good inside on our dates. I don't know if I can explain, it's one of those intangibles . . ."

Barb's demeanor grew serious. "You know he's daft in love with you."

"Yes, I can see it in his eyes."

"So that's it, Brad is the winner. Send him a telegram."

"Barb, this was just a game—not the basis for some big life decision. I'm not anywhere near ready to make a commitment to either of these two men. For the time being, it's going to be the status quo—nothing serious with Brad or Lance."

"You're really into this career thing, aren't you?"

"Yes. And I can't fully explain or comprehend this need that drives me. All I know is I want to feel the same exhilaration men experience—the sense of achievement that goes with success."

At this point in her career, Lorna felt like she was only on the third rung up the ladder.

"You'll see, Barb. One of these days I'll make my mark in life. I'll be feted as a woman of accomplishment. Then I'll be ready to settle down and do this family thing."

"I wish you luck," Barb said. "By the way, which guy are you seeing next?"

"I have a date with Lance tomorrow night."

Barb heard the clock downstairs chiming. "Hey, we ought to be leaving soon to make sure we get good seats."

"Good idea. Let's get going."

Chapter 20

July 30, 1951

When it came to women in general, nearly all of Lance's actions were ultimately directed by his southern compass. His patience was growing thin with Lorna. He had grown weary of playing the perfect suitor. The game of verbal foreplay and niceties was growing tedious. It had never taken him this long to seduce a woman before. The delay and the wait were irritating him. Tonight he would add to his list of conquests. He would turn on the fatal charm, wine and dine like never before. He would say all the right words and ply her with drink. If that didn't work he would resort to plan B. One way or another, he meant to have her. He had waited long enough.

"That outfit looks outstanding on you," Lance said, as he handed her a red rose in the Beulah Club lobby.

"Thank you," Lorna replied. She was dressed in a pink cocktail dress and Ruby Keeler dancing shoes with a matching ribbon across the instep.

Lance was dressed, as usual, impeccably. "I think this is going to be an exceptional evening," he said as he helped her into the car.

"I've been looking forward to it all week." True to form, Lorna sat by the door.

"Come over here just a little closer," he coaxed. "I feel like I need a megaphone to communicate with you."

Lorna gingerly scooted a few inches closer. "This is just fine. You know how people talk about women who drape themselves all over a man."

"No, what do they say?"

"If she acts that way in public, you can imagine how she behaves when they are alone. They equate that type of behavior with tramps."

"This isn't exactly the prim Victorian Era, you know." Lance turned his eyes toward the car's ceiling.

Lorna folded her arms. "And what exactly do you think was wrong with Victorian manners and morals?"

"Look," Lance said in exasperation. "I just wish you wouldn't act like it was our first date. Please don't be so . . . standoffish."

"You know perfectly well I date other men. How would you like it if I draped myself all over them and encouraged inappropriate behavior?"

"Yeah, I see what you mean. I wouldn't like it. I wouldn't like it at all."

"So, stop trying to pressure me."

"It's just that we've been seeing each other for months now. I think I'm falling for you, and it would be nice to know the feeling might be mutual."

Lorna repeated her mantra. "I like you Lance, but I can't let love complicate my life and interfere with my career."

Lance just shook his head in frustration.

The three distinctive camelback trusses of the Municipal Bridge loomed ahead. Lance's sleek and luxurious car slowly negotiated the bridge incline. It had been built in 1916 by the city of St. Louis to circumvent the Eads Bridge monopoly of the Terminal Railroad.

"Why is there such a sharp "S" curve on this end of the bridge?" Lorna asked.

"It was done because two train tracks for the lower deck converged from opposite directions. It was the only way to accommodate the support system needed for the upper deck. The serpentine offset posed no problem for quaint cars of an earlier era, but now it's a real danger for modern vehicles

with powerful V-8 engines."

"How dangerous?"

"An average of two or three drivers a year miss the sharp turn, crash through the barriers, and plunge to their deaths."

Lorna shook her head. "What a shame."

The bright lights of St. Louis glittered on the far side of the river.

"I've never crossed this bridge before," Lorna said. "Where are we going?"

"To the Casa-Loma ballroom, then to a restaurant named Favazios. Ever heard of it?"

"Favazios or the Casa-Loma?"

"Either one."

"I'm not familiar with Favazios. Heard of Casa-Loma, but I've never been there." Lorna felt an uneasy vibration. "That's odd. Why do I feel a slight shaking on the bridge?"

"There's a freight train on the deck below, probably a Mo-Pac."

"Mo-Pac?"

"Missouri Pacific."

"Oh."

"Tonight is a special night at the Casa-Loma. Ray Anthony and his orchestra are going to be there."

"Why is that so special?"

"Because the big bands are on their way out."

"Gee, it would be a shame if that happened," Lorna lamented.

"Benny Goodman, Les Brown, Duke Ellington, the Dorsey brothers—they're all in trouble," Lance noted.

"How is it possible?"

"The musicians got too greedy. James Caesar Petrillo, the dictatorial head of their union, called a strike for higher wages after the war. Union scale went up from around two to three dollars an hour, depending on the locale. Raises in big cities like Chicago, New York or L. A. were more. There weren't many places pulling in enough dough to pay twenty musicians in a typical band. The money just wasn't there."

"So one by one the big bands are all breaking up?"

"Yes, it's a shame—the end of an incredible era."

Lorna and Lance spent a couple of enjoyable hours at the Casa-Loma then went to the restaurant. A tuxedoed musician was softly playing a violin, and dim romantic lights caressed exquisite oil paintings on the walls. They were very good reproductions. Favazio's was a fashionable Italian restaurant in an ethnic neighborhood known as The Hill. The place positively reeked with old world charm and ambiance. Lorna didn't notice Lance palm a five dollar bill to the maître d' when he greeted them. The man knew from experience it meant he was supposed to make the night special. He escorted them to a table in a secluded corner. Then he deftly lit a candle to create a mood of romantic intimacy.

"We'll start off with some champagne, the house specialty," Lance directed.

The waiters were all men, smartly dressed and trained in all the subtle nuances that made the dining experience there a memorable one. The elegant decor was accented with silk adornments of green and red and white—the national colors of a people descended from the Etruscans and Romans. An antique parchment map of the Italian peninsula graced the anteroom. Next to it was a picture of the reigning pope, Pius XII.

Lance subtly made sure Lorna's cut-glass goblet was refilled every time it dipped below the halfway mark. She looked at him approvingly across the candlelit table. He looked dashingly handsome and debonair in gray linen slacks and a well-tailored navy blazer with ivory scrimshaw buttons.

"Is that any specific ship carved on those buttons?" Lorna asked.

"Yes, it's the Cutty Sark, the sleekest and fastest of those old graceful clipper ships."

"I've never seen anything like them."

"I had the original buttons replaced with these. The extra cost was fifty bucks."

"They're really quite . . . special."

"I'm glad you like them."

His suave manner cloaked ugly intentions.

The sumptuous five-course meal was heavenly with each serving more indescribable than the last. After the third course, Lorna discovered she had to speak slowly and more distinctly. When dinner was finished, they drove to Lance's apartment on Columbia Place.

A roll of thunder heralded an approaching storm.

Lance's apartment, plain on the outside, luxurious on the inside, had a crisp orderliness that was unusual for a bachelor. He soon had flames caressing logs in the fireplace and the radio tuned to a station that featured lush mood music. A well-stocked bar near the kitchenette signaled his fondness for spirits.

He had borrowed an Airedale puppy from one of his friends for the evening. He knew Lorna was an animal lover and told her the dog belonged to him. It didn't take much convincing to talk Lorna into stopping by his place briefly to see the animal before he took her home. She should have said no, but an alchemy of alcohol and masculine charm persuaded her to say otherwise.

The sound of thunder rumbled in the troubled western sky as a breezy cold front preceded the approach of the broody storm.

Lance said, "Remind me to take an umbrella with us when I drive you home." He had just closed the door behind them when the first drops of rain began to fall. At first the rain was intermittent. Nature was toying with the city.

Lorna bumped slightly into the doorjamb as she entered his living room, sensing with a ripple of unease that she was a bit tipsy. Lorna was vaguely aware of being inside an apartment that mugged her senses with rich leather, dark paneled walls and masculine colors. She lurched forward, nearly falling before Lance caught her. Her head felt so woozy she could hardly stand. She paused and stood in place a few seconds, her body draped over his as she waited for the dizziness to subside.

"Let me pour you another glass of wine," Lance offered, as he twisted the bottle's cork. "It's what they call a nightcap."

"I don't think so," Lorna said thickly, the Midwest in her voice blurred by Dom Perignon champagne. "The room seems to be a merry-go-round already."

"Nonsense, " Lance countered. "A little of this will actually help clear your head. Wine has a countervailing effect on champagne." He shoved the full glass into Lorna's unsteady hands. She reluctantly took a few more sips.

Lance crooned a compliment. "Did I tell you how positively stunning you look in that dress?"

"I don't remember, but thank you very m-much. I was hop-ping, er, hoping you'd like it."

Lance decided that Lorna had just about reached the crossover point, that level of inebriation in which a woman was drunk enough to lose inhibition, but not too drunk to ruin the fun. He couldn't help giving this succulent fruit, ripe for the plucking, a lusty once over. This was the first time all evening that his actions or mannerisms had vouchsafed his true intentions.

Lorna glanced nervously around the room. "Where's the puppy?"

"He's locked in the bathroom. Probably sleeping. I put newspapers on the floor. I'll show him to you in a minute."

Lance took hold of Lorna's hands. "I think I'm falling for you."

Lorna blinked and tried to clear her head. "You're very nice, and I like you a lot but—"

He leaned over, took her by the shoulders and smothered her with a passionate, demanding kiss. Lorna's normal defenses were impaired. The enemy was at the gate and her drawbridge of inhibitions was down. Momentarily caught up in the passion, she responded in kind. She snaked her arms around him and found his body to be warmer than she'd expected. His hands began to caress her face, her neck, her bare shoulders. She found herself being carried away by his smooth voice, his masculinity, his heart-stopping good looks. Lorna's impeccable self-control deserted her momentarily. A little warning signal didn't go off until his hands began to wander into forbidden territory below the top of her dress. He pulled her down to the couch. "I want you, Lorna. I want you now. Make love with me."

"Please don't do that, Lance. I'm not that kind of a girl," Lorna protested.

"But you're so wonderful, I just can't help myself."

One of his hands was now resting on her knee. She clumsily pushed it off.

"N-no, Lance. I mean it. Petting is out of bounds. I think you had better take me home now," she pleaded while pushing him away from her. She stood up with the intention of stopping the lovemaking before it went too far. She struggled to maintain her balance. A ripple of nausea washed over her body.

"I feel sick."

As Lance was protesting her action, trying to talk her into staying, she lost her balance and fell back on the couch. A pulsing throb pounded in her temple. She panicked with the realization she had consumed too much alcohol and was on the verge of dropping off into a state of unconsciousness.

"I think I had better get you to bed, Lorna. You're in no condition to be up and about." He boldly lifted her off the couch and took her proprietarily through the doorway into his bedroom. The room was dark but a burst of light crashed through the windows. Veins of lightning streaked across the sky, momentarily giving the room a surreal quality, signaling the arrival of the storm's full fury. A companion burst of thunder ominously reverberated throughout the room.

"Take me home, Lance," Lorna insisted. "I can't possibly stay here all night."

Lance wasn't listening. His hormones were doing his thinking for him now, and he began to move to the next stage of malicious intent. He tossed Lorna onto the bed, shucked his coat and ripped off his tie.

"I don't want to stay here. I want to go back to the Beulah Club," Lorna reiterated.

But Lance was caught up in a trance of sexual anticipation. He had no intention of taking her home. His marauding lips began to smother her with kisses.

"You're not just a big tease, are you? I bet you like to get men all hot and bothered and then leave them twisting in the wind. Well not tonight, baby." His tone was sharp and demanding.

"No, I, uh—please . . . "

His romantic kisses were replaced with those of a selfish, give-me-what-I-want urgency. His mouth savagely plundered Lorna's, mashing her lips against her teeth.

"Stop! Stop it."

Lance saw fear in her eyes, but he was no longer concerned about her feelings, just his needs. He had wanted Lorna from the first moment he laid eyes on her. He had planned and schemed like this with many a girl. He had always gotten his way. Never before had he needed to resort to such extremes, but if this was what it took, then so be it.

Lorna tried to get up, tried to escape from his clutches, but her strength and will had been stolen by Bacchus. Her senses were dulled, and she felt as if she was trying to swim in quicksand. The weight of his body pressed her into the mattress. Every little movement of resistance seemingly required a massive amount of energy.

"Stop. You can't do this," Lorna vainly protested. She began pounding him on his back. Her blows were mere pebbles pelting the walls of a stone fortress. She nearly passed out. The same bright colors swirled in her brain as when she'd been given ether to have her tonsils removed at the age of six. Lance was emboldened by Lorna's desperate resistance.

"I like a woman with spirit," he said as he shifted his leverage. The look on his face scared her. His cruel, dark eyes were as hard as granite.

"Get off me, you filthy vulture," Lorna spit out, her heart filled with rage and hate.

Her desperate pleas fell on deaf ears. Lance was lost in a world of primal sensation and was well beyond the point of reason. Lorna bucked and twisted, trying to thwart him. Her effort was valiant, but futile, as he straddled her with his crushing weight.

"No! No! No!"

She resisted with every ounce of energy in her body until it was completely drained. Her face turned to the window when she sensed the inevitable. Lightning flickers enabled her to see outside. A nearby Dutch elm was whipping back and forth, ravaged by the wanton, frenzied wind. The earth was being assaulted by a sky that exploded with crashing thunder and horizontal rain. She felt her legs being roughly pushed apart, a cruel prelude to her violation. Lorna averted her head and helplessly clawed the air. The ordeal, which was over in a matter of minutes, was endured with numbed detachment. He let out a sigh as his body convulsed. She finally pushed him off and rolled free, but only after his sordid act was concluded and his body went limp.

Lorna was disheveled, groggy and silent as Lance drove her back to the Beulah Club. The storm was easing, but plump raindrops continued to pelt the windshield. Lance stared straight ahead, impervious to her pain, as if hypnotized by the monotonous motions of the wiper blades. Back and forth in quick metronomic arcs. Whap. Whap.

The shame and horror of what had happened overwhelmed her. It was the first time in her life that she had experienced the feeling of helplessness, the shame of being stripped of one's dignity. Lorna turned her head, closed her eyes and wept, her body convulsing in uncontrollable sobs. She fought for composure, pulling herself together. Another stretch of silence.

"How could you do that to me, Lance, with no regard for my wishes or feelings?"

"Stop complaining. You wanted it as much as I did, but you just won't admit it. I just had to loosen you up a bit—free you from your outdated Puritanical sense of morality. I've never had a single complaint from any woman I've been with."

"I'm sure you haven't. You have it well rehearsed—say all the right things, impress the women with charm, shower them with gifts, take them to fancy and expensive places. Pretty soon they're falling all over you. How many notches do you have on your bedpost, Lance—ten? twenty? You won't get away with this. I'll have you up on charges. You RAPED me!"

Lance let out a laugh that chilled her to the bone. "No you won't. You're not going to drag your name through the mud in a futile war you can't possibly win."

"Yes, I will, you'll see."

Lance was impressed with her bravado.

"You won't."

"And why not?"

"Think about it. You have no proof. No witnesses. It will be your word against mine."

A shudder plowed through her body.

"My family is rich and powerful. My dad may not like what I do for a living, but he'll do everything possible to prevent you from dragging the family name down. He'll use all his resources to ensure the trial is all about ***you***. By the time our lawyers are through with you on the stand, it will be your reputation that's shot, not mine. They'll find witnesses who'll swear that you are nothing but a floozy. I'll claim you tried to blackmail me for money, and when I turned you down, you trumped up these rape charges. Think about it. You're a nobody, an out-of-towner. My family has been a pillar of society in these parts for nearly a hundred years." He flashed her a cruel smile. "You don't have a chance."

"You're despicable. You're really, REALLY despicable."

"I have to admit, you were my hardest conquest. I've always liked young, fresh-faced girls like yourself. Especially if they're nubile virgins. It's always more exciting when you take, er, a woman surrenders her virginity. You must really think you're hot stuff. All of that nonsense about a man having to marry you just to get into your pants."

Uncontrollable rage shook Lorna's bones an instant before she hauled off and slapped his face as hard as she could. The forcefulness of her actions shocked them both. "You're a contemptuous, self-centered slug . . . without any sense of decency. You don't have an ounce of integrity in your body. I can't believe you fooled me so easily. One of these days you'll get your just reward."

Lance reached over and grabbed her by the hair. He wanted to punch her in the face in retaliation, but he thought the better of it. There were no marks on her now, and if he got rough, it might push her over the edge of reason. In the unlikely event she did file charges, the fact that she had no bruises on her body would make her accusations even harder to prove. He slowly relaxed his grip. Lorna retreated to the far edge of the seat.

How could I have been so stupid?

The full fury of the storm was spent, and it moved east toward oblivion. Gone but not forgotten. Its gale force winds had left scars on the landscape that would exist for years to come.

Lorna angrily vaulted out of the car when Lance pulled to an abrupt halt in front of her residence hall. She slammed the door as hard as she could, rattling its hinges. Stumbling blindly past the front desk, she mounted the stairs without saying a word to the perplexed girl on duty. Laurie had copiously been engaged in a gossip-fest on the phone. She looked up just in time to catch a glimpse of Lorna as she hurried past. ***My, she looks ragged around the edges. Must have had a real doozy of a lover's spat***, she thought.

Gloria Hornback – Lorna's roommate

The hour was late but Gloria, wearing blue cotton PJs, was still awake. She was in bed, propped up against pillows, engrossed in a copy of Kathleen Windsor's ***Forever Amber***.

"What on earth happened to you," Gloria said with a gasp of astonishment when Lorna stormed into the room.

"Nothing!" was all that Lorna

muttered as she grabbed a bath towel and staggered across the hall to take a shower.

She felt dirty and couldn't wait to cleanse herself and rid her body of a sickening smell that made her skin crawl. It was a vile odor and Lorna feared it might never scrub away. Flotsam and jetsam. The residue of his barbaric territorial markings. She was still woozy and had to hold on to one side of the shower stall to maintain her balance. Maybe the stream of hot water would somehow scour her memory of the most abominable event in her brief lifetime. She scrubbed her skin pink, nearly rubbing it raw, as if punishing her self for allowing Lance to dupe her. The water pounded her body for what seemed an eternity before she realized that nothing would cleanse her of this ugliest and foulest of deeds. Her very soul had been bruised. Her life was a wreck—a shambles. "D—you, Lance. I hope you burn in hell for doing this to me."

Unbidden, a slew of unanswerable questions assaulted her brain. ***What if I become pregnant? How will I be able to stand working in the same office with Lance?*** There were no answers, only more pain. She sighed dejectedly, thinking about what a fool she had been.

When Gloria came looking to see if Lorna was all right, she found her bent at the waist with her head in a lavatory, retching miserably.

"Are you going to be okay? Anything I can do?" Gloria asked.

"No, uh, I think I'm feeling better now," Lorna said, her body still weak and shaky from the convulsions and aftermath of the ordeal.

"Did he hurt you, hit you, slap you around, that . . . that miserable creep?"

"I never want to see him again. I hate him; I hate the very ground Lance walks on," Lorna spouted, somewhat surprised by the vehemence of her loathing for a fellow human being. She cupped her hand and sipped some cool refreshing water to rinse the sour taste from her mouth.

"Let me help you back to the room," Gloria offered sympathetically.

"All right, as soon as I splash some water on my face."

With Gloria's arm around her waist, Lorna staggered to her room and sat on the edge of the bed. She clutched the collar of her terry cloth robe around her neck, and then crossed her arms, hugging herself with shaking hands. Gloria sat next to Lorna with an arm of comfort around her shoulder, offering solace.

"What happened between you two? I've never seen you this distraught the whole time we've known each other."

"He, he ra—, he raped m-me," Lorna stammered in a raw voice.

Gloria jumped to her feet. "Oh my GOD! I can't believe he would do something so awful. Where did it happen?"

Lorna hung her head and closed her eyes as another wave of nausea sent her reeling. "His apartment. It . . . happened in his apartment," she offered numbly.

"You need to call the police and then go to Christian Welfare Hospital," Gloria urged.

"No! Don't call the p-police."

"You can color me dumb, but I don't understand: why not?"

"I don't think I could handle the shame of this if it went public." There was a quaver in Lorna's voice.

"But you can't let him get away with it." Gloria's voice was adamant. "He deserves to go to jail."

Lorna disgustedly threw herself backward onto her pillow, rolled over and buried her face in her forearm. "It's no use. It . . . it's my word against his. There would be a trial. I can just imagine what humiliating questions Lance's rotten lawyer would ask. Everyone would know. I couldn't handle the public humiliation."

"Let me tell Bob. He'll go over there and beat the living daylights out of that worm," Gloria implored.

Lorna flopped over and jerked to an upright position. "No, Bob might get hurt. I couldn't live with that."

Gloria adjusted one of the dozen pink curlers on her head. "Bob can take care of himself."

"No, I'm afraid if he did do something like that, Lance might pay somebody to go after him. It's too risky."

"I still think you need to go to the police," Gloria insisted.

"It wouldn't do any good. Lance said the maître d' at the restaurant was beholden to him. Said he'd paid the man huge tips over the years. Said he'd lie for Lance on the stand. He'd claim he saw me drink too much and was practically begging for it, rubbing up against Lance with my hands all over him. And Lance would have the best lawyers in town. You know whom the jury would believe. By the time his lawyer was finished with me, I'd look like a wanton trollop, a greedy little gold-digging tart out to ruin Lance's reputation. They would claim I tried blackmail, and when he refused, I hauled him into court on trumped up charges. Wouldn't that be pathetic?"

"This is incomprehensible," Gloria said. "I can't believe some men can be so sadistic."

Lorna gave a shrug and exhaled in exasperation. "My first experience with sex, and it was ugly and sordid. God's grand design for love between man and woman, and it was awful."

"That wasn't God's plan," Gloria said. "His plan is sacred and beautiful, within the confines of matrimony. Sex is meant to be an affirmation of wedding vows. It's the greed and lust of some men who have twisted sex into something repulsive."

Bob Von Brock – Gloria's future husband

"I feel hollow, like a fruit that's been sucked dry. I . . . I hate men," Lorna said sourly.

"No you don't," Gloria amended. "You hate what's happened to you and the man who is responsible. Most men aren't like that heel. Bob would never, could never, do that to me or any other woman."

"How do you know?"

"Call it intuition. And from what you've told me about Brad Logan, I don't think he could either."

"Whatever I might have had with Brad is gone, ruined forever."

"If you feel anything for him, anything at all, you have to trust him enough to tell him."

Lorna began to sob uncontrollably. "You don't understand. I could never bring myself to tell him about this. I couldn't stand to see the hurt in his eyes."

"But it wasn't your fault."

"In a way it was. I should have never agreed to go to Lance's apartment. That was really pretty obvious. Besides, I should have chosen Brad over Lance a long time ago."

"You're not being fair with yourself, Lorna. You weren't ready to choose. You're not to blame."

"You've got to promise me you won't tell anyone about this, Gloria."

"Oh, Lorna, this is too big a burden for you to carry by yourself, all locked up inside you, eating away at your sanity."

Lorna grabbed Gloria's arm and squeezed. "I'll learn to cope. Promise me. Swear, swear you won't breathe a word of this to anyone—ever."

"I think you're making a mistake, but if that's what you want, wild horses couldn't drag it out of me."

"Promise?"

"I swear." She drew an invisible X over her heart.

I'm going to get through this, Lorna promised herself. She cried herself to sleep that night.

When Lorna missed her period the next month she knew she was pregnant.

CHAPTER 21

In 1888 the City Council of East St. Louis passed a controversial ordinance mandating downtown streets were to be raised to escape the frequent floods of the Mississippi River. The projected cost was a staggering nine hundred thousand dollars. Streets were to be raised an average of ten to twelve feet. The engineer in charge of the project made a miscalculation, resulting in the streets being raised six inches higher than what had been intended. This cost the city nearly a hundred thousand dollars more than what had been budgeted. The despondent engineer, his reputation ruined, committed suicide. Two years later the river left its banks once more. The only thing that saved the town from being ravaged was that six-inch mistake.

August 17, 1951

Brad thought his picnic date with Lorna at Jones Park had gone extremely well. He was on the verge of asking her to go steady. Or something like that. But just when the relationship seemed to be going somewhere, she inexplicably reverted to her old persona—cold and distant. He didn't have the slightest clue until he accidentally bumped into Lance at the Liberty Cafe.

Lance spotted Brad across the room, got up with his cup of coffee, and sat in the chair across from him. Before speaking, he stared at Brad for a few seconds with a cocky smile on his face.

"So you're Brad Logan, my so-called competition."

"Hello. I know who you are. You're Lance Troutman, the ***Journal*** reporter who has been dating Lorna Sanders."

"Ah, my reputation precedes me," he bragged.

Brad glared at him. "I've heard a lot about you, most of it bad."

The waitress refilled his cup of coffee.

"Could you pass the sugar please?"

Brad obligingly slid the glass container in his direction.

"I can see you don't have a very high opinion of me."

"That's an understatement."

"Well, you don't have to worry anymore," he said, plopping a couple of sugar cubes into his coffee.

Brad took the last bite of his club sandwich and washed it down with coffee. "What do you mean?"

"I broke up with her."

"Why would you do that?"

He finished a sip of coffee and looked up, his gaze locking on Brad. He didn't like the smug look on Lance's face.

"Let's just say I finally got what I wanted from her." Brad's Scottish blood began to rise. "Now that the chase is over I'm ready to move on to greener pastures—something new, something different."

"You're a liar." Brad's features hardened. "You either broke up with her because you couldn't get to first base, or she broke up with you because you didn't know how to act like a gentleman."

"You're wrong, Brad. I hit a home run with her; I scored."

His words fell on him like a ton of bricks. "I know her better than you do. She would never go to bed with a lecherous playboy," he said, slightly hot under the collar.

"Oh yeah. Well I'm going to let you in on a little secret. I've had plenty of women. Lorna might have been a little harder to . . . let's say, persuade, than most. But in the end, I had my way with her . . . at my apartment. I always get what I want."

"I still don't believe you. Lorna just isn't that kind of girl."

Lance took a big gulp of coffee from his cup. "Boy, do you have a lot to learn about women. You just haven't discovered how to say and do the right things that convince females to say ***yes*** and experience the pleasures that only a man can give them."

"You're lying—just trying to get my goat."

"Well let me tell you, buddy-boy. I've seen everything she's got, from her lacy white panties and bra to everything underneath."

"Shut up! That's a lot of bunk!"

"No it isn't. She even has a cute little birthmark on her stomach. Want me to describe it?"

"I don't want to hear anymore. You've made your point. What happens between a man and a woman is private. You must be a real low-life, sitting here bragging to me about your conquests."

"Hey, don't be such a sore loser. I may have got there first, but that should be no big deal. She's all yours now. I'm moving on. There's a new secretary at the office who is built like **Jane Russell.** She really knows how to fill out a sweater. I can't wait to have a go at her."

Lance's words rang in his head like the bell in the tower at Sacred Heart Church. He felt sick to his stomach. "Excuse me; I'm leaving. I can't stand to be around someone who has so little respect for women."

Jane Russell, star of *The Outlaw*

He got up to leave, but Lance wouldn't drop the matter. He grabbed his arm as he walked by his stool.

"Let it rest," Brad said sternly.

A malicious smile creased the man's face. "Hey, let me give you a few pointers on how to score with Lorna. Better than that, I'll tell you exactly how she likes it."

Brad couldn't contain himself any longer. A dam of emotions burst and he landed a haymaker flush on his face, producing a crunch-like sound of bone and cartilage. The blow knocked Lance backwards and the chair made a clatter as it fell over on the floor, disgorging its occupant in the process.

Lance had a pained expression on his face as he took out a handkerchief and gingerly pressed it to his blood-spurting nose.

"D—, Logan. You broke my nose!"

Seeing Lance flat and bleeding caused a strange sense of pleasure to wash over Brad. He raised a trembling fist and shook it at his tormentor. "Consider yourself lucky. Believe me, you deserved a lot more. You're a sorry excuse for a human being."

Lance slowly pulled himself to his feet, trying to get the bleeding to stop. "Say, you're really jealous aren't you. You must really have a thing for her."

"You've got it wrong, Lance. I feel sorry for you. Apparently you threw away the chance of a lifetime. You probably could have married the most wonderful girl on the planet. I pity you because you didn't have sense enough to honor and cherish the best thing that ever happened to you. I wonder how long it will take you to realize what you missed out on, what you might have had." Brad wanted to say more but he clamped his lips together, spun around, and left the restaurant.

After brooding about what Lance had told him, Brad decided to go over to the ***Journal,*** hoping to catch Lorna at the office. She was typing something at her desk when he walked in.

"Hello, Barb," Brad said at the front counter. He nervously raked his fingers through his hair. "Could you please tell Lorna I need to see her . . . immediately?"

Barb Edelblute could see he was angry and gave a halting glance at Lorna who nodded an ***okay*** as she got up and walked toward them.

"Hello, Brad. What do you want?" she said with a noticeable lack of enthusiasm in her voice.

He couldn't hide his irritation. "We need to talk."

"Not here. Not now," she said as she glanced around, seeing several co-workers who were staring.

"Yes, here and now," he replied vehemently.

"Can't this wait?"

"No."

"All right," she sighed. "If you insist. Let's go to the back where we'll have some privacy."

She wheeled and led him toward an office that had CONFERENCE ROOM stenciled in gold lettering on the frosted glass of the paneled door. They walked past a man who was editing copy. Brad was nearly oblivious to the clicking and chattering of office typewriters. A behive of activity. He confronted her as soon as they were inside and the door was closed.

"Guess who I just talked to?"

"From the look on your face it must have been Lance."

"Right. And you'll never guess what he told me."

"Yes I can. And I'll bet it wasn't pretty, was it?"

"It was ugly," he said massaging his sore knuckles.

"Did you two have a fight? You didn't hit him?"

"Don't worry, he deserved it."

"Did you believe what he told you?"

"Of course not. At least not until he started giving me vivid descriptions."

"So you think it's true?"

"I didn't want to. I refused to believe it. I kept telling myself he was making it all up to get a rise out of me."

"What changed your mind?"

"The details of your sordid little affair at his apartment."

"And you believe him?"

"Are you trying to tell me what Lance said isn't true, that he made it all up?"

"No, I'm just saying it might not have happened the way he told it."

"Oh, I'm sure he embellished the details. He relished that aspect. But did you, or did you not have sex with him?"

It was rape! That's what she wanted to say—but couldn't. "Y-yes . . . w-we had sex," she said with a look of dejection. She lowered her eyes to avert direct eye contact.

Brad's world imploded.

"And to think I thought you were special . . . different . . . pure and wholesome."

Lorna stepped forward and grabbed his arm. "Oh, Brad. I didn't mean for it to happen. You've got to believe me."

His willpower almost fled in the wake of her tantalizing fragrance, but he pushed her back. "I can't believe you threw it all away. I would have walked through fire for you. You betrayed my trust, my love."

"It's you I love, Brad. I know that now. Believe me, I didn't mean to hurt you. Down deep, I meant for you to be the first."

"Shut up! Just shut up!" His face tensed. "Do you think I want to hear that?" His voice was harsh and unforgiving. "***Now*** you tell me you love me. Only it's ***after*** Lance got what he wanted and is through with you. Do you really think telling me that changes anything?"

"I—"

"I'm devastated. I thought I knew you. We had a special bond, but you've destroyed it all. What might have been is gone forever."

She turned her back to him and started crying, but her emotions weren't about to get past his anger.

"Don't give up on our relationship, Brad," she pleaded. "You don't know the full story."

He spun her around and made her face him. He wanted his words to hurt her as much as her fling with Lance had wounded him. "I know enough. I know more than I want to know!"

She was sobbing now, her face in her hands. He grabbed her shoulders and made her look at him. "What were you thinking?"

He could feel her tense up as she flinched. "Brad, you don't understand." She fleetingly thought about trying to tell him the truth but decided he'd never believe it—not after what Lance had told him. Especially since she hadn't gone to the police to press charges. ***Gloria was right. I should have taken him to court.***

"I don't want to hear it. I don't want to see you anymore, Lorna. As much as it hurts me to say this, I've got to move on. I was so sure you were the one for me. We had so much going for us," Brad insisted, his voice ringing with anger and frustration.

"Please, Brad . . . I love you. I really do." Her voice trailed off, as if she suddenly realized the futility of her efforts. She wanted to tell him she had been raped, but she couldn't face the humiliation.

"And you'll ***never*** know how much I loved you," he said as he flung open the door so hard it slammed against the wall. He left without a backward glance, without a single thought of relenting, out of her life . . . forever. Brad stumbled outside, hardly aware of anything else except the crushing trauma of his breakup with Lorna.

Lorna was stunned by what had just transpired. She buried her face in her hands and was so absorbed with hurt and self-recrimination she didn't hear the toilet being flushed in the water closet adjacent to the conference facility. Priscilla Bartlett had gone there on the pretext to freshen her makeup. She nodded to herself, pleased at the success of her eavesdropping. ***Excellent gossip.***

As Lorna walked out the door she was seized by a dizzy spell. She paused and leaned back against the wall in the hallway. ***At least Brad doesn't know I'm pregnant***, Lorna whispered to her self, unaware that someone else was close enough to hear. A gloating Priscilla timed her exit so that the two of them nearly bumped into each other. Revenge would be sweet.

"I'm so sorry," Priscilla said, looking like the proverbial cat that had just eaten the canary. "But these walls are paper thin and I couldn't help but overhearing your conversation with Brad."

Lorna exhaled a disgusted sound. "Somehow you always seem to have an uncanny knack for being in the right place at the wrong time. I'll bet you'd really be good at blackmail. Too bad this newspaper doesn't print a trashy gossip column. You could probably win a Pulitzer in that category."

"Don't you look down your nose at me, you little tramp," Priscilla retorted, her eyeteeth looking much like the fangs on a pit viper.

"You never cease to amaze me," Lorna replied. "I'm surprised you didn't run out and sell tickets so everyone in the office could watch my quarrel with Brad."

Priscilla's tone switched from blue skies to storm. "Don't blame me for the sordid mess you've gotten yourself into." Priscilla could see that she was getting Lorna's goat so she dished out some more. "After all, you're the one who's knocked-up, not me. I'll bet when Mermelstein finds out about your condition you won't last two seconds around here. You're history, Miss Litchfield."

"I'll bet you just can't wait to tell him, can you?" Lorna tried to sound defiant, but her voice was filled with emotion and cracked in the middle of her sentence. "Now you can add tattletale and backstabbing to your resumé."

"Go back to Hicksville, have your bastard child, and go back to working at the library. You're a disgrace to the journalism profession."

Litchfield Public Library

Lorna had enough. She impetuously lashed out at Priscilla, slapping her so hard that it knocked her back against the wall. Priscilla's startled face grew lumpy and erupted with raspberry splotches.

"That's for all the rotten put-downs about my home town. I don't care to hear anything else from your vicious mouth. One of these days, Priscilla, your personality disorder is going to catch up with you." Lorna pivoted and walked away while a stunned Priscilla rubbed a cheek that was stinging like crazy.

The next morning, Maury Mermelstein called Lorna into his office. "I'm afraid we have something very unpleasant to talk about, Miss Sanders." He had a pencil turned sideways in his hand and he was nervously flipping the eraser end of it up and down with his thumb. The eraser made a dull tapping sound on the highly polished surface of his desk.

Lorna closed her eyes for a moment and shook her head. "I think I know what the drift of this conversation is going to be. You've had an eye-opening chat with that office snitch Priscilla Bartlett, haven't you?"

"Please, Miss Sanders. Don't try to make her the heavy in this little melodrama. She's only looking out for the best interests of this newspaper."

"Give me a break. I can see she's got the wool pulled over your eyes too."

Mermelstein adopted the look of a stern taskmaster. "I think it's safe to assume by your reaction that what Priscilla told me is true. Do you deny that you are an unmarried woman with child?"

Lorna swallowed her pride, bleakly looked down, and avoided his probing gaze. "Yes, yes, it's true. But I'm not showing and—"

"That's not the point. We have a reputation to maintain around here. Can you imagine if word got out that our society page reporter had behaved in an immoral manner and was expecting an illegitimate child? We could lose advertisers, revenue would go down . . ."

"But—"

"No buts about it." He leaned forward. "Under the circumstances your continued employment is out of the question."

Lorna sat there silently, her hands clasped in her lap, feeling worse with every word.

"I like you, Miss Sanders. You've more than exceeded my expectations. You were a quick learner, and you've done an excellent job. But I'm afraid I don't have any choice in the matter. Your employment is terminated here and now. I expect you to clean out your desk and leave the premises. I hope you'll be able to get your life straightened out and get past all of this."

"And what is going to happen to Lance? He's the father, you know. It's his shame too. Are you going to fire him as well?"

"Society doesn't work that way. Call it a double standard, if you will, but it's always the woman who bears the brunt of responsibility when these things happen. I guess it isn't fair, but I'm not telling you something you didn't already know. If I confront Lance, he'll just deny it."

"So he gets off, scot-free—no consequences, because he's a man."

"I'm sorry, Miss San—"

"Never mind. You're right, of course—about the way things work."

Mermelstein stood and extended his hand. "I really do wish you the best of luck in the future."

Lorna sat there, staring unseeingly at his blue Noxema jar, too stunned and disappointed to move. Finally she rose and gave him an unenthusiastic handshake. "I don't suppose there's any way I could come back to my job after the baby is born?"

"I'm afraid not. This is something I'd like to put to rest as quickly as possible. You'll be the subject of office gossip for months as it is. I hope you can understand my position."

"I understand. I was just hoping against hope. I appreciate everything you've done for me. I realize you went out on a limb when you hired me. I'm sorry I let you down."

"Apology accepted."

"Well, uh, if I don't see you again before I leave, thanks again for everything."

"Good-bye, Miss Sanders."

"Good-bye." Lorna opened Mermelstein's door, but then turned to ask a final question before she left. "Who is replacing me?"

He lowered his eyes. "Priscilla Bartlett," he said cheerlessly.

Lorna went back to her desk and cleaned out her personal effects, placing them in a brown paper bag. On her way out she stopped at the front desk to say good-bye to Barb Edelblute.

"You've been a good friend. I'm going to miss you," Lorna said as the two of them hugged.

"It breaks my heart to see you go. I'm going to miss you terribly. Be sure to keep in touch."

"I will, I promise."

Lorna left the office, her envisaged bright future in ruins. From the sidewalk, she gave a brief glance up at the window of the Spivey building where she knew Brad's office was located. A tear ran down her cheek and splashed on the toe of her shoe.

The next day, Brad was walking near his office building when he heard newsboy Johnny Moberly screaming something about the latest headline. Brad gave him a nickel and stared in utter disbelief at the bold print:

WALTERS ARRESTED FOR MURDER!

Don't tell me Knucky went out and killed Delonzo. Brad scanned the columns to discover the identity of the alleged victim. When he saw the name he couldn't believe it.

Ohmygosh!

CHAPTER 22

There were very few bank robberies in commercially and industrially rich East St. Louis. Old-timers said John Dillinger considered robbing one of the banks in East St. Louis, but the bridges and the railroads stopped him. The commercial pulse of America could be felt in that town. Though consisting of a mere thirteen square miles, it was criss-crossed with 550 miles of railroad tracks, increasing the possibility of being stopped by a train during the getaway. And since toll booths on the bridges made escape across the river hazardous, robbing banks there was risky business.

Wednesday, September 19, 1951

Knucky was arrested, fingerprinted, photographed and arraigned. His trial, a ***cause célèbre,*** was held at the county courthouse in Belleville. It was brick and stone with a facade of Doric columns and Greek pediments gracing its front. Cahokia had originally been the county seat, but its location on the flood plain created problems when there were heavy rains. Consequently, the seat of government was moved in 1814 up on the bluffs to a place whose name means ***beautiful town.*** The venerable building, constructed in 1861, was typical of most Midwest courthouses with its cavernous rooms, high ceilings, floors of Vermont marble and paneled walls—built in a stately manner to remind citizens of the law's authority and majesty. Its solemn decorum was meant to invoke strictures against boorish, clamorous behavior. The splendid courtrooms gave you a sense that history had visited there and left a rich backdrop for legal drama. Massive oak doors with polished brass handles led to courtroom number one. The room was bursting with curious spectators, their kibitzing a steady hum of innuendo and speculation.

Judge Kermit Croissant peered over a pair of half-frame cheaters he had pushed below the bridge of his nose. He was looking straight at their table with a stern legal face. Off to his side an American flag hung limp from its pole. Brad half expected him to shout ***Achtung***! in guttural German. The defendant, Knucky Walters, was seated between Morris Goldman and Brad. Goldman was the lead counsel. Knucky had insisted, over the vehement protests of Goldman, that Brad would be junior counsel in the murder trial. Knucky said Brad was his good luck charm, and he had a gut feeling somehow he would be the difference in helping him beat the rap. Alan Cox, a uniformed officer, was seated directly behind Knucky.

Belleville courthouse circa 1910– courtesy St. Clair County/Lebanon Historical Societies

"Defense has two preemptory challenges left," Judge Croissant said. "Does it wish to exercise those options?"

"The defense is satisfied with the composition of the jury," Goldman answered.

Brad had urged Goldman to be more discriminating with jury selection. He told him about a new method he had read about in law school where a lawyer could increase his chances of winning a case by being very selective during the ***voir dire*** process. It recommended asking pointed questions of prospective jurors to help reveal their prejudices and biases. Brad even gave him anecdotal evidence of how such tactics could tilt a jury in a certain direction. But Goldman was of the old school; he would have none of that.

"Thanks to my courtroom savvy, I have only lost one case in the last eight years. I can size up a person quickly by his demeanor and body language," he boasted.

"Okay, have it your way," Brad said in resignation.

Judge Croissant gave a curious glance at Steve Todd, the state's attorney trial shark, whose previous battles with Goldman led those in the courtroom to anticipate a blood-letting vendetta.

"The prosecution accepts this jury," he said in smug satisfaction.

They have a jury sympathetic to their case, Brad thought. ***That's one strike against us.***

Brad looked around the room. The gallery was jam-packed, and the place was lousy with reporters. He leaned over toward Knucky. "The evidence they presented to the grand jury was largely circumstantial. Now we'll see if they have anything else up their sleeves."

Knucky nodded in affirmation.

Judge Croissant sequestered the jury, and the trial began. "Is the prosecution ready to proceed in the case of the People versus Lloyd Walters?" Croissant tersely asked.

"Ready for the People," Todd said.

"Ready for the defendant," Goldman said in anticipation of Judge Croissant's question. He knew the judge liked to keep things moving and was trying to score brownie points.

"A word of caution is in order. If I catch any of you grandstanding, I'll hit you with a contempt citation faster than **Captain Marvel** can say Shazam. Mr. Todd, you may make your opening statement to the jury," Croissant instructed.

Todd, who had racked up a very impresssive string of convictions, looked calm, cool, efficient. "Good morning, ladies and gentlemen of the jury." He began a solemn recitation of statements as if they were unassailable facts. "We intend to show that the defendant, Lloyd Walters, had the motive, the opportunity, and the means to commit this vile crime. We contend that he went to the apartment of Mr. Troutman on the night of August 19th because he was angry about an article the deceased was going to publish about organized crime in East St. Louis. A heated argument ensued, and Mr. Walters shot and killed Mr. Troutman. We have witnesses who can place Mr. Walters at the scene of the crime just a half hour before the body was discovered."

The prosecutor whirled and dramatically pointed a finger at Knucky. "With collaborative evidence, we will prove he had both means and motive. We are also convinced that we have the murder weapon, a gun registered in the name of Mr. Walters." Todd pivoted back to face the jury. "Based on the evidence we intend to present, we will ask the jury to convict the defendant of second degree murder."

Brad was aware that most spectators were looking at Knucky in judgmental fashion.

JAMES STEWART

"Defense, it's your turn," Croissant instructed with Teutonic sternness.

Knucky passed Brad a hand-written note from Goldman that defied translation. Brad got up, walked over to him and leaned down so Goldman could inform him directly.

"You can tell the jury how we plan to contradict the D.A.'s case. Try not to screw it up," he said.

Goldman had earlier told Brad he would conduct the questioning and deliver the final summation. He considered the opening statement a mere formality.

"Is this going to take all day, gentlemen?" Croissant boomed at them.

Brad rose from the counsel's table and buttoned his coat. Goldman tugged at his arm.

"Hey, Logan, XYZ."

"Pardon?"

"Examine your zipper, you're flying at half mast."

Logan quickly sat down and pulled up his zipper. He stood again and approached a baker's dozen of citizens—twelve jurors, plus an alternate, in the jury box. He paused a few seconds to regain his composure. His mouth felt bone dry. He was afraid his first words would tumble out several octaves high in an embarrassing falsetto.

"May it please the court and members of the jury," he began, making deliberate eye contact with each juror. So far so good, he told himself. "I plan to be brief, but to the point. The prosecution would have you believe they have an open and shut case. It simply isn't so. The defense will show the evidence against our client is based on supposition and guesswork, but not fact. We will demonstrate that Mr. Walters had no reason to kill Mr. Troutman, and that the authorities, in their haste to solve the crime, rushed to judgment and came to the conclusion our client was guilty. This faulty hypothesis colored the entire investigation."

Brad placed one hand on the railing of the jury box. "We will prove," he said, pointing his finger at the prosecution team, "that they ignored any other signs of evidence which might have led them to conclude otherwise. They never looked in any other direction or considered alternative suspects."

Something in the gallery caught the corner of his eye, causing him to momentarily lose his concentration. He briefly turned his head from the jury and looked to the back of the room, pretending to be lost in thought. He was startled to see Lorna sitting there in a stunning navy outfit, her bright hazel eyes once again working their magic on him. She looked outstanding in a white derby with a small veil and navy ribbon band, tilted saucily on her head. He whirled around and refocused on the jury. ***It's over, Logan. Don't even think about it.*** He took a steadying breath.

"Policemen and prosecutors are led by their dogma, I'm sure unconsciously, to distort evidence in order to bolster their case. We believe our client has been framed for murder to gain control of his business interests. In order to successfully frame someone it is necessary to utilize either perjured testimony or contrived evidence. We expect to show that both tactics have been used in this case. According to law, whenever the prosecution resorts to reliance on circumstantial evidence, the court must instruct you that if the defense can propose a reasonable alternative that is equally or more believable, it is the sworn duty of the jury to accept the hypothesis and vote for acquittal. We ask that you not judge this man based on things you may have read about him in the newspaper. We believe you to be a fair-minded group of people, and when we show the lack of substance in the charges against our client, we expect an honest verdict of ***not*** guilty."

Brad looked for Lorna as he walked back to his chair, but she was gone. He later learned she had left the city and went back to Litchfield.

"Your Honor," Steve Todd blurted, "You should advise the jury that the defense alternative theory must be ***viable***."

Croissant peered down at Todd imperiously. "I think I know how to do my job," he snapped. "Of course I will so instruct the jurors. Anything less would border on incompetence. You don't think I'm a nincompoop do you?"

Famed defense lawyer Clarence Darrow

"No sir, sorry, Your Honor."

"Not exactly the eloquence of Clarence Darrow, but fairly creative, Logan," Goldman grudgingly admitted, as he took his seat.

Robert Then came forward and was the first witness to place his hand on the Bible and be sworn. He testified that on the evening of August 19, he received orders to go to the residence of Lance Troutman at Embassy Apartments, unit 102, in Columbia Place. He knocked on the front door, and there was no answer. The door was unlocked, so he went in, and he discovered the body on the living room floor. The man had apparently been shot. Lieutenant Then immediately notified the homicide squad, and detectives Sweeney and Sullivan were assigned to the case. He then waited until the detectives, fingerprint experts, and a deputy coroner arrived.

"Your witness," Steve Todd barked.

"How were you told to go to that particular address?" Goldman asked.

"I was instructed by the dispatch officer."

"In what manner?"

"I received a call over the police radio in my car."

"Is it a one-way radio—one that can receive messages only?"

"That's correct."

"What were his instructions?"

"I object, Your Honor," Todd interrupted. "This is improper cross-examination because it's irrelevant and immaterial."

Goldman countered: "Lieutenant Then testified he was 'instructed' to go to the Embassy Apartments in Columbia Place. I believe the rules allow me to bring out the full conversation once the prosecution enters it. I merely want the jury to hear the full extent of—"

"Objection overruled," Judge Croissant interrupted. "Continue Lieutenant Then."

"Well," Then said, "I was merely told to go to unit 102."

"Were you told what to look for?"

"Yes, a body."

"Anything said about how the dispatcher knew you might find a body there?"

"Yes. He said it had been called in by someone."

"Anything about ***how*** it had been reported?"

"I was told it was an anonymous tip."

"An anonymous tip. How convenient. Did they say whether it was a man's or a woman's voice?"

"They said it was a man."

"Was the victim already dead by the time you arrived?"

"I checked his carotid artery. No pulse."

"Thank you, Lieutenant Then. I have no more questions."

Steve Todd paraded a succession of witnesses to the stand, showing that the dead man's identity was Lance Troutman, and he had been shot in the chest with a single .32 caliber bullet. According to testimony, the slug was badly deformed from smashing into bone. Time of death was said to be between eight and ten P.M. on the evening of August 19th. It was established that the alleged murder weapon, a Colt revolver, was purchased by Lloyd Walters at Bakos' Hardware store on Collinsville Road. The serial number was 658331. The owner of the store produced records showing that the gun had been sold to Lloyd Walters three years earlier, and that Walters had signed the receipt. The sales slip was entered into the records and marked for evidence. Todd was adept at pausing at the right moment to let the jury hear murmurs and sounds of surprise coming from the gallery.

Brad whispered to Knucky, "I thought you said you didn't carry a gun."

Knucky shrugged. "I don't, but I've got an arsenal at home."

Morris Goldman asked to cross-examine concerning the autopsy report.

"Call Dr. C. C. Kane to the stand," Judge Croissant ordered.

Dr. Kane came forward, took the oath, and identified himself as Dr. C. C. Kane, the surgeon who had performed the autopsy on the body of Lance Troutman.

"When was the autopsy performed on Mr. Troutman?" Goldman asked.

Kane meticulously straightened his cuff links before answering. "On the morning of August twentieth."

"What time on the morning of the twentieth?"

"I started at eight o'clock."

"How did you establish the approximate time of death?"

"By rigor mortis and the state of food ingested into the stomach."

"Wouldn't the state of rigor mortis be difficult to determine twelve hours or more after Mr. Troutman was killed?"

"I checked the condition of the body that evening after it was brought to the morgue."

"And did you make written notes of your observations?"

"No, I merely made a mental note since I was planning to do the autopsy the next day."

"Isn't it true that authorities do not agree on the development of rigor, because of variables involved?"

"Uh, correct."

"So rigor develops faster in some bodies than others. Can you describe some of the variables?"

"A person under great emotional stress or anxiety might develop rigor more quickly. And rigor could develop sooner if there had been a struggle or significant physical activity before death."

"So the condition of the stomach contents was more of a determining factor in the time of death than the adLancement of rigor mortis?"

"Yes."

"How did you determine when Mr. Troutman consumed his last meal?"

"John Cange, the owner of Cange's Barbecue, said that he, Mr. Troutman, ate a dinner of barbecued chicken, potato salad, and baked beans around five o'clock that evening. This was confirmed by several other patrons who were at the establishment."

"You determined the approximate time of death according to the state of the digestive process?"

"Right."

"And to what degree of accuracy do you claim with your estimate?"

"It is fairly accurate, within two to two and one-half hours."

Goldman gave him a look of mild disdain. "Based on what?"

"Based on the fact that I have performed over three-hundred autopsies."

"Thank you, Dr. Kane. No further questions."

"Detective Sweeney is called to the stand," Steve Todd said. Sweeney came forward and was sworn.

"Detective Sweeney, how long have you been a member of the police force?"

"I first went to work as a motorcycle policeman for the park board in 1926. I was twenty years old at the time."

"When did you become a city policeman?"

"As soon as I turned twenty-one."

"Your honor, what does this line of questioning have to do with the specifics of this case?" Goldman objected.

"Where are you going with this, counselor?" Croissant asked Todd.

"I am trying to establish the experience and expertise of this witness, Your Honor."

"Very well, but get on with it. This is about as interesting as watching corn grow."

"How long did it take you to make detective?"

"Five years."

"So you have about twenty years of experience as a detective?"

"Uh, huh."

"Have you ever arrested someone for murder who was later found to be not guilty by a jury of his peers?"

"No, sir, it's never happened."

Hey, Goldman, you should be objecting to this infallibility line, Brad thought. A pretty courtroom reporter, whose fingers flew mutely over the keys of her machine, briefly distracted him.

"Could you please tell the court what you found on the floor, next to the deceased?"

"Before he died, Mr. Troutman scribbled a letter on the hardwood floor with his own blood."

"Here is a picture taken by a police photographer at the crime scene. Could you please describe what is shown?"

"It appears as if the victim was trying to write a capital letter 'B' before he died."

"Isn't it true that the defendant is widely recognized by the name Knucky, which begins with the letter 'B?"

"Yes!"

"Your Honor, I would like to introduce these photographs into evidence as exhibit number three."

"So ordered. The clerk will make the appropriate designation."

Prosecutor Todd forged on. "When you arrested Mr. Walters, did he have a weapon on him?"

"No, but we searched his house and found a .32 caliber Colt revolver."

"The same caliber as the bullet fired into the body of the deceased?"

"Correct."

"What else, in ***your*** opinion, pointed a finger of suspicion at Mr. Walters?"

"My partner and I talked to a cleaning lady who saw Mr. Walters leave the premises not long before Lieutenant Then discovered the body."

"Thank you, Detective Sweeney." He looked at Goldman. "You may cross examine."

Goldman confidently strode to the stand to confront the witness. Knucky tapped Brad's wrist, leaned over and told him he needed a cigarette.

"Detective Sweeney, we heard you testify that you have never falsely arrested anyone for murder."

"That's right."

"Isn't it true that ten years ago you arrested Jack Dawson for murder, a charge for which he was eventually acquitted?"

Sweeney, always so sure of himself, hesitated and hedged with his answer this time.

"Well, er . . . uh, I arrested him six months later on another charge, and that time he was convicted."

Goldman dramatically pointed an accusing finger. "But in that particular case someone else confessed to the crime."

"Uh, yes, I guess that's correct."

"You guess?"

Detective Robert "Tree" Sweeney

"Okay, that . . . ***is*** . . . correct."

"So you can't claim to be perfect. You do occasionally make mistakes?"

"Once."

"And isn't it possible this might be another one of your mistakes?"

"Not very likely!"

"But it is a possibility since you are not infallible?"

"Yes, it ***might*** be possible. It's also possible we could be invaded by Martians."

"Your Honor . . ."

"Knock off the wisecracks, Sweeney, unless you're looking for a contempt citation."

Sweeney looked down and stared at a scuffmark on his shoe. "Yes, Your Honor."

"Now, let's take another look at the photograph just submitted for evidence."

"Would you agree the letter 'B' is not completely formed?"

"Yes, the letter is incomplete."

"And why do you suppose that is?"

"I concluded the victim died before he was able to finish forming the letter."

"Please look at the letter again, Mr. Sweeney."

"Isn't it possible Mr. Troutman actually finished the letter and had drawn the letter 'P' instead?"

"That's not what I believe because the extra mark below the first half of the letter indicates he was trying to finish the letter 'B.'"

"Take a closer look, Mr. Sweeney. Isn't it possible the dying man, in his weakened condition, finished forming the letter 'P' and made the smudge mark as he expired?"

"It's possible, but when you add up all the other evi—"

"Thank you very much, Mr. Sweeney. I have no further questions."

Next the prosecution called a ballistics expert to the stand, Mildred Rongey. She had testified a number of times before and was perfectly relaxed as she took the chair. Dressed in a crisp cream-colored linen suit, Brad guessed the auburn-haired woman to be in her mid-thirties. She reminded him a little of **Rhonda Fleming.**

Actress Rhonda Fleming (author's collection)

"What's a twelve letter word for stubborn or disobedient?" Judge Croissant said to no one in particular.

A hushed silence fell on the proceedings. Members of the jury looked at each other with blank expressions. Goldman had his hand to his temple, eyes closed trying to think.

"It might be ***recalcitrant***, Your Honor," Brad suggested.

"That's it!" Croissant filled in the crossword letters. "Proceed with your witness, Mr. Todd."

Todd shrewdly acted as if there had been no interruption. "Miss Rongey, did you conduct tests on this gun, which belongs to the defendant?"

She crossed a shapely pair of gams and looked at the revolver handed to her by the state's attorney.

"Yes, those are my initials on the tag."

"Could you please tell us about the tests conducted on the bullet taken from the body of Mr. Troutman, and the gun we have here before us? What did spectrographic analysis of the bullet lead you to conclude?"

"I was able to determine that the bullet removed from the body was fired by a gun of similar make and model. I compared the bullet to a couple that were test-fired from ***this*** gun," she said, as she held it up for all to see."

"And what were the results?"

"The bullet taken from the deceased came from a gun possessing six lands and grooves with a twist to the left. That is consistent with this particular weapon—a .32 caliber Colt revolver."

"How do you know the bullet didn't come from something courtesy of Messrs. Smith & Wesson?"

"A Smith & Wesson has a twist to the right."

"In other words, a bullet from a Smith & Wesson spins clockwise to the right as it exits the gun's muzzle."

"Correct."

"What about the bullet markings?"

"According to the striations, there is a strong probability that the bullet was fired by the murder weapon."

"Objection! It has not been proved this gun is the murder weapon."

"Sustained."

"I'm finished with this witness, Your Honor."

Brad caught Knucky looking off to his right and tapped him on the shoulder. "Quit staring at the citizens. It's against the law to intimidate a jury."

Knucky frowned, then nodded and shifted his gaze to the witness stand.

"Your turn, defense," Judge Croissant snapped.

Goldman took his turn. "I'm curious, Miss Rongey. Just what are your qualifications as a ballistics expert?"

"Do you believe a woman couldn't possibly be a firearms expert? Is that it, Mr. Goldman?"

"I didn't say—"

"Let me put your mind at ease. I grew up on a ranch in Oklahoma. I have been around firearms all of my life. I was on our high school shooting team; in college, I placed second at nationals. I graduated from the University of Oklahoma with a degree in chemistry and biology. I attended the National Academy of Forensics in Baltimore, Maryland, and graduated second in my class. I have just accepted a position with the Federal Bureau of Investigation in Washington, D. C. Is that good enough for you, Mr. Goldman?"

Goldman was sorry he'd asked. He had been sandbagged— blindsided by Todd who purposely avoided bringing up her credentials because he knew Goldman would delve into it.

"That's very impressive, Miss Rongey. But let's get down to specifics. Ballistics isn't really a science, is it? Isn't it kind of like palm reading?"

"That isn't true. Palm reading is a game, child's play meant for entertainment. Ballistics ***is*** a science."

"But not an exact science, is it Miss Rongey?"

"It may not be what you consider ***exact***, but it is very accurate and reliable."

Goldman leaned toward the witness. "Isn't it true that the bullet you took from the body of the deceased was a dumdum?"

"Uh, yes, that's correct."

"And could you explain to the jury the characteristics of a dumdum?"

"Well, uh, it's a flat nosed bullet," she said reluctantly.

"Isn't it true that a soft lead bullet of this type deforms badly when it encounters flesh and bone?"

"Yes, it mushrooms, but I was able to determine with reasonable certainty the bullet probably came from the defendant's weapon."

"Oh, really." Everyone in the courtroom could tell from Goldman's tone and inflection he was on the verge of scoring points with the jury. "Well, then, to what degree of certainty can you say the bullet was fired from the defendant's gun? Is it a ninety percent probability?"

"No sir."

"Eighty percent?"

"No, not quite that high. It's approximately seventy-five percent."

"Is the figure arrived at the same way they roughly determine percentages on fingerprint matches—based on a certain number of matched pairs?"

"It's much more scientific than that, but in layman's terms, that would be an apt way of describing the process. Most of the time I can conclude with absolute certainty about a murder weapon."

Goldman took the gun from her, held it high, then walked over and stood next to the jury. "After all of the scientific examination and inquiry on this particular weapon, the best you can come up with is a seventy-five percent probability?"

"That's right."

"So you can tell us with certainty about the class characteristics, that the bullet was fired from a .32 caliber Colt. But you can't tell us there are enough similarities in the individual characteristics of Mr. Walters' gun to positively identify ***it*** as the murder weapon?"

"That would be correct, but in my opinion it's the murder weapon."

"No further questions, Your Honor."

"The witness may—"

"I'm sorry, Your Honor. I have one more question," Brad said.

Goldman looked puzzled. "Don't screw this up, Sonny," he growled as they passed each other.

"Miss Rongey, could you please estimate the number of weapons in our country that have six lands and grooves with a left twist?"

"I wouldn't know the exact number."

"Let's make a guesstimate. Twenty thousand?"

"Easily."

"Fifty thousand?"

"Probably more."

"One hundred thousand?"

"At least."

"One more question. Miss Rongey, if that were your father sitting beside Mr. Goldman, would you think it fair for him to be sent to prison on a seventy-five percent probability?"

"Objection!"

"Question withdrawn," he said before Croissant could rule. "Thank you, I have nothing more."

Judge Croissant looked at his watch. "It's almost noon. The court will recess until two o'clock. Jurors are reminded they are not to discuss this case among themselves, nor should they allow anyone else to discuss it in their presence. And it should go without saying that jurors are not to form any opinions about the case until the trial phase is completed and deliberations begin."

He rapped the gavel, stood up and went into his chambers.

Russ Maxwell emerged from the crush of spectators to snap a picture as Knucky was led back to his cell. (Croissant had denied a spirited effort at bail.) "Let's see some optimism. Smile, Mr. Walters," he said, an instant before the flash bulb melted from the jolt of electricity. The explosion of light blinded Knucky.

"I am smiling," he sourly replied. Unlike Al Capone, Walters didn't engage in banter with reporters or toss them interesting quotes.

Brad longingly searched the crowd for the woman in the white derby. She was probably gone forever. He had loved her so much. How would he ever find another to take her place, he wondered.

Outside, the wind was playing with the American flag, twisting it to and fro. Whip. Snap. Morris and Brad clambered down the seemingly endless sixteen granite steps, left the Belleville courthouse, and headed for a popular eatery, the Capitol Restaurant, located on The Square.

"I'm not ordering much," Morris announced. "My wife says I need to go on a diet, you know—fewer calories and more green stuff."

Brad looked at him and smiled. "I'm a meat and potatoes man myself. Never cared much for rabbit food."

Goldman responded with a nod and a grunt. Brad wasn't sure what it meant.

Brad settled for fries and a bowl of chili. Morris selected one of their kosher specialties—a pastrami sandwich on yellow-crusted rye. He also ordered a bowl of oyster soup, macaroni and cheese, fruit salad, a dish of lime Jell-O and a piece of chocolate cake.

He unbuttoned the vest of his elegant flannel suit. "Don't tell my wife, okay?"

"Mum's the word."

"That was a good question you put to the female ballistics expert, Logan."

"Thanks."

"But don't ever try to upstage me again." Goldman took out a panatela that had been clipped and lit up. He waved it at Brad. "Hand-rolled by a man in Cuba who's related to Batista."

"I honestly wasn't trying to upstage you, Morris. I was merely trying to keep things moving along to stay on the good side of Judge Croissant. That way we didn't have to redirect."

"That's a lame excuse."

"It's not an excuse; it's a reason. But don't worry, I'll check with you first next time."

"Fine! And remember, just because Croissant says 'jump,' I don't always ask, 'How high?' He doesn't control everything in court. You can't let him intimidate you or let his quirky mannerisms throw you off balance."

"He already did. They already have."

"His wife and daughter were killed in an auto accident a couple of years ago, and he hasn't been the same since."

"So that explains it," Brad said.

"Oddball behavior aside, he makes certain both sides get a fair trial."

"I guess in the end that's the most important thing."

"I suppose you're wondering why I let you make the opening statement?"

Brad scratched an itch over his left eyelid. "Sure, I thought about it."

"I was curious to see how you handled something impromptu. I also wanted to see if you had a knack for relating to jurors."

Brad was dying to ask him how he did but resisted the impulse.

The waitress brought the food to their table.

Brad politely thanked her. "The state's attorney seems to be tightening the noose of incriminating circumstances around Walters' neck," he said.

"All we've heard so far," Goldman said between bites on his sandwich, "is testimony about happenstance that won't withstand the scrutiny of our jury. I think things will start to turn around once we put on our defense."

"Let's hope so." Brad wondered if he wasn't being overly optimistic.

There was a pause in the conversation as Goldman gave him an odd look and then brushed a fly away from the table.

"You know, Brad, I have a sixth sense about some things. You don't like me, do you?"

"It isn't a matter of like or dislike. I'm . . . uncomfortable working with you."

Goldman held up a finger to call time out while he finished swallowing the last of his sandwich. "You think I'm an unethical, egotistical bum who is in league with crooks and milks the system for all it's worth? Come on, admit it."

Brad was nibbling on a fry dipped in Brooks tangy ketchup. "No, it's just that—"

"You may find this hard to believe, but I had ideals just like you when I started. Just wait until you've been in this business a few years and reality sets in. You'll see."

"They say you're a mouthpiece for the mob."

"That's baloney."

"So why is it you represent so many shady characters?"

"Look, Brad. It's like this. I didn't seek out these guys; they came to my office. Once the word got out I was good at what I do, they sought me out. The whole thing just kind of snowballed."

"Doesn't it bother your conscience, getting these guys off? Aren't you afraid you might be violating the spirit of the ABA's Cannon of Ethics?"

"I just do my job. It's not my fault if the prosecution presents a weak case. And look who's calling the kettle black. You're the one helping to defend Knucky."

"But only because I'm convinced he's innocent."

"A lawyer isn't supposed to be concerned about guilt or innocence." He absentmindedly tamped out his cigar in an ashtray. "You do your job and let the jury make that decision."

"I know it's the way the justice system works in theory, but I'm beginning to think the means are corrupting the end."

"You do what you have to do. You'll learn that the longer you're in this profession. Pretty soon you'll be on the same treadmill as the rest of us."

"Why do you do it? What motivates you, Morris? Money? Power? The challenge?"

"A little bit of all three. You lose your idealism fast in this business. It gets pushed out of the way by hard reality. Over the years I've developed a taste for certain things. I like expensive cars, flashy watches, European clothes and caviar. I have a lifestyle to maintain, and it takes lots of money. I also like to gamble for high stakes. That's my high. I gamble instead of doing drugs. Sometimes I win, and sometimes I lose."

"I hear you're part of a consortium that owns the Sands in Las Vegas."

Goldman took his glasses off, shook his head and massaged the bridge of his nose. "I don't discuss specifics when it comes to my financial life."

"Sorry, it was rude of me to bring it up."

Goldman finished his sandwich and was working on the Jell-O. He cocked his head and gave Brad a puzzled look. "You don't seem right, Logan. You're not still mooning over that dame at the ***Journal***, are you?"

"You know about that?"

"Yeah, Knucky filled me in. You better pull yourself together, or you're not going to be much help to me on this case."

"Sorry, I'll try to put all of that behind me." Brad didn't think he sounded very convincing. Memories of Lorna kept flowing back in snatches of soul-tormenting detail. Every fiber of his body missed the sound of her voice, the look of her face.

The sound of Morris' gruff voice brought his drifting attention back. "Say, how on earth did a square peg like you ever hook up with a rounder like Knucky? You two are polar opposites."

"We met by accident about a year ago when I went to the Club 501 to eat supper. We seemed to hit it off, and we've been friends ever since."

"But you don't seem his type. It's like the two of you have nothing in common."

"I know what you mean. But we always seem to enjoy each other's company. I think he likes me because he knows I don't want anything from him except friendship."

Goldman munched the last bite of his cake and swigged a sip from his bottle of **Falstaff** beer. "Friendship, now that's a rare commodity. I think I could probably count all of mine on one hand."

"I'll bet you have more than that if you really thought about it," Brad said.

"Don't I wish," Goldman responded. "Hey, I'll bet you a steak dinner the juror on the right, front row, the gentleman in the gray suit wearing glasses, gets picked foreman."

"What is it with these bets? Is everybody in town hooked on gambling? Make it a coffee and apple pie à la mode."

"Cheapskate!"

Johnny Weissmuller/Tarzan and Jane

"It has nothing to do with that. My church preaches against gambling because it's a vice."

"Yeah, yeah. Okay. Well . . . whom do you pick?"

"I think they'll choose the guy with the red tie who is a foreman at **Excelsior Tool and Die**."

"You're on."

"You know what, Morris? If Knucky didn't shoot Troutman, like he claims, how do you account for the bullet being a pretty good match for his gun?"

"I can't figure it. When it comes to murder, I don't believe in coincidences."

Brad looked at his watch. "Hey, we'd better get back to the courthouse or we'll be late. We don't want to do anything to irritate Judge Croissant."

"Once you get to know all of his little idiosyncrasies and pet peeves, he isn't so bad. He knows his law, and he seldom gets reversed. He has a fetish about that."

"All I know is when I'm in front of him I seem to get nervous—like a long tailed cat in a room full of rocking chairs."

Goldman picked up his cigar and lit up. He laid a ten spot on the table. "I'll get the tip," he insisted. Brad nodded and placed a bill and coins totaling a dollar eighty-nine next to his plate.

* * *

At two o'clock, promptly, recess was over, and Judge Croissant gaveled the assemblage to order. "Let's go. Time's a wastin'. Call your next witness, Mr. Todd."

The person who took the stand was a fingerprint expert, Leonard Van Camp, from the East St. Louis Police Department. He meticulously straightened the crease in his slacks after being seated.

"Mr. Van Camp, could you please explain to the court the definition of a latent fingerprint?"

"Yes, it is merely a print that has been lifted and removed from its original source and placed on a sheet of paper or a white card for easy identification."

"I have here a set of cards with latent fingerprints lifted from the scene of the crime," said the prosecutor. "Would you please carefully examine the print on card number eleven, which was lifted from the door knob of the deceased's apartment."

He handed the card to Van Camp, who carefully studied the print. Then he handed him another card.

"Now would you compare the first print with the one on this next card which is a print taken from the defendant, the day he was arrested, marked People's Exhibit number twelve."

The fingerprint expert carefully inspected the two cards.

"Is it true, sir, that fingerprints, like snowflakes, are unique—no two are exactly alike?" Todd asked.

"Yes, it's true."

Brad glanced over at Goldman and was surprised to see him doodling on his legal pad.

"Can you describe for us, in a general manner, what experts look for when trying to identify fingerprints?"

"Every fingerprint consists of distinguishing characteristics." Van Camp explained. "We use the system invented by Sir Edward Henry in 1895 that consists of markings and designs we refer to as loops, whorls, arches, deltas and so on. One of the things we do is count the number of ridges until we come to a peculiar branching of lines. For example, if both prints have seven ridges before reaching a distinctive arch or branch, that would be called one point of similarity."

"The ridge is the raised part of the skin which makes the print, and the lower portions are the furrows?" Todd interjected.

"Right."

"And if you have just one point of similarity, that would merely be a coincidence?"

"Yes."

"Please tell the court what you found when you examined these two sets of prints."

"They are identical—a perfect match in every aspect."

"So you can say with absolute certainty the print taken from the victim's front door belongs to Mr. Walters, the defendant?"

"I am one hundred percent sure of the match."

"Thank you, Mr. Van Camp," Todd said, with a Brer Rabbit smile of self-satisfaction.

Goldman surprised Brad by leaning behind Knucky and telling him to cross-examine. He frequently did this with his assistants when he was immersed in thought and did not wish to break his concentration. Naturally, it was only when he thought the questioning would be inconsequential.

"Tell us, Mr. Van Camp, were there other fingerprints lifted from the crime scene?" Brad asked.

"Yes, People's Exhibit numbers twelve, thirteen, fourteen and fifteen were also lifted from the crime scene."

"Could you identify the persons to whom those belong?"

"Exhibit number fourteen belongs to the deceased, Mr. Troutman. Number twelve was the cleaning lady's."

"What about Exhibit number fifteen?"

"That one belongs to Mr. Then, the officer who discovered the body."

"Were there any partial prints?"

"Yes, a few. But it was impossible to determine the owner of the prints."

"And, finally, number thirteen?" he asked.

"Exhibit number thirteen, a full print, did not match any other prints we had available to us."

"So this leaves us with the possibility someone else besides Mr. Walters might have killed Mr. Troutman?"

"Objection! Calls for a conclusion by the witness," Todd yelled.

"Sustained! Mr. Logan, don't try that one again," Croissant admonished. "They should have taught you that in Lawyering 101."

"Let me rephrase the question. Mr. Van Camp, the existence of an unidentifiable print indicates the presence of someone else in the room, does it not?"

"That is correct."

"Thank you. That is all."

He went back to the table, expecting to get royally chewed out by Goldman.

"You did okay, Logan. I would have said the same thing. At least you brought up the possibility in the minds of the jury someone else might have committed the crime. All we need is reasonable doubt."

The next witness was the cleaning lady who claimed she

could identify Mr. Walters as having been at the apartment on the night of the murder. Judge Croissant, looking slightly bored, exhaled on his glasses and began rubbing them with a handkerchief.

Pause.

"Mrs. Bennett," Todd said, "could you explain how you happened to be a witness to certain events at the apartment of Lance Troutman on the night of August 19th?"

"There are twelve apartments in the complex, and my husband is employed by the owners. He mows the grass and does general maintenance work. I also work there, but I am employed by seven of the gentlemen residents to do maid service in their apartments on a weekly basis."

"Why was your husband not a witness to these events?"

"He had gone home to get a part for a toilet that wasn't flushing properly."

"I see. How did you happen to be on the premises in the evening? Isn't the type of work you do performed more frequently during the day?"

"We do some of the work on Saturdays, but evening work is occasionally required because we both work at Model Laundry during the week. We keep the Sabbath holy. We do no work on the Lord's day."

"Did you see the defendant at the apartments on the night of August 19th?"

"Yes, I did."

"Had you ever seen this man prior to that evening?"

"Not in person, but I recognized him from pictures in the newspaper."

"What were you doing when you spotted the defendant?"

"I had just finished cleaning apartment 103 and was on my way over to apartment 108."

"Did he see you?"

"Oh, yes. He was very polite. Even tipped his hat to me and said, 'Good evening.' "

"Did you see him enter Mr. Troutman's apartment, unit 102?"

"I certainly did. He rang the electric bell and then went inside when Mr. Troutman opened the door."

"So you also saw Mr. Troutman?"

"That's right."

"Do you have any idea what time this was?"

"Yes, it was around seven-thirty in the evening."

"How can you be sure?"

"Because I have a regular habit of checking my watch every time I finish cleaning an apartment."

"Did you see or hear anything unusual after that?"

"No sir. My husband came back and was working on the toilet in the unit I was cleaning. I was running the vacuum sweeper."

"Thank you very much, Mrs. Bennett. I have no further questions," Todd said.

Brad leaned over toward Knucky. "She is a very solid witness for the prosecution." There was no reply.

Goldman strolled over to the witness.

"Mrs. Bennett, I see you are wearing glasses. Were you wearing your glasses that evening?"

"Yes, I generally wear them all the time."

"Were you wearing them when you allegedly saw the defendant?"

"I had momentarily taken them off because they had smudge marks, and I was getting ready to clean them."

"Could you tell us what your vision is without glasses?"

"If I remember correctly, about 20/80 in both eyes."

"So, how can you be sure it was Mr. Walters you saw going into Mr. Troutman's apartment?"

Pause.

There was tittering in the court that Judge Croissant ended with a light tapping of the gavel.

"Because after he greeted me, I finished the cleaning and put them back on. I clearly saw Mr. Walters and Mr. Troutman at the door of apartment 102."

"Did you see or hear the two men quarrel or argue?"

"No sir, I did not."

"And you didn't hear any shots?"

"No."

"So, for all you know, Mr. Walters went to see Mr. Troutman to sell him some raffle tickets?"

"Objection, Your Honor," Todd complained. "He's trying to put words in the mouth of the witness."

"Sustained."

"I'm finished with this witness," Goldman said.

The next person called to the stand was Marillyn Watts.

"Miss Watts, can you tell us where you were on the evening of July 12th, a little over a year ago?" Todd asked.

"I was eating dinner at the Club 501 with a friend of mine, Jim Vander Pluym."

"And did you see the defendant get into an argument with Mr. Troutman, the deceased?"

Goldman jumped to his feet. "Your honor, I object to this line of questioning. What bearing would a minor dispute that took place over a year ago have on the facts of this case? Besides, anything she has to contribute would be hearsay, unless she was part of the dispute."

Todd had anticipated the objection. "Your Honor, this line of questioning is intended to help establish a motive for the killing. The testimony of Miss Watts will show there was bad blood between Mr. Walters and Mr. Troutman."

Judge Croissant hesitated for a period, as if sifting through judicial procedure in his mind. "I'm going to allow this testimony because I believe it does have some bearing on the facts of this case."

"But, Your—"

"Are you challenging my ruling, Counselor?"

"Er, no sir."

"Fine, then let's move on."

"Thank you, Your Honor," Todd said with a smile of triumph.

"I ask you again, Miss Watts, did you see the two men get into an argument?"

"Yes, I did. I only noticed it because Mr. Walters got very loud and was yelling at Mr. Troutman."

"Could you tell what the argument was about?"

"No sir, I only knew that the two of them were very angry about something."

"Did you see either of them try to physically harm the other person?"

"No, it was confined to a verbal shouting match."

"What happened to Mr. Troutman later that evening?"

"He was in a car accident and ended up in a hospital. Mr.

Troutman told people someone from the Club 501 had laced his drink with knockout drops."

Goldman leaped to his feet again. "Objection—immaterial, irrelevant, prejudicial and improper. She is making a false allegation that cannot be substantiated in any manner. I move this part of the testimony be stricken from the record."

"Objection sustained. The jury will disregard Miss Watts' inflammatory statements alleging Mr. Walters, or one of his employees, tried to harm Mr. Troutman by placing knock-out drops in his drink."

Knucky leaned over to Brad and whispered: "That's unfair! They already heard what she had to say. They ain't gonna forget her testimony."

"You're right," Brad agreed, "the damage has been done. Say, how come you never told me the reporter in your story was Lance Troutman?"

"You never asked."

CHAPTER 23

East St. Louis was home port for the *Sprague*, the largest boat on the Mississippi River. It was used for hauling bauxite from Arkansas for the Aluminum Ore plant, the largest processsor of that mineral in the *world.* The city also led the nation in the production of roofing materials and baking powder. It also claimed the first paved road in the state of Illinois, the St. Clair County Turnpike (State Street), which went from downtown East St. Louis to Belleville.

Illinoistown Inn on St. Clair County Turnpike, circa 1866

It was 4:30 P.M. on Friday, the third afternoon of Walters' trial. Court had adjourned, and Brad was in his office, leaning back in his chair, feet propped up on his desk. He was massaging his temples, the faint beginnings of a headache. He knew the trial would probably end on Monday and despite spirited efforts by the defense to plant seeds of doubt with the jury, there was a good chance Knucky would be convicted of second-degree murder.

He wadded up an old office memo and tossed it into the wastebasket. ***Swish! Logan cans a spectacular shot with one-second left to give the Fighting Illini a dramatic victory over archrival Indiana. The crowd goes wild!***

Brad's masculine ego restored, he returned to matters at hand. He was nursing a deep anxiety. Brad knew that despite Walters' probable innocence in this matter, the man was likely responsible for the deaths of others who had challenged his domain. The fact that they were low-lifes—denizens of moral poverty—did little to salve his conscience. According to the Gospels, even a penitent thief had made it into heaven.

Yet, despite Walters' criminal activities, he had some redeeming qualities. Like Janus, the Roman god of doorways, he had two faces. He may not have been the best of husbands, but he was devoted to his kids. And Knucky could be kind and generous. Brad had learned that when one of his waitresses couldn't afford to buy her daughter a new dress for the school prom, Knucky gave her fifty dollars and told her not to worry about it. Montrose once told Brad on the QT that Knucky gave large sums anonymously to the Red Cross, Community Chest and Catholic Charities.

Brad was heartsick about the tangled mess that was East St. Louis politics. Most of the police and politicians were honest, but there were a significant number on the take. If there was a land clearance scheme, a public housing project, or a new school to be built, certain palms had to be greased. A commissioner would shepherd the contract through a council sub-committee and see to it that the "right" construction company was awarded the project. It was s.o.p. for the contractor and most sub-contractors to overcharge by approximately ten percent. Kickbacks were then made to a host of civic officials, policemen and union leaders who enriched themselves with graft.

He knew there was no telling how many people were on Walters' payroll. He had also learned 'Baldy' O'Malley was Walters' bagman. His primary responsibility was the weekly visit to tavern owners, "policy" kings, and vending/pinball machine sites to make collections. Then he made the rounds to Captain Jesse Shively and his "friends" in the various precincts on Monday to deliver their cut of those "contributions."

Brad once asked Montrose why the term ***policy*** was used for betting the numbers. He told him that runners, people who took the bets, coined the word. When asked why people were giving them money in exchange for tickets, they merely said they were collecting on insurance policies.

Honest graft, as some called it, was the matrix of East St. Louis politics. Municipal machinations were tricky, complex, and frequently a little bit different from what they seemed. Brad had read Lincoln Steffans' sensational muckraking book ***Shame of the Cities*** and knew this was the general scheme of things in most big towns and had been since the days of Boss Tweed in New York City. But that was small solace because this was happening in his back yard, right here in his own hometown.

He also realized anyone who threatened to buck the status quo and expose the system ran the risk of falling victim to an "engineered accident," or worse.

Brad closed his eyes and contemplated the moral conundrum. He let out a deep, slow sigh and decided to chuck it in and head for home. He opened his eyes, swung his feet off the desk and started to get up. At that moment, he saw Missola standing at the threshold of his open office door.

"Hello, good friend. I was just getting ready to leave. What can I do for you?"

Missola, dressed in her usual workaday attire, dust rag in

hand, was getting ready to start her cleaning chores.

"You looks awful, Mistuh Logan, like sumpin' the cat drug in."

"I know. I'm beat. It's been a long, hard day."

"Is ya still workin' on the Walters trial?" She finished tying a bow on her apron behind her back.

"Yes, and it's beginning to get me down."

Missola had an eager look on her face. "I brought you somethin', somethin' that might help." She handed him a manila folder. Curious, he took it from her and opened it.

"Carbon paper—what on earth . . . ?"

"It got lotsa names an' numbers, Mistuh Logan. I've had it over a year."

Brad got out of his chair, walked over to the window, and carefully holding the folder to avoid prints on the carbons, turned it to the light to try and read it. "Oops." The letters were backwards. He went over to his secretary's desk and took out a large hand mirror she used when combing her hair or freshening her makeup. Holding the mirror at an angle allowed him to read what was on the carbons. Sure enough, there was an indelible impresssion left by the typewriter keys. A look of stunned surprise came over his face.

"Missola, how on earth did you come to possess these documents? They appear to be exactly what I have been looking for; they're dynamite. We've been desperate for a decent break and here it is, gilt-edged and gift wrapped."

"Before I comes here to work, I was a cleanin' lady at City Hall an' the po-lice station."

East St. Louis City Hall (The police station was next to it on the south side)

"I never knew," he said.

"Didn't have no reason to tell ya. Didn't think it was impo'tant."

"Please go on. How did you obtain these two carbons?"

"I was workin' late one evenin' when Jack Rafferty, the po-lice com'ishner, comes to his office an' starts typin' somethin' on his sec'tary's machine. I thought this was strange cuz the man weren't good at typin'. He used dese two fingers," she said, holding up the index fingers on each hand. "An he was kind o' nervous the whole time, lookin' up an' turnin' his head to see if anybody might be comin'. After he left, I went in to his room, an' I found sev'ral carbon papers in the waste basket. They was fresh an' hadn't been used for nothin' else, so everythin' marked on 'em was right there. Figgered they might be impo'tant, so I put 'em in a folder an' took 'em home with me. Jus' figgered they might come in handy some time. Cullud folk need all the trump cards they can git. Had almost forgot 'bout em."

"Thank you, Missola." Brad grabbed hold and hugged her. "I think I've finally got this thing figured out. These documents are going to produce a storm that will make the tornado of 1896 look like a summer breeze."

Embarrassed, Missola pulled away. "Tain't nothin'." Then she turned and left the office, anxious to begin her routine.

Is it possible to find Rafferty's fingerprints on these carbons? Brad wondered. Unless he could find the chief's prints on the documents, they wouldn't mean much. He made two phone calls. The first was to Bakos Hardware to make an appointment to see the owner on Saturday at 10:00 A.M. Then he phoned Gene Moore, a friend of his at the police crime lab. Moore told him that by using iodine fumes, it was likely they could get a good set of prints from carbon paper. Next, Brad called Ed Bennett, the handyman at Lance's apartment complex, and asked him a few questions. Then he quickly did the subpoena paperwork for a judge to sign, and he dashed off to the lab.

"You did the work on this, so you get to ask the questions," Goldman whispered to Brad. "I hope you don't bite off more than you can chew." It was ten minutes after nine in the morning, the following Monday. "I just hope you know what you are doing. It's Walters' life and your career that are on the line."

"Defense calls John Rafferty, Chief of Police, to the stand."

There was a collective sucking noise as the large crowd on hand gasped and drew in its breath. Then a rising sound of murmurs and comments. Rafferty nervously walked to the witness stand and took the oath.

Brad stood and prepared to toss the incendiary grenade. He walked over and handed Steven Todd a folder containing typed copies of the carbons. Then he gave Judge Croissant another folder containing the original carbons plus copies. "Defense exhibit number four, Your Honor. I'd like these marked and entered in the record."

Croissant scrutinized the contents. He had difficulty concealing a look of astonishment. "So ordered." He handed the documents to the bailiff who walked them over to the clerk.

Brad crossed to John Rafferty and handed him yet another replica of the carbons.

"Mr. Rafferty, can you tell us why your fingerprints were found on the originals of these documents?"

Rafferty looked at the papers contemptuously. After a few seconds the color quickly drained from the police chief's face. His mouth crimped in annoyance.

"I have no idea how my fingerprints got on those carbons." He spoke in faint second generation Irish-accented English. "You can't prove ***I*** typed them." Reporters, seated behind the prosecution throughout the trial to get a better view of Walters' expressions and reactions, furiously scrambled their pens across their note pads.

Like a boxer in the ring, Brad had been biding his time, jabbing and back pedaling, waiting for an opening into which he could throw a hard right cross. Now he went on the attack. "You're wrong about that, Mr. Rafferty. We found a Negro cleaning lady who worked at your office. She'll testify she saw you typing with those carbons and that she found them in the wastebasket where you had thrown them away."

Rafferty dug in his heels. "It still doesn't prove anything. The carbons were mixed in with other trash so they could have been left there by anyone."

"Wrong, Mr. Rafferty. She'll testify those carbons were the only things in the waste basket because she had already cleaned that room."

Rafferty was dumbstruck and couldn't think of a rebuttal.

Attaboy, Logan. Keep him off balance. "The information on these pages proves you were distributing payoffs to a large number of public officials."

Rafferty looked at Logan with a sneer. "I resent this baseless accusation. Those payments were for services performed by those individuals above and beyond their regular duties."

"They also show you made regular payments to Lance Troutman, the man my client stands accused of killing." Brad turned an accusatory eye on the chief. "I think you're lying, Mr. Rafferty. I believe we're talking about graft, corruption and murder. My guess is the payoffs to Lance Troutman were made because he was blackmailing you."

"What possible reason would Troutman have to blackmail me?" He nervously tugged at a suddenly noose-tight collar.

"Simple. He found out from Mr. Torricelli about the construction kickbacks going on at City Hall. Troutman was planning to write a dynamite series of articles about it, but when Torricelli was murdered, he decided blackmail would be more lucrative."

"You're tilting at windmills. I guess the next nutty thing you're going to say is that it was me who killed Troutman instead of Knucky Walters."

"You read my mind. That was ***exactly*** my next sentence." The gasps and murmurs shuddering through the gallery caused Croissant to rap his gavel.

"What! I'm going to sue you for slander and defamation of character. When my lawyers get through with you, you'll be lucky to practice law in Slippery Rock."

"We'll see about that. Defense exhibit number five, Your Honor." Logan held high a slip of paper and passed out the necessary copies.

"Can you tell us what this is, Mr. Rafferty?"

"It looks like some kind of store receipt from Bakos Hardware."

"Can you tell the court whose signature is at the bottom?"

"It looks as if someone forged my name."

"I don't think we'll have any trouble proving it's ***your*** signature, Mr. Rafferty. And if you'll notice, it's for $42.95, payment for a .38 revolver, the exact make and model owned by Mr. Walters."

"Just a coincidence." Rafferty's intense eyes were icy, irate, menacing.

"That price also includes a box of flat-nosed bullets—the exact type used by Mr. Walters. Please don't patronize us by saying that's also a coincidence."

"So I bought a gun and some ammo—big deal. People buy guns and bullets all the time."

"I checked the records. You already own an Iver-Johnson revolver. You purchased ***this*** gun to kill Lance Troutman and put the blame on Walters." The courtroom was hushed.

Rafftery grimaced and twisted in his seat. "I've never been to that Troutman guy's apartment."

"Yes, you have. Ed Bennett, the handyman, was away on an errand the whole time Walters was there. But he came back. I asked him if he saw any cars different from those usually parked in the area. Bennett said he saw a red Mercury sedan, just like the one you drive."

"There are dozens and dozens of red Mercs in this town."

Rafferty's Mercury

"But Mr. Bennett said this one had a bright yellow sticker on the windshield—the kind issued to a handful of high-level City Hall employees with reserved parking spaces. That kind of narrows the field, doesn't it?"

Rafferty leaned forward with a smug expression. "I've got enough experience as police chief to know that still isn't enough evidence."

Brad tenaciously pressed on. "Remember the letter Troutman was trying to write with his own blood before he died?"

"Yes, I read about it in the police report."

"The prosecution thinks the dying man was trying to form a capital B to form the word ***Knucky.*** But that isn't right, is it, Mr. Rafferty?" All eyes were fixed on the witness.

"How would I know?"

"Because ***you*** are the one who shot him. He wasn't trying to form the letter B. It was an incomplete R signifying he was shot by you, Chief Rafferty."

Rafferty exploded. "That's untrue—pure, irresponsible conjecture on your part."

Reporters were scribbling feverishly. The courtroom grew noisy and Judge Croissant banged his gavel, calling for order.

Something caught Brad's eye from the back of the room. Hal Schaeffer, a crackerjack sleuth who did some work for his firm, had entered the chamber. Schaeffer walked over and gave a sheaf of papers to Morris Goldman. "Your Honor, may I have a moment to confer with my partner?"

"You have sixty seconds, counselor." Croissant fixed his eyes on a large wall clock on the left side of the courtroom.

Brad walked over and talked briefly with Goldman, nodding his head, as if pleased at what he was being told. Then he came back at Rafferty with a hard body blow.

"Your wrong about the lack of evidence, Chief Rafferty. The authorities found a number of fresh prints at the murder scene that didn't belong to either Walters or Troutman. I obtained a search warrant, and I've just been informed the authorities found the murder weapon at your home, with ***your*** prints on it."

Rafferty bristled. "Impossible! They couldn't have found that gun because . . . I . . . er . . ."

"Because you tossed it in the river. Is that what you were going to say?"

"No, uh . . ."

"Never mind. What they actually found were papers and ledgers with your fingerprints on them. That will give us even more information about the grafters at City Hall."

After a slight pause, savoring the moment fully, Brad delivered the coup de grâce. "I was also told your fingerprints on those pages matched the prints from Troutman's house that were on prosecution exhibit number thirteen."

Knockout!

Chief Rafferty, a slacken expression on his ashen face, slumped in the witness chair, totally defeated, thoroughly wrecked.

Pandemonium!

The room grew noisy with the stunning and unexpected turn of events. Croissant slammed the gavel so hard the head flew off and hit a surprised Stephen Todd in the chest.

The crowd quieted after Croissant screamed, ***Order***. "Your Honor, based on this new evidence and the testimony just presented, defense requests a directed acquittal, with prejudice, on the charge of second degree murder," Brad said.

Croissant looked at Steven Todd, who rose from his chair and brushed a lock of hair in place. "In light of this new evidence, the prosecution has no objection."

"Defense request is granted." Judge Croissant took his glasses off, turned and peered at the jury. "You are hereby dismissed. The court would like to thank all of you for performing your civic duty." He rapped his knuckles twice and announced, "Court is adjourned."

The room grew noisy as Walters' wife rushed to his side and gave him a hug. Blinding starbursts from camera flashbulbs captured the poignant moment. The court was clattery with excitement at the unexpected outcome of Walters' trial. Reporters from twelve area newspapers fired off dozens of questions at Logan, Goldman and Walters. Then they zoomed to the lobby phone booths to file their stories. Russ Maxwell wheeled and rapidly snapped additional shots of Goldman shaking Brad's hand and of Knucky giving Brad a bear hug. Next, he caught a downcast John Rafferty, head bowed, angered and tormented by the turn of events that would lead to his arrest for the Torricelli and Troutman murders. Maxwell turned and raced to the developing room at the ***Journal.***

"That was a lucky break for us, getting those carbon sheets from Brad's cleaning lady," Goldman said while lighting up a Havana victory cigar. It was later that same afternoon and they were at the Club 501—Brad, Morris, Knucky, Montrose and Roland. Knucky was treating everyone to drinks and a celebratory dinner. After placing their food orders, they lapsed into the traditional whys and wherefores of the trial.

"Can you believe Rafferty was so stupid as to type all of that incriminating evidence with specific names, dates and payoff amounts?" Montrose said.

"By keeping detailed records, he figured it would keep everybody in line." Goldman replied. "No one dared to pull a fast one because Rafferty had the goods on them."

Brad spoke up. "I think there was another reason. I think the fact that municipal corruption had been going on for seventy-five years without a single policeman or member of City Hall going to jail made them bold and slipshod. And I still think Rafferty and Delonzo are somehow connected."

"Why didn't you bring that out at the trial?" Knucky asked.

"Because all I know for sure is that Rafferty called Delonzo's home in St. Louis. I obtained that information from the phone company. They can trace long-distance calls but not local ones. But it doesn't prove anything."

"So this whole thing started with the Torricelli killing, is that right?" Knucky asked.

"That's correct," Brad said. "Rafferty hired Sizemore to kill Torricelli because he was going to blow the whistle on the contract kickbacks at City Hall."

"Why did he type the information?" Roland asked.

"So it wouldn't be in his handwriting in case something happened to it," said Goldman.

"Yeah, well now that it's all public knowledge, my union buddies ain't gonna like the new rules," Knucky said.

"People have short memories," Goldman said. "The same thing happened in St. Louis about ten years ago. From what I know, everything over there is back to the way it used to be."

"What made Lance so sure that someone connected to City Hall wouldn't put out a contract on him?" Roland asked.

"He probably made a deal with Rafferty that as long as he was on the payroll any other crooked dealings that came his way as a reporter would be covered up," Brad said.

Interior of a commission house at the Stock Yards

"So how did the phone number on that book of matches from Torricelli's house point you in the right direction?" Montrose asked.

"It had the police station and City Hall numbers written on it and the name ***Jack.*** I couldn't figure out who Jack was at the station or City Hall. The only prominent Jack I could think of was Jack Scoville, but he's at the **Stock Yards.** It was Missola who made me remember the names Jack and John are often used interchangeably."

Roland scratched his head. "So was there any connection between Troutman an' Torricelli?"

"When Torricelli found out he was being bypassed for contracts because he wouldn't play ball, he told officials at City Hall he was going to blow the whistle. Then he probably called Troutman and told him everything he knew, so that Troutman would write an exposé about what was going on. My guess is that he told Lance he had proof of the kickback scheme hidden in his house. As it turned out, all he had was a list that he had compiled. It contained the names of various local contractors, the amount of the contracts they were awarded, along with the dates. Torricelli had copies of his own bids and could prove he was the low bidder in about six instances."

Montrose looked puzzled. "Wouldn't that have been enough?"

"Probably not," Goldman intervened. "Officials might have claimed Torricelli's bid didn't meet the exacting standards they were looking for. Or they could say that he had a reputation for shoddy work, or that they were afraid he wouldn't get the project completed on time. There are lots of loopholes."

"Contracts don't always go to the lowest bidder, even when kickbacks aren't involved," Brad added.

Goldman finished a drink, poured himself another, and finished the explanation. "Rafferty and his cronies didn't know for sure what Torricelli had. But when word got around Torricelli was planning to rock the boat, a lot of people got worried. By itself, the information Torricelli had wasn't sufficient to get anybody convicted of fraud or bribery, but his complaining could have ultimately led to a grand jury inquiry. That would have spelled trouble."

"So when Sizemore killed Torricelli, he was told to make it look like a mob hit—a red herring for the authorities," Knucky said.

"Right," Goldman added with a hacking cough.

"After Torricelli was murdered, Lance probably decided that blackmail would be more profitable," Brad explained.

"So he put the squeeze on Rafferty for money, and the man ponied up," Montrose said.

"And that only became intolerable when Lance demanded even more money to keep quiet," Brad said.

Roland, who had been reading the label of his Stag beer, wanted to know what caused Lance to get greedy.

"It happened after Troutman heard Rafferty testify at the Kefauver hearings," Goldman volunteered. "When all the stuff came out about Rafferty's expensive country estate in rural O'Fallon, that's when Troutman upped the ante."

"Why did Troutman need money?" Montrose asked. "I thought his family was loaded."

"They are," Knucky explained. "But his father hated his irresponsible playboy lifestyle, so he cut off his allowance. On top of that he was a compulsive gambler. My boys tell me he was lousy at cards, an' lousy at handicapping the bangtails. He was in debt up to his eyeballs."

"What makes you two think Rafferty and Delonzo are in cahoots?" Roland asked.

"After Walters' warehouse was burned and Delonzo's car was blown up, the newspapers were full of speculation about rivalry between the two factions," Goldman explained.

"Yeah," Brad continued. "My guess is that if Delonzo was in charge of the East Side, he would widen the operations to include drugs and prostitution. Rafferty could see to it that only occasional raids and arrests were made, just to keep up appearances. After the guilty paid fines, then it would be back to business as usual."

"In return," Goldman jumped in, "Rafferty and his crew would get a cut or percentage."

"Won't all that change with Rafferty and the others going to jail?" Montrose asked.

"Nope," Brad answered. "Remember what was said at the Kefauver hearings. With nonpartisan elections in East St. Louis where the politicos merely run two slates of candidates, it doesn't matter who wins. Nothing changes. My guess is that this contest between Delonzo and Knucky is far from over."

"But how did Rafferty know the D.A. would go after Knucky if Troutman was found murdered?" Montrose wondered out loud.

Goldman held up a couple of fingers. "Two things. He knew nearly everyone in law enforcement remembered what happened to Jake Lingle back in the 1930s."

Jake Lingle – murdered Chicago reporter

"You mean the Chicago reporter who got himself killed?" Knucky asked.

"Yes," Morris continued. "Jake was a bought reporter. He was on the Capone payroll and received regular payments to insure that he wouldn't dig too deeply with his stories and investigations. When Jake started asking for more money, they killed him."

Roland's blue-gray eyes narrowed. "What does that have to do with Lance and Knucky?"

"Point number two," Brad continued the explanation. "The episode where Knucky had his bartender put KO drops in Lance's drink when he was snooping around for a story became the talk of the town. Everyone knew there was bad blood between Lance and Knucky."

Walters' eyes lit up. "So I would become a prime suspect because I had motive?"

"Correct," Brad said. "Rafferty knew the police would assume Knucky found out that Lance, inspired by the Kefauver hearings, was planning to do a series on crime in our city."

"And don't forget," Goldman said, "Lance was dating the female reporter who wrote an editorial calling for a cleanup of the city."

"Yeah," Roland said. "The dame Brad is sweet on."

Brad shook his head. "She's ancient history now."

Goldman went on. "The only things left were means and opportunity. To set things in motion, Rafferty had one of his police cronies anonymously tip one of Walters' informants that Lance was planning to do a less than flattering story on him. They knew it would set Knucky off. They counted on his famous temper to take it from there and send him looking for Lance."

"And I fell right into their trap," Knucky said, shaking his head. "What a sap. When I confronted Lance about the article, he denied it, of course."

"Why didn't Montrose or Roland go with you?" Brad asked.

"Lance is such a twerp, I wanted to handle it myself. I told them to wait in the car."

Brad waved some smoke away and leaned forward. "Then the two of you got into it?"

"Yeah, I called him a liar and we got into a fight. He was such a putz. I gave him one good clip on the chin, and he went down like some pug-ugly throwing a fight. He was bleeding and half unconscious when I left, but I didn't kill him."

"After Knucky drove away," Goldman said, "Rafferty went in and finished the job."

"So how did he make it look like Walters' gun was the murder weapon?" Montrose asked.

"It wasn't as hard as you think," Goldman said. "Remember Del Shinn, the ex-marine who was Walters' driver before Montrose?"

"Yeah, Knucky caught him lying about something one day and fired him on the spot. I thought Knucky was going to kill him," Roland said.

"Well, after that, he drifted over to St. Louis and started working for Delonzo."

"So?" Roland shrugged.

"Well, Del Shinn was with Knucky the day he bought his gun from Bakos' Hardware. He told Delonzo the exact type of gun Knucky owned and the kind of bullets he used. And Delonzo relayed that information to Rafferty."

"How did you and Brad figure it out?" Montrose asked.

Brad explained it was something Goldman had said that gave him a hunch about the guns. "His experience told him something like that had to be the reason for the similarity in the two weapons. Goldman said coincidences are rare when it comes to murder. I went over to Bakos and the owner told me he had recently sold a gun similar to Walters'. Guess who's name was on the receipt?"

"Rafferty's!" Montrose said without hesitation.

"You guessed it."

"What about the problem of matching the bullet to my gun?" Knucky asked.

Goldman leaned over and stuck a finger in Walters' chest. "He placed the muzzle right over his heart against one of his ribs. Rafferty figured the soft-lead, flat-nosed bullet would be deformed after shattering the bone, making that part of the evidence against Knucky inconclusive. But connected with everything else, it would probably result in a conviction."

"Can you believe it?" Knucky shook his head. "The sly old fox gettin' sent to the stir for a crime he didn't commit. I would'a been a laughing stock." Knucky stood up, put a hand on Brad's shoulder and looked Goldman straight in the eye. "Let's drink a toast." Everyone clinked their glasses and raised their drinks. "To the two best-damned, uh, darned lawyers on both sides of the river."

After a twenty-one day inquiry, helped by investigations from the FBI, a federal grand jury in East St. Louis handed down indictments against seven different city officials including two commissioners, the comptroller, the city clerk, the treasurer, the police chief and one other high ranking police official. There were thirty-seven counts of conspiracy to defraud, racketeering, malfeasance of office and accepting bribes. In addition, Rafferty was arraigned at the county courthouse and charged with two counts of murder by Assistant District Attorney, Steven Todd.

Knucky's new television

CHAPTER 24

Back in the old days all of the Captains of Industry were seduced into investing in the East St. Louis real estate bull market. The list of those who owned property or businesses in the city was a veritable Who's Who, including John Jacob Astor, J. P. Morgan, Andrew Mellon, Nelson Morris, Jay Gould, Philip Armour, Gustavus Swift and John D. Rockefeller.

It was one month after the trial and Knucky had been in his new moat home barely a week. He invited Brad to see the fourteen-acre lake on the day the Giants and Dodgers were scheduled for a playoff game to determine the National League Championship. Knucky had bought a new Capehart television with a fifteen-inch screen. Roland and Montrose were there, and the four of them watched the game in a large room off the kitchen. A pleasant fire crackled

in an impressive fireplace, casting dancing shadows on the stone hearth. Beer and pretzels were served.

"What kind of soda do ya want?" Knucky yelled from the kitchen.

1973 photo of Walters' fireplace in his famous moat home, courtesy H. Fiebig

"I'll have a Hires Root Beer or a Double Cola," Brad answered.

"Sorry, you'll have to settle for what my kids drink. All we have in the fridge is cream soda or **Whistle Orange.**"

"A Whistle will do just fine."

Little did they know this single game would turn out to be one of the most famous in the annals of baseball history. Both teams had finished the regular season with identical records, and the outcome of one game between the two teams would decide which would face the powerful New York Yankees in the World Series. The Giants had come from thirteen-and-a-half games back to finish dead even. A packed house of thirty-five thousand fans jammed the Polo Grounds that Monday afternoon on October 3.

Unlike Knucky, Montrose and Roland were avid baseball fans, and the three of them camped in front of the fireplace and discussed the vagaries of the past season. Montrose was wearing a brown collarless cardigan made popular by Chicago drummer, Buddy Rich. It was the first time Brad had seen him without a suit.

Brad and his friends watched the game on TV, but turned off Russ Hodges and loyally listened to the play-by-play on St. Louis KMOX radio. By the sixth inning, the Giants were trailing the Jackie Robinson-led Dodgers by a run. The Giants scored the tying run in the bottom of the seventh on a sacrifice fly.

"Who are you rooting for, Knucky?" Brad asked.

"Whoever wins," Knucky deadpanned.

But the Dodgers bounced back and scored three more runs to go up 4-1. So far, Don Newcomb had outpitched Sal Maglie. The Giants, down to their last three outs, put on a furious rally, and the score was now 4-2 with runners at second and third when Scotsman Bobby Thompson strode to the plate. Ralph Branca, a fire balling relief pitcher, was on the mound. The TV camera zeroed in on a tense Giant manager, Leo Durocher, chewing a plug of Bull Durham on the top step of the dugout.

"Thompson already has had a great day with two hits and a sacrifice fly," Brad commented.

"I hope they walk Thompson," Montrose offered. "That will bring up Willy Mays, and he could end the whole thing with a grand slam."

"That would be a pretty improbable ending," Roland countered.

Baseball history was in the making. The rookie Mays never got a chance. It was Thompson who had a rendezvous with destiny as he tomahawked a high pitch and sent it screaming into left field. Outfielder Andy Pafko helplessly watched the game-winner as it sailed over his head and into the seats. Baseball nirvana.

Harry Caray excitedly described the Shot Heard Round the World in his unique raspy voice—a high-pitched stream of delerium.

After the game was over, Knucky gave Brad a tour of the commodious, ultramodern house. The two-story brick structure had a modern kitchen, a large rathskeller, two massive stone fireplaces, nine bedrooms, eight bathrooms, a twelve horse stable and a three car garage. They went outside and walked around the grounds. Though late in the afternoon, there was plenty of light because the area didn't go off daylight saving time until the end of the month. The

TV test pattern used in 1951

Bobby Thompson and Ralph Branca (author's collection)

residence looked more like a fortress tensed for battle. It reminded Brad of a medieval castle, surrounded by water and crouched like some mythical beast, ready and waiting for the next marauder. Then the four men sat around and kibitzed while watching the news and other programs.

Around seven-thirty Knucky looked at his watch. "Holy smokes, I had no idea it was this late. I'm starvin'. Anybody else hungry?"

Everyone nodded in unison.

"I'll send Montrose into town. There's this new Italian restaurant named Zeppetella's on the north side of Collinsville that cooks something called pizza pie. I'm gonna order two—one sausage and one pepperoni. Have you ever eaten pizza before, Brad?" Knucky asked.

Broadcaster Harry Caray who described Thompson's "shot heard round the world"

"Never."

"You're gonna love it."

"I trust your judgment when it comes to food," Brad said.

"Roland, while Montrose goes for the pizza, I want you to go out and sweep the garage floor. My wife has been griping about us tracking dirt into the house."

"I thought that was the maid's job," Roland complained.

"Normally it is, but she got sick the day she was supposed to do it."

"Okay, boss. If you say so," Roland said with a frown.

* * *

A large dark sedan moved unnoticed down the gravel access road toward Walters' moat house. The car traveled at a snail's pace—only fifteen miles an hour. Its lights were doused. The driver was a trained professional and was adept at driving surreptitiously in the dark. The standard safety glass in the car had been replaced by specially made material that was developed for the military by Dupont Chemical of Delaware. The trunk was loaded with enough heavy-caliber blued steel and copper-jacketed lead to equip a small army. The four men in the car began to feel the adrenaline rush in anticipation of the job that lay ahead. Sal Delonzo was in the front seat, nervously puffing on a cigarette. He ran his hand through his hair and formed a cruel smile. The yearlong vendetta was about to come to an end. Walters' East Side house of cards was about to implode.

A few bits of gravel fell from the zigzag tire treads as the car rolled to a stop. Several metallic clicks broke the silence as the doors swung open. The men exited the vehicle and held the handles in the down position until metal touched metal as they silently pushed the doors closed. There were several more soft clicks as the men released the safety mechanisms on their weapons. In slightly crouched positions, Delonzo and his entourage began to move toward the light that was on in the garage.

* * *

Montrose had been gone about ten minutes, and Roland was still out sweeping with the broom.

"Excuse me, Brad." Knucky put out his cigarette in an ashtray choked with bent, white weeds. "I gotta go upstairs and take my blood pressure pill."

Brad was staring at a boxing match on TV; but his concentration drifted, and he thought about the insides of that electronic marvel. He used to love watching his father repair radios on the kitchen table in his spare time. Inside the wood veneer shell was a metal chassis full of glowing vacuum tubes with numbers on top like 6SN7 or 5AU4. The underside of the frame was a mass of twisted wires, rectifiers, resistors, and capacitors. It always amazed him that his father could make sense of such complicated components.

Knucky had been gone for several minutes when suddenly Brad heard a distant voice. "Brad, come here, quick!" It was half-shouted with a sound of immediate urgency.

"I'm coming," Brad said as he rushed up darkened stairs.

"I'm here in the bedroom at the end of the hall. Don't turn on the light."

Brad groped his way along the wall and found the bedroom that was in almost total darkness. He barely made out Walters' silhouette, standing on the far side of the room.

"What's up?"

Knucky grabbed his arm and pulled him over to the window overlooking the driveway. He had made a tiny chink in the curtains. The light over one of the garage doors was still on.

"See that out there? Look . . . a Lincoln Zephyr blocking the moat road."

Brad leaned over Walters' shoulder and cautiously peered out the crack. "I see five men down there, and they have something in their hands. I can't make out any of their faces."

"They probably caught Roland off guard. You can bet it's not members of the St. Louis Symphony carrying their violins," Knucky wisecracked.

"When do you think Montrose will get back?"

"Who knows, but we gotta do somethin' now, or else we're dead."

"Did you build one of those secret passageways to a hidden room like I suggested?"

"Sure did, its access is in the foyer."

"Then that's our salvation," Brad quipped.

* * *

Delonzo and his men subdued Roland, entered the house through the garage and quickly fanned out to find their prey. After a few minutes they met back in the kitchen.

"It's almost as if they disappeared," moaned Vinny.

"Nobody just disappears," Delonzo shot back. "Wait a minute. I almost forgot about what Earl Shelton and his brothers did to one of their hideouts. Check the walls for any cracks, seams or hollow spots. There might be a secret room."

Photo of the actual bar in Walters' house, courtesy H. Fiebig

Once again the men spread out, scrutinizing the walls and tapping on them with their knuckles for telltale hollow sounds.

Delonzo scoured the kitchen and then moved to the foyer. He was drawn to a gilded, full-length Florentine mirror that somehow seemed out of place. He studied the intricately sculptured nineteenth-century frame, adorned with two hideous gargoyles at the top on both sides. Keenly observant, he noticed a miniscule seam on the neck of one gargoyle. He firmly grasped the head and tried to turn it to the left. Nothing. Then he turned it clockwise and the head swiveled until it was staring at the ceiling. There was a distinct ***click*** and the left side of the mirror swung open revealing a pocket door, the kind that slides into the wall.

"Hey, boys, I've found it," he yelled, with a gleefully wicked smile on his face. Delonzo's henchmen came running, guns still drawn.

"You're about to witness the demise of Knucky Walters," Delonzo said. "Vinny, nudge the door with the muzzle of your Thompson and then empty it into the room as it opens."

Delonzo leaned forward in sadistic anticipation. "Trapped like the dirty rat that he is."

The weapon began chattering incessantly as the door slid into the wall. Vinny methodically moved the gun right to left, up and down, to make sure that a blistering pattern of fire would extinguish any lifeform staring at its business end. The trigger mechanism finally clicked as the last shell was ejected. Delonzo waved his hand expectantly to clear the smoke. Then his jaw dropped in abject disbelief as he stared into the room.

* * *

"We gotta get outta here," Knucky said excitedly. "Hiding in that secret room off the foyer won't work. I didn't realize until after it was built that it gives me the willies—some kinda phobia.

"Claustophobia."

"What?"

"Claustophobia," Brad replied. "Fear of being trapped in a small place."

They sped down the hall and stumbled on the stairs, making their way out the back door.

"Do you have a gun?" Brad asked.

"No time for that. Besides, a peashooter against cannons is useless. We gotta hide."

"Where?"

"In the woods," Knucky said, already sounding a bit winded.

Knucky closed the back door carefully so as not to alert the gang that they had been spotted.

"Who do you think they are, Delonzo's men?"

Knucky cocked his head to one side. "Delonzo and his Dago posse—I'd bet my life on it."

"Don't be morbid."

A shaft of moonlight enabled Brad to catch a glimpse of nervous excitement in Walters' eyes. "Let's hope we can clear the back yard and get to the boat before they see us," he said.

They safely made their way down the gangplank, untied the johnboat and scrambled aboard.

"I'll row," Brad whispered. "I've done it several times at Jones Park lagoon."

"Be my guest. I'm exhausted."

Brad grabbed the oars and quickly but quietly pulled them to the far side. They clambered out of the boat, the muddy ground beneath them sucking at their shoes, threatening to pull them off their feet. Knucky slipped on a slick spot and would have fallen on his knees if Brad hadn't caught him.

"Hurry," Brad said, pulling him along as they ducked low and zigzagged forward, commando-style. "We're almost there."

They reached the sanctuary of a dense stand of trees and stopped to catch their breaths, each leaning on a thick trunk. The trees were mostly deciduous—white oak, silver maple, gum, elm and poplar—interspersed with occasional scrub pines. Brad looked back at the house but didn't see anyone in the yard. He was surprised to find himself breathing rather hard. Normally he could run for miles with singular ease.

It must be fear constricting my blood vessels, forcing my lungs to work overtime. Knucky, meanwhile, was still wheezing.

"How long do you think we can hide in the woods?" Brad asked.

"I don't know."

They could hear voices coming from the yard, so they turned and peeked from the safety of the trees.

"They're not in the house," one of the men yelled.

"They must have sneaked out back."

"Look for a small boat!"

Knucky and Brad turned sideways behind their respective trees as someone let forth a burst of machine gun fire. Splinters and wood chips were flying everywhere as ear-splitting bullets ate limbs and bark and thudded into tree trunks. Suddenly there was a piercing voice. "We know you're out there, Walters. You're done for. We're coming to get ya."

Brad quickly scouted the area. "They'll have to double back and recross the moat bridge to come after us," he said.

"That will give us time to go deep enough into the woods where, hopefully, they won't find us."

"Yeah, let's get moving."

A string of clouds finished moving across the face of the bright moon, enabling Brad to see Knucky getting ready to yell back at them. Brad rushed over and clamped a hand over his mouth.

"Mmm, uhh," he gurgled.

"Quiet, Knucky," he admonished with a quelling look. "Now is not the time to let them know how tough you are."

He angrily pulled his hand away. "I'm not afraid of those goons."

"Knucky, we don't have any weapons," Brad reminded.

"Oh, yeah."

They started making their way deeper into the woods. Each step posed danger—a possible twisted ankle or bruised knee. A steady rain began to fall, pelting the autumn canopy.

"Great, even Mother Nature is against us," Knucky muttered.

"It could work to our advantage. The rain might also discourage our pursuers." A little of Mark Trail's outdoor savvy would also come in handy, Brad mused.

"I just thought of something," Knucky said in a strange voice.

"What?"

"Our wager. If we both get killed, we'll never know who won the bet about people showing up at our funerals."

"Let's try to think positive about this," Brad said.

As they started down a ravine, Knucky tripped on a vine and tumbled headlong to the bottom. A startled black rat snake, in search of a barn, slithered out of his path just before he abruptly slammed into a tree. By the time Brad reached him, he was holding his shoulder and moaning with pain.

"I think I busted my wing," he groaned.

Brad caught up with Knucky and crouched beside him. "Can you stand up?"

"I . . . I think so. Nothin' else is hurtin'."

Brad helped him get to his feet. His left shoulder was sagging noticeably. He ran his hand up and down Walters' arm, gently squeezing. "Does any of that hurt? Anything feel broken?"

"No, I . . . I think my arm is okay; it's just my shoulder."

"Your shoulder isn't broken. It's dislocated."

"What does that mean?"

"It means your ball joint came out of the socket."

"How do you know?"

"I took an anatomy class in pre-law so I would know what the doctors were talking about in medical malpractice or injury lawsuits."

"So do you also know how to fix it, Dr. Kildare?"

"Maybe."

Knucky looked incredulous. "You're not kidding."

"I think I can yank it back into place. That's all the doctor does."

"Will it stop the pain?"

"It'll still be plenty sore. Your muscles and ligaments have been strained; but it won't hurt as much as it does now."

"Let's do it."

"Are you sure?"

"I said, go ahead."

"Do you have something you can bite down on for the pain?"

"I don't need nothin'. Grab my arm an' pull."

"Okay." Brad gingerly grabbed hold of his arm just above the wrist. "Ready?"

"Ready."

Knucky turned his head as he started to pull.

Brad shot him a questioning look. It was dark again and Knucky didn't see it. "Are you sure?"

"Do it."

Brad yanked on his arm as hard as he could, and Knucky gave out a muffled yell. He turned and looked at Brad, his unseen pale face etched with pain.

"Did it work? It still hurts like blazes."

"Let me see." Brad got in front of him and saw that his shoulder was listing to port. "Sorry. I must not have pulled hard enough. I need more leverage."

"Great," Knucky said glumly.

"I know what. Grab hold of that tree and don't let go."

"Are you serious?"

"If you hold on tight, it'll work."

"What if it pulls my other joint outta whack?"

"You're right, that might happen. Let me think. I know. Get down on the ground and I can place my foot on your side for leverage."

"Yeah. That . . . that should do it. All right. Let's give it one more try," he said with a note of apprehension. Knucky lay on the ground and tried to wipe the rain out of his eyes.

Brad sat down, placed his foot on him for leverage and grabbed hold of his arm. "Ready?"

He clinched his teeth. "Give 'er a tug."

"On three. Here we go. One . . . two . . . **three**," he said, yanking as hard as he could. A sickening sound of stretching muscle and bone rubbing bone came from Walters' shoulder as it popped back into place. He mumbled a few more unmentionables.

"Sorry about that, kid."

"You don't have to apologize. You've got a lot of guts."

"Are you kiddin'? I almost fainted," he said with a coughing laugh.

"You were very brave. I don't think I could have done it."

"Boy, I sure could use a cup of coffee an' a cigarette."

"That will have to wait. Take your suit coat and shirt off."

"What for?"

"I'm going to make a sling out of your shirt. Then you can put your coat back on."

Knucky looked duly impressed as he placed his arm in the body of the shirt, buttoned it up, and then tied the long sleeves around his neck into a knot. Next, Brad helped him with his suit coat.

They crossed a small creek at the bottom of the ravine, sinking nearly to their ankles in muck and mire. Brad and Knucky struggled across moss-covered rocks in wet, muddy shoes and clambered up the incline to the other side, moving deeper into the trees. Navigating the woods at night was tougher than Brad thought. As diaphanous clouds floated in ghostly unison across the face of the full moon, their small forest alternately became light then once again enveloped in temporary darkness. They began to shiver as a light breeze murmured through the trees.

"Are your teeth chattering?" he asked Knucky.

"Yeah. Heckuva time for it to be rainin'. Yours?"

"Yeah, mine too. I don't know if it's from fear, cold, or both."

"We can sure use the rain, but I wish it had waited until morning."

Moonbeams and droplets on the leaves made the tree limbs glisten. When Brad looked up at the sagging branches, a shroud of shimmering silver greeted his sight. Every time the wind blew the sodden boughs they received an extra shower of plump droplets.

"I gotta pee again," Knucky exclaimed. "My prostate's been giving me trouble."

"Me too," Brad said.

"You've got prostate problems?" he said in a disbelieving tone.

"No, I mean I also need to pee."

"Oh."

They wandered apart a few yards, turned their backs to each other and relieved themselves.

"Are you up to going on?" Brad said when they finished.

"Sure, let's keep movin'."

"Hold on, Knucky. I just got grabbed by a Wait-A-Second bush."

He stopped and turned. "I ain't never heard of no such bush."

Brad pulled the prickly branch free of his coat sleeve. "Well, this one grabbed me as I went by and said, '*Wait a second.*' "

"Is that your new Brooks Brothers suit coat?"

"No. Thank goodness it's my old Robert Hall."

"Well, I'm ruining a perfectly good two-hundred dollar suit," he moaned.

Brad glanced back over his shoulder. "Let's stop a minute and listen to see if we hear anyone behind us."

"Good idea. God, am I tired."

"Shh. Hear anything?"

"No, do you?"

"Nothing." Brad looked around and only saw trees, straight and imposing, like Swiss Guards at the Vatican. "Let's just stay here and hope they don't find us."

"I'd sell my soul for a shot of whiskey right now," Knucky said.

"Me too, but old Beelzebub would have to fork over a cup of hot **Ovaltine** with a marshmallow floating on top. And on top of everything else, I'm starving. I wonder what happened to Montrose?"

Knucky shook his head. "I dunno, but I don't see what good he could do—one man against four or five."

"Say, how come we didn't hear your German shepherd barking when those men drove up?"

"I don't know," Knucky said. "They might have given him poisoned meat or shot him with a gun that had a silencer."

"I sure hope not. Your kids will be brokenhearted."

"That's for sure. Boy, am I lucky the wife and kids are visiting relatives in Herrin."

"We're both soaked to the gills from this rain. I hope we don't catch pneumonia," Brad said.

Walters' hair was plastered to his head, and he pushed it out of his eyes by running his hands through it. "I'm tired. I need ta sit a minute," he said.

They sat down on spongy ground at the base of a large oak tree and propped themselves against the trunk. The damp earth was rich with the smell of pine needles, musty leaves and rotting vegetation.

"How's your arm?"

"Hurts like h—uh, it hurts a lot." Knucky was shivering in the damp night air.

Suddenly the sky began to clear.

"I think we're deep enough in the woods. We can stay here," Brad said. He looked at Knucky and started laughing.

"What's so funny?"

Burt Lancaster

"You have smears of dirt and mud all over your face. I probably do, too."

"Yeah, you're a soggy mess," Knucky observed.

Brad raised his arm and used the coat sleeve to wipe a big splotch of water from his cheek. Had their situation not been so serious, it might have been comical. "I can't believe we're out here running from gangsters," Brad said. "I ought to send a summary of this to Damon Runyon. It might give him an idea for another story."

"Excuse me if I fail ta see the humor in any of this," Knucky answered dourly.

"I'm sorry." Brad thought for a moment and contemplated the gravity of their situation. There seemed to be no end to these merry-go-round gangland wars. At first it had been the Sheltons versus the Birger gang. Then Knucky wrested control from the Sheltons. Now Delonzo and his men were trying to rub out Walters and his associates. This was merely one battle, round three, brought on by what happened in round two, which would lead to yet another conflict, round four.

"Do you think we'll be able to find our way out of here?" Brad asked.

"If I remember right, these woods are only about a mile deep and then there should be a farm or some other signs of civilization," Knucky said.

All of a sudden their conversation was interrupted by the sound of muffled gunfire.

"That's coming from behind us," Brad said.

"Where's **J. Edgar Hoover** when you need him?" Knucky said in a droll manner. "Whadda ya think they're shootin' at?"

J. Edgar Hoover

"I have no idea, but it doesn't sound that far away. Maybe trying to wait it out in these woods wasn't such a good idea." Brad got to his feet and grabbed Walters' good hand and pulled him up. "Let's keep moving."

They trudged silently in tandem through the dense trees and brush. A startled doe and her faun bolted from their hiding place and sought refuge by putting distance between themselves and the human intruders. Brad and Knucky jumped back, their hearts thumping at the unexpected commotion. Before they could gather their wits, another animal streaked by them and disappeared into the undergrowth.

"What was that? I can't believe this place has so many critters," Knucky said.

"Probably a raccoon." The night seemed to be alive with creepy guttural sounds of animals foraging for food, reminding Brad of the evil forest in *The Wizard of Oz*.

They skirted a confusion of prickly briars, thickets and brambles. Brad held back several small branches of a tulip tree for Knucky. Moving forward, Brad stumbled on the trunk of a small fallen tree, sending its insect inhabitants scurrying. One knee went to the ground. ***Ouch!*** Something sharp bit through his slacks into his flesh. He pulled out a long thorn from a black locust tree.

"If that gets sore, ya might have to put an egg membrane poultice on it to draw out infection," Knucky cautioned.

"That's old fashioned, Knucky. I've got some of that Prid salve at home to put on it."

"Say, Brad. These guys aren't after you. It's me they want. If they catch up with us, they ain't gonna want to leave witnessses. Why don't we separate? You'd have a better chance of getting away. I'm just slowin' ya down."

As they continued to make their way through the gloomy night, breathing the damp pungent air and shivering in their soaked, mud-encrusted clothing, Brad explained why he wasn't going to leave him. "Not a chance, Knucky. We're in this together, fifty-fifty. With that arm of yours, you wouldn't have a prayer. Besides, you've got a wife and kids to think about."

Knucky was surprised by Brad's loyalty. "You're makin' a mistake, but thanks for stickin' with me. I won't forget this."

Brad's knee was still talking to him with pain and a warm ooze of blood. He tried to bolster their sagging spirits. "Hey, Knucky. Why did the chicken cross the road?"

"I don't know."

"To prove to possums and raccoons that it can be done."

Brad couldn't see Walters' face, but he heard him give a chuckle.

"Did you hear about the moron who drove in the Indy 500?"

"Nope. But I bet you're gonna tell me about it."

"He made five pit stops . . . three of them just to ask directions."

"If I were you, I wouldn't quit my day job," Knucky said.

"Yeah, I guess Jack Benny doesn't need to worry about any competition from me."

"Hey, I just thought of one," Knucky said with a slight smile.

"Let's hear it."

"There was this father who wanted to teach his son a lesson about the pitfalls of drinking. 'Watch this,' he told the youngster. He set two glasses on the table and filled one with water and the other with Jack Daniels. He dropped an earthworm in the water and it swam around, happy as could be. Then he plopped the worm in the hard liquor and it shriveled up and died. 'What conclusion can you draw from this demonstration?' he asked his son. The lad thought a minute and then piped up, 'If you drink you won't get worms.' "

With one hand cupped over their mouth to muffle the laughter, they exploded uproariously over that joke.

They plodded on. Brad bent a low-hanging limb upward so Knucky could more easily duck under it. Then Brad reached out and imperatively took hold of his good arm and said, "Shh, do you hear that? It's somebody talking. It sounds like we have company."

Their flight to freedom was halted by a chilling voice. "**Hold it right there, you two,**" the man ordered as he stepped out from behind the wide trunk of a tree. Joe,

Delonzo's enforcer, was brandishing a small but mean-looking gun.

"We've been outflanked," said Brad.

"Who are you?" Knucky angrily demanded.

"It's one of the guys who roughed me up by my car a few months ago," Brad said. "You work for Salvatore Delonzo, don't you?" Brad weighed his chances of lunging at the man and knocking the gun from his hands. He knew that once he took control and tied them up, they would be goners. He tensed his muscles and was getting ready to spring forward when his foot slipped in the mud, creating a squishy noise that brought Joe's eyes and gun quickly back to him. A bullet ripped into the ground next to his foot.

"Don't move!" Though thwarted, Brad was thankful he'd stopped just short of making a fatal error.

Joe was not alone. Two associates, Vince and Tony, were moving up fast. Their guns, unlike this man's, had long barrels. "Shut up and start moving toward the car over by the road," he ordered.

The other men surrounded Brad and Knucky. They quickly patted them down for a piece then nudged their ribs with cold gun muzzles and ordered them to keep moving.

"Where is it, Logan?" the man with the handgun asked.

"I don't know what you're talking about."

"Torricelli's ledger, the records with all the names and stuff in it."

Brad stared at the ground, trying to think of an answer.

"I asked you a question. Answer me, d—you."

"I gave it to the D.A. to help with the Rafferty prosecution."

"Maybe you did," Joe said. "But we think you kept a copy. Not everything he wrote in it is gonna come out in the newspapers."

"You didn't think I'd be dumb enough to just have it with me, do you?" Brad was stalling for time, trying to play out the string for as long as he could.

Joe went ahead and searched Brad's coat pocket. "I'll tell you where it is if you let us go." They stared each other down for a few seconds.

"You're gonna tell us one way or the other when we get back to the house," the man said, sneering.

"Okay, you win. It's back at Walters' place in the safe," he fibbed. "There isn't any need to kill us. Knucky is more than willing to share his empire. Besides, you'll need him to help you run it."

He ignored Brad's logic. "We've been trying to get Knucky for months. Too bad he didn't get out of town after we burned his warehouse to the ground. Now that we have him, he's history. So are you. That little book should be helpful. It might let us know who we can work with on the east side."

The one named Tony chimed in. "Yeah, and it'll come in handy in case we need to blackmail somebody if they try to get outta line."

They arrived at the car. Delonzo's men prodded their captives with their guns to get in the front seat.

"Okay, okay . . . we're getting in. Take it easy. Can't you see Walters' got a bad arm?"

"What happened? One of our bullets git him?"

"No, he fell and dislocated his shoulder."

"Too bad, but don't worry, it won't be bothering him much longer."

Brad helped Knucky get in the car and then followed him and sat next to the window. ***I hope Knucky has a plan because I have no idea how we're going to get out of this.***

The two men with the machine guns placed their weapons in the trunk and drew what appeared to be large caliber pistols from shoulder holsters. Then they climbed into the back seat. Joe, the one with the small gun, got in the front seat and drove. The other two men kept their pistols aimed at the back of their hostages' heads. Brad half expected one of the men to lean forward and garrote him with a piano wire. He decided to suppress his characteristic defiance and meekly act subjugated.

They made their way along the main road back to Walters' house. Brad watched with growing apprehension as the car crossed the moat bridge and parked next to the house. Another man greeted them as the car ground to a halt on the gravel driveway. The headlights of the car showed Sal Delonzo standing next to an inert body on the ground. Brad's heart sank. He could see it was Roland. He wasn't moving.

Knucky saw it too and threatened, "I'll get you guys for this."

They were ordered out of the car. Knucky winced as he bumped his bad arm on the doorpost. Brad's sadness was replaced with wonder as the man next to Delonzo reached down and pulled Roland to his feet.

"Don't worry," Delonzo said. "He's still very much alive."

"Yeah, but not for long," the driver of the car said.

"That's right," Delonzo replied. "As soon as we get what we want from the safe, all three of you are expendable. Even if there isn't any ledger, I'll bet there's a pile of dough in it."

"We don't plan to tell you anything else unless you let us go," Brad said with a false bravado.

"Just wait until Tony gets through using his knife. He's pretty good. He sure had that Indian blabbermouth begging for mercy."

He tossed Brad a sinister look. "The blade under the fingernails works every time. I've yet to see it fail," bragged the one named Joe, reveling in the perverted glee of sadism.

"So it was you guys who killed Wayne Littlefeather," Brad said.

"Custer got it right. The only good Indian is a dead one,"

Desk, paneling, curtains, clock at Walters' moat home, courtesy H. Fiebig

Tony answered.

"I think it was Sheridan who said that—not Custer," Brad said.

"Shaddup!" He smacked Brad on the cheek with the back of his hand.

"All right, everybody, let's go inside," Delonzo barked.

They were herded at gunpoint into the living room with Delonzo in front and the other four men in back. They made Knucky sit in an overstuffed chair while two men held on to each of Roland's arms. Brad's heart began to pound. What could they do? He came to the realization that if something didn't happen fast, they were dead men.

Brad looked at Knucky for an indication—a plan of action. He figured the old master of survival, the man renown for resourcefulness and solutions, had an ace up his sleeve. But all he saw on his face were scratch marks left by bushes and saplings, plus a scowl of moody silence. ***He thinks we're doomed.*** Then Brad glanced at Roland, looking to him for some sign. He caught a look of waiting expectancy in his eyes. When he realized that Brad had noticed, he winked an eye, his expression warning him to be ready. But ready for what? Surely he wasn't planning to jump these guys and wrest their guns from them.

"I sure could use a cigarette," Knucky said. His arm was still trussed up in Brad's makeshift sling.

"You won't need one where you're going," the one in a dark brown suit said.

"What the heck. Let the condemned man have one last request," Delonzo said as he shoved a cigarette into Walters' free hand.

Knucky mumbled "thanks" and stuck it between his lips. Delonzo lit it with his lighter, and Knucky took a deep drag and exhaled in ecstasy. Delonzo was rocking back and forth on the balls of his feet. "Now, what's the safe combination?" he demanded.

"Don't tell him unless there's a deal," Brad said defiantly.

"Okay, Tony. Let's see you work your knife magic," Delonzo said with an evil grin.

The one named Tony slid a thin black knife from his pants pocket. There was a gleaming flash as it sprang to life with an ominous click and a four-inch blade shot from the end of the knife.

"I did hard time up north at Joliet. You won't get anything outta me," Knucky said.

Delonzo thought for a second. "Not him. Do Logan, the young one." The man turned away from Knucky and walked over to Brad.

Knucky crossed himself quickly and prayed to an army of saints that he'd donate huge sums to Catholic Charities if his friend got out of this in one piece.

Brad bit down on his lower lip. His mouth was dry as he tried to swallow. The thought of the pain that Delonzo had promised made his knees weak.

The savage tension was broken by Delonzo's voice. "Wait a minute. Vinny, you'd better go outside and keep a lookout, just in case Walters' driver happens to show up."

"TOO LATE! Don't anybody move or Delonzo gets a bullet in the brain," came a booming bass warning from the kitchen doorway. Brad's heart jumped to his throat. It was Montrose, with Walters' dog at his side. The German shepherd's ears were laid back and his hackles stood out sharply as the dog bared its teeth and growled. Montrose had a menacing look on his face; his fierce white eyeballs glared from their black sockets. He was pointing a pistol the size of a bazooka at Delonzo's forehead. For a moment, he thought it was going to be some kind of Mexican standoff. Then all you-know-what broke loose.

Tony spun around and threw his knife at Montrose. Montrose shifted his aim and fired at Tony a split second before the blade found its mark, embedding itself in his muscular left shoulder. The bullet hit Tony in the chest, knocking him backwards. He moaned and collapsed on the floor in a heap.

One down.

Walters' dog Bruno rocketed toward Delonzo. He closed the distance in three bounds and with a powerful spring was on him, sinking his fangs into his left wrist as he tried to fend him off. Delonzo screamed in agony then smacked the dog in the head with his gun, sending him to the floor in a state of unconsciousness. Knucky, his German blood boiling, leaped to life and grabbed a brass candlestick from the table and crashed it into Delonzo's left leg, crushing the kneecap and sending him to the floor. He fired a wild shot at Knucky as he went down, nicking him on the ear. The impact with the floor sent the gun sprawling.

Two down.

As soon as the action started, Roland cocked his elbows and brought them back as hard as he could into the solar plexus of his captors as they prepared to fire at Montrose. They collapsed in rag-dollish manner, doubling over in pain, clutching their stomachs. A good right uppercut sent one of them to dreamland.

Three down.

Brad's man, Vinny, now pointed his gun at Roland who was dealing with Joe, his other captor. Brad sprang to life and grabbed Vinny by the forearm, spoiling his aim. The gun's blast reverberated in Brad's ear, but the large caliber slug went harmlessly into the ceiling. Roland pinned Joe's hand, tenaciously clinging to his gun, against the wall then crunched his jaw with a powerful swing of his elbow. The gun clattered to the floor, and the man let out a loud, painful-sounding groan as he sank into oblivion.

One left.

Robert Mitchum

Brad wrestled with Vinny for control of the gun. It wasn't much of a contest. Brad's hand closed like a vise on his opponent's arm and whipped it behind him. Brad was surprised at how weak the man was. He forced his arm into a hammerlock, shoved him against the wall, and used the old thumb trick in an effort to pry the gun out of his grasp. Several framed photos came crashing down on the hardwood floor. Brad struck a glancing judo blow to his opponent's throat, bruising his windpipe and causing him to grab his neck and gasp for air in big gulps, like a fish out of water. "Don't move a muscle!" Brad shouted in his best **Robert Mitchum** tough guy voice as he gained control of the gun. Actually, he sounded more like Burt Lancaster.

Game over. Victory for the home team!

Roland and Montrose made the men lie down on the floor with their hands behind their backs. Montrose took off his coat and pulled out the knife. He held a bloody handkerchief against the wound to stanch the bleeding.

Brad glanced over at Knucky. He had grabbed one of the guns from the floor and was standing over Sal Delonzo, letting loose with some garbled expletives and waving the gun at him in one of his patented volcanic outbursts.

Exterior shot of Walters' moat home, 1973 (Fiebig)

"Don't kill him, Knucky," Brad shouted.

Knucky glared at him uncomprehendingly. "Are you serious?" he said angrily. "After what he was planning to do to us?"

"Let the law take care of him. He'll get the chair for killing Wayne Littlefeather and ordering his men to set the warehouse fire that killed your man."

An old rage flickered in Walters' eyes. "He almost killed my dog, Bruno, this s.o.b.'s gonna pay." He smacked Delonzo across the face with a glancing blow from the gun. Then he cocked and pointed it above the bridge of his nose.

"He's not worth it; let him go," Brad yelled.

"No! He'll hire Goldman, and Morris will get him off."

"No he won't. I'll work with Sweeney and make sure that doesn't happen."

"It's no use, Brad. You're not gonna talk me out of this," he said, as he leaned over and pressed the gun muzzle hard against Delonzo's forehead.

Tension etched the corners of Brad's mouth. "If you kill him, it will be murder. You'll go to jail."

"I'll just say it was self-defense. Roland an' Montrose will back me up."

"But I won't. You know I can't lie about something like that. Not even for one of my best friends. Think of your wife and kids. Remember what out-of-control anger did to Captain Ahab."

Knucky righted himself and stood there for a while, trying to absorb everything Brad had just said. He was so angry the gun was shaking in his hands.

"You can't let him kill me," Delonzo cried, pleading with Brad to intervene and save his life. "It'll be pure murder. You can't let him do it," he said hysterically. Beads of sweat popped out on Delonzo's brow.

"Look at him. He's not so tough now that it's his turn to die."

"Knucky, I'm begging you," Brad said. "Please don't do this."

"Sorry, Brad. This scum deserves a bullet in the brain. Nobody invades my home an' gets away with it."

Brad watched in horror as Knucky took dead aim and pulled the trigger. Brad closed his eyes, turned his head, and said, "Oh, God." When he opened them, Knucky was standing with a grim smile on his face. Delonzo was lying there as a pool of liquid oozed from beneath his body. Brad's mouth dropped open in amazement. Delonzo was still alive, shaking with fright. Knucky had aimed the gun several inches above Delonzo's head. The liquid wasn't blood; it was urine. Delonzo had soiled his pants.

"I just wanted him to know some of the fear that I felt when I knew he was getting ready to kill me," Knucky said.

"I'm glad you didn't execute him." Brad put a friendly hand on his shoulder.

"Jeez, Brad." That classic wry, mocking look danced around Walters' face. "You really roughed up your man. What happened to that Christian compassion you're always talking about?"

"Are you kidding? All I could think about was survival."

The wail of police sirens filled the air and several black-and-whites screeched to a halt in Walters' driveway. The room was soon flooded with blue uniforms wearing Edwardsville police badges. A passing neighbor heard the gunfire and had called the police. Knucky and his men were disarmed. They were going to run everyone in until Brad identified himself and explained to the police that Delonzo and his men had invaded Walters' home and tried to kill all of them. Police were especially elated when he told them Delonzo had been responsible for two killings. Delonzo and his men were cuffed and hauled off to jail. Montrose was taken to the hospital. Knucky, Roland, and Brad followed the police to the station so officers there could take their statements.

"You were right about one thing, Knucky," Brad said.

"Yeah, how so?"

Brad licked some tomato sauce from his fingers. "This pizza pie is delicious."

CHAPTER 25

The East St. Louis stockyards led the *world* in the

horse and mule markets. When Benito Mussolini went to war against Ethiopia in the 1930s, he bought horses from East St. Louis to carry equipment for his army.

May 2, 1952

The year 1951 had been tumultuous. **Joe McCarthy** was under attack. Margaret Chase Smith of Maine, the country's first female U.S. Senator, drew criticism from her own Republican party for attacking McCarthy's smear tactics. Truman fired a recalcitrant MacArthur for insubordination. The smooth and crafty Sugar Ray Robinson defeated Jake LaMotta in the 13th round to capture the middleweight boxing crown. Matthew Ridgeway's forces recaptured Seoul, the capital of South Korea. It was the fourth time in the last nine months that the city had changed hands. Remington Rand unveiled a new computer called UNIVAC that was going to be used by the U.S. Bureau of Census. Governor Adlai Stevenson had to call out the Illinois National Guard to quell a race riot that occurred when a Negro family tried to move into the Chicago suburb of Cicero. **Lucille Ball, Roy Rogers** and Jack LaLanne had shows that made their debut on television. The Los Angeles Rams defeated the Cleveland Browns 24-17 for the NFL championship. The top Hollywood films were ***A Streetcar Named Desire, A Place in the Sun*** and. ***The African Queen.*** And thirty-two year-old J. D. Salinger was raising eyebrows with his provocative ***The Catcher in the Rye.***

Roy Rogers

The tumult in Brad's life was caused by the absence of a certain woman's love. "Time Marches On." That's what the man in the movie newsreel said. He pondered the complexities and ambiguities of relationships. Here it was: a third of the way into 1952 and the ache for her was still there. The units of time that measured his apartness from Lorna, though numbered in months, seemed like decades. He glanced at the cigar box next to him on the front seat of his car, drawing a deep breath as he did so. Random reminiscences of the dates they went on tortured his memory.

Walking down Collinsville Avenue one morning, Brad saw Lorna. His heart started pounding. He had not been able to get her out of his mind. She was starting to cross the street as the light was changing. When Brad got to the corner, the light had turned red. He ignored it and ran out into the street, oblivious to the honking horns and the outraged cries of motorists.

Brad reached the other side and hurried to catch up with her. He grabbed her shoulder. "Lorna . . . "

The woman turned. "I beg your pardon?"

It was a total stranger.

It had been nearly eight months since he last saw her. During the past few weeks he had lost his drive and initiative, the will to accomplish anything in his life at the office. Oh, how he missed her. He missed Lorna's smile and the way she tossed her head when she laughed. He missed her fragrance, her silky-smooth skin, the sparkle in her eye when she learned something new. He fell into a deep abyss of desperate loneliness, like that sad clown, Pagliacchi.

Brad found out from Gloria that Lorna was living with her Aunt and Uncle Sanders, away from prying eyes. Gloria said Lorna had trundled off to Olney, Illinois, to have the baby. When she had gone back to Litchfield, obviously pregnant, she became the object of juicy gossip and slurs. Scornful commentary burned her ears. She suffered the stares, the hushed whispers and the looks of moral superiority with a dignity far beyond her years. But, ultimately, the gossipmongers and the wagging tongues of townfolk became too much for her to bear. Gloria said the pregnancy ordeal was akin to wearing a Hester Prynne scarlet letter. Lorna's plan, she said, was to put the baby up for adoption and then try to cobble her life back together, piece by piece. Gloria had talked to Lorna on the phone a few times but had never asked about her address. She did remember Lorna saying her aunt and uncle were named Wilburn and Norma Sanders.

I'm glad she's giving up the baby. I wouldn't want it around forever reminding me of Lance, Brad thought. On this particular Tuesday morning, the first week of May, the blue sky above was filled with cottony clouds that were scooting eastward, caressed by gentle spring zephyrs. Brad inhaled the blossom-scented air deeply into his lungs, nearly intoxicated with its fragrance. His car was headed out of town, moving northeast on a trek to Olney. Brad was trying to figure out what he was going to say to Lorna. He mentally typed a speech, pulled the paper out of the roller, and started over. He visualized editing the new sheet, but it wasn't any better. Brad yanked it out and tore it up, muttering under his breath.

Senator McCarthy in action.

He flipped on the radio and in a pique of nostalgia wondered about its future. One by one the old programs were going off the air because of the increased popularity of television. ***The Inner Sanctum, Richard Diamond, Amos 'n' Andy, Johnny Dollar, Duffy's Tavern, Fibber McGee and Molly, The Whistler*** with his distinctive eight-note aria—all had been favorites. He turned the knob to find the news, hoping it would keep him from slipping into remorseful thought. The radio made those distinctive

Walter Winchell

squawking and squelching noises until he dialed the tuner and found the right station. But his relationship with Lorna kept intruding on the present, causing him to hear the news in disjointed segments. Bits and pieces. **Walter Winchell** was blasting away at Communist perfidy with his rat-a-tat-tat voice. Fighting . . . stalemated along the . . . parallel in the Korean conflict. A tuneful commercial: "Rinso white, Rinso white; happy little washday song." ***What if she never wants to see me again?*** George Hopper . . . gearing up for his . . . swim across the Mississippi with his . . . cuffed behind his back. This time he planned to tow a couple of . . . . Brad wished he had learned the truth sooner about Lance and Lorna.

Some fine lawyer you are, Logan.

The Cardinals lost to the . . . on a ninth inning home run by Duke. . . .

I shouldn't have let my pride stand in the way of my feelings.

When the signal began to fade, he turned the radio off and hummed a Frankie Laine tune. Brad was lost in contemplation, wondering whether the afternoon's events would bring joy or sorrow.

You'll never forgive yourself if you lose her, an inner voice mocked him.

He went to the public library in Olney and looked up the Sanders' address in a city directory. Then he drove to 2404 Elm Street. Brad was momentarily distracted by a dust devil that cut a diagonal path in front of his car. The funnel was about five feet high and there was grit, dead leaves, and grass bits swirling around in a frenzy. Bobbing and weaving like some ghostly apparition, it seemed to have a life of its own. Then it dashed across a vacant lot into a backyard where laundry was hanging on a line to dry. He smiled at clothespins that went helter-skelter as the turbulence plucked the laundry and tossed it on the ground haphazardly.

Another distraction. Several of the city's most famous residents, those unique white albino squirrels, were playfully chasing each other near the base of a sycamore tree.

It made Brad think about the magnificent sycamore tree in his front yard he had shinnied up as a youth. For him the tree stood like a sentinel, a benchmark for tracking time and the passing of seasons; his height and girth relative to its light colored trunk; his strength and agility in climbing sturdy branches that supported a tree swing. And when maturing glands brought forth puberty, the tree became a carving surface for displaying his adolescent passions with sets of initials.

That was back in those halcyon days when he worked on countless versions of who he would be when he grew up. Some of the possibilities had been **William Boyd**, Buck Rogers, Don Winslow of the Navy, Elliot Ness, President Roosevelt, Red Ryder, and writer H.P. Lovecraft.

Spring, showing off in resplendent fashion, was in full bloom. Crocus and hyacinths were pushing up through flowerbeds that were on either side of the porch steps. It was the time of forsythia and lilac, dogwood and red bud. The trees were sweet with bud and blossom, and the birds were either mating or busily building nests. Brad walked up the stairs leading to a large wooden porch. His heart was anxious and full of excitement. There was also a slight dread from the knowledge that words might fail him in this most important moment. Here he was, an untrained actor, ready to take center stage, about to play the greatest role in his life. He closed his eyes and said a quick prayer, trying to gather the courage to meet the daunting task that lay ahead. A sturdy oak door set with a large oval of beveled glass confronted him. He pushed the doorbell twice, its sound

William Boyd

muffled by the fortissimo beat of his pulsing heart.

A petite woman in a print housedress answered the door. Her flaxen hair, streaked with gray, was held in place by several strategically placed combs. "May I help you?" She had a sweet smile and roundish face—the kind that sold cake mixes on television commer-cials.

"Yes, ma'am. My name is Brad Logan, and I'm looking for Miss Sanders. We're friends and I was told she is living here."

"Is she expecting you?"

"I don't think so, but could you tell her it's important that I see her?"

"Have a seat on the porch swing, young man, and I'll go tell her you're here. What is your name again, please?"

"Brad . . . Brad Logan."

Brad went over and sat on the swing. His heart was tripping over fear and anticipation of what the next few moments might bring. A zillion things were whirling around in his brain.

The woman came back and opened the door. "She's out back, feeding the baby. Follow me around the side of the house." They negotiated a gray flagstone path to the rear. The back yard had a well-manicured privacy hedge. Lorna was sitting in a metal lawn chair under the benevolent shade of a weeping willow. Her face was ***au natural***, and she pleased Brad's eyes in a crisp periwinkle summer dress. She was fastening the front buttons, the baby having just finished nursing. A table model radio on the screened-in back porch was playing ***Charmaine*** by Montovani, his first big hit in America. Brad felt a lump forming in his throat.

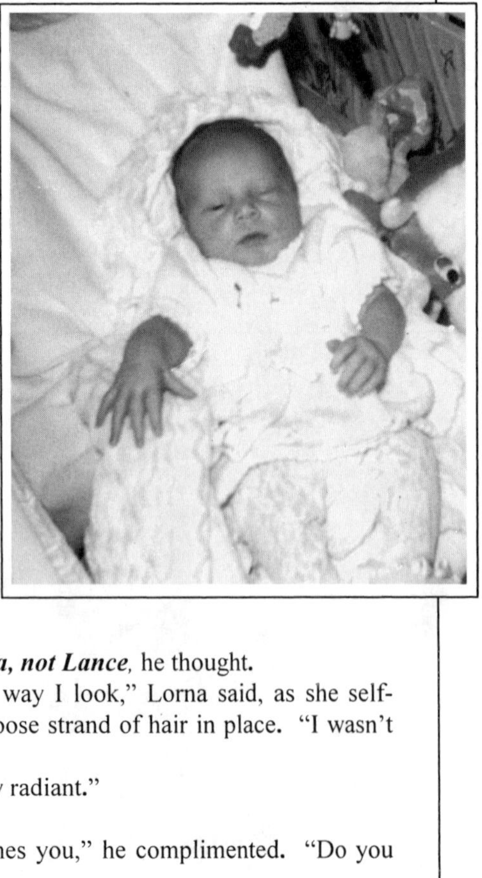

Brad whispered a prayer. "***Please, Lord, help me find the right words to say.***"

"She's a beautiful baby," he said.

Lorna's mouth formed a perfect oval but for several seconds nothing came out. "Uh, hello, Brad. Yes, she is something to behold."

"Obviously, she takes after her mother."

She looks like Lorna, not Lance, he thought.

"Please excuse the way I look," Lorna said, as she self-consciously pushed a loose strand of hair in place. "I wasn't expecting company."

"You look positively radiant."

"Thanks for lying."

"Motherhood becomes you," he complimented. "Do you have a name for her?"

"No, I decided that would be too painful. A lawyer is coming today with papers for me to sign. There is a couple in the area . . . schoolteachers, who want to adopt. He assured me they'll provide her with a good home. He should be here soon."

"Here, let me take the baby inside and burp her," Lorna's aunt offered. Lorna gently handed her aunt the baby, and she turned and walked back into the house.

"Why did you come?" Lorna asked. "I never expected to see you again."

Brad paused, searching his memory bank for just the right words. ***Because ever since the last time I saw you I felt like a part of me was missing. It's like my mind has been trapped in a fog, somewhere between ego and id.***

"Because in my heart of hearts, I miss you like crazy." There it was—plain, easy, forthright.

Lorna had thought about the possibility of Brad coming back to her and trying to make amends. But she decided that it was too late, that too many painful things had happened. She had resolved that she would start over and rebuild her life. She was only twenty-one, and there was plenty of time to achieve her career goals. She would listen to her parents and go back to college—let herself mend behind the sheltered walls of academia.

He leaned forward, took hold of her hands and gently kissed them. Tears were swimming on the rim of her eyelids. "I messed up pretty badly, didn't I? Are you still angry with me?" She tried to blink the tears back but several rivulets ran down her soft cheeks. He gently brushed them away with his fingers, and then kissed the top of her head.

"Hmmm. You smell nice," he said, "like that soft, scented breeze that just went by—yellow jasmine, mock orange, and honeysuckle." He hunched down beside her. "I was very hurt when I found out you were pregnant. I knew it was his. You have no idea how crushing that is to a man's ego."

"I've seen everything she's got, from her lace panties. . ."

"I didn't mean to hurt you. Please forgive me."

"I'm the one who needs to ask your forgiveness. I behaved badly," he said gently pushing a wisp of hair behind her ear. "I was tortured by the thought of you making love to Lance."

"You must think I'm a real hypocrite, telling you all those times about how I was saving myself for my husband on my wedding night?"

"I don't think that at all. There is no doubt in my mind that is what you fully intended. Gloria told me the truth about what really happened—how Lance purposely got you drunk and then took advantage. He was a moral lecher with a hole in his soul. You couldn't have known his mission in life was to deflower as many maidens as possible."

"I've seen everything she's got, from her lace panties. . ."

"I should have never agreed to go back to his apartment. I was looped—too much to drink." Lorna closed her eyes and shuddered at the memory. She opened them and stared at the ground. "I can't be your destiny, Brad. I don't deserve your love."

Brad gently cupped her chin with his hand and turned her head until her eyes lighted on his. "You deserve a lot more than you think you do. You deserve the best of everything. You deserve a love that will honor and cherish you, an enduring love that will last forever and a day. That is how long I will love you."

"It's too late. I'm sorry I ruined what we had. My reputation is in tatters. I guess I'm not much different from those girls at high school who ran off and married guys that were no good. I thought I was too smart, too sophisticated to be fooled by a playboy like Lance. I should have known you were the one as soon as I realized you made me smile inside every time we were together. Now I'm used goods—damaged merchandise. I just can't believe—"

"Ssh," Brad said, as he held her in a tender and warm embrace. "I don't ever want to hear you say, or even think, you're used goods. It's not your fault. Your innocence was stolen by a con artist—a charmer, a flim-flam Casanova. Besides, he didn't take the things I love about you the most: your smile, your laugh, your verve, your incredible voice."

Her watery eyes were filled with anguish and regret. He gently kissed a salty tear that ran down one of her cheeks. "What you need is a good hug."

Brad stood up and pulled Lorna out of her seat, drawing her close, making entrance to that magical realm of wisteria, enveloping and infusing her with his strength and warmth. He was trying to break through the barrier of doubt, trying to reach that place where she kept everything in guarded abeyance.

"Thanks, I needed that."

"I came here when I realized my anger and hurt would serve no purpose except to keep me apart from you. I came to say I dearly love you and want to marry you."

"You can't be serious, not after everything that's happened."

"Let me show you something," Brad said as he slipped a rubber band from an old Dutch Masters cigar box. "When I was a kid, I kept my treasures in here—my baseball cards, marbles, Jack Armstrong club membership certificate, a plastic arrowhead that glowed in the dark, and collectible cigar bands. I even had a booklet of official charts, codes and secrets as a member of Captain Midnight's squadron. Here, take a look."

Brad flipped open the lid and she peered inside. Her mouth was agape as she rummaged through the contents, finding an amazing array of dodads within its confines.

"Why . . . why these are pictures and momentos of things we did together on dates. Here's the pencil from the baseball game, the whistle from the box of Cracker Jack, a ticket stub from the Majestic Theater, several of my news articles from the ***Journal***, pictures of us at the race track and Jones Park. This is simply amazing. You're either a pack rat or more of a romantic than I had thought."

"Look over in the corner," he said.

She burrowed deeper and pulled out a gleaming gold wedding band.

"I want to get married, Lorna. Right now, as soon as we can."

She pressed the ring to her lips. She was tempted. Oh, how she was tempted. "I, I'd love to Brad, but it wouldn't be fair. I don't think you could ever forget everything that has happened. And your parents, they'd never accept me."

"When they get to know you, they'll think you're great."

"Let me finish. You've got a career to think about, and you know how people talk. No telling how long it is going to take me to get over having to give up my baby for adoption. I fear there will always be a melancholy—a big empty space in my heart that nothing will ever be able to replace. I couldn't ask you to endure that because there's no telling how long it might take me to get past the trauma. I may always feel a part of me is missing. We have too much history, and I'm afraid it would always come between us."

She reluctantly placed the ring back in the box.

Brad was stunned. "But I love you," he protested. "I've loved you from the first moment we met, and I always will."

"I know you do, and I love you too, but it won't work. There would always be a gulf between us, your belief that I had somehow betrayed your love."

"But—"

"Listen to me. The knowledge of what happened between Lance and me would eat away at you and slowly erode the bond of trust that is the keystone of a good marriage. I made a mistake, Brad. I'm just human. You probably reacted the way you did because of your upbringing. Marrying me would go against everything you've been taught in that little white church of yours. It's been drummed into your head to wed a girl who's pure, chaste. I'll never be able to walk down the aisle in a white dress."

Brad began to think perhaps Lorna was right. After all, what happened between Lorna and Lance had haunted him for months.

"This isn't going like I had planned," he said. His expression hardened with frustration in a futile effort to get through to her. He picked his brain for the phrase or sentence that would allay her fears and make things right between them. But he knew he couldn't turn back the clock. Perhaps certain remnants from the past couldn't be smoothed over.

"I've seen everything she's got, from . . ."

"I don't want to lose you again."

"Nor I you," she said. "But we need to face reality. Please get on with your life, just walk away—leave."

He stared in disbelief. "You want me to go?"

"Excuse me," Lorna's aunt interrupted. "Just wanted to let you know the baby is sleeping now. And there is a gentleman here with some papers for you to sign—a Mr. Andrew Theising."

"I . . . I guess I had better be going," Brad said, too stupefied to think of what else to say. "If you ever need anything, just give me a call. I'll always be there for you." He kissed her on the forehead. "I . . . well . . . goodbye."

"Thanks, I appreciate the offer."

Brad turned and with a clouded mind stumbled past a well-dressed man in a dark blue suit. Lorna sadly watched Brad walk out of her life a second time. Her heart was breaking. She loved him with every fiber of her being. She followed him with her eyes to the latticework arch of the arbor gate, half hoping he would come rushing back and sweep her up in his arms. He momentarily paused.

If he turns around, I'm going to him.

But there were no reconsidering actions. He continued walking until he was out of her sight.

Good-bye, my love, Lorna softly whispered.

"I'm sorry ma'am," the lawyer offered. "Have I come at a bad time? I could leave and return later this afternoon if this is inconvenient for you."

"No, it's all right," Lorna said. "There's no such thing as a 'good time' for doing what needs to be done."

"Yes ma'am. I understand how hard this must be for you," he offered apologetically. "If it's any solace, I can assure you the couple adopting your child is the very best. I have known both of their families for quite some time. You can rest assured they will take good care of her. She will be raised in a loving, caring, Christian environment."

Lorna nervously skimmed back her hair. "Do you know what they are planning to name my baby?"

"I'm sorry, I haven't any idea. But I do know they can't wait to get her."

"Once I sign the papers, when will you take her away?"

"I was hoping to take her immediately. The longer you have her, the harder it will be on both of you. The baby needs to get adjusted to her new environment as soon as possible. However, if you prefer, I could wait until tomorrow morning."

Lorna had a look of utter helplessness.

"I guess . . . I guess you're right. You can have her after I sign the papers. I'll just need one moment to say good-bye." Her voice cracked as it trailed off at the end.

The lawyer pulled some documents from a leather portfolio and showed them to Lorna.

"These are all fairly standard," he explained. "Your signature attests your willingness to give up any and all claims to the baby as your daughter."

"I can assure you that what you are doing is in the baby's best interests," the man said.

"Aunt Norma, would you please bring the baby here so I can give her to Mr. Theising? I want to see her one more time and kiss her good-bye."

"Please tell her new parents I love my baby very much, and that I only gave her up so she would have a better chance in life," Lorna said sadly.

"Yes, Miss Sanders, I'll be sure to do that."

"And don't forget to tell them she likes to sleep on her back."

"I'll tell them."

"And that she needs to be burped several times during a single feeding. She must have a small stomach."

"I'll be sure to mention it, ma'am."

Lorna's aunt came out with the baby. She was wide-awake and cooing tiny sounds of contentment. Lorna took the little bundle into her arms and gazed at the tiny angelic face. Lorna's eyes grew watery as she prepared to say her final farewell. She gave a tender squeeze. "Good-bye, sweet precious. You be a good girl with your new parents. I'll pray every day for your safety and good health. You grow up to be a woman of strong character. Have a good life and try to make a difference in this world. I love you very much, and I'll never forget you," Lorna said, as she lightly kissed her forehead. A face bathed in tears reflected her heartbreak. She reluctantly handed the baby back to her aunt.

"Where are the papers? I, I'm ready to sign." Her shaky voice mirrored her fragile emotional state.

The man handed her his portfolio with the papers on top.

"Just sign and date on the line with an X next to it," he said while handing her an expensive looking fountain pen.

Lorna found the signature line. She paused and briefly closed her eyes, bracing herself for one of the most difficult things she would ever do in life—giving up her own flesh and blood. The universe seemed at a standstill. Then she shakily began writing her name in cursive, L-o-r-n-a . . .

"***Wait***, there's something I have to say," Brad said, gently taking the pen from her trembling hands.

Lorna looked up with disbelieving eyes. "Brad, you came back . . . why?"

"I don't want you to give up the baby. I love you, and I can't stand to see you go through this agony. She will always be a part of you, and that is all I care about. Lance may have been her biological father, but her real father will be the one who gives her love. I plan to be the one who rubs her gums when she's teething, the one who walks the floor at night with her when she has colic, and the one who is there when she says her first word. I want to see her take her first steps, sing nursery rhymes to her, teach her to ride a bicycle and how to whistle. I'll be there to help her through those awkward teen years and walk her down the aisle when she marries that special young man in her life."

Lorna brushed a hand over her cheek as her heart skipped a beat. "Oh, Brad. I so much want to believe you. But you can't mean it. That would be taking on so much responsibility. Are you sure you want to do this?"

"I've never been more sure of anything. I want us to be together—a family." He took her hand and slipped the ring on her finger. Lorna looked as if her heart had just done a happy cartwheel. She exuberantly flung her arms around his neck and gave him a fervent kiss.

"I love you Brad. I have never been able to fully trust a man until now. I'm really sorry it took me so long to figure out what I really wanted."

"None of that matters anymore. Yesterday is yesterday. What's important is the moment—the here and now."

"Brad, you're my Gibraltar, my safe harbor, my other half. A part of me has loved you since the day we first met. The rest of me just had to catch up, get some things out of my system—that and a little growing up."

Brad tore the adoption papers in several pieces and handed Mr. Theising his portfolio.

"We're very sorry to have inconvenienced you. Thank you for your time and effort."

"I understand," he said. "I hope everything works out for the two of you."

"You mean the three of us," Brad corrected. "Please offer the other couple our sincerest regrets. I know they'll be terribly disappointed."

The lawyer placed his hat on his head then turned and left.

"Oh, Lorna, I'm so happy for you," her aunt gushed. "I'm going inside to fix some chicken and dumplings. I want Brad to stay for supper so we can get acquainted, now that he's going to be part of the family."

"Fine. I love chicken and dumplings," Brad said as she turned and climbed the back steps.

Lorna was smiling and holding the baby next to her. Brad encircled both of them lovingly with his arms. For the very first time he could see ***real*** love in Lorna's eyes.

She squared her shoulders and looked resolute. "I want you to know something, Brad Logan."

"I'm listening."

"I'm not saying ***yes*** out of desperation. I would never do that." She traced his lips with her fingers, loving their gentleness. "I don't believe in a sham relationship—the pale illusion of a marriage. I, too, long for a union of passion, trust and family building. I'm saying ***yes*** because I love you just as much as you love me. You won my heart, Lancelot. It was your looks, your humor, your sense of who you are—the ability of your heart to be beguiled by nature. I love the way you indulge in daydreams. You're like me . . . inclined to chase rainbows; you look at clouds and see cotton candy."

"Thanks for telling me. I think that was something I needed to hear. Your words confirm what Gloria suspected all along."

She stepped back with a quizzical look. "What did Gloria have to do with this?"

"Gloria called yesterday and said she had something to tell me—said it was something important about our relationship."

Lorna's misty eyes clouded with confusion. "What could she possibly have told you that would have made any difference in the way you felt about me?"

"Well, uh, it was actually more about how you felt about me."

"But I never told her my true feelings for you. I didn't tell anyone."

"Oh yes you did."

"Who?"

"Your diary."

Lorna's eyes widened. "She read my diary? Why that little snoop, I'll—"

"Believe me, she wasn't proud that she violated your privacy."

"She had no right."

"No she didn't, and she's suffered pangs of guilt about it ever since. But she also read the part you wrote about a week before your last date with Lance."

"I can't remember; I'm not sure what that would have been."

"It was where you confided to your diary your ambivalent feelings about the two of us."

"Oh, yes, I remember now. In fact, I think I can quote it nearly verbatim:

7-17 (or was it the 18th) -1951
Dear diary:

Well, it finally happened. I've met someone who means more to me than I think I'm ready to handle. Probably the man of my dreams—the one who makes my heart go ping; the man I want to spend the rest of my life with; the man I want to father my children.

My feelings for Brad seem to have crept up on me. I didn't mean for it to happen. I met him over a year ago, and it took me this long to figure it out. I guess I never realized love could be so complicated. The only problem is he probably wants to get married right away and start a big family. I'm afraid if I do that before I find out how far my abilities as a writer can take me, I'll always resent him for preventing me from achieving my goal. I don't want to look back thirty years from now and wonder what might have been. Yet I don't want to lose him either.

Darn! I guess it wouldn't be fair to ask him to wait five, six or seven years. I sense his growing frustration with what he perceives to be a lack of progress in our relationship. It would break my heart to see him give up on me and marry another. I'm afraid if I keep shutting him out, I'll end up a dried old prune like that spinster, Emily Dickinson. What should I do?

"That's just about what Gloria said to me, but not embellished with your detail. Don't let this diary thing come between you and your friendship with her. After all, it did result in us getting together."

"I, I suppose you're right," Lorna admitted.

"Do you miss your job at the ***Journal***?"

Lorna looked a bit ambivalent. "In a way I do. I was just beginning to hit my stride."

"You know those goals you confided to your diary?"

"Yes, but don't fret about it. I'm gladly willing to trade them for a loving husband and children."

"You don't understand. I don't want you to look back on this moment with an ounce of regret wondering ***what if.*** I don't want you to give up your dream."

She pressed her hand to her mouth, as if trying to comprehend what her ears had just heard. "What do you mean?"

"You can write at home and submit articles to magazines. You might even want to write a novel."

"But there isn't any way I would have time to keep up, what with taking care of the kids, grocery shopping, cooking, housekeeping chores . . ."

"Oh, yes there is. I'll be your helpmate and make sure you have some free time. You cook the meals; I'll do dishes. You do the dusting, I'll mop and run the vacuum cleaner."

"What about washing and ironing?"

"I'll wash, you iron?"

"You know how to do all that stuff?"

"I had to do some of it in college. What I don't know, I can learn."

Lorna's eyes sparkled. "And you would do this . . . for me?"

"You don't want to marry a man who wants less for you than himself. I don't want you to have doubts somewhere down the road with 'if onlys' or 'might have beens.' I've got enough love for you to last three lifetimes. I'll do whatever it takes to keep you happy and make our marriage work. I understand your dreams and ambitions."

Lorna gave him another kiss, tears of happiness running down her cheeks. She looked skyward. "Thank you, God!"

"I think my grandmother was right," Brad said.

Lorna shrugged. "About what?"

He leaned over and kissed the silky smoothness of her hair. "She once told me love is when you care for someone else more than you care for yourself."

"It sounds as if she was a very wise woman." Lorna lightly brushed her lips against his.

"I want to share life's great adventure with you and grow old in the comfort of each other's arms. As Browning aptly put it, 'the best is yet to be.' There's just one more thing," Brad said. "One teeny caveat."

"Uh oh, what's that?"

"I'm going to want at least three more."

"Three more?"

"Children! Don't forget, God said be fruitful and multiply. Children give purpose and meaning to life and help celebrate the love between man and woman."

She gave him an odd look. "You know, that could result in an uncommon amount of lovemaking."

"I can't wait to start trying."

"I'm anxious for you to meet Mom and Dad."

"Already have."

"What? . . . How?"

"I'm a traditionalist. I went to Litchfield yesterday to ask your father's permission to marry you."

"You didn't!"

"Uh huh."

"What did he say?"

"He said I wasn't good enough for you."

"That sounds like my daddy. What did you do to convince him?"

"Well, your grandfather liked me right off the bat. Said he was a good judge of horseflesh. Then your dad and I got into a discussion about religion. He decided that I was sufficiently grounded in doctrine so as not to be an embarrassment to the family."

"So, that was it?"

"Nope!"

"What else?"

"He said that if I didn't treat you right he'd come after me with a two-by-four. He also said I would have to stop hob-nobbing with known criminals such as Knucky Walters."

"Yep, that's my dad."

"I told him that wouldn't be a problem."

"Really . . . you mean it?"

"Yes, I do. Since I was planning to become fully domesticated, I figured living on the edge was too risky for a family man with responsibilities."

"Have you told Knucky Walters?"

"I plan to go see him in a few days. I'll just have to tell him about my new priorities. He'll understand. Underneath that walnut exterior of his beats the heart of a person with some streaks of decency."

Brad kissed the baby on her cheek and gave Lorna a slow, passionate kiss, thoroughly thrilled by her equally passionate response. Then he nuzzled her and inhaled the fragrance of her skin. The world seemed right. He was deliriously happy. ***Logan, you're the luckiest man in the world.***

"It's a big, wide, beautiful world out there and the sun is shining," Lorna said as she placed her hand in his, giving it a loving squeeze.

Lorna, shortly after her marriage to Brad

"Absolutely. It's a good day for new beginnings. Let's start thinking about what we should name our baby girl and get on with the rest of our lives. Whatever the future has in store for us, rain, shine or whatever, we can face it!"

"Can I have another one of your hugs?" she asked with a playful smile.

* * *

EPILOGUE

Brad patted Roland on the shoulder as he walked by his table at the Club 501. Roland looked up and smiled. He had been absorbed in a story from "True Detective" magazine.

"Let me know how it ends."

He nodded.

Strangely, Brad had grown fondly accustomed to the friendly, informal ambiance, the sights and smells, which were part and parcel of this place. He had learned after many visits the Club 501 was a switching yard of scuttlebutt about sports, jobs, local politics and neighborhood gossip. He looked around with a tinge of nostalgia, knowing it might be his last visit. He spotted an attorney he knew lounging against the bar, a drink in one hand, chatting with a presumed client. Larry Williamson, the bartender, was engaged in meaningful conversation with a shapely woman who had a cumulus halo of auburn around her face. A cocktail sat in front of her and she was puffing incessantly on a cigarette. It must have been a Raleigh because she was toying with one of those beige coupons included on the back of every pack. Brad cocked his head to hear a snatch of conversation. Of all things, they were discussing Freud. "I think Siggy needed a good analyst," he heard her say. She stabbed at the air, expressively using her hands to accentuate her language.

Brad's attention shifted elsewhere. A man with chubby hands and a paunch was glued to a stool at the bar, totally devoted to his cigarette and a bottle of gin he was caressing. Knucky was sitting at his usual booth, absentmindedly fingering some expensive-looking cigars. He seemed to be lost in contemplation, thinking undoubtedly about some knotty problem that required his attention. Brad was practically on top of him before he sensed his presence.

"Oh, hi, Brad. Have a seat." He made a vague gesture with his hands.

"What are you doing with those cigars? I've never seen you smoke one," Brad said.

"They're for the car."

"Come again."

"The glove box. I always keep a few expensive Havanas in there just in case."

"In case . . . what?"

"In case I get pulled over by a cop in a prowl car."

Brad shook his head in disbelief. "Knucky, Knucky. You play all the angles, don't you?"

"I'm just a good judge of human nature," he said, with the ghost of a twinkle in his eye.

"You never cease to amaze me."

"What brings ya here at this time of the day? It's only ten-thirty in the mornin'."

"I have something I wanted to tell you."

"Okay, shoot."

"I'm quitting my job with the firm," Brad said. "I just don't think I was cut out to be a trial lawyer."

Brad had purposely gone to the Club 501 to see Knucky. To tell him good-bye. The thing about quitting the job was his obtuse way of getting around to it.

Knucky frowned thoughtfully. "Whadda ya mean? Ya did just fine at my trial. Ya have everything it takes to be a great lawyer." He took a swig on his bottle of beer.

"Nice of you to say that. I'm just not cut out to make the little compromises with the truth that a lawyer sometimes has to do to win his case. I don't want to be one of those lawyers, who at the end of the day rationalizes his behavior by saying he did more good than harm. Beside, most litigators have their first heart attack sometime in the fifties."

"If you're afraid you'll end up like Goldman, I think you're mistaken. You got too many of those little voices inside you to let that happen. An ya don't have to worry about me corrupting you either. You're as honest as the day is long. It's not in ya. You'd always know where to draw the line."

"Thanks for the vote of confidence, but I don't want to be put in a position where I have to deal with those kinds of situational ethics. Remember when you told me about the crooks that shaved slivers of silver from coins?

"Yeah, what about it?"

"Every time I'm forced to twist the facts, exaggerate to finesse a jury, or leave a detail out to cloud the issues, I walk away with a guilty feeling. Like I'm pilfering the truth. A good lawyer has to do that, if he expects to win. As a litigator you are trained to confuse with euphemisms, seek out obscure loopholes, and conceal or hold back information that would harm your client. And I have a sense that increasingly our legal system is more about winning than anything else. I once read where Oliver Wendell Holmes said that in the American courtroom, what you get is the law, not justice. I didn't understand what he meant at the time, but I do now. And that's why I can't do it anymore."

"So you're gonna go into corporate or tax law? We'll still see each other regularly, won't we?"

"I'm afraid not."

"Why?"

"I got married by the justice of the peace yesterday."

"No kiddin'? To that female reporter you were nuts about?"

"Yes."

"That's what happens when ya wear your heart on your sleeve. You fall for the first split tail that comes along."

"Come on Knucky, I love her very much."

He coughed a small laugh. "I know ya do, kid, just joshin' ya. So what are ya gonna do for a livin'?"

"I plan to get a real job, teaching law at my alma mater at Champaign-Urbana. I think the university life will be a perfect fit for my family and me. No long hours, no questionable ethical decisions to make. No yelling and arguing in court . . ."

"And no decent salary," Knucky interrupted.

"It will be enough. Salaries are increasing. More and more young people are going to college these days. My kids will get a good education for little or no tuition. Besides, I think my life will be more pleasing to God in that capacity."

"So, no more excitement. No more livin' on the edge?"

"You know what they say: If you swim with the sharks long enough, you'll probably get bitten."

"But you love this town. It's in your blood. How can you leave?"

Brad shoved his hands into his pockets. "I'll always have a special place in my heart for East St. Louis, but I have to do what's best for my family."

"Aren't you going to miss getting beat up or shot at? Aren't you afraid you'll get bored?"

"I hardly think so. I'll be too busy. I plan to be active in church and civic organizations. And I want to do pro bono legal work for civil rights and the poor."

"It sounds to me like you're another Nick Carraway."

"Why is that?"

"At the end of ***The Great Gatsby***, Carraway goes back home to a simpler lifestyle."

"You finished it! You actually read the whole novel?"

Knucky had a cocky smile on his lips. "Sure did."

"Well, knock me down and fan me with a brick."

"So you're gonna leave good ol' East St. Louis. Think you'll miss it?"

"Yes. And I'm going to miss you, too. You've been a good friend."

"Now don't go gettin' all mushy. You'll probably be a lot better off gettin' away from characters like me. Sometimes I wish I could be more like you, kid. You've been a good influence."

"Why don't you quit? Give it up. Do it for your wife and kids. Surely you don't need the money."

"I've thought about it. Believe me, I've thought about it. But ya can't teach an old dog new tricks. People like me don't change. You are who ya are. I took a different turn at a crossroads a long time ago. I wouldn't know how to be anything else. It's what I've chosen. I don't know of a single person who ever reached my level in the syndicate and just walked away from it."

"You could be the first."

"Wouldn't that be somethin'? But everyone would just say I turned yellow or lost my nerve, or just lost it—period.

Besides, I wouldn't know what to do with myself."

"You could retire and move to Florida."

"I can just see myself, playing bingo and shuffleboard with all the other blue-haired geezers down there. Nope. That's not for me."

Brad smiled and shook his head. "If there's ever anything I can do for you, don't hesitate; contact me."

"Same for me," he said. "If you ever need anything . . ."

Knucky reached out his hand, and Brad shook it warmly. "Take care of yourself, old buddy."

"See ya around sometime," he said.

"My parents still live here. I'll be back from time to time, so we might see each other once in awhile."

"I'd like that. I'd like that a lot," he said.

Brad headed for the door then stopped and turned. "Give my best to Montrose."

"Sure thing. Aren't you forgetting something else, kid?"

"What's that?"

"Our little bet."

"Oh yeah. I'll put a little proviso in my will for someone to notify you if I die first," Brad said.

"What if I go ahead of you?"

"Don't worry. If that happens your obit will be in all the Illinois newspapers. I'll hear about it."

"So long, Brad."

"Good-bye, Knucky."

* * *

Brad never saw Knucky Walters again. Not ever. He meant to stop in and see him when he came back to town to visit his parents. But somehow he never got around to it. Two years later, both of his parents died—Brad's mother from heart disease and his father, just four months later, from a bleeding ulcer. Friends said Herb Logan grieved himself to death over the passing of his wife.

Lorna and Brad made a good life for themselves up in Urbana. They had three other kids, one boy and two more girls. Lorna did some free-lance writing and had several articles published in national magazines. Thus encouraged, she wrote a novel that sold. And six more in succession.

Knucky passed away in August of 1968 at the age of sixty-three. He died at Alexian Brothers Hospital in St. Louis, following an operation for a lesion on the larynx. He also suffered from heart and liver ailments. There were no more serious attempts to wrest his empire from him, although several of his associates suffered violent deaths from the hands of unknown persons for unknown reasons.

Walters' would have been pleased by the huge turnout at his Mass at St. Stephens Church in Caseyville. There were truckloads of flowers sent to Kassly's Funeral Home in Collinsville. Hundreds of mourners came to pay their last respects. Walters counted friends in the sporting arena and the world of entertainers, nightclub operators, gamblers, bartenders, waitresses and cab drivers. His funeral cortege was over a half-mile long.

Brad's parents were buried in St. Clair Memorial Cemetery near the juncture of Routes 50 and 161. He kept his word to Knucky. He visited his parents' grave once a year. When he finished paying his respects, Memorial Day, 1969, he drove over to Mount Carmel Cemetery on Signal Hill, only a few miles farther south. Walters' tombstone was nondescript and similar to many others in the garden of stone. As Brad looked upon the grave site, he could not help but remember those early days in his career and the conversations they once had. Those were good times and good memories. Knucky taught him a lot about human nature. And about power – who had it and who didn't. Brad missed the distinct pattern, sound, and rhythm of his voice. Knucky was a man with some serious flaws in his character, a bad person in many respects. But Brad always figured God wanted him to see the best in others. His grandmother Holmes said everyone has virtue. He found Knucky's friendship steadfast. He was there for Brad when he needed him. What more could one man ask, or expect, of another.

When Brad decided it was time to go, he waved a salute at Walters' tombstone and whispered, "So long, pal. At the very least, I hope you made it to the netherworld you call Purgatory." As he turned to leave the gravesite, his eye caught the name on the adjacent tombstone. He shook his head in amazement. Life is full of ironies. Truth is stranger than fiction. The name inscribed on the other headstone, a mere six feet away from Walters', was that of his old nemesis, detective Sweeney who died in 1967.

* * *

Gloria Hornback married Bob Von Brock and moved to Collinsville. They had four children. Bob worked as a computer technician for IBM until he died of a heart attack in 1996. She went on to earn her master's degree in gerontology and teaches part-time at Lindenwood College in Missouri.

Laurie McIntyre took training with TWA and worked as an international reservations agent in St. Louis. She transferred to Norfolk, Virginia, met her husband-to-be, and was promoted to supervisor.

Bob Sweeney continued to be anathema to criminals until 1956 when he resigned from the East St. Louis police force. He was being pressured to "take it easy" on the local hoodlums, and he quit rather than compromise his principles.

Montrose remained a driver until Walters' death in 1968. He became interested in politics and became an alderman. In 1971 he became the first black mayor of East St. Louis and was noted for his flamboyance and stylish manner of dress.

Roland Jones grew tired of Walters' temper tantrums and returned to his first love, wrestling, and became a promoter and referee on the professional circuit.

Missola played the numbers and one day bought a winning policy. She used the money as down payment for a three-bedroom bungalow with a white picket fence in Alta Sita.

ABOUT THE AUTHOR

This is Bill Nunes' 8th book, all self-published. The first 6 were nostalgia books about old East St. Louis. The 7th was *Southern Illinois: An Illustrated History*. He was born and reared in East St. Louis and attended the little white church described in the novel. The Brad Logan character is his alter ego and many of the details in the novel about Brad's home life parallel the author's. Bill and his wife are retired teachers.

Bill Nunes first met Lorna Sanders at that little white church, attended by both their families. They started dating when she was a high school senior at Collinsville in 1958. The two married in 1960 after finishing their sophomore year at Belleville Jr. College. They have two children, Steven and Laurie (can you find them in the novel?), and a grandchild, Evan Eure Jones.